MASS MEDIA RESEARCH

FROM THE WADSWORTH SERIES IN MASS COMMUNICATION

General

Media/Impact: An Introduction to Mass Media, Updated First Edition by Shirley Biagi

Media/Reader by Shirley Biagi

Mediamerica: Form, Content, and Consequence of Mass Communication, 4th, by Edward Jay Whetmore

The Interplay of Influence: Mass Media & Their Publics in News, Advertising, Politics, 2nd, by Kathleen Hall Jamieson and Karlyn Kohrs Campbell

Technology and Communication Behavior by Frederick Williams

When Words Collide: A Journalist's Guide to Grammar and Style, 2nd, by Lauren Kessler and Duncan McDonald

Interviews That Work: A Practical Guide for Journalists by Shirley Biagi

Computer Graphics Applications: An Introduction to Desktop Publishing & Design, Presentation Graphics, Animation by E. Kenneth Hoffman with Jon Teeple

Uncovering the News by Lauren Kessler and Duncan McDonald

Mastering the Message by Lauren Kessler and Duncan McDonald

Media Writing, 2nd, by Doug Newsom and James Wollert

Radio/Television/Cable/Film

Stay Tuned: A Concise History of American Broadcasting, 2nd, by Christopher H. Sterling and John M. Kittross

Movie History: A Survey by Douglas Gomery

Working Cinema: Learning from the Masters by Roy Paul Madsen

World Broadcasting Systems: A Comparative Analysis by Sydney W. Head

Broadcast/Cable Programming: Strategies and Practices, 3rd, by Susan Tyler Eastman, Sydney W. Head, and Lewis Klein

Immediate Seating: A Look at Movie Audiences by Bruce A. Austin

Radio Station Operations: Management and Employee Perspectives by Lewis B. O'Donnell, Carl Hausman, and Philip Benoit

Broadcast and Cable Selling, 2nd, by Charles Warner and Joseph Buchman

Advertising in the Broadcast and Cable Media, 2nd, by Elizabeth J. Heighton and Don R. Cunningham

Copywriting for the Electronic Media: A Practical Guide by Milan D. Meeske and R. C. Norris

Announcing: Broadcast Communicating Today by Lewis B. O'Donnell, Carl Hausman, and Philip Benoit

Modern Radio Production, 2nd, by Lewis B. O'Donnell, Philip Benoit, and Carl Hausman

Writing for Television and Radio, 5th, by Robert L. Hilliard

Writing the Screenplay: TV and Film by Alan A. Armer

Institutional Video: Planning, Budgeting, Production, and Evaluation by Carl Hausman

Video Communication: Structuring Content for Maximum Program Effectiveness by David L. Smith

Television Production Handbook, 4th, by Herbert Zettl

Electronic Moviemaking by Lynne S. Gross and Larry W. Ward

Audio in Media, 3rd, by Stanley R. Alten

Directing Television and Film, 2nd, by Alan A. Armer

Sight-Sound-Motion: Applied Media Aesthetics, 2nd, by Herbert Zettl

Electronic Cinematography: Achieving Photographic Control over the Video Image by Harry Mathias and Richard Patterson

MASS MEDIA RESEARCH
AN INTRODUCTION

THIRD EDITION

ROGER D. WIMMER
Paragon Research

JOSEPH R. DOMINICK
University of Georgia

Wadsworth Publishing Company
Belmont, California
A Division of Wadsworth, Inc.

Communications Editor: Kris Clerkin
Editorial Assistant: Nancy Spellman
Production Editor: Gary Mcdonald
Managing Designer: Andrew H. Ogus
Print Buyer: Karen Hunt
Permissions Editor: Robert M. Kauser
Designer: Vargas/Williams/Design
Copy Editor: Denise Cook-Clampert
Technical Illustrator: Susan Breitbard
Compositor: Thompson Type, San Diego
Cover: Vargas/Williams/Design
Signing Representatives: Tom Orsi and Mark Francisco

Printed in the United States of America

1 2 3 4 5 6 7 8 9 10 — 95 94 93 92 91

Library of Congress Cataloging-in-Publication Data

Wimmer, Roger D.
    Mass media research : an introduction / Roger D. Wimmer, Joseph R.
Dominick. — 3rd ed.
      p.   cm.
    Includes bibliographical references and index.
    ISBN 0-534-13962-0
    1. Mass media — Research.   I. Dominick, Joseph R.   II. Title.
P91.3.W47   1991
302.23′072 — dc20   90-12647
                                                                          CIP

To MMM, Joan & Meahgan

PREFACE

In the preface to the second edition of this book, we stated that the media in the United States constantly change, which then affects media researchers. This statement is still valid with the third edition. The media have continued to become more competitive, even in small markets. Owners and operators of electronic and print media continue to search for answers to attract the largest audience. Whether it's radio, television, cable, newspapers or magazines, the goal is to develop the most attractive product possible to increase consumer interest and steal audience or readers away from other outlets. Each medium continues to search for a new niche.

One new area of competition is in cable television, where the FCC has allowed new cable systems (build-overs) to be constructed in the same city. In many parts of the country, consumers now have a choice between cable systems. Once a monopoly, cable television will soon become as competitive as other mass media.

The increased competition, a need to develop more popular products, and various government regulations have further increased the need for research in the mass media. Media managers now use research data as part of their normal activity; few decisions are made without the aid of research.

The importance of research in the mass media should be a signal for mass media students. Understanding research fundamentals is becoming a prerequisite to working in the media. This book is intended to be the first step in the process of learning about mass media research.

Every chapter in this edition has been rewritten. The changes were made because of changes in the research field and suggestions from teachers, students, and others who have read the text. We always welcome suggestions for improvement.

The organization of the third edition is slightly different from the second edition. Part One includes four chapters about the fundamentals of research. Each chapter has been expanded and reorganized. Part Two includes a variety of research approaches and has been expanded to include longitudinal research and other qualitative methods. Part Three discusses data analysis procedures in three chapters, each of which has been significantly reorganized. Part Four discusses various research applications and includes an updated chapter on mass media effects research; and Part Five concerns analyzing and reporting research.

The chapters in each section conclude with problems and questions for further consideration. In addition, there are now four appendixes. Appendix 1 contains various statistical tables; Appendix 2 is a brief guide for conducting focus groups; Appendix 3 discusses some basic multivariate statistical procedures used in mass media research, and now includes a discussion of cluster analysis and multi-dimensional scaling; and Appendix 4 contains actual data from a Paragon Research (Denver, Colorado) study used in Chapter 17. These data may be used to conduct other analyses. The glossary at the end of the text contains words that are **boldface** where they are first introduced in the text.

We wish to thank the following people who reviewed the manuscript or provided insightful comments for this third edition: Fiona Chew, Syracuse University; Jack M. McLeod, University of Wisconsin–Madison; L. John Martin,

University of Maryland; and Dilnawaz A. Siddiqui, Clarion University of Pennsylvania. We also thank Denise Cook-Clampert for her superb job. We greatly appreciate her painstaking review of the manuscript. From Wadsworth, we thank Kris Clerkin, Nancy Spellman, and Gary Mcdonald for their helpful suggestions and patience in dealing with us.

If you find a **serious** problem in the text, please call one author — he will be more than happy to give you the home telephone number of the other.

Roger Wimmer
Denver, Colorado

Joseph Dominick
Athens, Georgia

CONTENTS

ix

ART TWO   RESEARCH APPROACHES   83

P ART THREE   DATA ANALYSIS   197

P ART FOUR   RESEARCH APPLICATIONS   259

PART FIVE   **ANALYZING AND REPORTING DATA   367**

MASS MEDIA RESEARCH

THE RESEARCH PROCESS

CHAPTER 1

SCIENCE AND RESEARCH

I n the introduction to their book, *No Way,* Davis and Park (1987) open by stating:

- It is impossible to translate a poem.
- It is impossible for the president of the United States to be less than 35 years old.
- It is impossible to send a message into the past.
- It is impossible for a door to be open and closed at the same time.

Some individuals involved in mass media would probably like to add another item to this list:

- It is impossible to learn how to conduct mass media *research.*

Davis and Park address the nature of the impossible in several areas. Their book is a collection of essays by authors who explain how some seemingly impossible statements and situations are not what they appear to be. For example, they say that the last item in their list (the open/closed door) sounds like pure logic but it isn't. A revolving door provides evidence that the "pure logic" is incorrect.

For some reason, probably related to a dislike for math, many people consider the word *research* and everything the word suggests as unpleasant. But *research* can be a valuable term. It can lead to uncovering the answers to "impossible" questions.

Several decades ago Richard Weaver (1953), a communications scholar, discussed the meanings of language and identified the differences between "god" and "devil" terms. A god term is positive and has connotations of strength, goodness, and significance; *democracy, innovation,* and *freedom* are god terms in the United States.

A devil term, on the other hand, represents a negative image and connotes weakness, evil, or impending doom; *communist, drug cartel,* and *inferior* are examples of devil terms.

One term that transcends both categories is *research.* Advertisers, for example, use *research* as a god term to sell products and services. Broadcast commercials and print advertisements include statements such as: "Research shows that 6 out of 10 doctors . . ." and "According to a recent survey, 80 out of 100 Cadillac owners preferred. . . ." The intention is to associate with the product a degree of importance based on the mere performance of research; research results alone are considered enough to convince consumers of the need for a product.

Research can also be a devil term, however, especially to those mass media students who consider statistics and research to be detours on the road to receiving a college degree. It is the intention of this book to help dispel the "devil" connotation of *research,* as well as demonstrate that mass media research does not fall into the realm of the impossible. In communications, research need not be viewed negatively; rather it should be regarded as a tool with which to search for answers.

Chapter 1, which introduces mass media research, includes discussions of the development of mass media research during the past 40 years, the methods used in collecting and analyzing information, and an expanded discussion of the scientific method of research. This chapter provides the foundation for topics discussed in greater detail in later chapters.

Two basic questions the beginning researcher must learn to answer are *how* and *when* to use research methods and statistical procedures. Developing methods and procedures are valuable tasks, but the focus for the majority of research students should be on applications. This book advocates the approach of the *applied data analyst* (researcher), not the statistician.

Although both statisticians and researchers are fundamental in producing research results, their specialties are different (keep in mind that one person may serve in both capacities). Statisticians generate statistical procedures or formulas called **algorithms**; researchers use these algorithms to investigate research questions and hypotheses. The results of this cooperative effort are used to advance our understanding of the mass media.

For example, the users of radio ratings information have complained for years about the instability of ratings information. The **ratings** and **shares** (Chapter 14) for stations in a given market often vary dramatically from one survey period to another without any apparent explanation. The users of radio ratings asked statisticians (and the Arbitron company) to help determine why this problem occurred and to offer suggestions for making syndicated radio audience information more reliable. The primary recommendations were to use larger sample sizes and more refined methods of selecting respondents. The statisticians and researchers worked together to solve a problem.

Since the early part of the 20th century, when there was almost no interest in audience size and/or the type(s) of people in the audience, the mass media industry has come to rely on research results for nearly every major decision it makes. This increased demand for information has created a need for more research organizations, both public and private, as well as an increase in research specialization. There are research directors who plan and supervise studies and act as liaisons to management; methodological specialists who provide statistical support; research analysts who design and interpret studies; and computer specialists who provide hardware and software support in data analysis.

The importance of research in mass media is partly due to the realization that gut feelings or reactions are not entirely reliable as bases for decisions. Although common sense is often accurate, media decision makers need additional, more objective information to evaluate problems, especially when hundreds of thousands of dollars are at stake. Thus, the past 50 years have witnessed the slow evolution of an approach combining research and intuition to create a higher probability of success in the decision-making process.

Research is not limited to decision-making situations. It is also widely used in theoretical areas to attempt to describe the media, to analyze media effects on consumers, to understand audience behavior, and so forth. Barely a day goes by without some reference in the media to audience surveys, public opinion polls, the status or growth of one medium or another, or the success of advertising or public relations campaigns. Research in all areas of the media continues to expand at a phenomenal rate.

THE DEVELOPMENT OF MASS MEDIA RESEARCH

Mass media research seems to have evolved in definable steps, and similar patterns have been followed in each medium's requirements for research (Figure 1.1). In Phase 1 of the research, there is an interest in the medium itself. What is it? How does it work? What technology does it involve? How is it similar or different to what we already have? What functions and/or services does it provide? Who will have access to the new medium? How much will it cost?

Once the medium is developed, the initial research phase is followed by Phase 2. In this phase, specific information about the uses and the users of the medium is accumulated. How do people use the medium in real life? Do they use it for information only or for entertainment? Do children use it? Do adults use it? Why? What gratifications does the new medium provide? What other types of information and entertainment does the new medium replace?

FIGURE 1.1   RESEARCH PHASES IN MASS MEDIA

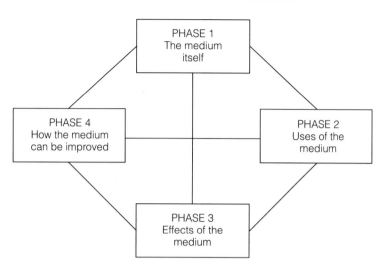

Were original projections about the use of the medium correct? What uses other than those that were projected are evident?

Phase 3 includes investigations of the social, psychological, and physical effects of the medium. How much time do people spend with the medium? Does it change people's perspectives about anything? What do the users of the medium want and expect to hear and/or see? Are there any harmful effects related to using the medium? Does the technology cause any harm? How does the medium help in people's lives? How does it hurt? Can the medium be combined with other media or technology to make it even more useful?

Phase 4 includes research related to how the medium may be improved, either in its use or through technological developments. Can the medium provide information and/or entertainment to more different types of people? How can new technology be used to perfect or enhance the sight or sound of the medium? Is there a way to change the content (programming) to be more valuable and/or entertaining?

Figure 1.1 is not intended to suggest that the research phases are linear — that when one phase is over, it is never considered again. In reality, once a medium is developed and established, research may be conducted simultaneously in all four phases. For example, although radio has been around for over 50 years, researchers are still investigating the medium itself (stereo AM), the uses of radio (specific moods generated by listening to radio), effects (potential health problems caused by living too close to radio antennas), and improvements (simulcasting television news programs on AM and/or FM so commuters can listen to their favorite news program in their cars).

Research is essentially never-ending. In most instances, a research project designed to answer one series of questions merely produces a new set of questions no one thought of before. This failure to produce a closure may be troublesome to some people, yet it is the essential nature of research.

Four different phases of research are defined in Figure 1.1. However, in some instances, as in private sector research, an additional research phase is always present: How can the medium make money? The largest percentage of research conducted in the private sector relates in some way to finance — how to save money, make money, take money away from another source, or keep others from making money.

At least four major events or social forces have contributed to the growth of mass media research. The first was World War I, which brought about a need to further understand the nature of propaganda. Researchers working from a stimulus–response point of view attempted to uncover the effects of the media on people (Lasswell, 1927). The media at that time were thought to exert a very powerful influence over their audiences, and several assumptions were made about what the media could and could not do. One theory of mass media, later named the "hypodermic needle" model of communication, basically suggested that mass communicators need only "shoot" messages at an audience and they would produce preplanned and almost universal effects. The belief was that all people behave in very similar ways when they encounter media messages, though we know now that individual differences among people rule out this rather simplistic view. However, as DeFleur and Ball-Rokeach (1982) note:

> These assumptions may not have been explicitly formulated at the time, but they were drawn from fairly elaborate theories of human nature, as well as the nature of the social order. . . . It was these theories that guided the thinking of those who saw the media as powerful.

A second contributor to the development of mass media research was the realization by advertisers in the 1950s and 1960s that research data were useful in devising ways to persuade potential customers to buy products and services. Consequently, they encouraged studies of message effectiveness, audience demographics and size, placement of advertising to achieve the highest level of exposure (efficiency), frequency of advertising necessary to persuade potential customers, and selection of the medium that

offered the best chance of reaching the target audience.

A third contributing social force was the increasing interest of citizens in the effects of the media on the public, especially on children. The direct result was an interest in research related to violence and sexual content in television programs and in commercials aired during children's programs. Researchers have expanded their focus to include the positive (prosocial) as well as the negative (antisocial) effects of television (Chapter 16). This phase was active in the late 1980s with the heated debate over pop music lyrics and videos, which are shown on MTV and elsewhere.

Increased competition among the media for advertising dollars has been a fourth contributor to the growth of research. Media management has grown more sophisticated, utilizing long-range plans, management by objectives, and increasing dependency on data to support the decision process. Even program producers seek relevant research data, a task usually assigned to the creative side of program development. In addition, the mass media are now headed full speed into audience fragmentation; we are experiencing a "demassification" of the mass media.

The competition among the media for audiences and advertising dollars continues to reach new levels of complexity. The media "survival kit" today includes information about consumers' changing values and tastes, shifts in demographic patterns, and developing trends in lifestyles. Audience fragmentation in the media has led to an increased desire for trend studies (fads, new behavior patterns), image studies (how people perceive the media and their environment), and segmentation studies (explanations of types or groups of people). Major research organizations, consultants, and media owners and operators now conduct research that was previously considered the sole property of marketing, psychology, and sociology. With the advent of increased competition and audience fragmentation, media managers are more frequently using marketing strategies in an attempt to discover their position in the marketplace, and when this position is isolated or identified, the medium is packaged as an "image" rather than a product. (Similarly, the producers of consumer goods such as soap and toothpaste try to sell the "image" of these products, since the products themselves are very similar, if not the same, from company to company.) This packaging strategy involves determining what the members of the audience think, how they use language, how they occupy their spare time, and so on. Information on these ideas and behavior patterns is then woven into the merchandising effort to make the medium seem to be part of the audience. Positioning thus involves taking information from the audience, transforming it into research data, and using it to market the medium (see Ries and Trout, 1986a, 1986b, for more information about positioning companies and products in the business and consumer worlds).

Much of the media research up to the early 1960s originated in psychology and sociology departments at colleges and universities. Researchers with backgrounds in the media were rare because the media themselves were young. But this situation has changed. Media departments in colleges and universities grew rapidly in the 1960s, and media researchers entered the scene. Today the field is no longer dominated by researchers from allied areas. In fact, the trend is to encourage cross-disciplinary studies in which media researchers invite participation from sociologists, psychologists, and political scientists. Because of the pervasiveness of the media, researchers from all areas of science are now actively involved in attempting to answer media-related questions.

In recent years, mass media research has entered new areas of inquiry. These areas include the various psychological and sociological aspects of mass media, such as physiological and emotional responses to television programs, commercials, and music played by radio stations. In addition, computer modeling and other sophisticated computer analyses are now com-

monplace in media research to determine such things as potential success for television programs (network or syndicated). Once considered folly by some, mass media research is now a legitimate and an esteemed field.

MEDIA RESEARCH AND THE SCIENTIFIC METHOD

Kerlinger (1986) defines scientific research as a systematic, controlled, empirical, and critical investigation of hypothetical propositions about the presumed relations among observed phenomena. This definition contains the basic terms necessary in defining the method of scientific research, and describes a procedure that has been accepted for centuries. In the 16th century, for example, Tycho Brahe conducted years of systematic and controlled observation to prove wrong many of Aristotle's theories of the universe.

However, regardless of its origin, all research begins with a basic question or proposition about a specific phenomenon. For example: Why do viewers select one television program over another? What sections of the newspaper do people read most often? What types of magazine covers attract the widest number of readers? Which types of advertising are most effective in selling specific types of products? Each of these questions could be answered to some degree with a well-designed research study. The difficulty, in many cases, is to determine which type of study, or which method of collecting data, is most appropriate to answer the specific question(s).

There are several possible approaches in answering research questions. Kerlinger (1986), using definitions provided nearly a century ago by C. S. Peirce, discussed four approaches to finding answers, or "methods of knowing": tenacity, intuition, authority, and science.

The user of the **method of tenacity** follows the logic that something is true because it has always been true. An example is the store owner who says, "I don't advertise because my parents did not believe in advertising." The basic idea is that nothing changes; what was good, bad, or successful before will continue to be so in the future.

In the **method of intuition**, the a priori approach, one assumes that something is true because it is "self-evident" or "stands to reason." Researchers who conduct telephone research encounter this method of knowing frequently. Many respondents assume (intuition) that all research projects involve some form of sales. This "fear," along with various consumer groups that wish to ban all forms of telephone contacts for sales, research, or solicitation, may be the downfall of telephone research in the near future.

The **method of authority** seeks to promote belief in something because a trusted source, such as a relative, news correspondent, or teacher, says it is true. The emphasis is on the source, not on the methods the source may have used to gain the information. The claim that "The world is going to end tomorrow because the *New York Times* editorial said so" is based on the method of authority.

The **scientific method** approaches learning as a series of small steps. That is, one study or one source provides only an *indication* of what may or may not be true; the "truth" is found only through a series of objective analyses. This means that the scientific method is self-correcting in that changes in thought or theory are appropriate when errors in previous research are uncovered. For example, scientists changed their ideas about the planets Saturn, Uranus, and Neptune when, on the basis of information gathered by the Voyager spacecraft, they uncovered errors in earlier observations. In communications, researchers discovered that the early perceptions of the power of the media (the "hypodermic needle" theory) were incorrect and, after numerous research studies, concluded that behavior and ideas are changed by a combination of communication sources and that people may react to the same message in different ways.

The scientific method may be inappropriate in many areas of life, such as evaluating works of art, choosing a religion, or forming friendships, but the method has been valuable in producing accurate and useful data in mass media research. The following section provides a more detailed look at this method of knowing.

CHARACTERISTICS OF THE SCIENTIFIC METHOD

Five basic characteristics, or tenets, distinguish the scientific method from other methods of knowing. A research approach that does not follow these tenets cannot be considered to be a scientific approach.

Scientific research is public. Scientific advancement depends on freely available information. A researcher (especially in the academic sector) cannot plead private knowledge, methods, or data in arguing for the accuracy of his or her findings; scientific research information must be freely communicated from one researcher to another. As Nunnally (1978, p. 8) noted:

> Science is a highly public enterprise in which efficient communication among scientists is essential. Each scientist builds on what has been learned in the past, day by day his or her findings must be compared with those of other scientists working on the same types of problems.

Researchers, therefore, must take great care in published reports to include information on their use of sampling methods, measurements, and data-gathering procedures. Such information allows other researchers to verify independently a given study and to support or refute the initial research findings. This process of **replication**, discussed in greater detail in Chapter 2, allows for correction or verification of previous research findings.

Researchers also need to save their descriptions of observations (data) and their research materials so that information not included in a formal report can be made available to other researchers on request. It is common practice to keep all raw research material for 5 years. This material is usually provided free as a courtesy to other researchers, or for a nominal fee if photocopying or additional materials are required.

Science is objective. Science tries to rule out eccentricities of judgment by researchers. When a study is undertaken, explicit rules and procedures are constructed and the researcher is bound to follow them, letting the chips fall where they may. Rules for classifying behavior are used so that two or more independent observers can classify particular patterns of behavior in the same manner. For example, if the attractiveness of a television commercial is being measured, researchers might count the number of times a viewer switches channels while the commercial is shown. This is considered to be an objective measure because a change in channel would be reported by any competent observer. Conversely, to measure attractiveness by observing how many people make negative facial expressions while the ad is shown would be a subjective approach, since observers may have different ideas of what constitutes a negative expression. However, an explicit definition of the term *negative facial expression* might eliminate the coding error.

Objectivity also requires that scientific research deal with facts rather than interpretations of facts. Science rejects its own authorities if their statements are in conflict with direct observation. As the noted psychologist B. F. Skinner (1953) wrote: "Research projects do not always come out as one expects, but the facts must stand and the expectations fall. The subject matter, not the scientist, knows best."

Science is empirical. Researchers are concerned with a world that is knowable and potentially measurable. (*Empiricism* is derived from the Greek word for "experience.") They must be able to perceive and classify what they study and to reject metaphysical and nonsensical explanations of events. For example, a newspaper publisher's claim that declining subscription rates are "God's will" would be rejected by scientists — such a statement cannot be perceived, classified, or measured.

This does not mean that scientists evade abstract ideas and notions — they encounter them every day. But they recognize that concepts must be strictly defined to allow for observation and measurement. Scientists must link abstract concepts to the empirical world through observations, which may be observed either directly or indirectly via various measurement instruments. Typically this linkage is accomplished by framing an **operational definition**.

Operational definitions are important in science, and a brief introduction necessitates some backtracking. There are basically two kinds of definitions. A **constitutive definition** defines a word by substituting other words or concepts for it. For example, "An artichoke is a green leafy vegetable, a tall composite herb of the *Cynara scolymus* family" is a constitutive definition of the concept "artichoke." In contrast, an operational definition specifies procedures to be followed in experiencing or measuring a concept. For example, "Go to the grocery store and find the produce aisle. Look for a sign that says 'Artichokes.' What's underneath the sign is one." Although an operational definition assures precision, it does not guarantee validity. An errant stock clerk may mistakenly stack lettuce under the artichoke sign and fool someone. This underlines the importance of considering both the constitutive and the operational definition of a concept in evaluating the trustworthiness of any measurement. A careful examination of the constitutive definition of artichoke would indicate that the operational definition might be faulty. For further discussion of operational definitions, see Chapter 5, *Psychometric Theory* (Nunnally, 1978), and *The Practice of Social Research, 5th* (Babbie, 1989).

Science is systematic and cumulative. No single research study stands alone, nor does it rise or fall by itself. Astute researchers always utilize previous studies as building blocks for their own work. One of the first steps taken in conducting research is to review the available scientific literature on the topic so that the current study will draw on the heritage of past research (Chapter 2). This review is valuable for identifying problem areas and important factors that might be relevant to the current study (see Cattell, 1966).

In addition, scientists attempt to search for order and consistency among their findings. In its ideal form, scientific research begins with a single, carefully observed event and progresses ultimately to the formulation of theories and laws. A **theory** is a set of related **propositions** that presents a systematic view of phenomena by specifying relationships among concepts. Researchers develop theories by searching for patterns of uniformity to explain the data that have been collected. When relationships among variables are invariant under given conditions (that is, when the relationship is always the same), researchers may formulate a law. Both theories and laws help researchers search for and explain consistency in behavior, situations, and phenomena.

Science is predictive. Science is concerned with relating the present to the future. In fact, scientists strive to develop theories because, for one reason, they are useful in predicting behavior. A theory's adequacy lies in its ability to predict a phenomenon or event successfully. If a theory suggests predictions that are not borne out by data analysis, that theory must be carefully reexamined and perhaps discarded. Conversely, if a theory generates predictions that are supported by the data, that theory can be used to make predictions in other situations.

RESEARCH PROCEDURES

The use of the scientific method of research is intended to provide an objective, unbiased evaluation of data. To investigate research questions and hypotheses systematically, both academic and private sector researchers follow a basic eight-step developmental chain of procedures. However, merely following the eight research steps *does not guarantee* that the research is good, valid, reliable or useful. An almost countless number of intervening variables (influences) can destroy even the most well-planned research project. It's similar to someone assuming he or she can bake a cake just by following the recipe. The cake may be ruined by an oven that doesn't work properly, spoiled ingredients, high or low altitude, or numerous other problems.

The typical eight-step research process includes:

1. Select a problem.
2. Review existing research and theory (when relevant).
3. Develop hypotheses or research questions.
4. Determine an appropriate methodology/research design.
5. Collect relevant data.
6. Analyze and interpret the results.
7. Present the results in appropriate form.
8. Replicate the study (when necessary).

Step 4 includes the decision of whether to use **qualitative research** (such as focus groups or one-on-one interviews using small samples) or a **quantitative research** (such as telephone interviews) where large samples are used to allow results to be generalized to the general population under study (see Chapter 7 for a discussion of qualitative research).

Steps 2 and 8 are optional in private sector research because in many instances research is conducted to answer a specific and unique question related to a future decision, such as whether to invest a large sum of money in a developing medium. In this type of project there generally is no previous research to consult, and there seldom is a reason to replicate (repeat) the study because a decision will be made on the basis of the first analysis. However, if the research provided inconclusive results, the study would be revised and replicated.

Each step in the eight-step research process depends on all the others to help produce a maximally efficient research study. Before a literature search is possible, a clearly stated research problem is required; to design the most efficient method of investigating a problem, the researcher needs to know what types of studies have been conducted, and so on. All the steps are interactive: the results or conclusions of any step have a bearing on other steps. For example, a literature search may refine and even alter the initial research problem; a study conducted previously by another company or business in the private sector might have similar effects.

TWO SECTORS OF RESEARCH: ACADEMIC AND PRIVATE

The practice of research is divided into two major sectors, academic and private. Academic and private research are sometimes referred to as "basic" and "applied" research. However, these terms are not used in this text since research in both sectors can be basic and/or applied. Both sectors of research are equally important, and in many cases the two work together to solve mass media problems.

Academic sector research is conducted by scholars from colleges and universities. It also *generally* means that the research has a *theoretical* or scholarly approach; that is, the results are intended to help explain the mass media and their effects on individuals. Some popular research topics in the theoretical area include the use of the media and various media-related items, such as video games, teletext, and multiple-channel cable systems; lifestyle analyses of consumers; media "overload" on consumers; alternatives to present media systems; and the effects of various types of programming on children.

Private sector research is conducted by nongovernmental businesses and industries or their research consultants. It is generally *applied* research; that is, the results are intended to be used in decision-making situations. Typical research topics in the private sector include analyses of media content and consumer preferences, acquisition research to determine whether to purchase additional businesses or facilities, public relations approaches to solve specific informational problems, sales forecasting, and image studies of the properties owned by the company.

There are other differences between academic and private sector research. For instance, academic research is public. Any other researcher or research organization that wishes to use the information gathered by academic researchers should be able to do so merely by asking the original researcher for the raw data. Most private sector research, on the other hand, generates **proprietary data**: the results are considered to be the sole property of the sponsoring agency and cannot generally be obtained by other researchers. Some private sector research, however, is released to the public soon after it has been conducted, such as opinion polls and projections of the future of the media; still other data are released after several years, although this practice is the exception rather than the rule.

Another difference between academic and private sector research involves the amount of time allowed to conduct the work. Academic researchers generally do not have specific deadlines for their research projects (except when research grants are received). Academicians usually conduct research at a pace that accommodates their teaching schedules. Private sector researchers, however, nearly always operate under some type of deadline. The time frame may be specified by management or by an outside agency that requires a decision from the company or business. For example, the Federal Communications Commission often indicates that a rule or regulation will be reviewed on a specific date and advises that any person, group, or entity may respond to the review. When an impending ruling may have an impact on a company's operation, the data required for the FCC hearing must be collected and analyzed in a very short time. Private sector researchers rarely have an opportunity to pursue research questions in a casual manner; a decision is generally waiting to be made on the basis of the research.

Also, academic research is *generally* less expensive to conduct than research in the private sector. This is not to say that academic research is "cheap"—it is not in many cases. But academicians do not need to have enormous sums of money to cover overhead costs for office rent, equipment, facilities, computer analysis, subcontractors, and personnel. Private sector research, whether it is done within a company or hired out to a research supplier, must take such expenses into account. The reduced cost is the primary reason why many of the large media companies and groups prefer to use academic researchers rather than professional research firms.

Despite these differences, it is important for beginning researchers to understand that academic research and private sector research are not completely independent of each other. The link between the two areas is important. Academicians perform many studies for the industry, and private sector groups conduct research that can be classified as theoretical (for example, the television networks have departments that conduct social research). Many college and university professors act as consultants to, and often conduct private sector research for, the media industry.

It is also important for all researchers to refrain from attaching to academic or private sector research such stereotypical labels as "unrealistic," "inappropriate," "pedantic," and "limited in scope." Research in both sectors, although differing occasionally in terms of cost and scope, uses similar methodologies and statistical analyses. In addition, both sectors have common research goals: to understand problems and to predict the future.

In conducting a study according to the scientific method, researchers need to have a clear understanding of what they are investigating, how the phenomenon can be measured or observed, and what procedures are required to test the observations or measurements. Conceptualization of the research problem in question and a logical development of procedural steps are necessary to have any hope of answering a research question or hypothesis. Chapter 2 discusses research procedures in more detail.

S U M M A R Y

In an effort to understand any phenomenon, researchers can follow one of several methods of inquiry. Of the procedures discussed in this chapter, the scientific approach is most applicable to the mass media because it involves a systematic, objective evaluation of information. Researchers first identify a problem, then investigate it, using a prescribed set of procedures known as the scientific method of research. In addition, the scientific method is the only learning approach that allows for self-correction of research findings; one study does not stand alone but must be supported or refuted by others.

The rapid growth of mass media research is mainly attributable to the rapidly developing technology of the media industry. Because of this growth in research, both applied and theoretical approaches have taken on more significance in the decision-making process of the mass media and in our understanding of the media.

Questions and Problems for Further Investigation

1. Obtain a recent issue of *Journal of Broadcasting & Electronic Media*, *Journalism Quarterly*, or *Public Opinion Quarterly*. How many articles fit into the research phases outlined in Figure 1.1?

2. What are some potential research questions that might be of interest to both academic and private sector researchers? Do not limit the questions to the area of effects research.

3. How might the scientific research approach be abused by researchers?

4. Theories are important in developing solid bodies of information; they are used as springboards to investigation. However, there are few universally recognized theories in mass media research. Why do you think this is true?

5. During the past several years, citizens' groups have claimed that television has a significant effect on viewers, especially with regard to violence and sexual content of programs. More recently, groups are criticizing song lyrics. How might these groups have collected data to support their claims? Which method of knowing would such citizens' groups be most likely to use?

References and Suggested Readings

Anderson, J. A. (1987). *Communication research: Issues and methods*. New York: McGraw-Hill.

Babbie, E. (1989). *The practice of social research* (5th ed.). Belmont, CA: Wadsworth.

Bowers, J. W., & Courtright, J. A. (1984). *Communication research methods*. Glenview, IL: Scott, Foresman.

Brown, J. A. (1980). Selling airtime for controversy: NAB self regulation and Father Coughlin. *Journal of Broadcasting, 24*(2), 199–224.

Carroll, R. L. (1980). The 1948 Truman campaign: The threshold of the modern era. *Journal of Broadcasting, 24*(2), 173–188.

Cattell, R. B. (Ed.). (1966). *Handbook of multivariate experimental psychology*. Skokie, IL: Rand McNally.

Davis, P. J., & Park, D. (1987). *No way: The nature of the impossible*. New York: W. H. Freeman.

DeFleur, M. L., & Ball-Rokeach, S. (1982). *Theories of mass communication* (2nd ed.). New York: David McKay.

Ferris, T. (1988). *Coming of age in the Milky Way*. New York: William Morrow.

Herzog, H. (1944). What do we really know about daytime serial listeners? In P. Lazarsfeld & F. Stanton (Eds.), *Radio research 1943–44*. New York: Duell, Sloan, & Pearce.

Hsia, H. J. (1988). *Mass communication research methods: A step-by-step approach*. Hillsdale, NJ: Lawrence Erlbaum.

Katz, E., & Lazarsfeld, P. F. (1955). *Personal influence*. New York: Free Press.

Kerlinger, F. N. (1986). *Foundations of behavioral research*. New York: Holt, Rinehart & Winston.

Klapper, J. (1960). *The effects of mass communication*. New York: Free Press.

Lasswell, H. D. (1927). *Propaganda technique in the World War*. New York: Alfred A. Knopf.

Lazarsfeld, P., Berelson, B., & Gaudet, H. (1948). *The people's choice*. New York: Columbia University Press.

Lowery, S., & DeFleur, M. L. (1988). *Milestones in mass communication research*. White Plains, NY: Longman.

Murphy, J. H., & Amundsen, M. S. (1981). The communication effectiveness of comparative advertising for a new brand on users of the dominant brand. *Journal of Advertising, 10*(1), 14–20.

Nunnally, J. C. (1978). *Psychometric theory*. New York: McGraw-Hill.

Ries, A., & Trout, J. (1986a). *Marketing warfare*. New York: McGraw-Hill.

Ries, A., & Trout, J. (1986b). *Positioning: The battle for your mind*. New York: McGraw-Hill.

Sharp, N. W. (1988). *Communications research: The challenge of the information age*. Syracuse, NY: Syracuse University Press.

Skinner, B. F. (1953). *Science and human behavior*. New York: Macmillan.

Sybert, P. J. (1980). MBS and the Dominican Republic. *Journal of Broadcasting, 24*(2), 189–198.

Weaver, R. M. (1953). *The ethics of rhetoric*. Chicago: Henry Regnery.

Williams, F. (1988). *Research methods and the new media*. New York: Free Press.

RESEARCH PROCEDURES

The scientific evaluation of any problem must follow a sequence of steps to increase the chances of producing relevant data. Researchers who do not follow a prescribed set of steps do not subscribe to the scientific method of inquiry and simply increase the amount of error present in the study. This chapter describes the process of scientific research, from identifying and developing a topic for investigation to replication of results. The first section briefly introduces the steps in the development of a research topic.

Objective, rigorous observation and analysis are characteristic of the scientific method. To meet this goal, researchers must follow the prescribed steps shown in Figure 2.1. This research model is appropriate to all areas of scientific research.

SELECTING A RESEARCH TOPIC

Selecting a research topic is not a concern for all researchers; in fact, only a few investigators in communications fields are fortunate enough to be able to choose and concentrate on a research area interesting to them. Many come to be identified with studies of specific types, such as focus group methodology, magazine advertising, or communications and the law. These researchers investigate small pieces of a puzzle in communications to obtain a broad picture of their research area.

In the private sector, researchers generally do not have the flexibility of selecting topics or questions to investigate. Instead, they conduct studies to answer questions raised by management or they address the problems/questions for which they are hired, as is the case with full-service research companies.

Although some private sector researchers are limited in the amount of input they can contribute to topic selection, they usually are given total control over how the question should be answered (that is, what research methodology should be used). The goal of private sector researchers is to develop a method that is fast, inexpensive, reliable, and valid. If all these criteria are met, the researcher has performed a valuable task.

However, selecting a topic is a concern for many beginning researchers, especially those writing term papers, theses, and dissertations. The problem is knowing where to start. Fortunately, there are virtually unlimited sources available in searching for a research topic; academic journals, periodicals, and newsweeklies, and everyday encounters can provide a wealth of ideas. Some of the primary sources are highlighted in this section.

Professional Journals

Academic communication journals, such as the *Journal of Broadcasting & Electronic Media*, *Journalism Quarterly*, and others listed in the box on page 17 are excellent resources for information. Although academic journals tend to publish research that is 12 to 24 months old (due to review procedures and backlog of articles), the articles may provide ideas for research topics. Most authors conclude their research by discussing problems encountered during the study and suggesting topics that need further investigation. In addition, some journal editors build issues around individual research themes, which often can help in formulating research plans.

FIGURE 2.1   STEPS IN THE DEVELOPMENT OF A RESEARCH PROJECT

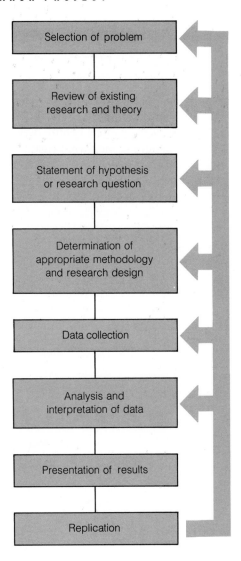

There are many high-quality journals covering various aspects of research. Some journals specialize in mass media research, and others include media research occasionally. The journals listed here provide a starting point in using academic journals for research ideas.

In addition to academic journals, professional trade publications offer a wealth of information relevant to mass media research. These include *Broadcasting*, *Advertising Age*, *Electronic Media*, *Television/Radio Age*, *Media Decisions*, *Editor & Publisher*, *CableVision*, and *Me-*

JOURNALS SPECIALIZING IN MASS MEDIA RESEARCH

- *Critical Studies in Mass Communication*
- *Journalism Quarterly*
- *Journal of Advertising*
- *Journal of Advertising Research*
- *Journal of Broadcasting & Electronic Media*
- *Journal of Consumer Research*
- *Public Relations Review*

JOURNALS OCCASIONALLY PUBLISHING MASS MEDIA RESEARCH

- *American Psychologist*
- *Communication Education*
- *Communication Monographs*
- *Communication Research*
- *Feedback* (from the Broadcast Education Association)
- *Human Communication Research*
- *Journalism Educator*
- *Journal of Communication*
- *Journal of Consumer Research*
- *Journal of Marketing*
- *Journal of Marketing Research*
- *Multivariate Behavioral Research*
- *Politics*
- *Public Opinion Quarterly*
- *Public Relations Quarterly*
- *Quarterly Journal of Speech*
- *Social Forces*
- *Sociology and Social Research*

dia and Marketing Management. Other excellent sources for identifying current topics in mass media are the weekly newsletters, such as *Media Industry Newsletter*, *Cable Digest*, and several publications from Paul Kagan and Associates.

Research abstracts, located in most college and university libraries, are also valuable sources for research topics. These volumes contain summaries of research articles published in nearly every academic journal. Of particular interest to media researchers are *Communication* *Abstracts*, *Psychological Abstracts*, *Sociological Abstracts*, and *Dissertation Abstracts*.

Magazines and Periodicals

Many educators feel that publications other than professional journals contain only "watered-down" articles written for the general public. To some extent this is true, but these articles tend to eliminate the tedious technical jargon and are often good sources for problems and hypotheses. In addition, more and more articles written by highly trained communications professionals are appearing in weekly and monthly publications such as *TV Guide*, *Time*, and *Newsweek*. These sources often provide interesting perspectives on complex problems in communication and many times raise interesting questions that media researchers can pursue.

Research Summaries

Professional research organizations irregularly publish summaries that provide a close look at the major areas of research in various fields. These summaries are often useful for obtaining information about research topics, since they survey a wide variety of studies. Good examples of summary research (also known as "meta-research") in communication include: *Television and Human Behavior*, by George Comstock and others; *The Effects of Mass Communication on Political Behavior*, by Sydney Kraus and Dennis Davis; and *Mass Communication: A Research Bibliography*, by Donald Hansen and J. Hershel Parsons. The *Communication Yearbook*, published annually between 1977 and 1989 by the International Communication Association, is a popular summary that contains a variety of media research. Another popular research source is the *Mass Communication Yearbook*, published by Sage Publications.

Everyday Situations

Each day we are confronted with various types of communication via broadcasting and print, interpersonal communication, public relations campaigns, and so forth. These confrontations can be excellent sources of research topics for the researchers who take an active role in analyzing them. What types of messages are produced? Why are they produced in a specific way? What effects are expected from the various types of communication? These and other questions may help develop a research idea. Significant studies based on questions arising from everyday encounters with the media and other forms of mass communication have covered investigations of television violence, layout of newspaper advertisements, advisory warnings on television programs, and approaches to public relations campaigns.

Archive Data

Data archives, such as the Inter-University Consortium for Political Research (ICPR) at the University of Michigan, the Simmons Target Group Index (TGI), the Gallup and Roper organizations, and the collections of Arbitron, Nielsen, and Birch media ratings data (Chapter 14), are valuable sources of ideas for researchers. The historical data are used by researchers to investigate questions different from those which the data were originally intended to address. For example, ratings books provide information about audience size and composition for a particular period in time, but other researchers may use the data for historical tracking, prediction of audiences in the future, the changes in popularity of types of stations and/or programs, and the relationship between audience ratings and advertising revenue generated by individual stations or an entire market. This process, known as **secondary analysis**, has become a major research approach because of the time and resource savings it affords.

Secondary analysis provides an opportunity for researchers to evaluate otherwise unavailable data. Becker (1981, p. 240) defines secondary analysis as

> [the] reuse of social science data after they have been put aside by the researcher who gathered them. The reuse of the data can be by the original researcher or someone uninvolved in any way in the initial research project. The research questions examined in the secondary analysis can be related to the original research endeavor or quite distinct from it.

ADVANTAGES OF SECONDARY ANALYSIS. Ideally every researcher should conduct a research project of some magnitude to learn about design, data collection, and analysis. Unfortunately, this ideal situation does not exist. Modern research is simply too expensive. In addition, because survey methodology has become so complex, it is rare to find one researcher, or even a small group of researchers, who are experts in all phases of large studies.

Secondary analysis is one research alternative that solves some of these problems. There is almost no expense involved in using available data. There are no questionnaires or measurement instruments to construct and validate, salaries for interviewers and other personnel are nonexistent, and there are no costs for subjects and special equipment. The only expenses entailed in secondary analysis are those for duplicating materials — some organizations provide their data free of charge — and computer time. Data archives are valuable sources for empirical data. In many cases, archive data provide researchers with information that can be used to help answer significant media problems and questions.

Secondary analysis has a bad connotation for some researchers, especially those who are unfamiliar with its potential (Becker, 1981). Although researchers can derive some benefits from developing questionnaires and conducting a research project using a small and often unrepresentative sample of subjects, this type of analysis rarely produces results that are externally valid (discussed later in this chapter). The argument here is that in lieu of conducting a small study that has limited (if any) value to other situations, researchers would benefit from using data that have been previously collected.

Another advantage of secondary analysis is that data allow researchers more time to further understand what has been collected (Tukey, 1969). All too often research is conducted and after a cursory analysis of the data for publication or report to management, the data are set aside, never to be touched again. It is difficult to completely analyze all data from any research study in just one or two studies, yet this procedure is followed in both the academic and private sectors.

Tukey (1969, p. 89) argues for data reanalysis especially for graduate students, but his statement applies to all researchers:

> There is merit in having a Ph.D. thesis encompass all the admitted steps of the research process. Once we recognize that research is a continuing, more or less cyclic process, however, we see that we can segment it in many places. Why should not at least a fair proportion of theses start with a reasonably careful analysis of previously collected and presumably already lightly analyzed data, a process usefully spread out over considerable time. Instant data analysis is — and will remain — an illusion.

Arguments for secondary analysis come from a variety of researchers (Glenn, 1972; Hyman, 1972; Tukey, 1969). It is clear that the research method provides excellent opportunities to produce valuable knowledge. The procedure, however, is not free from criticism.

DISADVANTAGES OF SECONDARY ANALYSIS. Researchers who use secondary analysis are limited to the types of hypotheses or research questions that can be investigated. The data already exist, and since there is no way to go back for further information, researchers must keep their analyses within the boundaries of the type of data originally collected.

Researchers conducting secondary analysis studies also may face the problems of using data that were poorly collected, inaccurate, or flawed. Many studies do not include information about the research design, sampling procedures, weighting of subjects' responses, or other peculiarities. Perhaps it is suspected that some of the data were fabricated. Large research firms tend to explain their procedures in detail.

Although individual researchers in mass media have begun to make their data more readily available (Reid, Soley, & Wimmer, 1981; Wimmer & Reid, 1982), not all follow adequate scientific procedures. This may seriously affect a secondary analysis.

Before selecting a secondary analysis approach, researchers need to consider the advantages and disadvantages. However, with the increased use of secondary analysis, some of the problems associated with research explanations and data storage are being solved. For an example of secondary analysis, see Becker, Beam, and Russial (1978).

DETERMINING TOPIC RELEVANCE

Once a basic research idea has been chosen or assigned, the next step is to ensure that the topic has merit. This step can be accomplished by answering eight basic questions.

Question 1: Is the Topic Too Broad?

Most research studies concentrate on one small area of a field; few researchers attempt to analyze an entire field in one study. There is a tendency, however, for researchers to choose topics that, while valuable, are too broad to cover in one study—for example, "the effects of television violence on children," or "the effects of mass media information on voters in a presidential election."

To avoid this problem, researchers usually write down their proposed title as a visual starting point and attempt to dissect the topic into small questions.

Question 2: Can the Problem Really Be Investigated?

Aside from considerations of broadness, a topic might prove unsuitable for investigation simply because the question being asked has no answer,

or at least cannot be answered with the facilities and information available. For example, a researcher who wants to know how people who have no television receiver react to everyday interpersonal communication situations must consider the problems of finding subjects without at least one television set in the home. Some may exist in remote parts of the country, but the question is basically unanswerable due to the current saturation of television. Thus the researcher must attempt to reanalyze the original idea in conformity with practical considerations. A. S. Tan (1977) solved this particular dilemma by choosing to investigate what people do when their television sets are turned off for a period of time. He persuaded subjects not to watch television for one week and to record their use of other media, their interactions with their family and friends, and so on.

Another point to consider is whether all terms of the proposed study are definable. Remember that all measurable variables must be operationally defined (Chapter 3). A researcher who is interested in examining youngsters' use of the media needs to come up with a working definition of the word *youngsters* to avoid confusion. Potential problems can be eliminated if an operational definition is stated: "Youngsters are children between the ages of 3 and 7 years."

One final consideration is to review available literature to determine whether the topic has been investigated. Were there any problems in previous studies? What methods were used to answer the research questions? What conclusions were drawn?

Question 3: Are the Data Susceptible to Analysis?

A topic does not lend itself to productive research if it requires collecting data that cannot be measured reliably and validly (Chapter 3). In other words, a researcher who wants to measure the effects of not watching television should consider whether the information about the subjects' behavior will be adequate and reliable, whether the subjects will answer truthfully, what value the data will have once gathered, and so forth. Researchers also need to have enough data to make the study worthwhile. It would be inadequate to analyze only 10 subjects in the "television turn-off" example, since the results could not be generalized with regard to the entire population.

Another consideration is the researcher's previous experience with the statistical method selected to analyze the data. That is, does he or she really understand the proposed statistical analysis? Researchers need to know how the statistics work and how to interpret the results. All too often researchers design studies involving advanced statistical procedures that they have never used. This tactic invariably creates errors in computation and interpretation. Research methods and statistics should not be selected because they happen to be popular or because a research director suggests a given method, but rather because they are appropriate for a given study and are understood by the person conducting the analysis. A common error made by beginning researchers is to select a statistical method without understanding what the statistic actually produces. Using a statistical method without understanding what the method produces is called the *law of the instrument*. It is much wiser to do simple frequencies and percentages and understand the results than to try to use a high-level statistic and end up totally confused.

Question 4: Is the Problem Significant?

Before a study is conducted, the researcher must determine whether it has merit, that is, whether the results will have practical or theoretical value. The first question to ask is, Will the results add knowledge to the information already available in the field? The goal of all research is to help further the understanding of the problems and questions in the field of study; if a study does not do this, it has little value beyond the experience the researcher acquires from conducting it. This does not mean that all research has to be earth-shattering. Many investigators, however, waste valuable time trying to develop monumental projects when in fact the smaller problems are of more concern.

A second question is, What is the *real* purpose of the study? This is important because it helps focus ideas. Is the study intended for a class paper, a thesis, a journal article, a management decision? Each of these projects has different requirements concerning background information needed, amount of explanation required, and detail of results generated. For example, applied researchers need to determine whether any useful action based on the data will prove to be feasible, as well as whether the study will answer the question(s) posed by management.

Question 5: Can the Results of the Study Be Generalized?

For a research project to have practical value — to be significant beyond the immediate analysis — it must have **external validity**; that is, one must be able to generalize from it to other situations. For example, a study of the effects of a small-town public relations campaign might be appropriate if plans are made to analyze such effects in several small towns, or if it is a case study not intended for generalization; however, such an analysis has little external validity.

Question 6: What Costs and Time Are Involved in the Analysis?

In many cases the cost of a research study is the sole determinant of the feasibility of a project. A researcher may have an excellent idea, but if costs would be prohibitive, the project must be abandoned. A cost analysis must be completed very early on. It does not make sense to develop specific designs and the data-gathering instrument for a project that will be canceled because of lack of funds. Sophisticated research is particularly expensive: costs may easily exceed $50,000 for one project.

A carefully itemized list of all materials, equipment, and other facilities required is necessary before beginning a research project. If the costs seem prohibitive, the researcher must determine whether the same goal can be achieved if costs are shaved in some areas. Another possibility to consider is financial aid from graduate schools, funding agencies, local governments, or other groups that subsidize research projects. In general, private sector researchers are not severely constrained by expenses; however, they must adhere to budget specifications provided by management.

Time is also an important consideration in research planning. Research studies must be designed in such a way that they can be completed in the amount of time available. Many studies have failed because not enough time was allotted for each research step, and in many cases, the pressure created by deadlines creates problems in producing reliable and valid results (for example, failure to provide alternatives if the correct sample of people cannot be located).

Question 7: Is the Planned Approach Appropriate to the Project?

The most marvelous research idea may be greatly, and often needlessly, hindered by a poorly planned method of approach. For example, a researcher who wished to measure any change in attendance at movie theaters that may have accompanied the increase in televison viewing in one city could mail questionnaires to a large number of people to determine how media habits have changed during the past few years. However, the costs of printing and mailing questionnaires, plus follow-up letters and possibly phone calls to increase the response rate, might prove prohibitive.

Could this study be planned differently to eliminate some of the expense? Possibly, depending on the purpose of the study and the types of question planned. The researcher could collect the data by telephone interviews to eliminate printing and postage costs. Some questions might need reworking to fit the telephone procedure, but the essential information could be collected. A close look at every study is required to plan the best approach. Every procedure in a research study should be considered from the standpoint of the **parsimony principle**, or Occam's razor. The principle, attributed to 14th-century philosopher William of Occam (also spelled Ockham), states that a person should not increase, beyond what is necessary, the number of entities required to explain anything, or make more assumptions than the minimum needed. Applying this to media research suggests that the simplest research approach is always the most efficient.

Question 8: Is There Any Potential Harm to the Subjects?

Researchers must carefully analyze whether the project may cause any physical or psychological harm to the subjects under evaluation. For example: Will respondents be frightened in any way? Will they be required to answer embarrassing questions or perform embarrassing acts that may create adverse reactions? Is there any possibility that the exposure to the research conditions will have lasting effects? Prior to the start of most public research projects involving human subjects, detailed statements explaining the exact procedures involved in the research are required to ensure that subjects will not be injured in any way. These statements are intended to protect unsuspecting subjects from being exposed to harmful research methods.

Underlying all eight steps in the research topic selection process is validity (Chapter 3). In other words, are all of the steps (initial idea to data analysis and interpretation) the *correct* ones to follow in trying to answer the question(s)?

REVIEWING THE LITERATURE

Researchers who conduct studies under the guidelines of scientific research *never* begin a research project without first consulting available literature. The review provides information about what was done, how it was done, and what results were generated. Experienced researchers consider the literature review as one of the most important steps in the research process because it not only allows them to learn from (and eventually add to) previous research data but also saves time, effort, and money. Failing to conduct a literature review is as detrimental to a project as failing to address any of the other steps in the research process.

Before any project is attempted, researchers ask the following questions:

1. What type of research has been done in the area?
2. What has been found in previous studies?
3. What suggestions do other researchers make for further study?
4. What has not been investigated?
5. How can the proposed study add to our knowledge of the area?
6. What research methods were used in previous studies?

Answers to these questions will usually help define a specific hypothesis or research question.

STATING A HYPOTHESIS OR RESEARCH QUESTION

After a general research area has been identified and the existing literature reviewed, the researcher must state the problem as a workable **hypothesis** or **research question**. A hypothesis is a formal statement regarding the relationship between variables, and it is tested directly. The predicted relationship between the variables is either true or false. On the other hand, a research question is a formally stated question intended to provide indications about something, and it is not limited to investigating relationships between variables. Research questions are generally used in situations where a researcher is unsure about the nature of the problem under investigation. The intent is merely to gather preliminary data. However, testable hypotheses are often developed from information gathered during the research question phase of a study.

For example, Singer and Singer (1981) provide an example of how a topic is narrowed, developed, and stated in simple terms. The authors were interested in whether television material enhances or inhibits a child's capacity for symbolic behavior. After a thorough review of available literature, Singer and Singer narrowed their study by seeking to answer three basic research questions.

1. Does television content enrich a child's imaginative capacities by offering materials and ideas for make-believe play?
2. Does television lead to distortions of reality for children?
3. Can intervention and mediation on the part of an adult while a child views a program, or immediately afterward, evoke changes in make-believe play, or stimulate make-believe play?

The information collected from this type of study could provide data to create testable hypotheses. For example, Singer and Singer might have collected enough valuable information from their preliminary study to test the hypotheses suggested below.

1. The amount of time a child spends in make-believe play is directly related to the amount of time spent viewing make-believe play on television.

2. A child's level of distortion of reality is directly related to the amount and type of television program the child views.
3. Parental discussions with children about make-believe play before, during, and after a child watches television programs involving make-believe play will increase the child's time spent involved in make-believe play.

The difference between the two sets of statements is that the research questions only pose general areas of investigation, whereas the hypotheses are testable statements about the relationship(s) between the variables. The only intent in the research question phase is to gather information to help the researchers define and test hypotheses in later projects.

RESEARCH AND EXPERIMENTAL DESIGN

Given the variety of research questions in mass media, different research approaches are required. Some questions call for a survey methodology via telephone or mail; others are best answered through in-person interviews. Still other problems necessitate a controlled laboratory situation to eliminate extraneous variables. The approach selected by the researcher depends on the goals and purpose of the study and how much money is available to conduct the analysis. Even projects that sound very simple may require a highly sophisticated and complex research approach.

The terms *research design* and *experimental design* have become interchangeable to refer to the process involved in developing or planning a research project. Some researchers prefer to use *research design* to describe nonlaboratory projects, and *experimental design* only for projects conducted in a laboratory setting. In this book, the terms are used interchangeably because countless arguments can be raised about whether or not a research project is an "experiment," and the relationship between "laboratory" and "experiment." That is, must an "experiment" be conducted in a controlled laboratory situation to be called an "experiment"?

Research and experimental design are essentially blueprints, or sets of plans, for collecting information. The ideal design collects a maximum amount of information with a minimal expenditure of time and resources. Depending on the circumstances, a design may be brief or very complicated; there are no specific guidelines concerning the amount of detail required for a design. However, all designs incorporate the steps in the process of collecting and analyzing the data.

Researchers must determine how the data will be collected and analyzed before beginning a research project. Attempting to force a study to follow a particular approach or statistic after the data have been gathered only invites error. For example, a director of marketing for a large shopping mall was interested in finding out more about the customers who shopped at the mall (for example, where they lived and how often they shopped at the mall). With very little planning, she designed a simple questionnaire to collect the information. However, the respondents' possible answers, or response choices, to each of the questions were inadequate and the questionnaire inappropriately designed for any type of summary analysis. Thus, the director of marketing was stuck with thousands of useless questionnaires.

All research—from very simple surveys of only a few people to nationwide studies covering complex issues—requires a design of some type. All procedures, including variables, samples, and measurement instruments, must be selected or designed in light of their appropriateness to the hypotheses or research questions, and all items must be planned in advance.

There are four characteristics of research design that should be noted if a study is to produce reliable and valid results (Haskins, 1968):

1. *Naturalistic setting*. For the results of any project to have external validity, the study must be conducted under normally encountered environmental conditions. This means that subjects should be unaware of the research situation, if possible; that phenomena should not be analyzed in a single session; and that normal intervening variables, such as noise, should be included in the study. Also, long-term projects are more conducive to a naturalistic atmosphere than short-term studies.

2. *Clear cause-and-effect relationships*. The reseacher must make every effort to control intervening or spurious independent/dependent variable relationships (Chapter 3). The results of a study can be interpreted with confidence *if and only if* all confounding effects are identified.

3. *Unobtrusive and valid measurements*. There should be no perceptible connection between the communication presented to subjects and the measurement instruments used. Subjects tend to answer questions differently if they can identify the purpose of the study. Also, the study should be designed to assess both immediate and long-term effects on the subjects.

To assure the validity of the measurements used, a sample should be large enough to allow detection of minor effects or changes (Chapter 4). Additionally, the selection of dependent variables should be based on their relevance to the study and the researcher's knowledge of the area, not on convenience.

4. *Realism*. A research design must above all be realistic. This necessitates a careful consideration of the availability of time, money, personnel to conduct the study, and researchers who are competent in the proposed research methodology and statistical analysis.

Once the research design has been properly developed, researchers should pretest as many phases of the project as possible. A pretest of the questionnaire, and a check for errors in the measurement instrument(s) and equipment will help determine if significant problems are present. A trial run, or **pilot study** (a small-scale version of the planned research project) is recommended, but is not always necessary or possible. The mall marketing director in the previous example could have saved a great deal of time and money by running a pilot study using 10 or 20 mall shoppers. She would have quickly discovered that the questionnaire did not produce the desired results.

RESEARCH SUPPLIERS AND FIELD SERVICES

Most researchers do not actually conduct every phase of every project they supervise. That is, although they usually design research projects, determine the sample to be studied, and prepare the measurement instruments, the researchers generally do not actually make the telephone calls or interview respondents in shopping malls. The researchers instead contract with a **research supplier** or a **field service** to perform these tasks.

Research suppliers provide a variety of services. A full-service supplier participates in the design of a study, supervises data collection, tabulates the data, and provides an analysis of the results. The company may offer work in any field (such as mass media, medical and hospital, or banking), or the company may specialize in one type of research work. In addition, some companies can execute any type of research method — **telephone surveys**, **one-on-one interviews**, **shopping center interviews (intercepts)** (Chapter 6), **focus groups** (Chapter 7) — or may concentrate on only one method.

Field services usually specialize in conducting telephone interviews, mall intercepts, one-on-one interviews, and recruiting respondents for **group administration** projects (Chapter 6) and focus groups, which are called **prerecruits** (the company prerecruits respondents to attend a research session). Although some field services offer help in questionnaire design and data tabulation, most concentrate on telephone interviews, mall interviews, and prerecruiting.

Field services usually have focus group rooms available (with two-way mirrors to allow clients to view the session), and test kitchens for projects involving food and cooking. Some field service facilities are gorgeous and elaborate, but others look as though the company just filed for bankruptcy protection under Chapter 11. Most field services lease space (or lease the right to conduct research) in shopping malls to conduct intercepts. Some field services are actually based in shopping malls.

Hiring a research supplier or field service is a simple process. The researcher calls the company, explains the project, and is given a price quote. A contract or project confirmation letter is usually signed. In some cases, the price quote is a flat fee for the total project. However, sometimes costs are based on **cost-per-interview** (**CPI**).

Before describing the CPI procedure, it is necessary to introduce the term **incidence** because it plays an important role in the research process. The term is used to describe the ease with which qualified respondents or subjects are (or can be) found for a research project. Incidence is given as a percentage of 100 — the lower the incidence, the more difficult it is to find a qualified respondent or group of respondents. **Gross incidence** is the percentage of qualified respondents reached of *all* contacts (such as telephone calls) made, and **net incidence** refers to the number of respondents or subjects who actually participate in a project.

For example, assume a telephone research study requires 100 female respondents between the ages of 18 and 49 who listen to the radio for at least 1 hour per day. The estimated gross incidence is 10%. A total of 1,818 calls will have to be made to recruit the 100 females, not 1,000 calls as some people may think. The number of calls required is *not* computed as the target sample size (100 in this example) divided by incidence (.10), or 1,000. The number of calls computed for gross incidence (1,000) must then be divided by the **acceptance rate**, or the percentage of the target sample that agrees to participate in the study.

The total calls required are 1,000 divided by .55 (a generally used acceptance percentage), or 1,818. Of the 1,818 telephone calls made, 10% (182) will qualify for the interview, but only 55% (100) will actually accept and complete the interview (net incidence).

Field services and research suppliers base

TABLE 2.1   CPI CHART

	Incidence							
	5	**6**	**7**	**8**	**9**	**10**	**20**	**30**
5 Minutes	44.25	38.00	34.00	30.75	28.50	26.50	14.25	10.25
10 Minutes	45.50	39.25	35.00	32.00	29.50	27.75	15.50	11.50
15 Minutes	46.50	40.50	36.25	33.00	30.75	29.00	16.75	12.50
20 Minutes	47.75	41.75	37.50	34.25	32.00	30.00	17.75	13.75
25 Minutes	49.00	42.75	38.50	35.50	33.00	31.25	19.00	15.00
30 Minutes	50.00	44.00	39.75	36.50	34.25	32.50	20.25	16.25

their charges on net incidence, not gross incidence. Many novice researchers fail to take this into account when they plan the financial budget for a project.

There is no "average" incidence rate in research. The figure differs depending on the complexity of the sample desired, the length of the research project, the time of year the study is conducted, and a variety of other problems. The lower the incidence, the higher the cost for a research project. That is a *guarantee*.

In addition, prices quoted by field services and research suppliers are based on an estimated incidence rate. Costs will be adjusted after a project is completed and the actual incidence rate is known. In most cases, a quote will be given with a plus or minus 10% "warning."

Let's go back to the CPI discussion. Assume a researcher wants to conduct a 400-person telephone study with adults who are between the ages of 18 and 49. A representative of the company will ask for the researcher's estimated incidence and the length of the interview (in minutes). The two figures determine the CPI. Most field services and research suppliers use a chart to compute the CPI; an example based on 1990 prices is shown in Table 2.1.

The table is easy to use. To find a CPI, first read down the left-hand side of the table for the length of the interview, then across for incidence. For example, the CPI for a 20-minute interview with an incidence of 10% is $30. A researcher conducting a 400-person telephone study with these "specs" will owe the field service or research supplier $12,000 (400 × $30) *plus* any costs for photocopying the questionnaire, mailing, and data tabulation (if requested). If the company analyzes the data and writes a final report, the total cost would be between $20,000 and $30,000.

Research projects involving prerecruits, such as focus groups and group administration, involve an additional cost: respondent co-op fees, or incentives. A telephone study respondent generally receives no payment for answering questions. However, when respondents are asked to leave their home to participate in a project, they are paid a co-op fee, usually between $25 and $100.

Costs escalate quickly in a prerecruit project. For example, assume a researcher wants to conduct a group session with 400 respondents instead of using a telephone approach. Instead of paying a field service or research supplier a CPI for a telephone interview, the payment is for recruiting respondents to attend a project

---

TABLE 2.1   CONTINUED

			Incidence				
	40	**50**	**60**	**70**	**80**	**90**	**100**
5 Minutes	8.25	7.00	6.50	6.00	5.75	5.50	5.00
10 Minutes	9.50	8.25	7.75	7.25	7.00	6.75	6.50
15 Minutes	10.50	9.50	9.00	8.50	8.00	8.00	7.75
20 Minutes	11.75	10.50	10.00	9.50	9.25	9.00	9.00
25 Minutes	13.00	11.75	11.25	10.75	10.50	10.25	10.00
30 Minutes	14.25	13.00	12.50	11.75	11.50	11.00	10.50

conducted at a specific location. Although most companies have separate rate cards for prerecruiting (they're usually a bit higher than the card used for telephone interviewing), assume the costs are the same. Recruiting costs, then, are $12,000 (400 × $30 CPI), with another $10,000 (*minimum*) for respondent co-op (400 × $25). Total costs so far are $22,000, about twice as much as a telephone study. However, more costs must be added to this figure: a rental fee for the room where the study will be conducted, refreshments for respondents, fees for assistants to check in respondents, and travel expenses (another $1,000–$4,000).

In addition, to have 400 people show up (4 sessions of 100 each), it is necessary to overrecruit since not every respondent will "show." In prerecruit projects, field services and research suppliers will overrecruit 25% to 100%. In other words, for a 400 "show rate," a company will prerecruit between 600 and 800 people. However, rarely does a prerecruit session hit the target sample size exactly. In many cases, the show rate falls short and a make-good is required (the project is repeated at a later date with another group of respondents to meet the target sample size). In some cases, more respondents than required show, which means that projected research costs may skyrocket.

In most prerecruit research projects, field services and research suppliers are paid on a "show-basis" only. That is, they receive payment only for respondents who show, not how many are recruited. If the companies were paid on a recruiting basis, they could recruit thousands of respondents for each project. The show-basis procedure also adds incentive for the companies to make sure that those who are recruited show up for the research session.

Although various problems with hiring and working with research suppliers and field services are discussed in Chapter 7, two important points are introduced here to help novice researchers when they begin to use these support companies.

1. *All suppliers and field services are not equal.* Any person or group with *any* qualifications can form a research supply company or field service. There are no formal requirements, no tests to take, and no national, state, or regional licenses to acquire. What's needed is a research shingle on the door, advertising in marketing and research trade publications, and (optional) membership in one or more of the *voluntary* research organizations.

Due to the lack of regulations in the research industry, it is the sole responsibility of the research user to determine which of hundreds of suppliers available are capable of conducting a professional, scientifically based research project. Experienced researchers develop a list of qualified companies, basically from the recommendations of other users (mass media researchers throughout the country are a very closely knit group of people who trade information almost daily).

2. *The researcher must maintain close supervision over the project.* This is true even with the very good companies, not because their professionalism cannot be trusted, but rather, to be sure that the project is answering the questions that were posed. Because of security considerations, a research supplier may never completely understand why a particular project is being conducted, and the researcher needs to be sure that the project will provide the exact information required.

DATA ANALYSIS AND INTERPRETATION

The time and effort required for data analysis and interpretation depends on the study's purpose and the methodology used. Analysis and interpretation may take several days to several months. In many private sector research studies involving only a single question, however, data analysis and interpretation may be completed in a few minutes. For example, a business or company may be interested in discovering the amount of interest in a new product or service. After a survey, for example, the question may be answered by summarizing only one or two items on the questionnaire that relate to demand for the product or service. In this case, interpretation is simply "go" or "no-go."

Every analysis should be carefully planned and performed according to guidelines designed for that analysis. Once the computations have been completed, the researcher must "step back" and consider what has been discovered. The results must be analyzed with reference to their external validity and the likelihood of their accuracy. Here, for example, is an excerpt from the conclusion drawn by Singer and Singer (1981).

> Television by its very nature is a medium that emphasizes those very elements that are generally found in imagination: visual fluidity, time and space flexibility and make-believe. . . . Very little effort has emerged from producers or educators to develop age-specific programming . . . it is evident that more research for the development of programming and adult mediation is urgently needed.

Researchers must determine through analysis whether their work is valid internally and externally. This chapter has touched briefly on the concept of external validity; an externally valid study is one whose results can be generalized to the population. To assess **internal validity**, on the other hand, one asks: Does the study really investigate the proposed research question?

Internal Validity

Control over research conditions is necessary to enable researchers to rule out all plausible rival explanations of results. Researchers are interested in verifying that "y is a function of x," or $y = f(x)$. Control over the research conditions is necessary to eliminate the possibility of finding that $y = f(b)$, where b is an extraneous variable. Any such variable that creates a rival explanation of results is known as an **artifact** (also referred to as extraneous variable). The presence of an artifact indicates a lack of internal validity: the study has failed to investigate its hypothesis.

Suppose, for example, that researchers discover through a study that children who view television for extended lengths of time have lower grade point averages in school than children who watch only a limited amount of television. Could an artifact have created this finding? It may be that children who view fewer hours of television also receive parental help with their school work: parental help (the artifact), not hours of television viewed, may be the reason for the difference in grade point averages between the two groups.

Sources of internal invalidity may arise from several places. Those most frequently encountered are described in the list below. Researchers should be familiar with these sources to achieve internal validity in the experiments they conduct (Campbell & Stanley, 1963; Cook & Campbell, 1979).

1. *History.* Various events occurring during a study may affect the subjects' attitudes, opinions, and behavior. For example, to analyze an oil company's public relations campaign for a new product, researchers first *pretest* subjects concerning their attitudes toward the company. The subjects are next exposed to an experimental promotional campaign (the *experimental treatment*); then a *posttest* is administered to determine whether changes in attitude occurred as a result of the campaign. Suppose the results indicate that the public relations campaign was a complete failure — that the subjects displayed a very poor perception of the oil company in the posttest. Before the results are reported, the researchers need to determine whether an intervening variable could have caused the poor

perception. An investigation discloses that during the period between tests, subjects learned from a television news story that the oil company was planning to raise gasoline prices by 20%. The news of the price increase — not the public relations campaign — may have acted as an artifact that created the poor perception. The longer the time period between a pretest and a posttest, the greater the possibility that history might confound the study.

The effects of history in a study can be devastating, as was shown during the late 1970s and early 1980s. Several broadcast companies and other private businesses perceived a need to develop Subscription Television (STV) in various markets throughout the country where cable television penetration was thought to be very low. An STV service allows a household to pick up, using a special antenna, pay television services similar to Home Box Office or Showtime. Several cities became prime targets for STV because both Arbitron and Nielsen reported very low cable penetration. Several companies conducted research in many of these cities, and results supported the Arbitron and Nielsen data. In addition, the research found that people who did not have access to cable television were very receptive to the idea of STV. However, it was discovered later that even as some of the studies were being conducted, cable companies in the target areas were expanding very rapidly and had wired many of the previously nonwired neighborhoods. What were once prime targets for STV soon became accessible to cable television. The major problem was that researchers attempting to determine the feasibility of STV failed to consider the historical changes (wiring of the cities) that could affect the results of their research. The net result was that many companies lost millions of dollars and STV soon faded from memory.

2. *Maturation.* Subjects' biological and psychological characteristics change during the course of a study. Growing hungry or tired or becoming older may influence the manner in which subjects respond to a research study. An example of how maturation can affect a research project was seen in the early 1980s when radio stations around the country began to test their music playlist in auditorium sessions (where listeners are invited to a large hotel ballroom to rate short segments of songs; Chapter 14). Some unskilled research companies tested up to 500 or 600 songs in one session and wondered why the songs after about the 400th one tested dramatically different from the other songs. Without a great deal of investigation, researchers discovered that the respondents were physically and emotionally drained once they reached 400 songs (about 2 hours), and merely wrote down *any* number just to complete the project.

3. *Testing.* Testing in itself may be an artifact, particularly when subjects are given similar pretests and posttests. A pretest may sensitize subjects to the material and improve their posttest scores regardless of the type of experimental treatment given to subjects. This is especially true when the same test is used for both situations. Subjects learn how to answer questions and to anticipate researchers' demands. To guard against the effects of testing, different pretests and posttests are required. Or, instead of being given a pretest, subjects can be tested for similarity (homogeneity) by means of a variable or set of variables that differs from the experimental variable. The pretest is not the only way to establish a *point of prior equivalency* (the groups were equal before the experiment) between groups — this can also be accomplished through sampling (randomization and matching).

4. *Instrumentation.* Also known as **instrument decay**, this term refers to the deterioration of research instruments or methods over the course of a study. Equipment may wear out, observers may become more casual in recording their observations, and interviewers who memorize frequently asked questions may fail to present them in the proper order. Some college entrance tests, such as the SAT and ACT, are

targets of debate by many researchers and/or statisticians. The complaints mainly address the concern that the current tests do not adequately measure knowledge of *today*, but rather what was *once* considered necessary and important.

5. *Statistical regression.* Subjects who achieve either very high or very low scores on a test tend to regress to the sample or population mean during following testing sessions. Often *outliers* (subjects whose pretest scores are far from the mean) are selected for further testing or evaluation. Suppose, for example, that researchers develop a series of television programs designed to teach simple mathematical concepts, and they select only subjects who score very low on a mathematical aptitude pretest. An experimental treatment is designed to expose these subjects to the new television series, and a posttest is given to determine whether the programs increased the subjects' knowledge of simple math concepts. The experimental study may show that indeed, after only one or two exposures to the new programs, math scores increased. But the higher scores on the posttest may not be due to the television programs; they may be a function of statistical regression. That is, regardless of whether the subjects viewed the programs, the scores in the sample may have increased merely because of statistical regression to the mean. The programs should be tested with a variety of subjects, not just those who score low on a pretest.

6. *Experimental mortality.* All research studies face the possibility that subjects will drop out for one reason or another. This is especially true in long-term studies. Subjects may become ill, move away, drop out of school, or quit work. This **mortality**, or loss of subjects, is sure to have an effect on the results of a study, since most research methods and statistical analyses make assumptions about the number of subjects used. It is always better, as mentioned in Chapter 4, to select more subjects than are actually required—within the budget limits of the study.

7. *Selection.* Most research designs compare two or more groups of subjects to determine whether differences exist on the dependent measurement. These groups must be randomly selected and tested for homogeneity to ensure that results are not due to the type of sample used.

8. *Demand characteristics.* The term **demand characteristics** is used to describe subjects' reactions to experimental conditions. Orne (1969) suggested that under some circumstances, subjects' awareness of the experimental purpose may be the sole determinant of how they behave; that is, subjects who recognize the purpose of a study may produce only "good" data for researchers.

People who become involved in research quickly learn about the many variations of demand characteristics. For example, research studies seeking to find out about respondents' listening and viewing habits always find subjects who report high levels of listening and viewing to PBS. However, when the same subjects are asked to name their favorite PBS programs, many cannot recall a single one (their TV favorite is usually something like *Wheel of Fortune*, while their radio favorite is something like the *American Top 40 Countdown*).

Cross-validating questions are often necessary to verify subjects' responses; by giving subjects the opportunity to answer the same question phrased in different ways, the researcher can spot discrepant, potentially error-producing responses. In addition, researchers can help control demand characteristics by disguising the real purpose of the study; however, researchers should use caution when employing this technique (Chapter 18).

In addition, most respondents who participate in research projects are eager to provide the information the researcher requests. They are flattered to be asked for their opinions. Unfortunately, this means that they will answer any type of question, even if the question is totally ambiguous, misleading, vague, or absolutely uninterpretable. For example, a recent telephone study was conducted by Paragon Research (where the senior author is president) with respondents in Pennsylvania who have area code 717. An interviewer using a telephone that did not have area codes blocked out (no access), unknowingly called area code 714 (Orange County, California). For nearly 20 minutes, the respondent in California answered questions about radio stations with *W* call letters — stations impossible for her to pick up on any radio. The problem was discovered in the questionnaire validation process. When called back, the "real" respondent at the 717 area code claimed to have never answered questions about local radio stations, and the computer printout of calls made for the project highlighted the erroneous telephone number.

9. *Experimenter bias.* Rosenthal (1969) discussed a variety of ways in which a researcher may influence the results of a study. Bias can enter through mistakes made in observation, data recording, mathematical computations, and interpretation. Whether experimenter errors are intentional or unintentional, they usually support the researcher's hypothesis and are considered bias (Walizer & Wienir, 1978).

Experimenter bias can also enter into any phase of a research project if the researcher becomes swayed by a client's wishes for how a project will turn out. The following example describes a situation that can cause significant problems for researchers if they do not remain totally objective throughout the entire project. The example is not included here to suggest that research *always* works this way, nor is it an endorsement of the situation.

Researchers are sometimes hired by individuals or companies to "prove a point" or to have "supporting information" for a decision (this is usually unknown to the researcher). For example, the program director at a television station may have a particular dislike for a program on the station and wants to "prove" his "theory" cor-

rect. A researcher is hired under the premise of finding out whether the audience likes or dislikes the program. In this case, it is very easy for the program director to intentionally or unintentionally sway the results just through the conversations with the researcher in the planning stages of the study. It is possible for a researcher to intentionally or unintentionally interpret the results in order to support the program director's desire to eliminate the program. The researcher may, for instance, have like/dislike numbers that are very close, but may give the "edge" to dislike because of the program director's influence.

Experimenter bias is a potential problem in all phases of research, and those conducting the study must be aware of problems caused by outside influences. Several procedures can help to reduce experimenter bias. For example, individuals who provide instructions to subjects and make observations should not be informed of the purpose of the study; experimenters and others involved in the research should not know whether subjects belong to the experimental group or the **control group** (this is called a **double blind experiment**); and automated devices such as tape recorders should be used whenever possible to provide uniform instructions to subjects. (See Chapter 5 for more information about control groups.)

Researchers can also ask clients not to discuss the intent of a research project beyond what type of information is desired. The program director should say only that information is desired about the like/dislike of the program and should not discuss what decisions will be made with the research. In cases where researchers *must* be told about the exact purpose of the project, or where the researcher is conducting the study independently, experimenter bias must be repressed at every phase.

10. *Evaluation apprehension.* Rosenberg's (1965) concept of **evaluation apprehension** is similar to demand characteristics, but it empha-

sizes that subjects are essentially *afraid* of being measured or tested. They are interested in receiving only positive evaluations from the researcher and from the other subjects involved in the study. Most people are hesitant to exhibit behavior that differs from the norm and will tend to follow the group, even though they may totally disagree with the others. The researcher's task is to try to eliminate this passiveness by letting subjects know that their individual responses are important.

11. *Causal time-order*. The organization of an experiment may in fact create problems with data collection and/or interpretation. It may be that results of an experiment are not due to the stimulus (independent) variable, but rather to the effect of the dependent variable. For example, respondents in an experiment about how advertising layouts in magazines influence their purchasing behavior may change their opinions when they read or complete a questionnaire after viewing several ads.

12. *Diffusion or imitation of treatments*. In situations where respondents participate at different times during one day or over several days, or groups of respondents are studied one after another, respondents may have the opportunity to discuss the project with someone else and contaminate the research project. This is a special problem with focus groups where one group often leaves the focus room while a new group enters.

13. *Compensation*. Sometimes individuals who work with a control group (the one that receives no experimental treatment) may unknowingly treat the group differently since the group was "deprived" of something. In this case, the control group is no longer legitimate.

14. *Compensatory rivalry*. In some situations, subjects who know they are in a control group may work harder or perform differently to out-perform the experimental group.

15. *Demoralization*. Control group subjects may literally lose interest in a project because they are not experimental subjects. These people may give up or fail to perform normally because they may feel demoralized or angry that they are not in the experimental group.

The sources of internal invalidity are complex and may arise in all phases of research. For this reason, it is easy to see why the results from a single study cannot be used to refute or support a theory or hypothesis. To try and control these artifacts, researchers use a variety of experimental designs and try to keep strict control over the research process so subjects and researchers will not intentionally or unintentionally influence the results. As Hyman (1954) recognized:

> All scientific inquiry is subject to error, and it is far better to be aware of this, to study the sources in an attempt to reduce it, and to estimate the magnitude of such errors in our findings, than to be ignorant of the errors concealed in our data.

External Validity

External validity refers to how well the results of a study can be generalized across populations, settings, and time (Cook & Campbell, 1979). The external validity of a study can be severely affected by the interaction in an analysis of variables such as subject selection, instrumentation, and experimental conditions (Campbell & Stanley, 1963). A study that lacks external validity cannot be projected to other situations. The study is only valid for the sample tested.

Most procedures to guard against external invalidity relate to sample selection. Cook and Campbell (1979) describe three considerations:

1. Use random samples.
2. Use heterogeneous samples and replicate the study several times.

3. Select a sample that is representative of the group to which the results will be generalized.

Using random samples rather than convenience or available samples (Chapter 4) allows researchers to gather information from a variety of subjects rather than those who may share similar attitudes, opinions, and lifestyles. As Chapter 4 discusses, a random sample means that everyone (within the guidelines of the project) has an equal chance of being selected for the research study.

Several replicated research projects using samples with a variety of characteristics (heterogeneous) allow researchers to test hypotheses and research questions and not worry that the results will only relate to one type of subject.

Selecting a sample that is representative of the group to which the results will be generalized is basic common sense. For example, the results from a study of a group of high school students cannot be generalized to a group of college students.

A fourth way to increase external validity is to conduct research over a long period of time. Mass media research is often designed as short-term projects: subjects are exposed to an experimental treatment and are immediately tested or measured. However, in many cases, the immediate effects of a treatment are negligible. In advertising, for example, research studies designed to measure brand awareness are generally based on only one exposure to a commercial or advertisement. It is well known that persuasion and attitude change rarely take place after only one exposure; they require multiple exposures over time. Logically, such measurements should be made over a period of weeks or months to take into account the sleeper effect: that attitude change may be minimal or nonexistent in the short run and still prove significant in the long run.

PRESENTING RESULTS

The format used in presenting results depends on the purpose of the study. Research intended for publication in academic journals follows a format prescribed by each journal; research conducted for management in the private sector tends to be reported in simpler terms, excluding detailed explanations of sampling, methodology, and review of literature. However, all presentations of results need to be written in a clear and concise manner appropriate to both the research question and the individuals who will read the report. A more detailed discussion of reporting is included in Chapter 18.

REPLICATION

One important point mentioned throughout this book is that the results of any single study are, by themselves, only *indications* of what might exist. A study provides information that says, in effect, "This is what may be the case." To be relatively certain of the results of any study, the research must be replicated. Too often, researchers conduct one study and report the results as if they are providing the basis for a theory or law. The information presented in this chapter, and in other chapters that deal with internal and external validity, argues that this cannot be true.

A research question or hypothesis requires investigation from many different perspectives before any significance can be attributed to the results of any one study. Research methods and designs must be altered to eliminate **design-specific results**, that is, results that are based on, hence specific to, the design used. Similarly, subjects with a variety of characteristics should be studied from many angles to eliminate **sam-**

ple-specific results; and statistical analyses need variation to eliminate method-specific results. In other words, all effort must be made to ensure that the results of any single study are not created by or dependent on a methodological factor; studies must be replicated.

Researchers overwhelmingly advocate the use of replication to establish scientific fact. Lykken (1968) and Kelly, Chase, and Tucker (1979) have identified four basic types of replication that can be used to help validate a scientific test.

- **Literal replication** involves the exact duplication of a previous analysis, including the sampling procedures, experimental conditions, measuring techniques, and methods of data analysis.
- **Operational replication** attempts to duplicate only the sampling and experimental procedures of a previous analysis, to test whether the procedures will produce similar results.
- **Instrumental replication** attempts to duplicate the dependent measures used in a previous study and to vary the experimental conditions of the original study.
- **Constructive replication** tests the validity of methods used previously by deliberately avoiding the imitation of the earlier study; both the manipulations and the measures used in the first study are varied. The researcher simply begins with a statement of empirical "fact" uncovered in a previous study and attempts to find the same "fact."

Although the process of replication has not been widely used in communications research, the trend seems to indicate that more and more mass media researchers consider it an invaluable step in producing scientific data (Wimmer & Reid, 1982).

RESEARCH HAZARDS

All researchers quickly discover that research projects do not always turn out the way they were planned. It seems that Murphy's Law — Anything that can go wrong will go wrong — holds true in any type of research. It is therefore necessary to be prepared for difficulties, however minor, in conducting a research project. Planning and flexibility are essential. Presented below are what are known as the TAT (They're Always There) laws. Although these "laws" are somewhat tongue-in-cheek, they are nonetheless representative of the problems one may expect to encounter in research studies.

1. A research project always takes longer than planned.
2. No matter how many people review a research proposal and say that it's perfect before you start, they will always have suggestions to make it better after the study is completed.
3. There are always errors in data entry.
4. The data errors that take the longest to find and correct are the most obvious.
5. Regardless of the amount of money requested for a research project, the final project always costs more.
6. A computer program never runs the first time.
7. A sample is always too small.
8. Regardless of how many times a pilot study or pretest is conducted to make sure that measurement instructions are clear, there will always be at least one subject who doesn't understand the directions.
9. All electronic equipment breaks down during the most crucial part of an experiment.
10. Subjects never tell you how they really feel or what they really think or do.

SUPPLEMENT ON INCIDENCE RATES AND CPI

Incidence rate is an important concept in research because it determines both the difficulty and cost of a research project. Table 2.1 (on pages 26–27) shows a standard CPI rate chart. These individual numbers are computed through a complicated series of steps. Without going into exact detail, this supplement explains the general procedure of how each CPI is computed.

As mentioned earlier, CPI is based on incidence and interview length. In prerecruiting, only incidence is considered, but CPIs are basically the same as those for telephone interviews. To determine a CPI, let's assume we wish to

TABLE 2.2   DETERMINING A CPI

Step		Explanation
1. Gross incidence:	1,000	Gross incidence figure. Simply $100 \div .10$.
2. Acceptance rate:	55%	Standard figure used. Use acceptance rate to determine how many calls are needed.
3. *Real* contacts necessary:	1,818	$1,000 \div .55$
4. Minutes per contact:	4	Number of minutes to find correct respondent (bad numbers, busy lines, etc.)
5. Total contact minutes:	7,272	$4 \times 1,818$
6. Productive minutes per hour:	40	Average number of minutes interviewers usually work in 1 hour (breaks, etc.)
7. Total contact hours:	182	$7,272 \div 40$
8. Total interview hours:	33	100×20 minutes
9. Total hours:	215	Contact + interview hours
10. Hourly rate:	$15	Industry standard
11. Total cost:	$3,225	$215 \times \$15$
12. CPI:	$32.25	$3,225 \div 100$ interviews

conduct a 100-person telephone study, with an incidence of 10% and an interview length of 20 minutes. The computation and an explanation of each step is shown in Table 2.2. In other words, 1,818 contacts are made. Of these, 10% will qualify for the interview (182) and 55% of these will accept (100). The total number of hours required to conduct the 100-person survey is 215, with a CPI of $32.25.

S U M M A R Y

This chapter has described the processes involved in identifying and developing a topic for research investigation. It was suggested that researchers consider several sources for potential ideas, including a critical analysis of everyday situations. The steps in developing a topic for investigation naturally become easier with experience; beginning researchers need to pay particular attention to material already available. They should not attempt to tackle broad research questions, but should try to isolate a smaller, more practical subtopic for study. They should develop an appropriate method of analysis and then proceed, through data analysis and interpretation, to a clear and concise presentation of results.

The chapter stresses that the results of a single survey or other research approach only provide indications of what may or may not exist. Before researchers can claim support for a research question or hypothesis, the study must be replicated a number of times to eliminate dependence on extraneous factors.

While conducting research studies, investigators must be constantly aware of potential sources of error that may create spurious results. Phenomena that affect an experiment in this way are sources of breakdowns in internal validity. If and only if differing and rival hypotheses are ruled out can researchers validly say that the treatment was influential in creating differences between the experimental and control groups. A good explanation of research results rules out intervening variables; every plausible rival explanation should be considered. However, even when this is accomplished, the results of one study can be considered only as indications of what may or may not exist. Support for a theory or hypothesis can be made only after the completion of several studies that produce similar results.

In addition, for a study to have substantive worth to the understanding of mass media, the results must be generalizable to subjects and groups other than those involved in the experiment. External validity can be best achieved through randomization of subject selection: there is no substitute for random sampling (Chapter 4).

Questions and Problems for Further Investigation

1. The focus of this chapter is on developing a research topic by defining a major problem area and narrowing the topic to a manageable study. Develop two different research projects in an area of mass media research. Use either an outline or a flowchart format.

2. Replication has long been a topic of debate in scientific research, but until recently, mass media researchers have not paid it a great deal of attention. Read the articles by Reid, Soley, and Wimmer (1981) and Wimmer and Reid (1982). Explain in your own words why replication has not been a major factor in mass media research. What could be done to correct the current situation in replication?

3. In an analysis of the effects of television viewing, it was found that the fewer the hours of television students watched per week, the higher were the scores achieved in school. What alternative

explanations or artifacts might explain such differences? How could these variables be controlled?

4. The fact that some respondents will answer any type of question, whether it is a legitimate question or not, is something novice researchers cannot relate to until they encounter it firsthand. Although it may not work, ask this question to a friend in another class or at a party: What effects do you think the sinking of Greenland into the Labrador Sea will have on the country's fishing industry?

References and Suggested Readings

Agostino, D. (1980). Cable television's impact on the audience of public television. *Journal of Broadcasting, 24*(3), 347–366.

Anderson, J. A. (1987). *Communication research: Issues and methods.* New York: McGraw-Hill.

Babbie, E. R. (1989). *The practice of social research* (5th ed.). Belmont, CA: Wadsworth.

Becker, L. B. (1981). Secondary analysis. In G. H. Stempel & B. H. Westley (Eds.), *Research methods in mass communications.* Englewood Cliffs, NJ: Prentice-Hall.

Becker, L. B., Beam, R., & Russial, J. (1978). Correlates of daily newspaper performance in New England. *Journalism Quarterly, 55,* 100–108.

Campbell, D. T., & Stanley, J. C. (1963). *Experimental and quasi-experimental designs for research.* Skokie, IL: Rand McNally.

Cohen, J. (1965). Some statistical issues in psychological research. In B. B. Wolman (Ed.), *Handbook of clinical psychology.* New York: McGraw-Hill.

Comstock, G., Chaffee, S., Katzman, N., McCombs, M., & Roberts, D. (1978). *Television and human behavior.* New York: Columbia University Press.

Cook, T. D., & Campbell, D. T. (1979). *Quasi-experimentation: Designs and analysis for field studies.* Skokie, IL: Rand McNally.

Glenn, N. (1972). Archival data on political attitudes: Opportunities and pitfalls. In D. Nimmo & C. Bonjean (Eds.), *Political attitudes and public opinion.* New York: David McKay.

Gribben, J., & Rees, M. (1989). *Cosmic coincidences: Dark matter, mankind, and anthropic cosmology.* New York: Bantam Books.

Haskins, J. (1968). *How to evaluate mass communication.* Chicago: Advertising Research Foundation.

Hyman, H. H. (1954). *Interviewing in social research.* Chicago: University of Chicago Press.

Hyman, H. H. (1972). *Secondary analysis of sample surveys.* New York: John Wiley.

Kelly, C. W., Chase, L. J., & Tucker, R. K. (1979). Replication in experimental communication research: An analysis. *Human Communication Research, 5,* 338–342.

Kraus, S., & Davis, D. (1967). *The effects of mass communication on political behavior.* University Park: Pennsylvania State University Press.

Lykken, D. T. (1968). Statistical significance in psychological research. *Psychological Bulletin, 21,* 151–159.

Orne, M. T. (1969). Demand characteristics and the concept of quasi-controls. In R. Rosenthal & R. L. Rosnow (Eds.), *Artifact in behavioral research.* New York: Academic Press.

Reid, L. N., Soley, L. C., & Wimmer, R. D. (1981). Replication in advertising research: 1977, 1978, 1979. *Journal of Advertising, 10,* 3–13.

Rosenberg, M. J. (1965). When dissonance fails: On eliminating evaluation apprehension from attitude measurement. *Journal of Personality and Social Psychology, 1,* 28–42.

Rosenthal, R. (1969). *Experimenter effects in behavioral research.* New York: Appleton-Century-Crofts.

Rubin, R. B., Rubin, A. M., & Piele, L. J. (1985). *Communication research: Stategies and sources.* Belmont, CA: Wadsworth.

Singer, D. G., & Singer, J. L. (1981). Television and the developing imagination of the child. *Journal of Broadcasting, 25,* 373–387.

Tan, A. S. (1977). Why TV is missed: A functional analysis. *Journal of Broadcasting, 21,* 371–380.

Tukey, J. W. (1969). Analyzing data: Sanctification or detective work? *American Psychologist, 24,* 83–91.

Walizer, M. H., & Wienir, P. L. (1978). *Research methods and analysis: Searching for relationships.* New York: Harper & Row.

Wimmer, R. D., & Reid, L. N. (1982). Willingness of communication researchers to respond to replication requests. *Journalism Quarterly, 59,* 317–319.

CHAPTER 3

ELEMENTS OF RESEARCH

C hapters 1 and 2 presented a brief overview of the research process. In this chapter, four basic elements of this process are defined and discussed: concepts and constructs, measurement, variables, and scales. To conduct and understand empirical research, it is necessary to understand these elements.

CONCEPTS AND CONSTRUCTS

A **concept** is a term that expresses an abstract idea formed by generalization from particulars. It is formed by summarizing related observations. For example, a researcher might observe that a public speaker becomes restless, starts to perspire, and continually fidgets with a pencil just before giving an address. The researcher might summarize these observed patterns of behavior and label them *speech anxiety*. On a more concrete level, the word *table* is a concept that represents a wide variety of observable objects, ranging from a plank supported by concrete blocks to a piece of furniture typically found in dining rooms. In mass media, terms such as *message length*, *media usage*, and *readability* are typically used as concepts.

Concepts are important for at least two reasons. First, they reduce the amount of detail researchers must take into account by combining particular characteristics or objects or people into more general categories. For example, a researcher may study families that own personal computers, modems, VCRs, CD players, cordless phones, and DAT players. To make it easier to describe these families, the researcher calls them "Taffies," and categorizes them under the concept of Technologically Advanced Families. Now, instead of describing each of the characteristics that make these families unique, the researcher has a general term that is more inclusive and convenient to use.

Second, concepts facilitate communication among those who have a shared understanding of them. Researchers use concepts to organize their observations into meaningful summaries and to transmit this information to their colleagues. Researchers who use the concept of "agenda setting" to describe a complicated set of audience and media activities will find that their colleagues will understand what is being discussed. Note that individuals must share an understanding of a concept if it is to be useful. Teenagers sometimes use the word *dweeb* to describe their acquaintances, and most teens understand perfectly what is meant by the concept. However, many adults have trouble understanding the concept.

A **construct** is a concept that has three distinct characteristics. First, it is a highly abstract notion that is usually broken down into dimensions represented by lower level concepts. In other words, a construct is a combination of concepts. Second, because of its abstraction, a construct usually can't be observed directly. Third, a construct is usually designed for some particular research purpose so that its exact meaning relates only to the context in which it is found. For example, the construct "involvement" has been used in many advertising studies (Pokrywczynski, 1986). It is a construct that is difficult to see directly, and it includes the concepts of attention, interest, and arousal. Researchers can only observe its likely or presumed manifestations. In some contexts

41

involvement means product involvement; in others it refers to involvement with the message or even with the medium. Its precise meaning depends on the larger research context.

To take another example, in mass communication research, the term *authoritarianism* represents a construct specifically defined to describe a certain type of personality; it comprises nine different concepts, including conventionalism, submission, superstition, and cynicism. Authoritarianism itself cannot be seen; its presence must be determined by some type of questionnaire or standardized test. The results of such tests indicate what authoritarianism might be and whether it is present under given conditions, but they do not provide exact definitions for the concept.

The empirical counterpart of a construct or concept is called a **variable**. Variables are important because they link the empirical world with the theoretical; they are the phenomena and events that can be measured or manipulated in research. Variables can have more than one value along a continuum. For example, the variable "satisfaction with cable TV programs" can take on different values — a person can be satisfied a lot, a little, or not at all — reflecting in the empirical world what the concept "satisfaction with cable TV programs" represents in the theoretical world.

Researchers attempt to test a number of associated variables to develop an underlying meaning or relationship among them. After suitable analysis, the important variables are retained while the others are discarded. These important variables are labeled **marker variables** since they seem to define or highlight the construct under study. After further analysis, new marker variables may be added to increase understanding of the construct and to permit more reliable predictions.

Concepts and constructs are valuable tools in theoretical research. But, as noted in Chapter 1, researchers also function at the observational, or empirical, level. To understand how this is done, it is necessary to examine variables and to know how they are measured.

Independent and Dependent Variables

Variables are classified in terms of their relationship with one another. It is customary to talk about **independent** and **dependent variables**: independent variables are systematically varied by the researcher, while dependent variables are observed and their values presumed to depend on the effects of the independent variables. In other words, the dependent variable is what the researcher wishes to explain. For example, assume that an investigator is interested in determining how the angle of a camera shot affects an audience's perception of the credibility of a television newscaster. Three different versions of a newscast are videotaped: one shot from a very low angle, another from a high angle, and a third from eye level. Groups of subjects are randomly assigned to view one of the three versions and to complete a questionnaire that measures credibility. In this experiment, the camera angle is the independent variable. Its values are systematically varied by the experimenter, who selects only three of the camera angles possible. The dependent variable to be measured is the perceived credibility of the newscaster. If the researcher's assumption is correct, the newscaster's credibility will vary according to the camera angle. (Note that the actual values of the dependent variable are not manipulated; they are simply observed or measured.)

Keep in mind that the distinction between types of variables depends on the purposes of the research. An independent variable in one study may be a dependent variable in another. Also, a research task may involve examining the relationship of more than one independent variable to a single dependent variable. For example, a study designed to examine the impact of type size and page layout on learning would encompass two independent variables (type size and layout) and one dependent variable (learning).

Moreover, in many instances multiple dependent variables are measured in a single study. This type of study, called a *multivariate analysis*, is discussed in Appendix 2.

Other Types of Variables

In nonexperimental research, where there is no active manipulation of variables, different terms are sometimes substituted for independent and dependent variables. The variable that is used for predictions or is assumed to be causal (analogous to the independent variable) is sometimes called the **predictor** or **antecedent variable**. The variable that is predicted or assumed to be affected (analogous to the dependent variable) is sometimes called the **criterion variable**.

Researchers often wish to account for or control variables of certain types for the purpose of eliminating unwanted influences. These **control variables** are used to ensure that the results of the study are due to the independent variables, not some other source. However, a control variable need not always be used to eliminate an unwanted influence. On occasion, researchers use a control variable such as age, sex, or socioeconomic status to divide subjects into specific relevant categories. For example, in studying the relationship between newspaper readership and reading ability, it is apparent that IQ will affect the relationship and must be controlled; thus, subjects may be selected on the basis of IQ scores, or placed in groups with similar scores.

One of the most difficult aspects of any type of research is trying to identify all the variables that may create spurious (false) or misleading results. Some researchers refer to this problem as "noise." Noise can occur even in very simple research projects. For example, a researcher designs a telephone survey that asks respondents to name the local radio station listened to the most during the past week. The researcher uses an open-ended question — that is, no specific response choices are provided; thus the interviewer writes down exactly what each respondent says in answer to the question. When the completed surveys are tabulated, the researcher notices that several people mentioned radio station WAAA. But if the city has a WAAA-AM and a WAAA-FM, which station gets the credit? The researcher cannot arbitrarily assign credit to the AM or the FM station; nor can credit be split, because such a practice may distort the actual listening pattern.

The researcher could attempt call-backs of everyone who said "WAAA," but this method is not suggested for two reasons: (1) the likelihood of reaching all the people who gave that response is low; and (2) even if the first condition is met, some respondents may not recall which station they mentioned originally. The researcher, therefore, is unable to provide a reliable analysis of the data because all possible intervening variables were not considered. (The researcher should have foreseen this problem, and the interviewers should have been instructed to find out in each case whether "WAAA" meant the AM or the FM station.)

Another type of research noise is created by people who unknowingly provide false information. For example, people who keep diaries for radio and television surveys may err in recording the station or channel they tune in; that is, they may listen to or watch station KAAA but incorrectly record KBBB (this problem is partially solved by the use of people meters — see Chapter 14). In addition, people often answer a multiple-choice or yes/no research question at random because they do not wish to appear ignorant or uninformed. To minimize this problem, researchers should construct their measurement instruments with great care. Noise is always present, but a large and representative sample should decrease the effects of some research noise. (In later chapters, noise is referred to as "error.")

Many simplistic problems in research are solved with experience. In many situations, however, researchers understand that total control over all aspects of the research is impossible, and the imposibility of achieving perfect control is accounted for in the interpretation of results.

efining Variables Operationally

r 1 it was stated that an operational ecifies procedures to be followed in or measuring a concept. Research

depends on observations, and observations cannot be made without a clear statement of what is to be observed. An **operational definition** is such a statement.

Operational definitions are indispensable in scientific research because they enable investigators to measure relevant variables. In any study, it is necessary to provide operational def-

---

ILLUSTRATIONS OF OPERATIONAL DEFINITIONS

	Variable	**Operational Definition**
Fcres Richards, Bermas, and Krugman (1989)	Reading of tobacco ads	Eye tracking behavior based on pupil and corneal reflection as measured by an Eye View Monitor System
Carroll (1989)	Television market size	Market ranking as listed in Arbitron Ratings Company, "Revised ADI Market Rankings, 1985–1986"
Lin and Atkin (1989)	TV viewing rules	A five-point scale that measured how frequently family rules were used to govern (1) amount of time the child watches TV; (2) types of shows the child is allowed to watch; (3) how late the child is allowed to watch
Wanta and Leggett (1988)	Clichés used by sports announcers	209 clichés as listed in Harold Evans's *Newsman's English*, various newspaper guidelines, and other clichés as suggested by reporters and journalism instructors contacted during the study
Bergen and Weaver (1988)	Journalists' job satisfaction	Response to the question "All things considered, how satisfied are you with your present job — would you say very satisfied, fairly satisfied, somewhat dissatisfied, very dissatisfied?"

initions for both independent and dependent variables. Table 3.1 contains examples of such definitions taken from research studies in mass communication.

Kerlinger (1986) identified two types of operational definitions, measured and experimental. A measured operational definition specifies how to measure a variable. For instance, a researcher investigating dogmatism and media use might operationally define *dogmatism* as a subject's score on the Twenty-Item Short Form Dogmatism Scale. An experimental operational definition explains how an investigator has manipulated a variable. Obviously, this type of definition is used when defining the independent variable in a laboratory setting. For example, in a study concerning the impact of television violence, the researcher might manipulate media violence by constructing two 8-minute films. The first film, labeled "the violent condition," might contain scenes from a boxing match. The second film, labeled "the nonviolent condition," could depict a swimming race. Or, to take another example, source credibility might be manipulated by alternately attributing an article on health to the *New England Journal of Medicine* and to the *National Enquirer*.

Operationally defining a variable forces the researcher to express abstract concepts in concrete terms. Occasionally, after unsuccessfully grappling with the task of making a key variable operational, the investigator may conclude that the variable as originally conceived is too vague or ambiguous and that redefinition is required. Because operational definitions are expressed so concretely, they can communicate *exactly* what the terms represent. For instance, a researcher might define political knowledge as the number of correct answers on a 20-item true/false test. And while it is possible to argue over the validity of the operational definition "Women possess more political knowledge than men," there is no confusion as to what the statement means.

Finally, there is no single infallible method for operationally defining a variable. No operational definition satisfies everybody. The inves-

tigator must decide which method is best suited for the research problem at hand.

MEASUREMENT

Mass media research, like all research, can be qualitative or quantitative. **Qualitative research** refers to several methods of data collection, which include focus groups, field observation, in-depth interviews, and case studies. Although there are substantial differences among these techniques, all involve what some writers refer to as "getting close to the data" (Chadwick, Bahr, & Albrecht, 1984).

Qualitative research has certain advantages. In most cases, it allows a researcher to view behavior in a natural setting without the artificiality that sometimes surrounds experimental or survey research. In addition, qualitative techniques can increase a researcher's depth of understanding of the phenomenon under investigation. This is especially true when the phenomenon has not been previously investigated. Finally, qualitative methods are flexible and allow the researcher to pursue new areas of interest. A questionnaire is unlikely to provide data about questions that were not asked, but a person conducting a field observation or focus group might discover facets of a subject that were not even considered before the study began.

There are, however, some disadvantages associated with qualitative methods. First of all, sample sizes are generally too small (sometimes as small as one) to allow the researcher to generalize the data beyond the sample selected for the particular study. For this reason, qualitative research is often used as a preliminary step to further investigation rather than the final phase of a project. The information collected from qualitative methods is often used to prepare a more elaborate quantitative analysis, although the qualitative data may in fact constitute all the information needed for a particular study.

Reliability of the data can also be a problem since single observers are describing unique events. Because a person doing qualitative research must become very closely involved with the respondents, loss of objectivity when collecting data is possible. If the researcher becomes too close to the study, the necessary professional detachment may be lost.

Finally, if qualitative research is not properly planned, the project may produce nothing of value. Qualitative research looks easy to conduct, but projects must be carefully planned to ensure that they focus on key issues.

Although this book is primarily about quantitative research, several qualitative methods are discussed in Chapter 7. For those who wish to know more about the other research techniques that make up qualitative analysis, two sources are Anderson (1987) and Lindlof (1987).

Quantitative research requires that the variables under consideration be measured. This form of research is concerned with how often a variable is present and generally uses numbers to communicate this amount. Quantitative research has certain advantages. One is that the use of numbers allows greater precision in reporting results. For example, the Violence Index (Gerbner, Gross, Morgan, & Signorielli, 1980), a quantitative measuring device, makes it possible to report the exact increase or decrease in violence from one television season to another, whereas qualitative research could only describe whether violence went up or down. Another advantage is that quantitative research permits the use of powerful methods of mathematical analysis. The importance of mathematics to mass media research is difficult to overemphasize. As pointed out by measurement expert J. P. Guilford (1954):

> The progress and maturity of a science are often judged by the extent to which it has succeeded in the use of mathematics. . . . Mathematics is a universal language that any science or technology may use with great power and convenience. Its vocabulary of terms is unlimited. . . . Its rules of operation . . . are unexcelled for logical precision.

For the past several years some friction has existed in the mass media field as well as in several other disciplines between those who have favored quantitative methods and those who preferred qualitative techniques. Recently, however, most researchers have come to realize that both qualitative and quantitative techniques are important in understanding any phenomenon. In fact, the term **triangulation**, commonly used by marine navigators, is frequently heard now in conversations about communication research. If a ship picks up signals from only one navigational aid, it is impossible to know the vessel's precise location. If, however, signals from more than one source are detected, elementary geometry can be used to pinpoint location. In the context of this book, *triangulation* refers to the use of both qualitative and quantitative methods to understand fully the nature of a research problem.

Although most of this book is concerned with skills relevant to quantitative research, it is not implied that quantitative research is in any sense "better" than qualitative research. Obviously, each technique has value, and different research questions and goals may make one or the other more appropriate in a given application. Over the past 30 years, however, quantitative research has become more and more common in mass media. Consequently, it is increasingly important for beginning researchers to familiarize themselves with common quantitative techniques.

The Nature of Measurement

The idea behind **measurement** is a simple one: a researcher assigns numerals to objects, events, or properties according to certain rules. Examples of measurement are everywhere: "She or he is a 10." "Unemployment increased by 1%." "The earthquake measured 5.5 on the Richter scale." Note that the definition contains three central concepts: numerals, assignment, and rules. A numeral is a symbol, such as V, X, C, or 5, 10,

100. A numeral has no implicit quantitative meaning. When it is given quantitative meaning, it becomes a number and can be used in mathematical and statistical computations. Assignment is the designation of numerals or numbers to certain objects or events. A simple measurement system might entail assigning the numeral 1 to the people who get most of their news from television, the numeral 2 to those who get most of their news from a newspaper, and the numeral 3 to those who get most of their news from some other source.

Rules specify the way that numerals or numbers are to be assigned. Rules are at the heart of any measurement system; if they are faulty, the system will be flawed. In some situations, the rules are obvious and straightforward. To measure reading speed, a stopwatch and a standardized message may be sufficient. In other instances, the rules are not so apparent. Measuring certain psychological traits such as "source credibility" or "attitude toward violence" calls for carefully explicated measurement techniques.

Additionally, in mass communication research and in much of social science research, investigators usually measure indicators of the properties of individuals or objects rather than the individuals or objects themselves. Concepts such as "authoritarianism" or "motivation for reading the newspaper" cannot be directly observed; they must be inferred from presumed indicators. Thus, if a person endorses statements such as "Orders from a superior should always be followed without question" and "Law and order are the most important things in society," it can be deduced that he or she is more authoritarian than someone who disagreed with the same statements.

Measurement systems strive to be isomorphic to reality. **Isomorphism** means identity or similarity of form or structure. In some research areas, such as the physical sciences, isomorphism is not a key problem, since there is usually a direct relationship between the objects being measured and the numbers assigned to them. For example, if an electrical current travels through Substance A with less resistance than it does through Substance B, it can be deduced that A is a better conductor than B. Testing a few more substances can lead to a ranking of conductors whereby the numbers assigned indicate the degree of conductivity. The measurement system is isomorphic to reality.

In mass media research, the correspondence is seldom that obvious. For example, imagine that a researcher is trying to develop a scale to measure the "persuasibility" of people in connection with a certain type of advertisement. She devises a test and administers it to five people. The scores are displayed in Table 3.2. Now imagine that an omniscient being is able to disclose the "true" persuasibility of the same five people. These scores are also shown in Table 3.2. For two people, the test scores correspond

TABLE 3.2   ILLUSTRATION OF ISOMORPHISM

Person	Test score	"True" score
A	1	0
B	3	1
C	6	6
D	7	7
E	8	12

exactly to the "true" scores. The other three scores miss the "true" scores, but there is a correspondence between the rank orders. Also note that the "true" persuasibility scores ranged from 0 to 12, while the measurement scale ranged from 1 to 8. To summarize, there is a general correspondence between the test and reality, but the test is far from an exact measure of what actually exists.

Unfortunately, the degree of correspondence between measurement and reality is rarely known in research. In some cases researchers are not even sure they are actually measuring what they are trying to measure. In any event, researchers must carefully consider the degree of isomorphism between measurement and reality. This topic is discussed in greater detail later in the chapter.

Levels of Measurement

Scientists have distinguished four different ways to measure things, or four different levels of measurement. The operations that can be performed with a given set of scores depend on the level of measurement achieved. The four levels of measurement are nominal, ordinal, interval, and ratio.

The **nominal level** is the weakest form of measurement. In nominal measurement, numerals or other symbols are used to classify persons, objects, or characteristics. For example, in the physical sciences, rocks can generally be classified into three categories: igneous, sedimentary, and metamorphic. A geologist who assigns a 1 to igneous, a 2 to sedimentary, and a 3 to metamorphic has formed a nominal scale. Note that the numerals are simply labels that stand for the respective categories; they have no mathematical significance. A rock that is placed in Category 3 does not have more "rockness" than those in Categories 2 and 1. Other examples of nominal measurement are numbers on football jerseys and license plates, and social security numbers. An example of nominal measurement in the area of mass communications would be classifying respondents according to the medium they depend on most for news. Those depending most on TV would be in Category 1, those depending most on newspapers would be in Category 2, and so on.

The nominal level, like all levels, possesses certain formal properties. Its basic property is that of equivalence. If an object is placed in Category 1, it is considered equal to all other objects in that category. Suppose a researcher is attempting to classify all the advertisements in a magazine according to primary appeal. If an ad has an economic appeal it is placed in Category 1, if it uses an appeal to fear, it is placed in Category 2, and so on. Note that all ads using "fear appeal" are considered equal even though they may differ on other dimensions, such as product type, size, or use of illustrations.

Another property of nominal measurement is that all categories are exhaustive and mutually exclusive. This means that each measure accounts for every possible option and that each measurement is appropriate to only one category. For instance, in the example of primary appeals in magazine advertisements, all possible appeals would need to be included in the analysis (exhaustive): economic, fear, morality, religion, and so on. Each advertisement would be placed in one and only one category (mutually exclusive).

Nominal measurement is frequently used in mass media research. For example, Hinkle and Elliot (1989) divided science coverage by supermarket tabloids and mainstream newspapers into medical coverage and hard technology stories and discovered that tabloids had far more medical stories. Weinberger and Spotts (1989) divided the use of humorous devices in British and American ads into six nominal categories — pun, understatement, joke, ludicrous, satire, and irony — and found that the use of humor was similar in both countries.

Even when it is measured at the nominal level, a variable may be used in higher order statistics by *transforming* it into another form. The results of this transformation process are known as **dummy variables**. For example, political party affiliation could be coded as follows:

Republican	1
Democrat	2
Independent	3
Other	4

However, this measurement scheme can be interpreted incorrectly to imply that a person classified as "Other" is three units "better" than a person classified as a "Republican." To measure political party affiliation and use the data in higher order statistics, the variable must be transformed into a more neutral form.

One way of transforming the variable to give equivalent value to each option is to recode it as a dummy variable that creates an "either/or" situation for each option: a person is either a "Republican" or something else. For example, a binary coding scheme could be used:

Republican	001
Democrat	010
Independent	100
Other	000

This scheme treats each affiliation equivalently and allows the variable to be used in higher order statistical procedures.

Note that the final category "Other" is coded using all zeros. A complete explanation for this practice is beyond the scope of this book; basically, however, its purpose is to avoid redundancy, since the number of individuals classified as "Other" is known from the data on the first three options. If, in a sample of 100 subjects, 25 are found to belong in each of the first three options, it is obvious that there will be 25 in the "Other" option. (For more information on the topic of dummy variable coding, see Kerlinger & Pedhazur, 1986.)

Objects measured at the **ordinal level** are generally ranked along some dimension, usually in a meaningful way, from smaller to greater. For example, one might measure the variable "socioeconomic status" by categorizing families according to class: lower, lower middle, middle, upper middle, or upper. A rank of 1 is assigned to lower, 2 to lower middle, 3 to middle, and so forth. In this situation, the numbers have some mathematical meaning: families in Category 3 have a higher socioeconomic status than families ranked 2. Note that nothing is specified with regard to the distance between any two rankings. Ordinal measurement has often been compared to a horse race without a stopwatch. The order in which the horses finish is relatively easy to determine, but it is difficult to calculate the difference in time between the winner and the runner-up.

An ordinal scale possesses the property of equivalence; thus in the previous example, all families placed in a category are treated equally, even though some might have greater incomes than others. It also possesses the property of *order* among the categories. Any given category can be defined as being higher or lower than any other category. Common examples of ordinal scales include rankings of football or basketball teams, military ranks, restaurant ratings, and beauty pageant finishing orders.

Ordinal scales are frequently used in mass communication research. Schweitzer (1989) ranked 16 factors that were important to the success of mass communication researchers. In a study of electronic text news, Heeter, Brown, Soffin, Stanley, and Salwen (1989) rank ordered audience evaluations of the importance of 25 different issues in the news and found little evidence for an agenda setting effect.

When a scale has all the properties of an ordinal scale and the intervals between adjacent points on the scale are of equal value, the scale is at the **interval level**. The most obvious example of an interval scale is temperature. The same amount of heat is required to warm an object from 30 to 40 degrees as to warm it from 50 to

60 degrees. Interval scales incorporate the formal property of *equal differences*; that is, numbers are assigned to the positions of objects on an interval scale in such a way that one may carry out arithmetic operations on the differences between them.

One disadvantage of an interval scale is that it lacks a true zero point, or a condition of nothingness. For example, it is difficult to conceive of a person having zero intelligence or zero personality. The lack of a true zero point means that the researcher cannot make statements of a proportional nature: someone with an IQ of 100 is not twice as smart as someone with an IQ of 50, and a person who scores 30 on a test of aggression is not three times as aggressive as a person who scores 10. Despite this disadvantage, interval scales are frequently used in mass communication research. Zohoori (1988) constructed a "motivations for using TV" scale by presenting respondents with a list of 11 reasons for viewing television. The response options ranged from "not at all like me," coded 1; "a little like me," coded 2; and "a lot like me," coded 3. Baren, Mok, Land, and Kang (1989) developed a five-point agree/disagree interval scale to measure a person's worth as seen by others by eliciting responses to seven statements such as "It's likely that I'd have this woman/man as a friend"; "It's fairly likely that this man/woman is punctual."

Scales at the **ratio level** of measurement have all the properties of interval scales plus one more: the existence of *true zero point*. With the introduction of this fixed zero point, ratio judgments can be made. For example, since time and distance are ratio measures, one can say that a car traveling at 50 miles per hour is going twice as fast as a car traveling at 25. Ratio scales are relatively rare in mass media research, although some variables, such as time spent watching television or number of words per story, are ratio measurements. For example, Gantz (1978) measured news recall ability by asking subjects to report whether they had seen or heard 10 items taken from the evening news. Scores could range from 0 to 10 on this test. Giffard (1984) counted the length of wire service reports related to 101 developed or developing nations. Theoretically, scores could range from zero (no coverage) to hundreds of words.

As we shall see in Chapter 12, researchers using interval or ratio data are able to use parametric statistics, which are specifically designed for these data. Procedures designed for use with "lower" types of data can also be used with data at a higher level of measurement. Statistical procedures designed for higher level data, however, are generally more powerful than those designed for use with nominal or ordinal levels of measurement. Thus, if an investigator has achieved the interval level of measurement, parametric statistics should generally be employed.

Statisticians disagree about the importance of the distinction between ordinal and interval scales and about the legitimacy of using interval statistics with data that may in fact be ordinal. Without delving too deeply into these arguments, it appears that the safest procedure is to assume interval measurement unless there is clear evidence to the contrary, in which case ordinal statistics should be employed. For example, for a research task in which a group of subjects ranks a set of objects, ordinal statistics should be used. If, on the other hand, subjects are given an attitude score constructed by rating responses to various questions, the researcher would be justified in using parametric procedures.

Most statisticians seem to feel that statistical analysis is performed on the numbers yielded by the measures, not the measures themselves, and that the properties of interval scales actually belong to the number system (Nunnally, 1978; Roscoe, 1975). Additionally, there have been several studies in which various types of data have been subjected to different statistical analyses. These studies suggest that the distinction between ordinal and interval data is not particularly crucial in selecting an analysis method (McNemar, 1962).

DISCRETE AND CONTINUOUS VARIABLES

Two forms of variables are used in mass media investigations. A **discrete variable** includes only a finite set of values; it cannot be divided into subparts. For instance, the number of children in a family is a discrete variable because the unit is a person. It would not make much sense to talk about a family size of 2.24 because it is hard to conceptualize 0.24 of a person. Political affiliation, population, and sex are other discrete variables.

A **continuous variable** can take on any value (including fractions) and can be meaningfully broken into smaller subsections. Height is a continuous variable. If the measurement tool is sophisticated enough, it is possible to distinguish between one person 72.113 inches tall and another 72.114 inches tall. Time spent watching television is another example. It is perfectly meaningful to say that Person A spent 3.12115 hours viewing while Person B watched 3.12114 hours. The *average* number of children in a family is a continuous variable. In this regard, it may be perfectly legitimate to talk about 0.24 of a person.

When dealing with continuous variables, it is sometimes necessary to keep in mind the distinction between the variable and the measure of the variable. If a child's attitude toward television violence is measured by counting his or her positive responses to six questions, there are only seven possible scores: 0, 1, 2, 3, 4, 5, and 6. It is entirely likely, however, that the underlying variable is continuous even though the measure is discrete. In fact, even if a fractionalized scale were developed, it would still be limited to a finite number of scores. As a generalization, most of the measures in mass communication research tend to be discrete approximations of continuous variables.

Variables measured at the nominal level are always discrete variables. Variables measured at the ordinal level are generally discrete, although there may be some underlying continuous measurement dimension. Variables measured at the interval or ratio level can be either discrete (number of magazine subscriptions in a household) or continuous (number of minutes per day spent reading magazines). Both the level of measurement and the type of variable under consideration are important in developing useful measurement scales.

SCALES

A **scale** represents a composite measure of a variable; it is based on more than one item. Scales are generally used with complex variables that do not easily lend themselves to single-item or single-indicator measurement. Some items, such as age, newspaper circulation, or number of radios in the house, can be adequately measured without scaling techniques. Measurement of other variables, such as attitude toward TV news or gratifications received from moviegoing, generally requires the use of scales.

Several different scaling techniques have been developed over the years. This section discusses only the better known methods.

Thurstone Scales

Thurstone scales are also called *equal-appearing interval scales* because of the technique used to develop them. They are typically used to measure the attitude toward a given concept or construct. To develop a Thurstone scale, a researcher first collects a large number (Thurstone recommended at least 100) of statements that relate to the concept or construct to be measured. Next, judges rate these statements along an 11-category scale in which each category expresses a different degree of favorableness toward the concept. After this laborious task, the items are ranked according to the mean or median ratings assigned by the judges. These values are then used to construct a questionnaire of 20–30 items that are chosen more or less evenly from across the range of ratings. The statements are worded so that a person can agree or disagree with them. The scale is then administered to a sample of respondents whose scores are determined by computing the mean or median value of the items agreed with. A person who disagrees with all the items has a score of zero.

One advantage of the Thurstone method is that it is an interval measurement scale. On the downside, this method is time-consuming and labor intensive. Thurstone scales are not often used in mass media research, but are common in psychology and education research.

Guttman Scaling

Guttman scaling, also known as *scalogram analysis*, is based on the idea that items can be arranged along a continuum in such a way that a person who agrees with an item or finds an item acceptable will also agree with or find acceptable all other items expressing a less extreme position. For example, here is a hypothetical four-item Guttman scale:

1. Indecent programming on TV is harmful to society.
2. Children should not be allowed to watch indecent TV shows.
3. Television station managers should not allow indecent programs on their stations.
4. The government should ban indecent programming from TV.

Presumably, a person who agrees with Statement 4 will also agree with Statements 1–3. Further, assuming the scale is valid, a person who agrees with Statement 2 will also agree with Statement 1, but will not agree with Statements 3 and 4. Because each score represents a unique set of responses, the number of items a person agrees with is the person's total score on a Guttman scale.

A Guttman scale also requires a great deal of time and energy to develop. Although they do not appear often in mass media research, Guttman scales are fairly common in political science, sociology, public opinion research, and anthropology.

Likert Scales

Perhaps the most commonly used scale in mass media research is the **Likert scale**, also called the *summated rating approach*. A number of statements are developed with respect to a topic, and respondents can strongly agree, agree, be neutral, disagree, or strongly disagree with the statements (see Figure 3.1). Each response option is weighted, and each subject's responses are added to produce a single score on the topic.

The basic procedure for developing a Likert scale is as follows:

1. Compile a large number of statements that relate to a specific dimension. Some statements are positively worded; some are negatively worded.
2. Administer the scale to a randomly selected sample of respondents.
3. Code the responses consistently so that high scores indicate stronger agreement with the attitude in question.
4. Analyze the responses and select for the final scale those statements that most clearly differentiate the highest from the lowest scorers.

Semantic Differential Scales

Another commonly used scaling procedure is the **semantic differential** technique. As originally conceived by Charles Osgood and his associates (Osgood, Suci, & Tannenbaum, 1957),

---

FIGURE 3.1   SAMPLE OF LIKERT SCALE ITEMS

1. Only U.S. citizens should be allowed to own broadcasting stations.

Response	Score assigned
_____ Strongly agree	5
_____ Agree	4
_____ Neutral	3
_____ Disagree	2
_____ Strongly disagree	1

2. Prohibiting foreign ownership of broadcasting stations is bad for business.

Response	Score assigned
_____ Strongly agree	1
_____ Agree	2
_____ Neutral	3
_____ Disagree	4
_____ Strongly disagree	5

Note: To maintain attitude measurement consistency, the scores are reversed for a negatively worded item. Question 1 is a positive item; Question 2 is a negative item.

this technique is used to measure the meaning an item has for an individual. Research indicated that three general factors — activity, potency, and evaluation — were measured by the semantic differential. Communication researchers were quick to adapt the evaluative dimension of the semantic differential for use as a measure of attitude.

To use the technique, a name or concept is placed at the top of a series of seven-point scales anchored by bipolar attitudes. Figure 3.2 shows an example of this technique as used to measure attitudes toward *Time* magazine. The bipolar adjectives that typically "anchor" such evaluative scales are pleasant/unpleasant, valuable/ worthless, honest/dishonest, nice/awful, clean/ dirty, fair/unfair, and good/bad. It is recommended, however, that a unique set of anchoring adjectives be developed for each particular measurement situation. For example, Markham (1968), in his study of the credibility of television newscasters, used 13 variable sets, including deep/shallow, ordered/chaotic, annoying/ pleasing, and clear/hazy. Robinson and Shaver (1973) present a collection of scales commonly used in social science research.

Strictly speaking, the semantic differential technique attempts to place a concept in semantic space through the use of an advanced statistical procedure called factor analysis. When

FIGURE 3.2   SAMPLE FORM FOR APPLYING THE SEMANTIC DIFFERENTIAL TECHNIQUE

Time magazine

biased	____:____:____:____:____:____:____	unbiased
trustworthy	____:____:____:____:____:____:____	untrustworthy
valuable	____:____:____:____:____:____:____	worthless
unfair	____:____:____:____:____:____:____	fair
good	____:____:____:____:____:____:____	bad

researchers borrow parts of the technique to measure attitudes, or images or perceptions of objects, persons, or concepts, they are not using the technique as originally developed. Consequently, perhaps a more appropriate name for this technique might be bipolar rating scales.

Reliability and Validity

Developing any scale and using it without prior testing is poor research. At least one pilot study should be conducted for any newly developed scale to ensure its **reliability** and **validity**. To be useful, a measurement must possess these two related qualities.

A measure is reliable if it consistently gives the same answer. Reliability in measurement is the same as reliability in any other context. For example, a reliable person is one who is dependable, stable, and consistent over time. An unreliable person is unstable and unpredictable and may act one way today and another way tomorrow. Similarly, if measurements are consistent from one session to another, they are reliable and can be believed to some degree.

In understanding measurement reliability, it is helpful to think of a measure as containing two components. The first represents an individual's "true" score on the measuring instrument. The second represents random error and does not provide an accurate assessment of what is being measured. Error can slip into the measurement process from several sources. Perhaps a question has been worded ambiguously, or a person's pencil slipped as he or she was filling out a measuring instrument. Whatever the cause, all measurement is subject to some degree of random error. Figure 3.3 illustrates this concept. As is evident, Measurement Instrument 1 is highly reliable — the ratio of the true component of the score to the total score is high. Measurement Instrument 2, however, is unreliable — the ratio of the true component to the total is low.

A completely unreliable measurement measures nothing at all. If a measure is repeatedly given to individuals and each person's responses at a later session are unrelated to that individual's earlier responses, the measure is useless. If the responses are identical or nearly identical each time the measure is given, the measure is reliable — it at least measures something — although not necessarily what the researcher intended (this problem is discussed below).

The importance of reliability should be obvious now. Unreliable measures cannot be used to detect relationships between variables. When the measurement of a variable is unreliable, it is composed mainly of random error, and random error is seldom related to anything else.

FIGURE 3.3   ILLUSTRATION OF "TRUE" AND "ERROR" COMPONENTS OF A SCALE

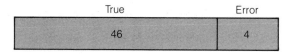

Measurement Instrument 1: Obtained Score = 50

True	Error
46	4

Measurement Instrument 2: Obtained Score = 50

True	Error
30	20

Reliability is not a unidimensional concept. It consists of three different components: stability, internal consistency, and equivalency.

Stability is the easiest of the components to understand. It refers to the consistency of a result or of a measure at different points in time. For example, suppose that a test designed to measure proofreading ability is administered during the first week of an editing class and again during the second week. The test possesses stability if the two results are consistent. Caution should be used whenever stability is used as a measure of reliability, since people and things can change over time. To use the previous example, it is entirely possible for a person to score higher the second time because some people might actually have improved their ability from week one to week two. In this case the measure is not really unstable; actual change has occurred.

An assessment of reliability is necessary in all mass media research and should be reported along with other facets of the research as an aid in interpretation and evaluation. One commonly used statistic for assessing reliability takes the form of a correlation coefficient denoted as r_{xx}. Chapter 9 provides a more detailed examination of the correlation coefficient, but for now we say only that r_{xx} is a number ranging from -1.00 to $+1.00$, used to gauge the strength of a relationship between two variables. When r_{xx} is high—that is, approaching ± 1.00—the relationship is strong. A negative number indicates a negative relationship (high scores on one variable are associated with low scores on the other), and a positive number indicates a positive relationship (a high score goes with another high score). In measuring reliability, a high, positive r_{xx} is desired.

One method that uses correlation coefficients to determine reliability is the *test–retest method*. This procedure measures the stability component of reliability. The same people are measured at two different points in time, and a coefficient between the two scores is computed. An r_{xx} that approaches $+1.00$ indicates that a person's score at Time A was similar to his or her score at Time B, showing consistency over time. There are two limitations to the test–retest technique. First, the initial administration of the measure might affect scores on the second testing. If the measuring device is a questionnaire, a person might remember responses from session to session, thus falsely inflating reliability. Second, the concept measured may change from Time A to Time B, thus lowering the reliability estimate.

Internal consistency involves examining the consistency of performance among the items composing a scale. If separate items on a scale assign the same values to the concept being measured, the scale possesses internal consistency. For instance, suppose a researcher designs a 20-item scale to measure attitudes toward newspaper reading. For the scale to be internally consistent, the total score on the first half of the test should highly correlate with the score on the second half of the test. This method of determining reliability is called the *split-half technique*. Only one administration of the measuring instrument is made, but the test is split into halves and scored separately. For example, if the test is in the form of a questionnaire, the even-numbered items might constitute one half and the odd-numbered items the other. A correlation coefficient is then computed between the two sets of scores. Since this coefficient is computed from a test that is only half as long as the final form, it is corrected by using the following formula:

$$r_{xx} = \frac{2(r_{oe})}{1 + r_{oe}}$$

where r_{oe} is the correlation between the odd and the even items.

Another common reliability coefficient is *alpha* (sometimes referred to as Cronbach's alpha), which uses the analysis of variance approach (Chapter 10) to assess the internal consistency of a measure.

The **equivalency** component of reliability assesses the relative correlation between two parallel forms of a test. Two instruments using different scale items are developed to measure the same concept. The two versions are then administered to the same group of people during a single time period and the correlation between the scores on the two forms of the test is taken as a measure of the reliability. The big problem with this method, of course, is developing two forms of a scale that are perfectly equivalent. The less parallel the two forms, the lower the reliability.

A special case of the equivalency component occurs when two or more observers judge the same phenomenon, as is the case in content analysis (Chapter 8). This type of reliability is called **intercoder reliability** and is used to assess the degree to which a result can be achieved or reproduced by other observers. Ideally, two individuals using the same operational measure and the same measuring instrument should end up with the same results. For example, if two researchers try to identify acts of violence in television content based on a given operational definition of *violence*, the degree to which their results are consistent is a measure of intercoder reliability. Disagreements reflect a difference either in perception or in the way the original definition was interpreted. Special formulas for computing intercoder reliability are discussed in Chapter 8.

In addition to being reliable, a measurement must be valid if it is to be of use in studying variables. A valid measuring device measures what it is supposed to measure. Or, to put it in familiar terms, determining validity requires an evaluation of the congruence between the operational definition of a variable and its conceptual or constitutive definition. Assessing validity requires some degree of judgment on the part of the researcher. In the following discussion of the major types of measurement validity, note that each one depends at least in part on the judgment of the researcher. Also, validity is almost never an all-or-none proposition; it is usually a matter of degree. A measurement rarely turns out to be totally valid or invalid. Typically it winds up somewhere in the middle.

There are four major types of validity, and each has corresponding techniques for evaluating the measurement method. They are: face validity, predictive validity, concurrent validity, and construct validity.

The simplest and most basic kind of validity, *face validity*, is achieved by examining the measurement device to see whether, on the face of it, it measures what it appears to measure. For example, a test designed to measure proofreading ability could include accounting problems, but this measurement would lack face validity. A test that asks people to read and correct certain paragraphs has more face validity as a measure of proofreading skill. Whether a measure possesses face validity depends to some degree on subjective judgment. To minimize subjectivity, the relevance of a given measurement should be independently judged by several experts.

Predictive validity is assessed by checking a measurement instrument against some future outcome. For example, scores on a test to predict whether a person will vote in an upcoming election can be checked against actual voting behavior. If the test scores allow the researcher to predict with a high degree of accuracy which people will actually vote and which will not, the test has predictive validity. Note that it is possible for a measure to have predictive validity and at the same time lack face validity. The sole factor in determining validity in the predictive method is the measurement's ability to correctly forecast future behavior. The concern is not what is being measured but whether the measurement instrument can predict something. Thus, a test to determine whether a person will become a successful mass media researcher could conceivably consist of geometry problems. If it predicts the ultimate success of a researcher reasonably well, the test has predictive validity but little face validity. The biggest problem associated with predictive validity is determining the criteria against which test scores are to be checked. What, for example, constitutes a "successful mass media researcher"? One who obtains an advanced degree? One who publishes research articles? One who writes a book?

Concurrent validity is closely related to predictive validity. In this method, however, the measuring instrument is checked against some present criterion. For example, it is possible to validate a test of proofreading ability by administering the test to a group of professional proofreaders and to a group of nonproofreaders. If the test discriminates well between the two groups, it can be said to have concurrent validity. Similarly, a test of aggression might discriminate between a group of children who are frequently detained after school for fighting and another group who have never been reprimanded for antisocial behavior.

The last form of validity, *construct validity*, is the most complex. In simplified form, construct validity involves relating a measuring instrument to some overall theoretic framework to ensure that the measurement is actually logically related to other concepts in the framework. Ideally, a researcher should be able to suggest various kinds of relationships between the property being measured and other variables. For construct validity to exist, the researcher must show that these relationships are in fact present. For example, an investigator might expect the frequency with which a person views a particular television newscast to be influenced by his or her attitude toward that program. If the measure of attitudes correlates highly with frequency of viewing, there is some evidence for the validity of the attitude measure. By the same token, construct validity is evidenced if the measurement instrument under consideration does *not* relate to other variables when there is no theoretic reason to expect such a relationship. Thus, if an investigator finds a relationship between a measure and other variables that is predicted by a theory and fails to find other relationships that are not predicted by a theory, there is evidence for construct validity. For example, Milavsky, Kessler, Stipp, and Rubens (1982) established the validity of their measure of respondent aggression by noting that, as expected, boys scored higher than girls and that high aggression scores were associated with high levels of parental punishment. In addition, aggression was negatively correlated with scores on a scale measuring prosocial behavior. Figure 3.4 summarizes the various types of validity.

FIGURE 3.4   TYPES OF VALIDITY

Judgment-based	**Criterion-based**	**Theory-based**
Face validity	Predictive validity Concurrent validity	Construct validity

FIGURE 3.5   RELATIONSHIP OF RELIABILITY AND VALIDITY

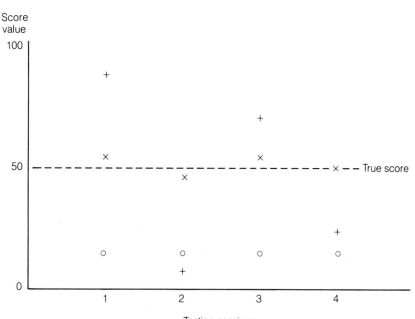

x = measure that is reliable and valid
o = measure that is reliable but not valid
+ = measure that is neither reliable nor valid

Before closing this discussion, it should be pointed out that reliability and validity are related. Reliability is necessary to establish validity, but it is not a sufficient condition — a reliable measure is not necessarily a valid one. Figure 3.5 demonstrates this relationship.

The ×'s represent a test that is both reliable and valid. The scores are consistent from session to session and lie close to the true value. The o's represent a measure that is reliable but not valid. The scores are stable from session to session but they are not close to the true score. The +'s represent a test that is neither valid nor reliable. Scores vary widely from session to session and are not close to the true score.

S U M M A R Y

Understanding empirical research requires a basic knowledge of concepts and constructs, variables, and measurement. Concepts summarize related observations and express an abstract notion that has been formed by generalizing from particulars. Connections among concepts form propositions which, in turn, are used to build theories. Constructs consist of combinations of concepts and are also useful in building theories.

Variables are phenomena or events that take on one or more different values. Independent variables are manipulated by the researcher; dependent variables are what the researcher attempts to explain. All variables are related to the observable world by means of operational definitions.

Researchers frequently use scales to measure complex variables. Thurstone, Guttman, Likert, and semantic differential scales are used in mass media research.

Measurement is the assignment of numerals to objects, events, or properties according to certain rules. There are four levels of measurement: nominal, ordinal, interval, and ratio. To be useful, a measurement must be both reliable and valid.

Questions and Problems for Further Investigation

1. Provide conceptual and operational definitions for the following items:
   a. Violence
   b. Artistic quality
   c. Programming appeal
   d. Sexual content
   e. Objectionable song lyrics
   Compare your definitions to those of others in the class. Would there be any difficulty in conducting a study using these definitions? Might you have demonstrated why so much controversy surrounds the topics, for example, of sex and violence on television?

2. What type of data (nominal, ordinal, interval, ratio) does each of the following concepts or measurements represent?
   a. Baseball team standings
   b. A test of listening comprehension
   c. A. C. Nielsen's list of the top 10 television programs
   d. Frequency of heads versus tails on coin flips
   e. Baseball batting averages
   f. A scale measuring intensity of attitudes toward violence
   g. VHF channels 2–13
   h. A scale for monitoring your weight over time

3. Try to develop a measurement technique that would examine each of the following concepts:
   a. Newspaper reading
   b. Aggressive tendencies
   c. Brand loyalty (to purchase of products)
   d. Television viewing

References and Suggested Readings

Anderson, J. (1987). *Communication research*. New York: McGraw-Hill.

Baran, S. B., Mok, J. J., Land, M., & Kang, T. Y. (1989). You are what you buy. *Journal of Communication, 39*(2), 46–55.

Bergen, L. A., & Weaver, D. (1988). Job satisfaction of daily newspaper journalists and organization size. *Newspaper Research Journal, 9*(2), 1–14.

Bloom, M. (1986). *The experience of research*. New York: MacMillan.

Carroll, R. (1989). Market size and TV news values. *Journalism Quarterly, 66*(1), 48–56.

Chadwick, B., Bahr, H., & Albrecht, S. (1984). *Social science research methods*. Englewood Cliffs, NJ: Prentice-Hall.

Emmert, P., & Barker, L. L. (1989). *Measurement of communication behavior*. White Plains, NY: Longman.

Fischer, P. M., Richards, J. V., Berman, E. J., & Krugman, D. M. (1989). Recall and eye-tracking study of adolescents viewing tobacco advertisements. *Journal of the American Medical Association, 261,* 840–889.

Gantz, W. (1978). How uses and gratifications affect recall of television news. *Journalism Quarterly, 55*(4), 664–672.

Gerbner, G., Gross, L., Morgan, M., & Signorielli, N. (1980). The mainstreaming of America: Violence profile no. 11. *Journal of Communication, 30*(3), 10–29.

Giffard, C. (1984). Developed and developing nations' news in U.S. wire service files to Asia. *Journalism Quarterly, 61*(1), 14–19.

Guilford, J. P. (1954). *Psychometric methods*. New York: McGraw-Hill.

Heeter, C., Brown, N., Soffin, S., Stanley, C., & Salwen, M. (1989). Agenda setting by electronic text news. *Journalism Quarterly, 66*(1), 101–106.

Hinkle, G., & Elliott, W. R. (1989). Science coverage in three newspapers and three supermarket tabloids. *Journalism Quarterly, 66*(2), 353–358.

Hsia, H. J. (1988). *Mass communication research methods*. Hillsdale, NJ: Lawrence Erlbaum.

Kerlinger, F. (1986). *Foundations of behavioral research* (3rd ed.). New York: Holt, Rinehart & Winston.

Kerlinger, F., & Pedhazur, E. (1986). *Multiple regression in behavioral research* (2nd ed.). New York: Holt, Rinehart & Winston.

Lin, C. A., & Atkin, D. J. (1989). Parental mediation and rulemaking for adolescent use of television and VCRs. *Journal of Broadcasting and Electronic Media, 33*(1), 53–69.

Lindlof, T. R. (Ed.). (1987). *Natural audiences: Qualitative research of media uses and effects*. Norwood, NJ: Ablex Publishing Company.

Markham, D. (1968). The dimensions of source credibility for television newscasters. *Journal of Communication, 18*(1), 57–64.

Mason, E. J., & Bramble, W. J. (1989). *Understanding and conducting research* (2nd ed.). New York: McGraw-Hill.

McNemar, Q. (1962). *Psychological statistics*. New York: John Wiley.

Milavsky, J., Kessler, R., Stipp, H., & Rubens, W. (1982). *Television and aggression*. New York: Academic Press.

Nunnally, J. (1978). *Psychometric theory*. New York: McGraw-Hill.

Osgood, C., Suci, G., & Tannenbaum, P. (1957). *The measurement of meaning*. Urbana: University of Illinois Press.

Pokrywczynski, J. (1986). *Advertising effects and viewer involvement with televised sports*. Unpublished doctoral dissertation, University of Georgia, Athens.

Robinson, J., & Shaver, P. (1973). *Measures of social psychological attitudes* (2nd ed.). Ann Arbor, MI: Institute for Social Research.

Roscoe, J. (1975). *Fundamental research statistics for the behavioral sciences*. New York: Holt, Rinehart & Winston.

Schweitzer, J. C. (1989). Factors affecting scholarly research among mass communication faculty. *Journalism Quarterly, 66*(2), 410–417.

Smith, M. J. (1988). *Contemporary communication research methods*. Belmont, CA: Wadsworth.

Wanta, W., & Leggett, D. (1988). Hitting paydirt: Capacity theory and sports announcers' use of clichés. *Journal of Communication, 38*(4), 82–89.

Weinberger, M. G., & Spotts, H. E. (1989). Humor in U.S. versus U.K. TV commercials. *Journal of Advertising, 18*(2), 39–44.

Williams, F., Rice, R., & Rogers, E. (1988). *Research methods and the new media.* New York: Free Press.

Zohoori, A. R. (1988). A cross-cultural analysis of children's television use. *Journal of Broadcasting and Electronic Media, 32*(1), 105–113.

CHAPTER 4

SAMPLING

his chapter describes the basics of the sampling methods that are widely used in mass media research. However, considering that sampling theory has become a distinct discipline in itself, there are some studies, such as nationwide surveys, that require a consultation of more technical discussions of sampling (for example, Blalock, 1972; Cochran, 1963; Kish, 1965; Raj, 1972).

POPULATION AND SAMPLE

One goal of scientific research is to describe the nature of a **population**, that is, a group or class of subjects, variables, concepts, or phenomena (Walizer & Wienir, 1978). In some cases this is achieved through the investigation of an entire class or group, such as a study of prime-time television programs during the week of September 10–16. The process of examining every member of such a population is called a **census**. In many situations, however, the chance of investigating an entire population is remote, if not nonexistent, due to time and resource constraints. Studying every member of a population is also generally cost prohibitive, and may in fact confound the research because measurements of large numbers of people often affect measurement quality.

The usual procedure in these instances is to select a **sample** from the population. A sample is a subset of the population that is taken to be representative of the entire population. An important word in this definition is *representative*. A sample that is not representative of the population, regardless of its size, is inade-

quate for testing purposes: the results cannot be generalized.

The sample selection process is illustrated using a Venn diagram (Figure 4.1); the population is represented by the larger of the two spheres. A census would test or measure every element in the population (A); a sample would measure or test a segment of the population (A_1). Although in Figure 4.1 it might seem that the sample is drawn from only one portion of the population, it is actually selected from every portion. Assuming that a sample is chosen according to proper guidelines and is representative of the population, the results from a study using the sample can be generalized to the population. However, generalizing results must proceed with some caution because of the error that is inherent in all sample selection methods. Theoretically, when a population is studied, only measurement error (that is, inconsistencies produced by the instrument used) will be present. However, when a sample is drawn from the population, the procedure introduces the likelihood of sampling error (that is, the degree to which measurements of the units or subjects selected differ from those of the population as a whole). Because a sample does not provide the exact data that a population would, the potential error must be taken into account.

A classic example of sampling error occurred during the 1936 presidential campaign. *Literary Digest* had predicted, based on the results of a sample survey, that Alf Landon would beat Franklin D. Roosevelt. Although the *Digest* sample included more than a million voters, it was composed mainly of affluent Republicans. Consequently, it inaccurately represented the population of eligible voters in that election.

FIGURE 4.1   A VENN DIAGRAM, AS USED IN THE PROCESS OF SAMPLE SELECTION

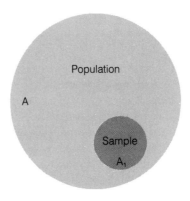

The researchers who conducted the study had failed to consider the population **parameters** (characteristics) before selecting their sample. Of course FDR was reelected in 1936, and it may be no coincidence that the *Literary Digest* went out of business shortly thereafter.

PROBABILITY AND NONPROBABILITY SAMPLES

A **probability sample** is selected according to mathematical guidelines whereby the chance for selection of each unit is known. A **nonprobability sample** does not follow the guidelines of mathematical probability. However, the most significant characteristic distinguishing the two types of samples is that probability sampling allows researchers to calculate the amount of sampling error present in a research study; nonprobability sampling does not.

In deciding whether to use a probability or a nonprobability sample, a researcher should consider four points.

1. *Purpose of the study.* Some research studies are not designed for generalization to the population, but rather to investigate variable relationships or to collect exploratory data for designing questionnaires or measurement instruments. A nonprobability sample is often appropriate in situations of these types.

2. *Cost versus value.* The sample should produce the greatest value for the least investment. If the cost of a probability sample is too high in relation to the type and quality of information collected, a nonprobability sample is a possible alternative.

3. *Time constraints.* In many cases researchers collecting preliminary information operate under time constraints imposed by sponsoring agencies, management directives, or publication guidelines. Since probability sampling is often time-consuming, a nonprobability sample may provide temporary relief.

4. *Amount of error allowed.* In preliminary or pilot studies, where error control is not a

prime concern, a nonprobability sample is usually adequate.

Probability sampling generally incorporates some type of systematic selection procedure, such as a table of random numbers, to ensure that each unit has an equal chance of being selected. However, it does not always guarantee a representative sample from the population, even when systematic selection is followed. It is possible to randomly select 50 members of the student body at a university in order to determine the average height of all students enrolled and, by extraordinary coincidence, end up with 50 candidates for the basketball team. Such an event is unlikely, but it is possible, and this possibility underscores the need to replicate any study.

Types of Nonprobability Samples

Nonprobability sampling is frequently used in mass media research, particularly in the form of available samples, samples using volunteer subjects, and purposive samples. Mall intercepts (Chapter 6) use nonprobability sampling. An **available sample** (also known as **convenience sample**) is a collection of readily accessible subjects for study, such as a group of students enrolled in an introductory mass media course, or shoppers in a mall. Although available samples can be helpful in collecting exploratory information and may produce useful data in some instances, the samples are problematic because they contain unknown quantities of error. Researchers need to consider the positive and negative qualities of available samples before using them in a research study.

Available samples are a subject of heated debate in many research fields. Critics argue that regardless of what results they may generate, available samples do not represent the population and therefore have no external validity. (This problem was discussed in Chapter 2.)

Proponents of the available sample procedure claim that if a phenomenon, characteristic, or trait does in fact exist, it should exist in *any* sample. In addition, Raj (1972) has contested the very notion of sample representativeness:

> Some writers suggest the use of a "representative" sample as a safeguard against the hazards of sampling. This is an undefined term which appears to convey a great deal but which is unhelpful. If it means the sample should be a miniature of the population in every respect, we do not know how to select such a sample.

Available samples can be useful in pretesting questionnaires or other preliminary (pilot study) work. They often help eliminate potential problems in research procedures, testing, and methodology before the final research study is attempted.

Subjects who constitute a **volunteer sample** also form a nonprobability sample, since the individuals are not selected mathematically. There is concern in all areas of research with regard to persons who willingly participate in research projects; these subjects differ greatly from nonvolunteers and may consequently produce erroneous research results. Rosenthal and Rosnow (1969) identified the characteristics of volunteer subjects on the basis of several studies and found that such subjects, in comparison with nonvolunteers, tend to exhibit higher educational levels, higher occupational status, greater need for approval, higher intelligence, and lower authoritarianism. They also seem to be more sociable, more "arousal-seeking," and more unconventional; they are more likely to be first children, and they are generally younger.

These characteristics mean that use of volunteer subjects may significantly bias the results of a research study and may lead to inaccurate estimates of various population parameters (Rosenthal & Rosnow, 1969). Also, available data seem to indicate that volunteers may more often than nonvolunteers provide data to support a researcher's hypothesis. In some cases volunteer subjects are necessary — for example, in comparison tests of products or services. However, volunteers should be used with caution because, as with available samples, there is an unknown quantity of error present in the data.

Although volunteer samples have been shown to be inappropriate in scientific research, the electronic media have begun to legitimize volunteers through the various polls conducted on radio and television stations, and the television networks. Local television news programs, for example, often report the results of the latest "viewer poll" about some local concern. MTV reports the results of a weekly artist popularity poll conducted by having viewers call an 800 telephone number. And ABC asks viewers to call a 900 number to vote on the "greatest moments" shown during the halftime of *Monday Night Football* (the survey votes cost viewers 95¢ each). Even though announcers occasionally say that the polls are not intended to be scientific in nature, the results are presented as such. Unwary listeners and viewers are being conned by the media. Such telephone polls are disturbing to legitimate scientific researchers.

A **purposive sample** includes subjects selected on the basis of specific characteristics or qualities and eliminates those who fail to meet these criteria. Purposive samples are often used in advertising studies: researchers select subjects who use a particular type of product and ask them to compare it with a new product. A purposive sample is chosen with the knowledge that it is not representative of the general population; rather it attempts to represent a specific portion of the population. In a similar method, the **quota sample**, subjects are selected to meet a predetermined or known percentage. For example, a researcher interested in finding out how VCR owners differ in their use of television from non-VCR-owners may know that 10% of a particular population owns a VCR. The sample the researcher selected, therefore, would be composed of 10% of VCR owners and 90% non-VCR-owners (to reflect the population characteristics).

Another nonprobability sampling method is to select subjects haphazardly on the basis of appearance or convenience, or because they seem to meet certain requirements (the subjects *look* educated). Haphazard selection involves researcher subjectivity and introduces error. Some haphazard samples give the illusion of a probability sample; these must be carefully approached. For example, interviewing every 10th person who walks by in a shopping center is haphazard, since not everyone in the population has an equal chance of walking by that particular location. Some people live across town, some shop in other centers, and so on.

Some researchers, research suppliers, and field services try to work around the problems associated with convenience samples in mall intercepts by using a procedure based on what is called "The Law of Large Numbers." Essentially, the researchers interview *thousands* of respondents instead of hundreds. The presumption (and sales approach used on clients) is that the large number of respondents eliminates the problems of convenience sampling. *It does not.* The large number approach is *still* a convenience sample. It is not a random sample as described in the first sentence of the next section.

Types of Probability Samples

The most basic type of probability sampling is the simple **random sample**, where each subject or unit in the population has an equal chance of being selected. If a subject or unit is drawn from the population and removed from subsequent selections, the procedure is known as random sampling *without replacement* — the most widely used random sampling method. Random sampling *with replacement* involves returning the subject or unit into the population so that it has a chance of being chosen another time. Sampling with replacement is often used in more complicated research studies such as nationwide surveys (Raj, 1972).

Researchers usually use a table of random numbers to generate a simple random sample. For example, a researcher who wants to analyze 10 prime-time television programs out of a total population of 100 programs to determine how the medium portrays elderly people can take a random sample from the 100 programs by numbering each show from 00 to 99 and then select-

ing 10 numbers from a table of random numbers, such as the brief listing in Table 4.1. First, a starting point in the table is selected at random. There is no specific way to choose a starting point; it is an arbitrary decision. The researcher then selects the remaining 9 numbers by going up, down, left, or right on the table — or even randomly throughout the table. For example, if it is decided to go down in the table from the starting point 44 until a sample of 10 has been drawn, the sample would include television programs numbered 44, 85, 46, 71, 17, 50, 66, 56, 03, and 49.

TABLE 4.1   RANDOM NUMBERS

38	71	81	39	18	24	33	94	56	48	80	95	52	63	01	93	62
27	29	03	62	76	85	37	00	44	11	07	61	17	26	87	63	79
34	24	23	64	18	79	80	33	98	94	56	23	17	05	96	52	94
32	44	31	87	37	41	18	38	01	71	19	42	52	78	80	21	07
41	88	20	11	60	81	02	15	09	49	96	38	27	07	74	20	12
95	65	36	89	80	51	03	64	87	19	06	09	53	69	37	06	85
77	66	74	33	70	97	79	01	19	44	06	64	39	70	63	46	86
54	55	22	17	35	56	66	38	15	50	77	94	08	46	57	70	61
33	95	06	68	60	97	09	45	44	60	60	07	49	98	78	61	88
83	48	36	10	11	70	07	00	66	50	51	93	19	88	45	33	23
34	35	86	77	88	40	03	63	36	35	73	39	(44)	06	51	48	84
58	35	66	95	48	56	17	04	44	99	79	87	85	01	73	33	65
98	48	03	63	53	58	03	87	97	57	16	38	46	55	96	66	80
83	12	51	88	33	98	68	72	79	69	88	41	71	55	85	50	31
56	66	06	69	44	70	43	49	35	46	98	61	17	63	14	55	74
68	07	59	51	48	87	64	79	19	76	46	68	50	55	01	10	61
20	11	75	63	05	16	96	95	66	00	18	86	66	67	54	68	06
26	56	75	77	75	69	93	54	47	39	67	49	56	96	94	53	68
26	45	74	77	74	55	92	43	37	80	76	31	03	48	40	25	11
73	39	44	06	59	48	48	99	72	90	88	96	49	09	57	45	07
34	36	64	17	21	39	09	97	33	34	40	99	36	12	12	53	77
26	32	06	40	37	02	11	83	79	28	38	49	44	84	94	47	32
04	52	85	62	24	76	53	83	52	05	14	14	49	19	94	62	51
33	93	35	91	24	92	47	57	23	06	33	56	07	94	98	39	27
16	29	97	86	31	45	96	33	83	77	28	14	40	43	59	04	79

Simple random samples for use in telephone surveys are often obtained by a process called **random digit dialing**. One method involves randomly selecting four-digit numbers (usually generated by a computer or through the use of a random numbers table) and adding them to the three-digit exchange prefixes in the city in which the survey is conducted. A single four-digit series may be used once, or it may be added to all the prefixes.

Unfortunately, a large number of the telephone numbers generated by this method of random digit dialing are invalid because some phones have been disconnected, some numbers generated have not yet been assigned, and for other reasons. Therefore, it is advisable to produce at least three times the number of telephone numbers needed; if a sample of 100 is required, at least 300 numbers should be generated to allow for invalid numbers.

A second random digit dialing method that tends to decrease the occurrence of invalid numbers involves adding from one to three random digits to a telephone number selected from a phone directory or list of phone numbers. One first selects a number from a list of telephone numbers (a directory or list purchased from a supplier). Assume that the number 448-3047 was selected from the list. The researcher could simply add a predetermined number, say 6, to produce 448-3053; or a predetermined two-digit number, say 21, to achieve 448-3068; or even a three-digit number, say 112, to produce 448-3159. Each variation of the method helps to eliminate many of the invalid numbers produced in pure random number generation, since telephone companies tend to distribute telephone numbers in series, or blocks. In this example, the block 30— is in use, and there is a good chance that random add-ons to this block will be residential telephone numbers.

As indicated here, random number generation is possible via a variety of methods. However, two rules are always applicable: (1) each unit or subject in the population must have an equal chance of being selected, and (2) the selection procedure must be free from subjective intervention by the researcher. The purpose of random sampling is to reduce sampling error; violating random sampling rules only increases the chance of introducing such error into a study.

Similar in some ways to simple random sampling is a procedure called **systematic sampling**, in which every *n*th subject or unit is se-

---

S I M P L E   R A N D O M   S A M P L E

Advantages

1. Detailed knowledge of the population is not required.
2. External validity may be statistically inferred.
3. A representative group is easily obtainable.
4. The possibility of classification error is eliminated.

Disadvantages

1. A list of the population must be compiled.
2. A representative sample may not result in *all* cases.
3. The procedure can be more expensive than other methods.

lected from a population. For example, to get a sample of 20 from a population of 100, or a **sampling rate** of 1/5, a researcher randomly selects a starting point and a **sampling interval**. Thus, if the number 11 is chosen, the sample will include the 20 subjects or items numbered 11, 16, 21, 26, and so on. To add further randomness to the process, the researcher may randomly select both the starting point and the interval. For example, an interval of 11 together with a starting point of 29 would generate the numbers 40, 51, 62, 73, and so on.

Systematic samples are frequently used in mass media research. They often save time, resources, and effort when compared to simple random samples. In fact, since the procedure so closely resembles a simple random sample, many researchers consider systematic sampling equal to the random procedure (Babbie, 1989). The method is widely used in selecting subjects from lists such as telephone directories, *Broadcasting/Cablecasting Yearbook*, and *Editor & Publisher*.

The degree of accuracy of systematic sampling depends on the adequacy of the **sampling frame**, or a complete list of members in the population. Telephone directories are inadequate sampling frames in most cases, since not all phone numbers are listed, and some people do not have telephones at all. However, lists that include all the members of a population have a high degree of precision. Before deciding to use systematic sampling, one should consider the goals and purpose of a study, as well as the availability of a comprehensive list of the population. If such a list is not available, systematic sampling is probably ill-advised.

One major problem associated with systematic sampling is that the procedure is susceptible to **periodicity**; that is, the arrangements or order of the items in the population list may bias the selection process. For example, consider the problem mentioned earlier of analyzing television programs to determine how the elderly are portrayed. Quite possibly, every 10th program listed may have been aired by ABC; the result would be a nonrepresentative sampling of the three networks.

Periodicity also causes problems when telephone directories are used to select samples. The alphabetical listing does not allow each person or household an equal chance of being selected. One way to solve the problem is to cut each name from the directory, place them in a "hat," and draw names randomly. Obviously, this would take days to accomplish and is not a real alternative. An easier way to use a directory is to tear the pages loose, mix them up, randomly

---

SYSTEMATIC SAMPLING

Advantages
1. Selection is easy.
2. Selection can be more accurate than in a simple random sample.
3. The procedure is generally inexpensive.

Disadvantages
1. A complete list of the population must be obtained.
2. Periodicity may bias the process.

select pages, and then randomly select names. Although this procedure doesn't totally solve the problem, it is generally accepted when simple random sampling is impossible. If periodicity is eliminated, systematic sampling can be an excellent sampling methodology.

Although a simple random sample is the usual choice in most research projects, some researchers don't wish to rely on randomness. In some projects, researchers want to *guarantee* that a specific subsample of the population is adequately represented. No such guarantee is possible using a simple random sample. A **stratified sample** is the approach used when adequate representation from a subsample is desired. The characteristics of the subsample (strata or segment) may include almost any variable: age, sex, religion, income level, or even individuals who listen to specific radio stations or read certain magazines. The strata may be defined by an almost unlimited number of characteristics; however, each additional variable or characteristic makes the subsample more difficult to find. Therefore, incidence drops.

Stratified sampling ensures that a sample is drawn from a homogeneous subset of the population, that is, from a population with similar characteristics. **Homogeneity** helps researchers to reduce sampling error. For example, consider a research study on subjects' attitudes toward two-way, interactive cable television. The investigator, knowing that cable subscribers tend to have higher achievement levels, may wish to stratify the population according to education. Before randomly selecting subjects, the researcher divides the population into three levels: grade school, high school, and college. Then, if it is determined that 10% of the population completed college, a random sample proportional to the population should contain 10% who meet this standard. As Babbie (1989, p. 190) noted:

> Stratified sampling ensures the proper representation of the stratification variables to enhance representation of other variables related to them. Taken as a whole, then, a stratified sample is likely to be more representative on a number of variables than a simple random sample.

Stratified sampling can be applied in two different ways. **Proportionate stratified sampling** includes strata with sizes based on their proportion in the population. If 30% of the population is adults 18–24, then 30% of the total

---

STRATIFIED SAMPLING

Advantages
1. Representativeness of relevant variables is ensured.
2. Comparisons can be made to other populations.
3. Selection is made from a homogeneous group.
4. Sampling error is reduced.

Disadvantages
1. A knowledge of the population prior to selection is required.
2. The procedure can be costly and time-consuming.
3. It can be difficult to find a sample if incidence is low.
4. Variables that define strata may not be relevant.

---

sample will be subjects in this age group. This procedure is designed to give each person in the population an equal chance of being selected. **Disproportionate stratified sampling** is used to oversample or overrepresent a particular stratum. The approach is used basically because the stratum is considered important for some reason: marketing, advertising, or other similar reasons. For example, a radio station that targets 25- to 54-year-olds may have ratings problems with the 25- to 34-year-old group. In a telephone study of 500 respondents, the station management may wish to have the sample represented as: years old, *70% 25–34, 20% 35–49,* and *10% 50–54.* This distribution would allow researchers to break the 25–34 group in smaller groups such as males, females, fans of specific stations, and other subcategories and still have reasonable sample sizes.

The usual sampling procedure is to select one unit or subject at a time. But this requires the researcher to have a complete list of the population. In some cases there is no way to obtain such a list. One way to avoid this problem is to select the sample in groups or categories; this procedure is known as **cluster sampling**. For example, analyzing magazine readership habits of people in the state of Wisconsin would be time-consuming and complicated if individual

subjects were randomly selected. With cluster sampling, one can divide the state into districts, counties, or zip code areas and select groups of people from these areas.

Cluster sampling creates two types of error: in addition to the error involved in defining the initial clusters, errors may arise in selecting from the clusters. For example, a zip code area may comprise mostly residents of a low socioeconomic status who are unrepresentative of the remainder of the state; if selected for analysis, such a group may confound the research results. To help control such error, it is best to use small areas or clusters, both to decrease the number of elements in each cluster and to maximize the number of clusters selected (Babbie, 1989).

In many nationwide studies, researchers use a form of cluster sampling called **multistage sampling**, in which individual households or persons are selected, not groups. Figure 4.2 demonstrates a four-stage sequence for a nationwide survey. First, a cluster of counties (or another specific geographic area) in the United States is selected. This cluster is narrowed by randomly selecting a county, district, or block group within the principal cluster. Next, individual blocks are selected within each area. Finally, a convention such as "the third household from the northeast corner" is established, and

CLUSTER SAMPLING

Advantages
1. Only part of the population need be enumerated.
2. Costs are reduced if clusters are well defined.
3. Estimates of cluster parameters are made and compared to the population.

Disadvantages
1. Sampling errors are likely.
2. Clusters may not be representative of the population.
3. Each subject or unit must be assigned to a specific cluster.

FIGURE 4.2   CENSUS TRACTS

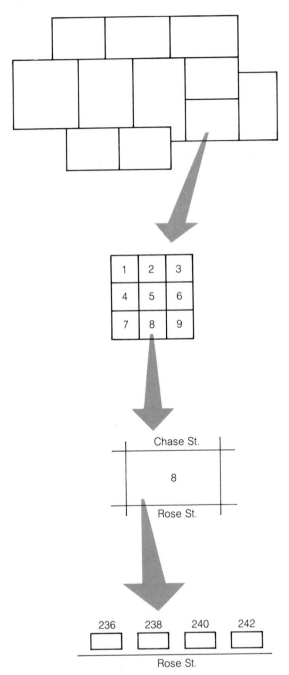

TABLE 4.2   EXAMPLE OF MATRIX FOR SELECTING RESPONDENTS AT RANDOM

	Number of people in household						
	1	**2**	**3**	**4**	**5**	**6**	**7**
Person to interview:	1	2	1	3	5	5	7
		1	3	4	3	2	6
			2	2	1	4	1
				1	2	6	4
					4	1	3
						3	2
							5

then the individual households in the sample can be identified by applying the selection formula in the stages just described.

In many cases researchers also need to randomly select an individual in a given household. In most cases researchers cannot count on being able to interview the person who happens to answer the telephone. Usually demographic quotas are established for a research study, which means that a certain percentage of all respondents must be of a certain sex or age. In this type of study, researchers determine which person in the household should answer the questionnaire by using a form of random numbers table, as illustrated in Table 4.2.

To get a random selection of individuals in the selected households, the interviewer simply asks each person who answers the telephone, "How many people are there in your home who are age 12 or older?" If the first respondent answers "Five," the interviewer asks to speak to the fifth oldest (the youngest in this case) person in the home. Each time a call is completed, the interviewer checks off on the table the number representing the person questioned. If the next household called also had five family members, the interviewer would move to the next number

in the 5 column and ask to talk to the third oldest person in the home.

The same table can be used to select respondents by sex. That is, the interviewer could ask, "How many males who are age 12 or older live in your home?" The interviewer could then ask for the "nth" oldest male, or female, according to the requirements of the survey.

Since the media are complex systems, researchers frequently encounter complicated sampling methods. These are known as *hybrid* situations. Consider some researchers attempting to determine the potential for videotext distribution of a local newspaper to cable subscribers. This problem requires investigating readers and nonreaders of the newspaper as well as cable subscribers and nonsubscribers. The research, therefore, requires random sampling from the following four groups:

Group A	Subscribers/Readers
Group B	Subscribers/Nonreaders
Group C	Nonsubscribers/Readers
Group D	Nonsubscribers/Nonreaders

The researchers must identify each subject as belonging to one of these four groups. If three variables were involved, sampling from eight groups would be required, and so on. In other words, researchers are often faced with very complicated sampling situations that involve numerous steps.

SAMPLE SIZE

Determining an adequate sample size is one of the most controversial aspects of sampling. How large must a sample be to provide the desired level of confidence in the results? Unfortunately, there is no simple answer. There are suggested sample sizes for various statistical procedures, but no single sample size formula or method is available for every research method or statistical procedure. For this reason, it is advisable to consult sampling texts for information concerning specific techniques (Cochran, 1963; Raj, 1972).

The size of the sample required for a study depends on at least one or more of the following seven points: (1) project type, (2) project purpose, (3) project complexity, (4) amount of error willing to be tolerated, (5) time constraints, (6) financial constraints, and (7) previous research in the area. Research designed as a preliminary investigation to search for general indications generally does not require a large sample. However, projects intended to answer significant questions (those designed to provide information for decisions involving large sums of money or decisions that may affect people's lives) require high levels of precision and, therefore, large samples.

A few general principles guide researchers in determining an acceptable sample size. These suggestions are not based on mathematical or statistical theory, but they should provide a starting point in most cases.

1.   A primary consideration in determining sample size is the research method used. Focus groups (Chapter 7) use samples of 6–12 people, but the results are not intended to be generalized to the population from which the respondents were selected. Samples of 25–50 are commonly used for pretesting measurement instruments, pilot studies, and for studies conducted only for heuristic value.

2.   A sample of 100 subjects per demographic group (such as adults 18–24 years old) is often used by researchers. This base figure is used to "back in" to a total sample size. For example, assume a researcher is planning to conduct a telephone study with adults 18–54. Using the normal mass media age spans of 18–24, 25–34, 35–44, and 45–54, the researcher would probably consider a total sample of 400 as satisfactory (100 per age group, or "cell"). However, the researcher may also wish to investigate the differences in opinions/attitudes among men and women, which produces a total of eight different demographic cells. In this case, a sample of 800 would probably be used — 100 for each of the cell possibilities.

3.   Sample size is almost always controlled by cost and time. Although researchers may wish to use a sample of 1,000 for a survey, the economics of such a sample are usually prohibitive. Research with 1,000 respondents can *easily* exceed $50,000. Most research is conducted using a sample that conforms to the project's budget. If a small sample is forced on a researcher by someone else (a client or project manager), the results must be interpreted accordingly — that is, with caution regarding the generalization of results.

4.   Multivariate studies (Appendix 2) always require larger samples than univariate studies because they involve the analysis of multiple response data (several measurements on the same subject). One guideline recommended for multivariate studies is: 50 = very poor; 100 = poor; 200 = fair; 300 = good; 500 = very good; 1,000 = excellent (Comrey, 1973). Other researchers suggest using a sample of 100 *plus* 1 subject for each dependent variable in the analysis (Gorsuch, 1974).

5. Researchers should always select a larger sample than is actually required for a study, since mortality must be compensated for. Subjects drop out of research studies for one reason or another, and allowances must be made for this in planning the sample selection. Subject mortality is especially prevalent in panel studies, where the same group of subjects is tested or measured frequently over a long period of time. In most cases, researchers can expect from 10% to 25% of the sample to drop out of a study before it is completed.

6. Information about sample size is available in published research. Consulting the work of other researchers provides a base from which to start. If a survey is planned and similar research indicates that a representative sample of 400 has been used regularly with reliable results, a sample larger than 400 may be unnecessary.

7. Generally speaking, the larger the sample used, the better. However, a large unrepresentative sample is as meaningless as a small unrepresentative sample, so researchers should not consider numbers alone. Quality is always more important in sample selection than mere size.

SAMPLING ERROR

Since researchers deal with samples from a population, there must be some way for them to compare the results of (or make inferences about) what was *found* in the sample to what *exists* in the target population. The comparison allows researchers to determine the accuracy of their data and involves the computation of error. All research involves error: **sampling error**, **measurement error**, and **random error** (also called unknown or uncontrollable error). Sampling error is also known as **standard error**. The different sources of error are additive. That is, total error is the sum of the three different sources. This section discusses sampling error in mass media research.

Sampling error occurs when measurements taken from a sample do not correspond to what exists in the population. For example, assume we wish to measure attitudes toward a new television program by 18- to 24-year-old viewers in Denver, Colorado. Further assume that all the viewers produce an average score of 6 on a 10-point program appeal measurement scale. Some viewers may dislike the program and rate the show a 1, 2, or 3, some find it mediocre and rate it 4, 5, 6, or 7, whereas the remaining viewers consider the show one of their favorites and rate it an 8, 9, or 10. The differences among the 18- to 24-year-old viewers provide an example of how sampling error may occur. If we asked each viewer to rate the show in a separate study and each one rated the program a 6, then no error exists. However, an error-free sample is unlikely.

Respondent differences do exist; some dislike the program, and others like it. Although the average program rating is 6 in the hypothetical example, it is possible to select a sample from the target population that does not match the average rating. A sample could be selected that includes only viewers who dislike the program. This would misrepresent the population because the average appeal score would be lower than the mean score. Computing the rate of sampling error allows researchers to have an idea concerning the risk involved in accepting research findings as "real."

Computing sampling error is appropriate only with probability samples. Sampling error cannot be computed with research using nonprobability samples because everyone did not have an equal chance of being selected. This is one reason why nonprobability samples are used only in preliminary research, or in studies where error rates are not considered important.

Sampling error computations are essential in research and are based on the concept of the **central limit theorem**. In its simplest form, the theorem states that the sum of a large number of independent and identically distributed random variables (or **sampling distributions**), has an approximate **normal distribution**. A theoretical sampling distribution is the set of all possible samples of a given size. This distribution of values is described by a bell-shaped curve, or *normal curve* (also known as a *Gaussian distribution*, after German mathematician and astronomer Karl F. Gauss who used the concept to analyze observational errors). The normal distribution is important in computing sampling error because sampling errors (a sampling distribution) made in repeated measurements tend to be normally distributed.

Computing standard error is a process of determining, with a certain amount of confidence, the difference between a sample and the target population. Error occurs by chance, or through some fault of the research procedure. However, when probability sampling is used, the incidence of error can be determined because of the relationship between the sample and the normal curve. A normal curve, as shown in Figure 4.3, is symmetrical about the mean or midpoint,

which indicates that an equal number of scores lie on either side of the midpoint.

In every normal distribution, the **standard deviation** defines a standard unit of distance from the midpoint of the distribution to the outer limits of the distribution. These standard deviation interval units (values) are used in establishing a **confidence interval** that is accepted in a research project. In addition, the standard deviation units indicate the amount of standard error. For example, using an interval (confidence interval) of + or − one standard deviation unit — 1 standard error — says that the probability is that 68% of the sample selected from the population will produce estimates within that distance from the population value (one standard deviation unit).

Researchers use a number of different confidence intervals. Greater confidence in results is achieved when they are tested at higher levels, such as 95%. The areas under the normal curve in Table 3 of Appendix 1 are used to determine other confidence intervals. For example, the 90% confidence interval (.45 on either side of the mean) corresponds to 1.645 standard er-

FIGURE 4.3   AREAS UNDER THE NORMAL CURVE

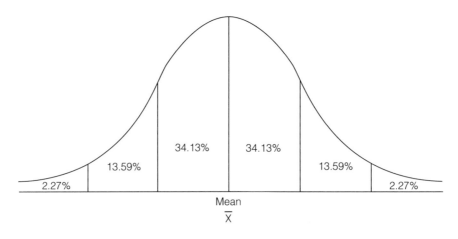

rors, the 95% interval corresponds to 1.96 standard errors, and the 99% interval corresponds to 2.576 standard errors. If the statistical data from the sample falls within the range set by the researcher, the results are considered significant.

Computing Standard Error

The essence of statistical hypothesis testing is to draw a sample from a target population, compute some type of statistical measurement, and compare the results to the theoretical sampling distribution. The comparison determines the frequency with which sample values of a statistic are expected to occur.

The *expected* value of a statistic is the mean of the sampling distribution. The standard error is the standard deviation of the sampling distribution. There are several ways to compute standard (sampling) error, but no single method is appropriate for all sample types or for all situations. In addition, error formulas vary in complexity. One error formula, designed for estimating audience sizes during certain time periods or for certain programs and for measuring cumulative audiences (see Chapter 14), uses the standard error of a percentage derived from a simple random sample. If the sample percent is designated as p, the size of the sample as n, and the estimated or standard error of the sample percentage as $SE(p)$, the formula is:

$$SE(p) = \sqrt{\frac{p(100 - p)}{n}}$$

Suppose a random sample of 500 households produces a **rating** (or estimate of the percentage of viewers; see Chapter 14) of 20 for a particular show. This means that 20% of those households were tuned in to that channel at that time. The formula can be used to calculate the standard error as follows:

$$SE(p) = \sqrt{\frac{20\,(80)}{500}}$$

$$= \sqrt{\frac{1{,}600}{500}}$$

$$= \sqrt{3.2}$$

$$= \pm 1.78$$

That is, the rating of 20 computed in the survey is subject to an error of $\pm$ 1.78 points; the actual rating could be as low as 18.22 or as high as 21.78.

Standard error is directly related to sample size. The error figure improves as the sample size is increased, but in decreasing increments. Thus, an increase in sample size does not provide a big gain, as illustrated by Table 4.3. As can be seen, even with a sample of 1,500, the

TABLE 4.3   FINDING ERROR RATE USING A RATING OF 20

Sample size	Error	Lower limit	Upper limit
600	± 1.63	18.37	21.63
700	± 1.51	18.49	21.51
800	± 1.41	18.59	21.41
900	± 1.33	18.67	21.33
1,000	± 1.26	18.74	21.26
1,500	± 1.03	18.97	21.03

TABLE 4.4   SAMPLING ERROR

Survey result is:		1% or 99%	5% or 95%	10% or 90%	15% or 85%	20% or 80%
Sample of:	25	4.0	8.7	12.0	14.3	16.0
	50	2.8	6.2	8.5	10.1	11.4
	75	2.3	5.0	6.9	8.2	9.2
	100	2.0	4.4	6.0	7.1	8.0
	150	1.6	3.6	4.9	5.9	6.6
	200	1.4	3.1	4.3	5.1	5.7
	250	1.2	2.7	3.8	4.5	5.0
	300	1.1	2.5	3.5	4.1	4.6
	400	.99	2.2	3.0	3.6	4.0
	500	.89	2.0	2.7	3.2	3.6
	600	.81	1.8	2.5	2.9	3.3
	800	.69	1.5	2.1	2.5	2.8
	1,000	.63	1.4	1.9	2.3	2.6
	2,000	.44	.96	1.3	1.6	1.8
	5,000	.28	.62	.85	1.0	1.1

Source: A Broadcast Research Primer. Washington, DC: National Association of Broadcasters, 1976, p. 19. Reprinted by permission.

standard error is only .75 better than with a sample of 500 computed above. A researcher would need to determine whether the increase in time and expense caused by an additional 1,000 subjects would justify such a proportionally small increase in precision.

Table 4.4 shows the amount of error at the 95% confidence level for measurements that contain dichotomous variables (such as "yes/no"). For example, with a sample of 1,000 and a 30% "yes" response to a question, the probable error due to sample size alone is ± 2.9. This means that we are 95% sure that our values for this particular question fall between 27.1% and 32.9%.

Sampling error is an important concept in all research areas because it provides an indication of the degree of accuracy of the research.

Research studies published by large audience measurement firms such as Arbitron and A. C. Nielsen are required by the Electronic Media Ratings Council to include simplified charts to assist in determining sampling error. In addition, each company provides some type of explanation about error, such as the Arbitron statement contained in every ratings book:

> Arbitron estimates are subject to statistical variances associated with all surveys using a sample of the universe. . . . The accuracy of Arbitron estimates, data and reports and their statistical evaluators cannot be determined to any precise mathematical value or definition.

Statistical error due to sampling is found in all research studies. Researchers must pay specific

TABLE 4.4   CONTINUED

Survey result is:	25% or 75%	30% or 70%	35% or 65%	40% or 60%	45% or 55%	50%
Sample of:	17.3	18.3	19.1	19.6	19.8	20.0
	12.3	13.0	13.5	13.9	14.1	14.2
	10.0	10.5	11.0	11.3	11.4	11.5
	8.7	9.2	9.5	9.8	9.9	10.0
	7.1	7.5	7.8	8.0	8.1	8.2
	6.1	6.5	6.8	7.0	7.0	7.1
	5.5	5.8	6.0	6.2	6.2	6.3
	5.0	5.3	5.5	5.7	5.8	5.8
	4.3	4.6	4.8	4.9	5.0	5.0
	3.9	4.1	4.3	4.4	4.5	4.5
	3.6	3.8	3.9	4.0	4.1	4.1
	3.0	3.2	3.3	3.4	3.5	3.5
	2.8	2.9	3.1	3.1	3.2	3.2
	1.9	2.0	2.1	2.2	2.2	2.2
	1.2	1.3	1.4	1.4	1.4	1.4

attention to the potential sources of error in any study. Producing a study riddled with error is tantamount to never having conducted the study at all. If the magnitude of error were subject to accurate assessment, researchers could simply determine the source of error and correct it. Since this is not possible, however, they must accept error as part of the research process, attempt to reduce its effects to a minimum, and remember always to interpret their results with regard to its presence.

SAMPLE WEIGHTING

In an ideal research study, a researcher has enough respondents or subjects with the required demographic, psychographic (why people behave in specific ways), or lifestyle characteristic. The ideal sample, however, is rare, due to the time and budget constraints of most research. Instead of canceling a research project because of sampling inadequacies, most researchers utilize a statistical procedure known as **weighting**, or sample balancing. That is, when subject totals in given categories do not reach the necessary population percentages, subjects' responses are multiplied (weighted) to allow for the shortfall. A single subject's responses may be multiplied by 1.3, 1.7, 2.0, or any other figure to reach the predetermined required level.

Subject weighting is a controversial data manipulation technique, especially in the area of broadcast ratings. The major question is just how much one subject's responses can be weighted and still be representative. Weighting is discussed in greater detail in Chapter 14.

S U M M A R Y

To make predictions about events, concepts, or phenomena, researchers must perform detailed, objective analyses. One procedure to use in such analyses is a census, in which every member of the population is studied. Conducting a census for each research project is impractical, however, and researchers must resort to alternative methods. The most widely used alternative is to select a random sample from the population, examine it, and make predictions from it that can be generalized to the population. There are several procedures for identifying the units that are to compose a random sample.

If the scientific procedure is to provide valid and useful results, researchers must pay close attention to the methods they use in selecting a sample. This chapter has described several types of samples commonly used in mass media research. Some are elementary and do not require a great deal of time or resources. Other sampling methods entail great expense and time. Researchers must decide whether costs and time are justified in relation to the results generated.

Sampling procedures must not be taken lightly in the process of scientific investigation. It makes no sense to develop a research design for testing a valuable hypothesis or research question and then nullify this effort by neglecting correct sampling procedures. These procedures must be continually scrutinized to ensure that the results of an analysis are not sample-specific; that is, results are not based on the type of sample used in the study.

Questions and Problems for Further Investigation

1. The use of available samples in research has long been a target for heated debate. Some researchers say that available samples are inaccurate representations of the population; others claim that if a concept or phenomenon exists, it should exist in an available sample as well as in a random sample. Which argument do you agree with? Explain your answer.

2. Many research studies use small samples. What are the advantages or disadvantages of this practice? Can any gain other than cost savings be realized by using a small sample in a research study?

3. What sampling technique might be appropriate for the following research projects?
   a. A pilot study to test whether people understand the directions to a telephone questionnaire.
   b. A study to determine who buys videocassette recorders.
   c. A study to determine the demographic makeup of the audience for a local television show.
   d. A content analysis of commercials during Saturday morning children's programs.
   e. A survey examining the differences between newspaper readership in high- and low-income households.

References and Suggested Readings

Babbie, E. R. (1989). *The practice of social research* (5th ed.). Belmont, CA: Wadsworth.

Blalock, H. M. (1972). *Social statistics*. New York: McGraw-Hill.

Cochran, W. G. (1963). *Sampling techniques*. New York: John Wiley.

Comrey, A. L. (1973). *A first course in factor analysis*. New York: Academic Press.

Fletcher, J. E. (Ed.). (1981). *Handbook of radio and TV broadcasting*. New York: Van Nostrand Reinhold.

Gorsuch, R. L. (1974). *Factor analysis*. Philadelphia: W. B. Saunders.

Kish, L. (1965). *Survey sampling*. New York: John Wiley.

Nunnally, J. C. (1978). *Psychometric theory*. New York: McGraw-Hill.

Raj, D. (1972). *The design of sample surveys*. New York: McGraw-Hill.

Rosenthal, R., & Rosnow, R. L. (1969). *Artifact in behavioral research*. New York: Academic Press.

Walizer, M. H., & Wienir, P. L. (1978). *Research methods and analysis*. New York: Harper & Row.

PART II

RESEARCH APPROACHES

C H A P T E R   5

EXPERIMENTAL RESEARCH

The mass media are complicated phenomena. Not only are there a variety of media presenting information to audience members, the audience uses these media in a variety of ways. Some people use the media for information, others use them for entertainment or just to pass time, creating a variety of research opportunities for investigators. A single research approach cannot be used because there are simply too many different situations that need investigation. Some situations require that subjects be studied under controlled conditions; other situations require telephone or in-person interviews.

This chapter describes the experimental method of research and its use in mass media investigations. The experimental method is the oldest approach in mass media research and continues to provide a wealth of information for researchers and critics of the media. We will discuss controlled laboratory experiments, then examine quasi-experimental designs, and conclude with a consideration of field experiments.

ADVANTAGES AND DISADVANTAGES OF LABORATORY EXPERIMENTS

There are several reasons why mass media researchers might select the experimental method.

1. *Evidence of causality.* First, experiments help establish cause and effect. Although philosophers of science might argue whether we can ever really prove a cause–effect link between two variables, the experiment is undoubtedly the best social science research method for establishing causality. The researcher controls the time order of the presentation of two variables and thus makes sure that the cause actually precedes the effect. In addition, the experimental method allows the investigator to control other possible causes of the variable under investigation.

2. *Control.* As suggested previously, control is another advantage of the experimental method. Researchers have control over the environment, the variables, and the subjects. Laboratory research allows investigators to isolate a testing situation from the competing influences of normal activity. Researchers are free to structure the experimental environment in almost any way. Lighting and temperature levels, proximity of subjects to measuring instruments, soundproofing, and nearly every other aspect of the experimental situation can be arranged and altered. Environmental control, however, has its drawbacks, and the artificially created environment of the laboratory is one of the main disadvantages of the technique.

Laboratory studies also allow researchers to control the number and types of independent and dependent variables selected and the way these variables are manipulated. Variable control strengthens internal validity and helps eliminate confounding influences. Appel, Weinstein, and Weinstein (1979), for example, were able to control almost every detail of their laboratory analysis of alpha brain wave activity while subjects viewed television commercials.

The experimental approach allows researchers to control subjects. This includes control over the selection process, assignment to the control or experimental group, and exposure to the experimental treatment. Researchers can place limits on the number of subjects participating in such a study and can choose specific types of subjects for exposure in varying degrees to the independent variable. For example, they may select subjects according to which medium they use for news information and vary each subject's exposure to commercials of different types to determine which is the most effective.

3. *Cost.* In relative terms, the cost of an experiment can be low when compared to other research methods. An advertising researcher, for example, can examine the impact of two different ad designs using an experimental design with as few as 40–50 subjects. A comparable test done in the field would be far more costly.

4. *Replication.* Finally, the experimental method aids in replication. The conditions of the study are typically clearly spelled out in the description of an experiment making it easier for others to replicate. In fact, classic experiments are often repeated, sometimes under slightly different conditions, to ensure that the original results were not idiosyncratic.

The experimental technique, however, is not perfect. It has two major disadvantages:

1. *Artificiality.* Perhaps the biggest problem with using this technique is the artificial nature of the experimental environment. The behavior under investigation must be placed in circumstances that afford proper control. Unfortunately, much behavior of interest to mass media researchers is altered when studied out of its natural environment. Critics claim that the sterile and unnatural conditions created in the laboratory produce results that have little direct application to real-world settings, where subjects are continually exposed to competing stimuli. Miller (1983) noted that critics of the laboratory method often resort to ambiguous and disjunctive arguments about the artificiality of the procedure, suggesting that contrasting the "real" world with the "unreal" world may, in fact, be merely a problem in semantics. The main point, he claimed, is that both laboratory and field methods investigate communication behavior, and if viewed in this way, it is meaningless to speak of behavior as "real" or "unreal": all behavior is real.

Miller also noted, however, that it is unsatisfactory and unscientific to dodge the problem of artificiality in laboratory procedures by including a disclaimer in a study indicating that the findings are applicable only to a particular audience, to the environmental conditions of the analysis, and to the period during which the study was conducted. Since external validity is a major goal of scientific research, a disclaimer of this nature is counterproductive. If researchers are not willing to expand their interests beyond the scope of a single analysis, such studies have only heuristic value; they make little or no contribution to the advancement of knowledge in mass media.

Many researchers have conducted field experiments in an attempt to overcome the artificiality of the laboratory. Although done in more natural surroundings, field experiments are prone to problems with control.

2. *Experimenter bias.* Experiments can have a problem with an experimenter bias (Chapter 2). Rosenthal and Jacobson (1966) discovered that experimenters who were told what findings were expected had results more in line with the research hypothesis than experimenters who were not told what to expect. To counteract this problem, some researchers use the double blind technique, in which neither the subjects nor the researchers know whether a given subject belongs to the control or the experimental group.

CONDUCTING EXPERIMENTAL RESEARCH

The experimental method involves both manipulation and observation. In the simplest form of an experiment, researchers manipulate the independent variable and then observe the responses of subjects on the dependent variable. Although every experiment is different, most researchers agree that eight steps are necessary in conducting an experiment.

1. *Select the setting.* Many experiments are best done in a laboratory or in another environment under the direct control of the researcher. Others are best done in more natural surroundings where the researcher has little, if any, control over the experimental situation. This latter type of experiment is called a field experiment and is discussed in more detail later in this chapter.

2. *Select the experimental design.* The appropriate design depends upon the nature of the hypothesis or research question, the types of variables to be manipulated or measured, the availability of subjects, and the amount of resources available.

3. *Operationalize the variables.* In the experimental approach, the independent variable(s) are generally operationalized in terms of the manipulation used to create them. Dependent variables are operationalized by constructing scales or rules for categorizing observations of behavior.

4. *Decide how to manipulate the independent variable.* To manipulate the independent variable (or variables), a set of specific instructions or events or stimuli are developed for presentation to the experimental subjects. There are basically two types of manipulations. In the **straightforward manipulation**, written materials, verbal instructions, or other stimuli are presented to the subjects. These items accomplish the task of manipulating the independent variable. For example, Baran et al. (1989) used a straightforward manipulation of their independent variable, product positioning. One group of subjects was presented with a "generic" shopping list containing items such as ice cream, frozen dinner, mustard, and coffee. Another group saw the "practical" list with items such as Borden's ice cream, Swanson's frozen dinner, French's mustard, and Maxwell House coffee. A third group was presented with the "upscale" list consisting of Haagen-Dazs ice cream, Lean Cuisine frozen dinner, Grey Poupon mustard, General Foods International Coffees, and similar items. Each group was then asked to make judgments about the character of the person to whom the list belonged. As predicted by the experimenters, the shopping lists had an impact on the way subjects evaluated the general goodness and responsibility of the lists' authors.

In a **staged manipulation**, researchers construct events and circumstances that enable them to manipulate the independent variable. Staged manipulations can be relatively simple or rather elaborate. They frequently involve the use of a confederate, a person who pretends to be a subject but who is actually part of the manipulation. For example, staged manipulations and confederates have been used in experiments to examine the impact of media aggression. In their study of cue properties of available targets, Berkowitz and Geen (1966) introduced each of their subjects to a confederate as part of their rather elaborate staged manipulation. Half of their subjects were introduced to a *Kirk* Anderson and half were introduced to a *Bob* Anderson. The confederate then evaluated a project completed by the subjects by administering a series of electric shocks. One group of subjects got a single shock and another group got a series of seven shocks. Half of the subjects then saw a violent film starring *Kirk* Douglas. The other half saw an exciting but nonviolent film. Following this, the tables were turned and the subjects were told to evaluate a project allegedly done by the confederate by giving either Bob or Kirk a series of electric shocks. The subjects who had received the seven shocks and seen the violent film, and who had been introduced to the confederate named Kirk, gave him a significantly larger mean number of shocks than did those subjects who also got seven shocks from the confederate named Bob.

In his study of the effects of televised courtroom coverage, Hoyt (1977) asked his subjects questions about a film they had just seen under three different staged conditions. One group answered questions in the presence of a TV camera at the front of the room. A second group answered questions with the camera concealed behind a full-length mirror, and a third group was questioned with no camera present. Hoyt found no differences in subjects' verbal behavior across the three conditions.

No matter what manipulation technique is used, a general principle for the experimenter to follow is to construct or choose a manipulation that is as strong as possible so that potential differences between the experimental groups are maximized. If, for example, an experimenter was trying to assess the effects of different degrees of newspaper credibility on audience perceptions of the accuracy of a story, one condition might attribute the story to the *New York Times* while another might attribute it to the *National Enquirer* or the *National Star*. A strong manipulation maximizes the chances that the independent variable will have an effect.

5. *Select and assign subjects to experimental conditions.* Recall from Chapter 2 that to ensure external validity, experimental subjects should be selected randomly from the population under investigation. The various random sampling techniques discussed in Chapter 4 are also appropriate for selecting subjects for experimental studies.

Random assignment is the most popular method of assigning subjects to experimental groups. If there are only two groups in the experiment, one way to achieve randomness is to flip a coin. If heads comes up, the subject goes to Group 1; if tails, Group 2. Experimental designs with more than two groups might use a table of random numbers to assign subjects. In a four-group design, a two-digit random number might be assigned to each subject. Those assigned 00–24 are placed in Group 1, 25–49 in Group 2, 50–74 in Group 3, and 75–99 in Group 4.

In some instances, randomization may not be possible and the experimenter might use a design where subjects are matched on relevant characteristics, or a repeated measures design

where subjects serve as their own controls (this is discussed more later in this chapter). Whatever method is used, the goal of subject assignment is to ensure internal validity by making certain that all groups are as similar as possible before the experimental manipulation takes place.

6. *Conduct a pilot study.* A pilot study with a small number of subjects will reveal any problems, and it will also allow the experimenter to make a **manipulation check** — a test to see if the manipulation of the independent variable actually had the intended effect. For example, suppose a researcher wanted to assess the effect of the viewer's involvement in a TV show on how well the viewer remembers the ads in the show. The experimenter constructs TV shows labelled high involvement (a cliff-hanger with lots of suspense), medium involvement (a family drama), and low involvement (a Senate committee hearing taped from C-SPAN). To check if these programs actually differ in involvement, the experimenter should measure the degree to which subjects were actually involved with the programs in each of the conditions. Such a check might include a self-report, an observational report (such as counting the number of times a subject looked away from the screen), or even a physiological measure. If the check shows that the manipulation was not effective, the experimenter can revamp the manipulation before the main experiment is conducted. (It's also not a bad idea to include a manipulation check in the main experiment itself.)

7. *Administer the experiment.* After the bugs are out and the manipulation checked, the main phase of data collection begins. Experimental manipulations are carried out on subjects either individually or in groups. The dependent variable is measured and subjects are debriefed. During debriefing, the experimenter explains the purpose and the implications of the research. If the manipulation required deception, the experimenter must explain why and how the deception was used. (See Chapter 18

for more about deception and other ethical problems of research.)

8. *Analyze and interpret the results.* The subjects' scores on the dependent variable(s) are tabulated, and the data are subjected to statistical analysis. Many of the statistics discussed in Chapters 10, 11, and 12 are used to analyze the results of experiments. Finally, the experimenter has to decide what the results mean. In some experiments, this may be the most difficult part to do.

EXPERIMENTAL DESIGN

When used in the context of experimental research, the word *design* can have two different meanings. In the first place, it can refer to the statistical procedures to be used to analyze the data. Hence, it is common to hear about an analysis of variance design or a repeated measures *t*-test design. On the other hand, *design* can refer to the total experimental plan or structure of the research. Used in this sense, it means selecting and planning the entire experimental approach to a research problem. This chapter uses the latter meaning of design. The appropriate statistical techniques for the various experimental designs discussed in this chapter are discussed in Part 3.

An experimental design does not have to be a complicated series of statements, diagrams, and figures; it may be as simple as:

Pretest → Experimental treatment → Posttest

Although other factors, such as variable and sample selection, control, and construction of a measurement instrument, enter into this design, the diagram does provide a legitimate starting point for research.

To facilitate the discussion of experimental design, the following notations are used to represent specific parts of a design (Campbell & Stanley, 1963):

- R   represents a random sample or random assignment.
- X   represents a treatment or manipulation of the independent variables so that the effects of these variables on the dependent variables can be measured.
- O   refers to a process of observation or measurement; it is usually followed by a numerical subscript indicating the number of the observation (O_1 = "observation 1").

A left-to-right listing of symbols, such as R O_1 X O_2, represents the order of the experiment. In this case, subjects are randomly selected or assigned to groups (R) and then observed or measured (O_1). Next, some type of treatment or manipulation of the independent variable is performed (X), followed by a second observation or measurement (O_2). Each line in experimental notation refers to the experience of a single group. A design such as the following:

$$R \quad O_1 \quad X \quad O_2$$
$$R \quad O_1 \qquad\quad O_2$$

indicates that the operations in the experiment are conducted simultaneously on two different groups. Notice that the second group, the control group, does not receive the experimental treatment.

An alternative notation system that provides a number of more complex notational schemes was developed by Haskins (1981). Researchers interested in a more detailed approach to research design notation should consult this paper.

Basic Experimental Designs

Each experimental design makes assumptions about the type of data the researcher wishes to collect, since different data require different research methods. Several questions need to be answered by the researcher before any type of design is constructed.

1. What is the purpose of the study?
2. What is to be measured or tested?
3. How many factors (independent variables) are involved?
4. How many levels of the factors (degrees of the independent variables) are involved?
5. What type of data is desired?
6. What is the easiest and most efficient way to collect the data?
7. What type of statistical analysis is appropriate for the data?
8. How much will the study cost?
9. How can these costs be trimmed?
10. What facilities are available for conducting the study?
11. What types of studies have been conducted in the area?
12. What benefits will be received from the results of the study?

The answer to each question has a bearing on the sequence of steps a study should follow. For example, if a limited budget is available for the study, a complicated, four-group research design must be excluded. Or, if previous studies have shown the "posttest only" design to be useful, another design may be unjustified.

Not all experimental designs are covered in this section; only the most widely used are considered. The sources listed at the end of the chapter provide more information about these and other designs.

PRETEST-POSTTEST CONTROL GROUP.   The pretest-posttest control group design is a fundamental and widely used procedure in all research areas. The design controls many of the rival hypotheses generated by artifacts; the effects of maturation, testing, history, and other sources are controlled because each group faces the same circumstances in the study. As shown in Figure 5.1, subjects are to be randomly selected or assigned, and each group is to be given a pretest. Only the first group, however, is to receive the experimental treatment. The difference between O_1 and O_2 for Group 1 is compared to the difference between O_1 and O_2 for Group 2. If a significant statistical difference is found, it is assumed that the experimental treatment was the primary cause.

POSTTEST-ONLY CONTROL GROUP.   When researchers are hesitant to use a pretest because

---

FIGURE 5.1   PRETEST-POSTTEST CONTROL GROUP DESIGN

R O_1 X O_2
R O_1 O_2

FIGURE 5.2   POSTTEST-ONLY CONTROL GROUP DESIGN

R   X O_1

R O_2

---

of the possibility of subject sensitization to the posttest, the design in Figure 5.1 can be altered to describe a posttest-only control group (Figure 5.2). Neither group has a pretest, but Group 1 is exposed to the treatment variable, followed by a posttest. The two groups are compared to determine if a statistical significance is present.

The posttest-only control group design is also widely used to control rival explanations. Both groups are equally affected by maturation, history, and so on. Also, both normally call for a *t*-test, a test to compare the significance between two groups, to determine whether a significant statistical difference is present (Chapter 12).

SOLOMON FOUR-GROUP DESIGN.   The Solomon four-group design (Figure 5.3) combines the first two designs and is useful if pretesting is

considered to be a negative factor. Each alternative for pretesting and posttesting is accounted for in the design, which makes it attractive to researchers. For example, consider the hypothetical data presented in Figure 5.4. The numbers in the figure represent college students' scores on a test of current events knowledge. The X represents a program of regular newspaper reading.

To determine if the newspaper reading had an effect, O_2 should be significantly different from O_1 and also significantly different from O_4. In addition, O_5 should be significantly different from O_6 and also from O_3. Assuming the 20-point difference shown in Figure 5.4 is significant, it appears that the independent variable in our example is indeed having an effect on current events knowledge. Note that other informative comparisons are also possible in this

---

FIGURE 5.3   SOLOMON FOUR-GROUP DESIGN

R O_1 X O_2

R O_3 O_4

R   X O_5

R O_6

FIGURE 5.4   HYPOTHETICAL DATA FOR SOLOMON FOUR-GROUP DESIGN

Group

1	R	20 (O_1)	X	40 (O_2)
2	R	20 (O_3)		20 (O_4)
3	R		X	40 (O_5)
4	R			20 (O_6)

design. To assess the possible effects of pretesting, O_4 can be compared with O_6. Comparing O_1 and O_3 allows the experimenter to check on the efficacy of randomization and any possible pretest–manipulation interaction can be detected by comparing O_2 and O_5.

The biggest drawback of the Solomon four-group design is a practical one. The design requires four separate groups, which means more subjects, more time, and more money. Further, some results produced from this design can be difficult to interpret. For example, what does it mean if O_2 is significantly greater than O_4, while O_5 is significantly less than O_6?

Factorial Studies

Research studies involving the simultaneous analysis of two or more independent variables are called **factorial designs**, and each independent variable is called a *factor*. The approach saves time, money, and resources and allows researchers to investigate the interaction between the independent variables. That is, in many instances, it is possible that two or more variables are *interdependent* in the effects they produce on the dependent variable, a relationship that could not be detected if two simple randomized designs were used.

The term *two-factor design* indicates that two independent variables are manipulated; a three-factor design includes three independent variables, and so on. (A one-factor design is a simple random design because only one independent variable is involved.) A factorial design for a study must have at least two factors or independent variables.

Factors may also have two or more levels. Therefore, the term 2×2 *factorial design* means "two independent variables, each with two levels." A 3×3 factorial design has three levels for each of the two independent variables. A $2 \times 3 \times 3$ factorial design has three independent variables: the first has two levels, and the second and third have three levels each.

To demonstrate the concept of levels, imagine that a television station manager would like to study the success of a promotional campaign for a new movie-of-the-week series. The manager plans to advertise the new series on radio and in newspaper. Subjects selected randomly are placed into one of the *cells* of the 2×2 factorial design in Figure 5.5. This allows for the testing of two levels of two independent variables, exposure to radio and exposure to newspapers.

Four groups are involved in the study: Group I is exposed to both newspaper and radio mate-

FIGURE 5.5 2 × 2 FACTORIAL DESIGN

	Radio	No radio
Newspapers	I	II
No newspapers	III	IV

rials; Group II is exposed only to newspaper; Group III is exposed only to radio; and Group IV serves as a control group and receives no exposure to either radio or newspaper. After the groups have undergone the experimental treatment, the manager can administer a short questionnaire to determine which medium, or combination of media, worked most effectively.

A 2 × 3 factorial design, which adds a third level to the second independent variable, is shown in Figure 5.6. This design demonstrates how the manager might investigate the relative effectiveness of full-color versus black and

white newspaper advertisements while also measuring the impact of the exposure to radio materials.

Say the television station manager wants to include promotional advertisements on television as well as using radio and newspaper. The third factor produces a 2 × 2 × 2 factorial design. This three-factor design (see Figure 5.7) shows the eight possibilities of a 2 × 2 × 2 factorial study. Note that the subjects in Group I are exposed to newspaper, radio, and television announcements, whereas those in Group VIII are not exposed to any of the announcements.

FIGURE 5.6   2 × 3 FACTORIAL DESIGN

	Radio	No radio
Full color newspaper ad	I	II
Black/white newspaper ad	III	IV
No newspaper	V	VI

FIGURE 5.7   2 × 2 × 2 FACTORIAL DESIGN

	Radio TV	Radio No TV	No radio TV	No radio No TV
Newspaper	I	II	III	IV
No newspaper	V	VI	VII	VIII

The testing procedure in the three-factor design is similar to that of previous methods. Subjects in all eight cells would be given some type of measurement instrument, and differences between the groups would be tested for statistical significance.

Other Experimental Designs

Research designs are as unique and varied as the questions and hypotheses they help answer. Designs of different types yield different types of information. If information about the effects of multiple manipulations is desired, a **repeated measures design** (several measurements of the same subject) is appropriate. In this design, instead of assigning different people to different manipulations, the researcher exposes the same subjects to multiple manipulations. The effects of the various manipulations appear as variations within the same person's performance rather than differences between groups of people.

One obvious advantage of the repeated measures design is that fewer subjects are necessary since each subject participates in all conditions. Further, since each subject in effect acts as his or her own control, the design is quite sensitive to detecting treatment differences. On the other hand, repeated measures designs are subject to carry-over effects—the effects of one manipulation may still be present when the next manipulation is presented. Another possible disadvantage stems from the fact that subjects experience all of the various experimental conditions and they may figure out the purpose behind the experiment. As a result, they may behave differently than they would if they were unaware of the study's goal.

If the experimenter thinks that the order of presentation of the independent variables in a repeated measures design will be a problem, a Latin square design can be used. Figure 5.8

FIGURE 5.8   LATIN SQUARE DESIGN

Subjects	Experimental conditions			
A	1	2	3	4
B	2	3	4	1
C	3	4	1	2
D	4	1	2	3

shows an example of a Latin square design for a repeated measures experiment with four subjects. Note that each of the subjects is exposed to all conditions and that each of the four conditions appears only once per row and once per column. The Latin square arrangement can also be used in a situation where repeated measures are made on independent groups rather than individual subjects.

LABORATORY RESEARCH EXAMPLE

An example from published literature is used here to illustrate the various facets of research design and the laboratory method. Cantor and Venus (1980) were interested in the effects of humor on the ability to recall radio commercials. It would have been possible to study this topic by conducting a survey or by launching a field experiment, but these researchers chose to investigate the problem under tightly controlled laboratory conditions. The authors were dissatisfied with the ambiguity of existing literature relating to humor and advertising and decided to investigate the problem using a broad research question: they tested the "effect of humor on the memorability and persuasiveness of a rigorously manipulated radio advertisement which was heard in a quasi-naturalistic setting." Here

FIGURE 5.9 DESIGN FOR THE CANTOR-VENUS STUDY

	Serious commercial		Humorous commercial	
	Serious intro	Humorous intro	Serious intro	Humorous intro
Male				
Female				

are the steps Cantor and Venus followed in their investigation:

STEP 1: SELECT THE SETTING. As just mentioned, Cantor and Venus chose the laboratory setting but tried to approximate a more natural listening condition.

STEP 2: SELECT THE EXPERIMENTAL DESIGN. After reviewing the available literature in the field and defining their research question, Cantor and Venus designed a 2 × 2 × 2 factorial study (Figure 5.9).

STEP 3: OPERATIONALIZE THE VARIABLES. One dependent variable, recall, was measured by a 10-question test regarding the information contained in the advertisements. A second dependent variable, impression of the product, was measured using a rating scale that ranged from −10 (extremely unfavorable) to +10 (extremely favorable). The operationalizations of the independent variables, serious vs. humorous commercial, serious intro vs. humorous intro and sex are described next.

STEP 4: DECIDE HOW TO MANIPULATE THE INDEPENDENT VARIABLES. The serious commercial involved two people talking about a fictitious magazine called *Newsline*. In the nonhumorous spot, a male and female simply talk politely about the magazine. In the humorous spot, the male keeps tearing articles out of the magazine while the woman is trying to read it. The serious intro to the commercial was a straight news report on the problem of prisoner exchange between nations; the humorous intro was a segment from Steve Martin's album, *Let's Get Small*. The operationalization of sex is self-evident.

STEP 5: SELECT AND ASSIGN SUBJECTS TO EXPERIMENTAL CONDITIONS. The authors recruited undergraduate students at the University of Wisconsin (59 male and 58 female) as subjects for the experiment and assigned them randomly to the four different exposure groups for each sex.

STEP 6: CONDUCT A PILOT STUDY. Although the published article does not mention a pilot study, probably for reasons of space, it is likely the authors did carry one out. In any case, a manipulation check was built into the final experiment, which disclosed that the humorous version of the ad and the humorous intro were perceived by subjects as funnier than the serious material.

STEP 7: ADMINISTER THE EXPERIMENT. Cantor and Venus first escorted subjects individually to a cubicle where they heard a radio message, then transferred them to another cubicle where they were exposed to the experimental treatments. Subjects were then taken to another room to fill out an instrument that measured recall and impressions of the product. Finally, all subjects were debriefed.

STEP 8: ANALYZE AND INTERPRET THE RESULTS. The authors selected the analysis of variance as the appropriate statistical technique to analyze their data (Chapter 12). They concluded that advertisers should be cautious in using humor as an attention getter and that humor had no impact on the evaluation of the advertised product.

QUASI-EXPERIMENTAL DESIGNS

The experimenter does not have the luxury of randomly assigning subjects to experimental conditions in many instances. Suppose, for example, a researcher knows that a local radio sta-

tion is about to be sold and she or he is interested in determining the effects of this change of ownership on employee morale. The researcher measures morale of a sample of employees at the station before and after the sale. At the same time, the researcher collects morale data from a sample of employees at a comparable station in the same community. This design is similar to the pretest-posttest control group design discussed on page 90, but it does not involve random assignment of subjects to experimental groups. To use Campbell and Stanley's (1963) terminology, it is a **quasi-experiment**. Quasi-experiments represent a valuable source of information but there are design faults that must be considered in the interpretation of the data.

This chapter discusses only two types of quasi-experimental designs, the pretest-posttest nonequivalent control group design and the interrupted time series design. For further information, consult Campbell and Stanley (1963) and Cook and Campbell (1979).

PRETEST-POSTTEST NONEQUIVALENT CONTROL GROUP DESIGN. This approach, illustrated in Figure 5.10, is the one used by the hypothetical researcher studying employee morale at radio stations. In this design, one group is exposed to the experimental manipulation and is compared

---

FIGURE 5.10   PRETEST-POSTTEST NONEQUIVALENT CONTROL GROUP DESIGN

O_1 X O_2

O_3 O_4

Note: The line dividing the two groups indicates that no random assignment occurred.

FIGURE 5.11   INTERRUPTED TIME SERIES DESIGN

O_1 O_2 O_3 O_4 O_5 X O_6 O_7 O_8 O_9 O_{10}

to a similar group not exposed. The pre- and posttest differences are compared to see if the experimental condition had an effect.

In the radio station example mentioned before, assume the pretest of employee morale showed that the workers at both radio stations had the same morale level before the sale. The posttest, however, showed that the morale of the employees at the sold station decreased significantly after the sale while the morale level at the other (control) station remained constant. This indicates that the station sale had an impact on morale. However, this may not be true. The two groups might have been different on other variables at the time of the pretest. For example, suppose the two groups of employees were of different ages. It is possible that the effect of the station sale on older employees produced the difference. The quasi-experimental design does not rule out this rival selection–treatment interaction explanation.

INTERRUPTED TIME SERIES DESIGN.   In this arrangement, diagrammed in Figure 5.11, a series of periodic measurements is made of a group. The series of measurements is interrupted by the experimental treatment and then measurements are continued.

This design can rule out several threats to internal validity. If there is a significant difference between O_5 and O_6, maturation can be ruled out by examining the scores for all the intervals prior to the manipulation. If maturation were occurring, it would probably produce differences between O_1 and O_2 and O_2 and O_3

and so on. If the only difference is between O_5 and O_6, then maturation is not a plausible explanation. The same logic can be applied to rule out the sensitizing effects of testing. The biggest threat to the internal validity in this design is history. It's possible that any apparent changes occurring after the experimental manipulation might be due to some other event that occurred at the same time as the experimental treatment.

FIELD EXPERIMENTS

Experiments conducted in a laboratory can be disadvantageous for many research studies because of certain problems they present: they are performed in controlled conditions that are unlike natural settings; they are generally considered to lack external validity; and they usually necessitate subject awareness of the testing situation. Because of these shortcomings, many researchers prefer to use field experiments (Haskins, 1968).

The exact difference between laboratory and field experiments has been a subject of debate for years, especially with regard to the "realism" of the situations involved. Many researchers consider field and laboratory experiments to be on opposite ends of the "realism" continuum. However, the main difference between the two approaches is the setting. As Westley (1989) pointed out:

> The laboratory experiment is carried out on the experimenter's own turf; the subjects come into

the laboratory. In the field experiment, the experimenter goes to the subject's turf. In general, the physical controls available in the labortory are greater than those found in the field. For that reason, statistical controls are often substituted for physical controls in the field.

The two approaches can also be distinguished by the presence or absence of rules and procedures to control the conditions and the subjects' awareness or unawareness of being subjects. If the researcher maintains tight control over the subjects' behavior and the subjects are placed in an environment they perceive to be radically different from their everyday life, the situation is probably better described as a laboratory experiment. On the other hand, if the subjects function primarily in their everyday social roles with little investigator interference or environmental restructuring, the case is probably closer to a field experiment. Basically, the difference between laboratory experiments and field experiments is one of degree.

Advantages of Field Experiments

The major advantage of field experiments is their external validity: since study conditions closely resemble natural settings, subjects usually provide a truer picture of their normal behavior and are not influenced by the experimental situation. For example, consider a laboratory study designed to test the effectiveness of two different versions of a television commercial. One group views Version A and the other views Version B. Both groups are then given a questionnaire to measure their willingness to purchase the advertised product. On the basis of these results, it may be concluded that Version B is more effective in selling the product. Although this may actually be the case, the validity of the experiment is questionable because the

subjects knew they were being studied (see the discussion of demand characteristics in Chapter 2). Another problem is that answering a questionnaire cannot be equated to actually buying a product. Furthermore, viewing commercials in a laboratory setting is different from the normal viewing situation, in which competing stimuli (crying children, ringing telephones, and so on) are often present.

In a field experiment, these commercials might be tested by showing Version A in one market and Version B in a similar, but different, market. Actual sales of the product in both markets might then be monitored to determine which commercial was the more successful in persuading viewers to buy the product. As can be seen, the results of the field experiment have more relevance to reality, but the degree of control involved is markedly less than is the case in the laboratory experiment.

Some field studies possess the advantage of being nonreactive. **Reactivity** is the influence that a subject's awareness of being measured or observed has on his or her behavior. Laboratory subjects are almost always aware of being measured. Although this is also the case in some field experiments, many can be conducted without subjects' knowledge of their participation.

Field experiments are useful for studying complex social processes and situations. In their study of the effects of the arrival of television in an English community, Himmelweit, Oppenheim, and Vince (1958) recognized the advantages of the field experiment for examining such a complicated topic. Since television has an impact on several lifestyle variables, the researchers employed a wide range of analysis techniques, including diaries, personal interviews, direct observation, questionnaires, and teachers' ratings of students, to document this impact. A topic area as broad as this does not easily lend itself to laboratory research.

Field experiments can be inexpensive. Most

studies require no special equipment or facilities. However, expenses increase rapidly with the size and scope of the study (Babbie, 1989).

Finally, the field experiment may be the only research option to use. For example, suppose a researcher is interested in examining patterns of communication at a television station before and after a change in management — a problem difficult if not impossible to simulate in a laboratory. The only practical option is to conduct the study in the field, that is, at the station.

Disadvantages of Field Experiments

The disadvantages of the field experiment are mostly practical ones. However, some research is impossible to conduct because of ethical considerations. The vexing question of the effects of television violence on young viewers provides a good example of this problem. Probably the most informative study that could be performed in this area would be a field experiment in which one group of children is required to watch violent television programs while another, similar group views only nonviolent programs. The subjects could be carefully observed over a number of years to check for any significant difference in the number of aggressive acts committed by the members of each group. However, the ethics involved in controlling the television viewing behavior of children and possibly encouraging aggressive acts, are extremely questionable. Therefore, scientists have resorted to laboratory and survey techniques to study this problem.

On a more practical level, field experiments often encounter external hindrances that cannot be anticipated. For example, a researcher may spend weeks planning a study to manipulate the media use of students in a summer camp, only to have the camp counselors or a group of parents scuttle the project because they do not want the children used as "guinea pigs." Also, it takes

time for researchers to establish contacts, secure cooperation, and gain necessary permissions before beginning a field experiment. In many cases this phase of the process may take weeks or months to complete.

Finally, and perhaps most important, researchers cannot control all the intervening variables in a field experiment. The presence of those extraneous variables affects the precision of the experiment and the confidence the researchers have in its outcome.

Types of Field Experiments

There are two basic categories of field experiments: those in which the researcher manipulates the independent variable(s), and those in which independent variable manipulation occurs naturally as a result of other circumstances. To illustrate the first type, suppose that a researcher is interested in investigating the effects of not being able to read a newspaper. A possible approach would be to select two comparable samples and not allow one to read any newspapers for a period of time; the second sample (the control group) would continue to read the newspaper as usual. A comparison could then be made to determine whether abstinence from newspapers has any effect in other areas of life, such as interpersonal communication. In this example, reading the newspaper is the independent variable that has been manipulated.

The second type of field experiment involves passive manipulation of independent variables. Suppose a community with no cable television system is scheduled to be wired for cable in the near future. In an attempt to gauge the effects of cable on television viewing and other media use, a researcher might begin studying a large sample of television set owners in the community long before the cable service is available. A few months after it is introduced, the researcher could return to the original sample, sort out the households that subscribed to cable and those that did not, and proceed from there to determine the effects of the cable service. In this case, there is no control over the independent variable (cable service); the researcher is merely taking advantage of existing conditions.

Note that in some field experiments, the experimenter is not able to randomly assign subjects to treatment groups. As a result, many field experiments are classified as quasi-experiments. As Cook and Campbell (1979) point out, the extent to which causal statements can be made from the results of these studies depends upon the ability to rule out alternative explanations. Consequently, researchers who use the field experiment technique must pay close attention to threats to the internal validity.

Examples of Field Experiments

Tan (1977) was interested in what people would do in a week without television. He recruited a sample of 51 adults and paid each of them $4 a day not to watch television for an entire week. Before depriving these subjects of television, Tan requested that they watch television normally for a 1-week period and keep a detailed diary of all their activities. At the start of the experimental week, Tan's assistants visited the subjects' homes and taped up the electrical plugs on their television sets to lessen temptation. Again, the subjects were requested to record their activities for the week. To maintain some control over the experiment, the assistants visited the subjects' homes periodically during the week to ensure that television was not being viewed.

One week later, the diaries completed during the week of deprivation were collected and the data compared to the week of normal television viewing. Tan discovered that when deprived of television, subjects turned more to radio and newspapers for entertainment and information. They also tended to engage in more social activities with their friends and family.

This study illustrates some of the strengths and weaknesses of field experiments. In the first place, they probably represent the only viable technique available to investigate this particular topic. A survey (Chapter 6) does not permit the researcher to control whether the subjects watch television, and it would be impossible in the United States to select a representative sample composed of people who do not own a television set. Nor would it be feasible to bring people into the laboratory for a whole week of television deprivation.

On the other hand, the ability of the field experimenter to control independent variables is not conclusively demonstrated here: Tan had no way to be sure that his sample actually avoided television for the entire week. Subjects could have watched at friends' homes or at local bars, or even at home by untaping the plugs. Moreover, Tan mentioned that several individuals who fell into the initial sample refused to go without television for only $4 per day. As a result, the nonprobability sample did not accurately reflect the general makeup of the community.

Field experiments are sometimes used to test the effectiveness of advertising campaigns. For example, Robertson et al. (1974) reported the results of a campaign designed to increase the use of auto safety belts. Six public service announcements were shown to households on one half of a dual cable system, while the households on the other half of the system served as a control group and were shown no messages. The researchers used traffic flow maps to select 14 observation sites likely to maximize the possibility of observing autos from the neighborhoods that were part of the message and no-message groups, respectively. Observing periods were arranged so that morning and afternoon traffic could be sampled.

The observers were strategically located to allow them to observe the drivers of the automobiles that passed their positions (some observers were in trees near key intersections). As a car approached, the driver's sex, apparent ethnic background, estimated age, and use of a safety belt were noted. The auto license number was recorded as the car drove away. With cooperation of the state department of motor vehicles, the license plate numbers were matched with the owners' names and addresses. These were then checked to see whether the person was or was not a subscriber to one of the dual cable systems. This process ultimately led to four different groups for analysis: Cable A households, where the messages were shown; Cable B households, the control group; noncable households in the same county; and out-of-county households. Observations were done before the safety belt campaign aired and for several months thereafter. The ads were scheduled so that an average TV viewer would see two or three messages per week.

The results of the observations revealed that the campaign had no measurable effect on safety belt use. Drivers in the half of the cable system that carried the messages were no more likely to use safety belts than were motorists in the control group or people not on the cable at all. In fact, the percentage of drivers using safety belts actually decreased during the time the announcements were aired.

This field experiment illustrates the considerable amounts of time, energy, and money that are necessary to conduct a study of this scope. Six different messages were produced, the cooperation of the cable system and the department of motor vehicles had to be secured, at least 14 observers were needed, and the data-gathering phase lasted for 9 months. The study also demonstrates some of the problems associated with field experiments. For example, the investigators could tell only that a person was or was not living in a household that was part of the cable system where the ads were shown; they had no way of knowing whether the driver had actually seen the announcements. Moreover, they had no way of knowing whether individuals in the control group had seen the messages while visiting friends or neighbors. Nor was it possible to assess the subjects' exposure to information about safety belt use in other media. Finally, motorists were observed only in their immediate neighborhoods. The study was not designed to observe safety belt use while driving on the highways.

Williams (1986) and her colleagues conducted an elaborate field experiment on the impact of television on a community. In 1973, she was able to identify a Canadian town that because of its peculiar geographic location was unable to receive television. This particular town, however, was due to acquire television service within a year. Given this lead time, the researchers were able to match the town with two others that were similar in population, area, income, transportation systems, education, and other variables. Residents of the three towns completed questionnaires that measured a large number of variables including aggressive behavior, personality traits, reading ability, creativity, sex-role perceptions, intelligence, and vocabulary.

Two years later, the research team went back to the three communities and residents completed a posttest with questions that measured the same variables as before. The design of this field experiment is illustrated in Figure 5.12. Note that it is a variation of the quasi-experimental, pretest-posttest nonequivalent control group design discussed earlier.

This field experiment provided a wealth of data. Among other things, the researchers found that the arrival of TV apparently slowed

FIGURE 5.12   DESIGN OF CANADIAN FIELD EXPERIMENT

Town	Time one	Time two
A	No TV reception	One TV channel
B	One TV channel	Two TV channels
C	Four TV channels	Four TV channels

down the acquisition of reading skills, lowered attendance at outside social events, fostered more stereotypical attitudes toward sex roles, and increased children's verbal and physical aggression.

Two rather ambitious field experiments were conducted by Milgram and Shotland (1973) with the cooperation of the CBS television network. The researchers arranged to have three different versions of the popular television series "Medical Center" constructed. One version depicted antisocial behavior that was punished (a jail sentence), another portrayed antisocial behavior that went unpunished, and a third contained prosocial (favorable) behavior. The antisocial behavior consisted of scenes of a distraught young man smashing a plastic charity collection box and pocketing the money.

In the first experiment, the researchers recruited subjects in two ways: ads placed in New York City newspapers promised a free transistor radio to anyone willing to view a 1-hour television show, and business reply cards containing the same message were passed out to pedestrians near several subway stops. Subjects were asked to report to a special television theater to view the program; upon arrival, each person was randomly assigned to one of four groups, and each group was shown a different program (the three described above plus a different nonviolent show used as a control). After viewing the

program (with no commercial interruptions) and completing a short questionnaire about it, the subjects were instructed to go to an office in a downtown building to receive their free radio.

The downtown office, monitored by hidden cameras, was part of the experiment. The office contained a plastic charity collection box with about $5 in it; a notice informed the subjects that no more transistor radios were available. Their behavior on reading the notice was to be the dependent variable: how many would emulate the antisocial act seen in the program and take the money from the charity box? Milgram and Shotland found no differences in antisocial behavior among the viewers of each group; no one broke into the charity box.

The second study tried to gauge the immediate effects of televised antisocial acts on viewers. Subjects were recruited from the streets of New York City's Times Square area and ushered into a room with a color television set and a plastic charity collection box containing $4.45. A hidden camera monitored the subjects' behavior, even though they were told that they would not be observed. Although this time some subjects broke into the box, once again, no differences emerged between the groups.

These two studies also demonstrate several positive and negative aspects of field experiments. In the first place, Milgram and Shotland had to secure the cooperation of CBS to conduct this expensive study. Second, volunteer subjects were used, and it is reasonable to assume that the sample was unrepresentative of the general population. Third, in the first experiment, the researchers did not control for the amount of time that passed between viewing the program and arriving at the testing center. Some participants arrived 24 hours after watching "Medical Center," while others came several days later. Clearly, the subjects' experiences during this interval may have influenced their responses. Finally, Milgram and Shotland reported that the second experiment had to be terminated early because some of the subjects started resorting to behavior that the researchers could not control.

On the plus side, the first experiment clearly shows the potential of the field experiment to simulate natural conditions and to provide a nonreactive setting. Upon leaving the theater after seeing the program, subjects had no reason to believe that they would be participating in another phase of the research. Consequently, their behavior at the supposed gift center was probably genuine and not a reaction to the experimental situation.

The Milgram and Shotland studies also raise the important question of ethics in field experiments. Subjects were observed without their knowledge and apparently were never told about the real purpose of the study, nor even that they were involved in a research study. Does the use of a hidden camera constitute an invasion of privacy? Does the experimental situation constitute entrapment? How about the subjects who stole the money from the charity box? Have they committed a crime? Field experiments can sometimes pose difficult ethical considerations, and these points must be dealt with *before* the experiment is conducted, not afterward, when harm may already have been inflicted on the subjects (see Chapter 18).

SUMMARY

Mass media researchers have a number of research designs from which to choose when analyzing a given topic. The laboratory experiment has been a staple in mass media research for several decades. Although criticized by many researchers as being artificial, the method offers a number of advantages that make it particularly useful to some researchers. Of specific importance is the researcher's ability to control the experimental situation and to manipulate experimental treatments.

This chapter also described the process of experimental design, the researcher's blueprint for conducting an experiment. The experimental design provides the steps the researcher will follow to accept or reject a hypothesis or research question. Some experimental designs are simple and take very little time to perform; others involve many different groups and numerous treatments.

Quasi-experimental designs are used when random selection and random assignment of subjects are not possible. Field experiments take place in natural settings, which aids the generalizability of the results but also introduces problems of control.

Questions and Problems for Further Investigation

1. Provide four research questions or hypotheses for any mass media area. Which of the designs described in this chapter is best suited to investigate the problems?

2. What are the advantages and/or disadvantages of each of the following four experimental designs?

   a.   X O_1
                     O_2
   b.   R   X O_1

c.   R O_1 X O_2
      R   X O_3
d.   R O_1 X O_2

3. The Cantor–Venus laboratory study on the effect of humor on radio advertisements was described in this chapter. In the same issue of the *Journal of Broadcasting* (Volume 24:1), Krull and Husson (pp. 35–47) investigated children's perceptions of television. Read this study and compare the authors' approach to the laboratory methods used by Cantor and Venus.

4. What research questions are best answered by field experiments?

References and Suggested Readings

Appel, V., Weinstein, S., & Weinstein, C. (1979). Brain activity and recall of TV advertising. *Journal of Advertising Research*, 19(4), 7–18.

Babbie, E. R. (1989). *The practice of social research* (5th ed.). Belmont, CA: Wadsworth.

Baran, S. J., Mok, J. J., Land, M., & Kang, T. K. (1989). You are what you buy. *Journal of Communication*, 39(2), 46–51.

Berkowitz, L., & Geen, R. (1966). Film violence and the cue properties of available targets. *Journal of Personality and Social Psychology*, 3, 525–530.

Bruning, J. L., & Kintz, B. L. (1987). *Computational handbook of statistics*. Chicago: Scott, Foresman.

Campbell, D. T., & Stanley, J. C. (1963). *Experimental and quasi-experimental designs and research*. Skokie, IL: Rand McNally.

Cantor, J., & Venus, P. (1980). The effects of humor on recall of a radio advertisement. *Journal of Broadcasting*, 24(1), 13–22.

Cook, T. D., & Campbell, D. T. (1979). *Quasi-experimentation: Designs and analysis for field studies*. Skokie, IL: Rand McNally.

Haskins, J. B. (1968). *How to evaluate mass communication*. New York: Advertising Research Foundation.

Haskins, J. B. (1981). A precise notational system for planning and analysis. *Evaluation Review*, 5(1), 33–50.

Himmelweit, H., Oppenheim, A. W., & Vince, P. (1958). *Television and the child*. London: Oxford University Press.

Hoyt, J. L. (1977). Courtroom coverage: The effects of being televised. *Journal of Broadcasting*, 21(41), 487–496.

Keppel, G. (1982). *Design and analysis: A researcher's handbook* (2nd ed.). Englewood Cliffs, NJ: Prentice-Hall.

Milgram, S., & Shotland, R. (1973). *Television and anti-social behavior*. New York: Academic Press.

Miller, D. C. (1983). *Handbook of research design and social measurement* (4th ed.). White Plains, New York: Longman.

Nunnally, J. C. (1978). *Psychometric theory* (2nd ed.). New York: McGraw-Hill.

Robertson, L., Kelley, A. B., O'Neill, B., Wixam, C. W., Elswirth, R. S., & Haddon, W. (1974). A controlled study of the effect of television messages of safety belt use. *American Journal of Public Health*, 64, 1074–1078.

Roscoe, J. T. (1975). *Fundamental research statistics for the behavior sciences*. New York: Holt, Rinehart & Winston.

Rosenberg, M. J. (1965). When dissonance fails: On eliminating evaluation apprehension from attitude measurement. *Journal of Personality and Social Psychology*, 1, 28–42.

Rosenthal, R. (1976). *Experimenter effects in behavioral research* (2nd ed.). New York: Irvington.

Rosenthal, R., & Jacobson, L. (1966). Teacher's expectancies: Determinants of pupils' IQ gains. *Psychological Reports*, 19, 115–118.

Rosenthal, R., & Rosnow, R. L. (1969). *Artifact in behavioral research*. New York: Academic Press.

Tan, A. (1977). Why TV is missed: A functional analysis. *Journal of Broadcasting, 21,* 371–380.

Walizer, M. H., & Wienir, P. L. (1978). *Research methods and analysis: Searching for relationships.* New York: Harper & Row.

Westley, B. H. (1989). The controlled experiment. In G. H. Stempel & B. H. Westley, *Research methods in mass communication.* Englewood Cliffs, NJ: Prentice-Hall.

Williams, T. M. (1986). *The impact of television.* New York: Academic Press.

CHAPTER 6

SURVEY RESEARCH

Surveys are now used in all areas of life. Businesses, consumer groups, politicians, and advertisers use them in their everyday decision-making processes. Some firms, such as Gallup and Harris, conduct public opinion surveys on a full-time basis.

The importance of survey research to the public at large is confirmed by the frequent reporting of survey results in the popular media. This is especially evident during campaign periods, when the public continually hears or reads about polls conducted to ascertain candidates' positions with the electorate.

The increased use of surveys has created changes in the way they are conducted and reported. More attention is now given to sample selection, questionnaire design, and error rates. This means that surveys require careful planning and execution; mass media studies using survey research must take into account a wide variety of decisions and problems. This chapter acquaints the beginning researcher with the basic steps of survey methodology.

DESCRIPTIVE AND ANALYTICAL SURVEYS

At least two major types of surveys are used by researchers: descriptive and analytical. A **descriptive survey** attempts to picture or document current conditions or attitudes, that is, to *describe* what exists at the moment. For example, the Department of Labor regularly conducts surveys on the amount of unemployment in the United States. Professional pollsters survey the electorate to learn its opinions of candidates or issues. Broadcast stations and networks contin-

ually survey their audiences to determine programming tastes, changing values, and lifestyle variations that might affect programming. In descriptive surveys of this type, researchers are interested in discovering the current situation in a given area.

Analytical surveys attempt to describe and explain *why* certain situations exist. In this approach two or more variables are usually examined to test research hypotheses. The results allow researchers to examine the interrelationships among variables and to draw explanatory inferences. For example, television station owners occasionally survey the market to determine how lifestyles affect viewing habits, or to determine whether viewers' lifestyles can be used to predict the success of syndicated programming. On a much broader scale, television networks conduct yearly surveys to determine how the public's tastes and desires are changing and how these attitudes relate to the perception viewers have of the three commercial networks.

ADVANTAGES AND DISADVANTAGES OF SURVEY RESEARCH

Surveys have certain well-defined advantages. First, they can be used to investigate problems in realistic settings. Newspaper reading, television viewing, and consumer behavior patterns can be examined where they happen, rather than in a laboratory or screening room under artificial conditions.

Second, the cost of surveys is reasonable considering the amount of information gathered. In addition, researchers can control expenses by selecting from four major types of surveys: mail, telephone, personal interview, and group administration.

A third advantage is that large amounts of data can be collected with relative ease from a variety of people. The survey technique allows the researcher to examine many variables (demographic and lifestyle information, attitudes, motives, intentions, and so on) and to use multivariate statistics (Appendix 2) to analyze the data. Also, geographic boundaries do not limit most surveys.

Finally, data helpful to survey research already exist. Data archives, government documents, census materials, radio and television rating books, and voter registration lists can be used as *primary* sources (main sources of data) or as *secondary* sources (supportive data) of information. With archive data, it is possible to conduct an entire survey study without ever developing a questionnaire or contacting a single respondent.

Survey research is not a perfect research methodology. The technique also possesses several disadvantages. The first and most important is that independent variables cannot be manipulated as in laboratory experiments. Without control of independent variable variation, the researcher cannot be certain whether the relations between independent and dependent variables are causal or noncausal. That is, a survey may establish that A and B are related, but it is impossible to determine solely from the survey results that A causes B. Causality is difficult to establish because many intervening and extraneous variables are involved. Time series studies help correct this problem sometimes, but not always.

A second disadvantage is that inappropriate wording and placement of questions within a questionnaire can bias results. The questions must be worded and placed to unambiguously elicit the desired information. This problem is discussed later in the chapter.

A third disadvantage of survey research, especially in telephone studies, is the potential problem of talking to the wrong people. For example, a respondent may claim to be 18 to 24, but may in fact be well over 30 years old.

Finally, some survey research is becoming more and more difficult to conduct. This is especially true with telephone surveys where answering machines, and respondents unwilling to participate, are creating very low incidence rates. Telemarketers (telephone salespeople) are essentially destroying mass media research. More and more people refuse to participate in legitimate studies for fear of attempts by the interviewer to try and sell something.

Even considering some of the problems, surveys can produce reliable and useful information. They are especially useful for collecting information on audiences and readership. General problems in survey research are discussed at the end of the chapter.

CONSTRUCTING QUESTIONS

Two basic considerations apply to the construction of good survey questions: (1) the questions must clearly and unambiguously communicate the desired information to the respondent, and (2) the questions should be worded to allow accurate transmission of respondents' answers to researchers.

Questionnaire design depends on choice of data collection technique. Questions written for a **mail survey** must be easy to read and understand, since respondents are unable to obtain explanations. **Telephone surveys** cannot use questions with long lists of response options; the respondent may forget the first few responses by the time the last ones have been read. Questions written for **group administration** must be concise and easy for the respondents to answer. In a **personal interview** the interviewer must tread lightly with sensitive and personal questions, which his or her physical presence might make the respondent less willing to answer. (These procedures are discussed in greater detail later in this chapter.)

The design of a questionnaire must always reflect the basic purpose of the research. A complex research topic such as media use during a political campaign requires more detailed questions than does a survey to determine a favorite radio station or magazine. Nonetheless, there are several general guidelines to follow regarding wording of questions and question order and length.

Types of Questions

Surveys can consist of two basic types of questions, open-ended and closed-ended. An **open-ended question** requires respondents to generate their own answers. For example:

What do you like most about your local newspaper?

_____

_____

What type of television program do you prefer?

_____

_____

What are the three most important problems in your community?

_____

_____

_____

Open-ended questions allow respondents freedom in answering questions and the chance to provide in-depth responses. Furthermore, they give researchers the opportunity to ask: "Why did you give that particular answer?" or "Could you explain your answer in more detail?" This flexibility to follow up on, or probe, certain questions enables the interviewers to gather information about the respondents' feelings and the motives behind their answers.

Also, open-ended questions allow for answers that researchers did not foresee in the construction of the questionnaire — answers that may suggest possible relationships with other answers or variables. For example, in response to the question, "What types of programs would you like to hear on radio?" the manager of a local radio station might expect to hear "news" and "weather" or "sports." However, a subject may give an unexpected response, such as "obituaries" (Fletcher & Wimmer, 1981). This will force the manager to reconsider his perceptions of some of the local radio listeners.

Finally, open-ended questions are particularly useful in a pilot version of a study. Researchers may not know what types of responses to expect from subjects, so open-ended questions are used to allow subjects to answer in any way they wish. From the list of responses provided by the subjects, the researcher then selects the most-often mentioned items and includes them in multiple-choice or forced-choice questions. Using open-ended questions in a pilot study generally saves time and resources, since all possible responses are more likely to be included on the final measurement instrument; there would be no reason to reconduct the analysis for failure to include an adequate number of responses or response items.

The major disadvantage associated with open-ended questions is the amount of time needed to collect and analyze the responses. Open-ended responses required interviewers to spend a lot of time writing down or typing answers. In addition, because there are so many types of responses, a content analysis (Chapter 8) of each open-ended question must be completed to produce data that can be tabulated. A content analysis groups common responses into categories, essentially making the question closed-ended. The content analysis results are then used to produce a codebook to code the open-ended responses. A **codebook** is essentially a menu or list of quantified responses. For example, "I hate television" may be coded as a 5 for input into the computer.

In the case of **closed-ended questions**, respondents select an answer from a list provided by the researcher. These questions are popular because they provide greater uniformity of response, and because the answers are easily quantified. The major disadvantage is that researchers often fail to include some important responses. Respondents may have an answer different from those that are supplied. One way to solve the problem is to include an "other" response followed by a blank space, to give respondents an opportunity to supply their own answer. The "other" responses are then handled just like an open-ended question—a content analysis of the responses is completed to develop a codebook. A pilot study or pretest of a questionnaire often solves most problems with closed-ended questions.

PROBLEMS IN INTERPRETING OPEN-ENDED QUESTIONS. Open-ended questions often provide a great deal of frustration. In many cases, respondents' answers are bizarre. Sometimes respondents don't understand a question and provide answers that are not relevant to anything. Sometimes interviewers have difficulty understanding respondents, or they may have problems with spelling what the respondents say. In these cases, researchers must interpret the answer and determine which code is appropriate.

The following examples are actual verbatim comments from telephone surveys conducted by Paragon Research in Denver, Colorado. They show that even the most well-planned survey questionnaire can produce a wide range of responses. The survey question asked: "How do you describe the programming on your favorite radio station?" Some responses were:

1. The station is OK, but it's geared to Jerry Atrics.
2. I only listen to the station because my poodle likes it.
3. The music is good, but sometimes it's too Tiny Booper.
4. It's great. It has the best floormat in the city.
5. The station is good, but sometimes it makes me want to vomit.
6. It's my favorite, but I really don't like it since my mother does.
7. My parrot is just learning to talk, and the station teaches him a lot of words.
8. My kids hate it, so I turn it up real loud.
9. It sounds great with my car trunk open.
10. My boyfriend forces me to listen.

General Guidelines

Before examining specific question types appropriate in survey research, some general do's and don'ts about writing questions are in order.

1. *Make questions clear.* This should go without saying, but many researchers become so closely associated with a problem that they can no longer put themselves in the respondents' position. What might be perfectly clear to researchers might not be nearly as clear to persons answering the question. For example, "What do you think of our company's rebate program?" might seem to be a perfectly sensible question to a researcher, but to respondents it might mean, "Is the monetary amount of the rebate too small?" "Is the rebate given on the wrong items?" "Does it take too long for the rebate to be paid?" or "Have the details of the program been poorly explained?" Questionnaire items must be phrased precisely so that respondents know what is being asked.

Making questions clear also requires avoiding difficult or specialized words, acronyms, and stilted language. In general, the level of vocabulary commonly found in newspapers or popular magazines is adequate for a survey. Questions should be phrased in everyday speech, and social science jargon and technical words should be eliminated. For example, "If you didn't have a premium channel, would you consider PPV?" might be better phrased: "If you didn't have a pay channel like Home Box Office or Showtime, would you consider a service where you pay a small amount for individual movies or specials you watch?"

The item, "Should the city council approve the construction of an interactive cable TV system?" assumes that respondents know what "interactive cable TV systems" are. A preferable option is: "An interactive cable television system is one in which viewers can send messages back to the cable company as well as receive normal television. Do you think the city council should approve such a system for this community?"

The clarity of a questionnaire item can be affected by double or hidden meanings in the words that are not apparent to investigators. For example, the question, "How many television shows do you think are a little too violent—most, some, few, or none?" contains such a problem. Some respondents who feel that all TV shows are extremely violent will answer "none" on the basis of the question's wording. These subjects reason that all shows are more than "a little too violent"; therefore, the most appropriate answer to the question is "none." Deleting the phrase "a little" from the question helps avoid this pitfall. In addition, the question inadvertently establishes the idea that *at least some* shows are violent. The question should read, "How many television shows, *if any*, do you think are too violent—most, some, few, or none?" Questions should be written so they are fair to all types of respondents.

2. *Keep questions short.* To be precise and unambiguous, researchers sometimes write long and complicated items. However, respondents who are in a hurry to complete a questionnaire are unlikely to take the time to study the precise intent of the person who drafted the items. Short, concise items that will not be misunderstood are best.

3. *Remember the purposes of the research.* It is important to include in a questionnaire only items that directly relate to what is being studied. For example, if the occupational level of the respondents is not relevant to the hypothesis, the questionnaire should not ask about it. Beginning researchers often add questions merely for the sake of developing a longer questionnaire. Keep in mind that parsimony in questionnaires is a paramount consideration.

4. *Do not ask double-barreled questions.* A **double-barreled question** is one that actually asks two or more questions. Whenever the word *and* appears in a question, the sentence structure should be examined to see whether more than one question is being asked. For example, "This product is mild on hands and gets out stubborn stains. Do you agree _____ or disagree _____?" Since a product that gets out stubborn stains might at the same time be highly irritating to the skin, a respondent could agree with the second part of the question while disagreeing with the first part. This question should be divided into two items.

5. *Avoid biased words or terms.* Consider the following item: "In your free time, would you rather read a book or just watch television?" The word *just* in this example injects a pro-book bias into the question because it implies that there is something less than desirable about watching television. In like manner, "Where did you hear the news about the president's new program?" is mildly biased against newspapers; the word *hear* suggests that "radio," "television," or "other people" is a more appropriate answer. Questionnaire items that start off with "Do you agree or disagree with so-and-so's proposal to . . ." almost always bias a question. If the name "Adolf Hitler" is inserted for "so-and-so," the item becomes overwhelmingly negative. By inserting "the President," a potential for both positive and negative bias is created. Any time a specific person or source is mentioned in a question, the possibility of introducing bias arises.

6. *Avoid leading questions.* A **leading question** is one that suggests a certain response (either literally or by implication) or contains a hidden premise. For example, "Like most Americans, do you read a newspaper every day?" suggests that the respondent should answer in the

affirmative or run the risk of being unlike most Americans. The question "Do you still use marijuana?" contains a hidden premise. This type of question is usually referred to as a *double bind*: regardless of how the respondent answers, an affirmative response to the hidden premise is implied — in this case, he or she has used marijuana at some point.

7. *Do not use questions that ask for highly detailed information.* The question "In the past 30 days, how many hours of television have you viewed with your family?" is unrealistic. Few respondents could answer such a question. A more realistic approach would be to ask, "How many hours did you spend watching television with your family yesterday?" A researcher interested in a 30-day period should ask respondents to keep a log or diary of family viewing habits.

8. *Avoid potentially embarrassing questions unless absolutely necessary.* Most surveys need to collect data of a confidential or personal nature, but an overly personal question may cause embarrassment and inhibit respondents from answering honestly. Two common areas with high potential for embarrassment are age and income. Many individuals are reluctant to tell their exact ages to strangers doing a survey. Instead of asking directly how old a respondent is, it is better to allow some degree of confidentiality by asking, "Now, about your age — are you in your 20s, 30s, 40s, 50s, 60s, . . . ?" Most respondents are willing to state what decade they fall in, and this information is usually adequate for statistical purposes. Interviewers might also say, "I'm going to read several age categories to you. Please stop me when I reach the category you're in."

Income may be handled in a similar manner. A straightforward, "What is your annual income?" often prompts the reply, "None of your business." It is more prudent to preface a reading of the following list with the question "Which of these categories includes your total annual income?"

———— More than $30,000
———— $15,000–$29,999
———— $8,000–$14,999
———— $4,000–$7,999
———— $2,000–$3,999
———— Under $2,000

These categories are broad enough to allow respondents some privacy but narrow enough for statistical analysis. Moreover, the bottom category, "Under $2,000," was made artificially low so that individuals who fall into the $2,000–$3,999 slot would not have to be embarrassed by giving the very lowest choice. The income classifications depend on the purpose of the questionnaire and the geographic and demographic distribution of the subjects. The $30,000 upper level in the example would be much too low in several parts of the country.

Other potentially sensitive areas include people's sex lives, drug use, religion, business practices, and trustworthiness. In all these areas, care should be taken to ensure respondents of confidentiality and even anonymity, when possible.

The simplest type of closed-ended question is one that provides a *dichotomous response*, usually "agree/disagree" or "yes/no." For example:

Television stations should editorialize.

———— Agree
———— Disagree
———— No opinion

While such questions provide little sensitivity to different degrees of conviction, they are the easiest to tabulate of all question forms. Whether they provide enough sensitivity is a question the researcher must seriously consider.

The *multiple-choice* question allows respondents to choose an answer from several options. For example:

In general, television commercials tell the truth . . .

_____ All of the time
_____ Most of the time
_____ Some of the time
_____ Rarely
_____ Never

Multiple-choice questions should include all possible responses. A question that excludes any significant response usually creates problems. For example:

What is your favorite television network?

_____ ABC
_____ CBS
_____ NBC

Subjects who favor PBS or Fox (although not _networks_ in the strictest sense of the word) cannot answer the question as presented.

Additionally, multiple-choice responses must be **mutually exclusive**: there should be only one response option per question for each respondent. For instance:

How many years have you been working in newspapers?

_____ Less than one year
_____ One to five years
_____ Five to ten years

Which blank should a person with exactly five years of experience check? One way to cor-rect this problem is to reword the responses, such as:

How many years have you been working in newspapers?

_____ Less than one year
_____ One to five years
_____ Six to ten years

Rating scales are also widely used in mass media research (see Chapter 3). They can be arranged horizontally or vertically:

There are too many commercials on TV.

_____ Strongly agree (translated as a 5 for analysis)
_____ Agree (translated as a 4)
_____ Neutral (translated as a 3)
_____ Disagree (translated as a 2)
_____ Strongly Disagree (translated as a 1)

What is your opinion of TV news?

Fair _____ _____ _____ _____ _____ Unfair
     (5) (4) (3) (2) (1)

Semantic differential scales (see Chapter 3) are another form of rating scale and are frequently used to rate persons, concepts, or objects. These scales use bipolar adjectives with seven scale points:

How do you perceive the term _public television_?

Good	_____	_____	_____	_____	_____	_____	_____	Bad
Happy	_____	_____	_____	_____	_____	_____	_____	Sad
Uninteresting	_____	_____	_____	_____	_____	_____	_____	Interesting
Dull	_____	_____	_____	_____	_____	_____	_____	Exciting

In many instances researchers are interested in the relative perception of several concepts or items. In such cases the *rank ordering* technique is appropriate:

> Here are several common occupations. Please rank them in terms of their prestige. Put a 1 next to the profession that has the most prestige, a 2 next to the one with the second most, and so on.
>
> ____ Police officer
> ____ Banker
> ____ Lawyer
> ____ Politician
> ____ TV reporter
> ____ Teacher
> ____ Dentist
> ____ Newspaper writer

Ranking of more than a dozen objects is not recommended because the process can become tedious and the discriminations exceedingly fine. Furthermore, ranking data imposes limitations on the statistical analysis that can be performed.

The **checklist question** is often used in pilot studies to refine questions for the final project. For example:

> What things do you look for in a new television set? (Check as many as apply.)
>
> ____ Automatic fine tuning
> ____ Remote control
> ____ Large screen
> ____ Cable ready
> ____ Console model
> ____ Portable
> ____ Stereo sound
> ____ Other _____

The most frequently checked answers may be used to develop a multiple-choice question; the unchecked responses are dropped.

Forced-choice questions are frequently used in media studies designed to gather information about lifestyles and are always listed in pairs. Forced-choice questionnaires are usually very long—sometimes dozens of questions—and repeat questions (in different form) on the same topic. The answers for each topic are analyzed for patterns, and a respondent's interest in that topic is scored. A typical forced-choice questionnaire might contain the following pairs.

> Select one statement from each of the following pairs of statements:
>
> ____ I enjoy attending parties with my friends.
> ____ I enjoy staying at home alone.
>
> ____ Gun control is necessary to stop crime.
> ____ Gun control can only increase crime.
>
> ____ If I see an injured animal, I always try to help it.
> ____ If I see an injured animal, I figure that nature will take care of it.

Respondents generally complain that neither of the responses to a forced-choice question is satisfactory, but they have to select one or the other. Through a series of questions on the same topic (violence, lifestyles, career goals), a pattern of behavior or attitude generally develops.

Fill-in-the-blank questions are used infrequently by survey researchers. However, some studies are particularly suited for fill-in-the-blank questions. In advertising copy testing, for example, they are often employed to test subjects' recall of a commercial. After seeing, hearing, or reading a commercial, subjects receive a script of the commercial in which a number of words have been randomly omitted (often every fifth or seventh word). Subjects are required to fill in the missing words to complete the commercial. Fill-in-the-blank questions can also be used in information tests. For example, "The senators from your state are _____ and _____." Or, "The headline story on the front page was about _____."

Tables, graphs, and figures are also used in survey research. Some ingenious questioning devices have been developed to help respondents more accurately describe how they think and feel. For example, the University of Michigan Survey Research Center developed the **feeling thermometer**, on which subjects can rate an idea or object. The thermometer, which is patterned after a normal mercury thermometer, offers an easy way for subjects to rate their degree of like or dislike in terms of "hot" or "cold." For example:

> How would you rate the coverage your local newspaper provided on the recent school board campaign? (Place an X near the number on the thermometer in Figure 6.1 that most accurately reflects your feelings; 100 indicates strong approval, and 0 reflects strong disapproval.)

FIGURE 6.1   A ''FEELING THERMOMETER'' FOR RECORDING A SUBJECT'S DEGREE OF LIKE OR DISLIKE

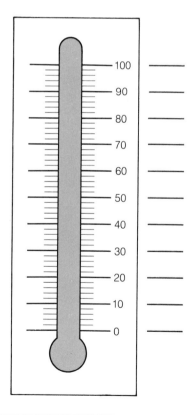

FIGURE 6.2   A SIMPLE PICTURE SCALE FOR USE WITH YOUNG CHILDREN

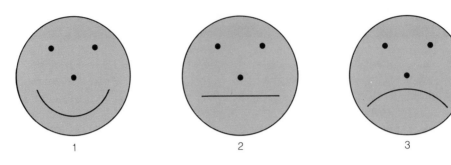

Some questionnaires designed for children use other methods to collect information. Since young children have difficulty in assigning numbers to values, one logical alternative is to use pictures. For example, the interviewer might read the question, "How do you feel about Saturday morning cartoons on television?" and present the faces in Figure 6.2 to elicit a response from a 5-year-old. Zillmann and Bryant (1975) present a similar approach in their "Yucky" scale.

QUESTIONNAIRE DESIGN

The approach used in asking questions as well as the physical appearance (in a self-administered questionnaire) can affect the response rate. Time and effort invested in developing a good questionnaire always pay off with more usable data. The following section offers some useful suggestions.

Introduction

One way to increase response rate in any type of survey is to prepare a persuasive introduction to the survey. Backstrom and Hursh-Cesar (1981)

suggest six principles for writing a successful introduction to a questionnaire; namely, the introduction should be short, realistically worded, nonthreatening, serious, neutral, and pleasant, but firm.

Generally speaking, there is no need to explain the purpose or value of a survey to respondents. It is also not necessary to tell respondents how long the survey will take to complete. In a telephone survey, telling the respondents that "the survey will take only a few minutes" gives them the opportunity to say they don't have that long to talk. An introduction should be short so the respondent can begin writing answers, or the interviewer can start asking questions. An effective introduction for a telephone survey is:

"Hello, my name is _____ with [**INSERT COMPANY NAME**]. We're conducting an opinion survey about radio in the Chicago area. We're not trying to sell anything, and this is not a contest or promotion. We're interested only in your opinions. For this survey, we need to talk to people who are between the ages of 25 and 49. Are you in this group? [IF 'YES,' CONTINUE. IF 'NO,' ASK FOR SOMEONE WHO IS. IF NO ONE IN AGE GROUP, **TERMINATE**]."

With some modifications, the same introduction is appropriate for a self-administered questionnaire. The introduction would include the second and fourth sentences and add at the end: "Please answer the questions as completely and honestly as possible."

The goal of the introduction in telephone surveys is to start the interview as quickly as possible so the respondent does not have a chance to say "No" and hang up. This may sound overly aggressive, but it works. The goal of the introduction in self-administered questionnaires is to make it as simple as possible.

Regardless of the survey approach used, a well-constructed introduction usually generates higher response rates than a simple "Please answer the following questions. . . ."

Instructions

All instructions necessary to complete the questionnaire should be clearly stated for respondents or interviewers. These instructions vary depending on the type of survey conducted. Mail surveys usually require the most specific instructions, since respondents are not able to ask questions about the survey. Respondents and interviewers should understand whether the correct response consists of circling, checking, placing in a specific order, or skipping an item.

Procedural instructions for respondents are often highlighted using a different typeface, capital letters, or some graphic device, perhaps arrows or lines. The following is an example from a mail survey:

Do you have a favorite radio station that you listen to most of the time?

_____ Yes   _____ No

↓

If yes, can you remember the names of any of the disc jockeys or newscasters who work for that station? *WRITE THE NAMES BELOW.*

_____

_____

_____

Some questionnaires require respondents to rank a list of items. In this case, the instructions must clearly describe which response represents the highest value:

Please rate the following magazines in order of importance to you. Place a 1 next to the magazine you prefer most, a 2 next to the magazine in second place, and so on up to 5.

_____ *Better Homes and Gardens*
_____ *Consumer Reports*
_____ *Omni*
_____ *Popular Science*
_____ *Reader's Digest*
_____ *Scientific American*

Fowler (1984) offers the following suggestions for putting together a self-administered questionnaire:

1. The questionnaire must be self-explanatory.
2. Questionnaires should be limited to closed-ended items. Checking a box or circling an answer should be the only task required.
3. The question forms should be few in number.
4. The questionnaire should be typed and laid out to ensure a clear and uncluttered product.
5. Instructions should be kept to a minimum. If people can be confused about what they are supposed to do, they will be.

The second point in Fowler's suggestions is strict. Respondents are usually able to answer open-ended questions with the same ease (or complication) as closed-ended questions.

Whether open-ended or closed-ended, all questions should be tested in a pretest to determine whether directions for answering questions are clear.

Procedural instructions for interviewers are often typed in capital letters and enclosed in parentheses, brackets, or boxes. For example, instructions for a telephone survey might look like this:

We'd like to start by asking you some things about television. First, what are your favorite TV shows?

> RECORD ALL NAMES OF TV SHOWS. PROBE WITH "ARE THERE ANY MORE?" TO GET AT LEAST THREE SHOWS.

1._____   3._____

2._____   4._____

Screener questions, or **filter questions**, which are used to eliminate unwanted respondents (or to include only respondents who have specific characteristics or answer questions in a specific manner), often require respondents or interviewers to skip one or more questions. Skips must be clearly specified. For example:

In a typical week, do you listen to AM radio?

_____ Yes
_____ No   [SKIP TO Q. 17]

A survey using this question might be designed to question only subjects who listen to AM radio. The screener question immediately determines if the subject falls into this group. If the respondent responds "No," the interviewer (or respondent if the survey is self-administered) skips a certain number of questions, or may terminate the survey immediately.

When interviewers are used, as is the case with telephone and one-on-one interviews, the questionnaires must have easy-to-follow instructions (including how many responses to

take for open-ended questions), simple skip patterns, and enough space to record answers (if survey responses are written down on paper). Telephone questionnaires must include everything an interviewer will say, including introductions, explanations, definitions, transitions, and pronunciations. The last point is particularly important because interviewers should sound like they know the topic. For example, the rock group INXS should have a phonetic spelling in parentheses, (*in excess*), following its first appearance in the questionnaire. Otherwise, some interviewer is *sure* to say something like: "Do you think music by the group 'Inks' should be played on your favorite radio station?"

All instructions should be clear and simple. A confusing questionnaire impairs the effectiveness of the interviewer, lowers the number of respondents who complete the test, and, in the long run, increases costs.

Question Order

All surveys flow better when the initial questions are simple and easy to answer. Researchers often include one or two "warm-up" questions about the topic under investigation so respondents become accustomed to answering questions and begin thinking about the survey topic. Preliminary questions can also serve as motivation to create interest in the questionnaire. Demographic data, personal questions, and other sensitive items should be placed at the end of the questionnaire to allow the interviewer to establish a rapport with each respondent, or for any suspicions to be alleviated in a self-administered questionnaire. Although some respondents may still refuse to answer personal items, or may hang up the telephone, at least the main body of data is already collected. Age and sex information are usually included in the first part of a questionnaire, so at least some respondent identification is possible.

The questionnaire should be organized in a logical sequence, proceeding from the general to the specific. Questions on similar topics should be grouped together, and the transitions between different question sections should be clear and logical.

Poor question order may bias a respondent's answers. For example, suppose that after several questions about the presence of violence in society, the respondent is asked to rank the major problems facing the country today from the following list:

_____ War
_____ Communism
_____ Violence on TV
_____ High prices
_____ Corrupt government
_____ Pollution

It is possible that violence on television might receive a higher ranking than it would if the ranking question had been asked before the series of questions on violence. Or, to take another example, suppose a public relations researcher is attempting to discover the public's attitudes toward a large oil company. If the questionnaire that began with attitudinal questions concerning oil spills and inflated profits asked respondents to rate certain oil companies, it is likely that the ratings of all the companies would be lower, due to general impressions created by the earlier questions.

There is no easy solution for the problem of question "contamination." Obviously, some questions have to be asked before others. Perhaps the best approach for researchers is to be sensitive to the problem and test for it in a pretest. If they think that question order A, B, C may have biasing effects, they should test another version using the order C, B, A. Completely neutral positioning is not always possible, however, and when bias may enter because of how responses are ordered, the list of items should be rotated. The word [ROTATE] after a question indicates that the interviewer must alter the order of responses for each respondent.

Different versions of question order can be printed for self-administered questionnaires.

Layout

The physical design of the questionnaire is another important factor in survey research. A badly typed, poorly reproduced questionnaire is not likely to attract many responses in a mail survey. Nor does a cramped questionnaire with 40 questions to a page help to instill respondents with a positive attitude. Response categories should be adequately spaced and presented in a nonconfusing manner. For example, the following format might lead to problems:

There are too many commercials on television.

Do you strongly agree _____ Agree _____
Have no opinion _____ Disagree _____
Strongly disagree _____ ?

A more effective and less confusing method is to provide a vertical ordering of the response choices:

There are too many commercials on television.

_____ Strongly agree
_____ Agree
_____ No opinion
_____ Disagree
_____ Strongly disagree

Some researchers recommend avoiding blanks altogether because respondents and interviewers tend to make large check marks or X's that cover more than one blank, making interpretation difficult. If blanks are perceived as a problem, boxes to check or numbers to circle are satisfactory. In any case, the response form should be consistent throughout the questionnaire. Format changes generally create confusion for both respondents and interviewers.

Finally, each question must have enough space for answers. This is especially true for open-ended questions. Nothing is more discouraging to respondents and interviewers than to be confronted with a presentation like the following.

Why do you go to the movies? _____
Who are your favorite movie stars? _____
What are your favorite television shows? __

If a research budget does not allow for enough paper, subjects should be asked to add further comments on the back of the survey.

Questionnaire Length

Questionnaire length is an important concern in any type of survey. One basic reason is that questionnaire length is directly related to completion rate. Long questionnaires cause fatigue and respondent mortality, and low completion rates. Shorter questionnaires guarantee higher completion rates.

There are no strict guidelines to help in deciding how long a questionnaire should be. The length depends on a variety of things. *Some* of these include:

1. Purpose of the survey
2. Type of problems or questions investigated
3. Age of respondents involved in the survey
4. Type and complexity of questions in the questionnaire
5. Location in the country where the study is conducted
6. Specific setting of the testing situation
7. Time of year
8. Time of day
9. Type of interviewer used (professional or amateur)

In most cases, questionnaire length is determined by trial and error. A survey developed with significantly less than 100% respondent completion is too long. The authors' experience during the past 10 years has shown the following time limits as *maximum*:

Self-administered in a group situation supervised by a researcher:	60 min.
One-on-one interviews:	60 min.
Telephone:	25 min.
Self-administered mail survey:	20 min.
Shopping center intercept:	15 min.

Telephone interviewing can be a difficult approach to use because there is a talent required in keeping people on the phone to answer questions. Professional interviewers can usually hold respondents' attention for about 25 minutes. There is a severe drop-off in incidence (respondents hang up) when an interview lasts more than 25 minutes.

PRETESTING

Without a doubt, the best way to discover whether a research instrument is adequately designed is to pretest it. That is, conduct a ministudy with a small sample to determine if the study approach is correct and for refining questions. Areas of misunderstanding or confusion can be easily corrected without wasting time or money.

There are several ways to pretest a questionnaire. When an acceptable draft of the questionnaire is completed, a focus group (Chapter 7) can be used to discuss the questionnaire with potential respondents. However, this is usually too expensive. The best pretest in telephone surveys is to have interviewers call 10–20 people and do a run-through. Any problems emerge quickly. Self-administered questionnaires should be pretested with the type of respondent who will participate in the actual study. Once again, any problems should be noticed immediately.

In any type of pretesting situation, it is appropriate to discuss the project with respondents after the questionnaire is completed. They can be asked if they understood the questions, whether questions were simple to answer, and so on. Respondents are always willing to help researchers.

GATHERING SURVEY DATA

Once a questionnaire is developed and one or more pretests or pilot studies have been conducted, the next step is to gather data from an appropriate group of respondents. There are four basic methods for doing this: the mail survey, the telephone survey, the personal interview, and group administration. Researchers can also use variations and combinations of these four methods, such as disk-by-mail surveys and mall interviews. Each procedure has definite advantages and disadvantages that must be considered before a choice is made. The remainder of this chapter highlights the characteristics of each method.

Mail Surveys

Mail surveys involve mailing self-administrable questionnaires to a sample of individuals. Stamped reply envelopes are enclosed to encourage respondents to mail completed questionnaires back to the researcher. Mail surveys are popular because they can secure a great deal of data with a minimum expenditure of time and money. At the outset, however, researchers should be aware that respondents are busy people with many demands on their time. Consequently, many people do not share the researcher's enthusiasm for questionnaires and often simply throw them away.

The general stages of a mail survey are discussed below. Even though the steps are listed in numerical sequence, many of these tasks are often accomplished in a different order or even simultaneously.

1. *Select a sample.* Sampling is generally done from a prepared frame (Chapter 4) that contains the names and addresses of potential respondents. The most common sampling frame used is the **mailing list**, a compilation of names and addresses in narrowly defined groupings that commercial firms sometimes prepare (see accompanying boxed material).

2. *Construct the questionnaire.* As discussed earlier, mail survey questionnaires must be concise and specific, since no interviewer is present to alleviate misunderstandings, answer questions, or give directions.

3. *Write a cover letter.* A brief note explaining the purpose and importance of the questionnaire usually increases response rates.

4. *Assemble the package.* The questionnaires, cover letters, and return envelopes are stuffed into mailing envelopes. Researchers sometimes choose to use bulk mail with first-class return envelopes. An alternate method is to send questionnaires first class and use business reply envelopes for responses. This method allows researchers to pay postage only for the questionnaires actually returned. Postal options always depend on the research budget.

5. *Mail the surveys.*

6. *Closely monitor the return rates.*

7. *Send follow-up mailings.* The first follow-up should be sent 2 weeks after the initial mailing, and a second (if necessary) 2 weeks after the first. The follow-up letters can be sent to the entire sample or only the subjects who failed to answer.

8. *Tabulate and analyze the data.*

ADVANTAGES.   Mail surveys cover a wide geographic area for a rather reasonable cost. They are often the only way to gather information from people who live in hard-to-reach areas of the country (or in other countries). Mail surveys also allow for selective sampling through the use of specialized mailing lists. In addition to those

OBTAINING SPECIALIZED LISTS

Several dozen firms specialize in providing sample lists to consumer product companies, advertisers, research firms, and others who use special lists for one reason or another. One significant use of lists is **data base marketing**, where manufacturers, wholesalers, or retailers purchase lists of target consumers and use direct mail or telemarketing for sales.

Some of the firms that provide lists are given below. Each company offers a variety: lists developed by random selection from telephone directories, lists developed from consumers who submit various product warranty cards, lists of businesses and professionals, and lists derived from an almost unlimited number of demographic and lifestyle characteristics.

Scientific Telephone Samples	Metromail	Survey Sampling
202 Fashion Lane	901 W. Bond Street	One Post Road
Suite 221	Lincoln, NE 68521	Fairfield, CT 06430
Tustin, CA 92680	402-465-4591	203-255-4200
714-731-8576		
	R. L. Polk	TeleMatch
MegaSample	6400 Monroe Blvd.	6501 Loisdale Ct., Suite 1101
200 Carleton Ave.	Taylor, MI 48180	Springfield, VA 22150
East Islip, NY 11730	313-292-3200	703-971-6400
516-277-7000		
	Donnelley Marketing	
National Demographics & Lifestyles	70 Seaview Ave.	
1621 18th Street, 3rd Floor	Stamford, CT 06904	
Denver, CO 80202	203-353-7000	
303-292-5000		

mentioned, lists are available that include only people with annual incomes exceeding $50,000, or consumers who have bought a car within the past year, or subscribers to a particular magazine, or residents of a specific zip code area. If researchers need to collect information from a highly specialized audience, the mail technique can be quite attractive.

Another advantage of the mail survey is that it provides anonymity, so that subjects are more likely to answer sensitive questions candidly. Questionnaires can be completed at home or in the office, affording subjects a certain sense of privacy. People can answer questions at their own pace and have an opportunity to look up facts or check past information. Mail surveys also eliminate interviewer bias, since there is no personal contact.

Probably the biggest advantage of this method, however, is its relatively low cost. Mail surveys do not require a large staff of trained workers. The only costs are for printing, mailing lists, envelopes, and postage. If the cost per completed questionnaire were to be computed, it is likely that the mail survey would prove to be the most inexpensive of all the survey methods. At a minimum, it can be said that researchers who are willing to spend time, energy, and money in a mail survey can usually ensure an above-average return rate.

DISADVANTAGES. First, mail questionnaires must be self-explanatory. There is no interviewer present to answer questions or to clear up misunderstandings. Mail surveys are also the slowest form of data collection. Returns start to trickle in around a week or so after the initial mailing and continue to arrive for several weeks thereafter. In fact, it may be months before some responses are returned. Many researchers simply set a cutoff date, after which returns are not included in the analysis.

Another problem with mail surveys is that researchers never know exactly who answers the questions. A survey sent to corporate executives, for example, may be completed by assistants. Furthermore, replies are often received only from people who are interested in the survey, and this injects bias into the results. Most researchers agree, however, that the biggest disadvantage of the mail survey is the typically low return rate. A typical survey (depending on the area and type of survey) will achieve a response rate of 20%–40%. This low return casts doubt on the reliability of the findings.

INCREASING RESPONSE RATES. A number of procedures for improving return rates have been investigated by survey researchers. There are no hard and fast guarantees. However, in a *meta-analysis* (the findings of several studies are treated as independent observations and combined to calculate an overall or average effect) of numerous studies concerning mail surveys, Fox, Crask, and Kim (1989) found that, on the average, response rates can be increased in a variety of ways. In descending order of importance, the authors found the following procedures to increase mail survey response rates: university sponsorship, stamped return postage as opposed to business reply, written prenotification of the survey sent to the respondent, postcard follow-up, first-class outgoing postage, questionnaire color (green paper as opposed to white), notification of cutoff date, and stamped outgoing postage as compared to metered

stamping. Offering monetary incentives also increases response rates, but the authors did not pursue this area since only a few studies offering incentives were available to them.

The authors further suggest that additional research is required to determine which combinations of the procedures, if any, can have an interactive effect to increase response rates even more than any single element does alone.

Telephone Surveys

Telephone surveys and personal interviews employ trained members of a research team to ask questions orally and record the responses. The respondents generally do not get a chance to see the actual questionnaire. Since telephone and personal interviewing techniques have certain similarities, much of what follows applies to personal interviews as well.

Telephone surveys seem to fill a middle ground between mail surveys and personal interviews. They offer more control and higher response rates than most mail surveys but are limited in the types of questions that can be used. They are generally more expensive than mail surveys but less expensive than face-to-face interviews. Because of these factors, telephone surveys seem to represent a compromise between the other two techniques, and this may account for their growing popularity in mass media research.

Interviewers are extremely important to both telephone and personal surveys. An interviewer ideally should function as a neutral medium through which the respondents' answers are communicated to the researcher. The interviewer's presence and manner of speaking should not influence respondents' answers in any way. Adequate training and instruction can minimize bias that the interviewer might inject into the data. For example, if he or she shows disdain or shock over an answer, it is unlikely that the respondent will continue to answer questions in a totally honest manner. Showing agreement with certain responses might prompt similar answers to other questions. Skipping questions, carelessly asking questions, and being impatient with the respondent might also cause problems. As an aid to minimizing interviewer bias, the National Association of Broadcasters has published the following recommendations to interviewers.*

1. Read the questions exactly as worded. Ask them in the exact order listed. Skip questions only when the instructions on the questionnaire tell you to. There are no exceptions to this.
2. Never suggest an answer, try to explain a question, or imply what kind of reply is wanted. Don't prompt in any way.
3. If a question is not understood, say, "Let me read it again," and repeat it slowly and clearly. If it is still not understood, report a "no answer."
4. Report answers and comments exactly as given, writing fully. If an answer seems vague or incomplete, probe with neutral questions, such as, "Will you explain that?" or, "How do you mean that?" Sometimes just waiting a bit will tell the respondent you want more information.
5. Act interested, alert, and appreciative of the respondent's cooperation. But never comment on his or her replies. Never express approval, disapproval, or surprise. Even an "Oh" can cause a respondent to hesitate or refuse to answer further questions. Never talk up or down to a respondent.
6. Follow all instructions carefully, whether you agree with them or not.
7. Thank each respondent. Leave a good impression for the next interviewer.

A general procedure for conducting a telephone survey follows. Again, the steps are presented in numerical order, but it is possible to address many tasks simultaneously.

1. *Select a sample.* Telephone surveys require researchers to specify clearly the geographic area to be covered and to identify the type of respondent to be interviewed in each household contacted. Many surveys are restricted to people over 18, heads of households, and so forth. The sampling procedure used depends on the purpose of the study (see Chapter 4).

2. *Construct the questionnaire.* Phone surveys require straightforward and uncomplicated response options. Ranking a long list of items is especially difficult over the telephone, and this task should be avoided. In addition, the length of the survey should not exceed 10 minutes for nonprofessional interviewers. Longer interviews require professionals who are capable of keeping people on the telephone.

3. *Prepare an interviewer instruction manual.* This document should cover the basic mechanics of the survey (what numbers to call, when to call, how to record times, and so on). It should also specify which household member to interview and should provide general guidelines on how to ask the questions and how to record the responses.

4. *Train the interviewers.* Interviewers need to practice going through the questionnaire to become familiar with all the items, response options, and instructions. It is best to train interviewers in a group using interview simulations that allow each person to practice asking questions. It is advisable to pretest interviewers as well as the questionnaire.

5. *Collect the data.* Data collection is most efficient when conducted from one central location (assuming enough telephone lines are available). Problems that develop are easier to remedy, and important questions raised by one interviewer can easily be communicated to the rest of the group. A central location also makes it easier for researchers to check (validate) the interviewers' work. The completion rate should also be monitored during this stage.

---

*From *A Broadcast Research Primer*, 1976, pp. 37–38. Reprinted with permission.

6. *Make necessary callbacks.* Additional calls (usually no more than two) should be made to respondents whose lines were busy or who did not answer during the first session. Callbacks done on a different day or night tend to have a greater chance of success in reaching someone willing to be interviewed.

Backstrom and Hursh-Cesar (1981) offer the following advice about callbacks.

About 95% of all telephone interviews are successfully completed within three calls. However, we have rules for the number of callbacks to make if the first call results in a busy signal or a no answer. . . . We generally permit only three calls — one original and two callbacks — but if any of these calls produce busy signals or [future interview] appointments, we allow up to five calls total. . . .

When the first call produces a busy signal, the rule is to wait one-half hour before calling again. If the first call produced a "no answer," wait 2 to 3 hours before calling again, assuming it will still be a reasonable hour to call. If evening calls produce no answer, call during the following day.

In addition, interviewers should keep track of the disposition or status of their sample numbers. Figure 6.3 contains a sample disposition sheet.

7. *Verify the results.* When all questionnaires have been completed, a small subsample of each interviewer's respondents should be called again to check that the information they provided was accurately recorded. Respondents should be told during the initial survey that they may receive an additional call at a later date. This tends to eliminate any confusion when subjects receive a second call. A typical procedure is to ask the subject's first name in the interview so that it can be used later. The interviewer should ask, "Was James called a few days

---

FIGURE 6.3   SAMPLE TELEPHONE INTERVIEW DISPOSITION SHEET

Phone number _____

Call #1 _____ #2 _____ #3 _____ #4 _____ #5 _____

    Date _____ Date _____ Date _____ Date _____ Date _____

    Time _____ Time _____ Time _____ Time _____ Time _____

Code

  1 Completed interview

  2 Answering machine

  3 Busy

  4 No answer

  5 Refusal

  6 Appointment to call again
     (when _____)

  7 Nonworking number (out of order, disconnected, nonexistent)

  8 Nonresidential number

  9 Reached but respondent not available (out of town, hospital, etc.)

 10 Reached but not interviewed (ineligible household, speech or physical problem, age disqualification)

ago and asked questions about television viewing?" The verification can begin from there, and need consist of only two or three of the original questions (preferably open-ended and sensitive questions, since interviewers are most likely to omit these).

8. *Tabulate the data.* Along with the normal data analysis, telephone researchers generally compute a response rate: how many completed interviews, how many refusals, how many no-answers, and how many disconnects.

ADVANTAGES.   The cost of telephone surveys tends to be reasonable. The sampling involves minimal expense, and there are no elaborate transportation costs. Callbacks are simple and economical. Wide Area Telephone Service (WATS) enables researchers to conduct telephone surveys on a nationwide basis from any location.

Compared to mail surveys, telephone surveys can include more detailed questions, and, as stated earlier, interviewers can clarify misunderstandings that might arise during the administration of the questionnaire.

The nonresponse rate of a telephone survey is generally low, especially when multiple callbacks are employed. In addition, phone surveys are much faster than mail. A large staff of interviewers can collect the data from the designated sample in a relatively short time. In summary, phone surveys tend to be fast, easy, and relatively inexpensive.

DISADVANTAGES.   First of all, researchers must recognize that much of what is called survey "research" by telephone is not research at all, but an attempt to sell people something. Unfortunately, many companies disguise their sales pitch as a "survey," and this has made respondents suspicious and even prompts some to terminate an interview before it has gotten started. Additionally, visual questions are prohibited. A researcher cannot, for example, hold up a pic-

ture of a product and ask if the respondent remembers seeing it advertised. A potentially severe problem is that not everyone in a community is listed in the telephone directory, the most often used sampling frame. Not everyone has a phone, and many people have unlisted phone numbers; also, some numbers are listed incorrectly, and others are too new to be listed. These problems would not be serious if the people with no phones or unlisted numbers were just like those listed in the phone book. Unfortunately, researchers generally have no way of checking for such similarities or differences, so it is possible that a sample obtained from a telephone directory may be significantly different from the population. (See Chapter 4 concerning random digit dialing.)

Finally, telephone surveys with low incidence rates require numerous calls to obtain the desired sample. The list below is an actual summary of calls made by Paragon Research from Denver, Colorado, for a midwest city radio study conducted in November, 1989. Respondents were 25- to 54-year-old adults who listen "at least sometimes" to country music on radio during a typical week.

Call breakdown		Incidence (%)
Total calls made	7,155	—
Completions	407	5.7
Ineligible	2,262	31.6
No answer	1,569	21.9
Refusals	1,296	18.1
Recordings	935	13.1
Busy/Nonworking	659	9.2
Business	27	<1.0

The telephone numbers used by Paragon Research were selected from a list prepared by a sample generation company (discussed earlier). The list specified households with at least one resident between the ages of 25 and 54.

With an average completion time of 15 minutes, the completed surveys took about 102 hours. The remaining 6,748 calls took an average of 1 minute each, or another 113 hours, which means the survey took a grand total of about 215 hours. It would take one person almost twenty-seven 8-hour workdays (no breaks, no lunch, and constant dialing or talking) to complete this survey!

Personal Interviews

Personal interviews usually involve inviting a respondent to a field service location or research office (called a *one-on-one interview*). Sometimes interviews are conducted at a person's place of work or at home. There are two basic types of interviews, structured and unstructured. In a **structured interview**, standardized questions are asked in a predetermined order; relatively little freedom is given to interviewers. In an **unstructured interview**, broad questions are asked, which allows interviewers freedom in determining what further questions to ask to obtain the required information. Structured interviews are easy to tabulate and analyze but do not achieve the depth or expanse of unstructured interviews. Conversely, the unstructured type elicits more detail but takes a great deal of time to score and analyze.

The steps in constructing a personal interview survey are similar to those for a telephone survey. The list below discusses instances in which the personal interview differs substantially from the telephone method.

1. *Select a sample.* Drawing a sample for a personal interview is essentially the same as sample selection in any other research method. In one-on-one interviews, respondents are selected on the basis of a predetermined set of screening requirements. In door-to-door interviews, a multistage sample is used to first select a general area, then a block or neighborhood, and finally randomly select a household from which a person will be chosen (Figure 4.2 on page 72).

2. *Construct the questionnaire.* Personal interviews are flexible: detailed questions are easy to ask, and the time taken to complete the survey can be greatly extended (many personal interviews last 30–60 minutes). Researchers can also make use of visual exhibits, lists, and photographs to ask questions, and respondents can be asked to sort photos or materials into categories, or to point to their answers on printed cards. Respondents can have privacy and anonymity by marking ballots, which can then be slipped into envelopes and sealed.

3. *Prepare an interviewer instruction guide.* The detail of an instruction guide depends on the type of interview. One-on-one interviewer guides are not very detailed because there is only one location, respondents are prerecruited by a field service, and times are arranged. Door-to-door interviewer guides contain information about the household to select, the respondent to select, and what to do in the event the target respondent is not at home. Interviewer guides often contain information about how to conduct the interview, how to dress, how to record data, and how questions should be asked.

4. *Train the interviewers.* Training is important because the questionnaires are longer and more detailed. Interviewers should receive instruction on establishing a rapport with subjects, administrative details (when to conduct the interviews, how long each will take, and how much the interviewers will be paid), and follow-up questions. Several practice sessions are necessary to ensure that the goal of the project is met and that interviewers follow the established guidelines.

5. *Collect the data.* Personal interviews are both labor and cost intensive. These problems are why most researchers prefer to use telephone or mail surveys. A personal interview project can take several days to several weeks to complete because turnaround is slow. One interviewer can only complete a handful of surveys each day. In addition, costs for salaries and expenses escalate quickly. It is not uncommon for

some research companies to charge as much as $1,000 per respondent in a one-on-one situation.

Data gathering is accomplished by either writing down answers or by audiotaping or videotaping the respondents' answers. Both methods are slow and detailed transcriptions and editing are often necessary.

6. *Make necessary callbacks.* Each callback requires an interviewer to return to a household originally selected or the location used for the original interview. Additional salary, expenses, and time are required.

7. *Verify the results.* As with telephone surveys, a subsample of each interviewer's completed questionnaires is selected for verification. Respondents can be called on the phone or re-interviewed in person.

8. *Tabulate the data.* Data tabulation procedures for personal interviews are essentially the same as with any other research method. A codebook must be designed, questionnaires are coded, and data input into a computer.

ADVANTAGES.   Many of the advantages of the personal interview technique have already been mentioned. It is the most flexible means of obtaining information, since the face-to-face situation lends itself easily to questioning in greater depth and detail. Furthermore, some information can be observed by the interviewer during the interview without adding to the length of the questionnaire. Additionally, the interviewers can develop a rapport with the respondents and may be able to get replies to sensitive questions that would remain unanswered in a mail or phone survey.

The identity of the respondent is known or can be controlled in the personal interview survey. Whereas in a mail survey it is possible that all members of a family might confer on an answer, in a face-to-face interview, this can usually be avoided. Finally, once an interview has begun, it is harder for respondents to terminate the interview before all the questions have been asked. In a phone survey, all the subject needs to do is to hang up.

DISADVANTAGES.   As mentioned, time and costs are the major drawbacks to the personal interview technique. Another major disadvantage is the problem of interviewer bias. The physical appearance, age, race, sex, dress, nonverbal behavior, and/or comments of the interviewer may prompt respondents to answer questions untruthfully. Moreover, the organization necessary for recruiting, training, and administering a field staff of interviewers is much greater than that required for other data collection procedures. If large numbers of interviewers are needed, it is usually necessary to employ field supervisors to coordinate their work, which in turn will make the survey even more expensive. Finally, if personal interviews are conducted during the day, most of the respondents will not be employed outside the home. If it is desirable to interview respondents with jobs outside the home, it is necessary to schedule interviews on the weekends or during the evening.

A hybrid of personal interviewing is intensive, or in-depth, interviewing, which is discussed in Chapter 7.

Mall Interviews

Although mall interviews are essentially a form of personal interview as just discussed, their recent popularity and widespread use warrant individual consideration.

During the late 1980s, mall intercepts became one of the most popular research approaches among marketing and consumer researchers (Hornik and Ellis, 1988). In 1986, Schleifer (1986) found that of all people who participated in a survey in 1984, 33% were mall intercepts. In addition, *Marketing News* (1983) stated that 90% of the market researchers it surveys in the United States use mall intercepts. Both of these figures have risen since the studies were conducted.

Although mall intercepts use convenience samples and sampling error cannot be determined, the method has become the standard for many researchers. It is rare to go into a shopping mall without seeing a man or woman with a clipboard trying to interview a shopper. The method has become commonplace, and some shoppers resent the intrusion. In fact, it is common for shoppers to take paths to avoid the interviewers they can so easily detect.

By the way, purposely avoiding an interviewer isn't necessary. There is another way out if you don't wish to take the time for the interview. Remember from previous discussions that all research requires specific types of people — a screener is developed to eliminate respondents who do not qualify. Nearly every questionnaire has security screening questions to eliminate respondents who work for a company in any way related to the company sponsoring the study, or anyone who works for a marketing research firm. The last part of the security screener is your way out. When the interviewer stops you, simply say, "I work for a marketing research company." Your chances of being recruited are very slim. We're not advocating the practice of lying here, just offering a suggestion. Mall interviewers are generally nice people. It's easier for them to hear the security bail-out than a caustic remark about their presence in the mall.

The procedures involved in conducting mall intercepts are the same as those for personal interviews. The only major difference is that it is necessary to locate the field service that conducts research in the particular mall of interest. Field services pay license fees to mall owners to allow them to conduct research on the premises. Not just any field service can conduct research in any mall.

ADVANTAGES.   Mall intercepts are a quick and inexpensive way to collect personal interview data.

DISADVANTAGES.   Most of the disadvantages have been discussed in other sections of the book. However, as a review, some of the major problems are: convenience sampling restricts the generalizability of the results, the length of

interviews must be short; and there is no control over data collection (researchers are at the mercy of the field service to conduct a proper job).

Disk-By-Mail Surveys

During the late 1980s, a high-tech form of mail surveys has been used that appears to offer promise in the future. The procedure is called **disk-by-mail surveys**, or **DBM**. The name of the survey approach essentially explains the procedure: respondents are sent computer disks that contain a self-administered questionnaire, and are asked to complete it by using a personal computer. This method obviously involves several new areas to consider when conducting a research project.

DBM surveys are essentially the same as a typical self-administered mail survey. The normal steps involved in problem definition, questionnaire design, and pretesting are used. However, there are several unique considerations researchers must address when using DBM.

TYPE OF STUDY.   Most DBM surveys are conducted with professionals or other business related samples. The reason is simple. Only about 20% of American households have personal computers. Sample selection would be time-consuming and costly. However, computer ownership will certainly increase in the future, and in-home DBM surveys may become commonplace. For the time being, DBM surveys are conducted with professionals who generally have access to personal computers in their workplace.

SAMPLE SELECTION.   Locating qualified respondents for DBM surveys is the same as for any other research project, except that in addition to the other screener questions, there must be one about the availability of a personal computer.

COMPUTER HARDWARE.   A typical self-administered mail survey requires that the respondent only have a writing instrument. DBM surveys complicate the process in several ways. First of all, computers can use one of several different operating systems, or languages, which run the computer (Chapter 17). Fortunately, the systems used by IBM and Apple are the most widely used. The problems with the two operating systems can be solved by preparing two different DBM disks, or by asking one of the groups of users to try and locate the other type of computer to complete the survey.

A second problem with the DBM method is whether to use a color or monochrome display to present the questionnaire. Not all color monitors are equal, and the color appearance may be drastically different from one monitor to another. A monochrome display is best to avoid problems.

The type of disk drive is a third problem. The screener must include questions about the type of drive (for example, 5.25 or 3.5) so respondents receive the correct disk format.

Another problem, and not necessarily the last, relates to problems respondents may have with the computer disks. Disks are fragile and may be damaged in the disk duplication process, in shipment, or by the respondent. Replacement disks may have to be sent to some respondents.

SUPPORT.   Because computer problems may occur, or respondents may be unable to complete the survey, most DBM surveys offer respondents a toll free number to call for assistance. This adds further costs to the project.

RELIABILITY AND VALIDITY.   Significant questions are raised about these two areas in relation to DBM surveys. Who actually completes the surveys? Are responses more or less accurate than those provided to interviewers or in typical mail interviews? Does the novelty of the approach have any effect on respondents?

As mentioned earlier, DBM surveys are a totally new approach in research. Not much is known about the procedure, but in all likelihood, DBM surveys will be used more frequently in the future.

Group Administration

Group administration combines the features of mail surveys and personal interviews. The group-administered survey takes place when a group of respondents is gathered together (pre-recruited by a field service) and given individual copies of a questionnaire, or asked to participate in a group interview (a large focus group). The session can take place in a natural setting, but is usually held at a field service location or a hotel ballroom. For example, respondents may be recruited to complete questionnaires about radio or television stations, students in a classroom may complete questionnaires about their newspaper reading habits, or an audience may be asked to answer questions after viewing a sneak preview of a new film.

The interviewer in charge of the session may or may not read questions to respondents. Reading questions aloud may help respondents who have reading problems, but this is not always necessary (it is possible to screen respondents for reading and/or language skills). The best approach is to have several interviewers present in the room so individual problems can be resolved without disturbing the other respondents.

Some group-administered sessions include audio and/or video materials for respondents to analyze. The session allows respondents to proceed at their own pace, and in most cases, interviewers allow respondents to ask questions, although this is not a requirement.

ADVANTAGES.   The group administration technique has certain advantages. In the first place, a group-administered questionnaire can be longer than the typical questionnaire used in a mail survey. Since the respondents are usually assembled for the express purpose of completing the questionnaire, the response rates are almost always quite high. The opportunity for researchers to answer questions and handle problems that might arise generally means that fewer items are left blank or answered incorrectly.

DISADVANTAGES. On the negative side, if a group-administered survey leads to the perception that the study is sanctioned by some authority, suspicion or uneasiness on the part of respondents might result. For example, if a group of teachers is brought together to fill out a questionnaire, some might think that the survey has the approval of the local school administration and that the results will be made available to their superiors. Also, the group environment makes it possible for interaction among the respondents; this has the potential for making the situation more difficult for the researcher to control. In addition, not all surveys can use samples that can be tested together in a group. Surveys often require responses from a wide variety of people, and mixing respondents together may bias the results.

Finally, group administration can be expensive. Costs usually include recruiting fees, co-op payments, hotel rental, refreshments, and salaries for interviewers. A typical list of costs for group sessions includes:

CPI:	$30–$50 per person
Co-op:	$25–$50 per person
Hotel:	$500 per night
Refreshments:	$2–$10 per person
Interviewers:	Variable
Travel expenses:	Variable

ACHIEVING A REASONABLE RESPONSE RATE

No matter what type of survey is conducted, it is virtually impossible to get a 100% response rate. Researchers have more control over the situation in some types of surveys (such as the personal interview) and less in others (such as the mail survey). But no matter what the situation, not all respondents will be available for interviews and not all will cooperate. Consequently, the researcher must try to achieve the highest response rate possible under the circumstances.

What constitutes an acceptable response rate? Obviously, the higher the response rate the better, since as more respondents are sampled, it becomes less likely that response bias is present. But is there a minimum rate that should be achieved? Not everyone would agree on an answer to this question, but there are some helpful data available. Several studies have calculated the average response rates for surveys of various kinds. A comparison with these figures can at least tell a researcher if a given response rate is above or below the norm. For example, Dillman (1978) noted that response rates for face-to-face interviews have dropped sharply in recent years. In the 1960s, the average rate was 80%–85%. More recently, the completion rates of general population samples interviewed by the face-to-face technique is about 60%–65%. Yu and Cooper (1983) studied the completion rates reported in 93 social science journal articles from 1965 to 1981. They found the completion rate for personal interviews to be 82% and for telephone surveys about 72%. Mail surveys had an average completion rate of about 47%. (Note that many of the personal interviews included in this study were done in the 1960s and early 1970s. This should be kept in mind when comparing these figures to Dillman's data mentioned above.)

Regardless of how good the response rate, the researcher is responsible for examining any possible biases in response patterns. Were females more likely to respond than males? Older respondents more likely than younger ones? Whites more likely than nonwhites? A significant lack of response from a particular group might weaken the strength of any inferences from the data to the population under study. To be on the safe side, the researcher should attempt to gather information from other sources about the people who did not respond; by comparing such additional data with those from respondents, it should be possible to determine whether underrepresentation introduced any bias into the results.

Using common sense will help increase the response rate. In phone surveys, respondents should be called when they are likely to be at home and receptive to interviewing. Don't call when people are likely to be eating or asleep. In a one-on-one situation, the interviewer should be appropriately attired. In addition, the researcher should spend time tracking down some of the nonrespondents and asking them why they refused to be interviewed or did not fill out the questionnaire. Responses such as "The interviewer was insensitive and pushy," "The questionnaire was delivered with postage due," and "The survey sounded like a ploy to sell something" can be quite illuminating.

Along with common sense, certain elements of the research design can have a significant impact on response rates. Yu and Cooper (1983) in their survey of 93 published studies discovered the following.

1. Monetary incentives increased the response, with larger incentives being the most effective. Nonmonetary incentives (for example, ballpoint pens) were also helpful.
2. Preliminary notification, personalization of the questionnaire, follow-up letter, and assertive "foot-in-the-door" personal interview techniques all significantly increased the response rate.
3. Things that were not significantly related to an increased response rate were a cover letter, assurance of anonymity, and stating a deadline.
4. Stressing the social utility of the study and appealing to the respondent to help out the researcher did not affect response rates.

GENERAL PROBLEMS IN SURVEY RESEARCH

Although surveys are valuable tools in mass media research, there are problems present in any survey. Experience in survey research confirms the following points.

1. Subjects or respondents are often unable to recall information about themselves or their activities. This inability may be caused by memory failure, nervousness related to being involved in a research study, confusion about the questions asked, or some other intervening factor. Questions that are glaringly simple to researchers may create severe problems for respondents.

For example, during focus group sessions, radio station managers often ask the moderator to ask respondents which radio stations they have set on their vehicle's radio. The managers are surprised to discover how many people not only do not know which stations are programmed on their radio buttons, but how many do not know how many buttons are on their radio. Radio general managers and program directors worry about the finite aspects of their radio station, and many average listeners don't know if they have five or six (or any) buttons on their radio!

2. Due to a respondent's feelings of inadequacy or lack of knowledge about a particular topic, they often provide "prestigious" answers rather than admit they don't know something. This is called **prestige bias**. An example of this was given earlier in the book where respondents claim to watch public TV and listen to public radio, when, in fact, they don't.

3. Subjects may purposely deceive researchers by giving incorrect answers to questions. Almost nothing can be done about respondents who knowingly lie. A large sample may discount this type of response. However, there is no acceptable and valid method to de-

termine whether a respondent's answers are truthful; the answers must be accepted as they are given.

4. Respondents often give elaborate answers to simple questions because they try to "figure out" the purpose of a study, and what the researcher is doing. People are naturally curious, but become more so when they are the focus of a scientific research project.

5. Surveys are often complicated by the inability of respondents to explain their true feelings, perceptions, and beliefs — not because they don't have any, but because they can't put them into words. The question "Why do you like to watch soap operas?" may be particularly difficult for some people. They may watch them every day, but respond only by saying "Because I like them." Probing respondents for further information may help, but not in every case.

Survey research can be an exciting process. It's fun to find out why people think certain ways, or what they do in certain situations. But researchers must continually be aware of obstacles that may hinder data collection, and deal with these problems. The United States is the most surveyed country in the world, and many citizens now refuse to take part in any type of research project. Researchers must convince respondents and subjects that their help is important in decision making and solving problems.

The face of survey research is continually changing. One-on-one and door-to-door interviews are now very difficult to accomplish. This means there is a greater emphasis on mail surveys, mall intercepts, and electronic data gathering procedures. In telephone surveys, for example, **computer-assisted telephone interviewing (CATI)** is now common.

CATI uses video display terminals operated by interviewers to present questions and accept respondent answers, thus eliminating the need for the traditional pencil-and-paper questionnaires. The computer displays the proper questions in the proper order, eliminating the possibility of the interviewer making an error by asking the wrong questions or skipping the right ones. The respondent's answers are entered by the interviewer through the keyboard, making data coding much easier. Groves and Mathiowetz (1984) found that there was little difference in results from using CATI and non-CATI techniques. The response rates, reactions of the interviewers and respondents, and quality of data were virtually equivalent. CATI interviews tended to take slightly more time, but this was balanced by the presence of fewer interviewer errors due to skipping questions. As new software is developed in this area, it seems likely that a greater proportion of surveys will use the CATI technique.

Other areas of change include computer-generated, voice-synthesized surveys where respondents answer by pushing Touch-Tone telephone buttons; 800 telephone numbers for recruited respondents to call to answer questions asked by an interviewer or computer; and various types of touch sensitive TV screens that present questionnaires to respondents. Survey research is changing *very* quickly.

SUPPLEMENT ON CODEBOOK DEVELOPMENT

Since most research data are analyzed by computer, questionnaire responses must be quantified. A project codebook is a column-by-column explanation of the responses and their corresponding code numbers.

For example, the following codebook was prepared for the data used in Chapter 17 of this book. For those readers interested in conducting further analysis, the raw data for the study are included in Appendix 4.

Column(s)	Variable
1–3	Respondent number

Column(s)	Variable
4	Age and sex
	1 = Male 18–24
	2 = Male 25–34
	3 = Female 18–24
	4 = Female 25–34
5	WAAA Listen
	1 = Yes
	2 = No
6	WAAA Morning Show Listener
	1 = Frequently
	2 = Sometimes
	3 = Never
7	WBBB Listen
	1 = Yes
	2 = No
8	WBBB Morning Show Listener
	1 = Frequently
	2 = Sometimes
	3 = Never
9	WCCC Listen
	1 = Yes
	2 = No
10	WCCC Morning Show Listener
	1 = Frequently
	2 = Sometimes
	3 = Never
11	WDDD Listen
	1 = Yes
	2 = No
12	WDDD Morning Show Listener
	1 = Frequently
	2 = Sometimes
	3 = Never
13	WEEE Listen
	1 = Yes
	2 = No
14	WEEE Morning Show Listener
	1 = Frequently
	2 = Sometimes
	3 = Never
15	WFFF Listen
	1 = Yes
	2 = No

Column(s)	Variable
16	WFFF Morning Show Listener
	1 = Frequently
	2 = Sometimes
	3 = Never
17	Favorite Station
	1 = Don't know/No answer
	2 = Other
	3 = WAAA
	4 = WBBB
	5 = WCCC
	6 = WDDD
	7 = WEEE
	8 = WFFF
	9 = WGGG

The following columns relate to why respondents listen to station WCCC. The possible answers are: 1 = Agree; 2 = Disagree; 3 = Don't know/No answer.

18	Amount of new or current music
19	Quality of new or current music
20	Amount of older music
21	Quality of older music
22	Morning show
23	Upbeat/energetic feeling
24	Contests and prizes
25	Because friends listen
26	Afternoon announcers
27	Involvement in local activities
28	Hear favorite songs frequently
29	Attitude toward its listeners
30	Morning show announcers
31	Pace or tempo of station
32	News and information
33	Traffic reports
34	To hear new music and artists
35	Variety of music played
36	Source of local information
37	Amount of music

Coding questionnaires consists of reading each question, referring to the codebook, and assigning the appropriate code for the respondent's answer(s). These data are then input into the computer for analysis.

S U M M A R Y

Survey research is an important and useful method of data collection. The survey is also one of the most widely used methods of media research, primarily due to its flexibility. Surveys, however, involve a number of steps. Researchers must decide whether to use a descriptive or an analytical approach; define the purpose of the study; review the available literature in the area; select a survey approach, a questionnaire design, and a sample; analyze and interpret the data; and finally, decide whether to publish or disseminate the results. These steps are not necessarily taken in that order, but all must be considered before a survey is conducted.

To ensure that all the steps in the survey process are in harmony, researchers should conduct one or more pilot studies to detect any errors in the approach. Pilot studies save time, money, and frustration, since an error that could void an entire analysis sometimes is overlooked until this stage.

Questionnaire design is also a major step in any survey. In this chapter, examples have been provided to show how a question or interviewing approach may elicit a specific response. The goal in questionnaire design is to avoid bias in answers. Question wording, length, style, and order may affect a respondent's answers. Extreme care must be taken when questions are developed to ensure that they are neutral. To achieve a reasonable response rate, researchers should consider including an incentive, notifying survey subjects beforehand, and personalizing the questionnaire. Also, researchers should mention the response rate in their description of the survey.

Finally, researchers are charged with selecting a survey approach from among four basic types: mail, telephone, personal interview, and group administration. Each approach has advantages and disadvantages that must be weighed before a decision is made. The type of survey will depend on the purpose of the study, the amount of time available to the researcher, and the funds available for the study. In the future, survey researchers may depend less on the face-to-face survey and more on computer-assisted telephone interviewing.

Questions and Problems for Further Investigation

1. Develop five questions or hypotheses that could be tested by survey research. What approaches could be used to collect data on these topics?

2. Nonresponse is a problem in all survey research. In addition, many people refuse to participate in surveys at all. Provide an example of a cover letter for a survey on television viewing habits. Include comments that might help increase the response rate.

3. Define a target group and design questions to collect information on the following topics.
   a. Political party affiliation
   b. Attitudes toward television soap operas
   c. Attitudes toward newspaper editorials
   d. Attitudes toward the frequency of television commercials
   e. Public television viewing habits

4. Locate one or more survey studies in journals related to mass media research. Answer the following questions in relation to the article(s).
   a. What was the purpose of the survey?
   b. How were the data collected?
   c. What type of information was produced?
   d. Did the data answer a particular research question or hypothesis?
   e. Were any problems evident with the survey and its approach?

5. Design a survey to collect data on a topic of your choice. Be sure to address the following points.
   a. What is the purpose of the survey? What is its goal?
   b. What research questions or hypotheses will be tested?
   c. Are any operational definitions required?
   d. Develop at least 10 questions relevant to the problem.
   e. Describe the approach to be used to collect data.
   f. Design a cover letter or interview schedule for the study.
   g. Conduct a pretest to test the questionnaire.

References and Suggested Readings

Babbie, E. R. (1990). *Survey research methods* (2nd ed.). Belmont, CA: Wadsworth.

Backstrom, C., & Hursh-Cesar, G. (1981). *Survey research*. New York: John Wiley.

Beville, H. (1985). *Audience ratings*. Hillsdale, NJ: Lawrence Erlbaum.

Brighton, M. (1981). Data capture in the 1980s. *Communicare: Journal of Communication Science, 2*(1), 12–19.

Chaffee, S. H., & Choe, S. Y. (1980). Time of decision and media use during the Ford–Carter campaign. *Public Opinion Quarterly, 44*, 53–70.

Dillman, D. (1978). *Mail and telephone surveys*. New York: John Wiley.

Erdos, P. L. (1974). Data collection methods: Mail surveys. In R. Ferber (Ed.), *Handbook of marketing research*. New York: McGraw-Hill.

Fletcher, J. E., & Wimmer, R. D. (1981). *Focus group interviews in radio research*. Washington, DC: National Association of Broadcasters.

Fowler, F. (1984). *Survey research methods*. Beverly Hills, CA: Sage Publications.

Fox, R. J., Crask, M. R., & Kim, J. (1989). Mail survey response rate. *Public Opinion Quarterly, 52*(4), 467–491.

Groves, R., & Mathiowetz, N. (1984). Computer-assisted telephone interviewing: Effects on interviewers and respondents. *Public Opinion Quarterly, 48*(1), 356–369.

Hornik, J., & Ellis, S. (1989). Strategies to secure compliance for a mall intercept interview. *Public Opinion Quarterly, 52*(4), 539–551.

Hsia, H. J. (1988). *Mass communication research methods: A step-by-step approach*. Hillsdale, NJ: Lawrence Erlbaum.

Kerlinger, F. N. (1986). *Foundations of behavioral research* (3rd ed.). New York: Holt, Rinehart & Winston.

Lavrakas, P. J. (1987). *Telephone survey methods: Sampling, selection, and supervision*. Beverly Hills, CA: Sage Publications.

Marketing News. (1983). Inflation adjusted spending is on rise for consumer research. *Marketing News, 17*(1), 13.

Miller, D. C. (1977). *Handbook of research design and social measurement*. New York: David McKay.

National Association of Broadcasters. (1976). *A broadcast research primer*. Washington, DC: NAB.

Oppenheim, A. N. (1966). *Questionnaire design and attitude measurement*. New York: Basic Books.

Poindexter, P. M. (1979). Daily newspaper non-readers: Why they don't read. *Journalism Quarterly, 56*, 764–770.

Rosenberg, M. (1968). *The logic of survey analysis*. New York: Basic Books.

Schleifer, S. (1986). Trends in attitudes toward and participation in survey research. *Public Opinion Quarterly, 50*(1), 17–26.

Sewell, W., & Shaw, M. (1968). Increasing returns in mail surveys. *American Sociological Review, 33*, 193.

Sharp, L., & Frankel, J. (1983). Respondent burden: A test of some common assumptions. *Public Opinion Quarterly, 47*(1), 36–53.

Singer, E., & Presser, S. (Eds.) (1989). *Survey research methods: A reader*. Chicago: University of Chicago Press.

Wakshlag, J. J., & Greenberg, B. S. (1979). Programming strategies and the popularity of television programs for children. *Journal of Communication, 6*, 58–68.

Walizer, M. H., & Wienir, P. L. (1978). *Research methods and analysis: Searching for relationships.* New York: Harper & Row.

Weisberg, H. F., & Bowen, B. D. (1977). *An introduction to survey research and data analysis.* New York: W. H. Freeman.

Williams, F., Rice, R. E., & Rogers, E. M. (1988). *Research methods and the new media.* New York: Free Press.

Wimmer, R. D. (1976). *A multivariate analysis of the uses and effects of the mass media in the 1968 presidential campaign.* Unpublished doctoral dissertation, Bowling Green University, Ohio.

Winkler, R. L., & Hays, W. L. (1975). *Statistics: Probability, inference and decision* (2nd ed.). New York: Holt, Rinehart & Winston.

Yu, J., & Cooper, H. (1983). A quantitative review of research design effects on response rates to questionnaires. *Journal of Marketing Research, 20*(1), 36–44.

Zillmann, D., & Bryant, J. (1975). Viewers' moral sanctions of retribution in the appreciation of dramatic presentations. *Journal of Experimental Social Psychology, 11,* 572–582.

CHAPTER 7

QUALITATIVE RESEARCH METHODS

The quantitative approaches discussed in the preceding chapters are not suitable for all research problems. There may be certain situations in which a different technique is appropriate. Qualitative research and its advantages and disadvantages were introduced in Chapter 3. This chapter outlines the major differences between the two methods and examines the most frequently used techniques of qualitative research.

AIMS AND PHILOSOPHY

Qualitative research differs from quantitative research along three main dimensions. First, the two methods have a different philosophy of reality. For a quantitative researcher, reality is objective; it exists apart from the researcher and is capable of being seen by all. In other words, it's out there. For the qualitative researcher, there is no one single reality. Each observer creates reality as part of the research process; it is subjective and exists only in reference to the observer. Further, the quantitative researcher believes that reality can be divided into component parts, and he or she gains knowledge of the whole by looking at these parts. On the other hand, the qualitative researcher examines the entire process believing that reality is holistic and cannot be subdivided.

Second, the two methods have different views of the individual. The quantitative researcher believes all human beings are basically similar and looks for general categories to summarize their behaviors or feelings. The qualitative investigator believes that human beings are all fundamentally different and cannot be pigeonholed.

Third, quantitative researchers aim to generate general laws of behavior and explain many things across many settings. In contrast, qualitative scholars attempt to produce a unique explanation about a given situation or individual. Whereas quantitative researchers strive for breadth, qualitative researchers strive for depth.

The practical differences between these approaches are perhaps most apparent in the research process. The following five major research areas describe significant differences between quantitative and qualitative research.

1. *Role of the researcher*. The quantitative researcher strives for objectivity and is separated from the data. The qualitative researcher is an integral part of the data; in fact, without the active participation of the researcher, no data exist.
2. *Design*. In quantitative methods, the design of the study is determined before it begins. In qualitative research, the design evolves during the research; it can be adjusted or changed as it progresses.
3. *Setting*. Quantitative researchers try to control contaminating and/or confounding variables by conducting their investigations in laboratory settings. Qualitative researchers conduct their studies in the field, in natural surroundings. They try to capture the normal flow of events, without trying to control the extraneous variables.
4. *Measurement instruments*. In quantitative research, these exist apart from the researcher. In fact, another party could use the instruments to collect data in the researcher's absence. In qualitative research, the investigator is the instrument; no other individual could fill in for the qualitative researcher.

5. *Theory building*. In the quantitative area, research is used to test theory and to ultimately support or reject it. In the qualitative area, theory is "data driven" and emerges as part of the research process, evolving from the data as they are collected.

These differences will become more apparent throughout this chapter. Four common qualitative techniques are discussed: field observations, focus groups, intensive interviews, and case studies.

FIELD OBSERVATIONS

Before 1980, **field observation** was rarely used in mass media research. Lowry (1979) reported that only 2%–3% of the articles published in journalism and broadcasting journals had employed the technique. Recently, however, field observations have become more common in the research literature (Anderson, 1987; Lindlof, 1987).

Field observation is useful for collecting data as well as for generating hypotheses and theories. Like all qualitative techniques, it is more concerned with description and explanation than it is with measurement and quantification.

As illustrated in Figure 7.1, field observations are classified along two major dimensions: (1) the degree to which the researcher participates in the behavior under observation; and (2) the degree to which the observation is concealed.

Overt observation is represented by Quadrant 1. In this situation, the researcher is identified as such when the study begins. Those under observation are aware that they are being studied. Further, the researcher's role is only to observe, refraining from participation in the process under observation. Quadrant 2 represents overt participation. In this arrangement, the researcher is also known to those being observed, but unlike Quadrant 1, the researcher goes beyond the observer role and becomes a participant in the situation. Quadrant 3 represents the situation where the researcher's role is limited to that of observer, but those under observation are not aware they are being studied. A study in which the investigator participates in the process under investigation, but is not identified as a researcher, is represented by Quadrant 4.

To illustrate the distinction between the var-

FIGURE 7.1   DIMENSIONS OF FIELD OBSERVATION

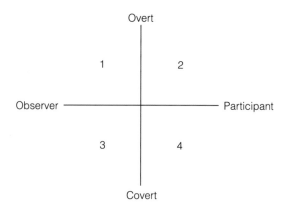

ious approaches, assume a researcher wants to observe and analyze the dynamics of writing comedy for television. The researcher could choose the covert observer technique and perhaps pretend to be doing something else (such as fixing a typewriter) while actually observing the TV writing team at work. Alternatively, the researcher could be introduced as someone doing a study of comedy writing and allowed to watch the team in action. If the research question is best answered by active participation, the investigator might be introduced as a researcher but would still participate in the writing process. If the covert participant strategy is used, the researcher might be introduced as a new writer just joining the group (such an arrangement might be made with the head writer who would be the only person to know the true identity of the researcher).

The choice of technique depends upon the research problem and the degree of cooperation available from the group or individual being observed, as well as ethical considerations. Covert participation may affect subjects' behavior and also raises the ethical question of deception. On the other hand, the information gathered may be more valid if subjects are unaware of being scrutinized.

Some examples of field observation studies in mass media research include Gieber's (1956) classic study of gatekeeping (information flow) in the newsroom and Epstein's (1974) description of network news operations. Pekurny (1980) used the overt participant approach in his study of NBC's "Saturday Night Live." He was given access to all phases of the program and took part in discussions with writers about how to structure a joke and about the suitability of some material for broadcast. Lemish (1987) used overt observation in her study of television viewing by infants and toddlers. Researchers visited the homes of 16 families and observed the viewing behavior of infants during 1- to 2-hour periods.

Lull (1982) conducted a mass observation study of the TV viewing habits of more than 90 families. Observers spent 2 days with the families and then returned to conduct interviews with each person they observed. Note that by using the two data sources (observations and interviews) Lull was "triangulating" to gain additional perspective on his data. He found that the interview data were only partially supported by the observations. Observers noted that the father was the primary controller of the TV set, but the interviews suggested the father's influence was somewhat less.

Advantages of Field Observations

Field observation is not an appropriate technique for every research question, owing to the lack of control and quantification, but it does possess several unique advantages. For one thing, many mass media problems and questions cannot be studied using any other methodology. Field observation often helps the researcher to define basic background information necessary to frame a hypothesis and to isolate independent and dependent variables. For example, a researcher interested in how creative decisions in advertising are made could observe several decision-making sessions to see what actually transpires. Field observations often make excellent pilot studies in that they identify important variables and provide useful preliminary information. In addition, since the data are gathered firsthand, observation is not dependent on the subjects' ability or willingness to report their behavior. For example, young children may lack the reading or verbal skills necessary to respond to a questionnaire concerning their play behavior, but such data are easily gathered by the observational technique.

A field observation is not always used as a preliminary step to other approaches, however. In many cases it alone is the only appropriate approach, especially when quantification is difficult. Field observation is particularly suitable for a study of the gatekeeping process in a network television news department, because quantification of gatekeeping is rather tenuous.

Field observation may also provide access to groups that would otherwise be difficult to observe or examine. For example, a questionnaire sent to a group of producers of X-rated movies is not likely to have a high return rate. An observer, however, may be able to establish enough mutual trust with such a group to persuade them to respond to rigorous questioning.

Field observation is usually inexpensive. In most cases, writing materials or a small tape recorder will suffice. Expenses increase if the problem under study requires a large number of observers, extensive travel, or special equipment (such as video recording machines).

Perhaps the most noteworthy advantage of field observation is that the study takes place in the natural setting of the activity being observed and can thus provide data rich in detail and subtlety. Many mass media situations, such as a family watching television, are complex and are constantly subjected to intervening influences. Field observation, because of the opportunity for careful examination, allows observers to identify these otherwise unknown variables.

Disadvantages of Field Observations

On the negative side, field observation is a bad choice if the researcher is concerned with external validity. This difficulty is partly due to the potentially questionable representativeness of the observations made and partly to problems in sampling. Observing the television viewing behavior of a group of children at a day-care center can provide valuable insights into the social setting of television viewing, but it probably has little correlation to what preschoolers do in other places and under different circumstances.

Moreover, since field observation relies heavily on a researcher's perceptions and judgments as well as on preconceived notions about the material under study, experimenter bias may unavoidably favor specific preconceptions of results, while observations to the contrary are ignored or distorted. This, primarily, is why one

observer is rarely used in a field observation study. Observations need to be *cross-validated* by second or third observers.

Finally, like field experiments, field observations suffer from the problem of reactivity. The very process of being observed may influence the behavior under study. Of course, reactivity can be a problem with other research methods, but it is most often mentioned as a criticism of field observation (Chadwick, Bahr, & Albrecht, 1984). Lull (1985), who provides some perspective on observer effects using data taken from an observational study of families' TV viewing behavior, found that the presence of an observer in the house did have some impact on family members. About 20% of parents and 25% of children reported that their overall behavior was affected by the presence of an observer. The majority of those who were affected thought that they became nicer or more polite and formal because of the observer's presence. When it came to differences in the key behavior under study, 87% said that the observer's presence had no effect on their TV viewing activity. Additionally, among those who reported an observer effect, there were no systematic differences in the distribution of changes. About the same number said that they watched more because of the observer as said they watched less. Obviously, additional studies of different groups in different settings are needed before this problem is fully understood, but Lull's data suggest that although reactivity is a problem with observational techniques, its impact may not be as drastic as some suggest.

In any case, at least two strategies are available to diminish the impact of selective perception and reactance. One is to use several observers to cross-validate the results. A second strategy has to do with the notion of triangulation — the supplementing of observational data by data gathered by other means (questionnaires, existing records, and so on). Accuracy is sought by using multiple data collection methods.

Field Observation Techniques

There are at least six stages in a typical field observation study: choosing the research site, gaining access, sampling, collecting data, analyzing data, and exiting.

CHOOSING THE RESEARCH SITE.   The choice of a research site depends upon the general nature of the research question. The area of inquiry usually suggests a behavior or a phenomenon of interest. Once that is identified, the next step is to select a setting in which the behavior or phenomenon occurs with sufficient frequency to make observation worthwhile. The setting should also accommodate the recording forms and instruments the observer plans to use. For example, if videotaping certain scenes is planned, there must be enough light available for the camera to operate.

Anderson (1987) suggests that the researcher select two or three possible research sites and then "hang around" (Anderson's terminology) each of them to discover their main advantages and disadvantages. He goes on to caution researchers that the site must be permanent and stable enough to permit observations over a period of time.

GAINING ACCESS.   Once the site is selected, the next step is to establish contact. Williamson, Karp, and Dalphin (1977) note that the degree of difficulty faced by researchers in gaining access to settings is a function of two factors: (1) how public the setting is, and (2) the willingness of the subjects in the setting to be observed. The easiest setting to gain access to is one that is open to the public and where people have little reason to keep their behavior secret (for example, TV watching in public places such as airports, bars, dormitory viewing rooms). The most difficult setting to gain access to is one where entry is restricted and where participants have good reason to keep their activities secret (for example, the behavior of hostage takers).

Observation of a formal group (such as a film production crew) often requires permission from management and perhaps union officials. School systems and other bureaucracies usually have a special unit to handle requests from researchers and to assist them in obtaining necessary permissions.

Gaining permission to conduct field observation research requires persistence and public relations skills. Researchers must determine how much to disclose about the nature of the research. In most cases it is not necessary to provide a complete explanation of the hypothesis and procedures, unless there may be objections to sensitive areas. Researchers interested in observing which family member actually controls the television set might explain that they are studying patterns of family communication. Once the contact has been made, it is necessary to establish a rapport with the subject(s). Bogdan and Taylor (1984) suggested the following techniques for building rapport: establish common interests with the participants; start relationships slowly; if appropriate, participate in common events and activities; and do not disrupt participants' normal routines.

SAMPLING.   Sampling in field observation is more ambiguous than in most other research approaches. In the first place, there is the problem of how many individuals or groups to observe. If the focus of the study is communication in the newsroom, how many newsrooms should be observed? If the topic is family viewing of television, how many families should be included? Unfortunately, there are no guidelines to help answer these questions. The research problem and the goals of the study are often used as indicators for sample size: if the results are intended for generalization to a population, one subject or group is probably inadequate.

Another problem is deciding what behavior episodes or segments to sample. The observer cannot be everywhere and see everything, so what is observed becomes a de facto sample of what is not observed. If an observer views one staff meeting in the newsroom, this meeting represents other, unobserved meetings; one conversation at the coffee machine is a sample of all such conversations. In many cases researchers cannot adhere closely to the principles of probability sampling, but they should keep in mind the general notion of representativeness.

Most field observations use purposive sampling: observers draw on their knowledge of the subject(s) under study and sample only from the behaviors or events that are relevant. In many cases, previous experience and study of the activity in question will suggest what needs to be examined. In a study of newsroom decision making, for example, researchers would want to observe staff meetings, since they are obviously an important part of the process. However, restricting the sampling to observations of staff meetings would be a mistake; many decisions are made at the water fountain, over lunch, and in the hallways. Experienced observers tend not to isolate a specific situation but rather to consider even the most insignificant situation for potential analysis. For most field observation, researchers need to spend some time simply getting the feel of the situation and absorbing the pertinent aspects of the environment before beginning a detailed analysis.

COLLECTING DATA. The traditional tools of data collection — the notebook and pen — have given way to radically new equipment in many cases, due to recent advances in electronics. For example, Bechtel, Achelpohl, and Akers (1972) installed television cameras in a small sample of households to document the families' television-viewing behavior. Two cameras, automatically activated when the television set was turned on, videotaped the scene in front of the set. However, while a camera is able to record more information than an observer with a notebook, Bechtel reported that problems in finding consenting families, maintaining the equipment, and interpreting tapes shot at low light levels made the project difficult.

Similarly, Anderson (1987) notes that although the advantages offered by audio and video recording are tempting, there are five major drawbacks to their use:

- Recording devices take time away from the research process because they need regular calibration and adjustment to work properly.
- The frame of the recording is different from the frame of the observer; a human observer's field of view is about 180°, whereas a camera's is about 60°.
- Recordings have to be catalogued, indexed, and transcribed, adding extra work to the project.
- Recordings take behavior out of context.
- Recordings tend to atomize (fragment) behavior and distract attention from the whole process.

Consequently, researchers must weigh the pros and cons carefully before deciding to incorporate recording equipment into the observational design.

Note taking in the covert participant situation requires special attention. Continually scribbling away on a notepad is certain to draw attention and suspicion to the note taker and might expose the researcher's real purpose in a particular setting. In a situation of this type, it is advisable to make mental notes and transcribe them at the first opportunity. If the researcher is initially identified as such, the problem of note taking is somewhat alleviated. Nonetheless, it is not recommended that the observer spend all of his or her time furiously taking notes. Subjects are already aware of being observed, and conspicuous note taking could make them more uneasy. Brief notes jotted down during natural breaks in a situation attract a minimum of attention and can be expanded at a later time.

The field notes constitute the basic corpus of data in any field study. In them, the observers record not only what happened and what was said, but also personal impressions, feelings, and interpretations of what was observed. A general procedure is to separate personal opinions from the descriptive narrative by enclosing the former in brackets.

How much should be recorded? It is always better to record too much information than too little. An apparently irrelevant observation made during the first viewing session might become significant during the course of the project. If the material is sensitive, or if the researcher does not wish it known that research is taking place, the notes may be written in abbreviated form or in code.

ANALYZING DATA. In field observation, data analysis consists primarily of filing and content analysis. Constructing a filing system is an important step in observation. The purpose of the filing system is to arrange raw field data in an orderly format to enable systematic retrieval later (the precise filing categories are determined by the data). Using the hypothetical study of decision making in the newsroom, filing categories might include the headings "Relationships," "Interaction — Horizontal," "Interaction — Vertical," and "Disputes." An observation may be placed in more than one category. It is a good idea to make multiple copies of all notes, and periodic filing of notes throughout the observation period will save time and confusion later.

A rough content analysis is performed to search for consistent patterns once all the notes have been ascribed to their proper files. Perhaps most decisions in the newsroom are made in informal settings such as hallways rather than in formal settings such as conference rooms. Perhaps most decisions are made with little superior-subordinate consultation. At the same time, deviations from the norm should be investigated. Perhaps all reporters except one are typically asked their opinions on the newsworthiness of events. Why the exception?

The overall goal of data analysis in field observation is to arrive at a general understanding of the phenomenon under study. In this regard, the observer has the advantage of flexibility. In laboratory and other research approaches, investigators must at some point commit themselves to a particular design or questionnaire. If it subsequently turns out that a crucial variable was left out, there is little that can be done. In field observation, the researcher can analyze data during the course of the study and change the research design accordingly.

EXITING. A participant must also have a plan for leaving the setting or the group under study. Of course, if the participant is known to everyone, exiting will not be a problem. Exiting from a setting that participants regularly enter and leave is also not a problem. Exiting can be difficult, however, when participation is covert. In some instances, the group may have become dependent on the researcher in some way and the departure may have a negative effect on the group as a whole. In other cases, the sudden revelation that a group has been infiltrated or taken in by an outsider might be unpleasant or distressing to some. The researcher has an ethical obligation to do everything possible to prevent psychological, emotional, or physical injury to those being studied. Consequently, leaving the scene must be handled with diplomacy and tact.

FOCUS GROUPS

The **focus group**, or group interviewing, is a research strategy for understanding audience/consumer attitudes and behavior. From 6 to 12 people are interviewed simultaneously, with a moderator leading the respondents in a relatively free discussion about the focal topic. The identifying characteristic of the focus group is *controlled group discussion*, which is employed to gather preliminary information for a research project, to help develop questionnaire items for survey research, or to understand the reasons behind a particular phenomenon.

A brief guide for conducting focus groups is contained in Appendix 3.

Advantages of Focus Groups

One advantage of focus groups is that they allow for the collection of preliminary information about a topic or phenomenon. Focus groups may be used in pilot studies to detect ideas that will be investigated further using another research method, such as a telephone survey, or another qualitative method.

A second important advantage is that focus groups can be conducted very quickly. The major portion of time is spent recruiting the respondents. A good research company that specializes in recruiting for focus groups can usually recruit respondents in about 7–10 days, depending on the type of person required.

The cost of focus groups also makes the approach an attractive research method; most focus groups can be conducted for about $1,000–$3,000 per group, depending on the type of respondent required for the group, the part of the country in which the group is conducted, and the moderator or company used to conduct the group. When respondents are difficult to recruit, or the topic requires a specially trained moderator, a focus group may cost several thousand dollars. The price, however, is not excessive if the groups provide valuable data for future research studies.

Researchers also like focus groups because of the flexibility in question design and follow-up. In conventional surveys, interviewers work from a rigid series of questions and are instructed to follow explicit directions in asking the questions. A moderator in a focus group, on the other hand, works from a list of broad questions as well as more refined probe questions; hence, follow-up on important points raised by participants in the group is easy. The ability to clear up confusing responses from respondents makes focus groups valuable in the research process.

Most professional focus group moderators or research companies use a procedure known as an *extended focus group*, in which respondents are required to complete a written questionnaire before the start of the group. The pregroup questionnaire, which basically covers the material that will be discussed during the group session, serves to "force" the respondents to commit to a particular answer or position before entering the group session. This commitment eliminates one potential problem created by group dynamics, namely, the person who does not wish to offer an opinion because he or she is in a minority.

Finally, focus group responses are often more complete and less inhibited than those from individual interviews. One respondent's remarks tend to stimulate others to pursue lines of thinking that might not have been brought out in an individual situation. With a competent moderator, the discussion can have a beneficial snowball effect, as one respondent comments on the views of another. A skilled moderator can also detect the opinions and attitudes of those who are less articulate by noting facial expressions and other nonverbal behavior while others are speaking.

Disadvantages of Focus Groups

Focus group research is not totally free from complications; the approach is far from perfect. Some of the problems are discussed here, while others are included later in Appendix 3.

Some groups become dominated by a self-appointed group leader who monopolizes the conversation and attempts to impose her or his opinion on the other participants. Such a person usually draws the resentment of the other participants and may have an extremely adverse effect on the performance of the group. The moderator needs to control such situations tactfully before they get out of hand.

Gathering quantitative data is inappropriate for a focus group. If quantification is important, it is wise to supplement the focus group with other research tools that permit more specific questions to be addressed to a more representative sample. Many people unfamiliar with focus group research incorrectly assume that the method will answer questions of "how many" or "how much." Focus group research is intended to gather qualitative data to answer questions such as "why" or "how." Many times people who hire a person or company to conduct a focus group are disgruntled with the results because they expected exact numbers and percentages. Focus groups do not provide such information.

As suggested earlier, focus groups depend heavily on the skills of the moderator, who must know when to probe for further information, when to stop respondents from discussing irrelevant topics, and how to get all respondents involved in the discussion. All these things must be accomplished with professionalism and care, since one sarcastic or inappropriate comment to a respondent may have a chilling effect on the group's performance.

There are other drawbacks, as well. The small focus group samples are composed of volunteers and do not necessarily represent the population from which they were drawn, the recording equipment or other physical characteristics of the location may inhibit respondents, and if the respondents are allowed to stray too far from the topic under consideration, the data produced may not be useful.

Methodology of Focus Groups

There are seven basic steps in focus group research.

1. *Define the problem.* This step is similar in all types of scientific research: a well-defined problem is established, either on the basis of some previous investigation or out of curiosity. For example, many television production companies that produce pilot programs for potential series will conduct 10–50 focus groups with target viewers to determine their reactions to each concept.

2. *Select a sample.* Because focus groups are small, researchers must define a narrow audience for the study. The type of sample depends on the purpose of the focus group: the sample might consist of consumers who use a particular type of laundry detergent, men aged 18–34 who listen to a certain type of music, or teenagers who purchase more than 10 record albums a year.

3. *Determine the number of groups necessary.* To help eliminate part of the problem of selecting a representative group, most researchers conduct two or more focus groups on the same topic. Results can then be compared to determine whether any similarities or differences exist; or, one group may be used as a basis for comparison to the other group. A focus group study using only one group is rare, since there is no way to know if the results are group-specific or characteristic of a wider audience.

4. *Prepare the study mechanics.* A more detailed description of the mechanical aspects of focus groups is in Appendix 3; suffice it to say here that this step includes arranging for the recruitment of respondents (by telephone or possibly by shopping center intercept), reserving the facilities at which the groups will be conducted, and deciding what type of recording (audio and/or video) will be used. The moderator must be selected and briefed about the purpose of the group. In addition, the researcher needs to determine the amount of co-op money each respondent will receive for participating. Respondents usually receive between $10 and $50 for attending, although professionals such as doctors and lawyers may require up to $100 or more for co-op.

5. *Prepare the focus group materials.* Each aspect of a focus group must be planned in detail; nothing should be left to chance — in particular, the moderator must not be allowed to wing it. The screener questionnaire is developed to produce the correct respondents; recordings and other materials the subjects will hear or see are prepared; any questionnaires the subjects will complete are produced (including the presession questionnaire); and a list of questions is developed for the presession questionnaire and the moderator's guide.

Generally a focus group session begins with some type of shared experience, so that the individuals have a common base from which to start the discussion. The members may listen to or view a tape or examine a new product, or they may simply be asked how they answered question 1 on the presession questionnaire.

The existence of a moderator's guide (Appendix 3) does not mean that the moderator cannot ask questions not contained in the guide. Quite the opposite is true. The significant quality of a focus group is that it allows the moderator to probe comments that respondents make during the session. A professional moderator is often able to develop a line of questioning that no one thought about before the group began, and many times the questioning provides extremely important information. Professional moderators who have this skill receive very substantial fees for conducting focus groups.

6. *Conduct the session.* Focus groups may be conducted in a variety of settings, from professional conference rooms equipped with two-way mirrors to hotel rooms rented for the occasion. In most situations, a professional conference room is used. Hotel and motel rooms are used when a focus facility is not located close by.

7. *Analyze the data and prepare a summary report.* The written summary of focus group interviews depends on the needs of the study and the amount of time and money available. At one extreme, the moderator/researcher may simply write a brief synopsis of what was said and offer an interpretation of the subjects' responses. For a more elaborate content analysis, or a more complete description of what happened, the sessions can be transcribed so that the moderator/researcher can scan the comments and develop a category system, coding each comment into the appropriate category. For example, a researcher who notices that most respondents focus on the price of a new product can establish a content category labeled "Price," code all statements in the transcript referring to price, and arrange these statements under the general heading. The same technique is followed for other content categories. When the coding is completed, the researcher makes summary statements about the number, tone, and consistency of the comments that fall into each category. Needless to say, this approach requires some expenditure of time and money on the researcher's (or client's) part.

INTENSIVE INTERVIEWS

Intensive interviews, or in-depth interviews, are essentially a hybrid of the one-on-one personal interview approach discussed in Chapter 6. Intensive interviews are unique in that they

- Generally use smaller samples.
- Provide very detailed information about the reasons why respondents give specific answers. Elaborate data concerning respondents' opinions, values, motivations, recollections, experiences, and feelings are obtained.
- Allow for lengthy observation of respondents' nonverbal responses.
- Are usually very long. Unlike personal interviews used in survey research that may last only a few minutes, an intensive interview may last several hours, and may take more than one session.
- Are customized to individual respondents. In a personal interview, all respondents are asked the same questions. Intensive interviews allow interviewers to form questions based on each respondent's answers.
- Can be influenced by the interview climate. To a greater extent than with personal interviews, the success of intensive interviews depends on the rapport established between the interviewer and respondent.

Advantages and Disadvantages of Intensive Interviews

As is probably obvious, the biggest advantage of the in-depth interview is the wealth of detail that it provides. Further, when compared to more traditional survey methods, intensive interviewing provides more accurate responses on sensitive issues. The rapport between respondent and interviewer makes it easier to approach certain topics that might be taboo in other approaches. In addition, there may be certain groups for which intensive interviewing is the only practical technique. For example, a study of the media habits of U.S. senators would be hard to do as an observational study. Also, it would be difficult to get a sample of senators to take the time to respond to a survey questionnaire. But in some cases, such persons might be willing to talk to an interviewer.

On the negative side, generalizability is sometimes a problem. Intensive interviewing is typically done with a small, nonrandom sample. Further, since interviews are usually non-standardized, each respondent may answer a slightly different version of a question. In fact, it is very likely that a particular respondent may answer questions not asked of any other respondent. Another disadvantage of in-depth interviews is that they are especially sensitive to interviewer bias. In a long interview, it's possible for a respondent to learn a good deal of information about the interviewer. Despite practice and training, some interviewers may inadvertently communicate their attitudes through loaded questions, nonverbal cues, or tone of voice. The effect this may have on the validity of the respondent's answers is hard to gauge. Finally, intensive interviewing presents problems in data analysis. A researcher given the same body of data taken from an interview may wind up with interpretations significantly different from the original investigator.

Procedures

The procedures for conducting intensive interviews are similar to those used in personal interviews in reference to problem definition, respondent recruiting, and data collection and analysis. The primary differences with intensive interviews are:

- Co-op payments are usually higher, generally from $50–$1,000.
- The amount of data is tremendous. Analysis may take several weeks to several months.
- Interviewers get extremely tired and bored. Interviews must be scheduled several hours apart, which makes data collection take much longer.
- It is very difficult to arrange intensive interviews because of the time required. This is especially true with respondents who are professionals.
- Small samples do not allow for generalization to the target population.

Examples of Intensive Interviews

In their study of violence on television, Baldwin and Lewis (1972) conducted interviews that ranged from 1 to 4 hours in length with a sample of Hollywood writers, producers, and directors. They followed the semistructured approach and worked from an outline of topics. The subjects were people responsible for the content of a prime-time series most likely to contain violence. The researchers sent letters explaining the project to the respondents and followed up with a phone call. None of their respondents refused an interview.

Graber (1988) conducted intensive interviews with 21 registered voters about their use of information media. The respondents were drawn randomly from the voter registration list and were contacted by the researchers. The final sample was selected to represent a fourfold typology based on the respondents' interest in politics and access to the media. Interviews averaged 2 hours in length, and each respondent was interviewed for a total of 20 hours.

Swenson (1989) recruited respondents for her study of TV news viewers by placing classified ads in the local newspapers. After finding eight individuals who fit the study criteria, the researcher then conducted five interview sessions averaging about 2–3 hours in length with each respondent.

CASE STUDIES

The **case study** method is another common qualitative research technique. Simply put, a case study uses as many data sources as possible to investigate systematically an individual, group, organization, or event. Case studies are performed when a researcher desires to understand or explain a phenomenon. Case studies are frequently used in medicine, anthropology, clinical psychology, management science, and history. Sigmund Freud wrote case studies of his patients; economists wrote case studies of the cable TV industry for the FCC; the list is endless.

On a more formal level, Yin (1989) defines a case study as an empirical inquiry that uses multiple sources of evidence to investigate a contemporary phenomenon within its real-life context in which the boundaries between the phenomenon and its context are not clearly evident. This definition highlights how a case study differs from other research strategies. For example, an experiment separates phenomenon from real-life context. The context is controlled by the laboratory environment. The survey technique tries to define the phenomenon under study narrowly enough to limit the number of variables to be examined. Case study research includes both single and multiple cases. Comparative case study research, frequently used in political science, is an example of the multiple case study technique.

Merriam (1988) lists four essential characteristics of case study research:

1. *Particularistic*. This means that the case study focuses on a particular situation, event, program, or phenomenon, making it a good method for studying practical real-life problems.
2. *Descriptive*. The final result of a case study is a detailed description of the topic under study.

3. *Heuristic*. A case study helps people to understand what's being studied. New interpretations, new perspectives, new meaning, and fresh insights are all goals of a case study.
4. *Inductive*. Most case studies depend on inductive reasoning. Principles and generalizations emerge from an examination of the data. Many case studies attempt to discover new relationships rather than verify existing hypotheses.

Advantages of Case Studies

The case study method is most valuable when the researcher wants to obtain a wealth of information about the research topic. Case studies provide tremendous detail. Many times researchers want such detail when they don't know exactly what they are looking for. The case study is particularly advantageous to the researcher who is trying to find clues and ideas for further research (Simon, 1985). This is not to suggest, however, that case studies are to be used only at the exploratory stage of research. The method can also be used to gather descriptive and explanatory data.

The case study technique can suggest *why* something has occurred. For example, in many cities in the mid-1980s, cable companies asked to be released from certain promises made when negotiating for a franchise. To learn why this occurred, a multiple case study approach, examining several cities, could have been used. Other research techniques, such as the survey, might not be able to get at all the possible reasons behind this phenomenon. Ideally, case studies should be used in combination with theory to achieve maximum understanding.

The case study method also affords the researcher the ability to deal with a wide spectrum of evidence. Documents, historical artifacts, systematic interviews, direct observations, and even traditional surveys can all be incorporated into a case study. In fact, the more data sources that can be brought to bear in a case, the more likely it is that the study will be valid.

Disadvantages of Case Studies

There are three main criticisms. The first has to do with a general lack of scientific rigor in many case studies. Yin (1989) points out that "too many times, the case study investigator has been sloppy, and has allowed equivocal evidence or biased views to influence the . . . findings and conclusions" (p. 21). It is easy to do a sloppy case study; rigorous case studies require a good deal of time and effort.

The second criticism is that the case study is not easily open to generalization. If the main goal of the researcher is to make statistically based normative statements about the frequency of occurrence of a phenomenon in a defined population, some other method may be more appropriate. This is not to say that the results of all case studies are idiosyncratic and unique. In fact, if generalizing theoretic propositions is the main goal, the case study method is perfectly suited to the task.

Finally, like participant observation, case studies are likely to be time-consuming and may occasionally produce massive quantities of data that are hard to summarize. Consequently, fellow researchers are forced to wait years for the results of the research, which too often are poorly presented. Some authors, however, are experimenting with nontraditional methods of reporting to overcome this last criticism (see Peters & Waterman, 1982).

Conducting a Case Study

The precise method of conducting a case study has not been as well documented as the more traditional techniques of the survey and the experiment. Nonetheless, there appear to be five distinct stages in carrying out a case study: design, pilot study, data collection, data analysis, and report writing.

DESIGN.   The first concern in a case study is what to ask. The case study is most appropriate for questions that begin with "how" or "why." A research question that is clear and precise will focus the remainder of the efforts in a case study. A second design concern is what to analyze. What exactly constitutes a "case"? In many instances, a case may be an individual, several individuals, or an event or events. If information is gathered about each relevant individual, the results are reported in the single or multiple case study format; in other instances, however, the precise boundaries of the case are harder to pinpoint. A case might be a specific decision, a particular organization at a certain point in time, a program, or some other discrete event. One rough guide for determining what to use as the unit of analysis is the available research literature. Since researchers want to compare their findings with the results of previous research, it is sometimes a good idea not to stray too far from what was done in past research.

PILOT STUDY.   Before the pilot study is conducted, the case study researcher must construct a study **protocol**. This document contains the procedures to be used in the study and also includes the data-gathering instrument or instruments. A good case study protocol contains the procedures necessary for gaining access to a particular person or organization and the methods for accessing records. It also contains the schedule of data collection and addresses the problems of logistics. For example, the protocol should note whether a copy machine will be available in the field to duplicate records, whether office space is available to the researchers, and what will be needed in the way of supplies. The protocol should also list the questions central to the inquiry and the possible sources of information to be tapped in answering these questions. If interviews are to be used in the case study, the protocol should contain the questions to be asked.

Once the protocol has been developed, the researcher is ready to go into the field for the pilot study. A pilot study is used to refine both the research design and the field procedures. Variables that were not foreseen during the design phase can crop up during the pilot study, and problems with the protocol or with study logistics can also be uncovered. The pilot study also allows the researchers to try different data-gathering approaches and to observe different activities from several trial perspectives. The results of the pilot study are used to revise and polish study protocol.

DATA COLLECTION. At least four sources of data can be used in case studies. Documents, which represent a rich data source, may take the form of letters, memos, minutes, agendas, historical records, brochures, pamphlets, posters, and so on. A second source is the interview. Some case studies make use of survey research methods and ask respondents to fill out questionnaires, others may use intensive interviewing.

Observation/participation is the third data collection technique. The same general comments made about this technique earlier in this chapter apply to the case study method as well. The last source of evidence used in case studies is the physical artifact — a tool, a piece of furniture, or even a computer printout. Although artifacts are commonly used as a data source in anthropology and history, they are seldom used in mass media case study research. (They are, however, frequently used in legal research concerning the media.)

Most case study researchers recommend using multiple sources of data, thus affording triangulation of the phenomenon under study (Rubin, 1984). In addition, multiple sources help the case study researcher improve the reliability and validity of the study. Not surprisingly, a study of the case study method found that the ones that used multiple sources of evidence were rated higher than those relying on a single source (Yin, Bateman, & Moore, 1983).

DATA ANALYSIS. Unlike more quantitative research techniques, there are no specific formulas or "cookbook" techniques to guide the researcher in analyzing the data. Consequently, this stage is probably the most difficult in the case study method. Although it is hard to generalize to all case study situations, Yin (1989) has suggested three broad analytic strategies: pattern matching, explanation building, and time series.

In the pattern-matching strategy, an empirically based pattern is compared with a predicted pattern or several alternative predicted patterns. For instance, suppose a newspaper is about to institute a new management tool: a regular series of meetings between top management and reporters, excluding editors. Based on organizational theory, a researcher might predict certain outcomes, namely, more stress between editors and reporters, increased productivity, weakened supervisory links, and so on. If analysis of the case study data indicates that these results did in fact occur, some conclusions about the management change can be made. If the predicted pattern did not match the actual one, the initial study propositions would have to be questioned.

In the analytic strategy of explanation building, the researcher tries to construct an explanation about the case by making statements about the cause or causes of the phenomenon under study. This method can take several forms. Typically, however, an investigator drafts an initial theoretical statement about some process or outcome, compares the findings of an initial case study against the statement, revises the statement, analyzes a second comparable case, and repeats this process as many times as necessary. For example, to explain why some new communication technologies are failing, a researcher might suggest lack of managerial expertise as an initial proposition. But an investigator who examined the subscription television industry might find that lack of management expertise is only part of the problem — inadequate market research is also contributory.

Armed with the revised version of the explanatory statement, the researcher would next examine the direct broadcast satellite industry to see whether this explanation needs to be further refined, and so on, until a full and satisfactory answer is achieved.

In the analytic strategy of time series analysis, the investigator tries to compare a series of data points to some theoretic trend that was predicted before the research, or to some rival trend. If, for instance, several cities have experienced newspaper strikes, a case study investigator might generate predictions about the changes in information-seeking behaviors of residents in these communities and conduct a case study to see whether these predictions were supported.

REPORT WRITING. The case study report can take several forms. The report can follow the traditional research study format: problem, methods, findings, and discussion. Or it can use a nontraditional technique. Some case studies are best suited for a chronological arrangement, whereas case studies that are comparative in nature can be reported from that perspective. No matter what form is chosen, the researcher must consider the intended audience of the report. A case study report written for policy makers would be done in a style different from one that was to be published in a scholarly journal.

Examples of Case Studies

Browne (1983) conducted a comparative case study of the newsroom practices at the Voice of America, the BBC, and Deutsche-Welle, three of the world's largest international radio stations. Browne's study illustrated how multiple sources of evidence are used in the case study technique. He interviewed 55 staff members of the three stations, sat in on editorial meetings, observed actual newsroom practices, and had access to corporate documents. He found that all three stations had common problems, particularly in

their relationships with their foreign language services.

Dimmick and Wallschlaeger (1986) conducted a case study of new media ventures by television network parent companies. They depended primarily upon published documents, particularly annual reports, to reach their conclusion that companies most dependent on network television profits were most active in new media ventures. In his case study of the American Forces Network in Europe, Craig (1986) used available documents and interviews with network personnel as his data. Craig's research was aided by the fact that he had formerly served with the American Forces Network. Stipp, Hill-Scott, and Dorr (1987) used the case study approach in their analysis of the making of the "Mr. T" cartoon series. Working with a social science advisory panel, the authors observed meetings with producers and writers, and examined story treatments, scripts, and storyboards. Additionally, the researchers were able to work directly with the series production staff.

S U M M A R Y

This chapter discusses four alternatives to laboratory and survey research: field observations, focus groups, intensive interviews, and case studies. *Field observation* involves the study of a phenomenon in natural settings. The researcher may be a detached observer or a participant in the process under study. The main advantage of this technique is its flexibility; it can be used to develop hypotheses, to gather preliminary data, or to study groups that would otherwise be inaccessible. Its biggest disadvantage is the difficulty in achieving external validity.

The *focus group*, or group interviewing, is used to gather preliminary information for a research study or to gather qualitative data concerning a research question. The advantages of the focus group method are the ease of data collection and the depth of information that can be gathered. Among the disadvantages: the quality of information gathered during focus groups depends heavily on the group moderators' skill; focus groups can only complement other research because they provide qualitative not quantitative data.

Intensive interviewing is used to gather extremely detailed information from a small sample of respondents. The wealth of data that can be gathered with this method is its primary advantage. Because intensive interviewing is usually done with small, nonrandom samples, however, generalizability is sometimes a disadvantage. Interviewer bias can also be a disadvantage.

The *case study* method draws from as many data sources as possible to investigate an event. Case studies are particularly helpful when a researcher desires to explain or understand some phenomenon. Some problems with case studies are that they can lack scientific rigor, they can be time-consuming to conduct, and the data they provide can be difficult to generalize from and to summarize.

Questions and Problems for Further Investigation

1. Develop a research topic that would be appropriate for a study by:
   a. Intensive interview
   b. Field observation
   c. Case study
2. Suggest three specific research topics that would be best studied by the technique of covert participation. Would any ethical problems be involved?
3. Select a research topic that is suitable for study using the focus group method, then assemble six or eight of your classmates or friends and conduct a sample interview. Select an appropriate method for analyzing the data.
4. Examine recent journals in the mass media research field and identify instances where the case study method was used. For each example, spec-

ify the sources of data used in the study, how the data were analyzed, and how the study was reported.

References and Suggested Readings

Anderson, J. A. (1987). *Communication research.* New York: McGraw-Hill.

Babbie, E. R. (1989). *The practice of social research* (5th ed.). Belmont, CA: Wadsworth.

Baldwin, T., & Lewis, C. (1972). Violence in television: The industry looks at itself. In E. Rubinstein, G. Comstock, & J. Murray (Eds.), *Television and social behavior* (Vol. I). Washington, DC: U.S. Government Printing Office.

Bechtel, R., Achelpohl, C., & Akers, R. (1972). Correlates between observed behavior and questionnaire responses on television viewing. In E. Rubinstein, G. Comstock, & J. Murray (Eds.), *Television and social behavior* (Vol. IV). Washington, DC: U.S. Government Printing Office.

Bickman, L., & Hency, T. (1972). *Beyond the laboratory: Field research in social psychology.* New York: McGraw-Hill.

Bogdan, R., & Taylor, S. (1984). *Introduction to qualitative research methods* (2nd ed.). New York: John Wiley.

Browne, D. (1983). The international newsroom. *Journal of Broadcasting, 27*(3), 205–231.

Calder, B. J. (1977). Focus groups and the nature of qualitative marketing research. *Journal of Marketing Research, 14,* 353–364.

Chadwick, B., Bahr, H., & Albrecht, S. (1984). *Social science research methods.* Englewood Cliffs, NJ: Prentice-Hall.

Cox, K. D., Higginbotham, J. B., & Burton, J. (1976). Applications of focus group interviewing in marketing. *Journal of Marketing, 40,* 77–80.

Craig, R. S. (1986). The American Forces Network, Europe: A case study in military broadcasting. *Journal of Broadcasting and Electronic Media, 30*(1), 33–46.

Dimmick, J., & Wallschlaeger, M. (1986). Measuring corporate diversification: A case study of new media ventures by television network parent companies. *Journal of Broadcasting and Electronic Media, 30*(1), 1–14.

Elliot, S. C. (1980). Focus group research: A workbook for broadcasters. Washington, DC: National Association of Broadcasters.

Epstein, E. J. (1974). *News from nowhere*. New York: Vintage.

Fletcher, A., & Bowers, T. (1983). *Fundamentals of advertising research* (2nd ed.). Columbus, OH: Grid.

Fletcher, J. E., & Wimmer, R. D. (1981). *Focus group interviews in radio research*. Washington, DC: National Association of Broadcasters.

Geiber, W. (1956). Across the desk: A study of 16 telegraph editors. *Journalism Quarterly, 33,* 423–432.

Graber, D. A. (1988). *Processing the news* (2nd ed.). White Plains, NY: Longman.

Lemish, D. (1987). Viewers in diapers: The early development of television viewing. In T. R. Lindlof (Ed.), *Natural audiences*. Norwood, NJ: Ablex.

Lindlof, T. R. (1987). *Natural audiences: Qualitative research of media uses and effects*. Norwood, NJ: Ablex.

Lowry, D. (1979). An evaluation of empirical studies reported in seven journals in the '70s. *Journalism Quarterly, 56,* 262–268.

Lull, J. (1982). How families select television programs. *Journal of Broadcasting, 26*(4), 801–812.

Lull, J. (1985). Ethnographic studies of broadcast media audiences. In J. Dominick & J. Fletcher (Eds.), *Broadcasting research methods*. Boston: Allyn & Bacon.

Merriam, S. B. (1988). *Case study research in education*. San Francisco: Jossey-Bass.

Pekurny, R. (1980). The production process and environment of NBC's *Saturday Night Live. Journal of Broadcasting, 24,* 91–100.

Peters, J. J., & Waterman, R. (1982). *In search of excellence*. New York: Harper & Row.

Reid, L. N., Soley, L. C., & Wimmer, R. D. (1981). Replication in advertising research: 1977, 1978, 1979. *Journal of Advertising, 10,* 3–13.

Reynolds, F. D., & Johnson, D. K. (1978). Validity of focus group findings. *Journal of Advertising Research, 18,* 21–24.

Robertson, L., Kelley, A. B., O'Neill, B., Wixom, C. W., Elswirth, R. S., & Haddon, W. (1974). A controlled study of the effect of television messages of safety belt use. *American Journal of Public Health, 64,* 1074–1084.

Rubin, H. (1984). *Applied social research*. Columbus, OH: Charles E. Merrill.

Simon, J. (1985). *Basic research methods in social science* (3rd ed.). New York: Random House.

Stipp, H., Hill-Scott, K., & Dorr, A. (1987). Using social science to improve children's television. *Journal of Broadcasting and Electronic Media, 31*(4), 461–473.

Swenson, J. D. (1989). *TV news viewers: Making sense out of Iran-Contra*. Unpublished doctoral dissertation, University of Chicago, Chicago.

Szybillo, G., & Berger, R. (1979). What advertising agencies think of focus groups. *Journal of Advertising Research, 19*(3), 29–33.

Tull, D., & Hawkins, D. (1987). *Marketing research* (4th ed.). New York: Macmillan.

Westley, B. H. (1989). The controlled experiment. In G. H. Stempel & B. H. Westley (Eds.), *Research methods in mass communication* (2nd ed.). Englewood Cliffs, NJ: Prentice-Hall.

Williamson, J. B., Karp, D. A., & Dalphin, J. R. (1977). *The research craft*. Boston: Little, Brown.

Wimmer, R. D., & Reid, L. N. (1982). Researchers' response to replication requests. *Journalism Quarterly, 59*(2), 317–320.

Woodside, A., & Fleck, R. (1979). The case approach to understanding brand choice. *Journal of Advertising Research, 19*(2), 23–30.

Woodward, B., & Bernstein, C. (1974). *All the president's men*. New York: Simon & Schuster.

Yin, R. (1989). *Case study research* (2nd ed.). Newbury Park, CA: Sage Publications.

Yin, R., Bateman, P., & Moore, G. (1983). *Case studies and organizational innovation*. Washington, DC: Cosmos Corporation.

C H A P T E R   8

CONTENT ANALYSIS

The chapters in Part II up to this point have concentrated on more general approaches used in mass media investigation. This chapter moves to content analysis, a specific research approach used frequently in all areas of the media. The method is popular with mass media researchers because it provides an efficient way to investigate the content of the media such as the number and types of commercials or advertisements in broadcasting or in the print media. Beginning researchers will find content analysis a valuable tool in answering many mass media questions.

Modern content analysis can be traced back to World War II, when allied intelligence units painstakingly monitored the number and types of popular songs played on European radio stations. By comparing the music played on German stations with that on other stations in occupied Europe, the allies were able to measure with some degree of success the changes in troop concentration on the continent. In the Pacific theater, communications between Japan and various island bases were carefully tabulated; an increase in message volume usually meant that some new operation involving that particular base was planned.

About this time, content analysis was used in attempts to verify the authorship of historical documents. These studies (see Yule, 1944) were primarily concerned with counting words in documents of questionable authenticity and comparing their frequencies with the same words in documents whose authors were known. These literary detective cases demonstrated the usefulness of quantification in content analysis.

After the war, content analysis was used by researchers studying propaganda in newspapers and radio. In 1952 Bernard Berelson published *Content Analysis in Communication Research*, which signaled that the technique had gained recognition as a tool for media scholars.

Since that time, the method has achieved wide popularity. In 1968, Tannenbaum and Greenberg reported that content analysis of newspapers was the largest single category of master's theses in mass communication. A later publication (Comstock, 1975) listed more than 225 content analyses of television programming. Recent concern over the portrayal of violence on television and the treatment of women and minority groups in print and television advertising and in music videos has further popularized the content analysis technique among mass media researchers. From 1977 to 1985, 21% of the quantitative studies published in the *Journal of Broadcasting and Electronic Media* were content analyses (Moffett & Dominick, 1987).

DEFINITION OF CONTENT ANALYSIS

Many definitions of content analysis exist. Walizer and Wienir (1978) defined it as any systematic procedure devised to examine the content of recorded information, Krippendorf (1980) defined it as a research technique for making replicable and valid references from data to their context. Kerlinger's (1986) definition is fairly typical: content analysis is a method of studying and analyzing communication in a systematic, objective, and quantitative manner for the purpose of measuring variables.

Kerlinger's definition involves three concepts that require elaboration. First, content analysis is *systematic*. This means that the content to be analyzed is selected according to explicit and consistently applied rules: sample **157** selection must follow proper procedures, and each item must have an equal chance of being included in the analysis. The evaluation process, also, must be systematic: all content under consideration is to be treated in exactly the same manner. There must be uniformity in the coding and analysis procedures, as well as in the length of time coders are exposed to the material. Systematic evaluation simply means that one and only one set of guidelines for evaluation is used throughout the study. Alternating procedures in an analysis is a sure way to confound the results.

Second, content analysis is *objective*. That is, the personal idiosyncrasies and biases of the investigator should not enter into the findings; if replicated by another researcher, the analysis should yield the same results. Operational definitions and rules for classification of variables should be explicit and comprehensive enough that other researchers who repeat the process will arrive at the same decisions. Unless a clear set of criteria and procedures is established that fully explains the sampling and categorization methods, the researcher does not meet the requirement of objectivity, and the reliability of the results may be called into question. Perfect objectivity is seldom achieved in a content analysis, however. The specification of the unit of analysis and the precise makeup and definition of relevant categories are areas in which individual researchers must exercise subjective choice. (Reliability is discussed at length later in the chapter.)

Third, content analysis is *quantitative*. The goal of content analysis is the accurate representation of a body of messages. Quantification is important in fulfilling that objective, since it aids researchers in the quest for precision. The statement "Seventy percent of all prime time programs contain at least one act of violence" is more precise than "Most shows are violent." Additionally, quantification allows researchers to summarize results and report them with greater parsimony. If measurements are to be made over intervals of time, comparisons of the numerical data from one time period to another can help to simplify and standardize the evaluation procedure. Finally, quantification gives researchers additional statistical tools to use that can aid in interpretation and analysis.

USES OF CONTENT ANALYSIS

Over the past decade the symbols and messages contained in the mass media have become increasingly popular research topics in both the academic and private sectors. The American Broadcasting Company conducts systematic comparative analyses of the three networks' evening newscasts to see how ABC's news coverage compares to that of its competitors. The national Parent-Teachers' Association has offered do-it-yourself training in rough forms of content analysis so that local members can monitor television violence levels in their viewing areas. Citizens' groups, such as the National Coalition on Television Violence, keep track of TV content. Public relations firms use content analysis to monitor the subject matter of company publications, and some labor unions now perform content analyses of the mass media to examine their own images. The *Media Monitor* publishes periodic studies of how the media treat social and political issues.

Content analysis in the mass media often makes use of **medium variables**, the aspects of content that are unique to the medium under consideration. For example, in newspapers and magazines such variables include typography, layout, and makeup; in television, they include shot duration, editing pace, shot selection, scene location, and camera angle. A discussion of medium variables as they relate to television news is contained in Adams and Schreibman (1978).

Although it is difficult to classify and categorize studies as varied and diverse as those using content analysis, they are generally employed for one of five purposes. A discussion of these aims will help illustrate some of the ways in which this technique can be applied.

Describing Communication Content

Several recent studies have catalogued the characteristics of a given body of communication content at one or more points in time. These studies exemplify content analysis used in the traditional, descriptive manner: to identify what exists. For example, Signorielli (1989) described the portrayal of the mentally ill in TV programs from 1967 to 1985. In like manner, Lowry and Towles (1989) analyzed the way sex, contraception, and sexually transmitted diseases are portrayed on soap operas. Similar analyses describe trends in content over time, such as Mayerle and Rarick's (1989) description of the image of education in prime-time network TV from 1948 to 1988.

These descriptive studies can also be used to study societal change. For example, changing public opinion on various controversial issues could be gauged by means of a longitudinal study (see Chapter 9) of letters to the editor or newspaper editorials. Statements about what values are judged to be important by a society could be inferred by a study of the nonfiction books on the best-seller list at different points in time.

Chadwick, Bahr, and Albrecht (1984) suggest that content analysis is useful in the analysis of projective personality tests such as the Rorschach and the Thematic Apperception tests. Subjects' responses to these tests can be content analyzed for characteristics suggesting certain personality traits. For example, Attkisson, Handler, and Shrader (1969) used content analysis to assess the validity of the Draw-A-Man test in determining religious values. The size, position, and details of the drawings were compared with subjects' religious beliefs.

Testing Hypotheses of Message Characteristics

A number of analyses attempt to relate certain characteristics of the source of a given body of message content to characteristics of the messages that are produced. As Holsti (1969) pointed out, this category of content analysis has been used in many studies that test hypotheses of form: "If the source has characteristic A, then messages containing elements x and y will be produced; if the source has characteristic B, then messages with elements w and z will be produced." Merritt and Gross (1978), for example, found that female editors of women's lifestyle pages were more likely than male editors to use stories about the women's movement. A study of local television newscasts revealed that the eyewitness format broadcast more news in the violent and human interest categories (Dominick, Wurtzel, & Lometti 1975). Benze and Declercq (1985) analyzed 113 TV commercials by 23 male and 23 female political candidates. They found that ads for female candidates were less likely to stress strength and more likely to stress compassion. Soderland, Surlin, and Romanow (1989) compared the gender of anchors and reporters on private and government operated stations in Canada and found that females were far more likely to serve as anchors on the government stations.

Comparing Media Content to the "Real World"

Many content analyses may be described as reality checks, in which the portrayal of a certain group, phenomenon, trait, or characteristic is assessed against a standard taken from actuality. The congruence of the media presentation and the situation that exists is then discussed. Probably the earliest study of this type was by Davis (1951), who found that crime coverage in Colorado newspapers bore no relationship to changes in state crime rates. DeFleur (1964) compared television's portrayal of the work world with job data taken from the U.S. census. More recently, the National Commission on the Causes and Prevention of Violence used content analysis data collected by Gerbner (1969) to compare the world of television violence with real-life violence. Lowry (1981) compared alcohol consumption patterns shown on prime-time TV with those that exist in real life, and concluded that TV portrays drinking as being more prevalent than it is in real life and as having fewer negative consequences than it does in real life. Trujillo and Ekdom (1987) examined the portrayal of American industry on TV and found that, when compared to government statistics, the service and public administration industries were overrepresented, whereas the manufacturing segment was underrepresented.

Assessing the Image of Particular Groups in Society

An ever-growing number of content analyses have focused on exploring the media image of certain minority or otherwise notable groups. In many instances, these studies are conducted to assess changes in media policy toward these groups, to make inferences about the media's responsiveness to demands for better coverage, or to document social trends. For example, as part of a license renewal challenge, Hennessee and Nicholson (1972) performed an extensive analysis of the image presented of women by a New York television station, Greenberg (1983) completed a lengthy content analysis of the image of Mexican-Americans in the mass media. More recently, Unger and Stearns (1986) studied the representation of African-Americans in television and magazine advertising and Gilly (1988) performed a cross-cultural content study that compared sex roles in advertising in Mexico, Australia, and the United States. She found that ads were the most stereotyped in Mexico and the least stereotyped in Australia.

Establishing a Starting Point for Studies of Media Effects

The use of content analysis as a starting point for subsequent studies is relatively new. The best-known example is **cultivation analysis**, whereby the dominant message and themes in media content are documented by systematic

procedures, and a separate study of the audience is conducted to see whether these messages are fostering similar attitudes among heavy media users. Gerbner, Gross, Signorielli, Morgan, and Jackson-Beeck (1979) discovered that heavy viewers of television tend to be more fearful of the world around them. In other words, television content — in this case, large doses of crime and violence — may cultivate attitudes more consistent with its messages than with reality. Other work that has used a similar framework includes DeFleur and DeFleur's (1967) study of the possible effects of occupational stereotypes in television programs and Dominick's (1973) study of the influence of television crime on the viewers' perception of actual crime.

A second example of this approach was summarized by Zillmann and Bryant (1983). These investigators examined the effects of the most common forms of humor used in educational TV programs. Among other things, they found that for a child audience, humor that is unrelated to the educational message fosters superior information gain.

LIMITATIONS OF CONTENT ANALYSIS

Content analysis alone cannot serve as a basis for making statements about the effects of content on an audience. A study of Saturday morning cartoon programs on television might reveal that 80% of these programs contain commercials for sugared cereal, but this finding alone does not allow researchers to claim that children who watch these programs will want to purchase sugared cereals. To make such an assertion, an additional study of the viewers would be necessary (as in cultivation analysis). Content analysis cannot serve as the sole basis for claims about media effects.

Also, the findings of a particular content analysis are limited to the framework of the categories and definitions used in that analysis. Different researchers may use varying definitions and category systems to measure a single concept. In mass media research, this problem is most evident in studies of televised violence. Some researchers rule out comic or slapstick violence in their studies, whereas others consider it an important dimension. Obviously, great care must be exercised in comparing the results of different content analysis studies. Researchers who use different tools of measurement will naturally arrive at different conclusions.

Another potential limitation of content analysis is a lack of messages relevant to the research. There are many topics or characters that receive relatively little exposure in the mass media. For example, a study of how Asians are portrayed in U.S. television commercials would be difficult because characters of this ethnicity are rarely seen (of course, this fact in itself might be a significant finding). A researcher interested in such a topic must be prepared to examine a large body of media content to find sufficient quantities for analysis.

Finally, content analysis is frequently time-consuming and expensive. The task of examining and categorizing large volumes of content is often laborious and tedious. Plowing through 100 copies of the *New York Times* or 50 issues of *Newsweek* involves large chunks of time and a corresponding degree of patience. In addition, if television content is selected for analysis, some means of preserving the programs for detailed examination is necessary. Typically, researchers videotape programs for analysis, but this requires access to a recorder and large supplies of videotape, materials not all researchers can afford.

STEPS IN CONTENT ANALYSIS

In general, a content analysis is conducted in several discrete stages. Although the steps are listed here in sequence, they need not be followed in the order given. In fact, the initial stages of analysis can easily be combined. Nonetheless, the following steps may be used as a rough outline.

1. Formulate the research question or hypothesis.
2. Define the population in question.
3. Select an appropriate sample from the population.
4. Select and define a unit of analysis.
5. Construct the categories of content to be analyzed.
6. Establish a quantification system.
7. Train coders and conduct a pilot study.
8. Code the content according to established definitions.
9. Analyze the collected data.
10. Draw conclusions and search for indications.

Formulating a Research Question

One problem to avoid in content analysis is the "counting-for-the-sake-of-counting" syndrome. The ultimate goal of the analysis must be clearly articulated, to avoid aimless exercises in data collection that have little utility for mass media research. For example, by counting the punctuation marks that are used in the *New York Times* and *Esquire* it would be possible to generate a statement such as: "*Esquire* used 45% more commas, but 23% fewer semicolons than the *New York Times*." The value of such information for mass media theory or policy making, however, is dubious. Content analysis should not be conducted simply because the material exists and can be tabulated.

As with other methods of mass media research, content analyses should be guided by well-formulated research questions or hypotheses. A basic review of the literature is a required step. The sources for hypotheses are the same as for other areas of media research. It is possible to generate a research question based on existing theory, prior research, or practical problems, or as a response to changing social conditions. For example, a research question might ask whether the growing visibility of the women's movement has produced a change in the way women are depicted in advertisements. Or, a content analysis might be conducted to determine whether the public affairs programming of group-owned television stations differs from that of other stations. Well-defined research questions or hypotheses enable the development of accurate and sensitive content categories, which in turn helps to produce more valuable data.

Defining the Universe

This stage is not as grandiose as it sounds. To "define the universe" is to specify the boundaries of the body of content to be considered, which requires an appropriate operational definition of the relevant population. If researchers are interested in analyzing the content of popular songs, they must define what is meant by a *popular* song. All songs listed in *Billboard*'s "Hot 100" chart? The top 50 songs? The top 10? What time period will be considered? The past 6 months? This month? A researcher who intends to study the image of minority groups on television must define *television*. Is it evening programming, or does it also include daytime shows? Will the study examine news content or confine itself to dramatic offerings? Basically, two dimensions are used to determine the appropriate universe for a content analysis: the topic area and the time period. The specification of the topic area should be logically consistent with the research question and related to the goals of the study. For example, if a researcher plans a study of the United States' relationship with Nicaragua, should it include the Iran–Contra hearings? The time period to be examined should be sufficiently long so that the phenomenon under study has ample chance to occur.

By clearly specifying the topic area and the time period, the researcher is providing a basic requirement of content analysis: a concise statement that spells out the parameters of the investigation. For example:

> This study considers TV commercials broadcast in prime time in the New York City area from September 1, 1990, to October 1, 1990.

Or:

> This study considers the news content on the front pages of the *Washington Post* and the *New York Times*, excluding Sundays, from January 1 to December 31 of the past year.

Selecting a Sample

Once the universe has been defined, a sample is selected. Although many of the guidelines and procedures discussed in Chapter 4 are applicable here, the sampling of content involves some special considerations. On one hand, some analyses are concerned with a relatively finite amount of data, and it may be possible to conduct a census of the content. Thus, Wurtzel (1975) was able to perform a census of 2 years of public access television programming in New York, and Wimmer and Haynes (1978) conducted a census of 7 years' worth of articles published in the *Journal of Broadcasting*. On the other hand, in the more typical situation, the researcher has such a vast amount of content available that a census is not practical. Thus, a sample must be drawn.

Most content analysis in mass media involves multistage sampling. This process typically involves two stages (although it may entail three). The first stage is usually to take a sampling of content sources. For example, a researcher interested in the treatment of the nuclear freeze movement by American newspapers would first need to sample from among the 1,650 or so newspapers published each day. The researcher may decide to focus primarily on the way big city dailies covered the story and opt to analyze only the leading circulation newspapers in the 10 largest American cities. To take another example, a researcher interested in the changing portrayal of the elderly in magazine advertisements would first need to sample from among the thousands of publications available. In this instance, the researcher might select only the top 10, 15, or 25 mass circulation magazines. Of course, it is also possible to sample randomly if the task of analyzing all the titles is too overwhelming. A further possibility is to use the technique of stratified sampling discussed in Chapter 4. For example, the researcher studying the nuclear freeze movement might wish to stratify the sample by circulation size and sample from within strata composed of big city papers, medium city papers, and small city papers. The magazine researcher might stratify by type of magazine: news, women's interests, men's interests, and so on. A researcher interested in television content might stratify by network or by program type.

When the sources have been identified, the dates can be selected. In many studies, the time period from which the issues are to be selected is determined by the goal of the project. If the goal is to assess the nature of news coverage of the Iran–Contra hearings, then the sampling period is fairly well defined by the actual duration of the story. If the research question is directed toward changes in the media image of San Francisco following the earthquake in October, 1989, then content should be sampled before, at the time of, and after the disaster. But within this period, what editions of newspapers and magazines and which television programs will be selected for analysis? It would be a tremendous amount of work to analyze each copy of *Time*, *Newsweek*, and *U.S. News and World Report* over a 5-year period. It is possible to sample from within that time period and obtain a representative group of issues. A simple random sample of the calendar dates involved is one possibility: after a random start, every *n*th issue of a publication is selected for the sample. This

method cannot be used without planning, however. For instance, if the goal is 50 edition dates, and an interval of 7 is used, the sample might include 50 Saturday editions (periodicity). Since news content is not randomly distributed over the days of the week, the sample will not be representative.

Another technique for sampling edition dates is to stratify by week of the month and by day of the week. A sampling rule that no more than two days from one week can be chosen is one way to ensure a balanced distribution across the month. Another procedure is to construct a *composite week* for each month in the sample. For example, a study might use a sample of one Monday, drawn at random from the four or five possible Mondays in the month, one Tuesday drawn from the available Tuesdays, and so on, until all weekdays have been included. How many edition dates should be selected? Obviously, this depends on the topic under study. If an investigator is trying to describe the portrayal of Mexican-Americans on prime-time television, a large number of dates would have to be sampled to ensure a representative analysis. If there is an interest in analyzing the geographic sources of news stories, a smaller number of dates would be needed, since almost every story would be relevant. The number of dates should be a function of the incidence of the phenomenon in question: the lower the incidence, the more dates that will have to be sampled.

There are some rough guidelines for sampling in the media. Stempel (1952) drew separate samples of 6, 12, 18, 24, and 48 issues of a newspaper and compared the average content of each of the sample sizes in a single subject category against the total for the entire year. He found that each of the five sample sizes was adequate and that increasing the sample beyond 12 issues did not significantly improve upon accuracy. In television, Gerbner, Gross, Jackson-Beeck, Jeffries-Fox, and Signorielli (1977) demonstrated that at least for the purpose of measuring violent behavior, a sample of one week of fall programming and various sample dates drawn throughout the year will produce comparable results. As a general rule, however, the larger the sample the better—within reason, of course. If too few dates are selected for analysis, the possibility of an unrepresentative sample is increased. Larger samples, if chosen randomly, usually run less risk of being atypical.

There may be times, however, when purposive sampling is useful. As Stempel (1989) points out, a researcher might learn more about newspaper coverage of South Africa by examining a small sample of carefully selected papers (those that subscribe to the international-national wire service and/or have correspondents in South Africa) than by studying a random sample of 100 newspapers.

Another problem to examine during the sampling phase relates to systematic bias in the content itself. For example, a study of the amount of sports news in a daily paper might yield inflated results if the sampling were done only in April, when three or more professional sports are simultaneously in season. A study of marriage announcements in the Sunday New

York Times for the month of June from 1932 to 1942 revealed no announcement of a marriage in a synagogue (Hatch & Hatch, 1947). It was later pointed out that the month of June usually falls within a period during which traditional Jewish marriages are prohibited. Researchers familiar with their topics can generally detect and guard against this type of distortion.

Once the sources and the dates have been determined, there may be one further stage of sampling. A researcher might wish to confine his or her attention to a selection of content within an edition. For example, an analysis of the front page of a newspaper is valid for a study of general reporting trends but is probably inadequate for a study of social news coverage. Figure 8.1 provides an example of multistage sampling in content analysis.

Selecting the Unit of Analysis

The **unit of analysis** is the thing that is actually counted. It is the smallest element of a content analysis, but it is also one of the most important. In written content, the unit of analysis might be

---

FIGURE 8.1   MULTISTAGE SAMPLING IN A HYPOTHETICAL CONTENT ANALYSIS STUDY

Research Question: Have there been changes in the type of products advertised in men's magazines from 1980 to 1990?

Sampling Stage 1: Selection of Titles
Men's magazines are defined as those magazines whose circulation figures show that 80% or more of their readers are men. These magazines will be divided into two groups: large and medium circulation.
    Large circulation: reaches more than 1,000,000 men.
    Medium circulation: reaches between 500,000 and 999,999 men.
From all the magazines that fall into these two groups, three will be selected at random from each division, for a total of six titles.

Sampling Stage 2: Selection of Dates
Three issues from each year will be chosen at random from clusters of four months. One magazine will be selected from the January, February, March, April issues, etc. This procedure will be followed for each magazine, yielding a final sample of 30 issues per magazine, or 180 total issues.

Sampling Stage 3: Selection of Content
Every other display ad will be tabulated, regardless of size.

a single word or symbol, a theme (a single assertion about one subject), or an entire article or
story. In television and film analyses, units of
analysis can be characters, acts, or entire programs. Specific rules and definitions are required for determining these units to allow for
greater agreement between coders and fewer
judgment calls.

Certain units of analysis are simpler to
count than others. It is easier to determine the
number of stories on the "CBS Evening News"
that deal with international news than the number of acts of violence in a week of network
television because a story is a more readily distinguishable unit of analysis than an act. The
beginning and ending of a news story are fairly
easy to see, but suppose that a researcher trying
to catalog violent content was faced with a long
fistfight between three characters? Is the whole
sequence one act of violence, or is every blow
considered an act? What if a fourth character
joins in? Does it then become a different act?

Operational definitions of the unit of analysis should be clear-cut and thorough; the criteria
for inclusion should be apparent and easily observed. These goals cannot be accomplished
without effort and some trial and error. As a
preliminary step, researchers must form a rough
draft of a definition and then sample representative content to see whether problems exist.
This procedure usually results in further refinement and modification of the operational definition. Table 8.1 presents typical operational definitions of units of analysis taken from mass
media research.

Constructing Categories for Analysis

At the heart of any content analysis is the category system used to classify media content. The
precise makeup of this system, of course, varies
with the topic under study. As Berelson (1952)
pointed out, "Particular studies have been productive to the extent that the categories were
clearly formulated and well-adapted to the
problem and the content."

To be serviceable, all category systems
should be mutually exclusive, exhaustive, and
reliable. A category system is mutually exclusive if a unit of analysis can be placed in one and
only one category. If the researcher discovers
that certain units fall simultaneously into two
different categories, the definitions of those categories must be revised. For example, suppose
researchers attempted to describe the ethnic
makeup of prime-time television characters using the following category system: (1) African-
American, (2) Jewish, (3) white, (4) Native
American, and (5) other. Obviously, a Jewish
person would fall into two categories at once,
thus violating the exclusivity rule. Or, to take
another example, a researcher might start with
the following categories in an attempt to describe the types of programming on network
television: (1) situation comedies, (2) children's
shows, (3) movies, (4) documentaries, (5) ac-
tion/adventure programs, (6) quiz and talk
shows, and (7) general drama. This list might
look acceptable at first glance, but a program
such as "Matlock" raises questions. Is it to be
placed in the action/adventure category or in
general drama? Definitions must have a high
degree of specificity to handle problems such
as this.

In addition to exclusivity, content analysis
categories must have the property of **exhaustivity**: there must be an existing slot into which
every unit of analysis can be placed. If investigators suddenly find a unit of analysis that does
not logically fit into a predefined category, they
have a problem with their category system.
Taken as a whole, the category system should
account for every unit of analysis. Achieving
exhaustivity usually is not a great problem in
mass media content analysis. If one or two unusual instances are detected, a category labeled
"other" or "miscellaneous" usually solves the
problem. (If too many items fall into this category, however, a reexamination of the original
category definitions is called for; a study with
10% or more of its content in the "other" category
is probably overlooking some relevant content

TABLE 8.1   EXAMPLES OF UNITS OF ANALYSIS

Researchers	Title	Universe	Sample	Unit
Brown & Campbell (1986)	Race and gender in music videos	Music videos appearing on MTV and Black Entertainment TV (BET) in 1984	75 videos aired on MTV on two nights and 37 videos from the "Video Soul" program on BET	(1) All lead performers in each video and (2) predominant theme of the video
Swayne & Greco (1987)	Portrayal of older Americans in television commercials	All network ads airing in November 1985	814 ads contained in 36 hours of network programming from 10–12 noon, 2–4 pm, and 8–10 pm, for all days of the week	Persons over 65 as judged by appearance, ambulatory aids, and presence of grandchildren
Pasadeos & Renfro (1988)	Rupert Murdoch's style and the *New York Post*	Newspaper content in the *New York Post* and *New York Daily News*, 1976–1983	12 issues of the *Post* and *Daily News* from the constructed 6-day weeks in 1976, 1977, 1979, and 1983	(1) Space given to headlines, body copy, illustrations, masthead, ads, and (2) "sensational" content
Gross & Sheth (1989)	Time-oriented advertising	Issues of *Ladies' Home Journal*, 1980–1988	Three issues randomly selected from each decade	The appeal of each ad (whether time-oriented or not)
Potter & Ware (1989)	Frequency and context of pro-social acts on prime-time TV	Dramatic programs on network prime-time TV during the 1987 season	All dramatic shows (88 hours) on the three networks for two randomly selected weeks	All prosocial acts: "any attempt by the character to help another character"

characteristic.) An additional way to assure exhaustivity is to dichotomize or trichotomize the content: attempts at problem solving might be defined as aggressive and nonaggressive; statements might be placed in positive, neutral, and negative categories. The most practical way to determine whether a proposed categorization system is exhaustive is to pretest it on a sample of content. If unanticipated items appear, the original scheme requires changes before the primary analysis can begin.

The categorization system should also be reliable; that is, different coders should agree in the great majority of instances about the proper category for each unit of analysis. This agreement is usually quantified in content analysis and is called **intercoder reliability**. Precise category definitions generally increase reliability, while sloppily defined categories tend to lower it. Pretesting the category system for reliability is highly recommended before beginning to process the main body of content. Reliability is crucial in content analysis, as discussed in more detail later in this chapter.

The question of how many categories to include may arise in constructing category systems. Common sense, pretesting, and practice with the coding system are valuable guides to aid the researcher in steering between the two extremes: developing a system with too few categories (so that essential differences are obscured) and defining too many categories (so that only a small percentage falls into each, thus limiting generalizations). As an illustration of too few categories, consider Wurtzel's (1975) study of programming on public access television. One of the preliminary categories was labeled "informational," and the data indicated that more than 70% of the content fell into this classification. As a result, Wurtzel subdivided the category into seven informational headings (ethnic, community, health, consumer, etc.). An example of the opposite extreme is the attempt made by Dominick, Richman, and Wurtzel (1979) to describe the types of problems encountered by characters in prime-time television shows popular with children. They originally developed seven categories, including problems that dealt with romance, problems between friends, and other emotional problems arising out of relationships (with siblings, co-workers, or others). Preliminary analysis, however, indicated that only a small fraction of problems fell into the "friendship" and "other

emotional" slots. Consequently, these three categories were combined into a single classification labeled "problems dealing with romance, sentiment, and other emotions." As a general rule, many researchers suggest that too many initial categories are preferable to too few, since it is usually easier to combine several categories than it is to subdivide a large one after the units have been coded.

Establishing a Quantification System

Quantification in content analysis can involve all four of the levels of data measurement discussed in Chapter 3, although usually only nominal, interval, and ratio data are used. At the nominal level, researchers simply count the frequency of occurrence of the units in each category. Gantz, Gartenberg, and Rainbow (1980) employed nominal measurement to determine the percentage of elderly people appearing in different categories of magazine advertisements: 14% in "corporate image" advertisements, 12% liquor, 11% travel, and so on. The topics of conversation on daytime television, the themes of newspaper editorials, and the occupation of prime-time television characters can all be quantified by means of nominal measurement.

At the interval level, it is possible to develop scales for coders to use to rate certain attributes of characters or situations. For example, in a study dealing with the images of women in commercials, each character might be rated by coders on several scales, such as:

independent __:__:__:__:__ dependent
dominant __:__:__:__:__ submissive

Scales such as these add depth and texture to a content analysis and are perhaps more interesting than the surface data obtained through nominal measurement. However, rating scales inject subjectivity into the analysis and may lower intercoder reliability unless careful training is undertaken. Chang (1975), for example, constructed an interval scale based on the degree of liking movie critics had for certain films.

Ratio level measurements in mass media research generally are applied to space and time. In the print media, column-inch measurements are used to analyze editorials, advertisements, and stories about particular events or phenomena. In television and radio, ratio level measurements are made concerning time: the number of commercial minutes, the types of programs on the air, the amount of the program day devoted to programs of various types, and so on.

Coding the Content

Placing a unit of analysis into a content category is called **coding**. It is the most time-consuming and least glamorous part of a content analysis. Individuals who do the coding are called *coders*. The number of coders involved in a content analysis is typically small; a brief examination of a sampling of recent content analyses indicates that typically two to six coders are used.

Careful training of coders, which usually results in a more reliable analysis, is an integral task in any content analysis. Although the investigator may have a firm grasp of the operational definitions and the category schemes, coders may not share this close knowledge. Consequently, they must become thoroughly familiar with the study's mechanics and peculiarities. To this end, researchers should plan several lengthy training sessions in which sample content is examined and coded. These sessions are used to revise definitions, clarify category boundaries, and revamp coding sheets until the coders are comfortable with the materials and procedure. Detailed instruction sheets should also be provided to coders.

Next, a pilot study is done to check intercoder reliability. The pilot study should be conducted with a fresh set of coders who are given some initial training to impart familiarity with the instructions and methods of the study. Some would argue that fresh coders are to be preferred for this task because intercoder reliability between coders who have worked for long periods of time developing the coding scheme might be artificially high. As Lorr and McNair (1966) suggest, "Interrater agreement for a new set of judges given a reasonable but practical amount of training . . . would represent a more realistic index of reliability."

To facilitate coding, standardized sheets are usually used. These sheets allow coders to classify the data by simply placing check marks or slashes in predetermined spaces. Figure 8.2 is an example of a standardized coding sheet and Figure 8.3 illustrates the coder instruction sheet that accompanied it. If data are to be tabulated by hand, the coding sheets should be constructed to allow for rapid tabulation. Some studies code data on 4 inch × 6 inch index cards, with information recorded across the top of the card. This enables researchers to sort the information quickly into categories. Templates are available to speed the measurement of newspaper space. Researchers who work with television generally videotape the programs and allow coders to stop and start the tape at their own pace while coding data. If a tape machine is not available, the coding procedure has to be simplified, because the coders have no opportunity for a second look.

When a computer is used in tabulating data, the data are usually transferred directly to computer coding sheets or perhaps mark-sense forms or optical scan sheets (answer sheets scored by computer). These forms save time and reduce data errors.

Computers are useful not only in the data tabulation phase of a content analysis, but also in the actual coding process. Computers will perform with unerring accuracy any coding task in which the classification rules are unambiguous. Computers can do simple tasks such as recognizing words or even syllables as they occur in a sample of text, with extreme speed. Wilhoit and Sherrill (1968), for example, instructed a computer to recognize the names of U.S. senators as they appeared in wire service copy. Of course the drawback to this approach is that the body of copy to be scanned must be in computer-readable form. In many instances,

---

FIGURE 8.2   STANDARDIZED CODING SHEET FOR STUDYING TV CARTOONS

Character Descriptive Code Sheet

Program name _____

A. Character number _____

B. Character name
   or description _____

C. Role   1-Major   3-Other (individual)
           2-Minor   4-Other (group)

D. Species
   1-Human   4-Robot   7-Other (specify):
   2-Animal   5-Animated object
   3-Monster/Ghost   6-Indeterminate

   _____

E. Sex

   1-Male   2-Female   3-Indeterminate   4-Mixed (group)

F. Race

   1-White   4-Robot   7-Other (specify):

   2-African-American   5-Native American

   3-Animal   6-Indeterminate

   _____

G. Age

   1-Child   3-Adult   5-Indeterminate

   2-Teenager   4-Mature adult   6-Mixed (group)

---

transcribing the original copy into the necessary format would require far more effort than counting the data manually. This situation may change, however, with the advent of teletext or viewdata systems, which supply copy that is already machine-readable, or with the arrival of high-speed scanning devices. In any case, the use of computers in content analysis is now widely accepted. For more information, consult Gerbner, Holsti, Krippendorf, Paisley, and Stone (1969) or Krippendorf (1980).

Television content can be coded with computer assistance by using event recorders that tabulate frequency and duration data. Coders push a series of buttons corresponding to the appropriate unit of analysis and their responses are electronically recorded. Bryant, Hezel, and Zillmann (1979) used such an arrangement to code humorous events in children's educational TV programs.

Analyzing the Data

The descriptive statistics discussed in Chapters 10, 11, and 12 and in Appendix 2, such as percentages, means, modes, and medians, are

Character Descriptive Code Sheet Instructions

Code all characters that appear on the screen for at least 90 seconds and/or speak more than 15 words (include cartoon narrator when applicable). Complete one sheet for each character to be coded.

A. Character number: code two-digit program number first (listed on page 12 of this instruction book), followed by two-digit character number randomly assigned to each character (starting with 01).

B. Character name: list all formal names, nicknames, or dual identity names (code dual identity behavior as one character's actions). List description of character if name is not identifiable.

C. Role
   1-*Major*: major characters share the majority of dialogue during the program, play the largest role in the dramatic action, and appear on the screen for the longest period of time during the program.
   2-*Minor*: all codeable characters that are not identified as major characters.
   3-*Other (individual)*: one character that does not meet coding requirements but is involved in a behavioral act that is coded.
   4-*Other (group)*: two or more characters that are simultaneously involved in a behavioral act but do not meet coding requirements.

D. Species
   1-*Human*: any character resembling man, even ghost or apparition if it appears in human form (e.g., the Ghostbusters)
   2-*Animal*: any character resembling bird, fish, beast, or insect; may or may not be capable of human speech (e.g., muppets, smurfs, Teddy Ruxpin)
   3-*Monster/Ghost*: any supernatural creature (e.g., my pet monster, ghosts)
   4-*Robot*: mechanical creature (e.g., transformers)
   5-*Animated object*: any inanimate object (e.g., car, telephone) that acts like a sentient being (speaks, thinks, etc.). Do not include objects that "speak" through programmed mechanical means (e.g., recorded voice playback through computer).
   6-*Indeterminate*
   7-*Other*: if species is mixed within group, code as mixed here and specify which of the species are represented.

E. 1-Male   2-Female   3-Indeterminate: use this   4-Mixed (group only)
                           category sparingly (if
                           animal has low masculine
                           voice, code as male).

Note: The remainder of the instructions continue in this format.

appropriate for content analysis. If hypothesis tests are planned, common inferential statistics (results are generalized to the population) are acceptable. The chi-square test is the most commonly used, since content analysis data tend to be nominal in form; however, if the data meet the requirements of interval or ratio levels, a *t*-test, ANOVA, or Pearson's *r* may be appropriate. Other statistical analyses are discussed by Krippendorf (1980), such as discriminant analysis, cluster analysis, and contextual analysis.

Interpreting the Results

If an investigator is testing specific hypotheses concerning the relationships between variables, the interpretation will be fairly evident. However, if the study is descriptive, questions about the meaning or importance of the results may arise. Researchers are often faced with a "fully/ only" dilemma. Suppose, for example, that a content analysis of children's television programs reveals that 30% of the commercials were for snacks and candy. What is the researcher to conclude? Is this a high or a low amount? Should the researcher report, "*Fully* 30% of the commercials fell into this category," or should the same percentage be presented as: "*Only* 30% of the commercials fell into this category"? Clearly, the investigator needs some benchmark for comparison. Thirty percent may indeed be a high figure when compared to commercials for other products or for those shown during adult programs.

In a study done by one of the authors, the amount of network news time devoted to the various states was tabulated. It was determined that California and New York receive 19% and 18% respectively, of non-Washington, DC, national news coverage. By themselves, these numbers are interesting, but their significance is somewhat unclear. In an attempt to aid interpretation, each state's relative news time was compared to its population, and an "attention index" was created by subtracting the ratio of each

state's population to the national population from its percentage of news coverage. This provided a listing of states that were either "overcovered" or "under-covered" (Dominick, 1977). To aid in their interpretation, Whitney, Fritzler, Jones, Mazzarella, and Rakow (1989) created a more sophisticated "attention ratio" in their replication of this study.

RELIABILITY

The concept of reliability is crucial to content analysis. If a content analysis is to be objective, its measures and procedures must be reliable. Reliability is present when repeated measurement of the same material results in similar decisions or conclusions. Intercoder reliability refers to levels of agreement among independent coders who code the same content using the same coding instrument. If the results fail to achieve reliability, something is amiss with the coders, the coding instructions, the category definitions, the unit of analysis, or some combination of these. To achieve acceptable levels of reliability the following steps are recommended.

1. *Define category boundaries with maximum detail.* A group of vague or ambiguously defined categories makes reliability extremely difficult to achieve. Examples of units of analysis and a brief explanation for each are necessary for coders to fully understand the procedure.

2. *Train the coders.* Training sessions in using the coding instrument and the category system conducted before the data are collected can help to eliminate methodological problems. During these sessions, the group as a whole should code sample material; afterward, they should discuss the results as well as the purpose of the study. Disagreements should be analyzed as they occur. The end result of the training sessions is a bible of detailed instructions and coding examples, and each coder should receive a copy.

3.   *Conduct a pilot study.* Select a subsample of the content universe under consideration and let independent coders categorize it. These data are useful for two reasons: poorly defined categories can be detected, and chronically dissenting coders can be identified. To illustrate these problems, consider Tables 8.2 and 8.3.

In Table 8.2, the definitions for Categories I and IV appear satisfactory. All four coders placed Units 1, 3, 7, and 11 in the first category; in Category IV, Item 14 is classified consistently by three of the four coders and Items 4 and 9 by all four coders. The confusion apparently lies in the boundaries between Categories II and III. Three coders put Items 2, 6, and/or 13 in Category II and three placed some or all of these numbers in Category III. The definitions of these two categories require reexamination and perhaps revision because of this ambiguity.

Table 8.3 illustrates the problem of the chronic disagreer. Coders A and B agree seven times out of eight. Coders B and C, however,

TABLE 8.2   DETECTING POORLY DEFINED CATEGORIES FROM PILOT STUDY DATA*

	Categories			
Coders	**I**	**II**	**III**	**IV**
A	1,3,7,11	2,5,6,8,12,13	10	4,9,14
B	1,3,7,11	5,8,10,12	2,6,13	4,9,14
C	1,3,7,11	2,8,12,13	5,6,10	4,9,14
D	1,3,7,11	5,6	2,8,10,12,13,14	4,9

*Arabic numerals refer to items.

TABLE 8.3   IDENTIFYING A CHRONIC DISSENTER FROM PILOT STUDY DATA*

	Coders		
Items	**A**	**B**	**C**
1	I	I	II
2	III	III	I
3	II	II	II
4	IV	IV	III
5	I	II	II
6	IV	IV	I
7	I	I	III
8	II	II	I

*Roman numerals refer to categories.

agree only two times out of eight, and Coders A and C agree only once. Obviously, Coder C is going to be a problem. As a rule, the investigator would carefully reexplain to this coder the rules used in categorization and examine the reasons for his or her consistent deviation. If the problem persists, however, it may be necessary to dismiss the coder from the analysis.

Assuming that the initial test of reliability yields satisfactory results, the main body of data is coded. When the coding is complete, it is recommended that a subsample of the data, probably between 10% and 25%, be reanalyzed by independent coders to calculate an overall intercoder reliability coefficient.

Intercoder reliability can be calculated by several methods. Holsti (1969) reported a formula for determining the reliability of nominal data in terms of percentage of agreement:

$$\text{Reliability} = \frac{2M}{N_1 + N_2}$$

where M is the number of coding decisions on which two coders agree, and N_1 and N_2 refer to the total number of coding decisions by the first and second coder, respectively. Thus, if two coders judge a subsample of 50 units and agree on 35 of them, the calculation is:

$$\text{Reliability} = \frac{2(35)}{50 + 50} = .70$$

This method is straightforward and easy to apply, but it is criticized because it does not take into account the occurrence of some coder agreement strictly by chance, an amount that is a function of the number of categories in the analysis. For example, a two-category system should obtain 50% reliability simply by chance; a five-category system would generate a 20% agreement by chance; and so on. To take this into account, Scott (1955) developed the *pi* index, which corrects for the number of categories used and also for the probable frequency of use.

$$pi = \frac{\substack{\% \text{ observed} \\ \text{agreement}} - \substack{\% \text{ expected} \\ \text{agreement}}}{1 - \% \text{ expected agreement}}$$

A hypothetical example will demonstrate the use of this index. Suppose that two coders are assigning magazine advertisements to the six categories shown and obtain the following distribution.

Category	Percent of All Ads
1 Prestige appeal	30%
2 Economic appeal	20%
3 Affiliation appeal	20%
4 Fear appeal	15%
5 Utilitarian appeal	10%
6 Other appeal	5%

First, the percentage of expected agreement must be calculated. This is the sum of the squared percentages of all categories. Thus, % expected agreement $= (.3)^2 + (.2)^2 + (.2)^2 + (.15)^2 + (.1)^2 + (.05)^2 = .20$. If the coders agree on 90% of their classifications (% observed agreement), *pi* can be calculated as follows:

$$pi = \frac{.90 - .20}{1 - .20} = .875$$

Fless (1971) extended this notion to cases of the same content seen simultaneously by a number of coders.

Estimating reliability with interval data requires certain care. Several studies have used the correlation method called the Pearson r, a method that investigates the relationship between two items. The Pearson r can range from -1.00 to $+1.00$. In estimating reliability in content analysis, however, if this measure has a high value, it may indicate either that the coders were in agreement or that their ratings were associated in some systematic manner.

For example, suppose an interval scale ranging from 1 to 10 is used to score the degree of favorability of a news item to some person or topic (a score of 1 represents very positive; 10 represents very negative). Assume that two coders are independently scoring the same 10 items. Table 8.4 illustrates two possible outcomes. In Situation I, the coders agree on every item, and r equals 1.00. In Situation II, the coders disagree on every item by three scale positions, yet r still equals 1.00. Clearly, the uses of this estimate are not equally reliable in the two situations.

Krippendorf (1980) circumvents this dilemma by presenting what might be termed an "all-purpose reliability measure," *alpha*, which can be used for nominal, ordinal, interval, and ratio scales and for more than one coder. Although somewhat difficult to calculate, *alpha* is the equivalent of Scott's *pi* at the nominal level with two coders and represents an improvement over r in the interval situation.

What is an acceptable level of intercoder reliability? This depends on the research context and the type of information coded. In some instances little coder judgment is needed to place units into categories (for example, counting the number of words per sentence in a newspaper story or tabulating the number of times a network correspondent contributes a story to the evening news), and coding becomes a mechanical or clerical task. In this context, one would expect a fairly high degree of reliability, perhaps approaching 100%, since coder disagreements would probably be the result of carelessness or fatigue. If, however, a certain amount of interpretation is involved, reliability estimates are typically lower. In general, the greater the amount of judgmental leeway given to coders, the lower the reliability coefficients will be. As a rule of thumb, most published content analyses typically report a minimum reliability coefficient of about 90% or above when using Holsti's formula, and about .75 or above when using *pi* or *alpha*.

Note that the previous discussion assumed that at least two independent coders categorized the same content. In some situations, however, *intracoder* reliability might also be assessed. These circumstances occur most frequently when only a few coders are used because extensive training must be employed to ensure the detection of subtle message elements. To test

---

TABLE 8.4 FALSE EQUIVALENCE AS A RELIABILITY MEASURE WHEN r IS USED

	Situation I			Situation II	
Items	**Coder 1**	**Coder 2**	**Items**	**Coder 1**	**Coder 2**
1	1	1	1	1	4
2	2	2	2	2	5
3	3	3	3	3	6
4	3	3	4	3	6
5	4	4	5	4	7
6	5	5	6	5	8
7	6	6	7	6	9
8	6	6	8	6	9
9	7	7	9	7	10
10	7	7	10	7	10
	$r = 1.00$			$r = 1.00$	

intracoder reliability, the same individual codes a set of data twice, at different times, and the reliability statistics are computed using the two sets of results.

VALIDITY

In addition to being reliable, a content analysis must yield valid results. As indicated in Chapter 3, validity is usually defined as the degree to which an instrument actually measures what it sets out to measure. This raises special concerns in content analysis. In the first place, validity is intimately connected with the procedures used in the analysis. If the sampling design is faulty, if categories overlap, or if reliability is low, the results of the study probably possess little validity.

Additionally, the adequacy of the definitions used in a content analysis bears directly on the question of validity. For example, a great deal of content analysis has focused on the depiction of televised violence; different investigators have offered different definitions of what constitutes a violent act. The question of validity emerges when one tries to decide whether each of the various definitions actually encompasses what one might logically refer to as violence. The continuing debate between Gerbner and the television networks vividly illustrates this problem. The definition of violence propounded by Gerbner and his associates in 1977 includes accidents, acts of nature, or violence that might occur in a fantasy or a humorous setting. However, network analysts do not consider these phenomena to be acts of violence (Blank, 1977). Both Gerbner and the networks offer arguments in support of their decisions. Which analysis is the more valid? The answer depends in part on the plausibility of the rationale that underlies the definitions.

This discussion relates closely to a technique traditionally called *face validity*. This validation technique assumes that an instrument adequately measures what it purports to measure if the categories are rigidly and satisfactorily defined and if the procedures of the analysis have been adequately conducted. Most descriptive content analyses usually rely on face validity, but other techniques are available.

The use of *concurrent validity* in content analysis is exemplified in a study by Clarke and Blankenburg (1972). These investigators attempted a longitudinal study of violence in television shows dating back to 1952. Unfortunately, few copies of the early programs were available, and the authors were forced to use program summaries in *TV Guide*. To establish that such summaries would indeed disclose the presence of violence, the authors compared the results of a subsample of programs coded from these synopses to the results obtained from a direct viewing of the same programs. The results were sufficiently related to convince the authors that their measurement technique was valid. However, this method of checking validity is only as good as the criterion measurement: if the direct viewing technique is itself invalid, there is little value in showing that synopsis coding is related to it.

Only a few studies have attempted to document *construct validity*. One instance involves the use of sensationalism in news stories. This construct has been measured by semantic differentials and factor analysis (Appendix 2), in an attempt to isolate its underlying dimensions, and related to relevant message characteristics (Tannenbaum, 1962; Tannenbaum & Lynch, 1960). Another technique that investigators occasionally use is *predictive validity*. For example, certain content attributes from wire stories might allow a researcher to predict which items will be carried by a newspaper and which will not.

In summary, several different methods to assess validity are used in content analysis. The most common is face validity, which is appropriate for some studies. It is recommended, however, that the content analyst also examine other methods to establish the validity of a given study.

EXAMPLES OF CONTENT ANALYSIS

Table 8.5, which summarizes four recent content analyses, lists the purpose of the analysis, the sample, the unit of analysis, illustrative categories, and the type of statistic used for each study.

S U M M A R Y

Content analysis is a popular technique in mass media research. Many of the steps involved in laboratory and survey studies are also found in content analysis; in particular, sampling procedures need to be objective and detailed, and

TABLE 8.5   EXAMPLES OF CONTENT ANALYSIS STUDIES

Researchers	Purpose of study	Sample	Units of analysis	Representative categories	Statistic
Lester (1988)	To comparatively analyze the use of mug shots by five U.S. newspapers	Each copy of five newspapers during a 5-day week for each month in 1986	Each mug shot: a head and shoulders portrait of a person	Size, page location, racial composition, sexual composition, subject	Percentages
Giffard & Cohen (1989)	To examine effects of South African censorship on American network news coverage	Abstracts of all network newscasts from January 1982 to May 1987	Each news report that dealt with South Africa	Length of report, location, presence of fresh video or file footage, and theme of report	Percentages
Copeland (1989)	To determine if males and females are "framed" differently in TV programs	Composite week of prime-time network entertainment programs	A continuous TV shot that contained only one person	Amount of screen space given to body compared to space given to face	Analysis of variance
Soley & Reid (1988)	To gauge the amount of nudity in magazine ads	Randomly selected ads from 1964 and 1984 issues of six magazines chosen to represent three reader categories	Adult models in ads	Degree of dress or undress, sex of model	Z-test for proportions, chi-square

operational definitions are mandatory. Coders must be carefully trained to ensure accurate data. Interpreting a content analysis, however, requires more caution: no claims about the impact of the content can be drawn from an analysis of the message in the absence of study that examines the audience. In the future, the computer will become an integral part of many content analyses.

Questions and Problems for Further Investigation

1. Define a unit of analysis that could be used in a content analysis of:
   a. Problem-solving on television
   b. News emphasis in a daily and a weekly newspaper
   c. Changes in the values expressed by popular songs
   d. The role of women in editorial cartoons

2. Using the topics in Question 1, define a sample selection procedure that would be appropriate for each.

3. Generate two content analyses that could be used as preliminary tests for an audience study.

4. Conduct a brief content analysis of one of the topics listed below. (Train a second individual in the use of the category system that you develop and have this person independently code a subsample of the content.)
   a. Similarities and differences between local newscasts on two television stations
   b. Changes in the subject matter of movies from 1980 to 1990
   c. The treatment of the elderly on network television

5. Using the topic selected in Question 4, compute a reliability coefficient for the items that were scored by both coders.

References and Suggested Readings

Adams, W., & Schreibman, F. (1978). *Television network news: Issues in content research*. Washington, DC: George Washington University.

Attkisson, C., Handler, L., & Shrader, R. (1969). The use of figure drawing to assess religious values. *Journal of Psychology, 71*, 27–31.

Benze, J., & Declercq, E. (1985). Content of television political spot ads for female candidates. *Journalism Quarterly, 62*(2), 278–283.

Berelson, B. (1952). *Content analysis in communication research*. New York: Free Press.

Blank, D. (1977). The Gerbner violence profile. *Journal of Broadcasting, 21*, 273–279.

Brown, J. D., & Campbell, K. (1986). Race and gender in music videos. *Journal of Communication, 36*(1), 94–106.

Bryant, J., Hezel, R., & Zillmann, D. (1979). Humor in children's educational television. *Communication Education, 28*(4), 49–59.

Chadwick, B., Bahr, H., & Albrecht, S. (1984). *Social science research methods*. Englewood Cliffs, NJ: Prentice-Hall.

Chang, W. (1975). A typology study of movie critics. *Journalism Quarterly, 52*(4), 721–725.

Clarke, D., & Blankenburg, W. (1972). Trends in violent content in selected mass media. In G. Comstock & E. Rubinstein (Eds.), *Television and social behavior: Media content and control*. Washington, DC: U.S. Government Printing Office.

Comstock, G. (1975). *Television and human behavior: The key studies*. Santa Monica, CA: Rand Corporation.

Copeland, G. A. (1989). Face-ism and primetime television. *Journal of Broadcasting and Electronic Media, 33*(2), 209–214.

Davis, F. (1951). Crime news in Colorado newspapers. *American Journal of Sociology, 57*, 325–330.

DeFleur, M. (1964). Occupational roles as portrayed on television. *Public Opinion Quarterly, 28*, 57–74.

DeFleur, M., & DeFleur, L. (1967). The relative contribution of television as a learning source for children's occupational knowledge. *American Sociological Review, 32*, 777–789.

Dominick, J. (1973). Crime and law enforcement on prime time television. *Public Opinion Quarterly, 37*, 241–250.

Dominick, J. (1977). Geographic bias in national TV news. *Journal of Communication, 27*, 94–99.

Dominick, J., Richman, S., & Wurtzel, A. (1979). Problem-solving in TV shows popular with children: Assertion vs. aggression. *Journalism Quarterly, 56,* 455–463.

Dominick, J., Wurtzel, A., & Lometti, G. (1975). Television journalism vs. show business: A content analysis of eyewitness news. *Journalism Quarterly, 52,* 213–218.

Fless, J. L. (1971). Measuring nominal scale agreement among many raters. *Psychological Bulletin, 76,* 378–382.

Gantz, W., Gartenberg, H., & Rainbow, C. (1980). Approaching invisibility: The portrayal of the elderly in magazine advertisements. *Journal of Communication, 30,* 56–60.

Gerbner, G. (1969). The television world of violence. In D. Lange, R. Baker, & S. Ball (Eds.), *Mass media and violence.* Washington, DC: U.S. Government Printing Office.

Gerbner, G., Gross, L., Jackson-Beeck, M., Jeffries-Fox, S., & Signorielli, N. (1977). One more time: An analysis of the CBS "Final Comments on the Violence Profile." *Journal of Broadcasting, 21,* 297–304.

Gerbner, G., Gross, L., Signorielli, N., Morgan, M., & Jackson-Beeck, M. (1979). The demonstration of power: Violence profile no. 10. *Journal of Communication, 29,* 177–198.

Gerbner, G., Holsti, O., Krippendorf, K., Paisley, W., & Stone, P. (1969). *The analysis of communication content.* New York: John Wiley.

Giffard, C. A., & Cohen, L. (1989). South African TV and censorship: Does it reduce negative coverage? *Journalism Quarterly, 66*(1), 3–10.

Gilly, M. C. (1988). Sex roles in advertising. *Journal of Marketing, 52*(2), 75–85.

Greenberg, B. (1983). *Mexican-Americans and the mass media.* Norwood, NJ: Ablex Publishers.

Gross, B. L., & Sheth, J. N. (1989). Time-oriented advertising: A content analysis of U.S. magazine advertising, 1890–1988. *Journal of Marketing, 53*(4), 76–83.

Hatch, D., & Hatch, M. (1947). Criteria of social status as derived from marriage announcements in the *New York Times. American Sociological Review, 12,* 396–403.

Hennessee, J., & Nicholson, J. (1972, May 28). NOW says: TV commercials insult women. *New York Times Magazine,* pp. 12–14.

Hinkle, G., & Elliott, W. (1989). Science coverage in three newspapers and three supermarket tabloids. *Journalism Quarterly, 66*(2), 353–358.

Holsti, O. (1969). *Content analysis for the social sciences and humanities.* Reading, MA: Addison-Wesley.

Kerlinger, F. (1986). *Foundations of behavioral research* (3rd ed.). New York: Holt, Rinehart & Winston.

Krippendorf, K. (1980). *Content analysis: An introduction to its methodology.* Beverly Hills, CA: Sage Publications.

Lester, P. M. (1988). Front page mugshots: A content analysis of five U.S. newspapers in 1986. *Newspaper Research Journal, 9*(3), 1–10.

Lorr, M., & McNair, D. (1966). Methods relating to evaluation of therapeutic outcome. In L. Gottschalk & A. Auerbach (Eds.), *Methods of research in psychotherapy.* Englewood Cliffs, NJ: Prentice-Hall.

Lowry, D. (1981). Alcohol consumption patterns and consequences on prime time network TV. *Journalism Quarterly, 58*(1), 3–9.

Lowry, D. T., & Towles, D. E. (1989). Soap opera portrayals of sex, contraception and sexually transmitted diseases. *Journal of Communication, 39*(2), 76–83.

Mayerle, J., & Rarick, D. (1989). The image of education in prime time network television series. *Journal of Broadcasting and Electronic Media, 33*(2), 139–157.

Merritt, S., & Gross, H. (1978). Women's page lifestyle editors: Does sex make a difference? *Journalism Quarterly, 55,* 508–514.

Moffett, E. A., & Dominick, J. R. (1987). Statistical analysis in the *Journal of Broadcasting,* 1970–1985. *Feedback, 28*(2), 13–20.

Pasadeos, Y., & Renfro, P. (1988). Rupert Murdoch's Style: *The New York Post. Newspaper Research Journal, 9*(4), 25–34.

Potter, W. J., & Ware, W. (1989). The frequency and context of prosocial acts on primetime TV. *Journalism Quarterly, 66*(2), 359–366.

Scott, W. (1955). Reliability of content analysis: The case of nominal scale coding. *Public Opinion Quarterly, 17,* 321–325.

Signorielli, N. (1989). The stigma of mental illness on television. *Journal of Broadcasting and Electronic Media, 33*(3), 325–331.

Soderlund, W. C., Surlin, S. H., & Romanow, W. I. (1989). Gender in Canadian local television news. *Journal of Broadcasting and Electronic Media, 33*(2), 187–196.

Soley, L. C., & Reid, L. N. (1988). Taking it off: Are models in magazine ads wearing less? *Journalism Quarterly, 65*(4), 960–966.

Stempel, G. (1952). Sample size for classifying subject matter in dailies. *Journalism Quarterly, 29,* 333–334.

Stempel, G. H. (1989). Content analysis. In G. H. Stempel & B. H. Westley, *Research methods in mass communication.* Englewood Cliffs, NJ: Prentice-Hall.

Swayne, L. E., & Greco, A. J. (1987). The portrayal of older Americans in television commercials. *Journal of Advertising, 16*(1), 47–54.

Tannenbaum, P. (1962). Sensationalism: Some objective message correlates. *Journalism Quarterly, 39,* 317–323.

Tannenbaum, P., & Greenberg, B. (1968). Mass communication. *Annual Review of Psychology, 19,* 351–386.

Tannenbaum, P., & Lynch, M. (1960). Sensationalism: The concept and its measurement. *Journalism Quarterly, 37,* 381–392.

Trujillo, N., & Ekdom, L. R. (1987). A 40-year portrait of the portrayal of industry on prime-time television. *Journalism Quarterly, 64*(2), 368–375.

Unger, L. S., & Stearns, J. M. (1986). The frequency of blacks in magazine and television advertising. In R. L. King (Ed.), *Marketing in an environment of change.* Charleston, SC: Southern Marketing Association.

Walizer, M. H., & Wienir, P. L. (1978). *Research methods and analysis.* New York: Harper & Row.

Whitney, D. C., Fritzler, M., Jones, S., Mazzarella, S., & Rakow, L. (1989). Source and geographic bias in network television news: 1982–1984. *Journal of Broadcasting and Electronic Media, 33*(2), 159–174.

Wilhoit, G., & Sherrill, K. (1968). Wire service visibility of U.S. Senators. *Journalism Quarterly, 45,* 42–48.

Wimmer, R., & Haynes, R. (1978). Statistical analyses in the *Journal of Broadcasting. Journal of Broadcasting, 22,* 241–248.

Wurtzel, A. (1975). Public access cable television: Programming. *Journal of Communication, 25,* 15–21.

Yule, G. (1944). *The statistical study of literary vocabulary.* Cambridge, England: Cambridge University Press.

Zillmann, D., & Bryant, J. (1983). Uses and effects of humor in educational ventures. In P. McGhee & J. Goldstein (Eds.), *Handbook of humor research* (Vol. II). New York: Springer-Verlag.

LONGITUDINAL RESEARCH

n **cross-sectional research** data are collected from a representative sample at only one point in time. Most of the research discussed to this point has been cross sectional. **Longitudinal research** involves the collection of data at different points in time. Although longitudinal investigations appear relatively infrequently in mass communication research, several longitudinal studies have been among the most influential and provocative in the field.

Of the 14 studies Lowery and DeFleur (1988) consider to be milestones in the evolution of mass media research, four represent the longitudinal approach: Lazarsfeld, Berelson, and Gaudet, *The People's Choice* (1944), which introduced the two-step flow model; Katz and Lazarsfeld, *Personal Influence* (1955), which examined the role of opinion leaders; the Surgeon General's Report on Television and Social Behavior, particularly as used in the study by Lefkowitz, Eron, Walder, and Huesmann (1972), which found evidence suggesting that viewing violence on television caused subsequent aggressive behavior; and the 10-year update of this report (Pearl, Bouthilet, & Lazar, 1982), which cited the longitudinal studies that further affirmed the link between TV violence and aggression. Other longitudinal studies also figure prominently in the field, including the elaborate panel study done for NBC by Milavsky, Kessler, Stipp, and Rubens (1982), the cross-national comparisons cited in Huesmann and Eron (1986), and the studies of mass media in elections as summarized by Peterson (1980). Thus although not widely used, the longitudinal method can produce results that are both theoretically and socially important.

DEVELOPMENT

Longitudinal studies have a long history in the behavioral sciences; in psychology in particular, they have been used to trace the development of children and the clinical progress of patients. In medicine, longitudinal studies have been widely used to study the impact of disease and treatment methods. The pioneering work in political science was done by sociologists studying the 1924 election campaign. Somewhat later, Newcomb (1943) conducted repeated interviews of Bennington College students from 1935 to 1939 to examine the impact of a liberal college environment on respondents who came from conservative families.

In the mass communication area, the first major longitudinal study was that of Lazarsfeld, Berelson, and Gaudet (1944) during the 1940 presidential election. Lazarsfeld pioneered the use of the panel technique in which the same individuals are interviewed several times. Lazarsfeld also developed the use of the 16-fold table, one of the earliest statistical techniques to attempt to derive causation from longitudinal survey data. Another form of longitudinal research, **trend studies** (in which different people are asked the same question at different points in time) began showing up in mass media research in the 1960s. One of the most publicized trend studies was the continuing survey of media credibility done by the Roper organization. Trend studies by Gallup and Harris, among others, also gained notoriety during this time.

More recently, the notion of cohort analysis, a method of research development by demographers, has achieved some popularity. **Cohort analysis** involves the study of specific populations, usually all those born during a given period, as they change over time. Other significant developments in the longitudinal area have taken place in analysis methods as more sophisticated techniques for analyzing longitudinal data were developed. **Cross-lagged correlation** was widely discussed during the 1960s and 1970s. Cross-lagged correlations are done when information about two variables is gathered from the same sample at two different times. The correlations between variables at the same point in time are compared with the correlations at different points in time. Two other forms of analysis have had relevance in longitudinal studies: path analysis and log–linear models. Path analysis is used to chart directions in panel data. Log–linear models are used with categorical panel data and involve the analysis of multivariate contingency tables. LISREL (LInear Structural RELations), a model developed by Joreskog (1973), is another statistical technique that has broad application in longitudinal analysis.

TYPES OF LONGITUDINAL STUDIES

The three main types of longitudinal studies are the trend study, the cohort analysis, and the panel study. Each will be discussed in turn.

Trend Studies

The trend study is probably the most common longitudinal study in mass media research. Recall that a trend study samples different groups of people drawn at different times from the same population. Trend studies are common around presidential election time. Suppose that 3 months before an election a sample of adults is drawn; 57% report that they intend to vote for Candidate A and 43% for Candidate B. A month later a different sample, drawn from the same population, shows a change: 55% report that they are going to vote for A and 45% for B. This is a simple example of a trend study. Trend studies provide information about net changes at an aggregate level. In the example, we know that in the period under consideration, Candidate A lost 2% of his support. We don't know how many people changed from B to A or from A to B, nor do we know how many stayed with their original choice. We only know that the net result was a 2-point loss for A. To determine both the gross and the net change, a panel study would be necessary.

ADVANTAGES. Trend studies are valuable in describing long-term changes in a population. They can establish a pattern over time to detect shifts and changes in some event. Economists, for example, compile trend studies that chart fluctuations in the employment rate and wholesale prices.

Another advantage of trend studies is that they can be based on a comparison of survey data originally constructed for other purposes. Of course, in utilizing such data, the researcher needs to recognize any differences in question wording, context, sampling, or analysis techniques that might differ from one survey to the next. Hyman (1987) provides extensive guidance on the secondary analysis of survey data. The growing movement to preserve data archives and the ability of microcomputer networks that make retrieval and sharing much easier suggest that this technique will gain in popularity. Secondary analysis saves time, money, and personnel; it also makes it possible to understand long-term change. In fact, mass media researchers might want to consider what socially significant data concerning media behaviors should be collected and archived at regular intervals. Economists have developed regular trend indicators to gauge the health of the economy, but mass communication scholars have developed almost no analogous social indicator of media or audience conduct.

DISADVANTAGES. Trend analysis is only as good as the underlying data. If the data are unreliable, then false trends will show up in the results. Second, to be most valuable, trend analysis must be based on consistent measures. Changes in the way indexes are constructed or the way questions are asked will produce results that are not comparable over time.

EXAMPLES OF TREND STUDIES. Both university and commercial research firms have asked some of the same questions for many national and statewide trend studies. For example, in the United States, a question about satisfaction with the president's performance has been asked hundreds of times dating back to the administration of Harry Truman. *Public Opinion Quarterly* has a regular section entitled "The Polls," which allows researchers to construct trend data on selected topics. In recent issues, the following trend data have appeared: (1) a 48-year sampling of attitudes about a woman's place and role; (2) 10-year trend data about attitudes toward U.S. intervention in Central America; and (3) a 7-year compilation of American attitudes toward Israeli–Palestinian relations. Of specific interest in the field of mass media research are the trend data on changing patterns of media credibility, compiled for more than 3 decades by the Roper organization. Among other well-known trend studies are the Violence Index constructed by Gerbner and his associates (Gerbner, Gross, Signorielli, Morgan, & Jackson-Beeck, 1979), the 15-year study of the economics of network ratings by Atkin and Litman (1986), and the 60-year study of trends in research about children and the mass media by Wartella and Reeves (1985).

Cohort Analysis

To the Romans, a "cohort" was one of the 10 divisions of a military legion. For research purposes, a *cohort* is any group of individuals who are linked in some way or who have experienced the same significant life event within a given period of time. Usually the "significant life event" is birth, in which case the group is termed a birth cohort. There are, however, many other kinds of cohorts, including marriage (for example, all those married between 1980 and 1985), divorce (for example, all those divorced between 1985 and 1990), educational (the class of 1990), and others (all those who attended college during the Vietnam era).

Any study in which there are measures of some characteristic of one or more cohorts at two or more points in time is a cohort analysis. Cohort analysis attempts to identify a *cohort effect:* Are changes in the dependent variable due to aging or are they present because the sample members belong to the same cohort? To illustrate, suppose that 50% of college seniors reported that they regularly read news magazines, whereas only 10% of college freshmen in the same survey made this report. How might the difference be accounted for? One possible explanation is that freshmen change their reading habits as they progress through college. Another is that this year's freshman class is composed of people with reading habits different from those who were enrolled 3 years ago.

There are two ways to distinguish between these explanations. One way involves questioning the same students during their freshman year and again during their senior year and comparing their second set of responses to those of a group of current freshmen. (This is the familiar panel design, which is discussed in detail below.) Or, a researcher can take two samples of the student population, at Time 1 and Time 2. Each survey has different participants—the same people are not questioned again as in a panel study—but each sample represents the same group of people at different points in their college career. Although we have no direct information about which individuals changed their habits over time, we do have information on how the cohort of people who entered college at Time 1 had changed by the time they became seniors. If 15% of the freshmen at Time 1 read news magazines and if 40% of the seniors at Time 2 read them, we can deduce that students change their reading habits as they progress through college.

Typically, a cohort analysis involves data in more than one cohort, and a standard table for presenting the data from multiple cohorts was proposed by Glenn (1977). Table 9.1 is such a table. It displays news magazine readership for a number of birth cohorts. Note that the column variable (read down) is age, and the row variable (read across) is the year of data collection. Because the interval between any two periods of measurement (that is, surveys) corresponds to the age class intervals, cohorts can be followed over time. When the intervals are not equal, the progress of cohorts cannot be followed with precision.

Three different types of comparisons can be made from such a table. Reading down a single column is analogous to a cross-sectional study and represents comparisons among different age cohorts at one point in time (intercohort differences). Trends at each age level that occur when cohorts replace one another can be seen by reading across the rows. Third, reading diagonally toward the right reveals changes in a single co-

TABLE 9.1   PERCENTAGE WHO REGULARLY READ NEWS MAGAZINES

	Year		
Age	**1982**	**1986**	**1990**
18–21	15	12	10
22–25	34	32	28
26–29	48	44	35

TABLE 9.2   COHORT TABLE SHOWING PURE AGE EFFECT

	Year		
Age	**1982**	**1986**	**1990**
18–21	15	15	15
22–25	20	20	20
26–29	25	25	25
Average	20	20	20

hort from one point in time to another (an intra-cohort study). Thus Table 9.1 suggests that news magazine reading increases with age (reading down each column). In each successive time period, the percentage of younger readers has diminished (reading across the rows), and the increase in reading percentage as each cohort ages is about the same (reading diagonally to the right).

The variations in the percentages in the table can be categorized into three different kinds of effects (for the moment we will assume that there is no variation due to sampling error or to changing composition in each cohort as it ages).

First, there are the influences produced by the sheer fact of maturation or growing older, called age effects. Second, there are the influences associated with members in a certain birth cohort (cohort effects), and finally there are the influences associated with each particular time period (period effects).

To recognize these various influences at work, examine the hypothetical data in Tables 9.2, 9.3, and 9.4. Again, let us assume that the dependent variable is the percentage of the sample who regularly read a news magazine. Table 9.2 demonstrates a "pure" age effect. Note that the rows are identical, and the columns show

TABLE 9.3 COHORT TABLE SHOWING PURE PERIOD EFFECT

		Year	
Age	1982	1986	1990
18–21	15	20	25
22–25	15	20	25
26–29	15	20	25
Average	15	20	25

TABLE 9.4 COHORT TABLE SHOWING PURE COHORT EFFECT

		Year	
Age	1982	1986	1990
18–21	15	10	5
22–25	20	15	10
26–29	25	20	15
Average	20	15	10

the same pattern of variation. Apparently it doesn't matter when a person was born or in which period he or she lived. As the individual gets older, news magazine readership increases. For ease of illustration, Table 9.2 illustrates a linear effect, but this is not necessarily the only effect possible. For example, readership might increase from the first age interval to the next and increase from the second to the third.

Table 9.3 demonstrates a "pure" period effect. There is no variation by age at any period — the columns are identical, and the variations from one period to the next are identical. Furthermore, the change in each cohort (read diagonally to the right) is the same as the average change in the total population. The data in this table suggest that year of birth and maturation have little to do with news magazine reading. In this hypothetical case, the time period seems to be most important. Knowing when the survey was done enables the researcher to predict the variation in news magazine reading.

A "pure" cohort effect is illustrated in Table 9.4. Here the cohort diagonals are constant and the variation from younger to older respondents is in the opposite direction from the variation from earlier to later survey periods. In this table, the key variable seems to be date of birth. Among those who were born between 1959 and 1962, news magazine readership was 15% regardless of their age or when they were surveyed.

Of course in actual data, these pure patterns rarely occur. Nonetheless an examination of Tables 9.2, 9.3, and 9.4 can help develop a sensitivity to the patterns one can detect in analyzing cohort data. In addition, the tables illustrate the logic behind the analysis. Glenn (1977) and Mason, Mason, Winsborough, and Poole (1973) also present tables showing pure effects.

ADVANTAGES. Cohort analysis is an appealing and useful technique because it is highly flexible. It provides insight into the effects of maturation, social, cultural, and political change. In addition, it can be used with either original or secondary data. In many instances, a cohort analysis can be less expensive than experiments or surveys.

DISADVANTAGES. The major disadvantage of cohort analysis is that the specific effects of age, cohort, and period are difficult to untangle through purely statistical analysis of a standard cohort table. In survey data, much of the variation in percentages among cells is due to sampling variability. There are no uniformly accepted tests of significance appropriate to a cohort table that allow researchers to estimate the probability that the observed differences are due to chance. Moreover, as a cohort grows older, many of its members die. If the remaining cohort members differ in regard to the variable under study, the variation in the cohort table may simply reflect this change. Finally, as Glenn (1977) points out, no matter how a cohort table is examined, three of the basic effects — namely, age, cohort, and period — are confounded. Age and cohort effects are confounded in the columns, age and period effects in the diagonals, and cohort and period effects in each row. Even the patterns of variations in the "pure" cohort Tables 9.2, 9.3, and 9.4 could be explained by a combination of influences.

Several authors have developed techniques to try to sort out these effects. Two of the most useful are Palmore's (1978) triad method and the constrained multiple regression model (Rentz, Reynolds, & Stout, 1983). If the researcher is willing to make certain assumptions, these methods can provide some tentative evidence about the probable influences of age, period, and cohort. Moreover, in many cases there is only one likely or plausible situation explanation for the variation. Nonetheless, a researcher should exercise caution in attributing causation to any variable in a cohort analysis. Theory and evidence from outside sources should also be utilized in any interpretation.

A second disadvantage of the technique is sample mortality. If a long time period is involved or if the specific sample group is hard to reach, the researcher may have some empty cells in the cohort table or some that contain too few members for meaningful analysis.

EXAMPLES OF COHORT ANALYSIS.   Cohort analysis is widely used in advertising and marketing research. For example, Rentz et al. (1983) conducted a cohort analysis of consumers born in four time periods: 1931–1940, 1941–1950, 1951–1960, and 1961–1970. Soft drink consumption was the dependent variable. Multiple regression analysis was employed to help separate the three possible sources of variation. The results indicated a large cohort effect suggesting that soft drink consumption will not decrease as successive cohorts age. Cohort analysis is also useful in the study of public opinion. Cassell (1977) conducted a cohort analysis of political party identification of Southern whites. The data indicated that both younger and older cohorts showed some movement from Democratic affiliation to the independent position. More recently, Wood (1986) outlined the use of cohort analysis in marketing and demonstrated how *Time* examined cohort data to chart trends in its subscribership. Rosengren and Windahl (1989) used cohort analysis as part of their in-depth longitudinal study of TV usage by Swedish youngsters. Among other things, they found a slight cohort effect but noted that age seemed to be the prime determinant of habitual television viewing.

Panel Studies

The measurement of the same sample of respondents at different points in time represents the panel design. Unlike trend studies, **panel studies** can reveal information about both net and gross changes in the dependent variable. For example, a study of voting intentions might reveal that between Time 1 and Time 2, 20% of the panel switched from Candidate A to Candidate B and 20% switched from Candidate B to Candidate A. Whereas a trend study would show only a net change of zero, the panel study would show a high degree of volatility in voting intention as the gross changes simply canceled each other out.

Similar to trend and cohort studies, panel studies can make use of mail questionnaires, telephone interviews, or personal interviews. Television networks, advertising agencies, and marketing research firms use panel studies to track changes in consumer behavior. Panel studies can reveal shifting attitudes and patterns of behavior that might go unnoticed with other research approaches; thus trends, new ideas, fads, and buying habits are among the variables investigated. For a panel study on the effectiveness of political commercials, for example, all members of the panel would be interviewed periodically during a campaign to determine if and when each respondent makes a voting decision.

Depending on the purpose of the study, researchers can use either a *continuous panel*, consisting of members who report specific attitudes or behavior patterns on a regular basis, or an *interval panel*, whose members agree to complete a certain number of measurement instruments (usually questionnaires) only when the information is needed. Panel studies produce data suitable for sophisticated statistical analysis and enable researchers to predict cause-and-effect relationships.

ADVANTAGES.   Panel data are particularly useful in answering questions about the dynamics of change. For example, under what conditions do voters change political party affiliation? What are the respective roles of mass media and friends in changing political attitudes? Moreover, repeated contacts with the respondents may help reduce suspicions, so that later interviews yield more information than the initial encounters. Of course, the other side to this benefit is the sensitization effect, discussed below.

Finally, panel studies help solve the problems normally encountered when defining a theory on the basis of a one-shot case study. Since the research progresses over a period of time, the researcher can allow for the influences of competing stimuli on the subject.

DISADVANTAGES. On the negative side, panel members are often difficult to recruit because of unwillingness to fill out questionnaires or submit to interviews several times. The number of initial refusals in a panel study fluctuates depending on the amount of time required, the prestige of the organization directing the study, and the presence or absence of some type of compensation. One analysis of the refusal rates in 12 marketing panel studies found a range of 15%–80%, with a median of about 40% (Carman, 1974).

Once the sample has been secured, the problem of mortality emerges. Some panel members will drop out for one reason or another. Because the strength of panel studies lies in interviewing the same people at different times, this advantage diminishes as the sample size decreases. Another serious problem is that respondents often become sensitized to measurement instruments after repeated interviewing, thus making the sample atypical (Chapter 4). For example, panelists who know in advance that they will be interviewed about public television watching might alter their viewing patterns to include more PBS programs (or fewer). Respondent error is always a problem in situations that depend on self-administered measurement instruments. If panelists are asked to keep a diary over a certain period of time, some may not fill it out until immediately before it is due. And, of course, panel studies require much more time and can be quite expensive.

EXAMPLES OF PANEL STUDIES. Perhaps the most famous example of the panel technique in mass media research is the collection of national television audience data by the A. C. Nielsen Company. Nielsen's sample consists of approximately 4,000 households located across the United States. These homes are equipped with Peoplemeters, devices which record when the television set is turned on, the channel that is tuned in, and who is watching. (Chapter 14 contains more information about people meters). Other panels are maintained by such commercial research organizations as Market Facts, Inc., National Family Opinion, Inc., and the Home Testing Institute.

Outside the marketing area, a well-publicized panel study was carried out with the support of the National Broadcasting Company (Milavsky et al., 1982). The overall purpose of this study was to isolate any possible causal influence of the viewing of violence on television on aggression among young people. Three panel studies were conducted, with the most ambitious involving boys aged 7–12. In brief, the methodology in the boys' study involved collecting data on aggression, TV viewing, and a host of sociological variables on six different occasions from children in Minneapolis, Minnesota, and Fort Worth, Texas. About 1,200 boys participated in the study. The time lags between each wave of data collection were deliberately varied so that the effects of TV viewing could be analyzed over different durations. Thus, there was a 5-month lag between the first and second waves, a 4-month lag between Waves 2 and 3, and a 3-month lag between Waves 3 and 4. The lag between Waves 1 and 6 constituted the longest time lapse (3 years). As is the case in all panel studies, the NBC study suffered from attrition. The particular design, however, magnified the effects of attrition. When a respondent left the sixth grade, he left the panel. Consequently, only a small number of children were available for the analysis of long-term effects. In fact, only 58 boys had valid aggression and TV viewing data in all six waves. The year-to-year losses reported by the NBC team illustrate the impact of year-to-year attrition on a sample of this age group. About 7% of the sample was lost in the first year, approximately 37% in the first 2 years, and 63% over all 3 years.

The study also illustrates how a panel design influences the statistical analysis. The most powerful statistical test would have incorporated data from all six waves and simultaneously examined all the possible causal relationships. This was impossible, however, because due to the initial study design and subsequent attrition, the sample size fell below minimum standards. Instead, the investigators worked with each of the 15 possible wave pairs in the sample. The main statistical tests used the analytical technique of partial regression coefficients to remove the impact of earlier aggression levels. In effect, the researchers sought to determine whether TV viewing at an earlier time added to the predictability of aggression at a later time, once the aggression levels present before the test began had been statistically discounted. After looking at all the resulting coefficients for all the possible wave pairs, the investigators concluded that there was no consistently statistically significant relationship between watching violent TV programs and later aggression. Nonetheless, they did find a large number of small but consistently positive coefficients that suggested the possibility of a weak relationship that might not have been detected by conventional statistical methods. Upon further analysis, however, the researchers concluded that these associations were due to chance.

Since their initial publication, the NBC data have been the topic of at least three reanalyses and reinterpretations (Cook, Kendizierski, & Thomas, 1983; Kenny, Milavsky, Kessler, Stipp, & Rubens, 1984; Turner, Hesse, & Peterson-Lewis, 1986). Concerns were raised over various aspects of the methodology and the appropriateness of conventional standards of statistical significance in light of small samples and skewed aggression measures. It is likely that more reanalyses will follow. Nonetheless, this study has value for anyone interested in longitudinal research. Many of the problems involved in panel studies and the compromises involved in doing a 3-year study are discussed in great detail.

The panel technique continues to be a popular one for studying the impact of TV violence. Singer, Singer, Desmond, Hirsch, and Nicol (1988) used this technique to examine the effects of family communication patterns, parental mediation, and TV viewing on children's perceptions of the world and their aggressive behavior. Ninety-one first and second graders were interviewed during the first phase of the study. One year later, 66 of the original sample were reinterviewed. Concerned about the effects of attrition, the researchers compared their final sample with the original on a wide range of demographic variables and found that attrition did not cause any significant differences between the two groups. Singer et al. found that family communication patterns during the first phase were strong predictors of children's cognitive scores, but were only weakly related to emotional and behavioral variables. The influence of TV viewing on aggression was greatest among heavy viewers who were least exposed to parental mediation.

The Rosengren and Windahl study (1989) mentioned earlier arrived at a similar conclusion from their panel study of Swedish schoolchildren. The investigators interviewed their main panel participants in 1976, 1978, and 1980. This study is remarkable for its low attrition rate: About 86 percent of those in the original 1976 survey were also in the 1980 survey. The researchers found that the relationship between TV violence and antisocial behavior was greatest among those children who were heavy viewers (more than 15 hours a week) of TV.

SPECIAL PANEL DESIGNS

Panel data can be expensive to obtain. Moreover, analysis cannot begin until at least two waves of data are available. For many panel studies, this may take years. Researchers who have limited time and resources might consider one of the alternatives discussed next.

Schulsinger, Mednick, and Knop (1981) outlined a research design called a **retrospective panel**. In this method, the respondent is asked to recall facts or attitudes about education, occupations, events, situations, and so on, from the past. These recalled factors are then compared with a later measure of the same variable, thus producing an instant longitudinal design. Belson (1978) used a variation of this design in his study of the effects of exposure to violent TV shows on the aggressive behavior of teenage boys when he asked his respondents to recall when they first started watching certain violent TV programs.

With this technique, obviously there will be problems. Many people have faulty memories; some will deliberately misrepresent the past; and others will try to give a socially desirable response. Only a few research studies have examined the extent to which retrospective panel data might be misleading. Powers, Goudy, and Keith (1978) reanalyzed data from a 1964 study of adult men. In 1974 all the original respondents who could be located were reinterviewed and asked about their answers to the 1964 survey. In most instances, the recall responses presented respondents in a more favorable light than did their original answers. Interestingly enough, using the 1974 recall data produced virtually the same pattern of correlations as using the 1964 data, suggesting that recall data might

be used, albeit with caution, in correlational studies. In 1974 Norlen (1977) reinterviewed about 4,700 persons originally questioned in 1968. Of those reinterviewed, 464 had originally reported that they had written a letter to the editor of a newspaper or magazine, but in 1974 about a third of this group denied ever having written to a newspaper or magazine. Clearly, the savings in time and money accrued by using retrospective data must be weighted against possible losses in accuracy.

A **follow-back panel** selects a cross-sectional sample in the present and uses archival data from an earlier point in time to create the longitudinal dimension of the study. The advantages of such a technique are clearly seen. Changes that occurred over a great many years can be analyzed in a short time period. This design is also useful in studying rare populations, since the researcher can assemble a sample from baseline investigations conducted earlier, probably at great expense. The disadvantages are also obvious. The follow-back panel depends on archival data, and many of the variables that interest mass media researchers are not contained in archives. In addition, the resulting sample in a follow-back design may not represent all possible entities. For example, a follow-back study of the managerial practices of small radio stations will not represent stations that went out of business and no longer exist.

A **catch-up panel** involves the selection of a cross-sectional study done in the past and locating all possible units of analysis for observation in the present. The catch-up design is particularly attractive if the researcher has a rich source of baseline data in the archive. Of course, this is usually not the case, since most data sources lack enough identifying information to allow the investigator to track down the respondents. When the appropriate data exist, however, the catch-up study can be highly useful. In effect, Lefkowitz et al. (1972) used a catch-up technique in their study of TV watching and child aggression. After a lapse of 10 years, the investigators tracked down 735 of 875 youths who had participated in a survey of mental health factors when they were in the third grade. These individuals were recontacted and asked questions similar to those they had answered as young children. Huesmann and his colleagues (Huesmann, 1986) caught up with this panel one more time when the panel members were 30 years old. After reinterviewing 409 subjects from the original pool of 875, the authors concluded that this 22-year panel study demonstrated that viewing media violence can have harmful lifelong consequences.

Another problem associated with the catch-up panel involves comparability of measures. If the earlier study was not constructed to be part of a longitudinal design, the original measurement instruments will have to be modified. For example, a study of 10-year-olds might have used teacher ratings to measure aggressiveness; such a measure would not be appropriate with 20-year-olds, however. Finally, the researcher in the catch-up situation is confined to the variables measured in the original study. In the intervening time, new variables might have been identified as important, but if those variables were not measured during the original survey, they are unavailable to the researcher. Figure 9.1 shows the similarities and differences in retrospective, follow-back, and catch-up panel designs.

ANALYZING CAUSATION IN PANEL DATA

The panel design provides an opportunity for the researcher to make statements about the causal ordering among different variables. There

---

FIGURE 9.1   COMPARISON OF RETROSPECTIVE, FOLLOW-BACK, AND CATCH-UP DESIGNS

Retrospective
   Step 1: Select current sample.
   Step 2: Interview sample about past recollections concerning topic of interest.
   Step 3: Collect current data on topic of interest.
   Step 4: Compare data.

Follow-back
   Step 1: Select current sample.
   Step 2: Collect current data on topic of interest.
   Step 3: Locate archival data on sample regarding topic of interest.
   Step 4: Compare data.

Catch-up panel
   Step 1: Locate archival data on topic of interest.
   Step 2: Select current sample by locating as many respondents as possible for whom data exist in the archive.
   Step 3: Collect current data on topic of interest.
   Step 4: Compare data.

are three necessary conditions for determining cause and effect. The first is time order. Causation is present if, and only if, the cause precedes the effect. Second, causation can occur only if some tendency for change in A results in change in B. In other words, there is an association between the two variables. Third, before attributing effects to causes, it is necessary to rule out all other alternative causes. Cross-sectional surveys, for which the data are collected at a single point in time, can fulfill only two of these three criteria. A cross-sectional survey allows the researcher to say that Variables A and B are associated. A skillfully constructed questionnaire and statistical controls such as partial correlation can help the researcher rule out alternative explanations. Nonetheless, only if the time order between A and B is evident can statements of cause be inferred. For example, a person's education typically is acquired before occupational status. Thus, the statement that education is a cause of occupational status (all other things equal) can be inferred. If there is no distinguishable temporal sequence in the data (as is the case with viewing of violence on TV and aggressive behavior), causal statements are conjectural. In a panel study, however, the variables are measured across time, making causal inferences more defensible.

There are many statistical techniques available for determining a causal sequence in panel data. A detailed listing and explanation of the computations involved is beyond the scope of this book. Nonetheless, some of the following references will be helpful to readers who desire more detailed information. Kessler and Greenberg (1981) discuss common methods for analyzing panel data measured at the interval level. Markus (1979) gives computational methods for data measured at the interval level and also discusses ways to analyze dichotomous panel data, including the increasingly popular log–linear technique. Asher (1976) provides a detailed dis-

cussion of path analysis. McCullough (1978) compares four methods of analysis for panel data: Lazarsfeld's 16-fold table, Coleman's mathematical model, cross-lagged panel correlation, and path analysis. Finally, the most mathematically sophisticated technique, linear structural equations, or LISREL, is discussed in Joreskog (1973), Long (1976), and Wheaton, Muthen, Alwin, and Summers (1977). Since it appears that the LISREL method has much to recommend it (the LISREL technique was used in the NBC panel study discussed above), researchers who intend to do panel studies should be familiar with its assumptions and techniques.

LONGITUDINAL DESIGN IN EXPERIMENTS

Although the preceding discussion was concerned with survey research, experimental research has a longitudinal dimension that should not be overlooked. Many research designs are based on a single exposure to a message, with the dependent variable measured almost immediately afterward. This procedure might be appropriate in many circumstances, but a longitudinal treatment design may be necessary to measure subtle, cumulative media effects. Furthermore, delayed assessment is essential to determine the duration of the impact of certain media effects (for example, How long does it take a persuasive effect to decay?). Bryant, Carveth, and Brown (1981) illustrated the importance of the longitudinal design to the experimental approach. In investigating TV viewing and anxiety, they divided their subjects into groups and assigned to each a menu of TV shows that could be watched. Over a 6-week period, one group was assigned a light viewing schedule, while a second was directed to watch a large number of shows that depicted a clear triumph of justice. A third group was assigned to view a large number of shows in which justice did not triumph. One of the dependent variables was also measured over time. The investigators obtained voluntary viewing data by having students fill out diaries for another 3 weeks. The results of this study indicated that the cumulative exposure to TV shows in which justice does not prevail seemed to make some viewers more anxious, thus offering some support to Gerbner's cultivation hypothesis.

A study by Zillmann and Bryant (1982) also showed the importance of the longitudinal dimension in assessing the cumulative effects of continued exposure. One experimental group watched nearly 5 hours of pornographic films over a 6-week period. A second group saw about 2.5 hours over the same period, while a control group saw nonerotic films. Those exposed to the larger dose of pornography showed less compassion toward women as rape victims and toward women in general. Clearly, the longitudinal design can be of great value in experimental research.

S U M M A R Y

Longitudinal research involves the collection of data at different points in time. There are three different types of longitudinal study: trend, cohort, and panel. A trend study asks the same questions of different groups of people at different points in time. A cohort study measures some characteristic of a sample whose members share some significant life event (usually time of birth) at two or more points in time. In a panel study the same respondents are measured at least twice. One of the advantages of the panel design is that it allows the researcher to make statements about the causal ordering of the

study variables, and several different statistical methods are available for this task.

Questions and Problems for Further Investigation

1. Search recent issues of scholarly journals for examples of longitudinal studies. Which of the three designs discussed in this chapter was used? Try to find additional longitudinal studies done by commercial research firms. What design was most used?

2. What are some mass media variables that would be best studied using the cohort method?

3. What are some possible measures of media or audience characteristics that might be regularly made and stored in a data archive for secondary trend analysis?

4. How might a panel study make use of laboratory techniques?

References and Suggested Readings

Asher, H. (1976). *Causal modeling.* Beverly Hills, CA: Sage Publications.

Atkin, D., & Litman, B. (1986). Network TV programming: Economics, audiences, and the ratings game, 1971–1986. *Journal of Communication, 36*(3), 32–50.

Belson, W. (1978). *Television violence and the adolescent boy.* Hampshire, England: Saxon House.

Bryant J., Carveth, R., & Brown, D. (1981). Television viewing and anxiety. *Journal of Communication, 31*(1), 106–119.

Carman, J. (1974). Consumer panels. In R. Ferber (Ed.), *Handbook of marketing research.* New York: McGraw-Hill.

Cassell, C. (1977). Cohort analysis of party identification among Southern whites, 1952–72. *Public Opinion Quarterly, 41*(1), 28–33.

Cook, T., Kendizierski, D., & Thomas, S. (1983). The implicit assumptions of television research. *Public Opinion Quarterly, 47*(2), 161–201.

Gerbner, G., Gross, L., Signorielli, N., Morgan, M., & Jackson-Beeck, M. (1979). The demonstration of power: Violence profile no. 10. *Journal of Communication, 29*(3), 177–196.

Glenn, N. (1977). *Cohort analysis.* Beverly Hills, CA: Sage Publications.

Huesmann, L. R. (1986). Psychological processes promoting the relation between exposure to media violence and aggressive behavior by the viewer. *Journal of Social Issues, 42*(3), 125–139.

Huesmann, L. R., & Eron, L. D. (1986). *Television and the aggressive child.* Hillsdale, NJ: Lawrence Erlbaum.

Hyman, H. (1987). *Secondary analysis of sample surveys.* Middletown, NY: Wesleyan University Press.

Joreskog, K. (1973). A general method for estimating a linear structural equation system. In A. Goldberger & O. Duncan (Eds.), *Structural equations models in the social sciences.* New York: Seminar Press.

Katz, E., & Lazarsfeld, P. (1955). *Personal influence.* New York: Free Press.

Kenny, D., Milavsky, J. R., Kessler, R. C., Stipp, H. H., & Rubens, W. S. (1984). The NBC study and television violence. *Journal of Communication, 34*(1), 176–188.

Kessler, R., & Greenberg, D. (1981). *Linear panel analysis.* New York: Academic Press.

Lazarsfeld, P., Berelson, B., & Gaudet, H. (1944). *The people's choice.* New York: Columbia University Press.

Lefkowitz, M., Eron, L. D., Walder, L. O., & Huesmann, L. R. (1972). Television violence and child aggression. In E. Rubinstein, G. Comstock, & J. Murray (Eds.), *Television and adolescent aggressiveness.* Washington, DC: U.S. Government Printing Office.

Long, J. (1976). Estimation and hypothesis testing in linear models containing measurement error. *Sociological Methods and Research, 5*, 157–206.

Lowery, S., & DeFleur, M. (1988). *Milestones in mass communication research* (2nd ed.). White Plains, NY: Longman.

Markus, G. (1979). *Analyzing panel data.* Beverly Hills, CA: Sage Publications.

Mason, K., Mason, W., Winsborough, H., & Poole, W. K. (1973, April). Some methodological issues in cohort analysis of archival data. *American Sociological Review*, pp. 242–258.

McCullough, B. (1978). Effects of variables using panel data. *Public Opinion Quarterly, 42*(2), 199–220.

Milavsky, J., Kessler, R. C., Stipp, H. H., & Rubens, W. S. (1982). *Television and aggression.* New York: Academic Press.

Newcomb, T. (1943). *Personality and social change.* New York: Dryden.

Norlen, V. (1977). Response errors in the answers to retrospective questions. *Statistik Tidskrift, 4*, 331–341.

Palmore, E. (1978). When can age, period and cohort effects be separated? *Social Forces, 57*, 282–295.

Pearl, D., Bouthilet, L., & Lazar, J. (1982). *Television and behavior: Ten years of scientific progress and implications for the eighties.* Washington, DC: Government Printing Office.

Peterson, T. (1980). *The mass media election.* New York: Praeger.

Powers, E., Goudy, W., & Keith, P. (1978). Congruence between panel and recall data in longitudinal research. *Public Opinion Quarterly, 42*(3), 380–389.

Rentz, J., Reynolds, F., & Stout, R. (1983, February). Analyzing changing consumption patterns with cohort analysis. *Journal of Marketing Research, 20*, 12–20.

Rosengren, K. E., & Windahl, S. (1989). *Media matter.* Norwood, NJ: Ablex Publishing.

Schulsinger, F., Mednick, S., & Knop, J. (1981). *Longitudinal research.* Boston: Nijhoff Publishing.

Singer, J. L., Singer, D. G., Desmond, R., Hirsch, B., & Nicol, A. (1988). Family mediation and children's cognition, aggression and comprehension of television. *Journal of Applied Developmental Psychology, 9*(3), 329–347.

Turner, C. W., Hesse, B. W., & Peterson-Lewis, S. (1986). Naturalistic studies of the long-term effects of television violence. *Journal of Social Issues, 42*(3), 51–73.

Wartella, E., & Reeves, B. (1985). Historical trends in research on children and the media, 1900–1960. *Journal of Communication, 35*(2), 118–133.

Wheaton, B., Muthen, D., Alwin, D. F., & Summers, G. F. (1977). Assessing reliability and stability in panel models. In D. Heise (Ed.), *Sociological methodology, 1977.* San Francisco: Jossey-Bass.

Wood, W. (1986, February). Get to know your cohort. *Marketing and Media Decisions*, pp. 144–145.

Zillmann, D., & Bryant, J. (1982). Pornography, sexual callousness and the trivialization of rape. *Journal of Communication, 32*(4), 10–21.

INTRODUCTION TO STATISTICS

Statistics is the science that uses mathematical methods to collect, organize, summarize, and analyze data. Statistics cannot perform miracles. If a research question or hypothesis is misdirected, poorly phrased, or ambiguous, or if a study uses sloppy measurement and design and the project contains numerous errors, statistics alone will not help. Statistics provide valid and reliable results only when the data collection and research methods follow established scientific procedures.

The science of statistics has expanded rapidly since the development of mini- and microcomputers. Only a few decades ago researchers spent weeks and months generating statistical data by executing handwritten calculations. In the 1950s, a Ph.D. was awarded to an Illinois student whose dissertation consisted merely of hand calculating a multivariate statistical procedure called factor analysis (Appendix 2). What once took weeks or months now takes only seconds or minutes.

Much of the groundwork for statistics was developed in 1835 by Lambert Adolphe Quetelet (kay-tuh-lay), a Belgian mathematician and astronomer, with his paper titled *On Man and the Development of His Faculties*. In addition to other techniques, Quetelet developed the ideas behind the normal distribution and developed the basics of probability theory from preliminary work by French mathematician and physicist Pierre-Simon Laplace and others. Quetelet's background is similar to others who were instrumental in the development of statistics. Almost all were renaissance men who were involved in areas such as astronomy, mathematics, physics, and philosophy. Luckily for us, we need only concentrate in one area.

Part III, humorously subtitled *On Students and the Purging of Their Statistical Anxieties*, focuses on the statistical procedures used by mass media researchers. This chapter provides an introduction to descriptive statistics.

DESCRIPTIVE STATISTICS

Descriptive statistics are intended to reduce data sets to allow for easier interpretation. If you asked 100 people how long they listened to the radio yesterday and recorded all 100 answers at random on a sheet of paper, you would be hard pressed to draw conclusions from a simple examination of that paper. Data analysis would be easier if they were organized in some fashion. In this regard, descriptive statistics are useful.

During the course of a research study, investigators typically collect data that are the results of measurements or observations of the people or items in the sample. These data usually have little meaning or usefulness until they are displayed or summarized using one of the techniques of descriptive statistics. Mass media researchers use two primary methods to make their data more manageable: data distribution and summary statistics.

Data Distribution

One way researchers can display their data is by distributing them in tables or graphs. A **distribution** is simply a collection of numbers. Table 10.1 is a hypothetical distribution of 20 respondents' answers to the question, "How many hours did you listen to the radio yesterday?" It would be difficult, however, to draw any conclusions **199** or make any generalizations from this collection of unordered scores.

As a preliminary step toward making these numbers more manageable, the data may be arranged in a **frequency distribution**, that is, a table of each score, ordered according to magnitude, and its actual frequency of occurrence. Table 10.2 presents the data from the hypothetical survey in a frequency distribution.

Now the data begin to show a pattern. Note that the typical frequency distribution table consists of two columns. The first, on the left, contains all the values of the variable under study, and the second, on the right, shows the number of occurrences of each value. The sum of the frequency column is the number (N) of persons or items that make up the distribution.

A frequency distribution can also be constructed using grouped intervals, each of which contains several score levels. Table 10.3 shows

TABLE 10.1   DISTRIBUTION OF RESPONSES TO ''HOW MANY HOURS DID YOU LISTEN TO THE RADIO YESTERDAY?''

Respondent	Hours listened	Respondent	Hours listened
A	0.0	K	0.0
B	2.5	L	2.0
C	1.0	M	1.0
D	2.0	N	3.0
E	0.0	O	0.5
F	0.5	P	0.5
G	1.0	Q	1.0
H	1.0	R	1.0
I	1.5	S	1.0
J	0.5	T	0.0

TABLE 10.2   FREQUENCY DISTRIBUTION OF RESPONSES TO ''HOW MANY HOURS DID YOU LISTEN TO THE RADIO YESTERDAY?''

Hours	Frequency ($N = 20$)
0.0	4
0.5	4
1.0	7
1.5	1
2.0	2
2.5	1
3.0	1

the data from the radio listening survey with the scores grouped together in intervals. This table is a more compact frequency distribution than Table 10.2, but the scores have lost their individual identity.

Other columns can be included in frequency distribution tables. For example, the data can be transformed into proportions or percentages. To obtain the percentage of a response, simply divide the frequency of the individual responses by N — the total number of responses in the distribution. Percentages allow comparisons to be made between different frequency distributions that are based on different values of N.

Some frequency distributions include the cumulative frequency (cf). This column is con-structed by adding the number of scores in one interval to the number of scores in the intervals above it. Table 10.4 displays the frequency distribution from Table 10.2 with the addition of a percentage column, a cumulative frequency column, and a column showing cumulative frequency as a percentage of N.

Sometimes it is desirable to present data in graph form. The graphs shown on the following pages contain the same information as frequency distributions. Graphs usually consist of two perpendicular lines, the *x-axis* (horizontal) and the *y-axis* (vertical). Over the years, statis-ticians have developed certain conventions re-garding graphic format. One common conven-tion is to list the scores along the *x-axis* and the

TABLE 10.3   FREQUENCY DISTRIBUTION OF RADIO LISTENING SCORES GROUPED IN INTERVALS

Hours	Frequency
0.00–0.50	8
0.51–1.50	8
1.51–3.00	4

TABLE 10.4   FREQUENCY DISTRIBUTION OF RADIO LISTENING SCORES

Hours	Frequency	Percentage	cf	cf percentage of N
0.0	4	20	4	20
0.5	4	20	8	40
1.0	7	35	15	75
1.5	1	5	16	80
2.0	2	10	18	90
2.5	1	5	19	95
3.0	1	5	20	100
	$N = 20$	100%		

frequency or relative frequency along the y-axis. Thus, the height of a line or bar indicates the frequency of a score.

One common form of graph is the **histogram**, or **bar chart**, in which frequencies are represented by vertical bars. Figure 10.1 is a histogram constructed from the data in Table 10.1. Note that the scores across the x-axis are actually the midpoints of half-hour intervals: the first category extends from 0 to 0.2499 hour, the second from 0.25 to 0.7499 hour, and so on.

If a line is drawn from the midpoint of each interval at its peak along the y-axis to each adjacent midpoint/peak, the resulting graph is called a **frequency polygon**. Figure 10.2 shows a frequency polygon superimposed onto the histogram from Figure 10.1. As can be seen, the two figures display the same information.

A **frequency curve** is similar to a frequency polygon except that points are connected by a continuous, unbroken curve instead of by lines. Such a curve assumes that any irregularities shown in a frequency polygon are simply due to

chance and that the variable being studied is distributed continuously over the population. Figure 10.3 superimposes a frequency curve onto the frequency polygon shown in Figure 10.2.

Frequency curves are described in relation to the **normal curve**, a symmetrical bell curve whose properties are discussed more fully later in this chapter. Figure 10.4 illustrates the normal curve and shows the ways in which a frequency curve can deviate from it. These patterns of deviation are referred to as skewness.

Skewness refers to the concentration of scores around a particular point on the x-axis. If this concentration lies toward the low end of the scale, with the tail of the curve trailing off to the right, the curve is called a *right skew*. Conversely, if the tail of the curve trails off to the left, it is a *left skew*. If the halves of the curve are identical, it is *symmetrical*, or normal.

A normal distribution of data is free from skewness. If data produce a curve that deviates substantially from the normal curve, the data

FIGURE 10.1   HISTOGRAM OF RADIO LISTENING SCORES

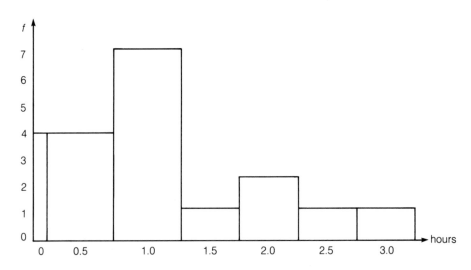

FIGURE 10.2   FREQUENCY POLYGON OF RADIO LISTENING SCORES SUPERIMPOSED ON THE HISTOGRAM OF THE SAME SCORES

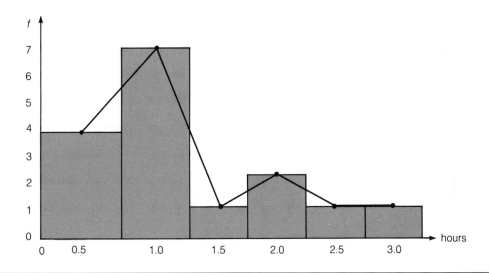

FIGURE 10.3   FREQUENCY CURVE (SHADED) OF RADIO LISTENING SCORES SUPERIMPOSED ON THE FREQUENCY POLYGON OF THE SAME SCORES

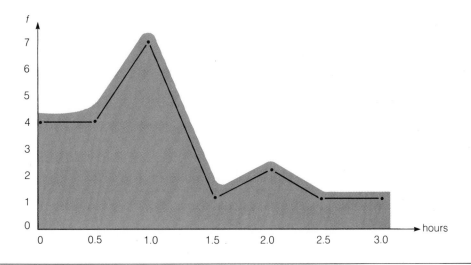

FIGURE 10.4 SKEWNESS AND THE NORMAL CURVE

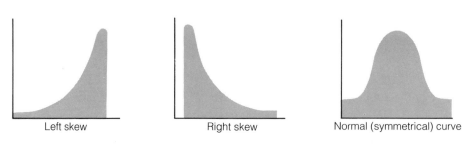

| Left skew | Right skew | Normal (symmetrical) curve |

may have to be transformed in some way (discussed later in this chapter) to achieve a more normal distribution.

Summary Statistics

The data in Table 10.1 (page 200) can be condensed still further through the use of **summary statistics**. These statistics help make data more manageable by measuring two basic tendencies of distributions: central tendency and dispersion or variability.

Central tendency statistics answer the question, What is a typical score? They provide information about the grouping of the numbers in a distribution by calculating a single number that is characteristic of the entire distribution. Exactly what constitutes a "typical" score depends on the level of measurement and the purpose for which the data will be used.

For every distribution, three types of characteristic numbers can be identified. One is the **mode** (Mo), or the score or scores occurring most frequently. Calculation is not necessary to determine the mode; it is found by inspecting the distribution. For the data in Table 10.1, the mode is 1.0. Although easy to determine, the mode has some serious drawbacks as a descriptive statistic. It focuses attention on only one

possible score and can thus camouflage important facts about the data when considered in isolation. This is illustrated by the data in Table 10.5: the mode is 70, but the most striking feature about the numbers is the way they cluster around 30.

A second characteristic score is the **median** (Mdn), which is the midpoint of a distribution: half the scores lie above it, and half lie below it. If the distribution has an odd number of scores, the median is the middle score; if there is an even number, the median is a hypothetical score halfway between the two middle scores. To determine the median, one must order the scores from smallest to largest and locate the midpoint by inspection. For example, here are nine scores:

0   2   2   5   ⑥   17   18   19   67

The median score is 6, since there are four scores above this number and four below it. Now consider these numbers:

0   2   2   5   6   ↑   17   18   19   67   75
                    11.5

No score neatly bisects this distribution; to determine the median, the two middle scores must be added and divided by 2:

TABLE 10.5   THE MODE AS A POTENTIALLY MISLEADING STATISTIC

Score	f
70	2
35–69	0
34	1
33	1
32	1
31	1
30	1
29	1
28	1
27	1
26	1

$$\text{Mdn} = \frac{6 + 17}{2} = 11.5$$

When many scores in the distribution are the same, computing the median becomes a bit more complicated. Statistics texts should be consulted for precise directions.

The third type of central tendency statistic is the **mean**. The mean is probably the most familiar summary statistic; it represents the average of a set of scores. Mathematically speaking, the mean is defined as the sum of all scores divided by N, or the total number of scores. Since the mean is widely used in both descriptive and inferential statistics, it is described here in greater detail.

As a first step, some basic statistical notation is required:

X = any score in a series of scores
$\overline{X}$ = the mean (read "X-bar"; M is also commonly used to denote the mean)
Σ = the sum (symbol is Greek capital letter **sigma**)
N = the total number of scores in a distribution

Using these symbols, the formula for the calculation of the mean is:

$$\overline{X} = \frac{\Sigma X}{N}$$

This equation indicates that the mean is the sum of all scores (ΣX) divided by the number of scores (N). Using the data in Table 10.1, the mean is:

$$\overline{X} = \frac{20}{20}$$
$$= 1.00$$

If the data are contained in a frequency distribution, a slightly different formula is used to calculate the mean:

$$\overline{X} = \frac{\Sigma f X}{N}$$

In this case, X represents the midpoint of any given interval, and f is the frequency of that interval. Table 10.6 uses this formula to

TABLE 10.6 CALCULATION OF MEAN FROM FREQUENCY DISTRIBUTION

Hours	f	fx
0.0	4	0.0
0.5	4	2.0
1.0	7	7.0
1.5	1	1.5
2.0	2	4.0
2.5	1	2.5
3.0	1	3.0
	$N = 20$	$\Sigma fX = 20$

$$\overline{X} = \frac{20}{20} = 1.00$$

calculate the mean of the frequency distribution in Table 10.2 (page 200).

Unlike the mode and the median, the mean takes into account all the values in the distribution, making it especially sensitive to extreme scores or "outliers." Extreme scores draw the mean in their direction. For example, suppose Table 10.1 contained another response, from Respondent U, who reported 12 hours of radio listening. The new mean would then be approximately 1.52 hours, an increase of more than 50% due to the addition of a single large score.

The mean may be thought of as the score that would be assigned to each individual if the total were to be evenly distributed among all members of the sample. It is also the only measure of central tendency that can be defined algebraically. As will be seen later, this allows the mean to be used in a wide range of situations. It also suggests that the data used to calculate the mean should be at the interval or ratio level (Chapter 3).

Two factors must be considered when deciding which of the three measures of central tendency to report for a given set of data. First of all, the level of measurement used may determine the choice: if the data are at the nominal level,

only the mode is meaningful; with ordinal data, either the mode or the median may be used. All three measures are appropriate for interval and ratio data, however, and it may be desirable to report more than one.

Second, the purpose of the statistic is important. If the ultimate goal is to describe a set of data, the measure that is most typical of the distribution should be used. To illustrate, suppose the scores on a statistics exam were 100, 100, 100, 100, 0, and 0. To say that the mean grade was 67 does not accurately portray the distribution; the mode would provide a more characteristic description.

The second type of descriptive statistics is used to measure **dispersion**, or variation. Measures of central tendency determine the typical score of a distribution; dispersion measures describe the way in which the scores are spread out about this central point. Dispersion measures can be particularly valuable when comparing different distributions. For example, suppose the average grades for two classes in research methods are exactly the same; however, one class has several excellent students and many poor students, while in the other class, all students are just about average. A measure of dispersion must be employed to reflect this difference. In many cases, an adequate description of a data set can be achieved by simply reporting a measure of central tendency (usually the mean) and an index of dispersion.

There are three measures of variation or dispersion; the simplest, **range** (R), is the difference between the highest and lowest scores in a distribution of scores. The formula used to calculate the range is:

$$R = X_{hi} - X_{lo}$$

where X_{hi} = the highest score and X_{lo} = the lowest score. The range is sometimes reported simply as "the range among scores was 40."

Since the range uses only two scores out of the entire distribution, it is not particularly descriptive of the data set. Additionally, the range often increases with sample size, since larger samples tend to include more extreme values. For these reasons, the range is seldom used in mass media research as the sole measure of dispersion.

A second measure, **variance**, provides a mathematical index of the degree to which scores deviate from, or are at variance with, the mean. A small variance indicates that most of the scores in the distribution lie fairly close to the mean; a large variance represents scores that are widely scattered. Thus, variance is directly proportional to the degree of dispersion.

To compute the variance of a distribution, the mean is subtracted from each score; these *deviation scores* are then squared, and the squares are summed and divided by N. The formula for variance (usually symbolized as S^2, although many textbooks use a different notation) is:

$$S^2 = \frac{\Sigma(X - \overline{X})^2}{N}$$

(In many texts, the expression $(X - \overline{X})^2$ is symbolized by x^2.) The numerator in this formula,

$\Sigma(X - \overline{X})^2$, is called the *sum of squares*. Although this quantity is usually not reported as a descriptive statistic, the sum of squares is used in the calculation of several other statistics. An example using this variance formula is found in Table 10.7.

This equation may not be the most convenient formula for calculating variance, especially if N is large. A simpler, equivalent formula is:

$$S^2 = \frac{\Sigma X^2}{N} - \overline{X}^2$$

The expression ΣX^2 means to square each score and sum the squared scores. (Note that this is not the same as $(\Sigma X)^2$, which means to sum all the scores and then square the sum.) An example of this formula is shown in Table 10.8, using the data from Table 10.7. Not surprisingly, S^2 is the same in both cases.

Variance is a commonly used and highly valuable measure of dispersion. In fact, it is at the heart of one powerful technique, analysis of variance (Chapter 12), which is widely used in inferential statistics. However, variance does have one minor inconvenience: it is expressed in terms of squared deviations from the mean rather than in terms of the original measurements. To obtain a measure of dispersion that is calibrated in the same units as the original data, it is necessary to take the square root of the variance. This quantity, called the **standard deviation**, is the third type of dispersion measure. The standard deviation is a more meaningful term than variance since it is expressed in the same units as the measurement involved to compute it.

To illustrate, assume a research project involves a question on household income that produces a variance of $90,000 — interpreted as 90,000 "squared dollars." Because the concept of "squared dollars" is confusing to work with, a researcher would probably choose to report the standard deviation: 300 "regular dollars" (300

TABLE 10.7   CALCULATION OF VARIANCE: X = SCORE

X	$\overline{X}$	$X - \overline{X}$	$(X - \overline{X})^2$
0.0	1.00	−1.00	1.00
0.0	1.00	−1.00	1.00
0.0	1.00	−1.00	1.00
0.0	1.00	−1.00	1.00
0.5	1.00	−0.5	.25
0.5	1.00	−0.5	.25
0.5	1.00	−0.5	.25
0.5	1.00	−0.5	.25
1.0	1.00	0	0
1.0	1.00	0	0
1.0	1.00	0	0
1.0	1.00	0	0
1.0	1.00	0	0
1.0	1.00	0	0
1.0	1.00	0	0
1.5	1.00	0.5	.25
2.0	1.00	1.00	1.00
2.0	1.00	1.00	1.00
2.5	1.00	1.50	2.25
3.0	1.00	2.00	4.00

$$S^2 = \frac{\Sigma(X - \overline{X})^2}{N} = \frac{13.5}{20} = 0.675$$

$= \sqrt{90,000}$). Usually symbolized as S (or SD), standard deviation is computed using either of the formulas shown below:

$$S = \sqrt{\frac{\Sigma(X - \overline{X})^2}{N}}$$

$$S = \sqrt{\frac{\Sigma X^2}{N} - \overline{X}^2}$$

Note that these two equations correspond to the respective variance formulas described above.

Standard deviation represents a given dis-tance of the scores from the mean of a distribution. This figure is especially useful in describing the results of standardized tests. For example, modern intelligence tests are constructed to yield a mean of 100 and a standard deviation of 15. A person with a score of 115 falls one standard deviation above the mean; a person with a score of 85 falls one standard deviation below the mean.

The notions of variance and standard deviation are easier to understand if they are visualized. Figure 10.5 contains two sets of frequency curves. Which curve in each set would have the larger S^2 and S?

TABLE 10.8   CALCULATION OF VARIANCE USING AN ALTERNATE FORMULA: X = SCORE

X	X^2
0.0	0
0.0	0
0.0	0
0.0	0
0.5	0.25
0.5	0.25
0.5	0.25
0.5	0.25
1.0	1.00
1.0	1.00
1.0	1.00
1.0	1.00
1.0	1.00
1.0	1.00
1.0	1.00
1.5	2.25
2.0	4.00
2.0	4.00
2.5	6.25
3.0	9.00
	$\Sigma X^2 = 33.50$

$$S^2 = \frac{\Sigma X^2}{N} - \overline{X}^2 = \frac{33.50}{20} - (1.00)^2 = 1.675 - 1.00 = 0.675$$

By determining the mean and standard deviation of a set of scores or measurements, it is possible to compute **standard scores** (z *scores*) for any distribution of data. Standard scores allow researchers to compare scores or measurements obtained from totally different methods; they allow for "apples and oranges" comparisons. This is possible because all standard score computations are based on the same metric; they all have a mean of 0 and a standard deviation of 1.0.

Standard scores are easy to compute and in-terpret. The formula for computing standard scores is simply the score minus the mean, divided by the standard deviation:

$$z = \frac{X - \overline{X}}{S}$$

Interpretation is easy because each score simply represents how many standard deviation units an individual is above or below the mean.

The computation of standard scores and the ability to compare different measurements or

FIGURE 10.5   VARIANCE AS SEEN IN FREQUENCY CURVES

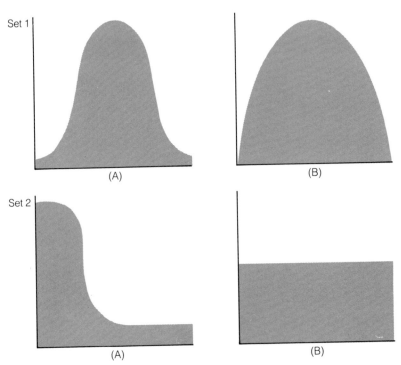

Which curve in each set represents the distribution with the larger S^2 and S?

Answers: Set 1 (B); Set 2 (A)

methods can be demonstrated by a brief example. Suppose that two roommates are in different sections of a media research course. On a particular day, each section is given a different exam, and both students score 73. However, the first roommate receives a letter grade of C, while the second roommate receives an A. How can this be? To understand how the professors arrived at the different grades, it is necessary to look at each section's standard scores.

Table 10.9 shows the hypothetical data for the two research sections. Each section contains 20 students. Scores in the first roommate's section range from a low of 68 to a high of 84 (range

= 16), whereas the scores in the second roommate's section range from a low of 38 to a high of 73 (range = 35). The differences in scores can be due to a variety of things including the difficulty of the tests, the ability of students in each section, and the teaching approach used by the professors.

The mean score in the first roommate's section is 74.6, with a standard deviation of 4.9 (43.9 and 7.5, respectively, in the other section). Assuming the professors strictly followed the normal curve (further discussed later in the chapter), it is easy to see why a score of 73 can have two different grades. The first roommate's

TABLE 10.9   z-SCORE HYPOTHETICAL DATA

	First Roommate's Section				Second Roommate's Section		
	Scores	(Computation)	z Score	Scores	(Computation)	z Score	
B grade	84	$(84 - 74.6)/4.9 =$	1.9	73	$(73 - 43.9)/7.5 =$	3.9	A grade
	81	$(81 - 74.6)/4.9 =$	1.3				
	81	$(81 - 74.6)/4.9 =$	1.3	50	$(50 - 43.9)/7.5 =$	.8	
				50	$(50 - 43.9)/7.5 =$	.8	
C grade	79	$(79 - 74.6)/4.9 =$	.9	47	$(47 - 43.9)/7.5 =$	.4	
	79	$(79 - 74.6)/4.9 =$	.9	46	$(46 - 43.9)/7.5 =$	.3	
	79	$(79 - 74.6)/4.9 =$	.9	45	$(45 - 43.9)/7.5 =$	.2	
	78	$(78 - 74.6)/4.9 =$	.7	43	$(43 - 43.9)/7.5 =$	$-.1$	
	77	$(77 - 74.6)/4.9 =$	.5	43	$(43 - 43.9)/7.5 =$	$-.1$	
	77	$(77 - 74.6)/4.9 =$	.5	42	$(42 - 43.9)/7.5 =$	$-.2$	
	75	$(75 - 74.6)/4.9 =$	.1	41	$(41 - 43.9)/7.5 =$	$-.4$	C grade
	73	$(73 - 74.6)/4.9 =$	$-.3$	41	$(41 - 43.9)/7.5 =$	$-.4$	
	71	$(71 - 74.6)/4.9 =$	$-.7$	41	$(41 - 43.9)/7.5 =$	$-.4$	
	71	$(71 - 74.6)/4.9 =$	$-.7$	40	$(40 - 43.9)/7.5 =$	$-.5$	
	71	$(71 - 74.6)/4.9 =$	$-.7$	40	$(40 - 43.9)/7.5 =$	$-.5$	
	70	$(70 - 74.6)/4.9 =$	$-.9$	40	$(40 - 43.9)/7.5 =$	$-.5$	
	70	$(70 - 74.6)/4.9 =$	$-.9$	40	$(40 - 43.9)/7.5 =$	$-.5$	
	70	$(70 - 74.6)/4.9 =$	$-.9$	40	$(40 - 43.9)/7.5 =$	$-.5$	
D grade	69	$(69 - 74.6)/4.9 =$	-1.1	39	$(39 - 43.9)/7.5 =$	$-.6$	
	68	$(68 - 74.6)/4.9 =$	-1.3	38	$(38 - 43.9)/7.5 =$	$-.8$	
	68	$(68 - 74.6)/4.9 =$	-1.3	38	$(38 - 43.9)/7.5 =$	$-.8$	

Mean 74.6   Mean 43.9

S 4.9   S 7.5

Note: The distribution of scores in each section is not normal (discussed later). In reality, the professors might transform the scores to produce a more normal distribution, or they might set grade cut-offs at other scores to spread the grades out.

performance is about average in comparison to the other students in the section. The second roommate is clearly well above the performance of the other students.

When any collection of raw scores is transformed into z scores, the resulting distribution possesses certain characteristics. Any score below the mean becomes a negative z score, any score above the mean is positive. The mean of a distribution of z scores is 0, which is also the z score assigned to a person whose raw score equals the mean. As mentioned, the variance and the standard deviation of a z-score distribution are both 1.00, (the mean is 0). Standard scores are expressed in units of the standard deviation; thus, a z score of 3.00 means that the score is three standard deviation units above the mean.

Standard scores are used frequently in all types of research because they allow researchers to directly compare the performance of different subjects on tests using different measurements (assuming the distributions have similar shapes). Assume for a moment that the apple harvest for a certain year was 24 bushels per acre, compared to an average annual yield of 22 bushels per acre with a standard deviation of 10. During the same year, the orange crop yielded 18 bushels per acre, compared to an average of 16 bushels with a standard deviation of 8. Was it a better year for apples or oranges? The standard score formula reveals a z score of .20 for apples and .25 for oranges. Relatively speaking, oranges had a better year.

The Normal Curve

An important tool in statistical analysis is the normal curve, which was briefly introduced in Chapter 4. Standard scores not only enable comparisons to be made between dissimilar measurements, but, when used in connection with the normal curve, they also allow statements to be made regarding the frequency of occurrence of certain variables. Figure 10.6 shows an example of the familiar normal curve. The curve is symmetrical and achieves maximum height at its mean, which is also its median and its mode. Also note that the curve in Figure 10.6 is calibrated in standard score units. When the curve is expressed in this way, it is called a *standard normal curve* and possesses all of the properties of a z-score distribution.

Statisticians have studied the normal curve closely in order to describe its properties. The most important of these is the fact that a fixed

FIGURE 10.6   THE NORMAL CURVE

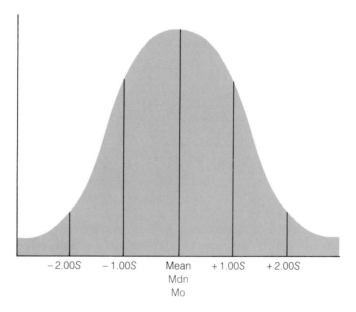

proportion of the area below the curve lies between the mean and any unit of standard deviation. The area under a certain segment of the curve is representative of the frequency of the scores that fall therein. From Figure 10.7, which portrays the areas contained under the normal curve between several key standard deviation units, it can be determined that roughly 68% of the total area, hence of the scores, lies within $+1$ and -1 standard deviation from the mean; about 95% lies within $+2$ and -2 standard deviations, and so forth. This knowledge, together with the presence of a normal distribution, allows researchers to make useful predictive statements. For example, suppose that television viewing is normally distributed with a mean of 2 hours per day and a standard deviation of 0.5 hour. What proportion of the population watches between 2 and 2.5 hours of TV? First, the raw scores are changed to standard scores:

$$\frac{2 - 2}{0.5} = 0 \text{ and } \frac{2.5 - 2}{0.5} = 1.00$$

Figure 10.7 shows that approximately 34% of the area below the curve is contained between the mean and one standard deviation. Thus, 34% of the population watches between 2 and 2.5 hours of television daily.

The same data can be used to find the proportion of the population that watches more than 3 hours of television per day. Again, the first step is to translate the raw figures into z scores. In this case, 3 hours corresponds to a z score of 2.00. A glance at Figure 10.7 shows that approximately 98% of the area under the curve falls below a score of 2.00 (50% in the left half of the curve plus about 48% from the mean to the 2.00 mark). Thus, only 2% of the population views more than 3 hours of television daily.

Table 3 in Appendix 1 contains all the areas under the normal curve between the mean of the

FIGURE 10.7   AREAS UNDER THE NORMAL CURVE

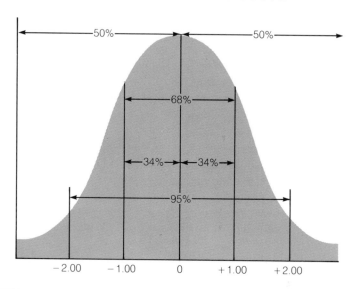

curve and some specified distance. To use this table, we match the row and the column represented by some standard score. For example, let's assume that the standard score of a normally distributed variable is 1.79. In Table 3 first find the row labeled 1.7. Next find the column labeled .09. At the intersection of the 1.7 row and .09 column is the number .4633. The area between the mean of the curve (the midpoint) and a standard score of 1.79 is .4633, or roughly 46%. To take another example, what is the distance from the midpoint of the curve to the standard score of −1.32? According to Table 3, 40.66% of the curve lies between these two values. Note that the area is always positive even though the standard score was expressed as a negative value.

To make this exercise more meaningful, let's go back to our example of the two roommates. Let's assume that the scores were normally distributed in the class that had a mean of 72 and a standard deviation of 5.0. The instructor decided to assign C's to 50% of the class. What numerical scores would receive these grades? To begin, remember that "50% of the grades" actually means "25% above the mean and 25% below the mean." What standard deviation unit corresponds to this distance? To answer this question, it is necessary to reverse the process performed above. Specifically, the first thing that we must do is examine the *body* of Table 3 in Appendix 1 for the value .2500. Unfortunately, it does not appear. There are, however, two numbers bracketing it, .2486 and .2517. Since .2486 is a little closer to .2500, let's use it as our area. Examining the row and column that

intersect at .2486, we find that it corresponds to 0.67 standard deviation unit. Now we can quickly calculate the scores that receive C's. First we find the upper limit of the C range by taking the mean (72) and adding to it 0.67 × 5 or 3.35. This yields 75.35, which represents the quarter of the area above the mean. To get the lower limit of the range, we take the mean (72) and subtract from it 0.67 × 5, or 72 − 3.35. This gives us 68.65. After rounding, we find that all students who scored 69–75 would receive the C grade.

The normal curve is important because many of the variables mass media researchers encounter are distributed in a normal manner, or normally enough that minor departures can be overlooked. Furthermore, the normal curve is an example of a probability distribution that becomes important in inferential statistics. Finally, many of the more advanced statistics discussed in later chapters assume normal distribution of the variable(s) under consideration.

SAMPLE DISTRIBUTIONS

For this section, it is necessary to introduce some new symbols to differentiate those statistics that indicate population parameters, or characteristics, from those used to describe a sample, as shown below.

A **sample distribution** is the distribution of some characteristic measured on the individuals or other units of analysis that were part of a sample. If a random sample of 1,500 college students were asked how many movies they at-

Characteristic	Sample statistic	Population parameter
Average	$\overline{X}$ (or M)	μ (mu)
Variance	S^2	σ^2 (sigma squared)
Standard deviation	S (or SD)	σ (sigma)

tended in the last month, the resulting distribution of the variable "number of movies attended" would be a sample distribution, with a mean ($\overline{X}$) and variance (S^2). It is theoretically possible (though not practical) to ask the same question of every college student in the United States. This would create a **population distribution** with a mean (μ) and variance (σ^2). Ordinarily, the precise shape of the population distribution and the values of μ and σ^2 are unknown and are estimated from the sample. This estimate is called a **sampling distribution**.

In any sample drawn from a specified population, the mean of the sample, $\overline{X}$, will probably differ somewhat from the population mean, μ. For example, suppose that the average number of movies seen by each college student in the United States during the past month was exactly 3.8. It is unlikely that a random sample of 10 students from this population would produce a mean of exactly 3.8. The amount that the sample mean differs from μ is called *sampling error* (Chapter 4). If more random samples of 10 were selected from this population, the values calculated for X that are close to the population mean would become more numerous than the values of X that are greatly different from μ. If this process were duplicated an infinite number of times and each mean placed on a frequency curve, the curve would form a sampling distribution.

Once the sampling distribution has been identified, statements about the *probability* of occurrence of certain values are possible. There are many ways to define the concept of probability. Stated simply, the probability that an event will occur is equal to the relative frequency of occurrence of that event in the population under consideration (Roscoe, 1975). To illustrate, suppose a large urn contains 1,000 table tennis balls, of which 700 are red and 300 white. The probability of drawing a red ball at random is 700/1,000, or 70%. It is also possible to calculate probability when the relative frequency of occurrence of an event is determined theoretically. For example, what is the probabil-

ity of randomly guessing the answer to a true/false question? One out of two, or 50%. What is the probability of guessing the right answer on a four-item multiple-choice question? One out of four, or 25%. Probabilities can range from zero (no chance) to one (a sure thing). The sum of all the probable events in a population must equal 1.00, which is also the sum of the probabilities that an event will and will not occur. For instance, when a coin is tossed, the probability of it landing face up ("heads") is .50 and the probability of it not landing face up ("tails") is .50 (.50 + .50 = 1.00).

There are two important rules of probability. The "addition rule" states that the probability that any one of a set of mutually exclusive events will occur is the sum of the probabilities of the separate events. (Two events are mutually exclusive if the occurrence of one precludes the other. In the table tennis ball example, the color of the ball is either red or white; it cannot be both.) To illustrate the addition rule, consider a population in which 20% of the people read no magazines per month, 40% read only one, 20% read two, 10% read three, and 10% read four. What is the probability of selecting at random a person who reads at least two magazines per month? The answer is .40 (.20 + .10 + .10), the sum of the probabilities of the separate events.

The "multiplication rule" states that the probability of a combination of independent events occurring is the product of the separate probabilities of the events. (Two events are independent when the occurrence of one has no effect on the other. For example, getting "tails" on a flip of a coin has no impact on the next flip.) To illustrate the multiplication rule, calculate the probability that an unprepared student will correctly guess the right answers to the first four questions on a true/false test. The answer is the product of the probabilities of each event: .5 (chance of guessing right on Question 1) times .5 (chance of guessing right on Question 2) times .5 (chance of guessing right on Question 3) times .5 (chance of guessing right on Question 4) = .0625.

The notion of probability is important in inferential statistics because sampling distributions are a type of probability distribution. When the concept of probability is understood, a formal definition of "sampling distribution" is possible. A sampling distribution is *a probability distribution of all possible values of a statistic that would occur if all possible samples of a fixed size from a given population were taken*. For each outcome, the sampling distribution determines the probability of occurrence. For example, assume that a population consists of six college students. Their film viewing for the last month was as follows:

Student	Number of films seen
A	1
B	2
C	3
D	3
E	4
F	5

$$\mu = \frac{1 + 2 + 3 + 3 + 4 + 5}{6} = 3.00$$

Suppose a study is made using a sample of two ($N = 2$) from this population. As is evident, there is a limit to the number of combinations that can be generated, assuming that sampling is done without replacement. Table 10.10 shows the possible outcomes.

The mean of this sampling distribution is equal to μ, the mean of the population. The likelihood of drawing a sample whose mean is 2.0 or 1.5 or any other value is found simply by reading the figure in the far right-hand column.

Table 10.10 is an example of a sampling distribution determined by empirical means. Many sampling distributions, however, are not derived by mathematical calculations but are determined theoretically. For example, sampling distributions often take the form of a normal curve. When this is the case, the researcher can make use of everything that is known about the properties of the normal curve. This can be illustrated by a hypothetical example using dichotomous data, or data with only two possible values. (This type of data is chosen because it makes the mathematics less complicated. The same logic applies to continuous data, but the computations are elaborate.) Consider the case of a television rating firm attempting to estimate

---

TABLE 10.10 GENERATING A SAMPLING DISTRIBUTION POPULATION = (1, 2, 3, 3, 4, 5) N = 2

$\overline{X}$	Number of possible sample combinations producing this $\overline{X}$	Probability of occurrence
1.5	2 (1,2) (2,1)	2/30 or .07
2.0	4 (1,3) (1,3) (3,1) (3,1)	4/30 or .13
2.5	6 (1,4) (2,3) (2,3) (3,2) (3,2) (4,1)	6/30 or .20
3.0	6 (1,5) (2,4) (3,3) (3,3) (4,2) (5,1)	6/30 or .20
3.5	6 (2,5) (3,4) (3,4) (4,3) (4,3) (5,2)	6/30 or .20
4.0	4 (3,5) (3,5) (5,3) (5,3)	4/30 or .13
4.5	2 (4,5) (5,4)	2/30 or .07
		1.00

Total number of possible sample combinations = 30

from the results of a sample the total number of people in the population who saw a given program. One sample of 100 people might produce an estimate of 40%, a second an estimate of 42%, and a third an estimate of 39%. If, after a large number of samples have been taken, the results are expressed as a sampling distribution, probability theory predicts that it would have the shape of the normal curve with a mean equal to μ. This distribution is shown in Figure 10.8. Interestingly enough, if a person draws samples of size N repeatedly from a given population, the sampling distribution of the means of these samples, assuming N is large enough, will almost always be normal. This holds even if the population itself is not normally distributed. Furthermore, the mean of the sampling distribution will equal the population mean — the parameter.

In earlier discussions of the normal curve, the horizontal divisions along the base of the curve were expressed in terms of standard deviation units. With sampling distributions, this unit is called the *standard error of the mean* (*SE*) and serves as a criterion for determining the probable accuracy of an estimate. As is the case with the normal curve, roughly 68% of the sample will fall within $\pm$ 1 standard error of the population mean, and about 95% will fall within $\pm$ 2 standard errors.

In most actual research studies, a sampling distribution is not generated by taking large numbers of samples and computing the probable outcome of each, and the standard error is not computed by taking the standard deviation of a sampling distribution of means. Instead, a researcher takes only one sample and uses it to estimate the population mean and the standard error. The process of inference from only one sample works in the following way: the sample mean is used as the best estimate of the population mean, and the standard error is calculated

FIGURE 10.8   HYPOTHETICAL SAMPLING DISTRIBUTION

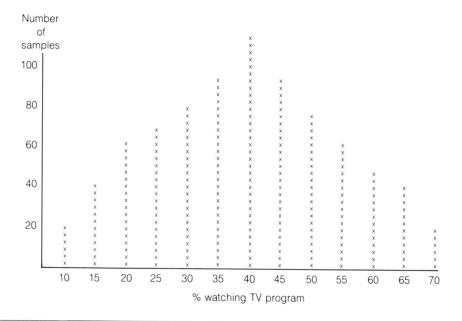

from the sample data. Suppose that in the foregoing example, 40 out of a sample of 100 people were watching a particular program. The mean, in this case symbolized as *p* because the data are dichotomous, is 40% (dichotomous data require this unique formula). The formula for standard error in a dichotomous situation is calculated as:

$$SE = \sqrt{\frac{pq}{N}}$$

where *p* = the proportion viewing, *q* = 1 − *p*, and *N* = the number in the sample. In the example, the standard error is

$$\sqrt{\frac{(.4)\,(.6)}{100}} = \sqrt{\frac{.24}{100}} = .048 \text{ or } 4.8\%$$

Standard error is used in conjunction with the **confidence interval** (CI) set by the researcher. Recall from Chapter 4 that a confidence interval establishes an interval in which researchers state, with a certain degree of probability, that the statistical result found will fall within the interval. Using the previous example, this means that at the 68% confidence interval, 68% of all possible samples taken will fall within the interval of 35.2 (40 − 4.8) and 44.8 (40 + 4.8), and at the 95% confidence level, 95% of all samples will fall between 30.4 (40 − 9.6) and 49.6 (40 + 9.6).

The most commonly used confidence level is .95, which is expressed by the following formula:

$$.95CI = p \pm 1.96SE$$

where *p* is the proportion obtained in the sample, *SE* is the standard error, and 1.96 is the specific value to use for encompassing exactly 95% of the scores in a normal distribution.

As an example, consider that a television ratings firm sampled 400 people and found that 20% of the sample was watching a certain program. What is the .95 confidence interval estimate for the population mean? The standard error is equal to the square root of [(.20)(.80)]/400, or .02. Inserting this value into the formula above yields a confidence interval of .20 ± (1.96) (.02), or .16 − .24. In other words there is a .95 chance that the population average lies between 16% and 24%. There is also a 5% chance of error, that is, that μ lies outside this interval. If this 5% chance is too great a risk, it is possible to compute a .99 confidence interval estimate by substituting 2.58 for 2 in the formula (in the normal curve, 99% of all scores fall within ± 2.58 standard errors of the mean). For a discussion of confidence intervals using continuous data, the reader should consult Hays (1973).

The concept of sampling distribution is important to statistical inference. Confidence intervals represent only one way in which sampling distributions are used in inferential statistics. They are also an important feature of *hypothesis testing*, in which the probability of a specified sample result is determined under assumed population conditions (Chapter 11).

DATA TRANSFORMATION

Most statistical procedures are based on the assumption that the data are normally distributed. Although many statistical procedures are "robust" or conservative in their requirement of normally distributed data, in some instances the results of studies using data that show a high degree of skewness may be invalid. The data used for any study should be checked for normality, a procedure accomplished very easily with most computer programs (Chapter 17).

Most non-normal distributions are caused by outliers. When such anomalies arise, researchers can attempt to transform the data to achieve normality. Basically, transformation involves performing some type of mathematical adjustment to *each score* to try and bring the outliers closer to the group mean. This may take the form of multiplying or dividing each score by a certain number, or even taking the square root or log of the scores. It makes no difference what procedure is used (although some methods are more powerful than others), as long as the same method is employed for all the data.

There are a variety of transformation methods from which to choose, depending on the type of distribution found in the data. Rummel (1970) describes these procedures in great detail.

S U M M A R Y

This chapter has introduced some of the more common descriptive and inferential statistics used by mass media researchers. Little attempt has been made to explain the mathematical derivations of the formulas and principles presented; rather, the emphasis here (as throughout the book) has been placed on understanding the reasoning behind these statistics and their applications. Unless researchers understand the logic underlying such concepts as mean, standard deviation, and standard error, the statistics themselves will be of little value.

Questions and Problems for Further Investigation

1. Find the mean, variance, and standard deviation for the following sets of data (answers appear later):
   Group 1   5, 5, 5, 6, 7, 5, 4, 8, 4, 5, 8, 8, 7, 6, 3, 3, 2, 5, 4, 7
   Group 2   19, 21, 22, 27, 16, 15, 18, 24, 26, 24, 22, 27, 16, 15, 18, 21, 20

2. From a regular deck of playing cards, what is the probability of randomly drawing an ace? An ace *or* a nine? A spade *or* a face card?

3. Assume that scores on the Miller Analogies Test are normally distributed in the population with a μ of 50 and a population standard deviation of 5. What is the probability that:
   a. Someone picked at random will have a score between 50 and 55?
   b. Someone picked at random will score 2 standard deviations above the mean?
   c. Someone picked at random will have a score of 58 or higher?

4. Assume a population of scores consisting of the following: 2, 4, 5, 5, 7, and 9. Generate the sampling distribution of the mean if $N = 2$ (sampling without replacement).

Answers to Question 1:
   Group 1 $X = 5.4, S = 1.4, SD = 1.2$
   Group 2 $X = 20.6, S = 15.4, SD = 3.9$

References and Suggested Readings

Blalock, H. M. (1972). *Social statistics.* New York: McGraw-Hill.

Champion, D. J. (1981). *Basic statistics for social research.* Boston: Houghton Mifflin.

Hays, W. L. (1973). *Statistics for the social sciences.* New York: Holt, Rinehart & Winston.

Nunnally, J. (1978). *Psychometric theory.* New York: McGraw-Hill.

Roscoe, J. T. (1975). *Fundamental research statistics for the behavioral sciences.* New York: Holt, Rinehart & Winston.

Rummel, R. J. (1970). *Factor analysis.* Chicago: Northwestern University Press.

Siegel, S. (1956). *Nonparametric statistics for the behavioral sciences.* New York: McGraw-Hill.

Williams, F. (1979). *Reasoning with statistics.* New York: Holt, Rinehart & Winston.

HYPOTHESIS TESTING

It is a rare occurrence for a scientist to begin a research study without a problem or question to test. This is similar to holding a cross-country running race without telling the runners where to start. Both situations need an initial step: for the cross-country race, a starting line is required; the research study needs a statement or question to test. This chapter describes the procedures of developing research questions and the steps involved in testing them.

RESEARCH QUESTIONS AND HYPOTHESES

Mass media research utilizes a variety of approaches to help answer questions. Some research is informal and seeks to solve relatively simple problems; some is based on theory and requires formally worded questions. All researchers, however, must start with some tentative generalization regarding a relationship between two or more variables. These generalizations may take two forms: *research questions* and *statistical hypotheses*. The two are identical except for the aspect of prediction: hypotheses predict an experimental outcome; research questions do not.

Research Questions

Research questions are often used in problem- or policy-oriented studies where researchers are not specifically interested in testing the statistical significance of their findings. For instance, researchers analyzing television program preferences or newspaper circulation would probably be concerned only with discovering general indications, not with gathering data for statistical testing. However, research questions can be tested for statistical significance. They are not merely weak hypotheses; they are valuable tools for many types of research.

Research questions are frequently used in areas that have been studied only marginally, or not at all. Studies of this nature are classified as *exploratory research* because investigators have no idea what may be found. They do not have enough prior information to make predictions. Exploratory research is intended to search for data *indications* rather than to attempt to determine *causality* (Tukey, 1962). The goal is to gather preliminary data, to be able to refine research questions, and possibly to develop hypotheses.

Research questions may be stated as simple questions about the relationship between two or more variables, or about the components of a phenomenon. For example, researchers might ask "How do high-technology firms perceive and use advertising?" (Traynor & Traynor, 1989) or "How do television and radio programs influence children's creativity as measured by a standardized test?" (Runco & Pezdek, 1984). Slater and Thompson (1984) posed several research questions about the attitudes of parents concerning warning statements that precede some television shows: "Do parents indicate that they frequently see the warning statements?" "Do the warnings influence parents' decisions about the suitability of a program for their child's viewing?" "Do parents advocate the imposition of a movie-type rating system for TV programs?"

In countless situations, however, researchers develop studies on the basis of existing theory and are thus able to attempt predictions about the outcome of the work. Brody (1984) hypothesized that access to the diverse offerings of cable television would produce a decline in borrowing books from the library. His data revealed support for this hypothesis in one cable market but not in another. Stroman and Seltzer (1985) hypothesized that persons relying on the newspaper for most of their news about crime would differ from those who rely on television news in their perceptions of the causes of crime. The hypothesis was supported by the data: TV news viewers said that flaws in the court system were a major contributing factor to crime, whereas newspaper readers cited poverty as a main cause.

To facilitate the discussion of research testing, the remainder of this chapter uses only the word *hypothesis*. But recall that research questions and hypotheses are identical except for the absence of the element of prediction in the former.

Purpose of Hypotheses

Hypotheses offer researchers a variety of benefits. First, they *provide direction* for a study. As indicated at the opening of the chapter, research begun without hypotheses offers no starting point; there is no indication of the sequence of steps to follow. Hypothesis development is usually the culmination of a rigorous literature review and emerges as a natural step in the research process. Without hypotheses, research would lack focus and clarity.

A second benefit of hypotheses is that they *eliminate trial-and-error research*, that is, the haphazard investigation of a topic in the hope of finding something significant. Hypothesis development requires researchers to isolate a specific area for study. Trial-and-error research is time-consuming and wasteful. The development of hypotheses eliminates this waste.

Hypotheses also *help rule out intervening*

and confounding variables. Since hypotheses focus research to precise testable statements, other variables, whether relevant or not, are excluded. For instance, researchers interested in determining how the media are used to provide consumer information must develop a specific hypothesis stating what media are included, what products are being tested for what specific demographic groups, and so on. Through this process of narrowing, extraneous and intervening variables are eliminated or controlled. This does not mean that hypotheses eliminate all error in research; nothing can do that. Error in some form is present in every study (Chapter 4).

Finally, hypotheses *allow for quantification of variables*. As stated in Chapter 3, any concept or phenomenon is capable of quantification if put into an adequate operational definition. All terms used in hypotheses must have an operational definition. For example, to test the hypothesis "there is a significant difference between recall of television commercials for subjects exposed to low-frequency and high-frequency broadcasts," researchers would need operational definitions of *recall*, *low-frequency*, and *high-frequency*. Words incapable of quantification cannot be included in a hypothesis.

In addition, some concepts have a variety of definitions. One example of this is *violence*. The complaint of many researchers is not that violence is incapable of quantification, but rather that it is capable of being operationally defined in more than one way. Therefore, before comparing the results of studies of media violence, it is necessary to consider the definition of *violence* used in each study. Contradictory results may be due to the definitions used, not to the presence or absence of violence.

Criteria for Good Hypotheses

A useful hypothesis should possess at least four essential characteristics: it should be compatible with current knowledge in the area; it should follow logical consistency; it should be in its most parsimonious form; and it should be testable.

That hypotheses must be in harmony with current knowledge is obvious. If available literature strongly suggests one point of view, researchers who develop hypotheses that oppose this knowledge without basis only slow the development of the area. For example, it has been demonstrated beyond a doubt that most people get their news information from television. It would be rather ludicrous for a researcher to develop a hypothesis suggesting that this is not true. There is simply too much evidence to the contrary.

The criterion of logical consistency means that if a hypothesis suggests that $A = B$ and $B = C$, then A must also be equal to C. That is, if reading the *New York Times* implies a knowledge of current events, and a knowledge of currents events means greater participation in social activities, then readers of the *New York Times* should exhibit greater participation in social activities.

It should come as no surprise that hypotheses must be in their most parsimonious form. The concept of "the simpler, the better" (Occam's razor) is stressed throughout this book. A hypothesis such as "Intellectual and psychomotor creativity possessed by an individual positively coincides with the level of intelligence of the individual as indicated by standardized evaluative procedures measuring intelligence" is not exactly parsimonious. Stated simply, the same hypothesis could read: "Psychomotor ability and IQ are positively related."

Most researchers would agree that developing an untestable hypothesis is unproductive. But there is a fine line between what is and what is not testable. The authors agree that untestable hypotheses will probably create a great deal of frustration, and the information collected and tested will probably add nothing to the development of knowledge. However, the situation here is similar to some teachers who say (and really mean) on the first day of class, "Don't ever be afraid to ask me a question because you think it's stupid. The only stupid question is the one that's not asked."

The authors consider hypothesis development in the same fashion. It's much better to form an untestable hypothesis than none at all. The developmental process itself is a valuable experience, and researchers will no doubt soon find their error. The untestable ("stupid") hypothesis may eventually become a respectable research project. The suggestion here is not to try and develop untestable hypotheses, but rather accept the fact when it happens, correct it, and move on. Beginning researchers should not try to solve the problems of the world. Take small steps.

What are some unrealistic and/or untestable hypotheses? Read the list of hypotheses below (some relate to areas other than mass media) and determine what is wrong with each one. Feldman (1987) was used in preparing some of these statements.

1. Watching too many soap operas on television creates antisocial behavior.
2. Clocks run clockwise because most people are right-handed.
3. High school students with no exposure to television earn higher grades than those who watch television.
4. Students who give apples to teachers tend to earn higher grades.
5. People who read newspapers wash their hands more frequently than those who do not read newspapers.
6. Movies rated XXX are 10 times worse than movies rated XX, and 20 times worse than movies rated X.
7. College students who cut classes have more deceased relatives than students who attend classes.
8. Einstein's theory of relativity would not have been developed if he had access to television.

9. Nike shoe sales would be higher if Bo Jackson "knew" hockey.
10. World opinion of a unified Germany would be different if the Berlin wall were torn down in 1993.

The Null Hypothesis

The **null hypothesis** (also called the "hypothesis of no difference") asserts that the statistical differences or relationships being analyzed are due to chance or random error. The null hypothesis (H_0) is the logical alternative to the research hypothesis (H_1). For example, the hypothesis "The level of attention paid to radio commercials is positively related to the amount of recall of the commercial" has its logical alternative (null hypothesis), "The level of attention paid to radio commercials is *not* related to the amount of recall of the commercial."

In practice, researchers rarely state the null hypothesis. Since every research hypothesis does have its logical alternative, stating the null form is redundant (Williams, 1979). However, the null hypothesis is always present and plays an important role in the rationale underlying hypothesis testing.

TESTING HYPOTHESES FOR STATISTICAL SIGNIFICANCE

In hypothesis testing, or significance testing, the researcher either rejects or accepts the null hypothesis. That is, if H_0 is accepted (supported), it is assumed that H_1 is rejected; and if H_0 is rejected, H_1 must be accepted.

To determine the statistical significance of a research study, the researcher must set a **probability level**, or significance level, against which the null hypothesis is tested. If the results of the study indicate a probability lower than this level, the researcher can reject the null hypothesis. If the research outcome has a high probability, the researcher must support (or, more precisely, fail to reject) the null hypothesis. In reality, since the null hypothesis is not generally stated, acceptance and rejection apply to the research hypothesis, not to the null hypothesis.

The probability level is expressed by a lowercase letter p (indicating probability), followed by a "less than" or "less than or equal to" sign, and then a value. For example, "$p \leq .01$" means that the null hypothesis is being tested at the .01 level of significance and that the results will be considered statistically significant if the probability is equal to or lower than this level. A .05 level of significance indicates that the researcher has a 5% chance of making a wrong decision about rejecting the null hypothesis (or accepting the research hypothesis). Establishing a level of significance depends on the amount of error researchers are willing to accept (in addition to other factors peculiar to the particular research study). The question of error is discussed in greater detail later in the chapter.

It is common practice in mass media research studies to set the probability level at .01 or .05, which means that either one or five times out of 100, the results of the study are based on random error or chance. There is no logical reason for using these figures; the practice has been followed for many years, basically because Sir Ronald A. Fisher, who developed the concept of significance testing, formulated tables based on the areas under the normal curve defined by these points. In many research areas, however, the researchers set the significance level according to the purpose of the study rather than by general convention. Some studies use .10 or .20 depending on the goals of the research. In exploratory research especially, more liberal levels are generally used; these are made more restrictive as further information is gathered.

In a theoretical sampling distribution, the proportion of the area in which the null hypothesis is rejected is called the **region of rejection**. This area is defined by the level of significance chosen by the researcher. If the .05 level of significance is used, then 5% of the sampling distribution becomes the critical region. Conversely, the null hypothesis is retained in the region between the two rejection values (or levels).

As Figure 11.1 shows, the regions of rejection are located in the tails or outer edges of the sampling distribution. The terms *one-tail testing* and *two-tail testing* refer to the type of prediction made in a research study. A one-tail test predicts that the results will fall in only one direction — either positive or negative. This approach is more stringent than the two-tail test, which does not predict a direction. Two-tail tests are generally used when little information is available about the research area. One-tail tests are used when researchers have more knowledge of the area and are able to more accurately predict the outcome of the study.

Consider, for example, a study of the math competency of a group of subjects who receive a special type of learning treatment, possibly a series of television programs on mathematics. The hypothesis is that the group, after viewing the programs, will have scores on a standardized math test significantly different from those of the remainder of the population, which has not seen the programs. The level of significance is set at .05, indicating that for the null hypothesis to be rejected, the sample's mean test score must

fall outside the boundaries in the normal distribution that are specified by the statement, "$p \leq$ .05." These boundaries, or values, are determined by a simple computation. First, the critical values of the boundaries are found by consulting the normal distribution table (see Areas Under the Normal Curve, Appendix 1, Table 3).

In Figure 11.1, the area from the middle of the distribution, or μ, the hypothesized mean (denoted by a dotted line), to the end of the tails is 50%. At the .05 level, using a two-tail test, there is a 2.5% (.0250) area of rejection tucked into each tail. Consequently, the area from the middle of the distribution to the region of rejection is equal to 47.5% (50% − 2.5% = 47.5%). It follows that the corresponding z values that will define the region of rejection are those that cut off 47.5% (.4750) of the area from μ to each end of the tail. To find this z value, use Table 3 of Appendix 1 (Areas Under the Normal Curve). This table provides a list of the proportions of various areas under the curve as measured from the midpoint of the curve out toward the tails. The far left column displays the first two digits of the z value. The row across the top of the table contains the third digit. For example, find the 1.0 row in the left-hand column. Next, find the entry under the .08 column in this row. The tabled entry is .3599. This means that 35.99%

FIGURE 11.1   REGIONS OF REJECTION FOR $p \leq .05$ (TWO-TAIL)

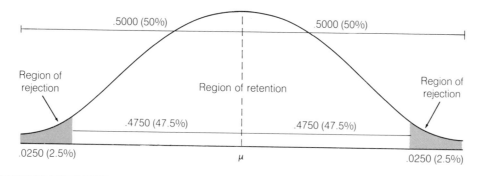

of the curve is found between the midpoint and a z value of 1.08. Of course, another 35.99% lies in the other direction, from the midpoint to a z value of -1.08. In our current example, it is necessary to work backwards. We know the areas under the curve that we want to define (.4750 to the left and right of μ) and need to find the z values. An examination of the body of Table 3 shows that .4750 corresponds to a z value of ± 1.96.

These values are then used to determine the region of rejection:

$$-1.96\,\alpha_m + \mu = \text{lower boundary}$$
$$+1.96\,\alpha_m + \mu = \text{upper boundary}$$

where α_m = the standard deviation of the distribution and μ = the population mean. Assume that the population mean for math competency is 100 and the standard deviation is 15. Thus, the sample group must achieve a mean math competency score either lower than 70.60 or higher than 129.40 for the research study to be considered significant:

$$-1.96(15) + 100 = 70.60$$
$$+1.96(15) + 100 = 129.40$$

If a research study produces a number between 70.60 and 129.40, the null hypothesis cannot be rejected; the instructional television programs had no significant effect on math levels. Using the normal distribution to demonstrate these boundaries, the area of rejection is illustrated in Figure 11.2.

Error

As with all steps in the research process, testing for statistical significance involves error. Two types of error particularly relevant to hypothesis testing are known as **Type I error** and **Type II error**. Type I error is the rejection of a null hypothesis that should be accepted, and Type II error is the acceptance of a null hypothesis that should be rejected. These error types are represented in Figure 11.3.

The probability of making a Type I error is equal to the established level of significance and is therefore under the direct control of the researcher. That is, to reduce the probability of Type I error, the researcher can simply set the level of significance closer to zero.

Type II error, often signified by the symbol β, is a bit more difficult to conceptualize. The

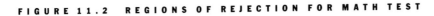

FIGURE 11.2 REGIONS OF REJECTION FOR MATH TEST

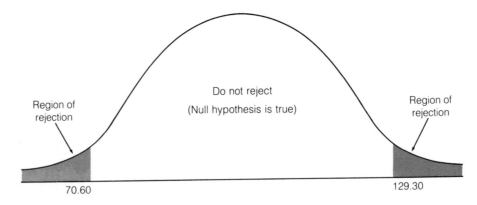

Region of rejection

Do not reject

(Null hypothesis is true)

Region of rejection

70.60

129.30

researcher does not have direct control over Type II error; instead, Type II error is controlled, although indirectly, by the design of the experiment. In addition, the level of Type II error is inversely proportional to the level of Type I error: as Type I error decreases, Type II error increases, and vice versa. The potential magnitude of Type II error depends in part on the probability level and in part on which of the possible alternative hypotheses actually is true. Figure 11.4 shows the inverse relationship between the two types of error.

As mentioned earlier, most research studies do not state the null hypothesis, since it is generally assumed. There is a way to depict Type I and Type II errors without considering the null hypothesis, however, and this approach may help to demonstrate the relationship between Type I and Type II errors.

As Figure 11.5 demonstrates, the research hypothesis is used to describe Type I and Type II errors instead of the null hypothesis. To use the table, start at the desired row on the left side and then read the column entry that completes the hypothesis to be tested. For example: "Significant difference found where none exists = Type I error."

One final way to explain Type I and Type II errors is by using a hypothetical example. Consider a research study to determine the effects of a short-term public relations campaign promoting the use of safety belts in automobiles. Suppose that the effort was highly successful and indeed changed the behavior of a majority of the subjects exposed to the campaign (this information is of course unknown to the researcher). If the researcher finds that a significant effect was created by the campaign, the conclusion is a correct one; if the researcher does not find a significant effect, a Type II error is committed. On the other hand, if the campaign actually had no effect, but the researcher concludes that the campaign was successful, a Type I error is committed.

The Importance of Significance

The concept of significance testing causes problems for many people. The main reason for this is that too many researchers overemphasize the importance of significance. When researchers find that the results of a study are nonsignificant, it is not uncommon to "talk around" the results — to de-emphasize the finding that the

---

FIGURE 11.3   TYPE I AND TYPE II ERRORS

	Reject H_0	Accept H_0
H_0 is true	Type I error	Correct
H_0 is false	Correct	Type II error

FIGURE 11.4   INVERSE RELATIONSHIP BETWEEN TYPE I AND TYPE II ERRORS

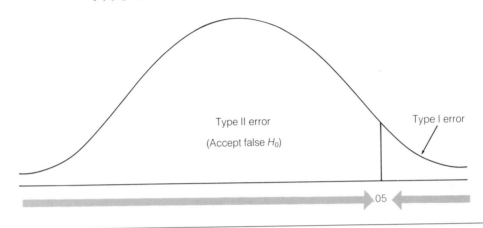

Type II error

(Accept false H_0)

Type I error

.05

FIGURE 11.5   USE OF THE RESEARCH HYPOTHESIS TO DISTINGUISH BETWEEN TYPE I AND TYPE II ERRORS

	Where one exists	Where none exists
Significant difference found	Correct	Type I error
No significant difference found	Type II error	Correct

results were not significant. But there is really no need to follow this course of action.

There is no difference in value between a study that finds significant results and a study that does not. Both studies provide valuable information. Discovering that some variables are not significant is just as important as determining what variables are significant. The nonsig-

nificant study can save time for other researchers working in the same area by ruling out worthless variables. Nonsignificant research is important in collecting information about a theory or concept.

Also, there is nothing wrong with the idea of proposing a null hypothesis as the research hypothesis. For example, a researcher could formulate the following hypothesis: "There is no significant difference in comprehension of program content between a group of adults (age 18–49) with normal hearing that views a television program with closed-captioned phrases and a similar group that views the same program without captions." A scientific research study does not always have to test for significant relationships; it can also test for nonsignificance. However, sloppy research techniques and faulty measurement procedures can add to the error variance in a study and contribute to the failure to reject a hypothesis of no difference as well as jeopardize the entire study. This is a danger in using a null hypothesis as a substantive hypothesis.

Power

The concept of **power** is intimately related to Type I and Type II errors. Power refers to the probability of rejecting the null hypothesis when it is true. In other words, power indicates the probability that a statistical test of a null hypothesis will result in the conclusion that the phenomenon under study actually exists (Cohen, 1969).

Statistical power is a function of three parameters: probability level, sample size, and effects size. As we know, the probability level is under the direct control of the researcher and predetermines the probability of committing a Type I error. Sample size refers to the number of subjects utilized in an experiment. The most difficult concept is *effects size*. Basically, the effects size is the degree to which the null hypothesis is rejected; this can be stated either in general terms (such as *any* nonzero value) or in exact terms (such as .40). That is, when a null hypothesis is false, it is false to some degree; researchers can state that the null hypothesis is false and leave it at that, or they can specify exactly how false it is. The larger the effects size, the greater the degree to which the phenomenon

under study is present (Cohen, 1969). However, researchers seldom know the exact value of effects size. When such precision is lacking, researchers can use one of three alternatives.

1. Estimate the effects size, based on knowledge in the area of investigation or indications from previous studies in the area, or simply state the size as "small," "medium," or "large." (Cohen describes these values in greater detail.)
2. Assume an effects size of "medium."
3. Select a series of effects sizes and experiment.

When the probability level, sample size, and effects size are known, researchers can consult power tables (published in statistics books) to determine the level of power present in their study.

Power tables consist of sets of curves representing different sample sizes, levels of significance (.05 and so on), and types of tests (one- or two-tail). For example, in a two-tail test, with a probability of .05, and sample of 10, the probability of rejecting the null hypothesis (assume it's false) is .37 (Type I error), and the probability of accepting or retaining the hypothesis is .63 (Type II error). The power tables show that by increasing the sample size to 20, the probability of rejecting the null hypothesis jumps to .62, and the probability of retaining the hypothesis drops to .38.

A determination of power is important for two reasons. First and most important, if a low power level prevents researchers from attaining statistical significance, a Type II error may result. If the power of the statistical test is increased, however, the results may be made significant.

Second, a high power level may help in interpretation of research results. If an experiment just barely reaches the significance level but has high power, researchers can place more faith in the results. Without power figures, the researchers would have to be more hesitant in their interpretations.

Consideration of statistical power should be a step in all research studies. Although power is only an approximation, computation of the value helps control Type II error. In addition, as power increases, there is no direct effect on Type I error; power acts independently of Type I error. Since the mid-1970s, researchers have paid closer attention to statistical power.

Chase and Tucker (1975) conducted power analyses on articles published in nine communications journals. The authors found that 82% of the 46 articles analyzed had an average power for medium effects of less than .80 (the recommended minimum power value). In addition, more than half the articles had an average power of less than .50, which suggests a significant increase in the probability of Type II error.

S U M M A R Y

Hypothesis development in scientific research is important because the process refines and focuses the research, excluding extraneous variables and permitting the quantification of variables. Rarely will researchers conduct a project without developing some type of research question or hypothesis. Research without this focus usually proves to be a waste of time (although some people may argue that many inventions, theories, and new information have been found without the focus provided by a research question or hypothesis).

An applicable hypothesis must be compatible with current related knowledge, and it must be logically consistent. It should also be stated as simply as possible and, generally speaking, it should be testable. Hypotheses must be tested for statistical significance. This testing involves error, particularly Type I and Type II error. Error must be considered in all research. An understanding of error such as Type I and Type II will

not make research foolproof, but it will make the process somewhat easier because researchers must pay closer attention to the elements involved in the project.

Too much emphasis is oftentimes placed on significance testing. It is possible that a nonsignificant test may add information to an available body of knowledge simply by finding what "does not work" or "should not be investigated." However, some nonsignificant research projects may be more valuable if the statistical power is analyzed.

Questions and Problems for Further Investigation

1. Develop three research questions and three hypotheses in any mass media area that could be investigated or tested.

2. What is your opinion about using very conservative levels of significance (.10 or greater) in exploratory research?

3. Conduct a brief review of published research in mass media. What percentage of the studies report the results of a power analysis calculation?

4. Explain the relationship between Type I and Type II errors.

5. Under what circumstances might a researcher use a probability level of .001?

6. If a researcher's significance level is set at $\alpha = .02$ and the results of the experiment indicate that the null hypothesis cannot be rejected, what is the probability of a Type I error?

References and Suggested Readings

Benze, J., & Declerq, E. (1985). Content of television spot ads for female candidates. *Journalism Quarterly, 62*(2), 278–283.

Brody, E. (1984). Impact of cable television on library borrowing. *Journalism Quarterly, 61*(3), 686–688.

Chase, L. J., & Tucker, R. K. (1975). A power-analytic examination of contemporary communication research. *Speech Monographs, 42*, 29–41.

Cohen, J. (1969). *Statistical power analysis for the behavioral sciences*. New York: Academic Press.

Doolittle, J. C. (1979). News media use by older adults. *Journalism Quarterly, 56*(2), 311–317.

Feldman, D. (1987). *Why do clocks run clockwise?* New York: Harper & Row.

Holly, S. (1979). Women in management of weeklies. *Journalism Quarterly, 56*(4), 810–815.

Joslyn, R. A. (1981). The impact of campaign spot advertising on voting decisions. *Human Communication Research, 7*(4), 347–360.

Roscoe, J. T. (1975). *Fundamental research statistics for the behavioral sciences*. New York: Holt, Rinehart & Winston.

Runco, M., & Pezdek, K. (1984). The effects of TV and radio on children's creativity. *Human Communication Research, 11*(1), 109–120.

Ryan, M. (1979). Reports, inferences and judgments in news coverage of social issues. *Journalism Quarterly, (56)*3, 497–503.

Slater, D., & Thompson, T. (1984). Attitudes of parents concerning televised warning statements. *Journalism Quarterly, 61*(4), 853–859.

Stroman, C., & Seltzer, R. (1985). Media use and perception of crime. *Journalism Quarterly, 62*(2), 340–345.

Traynor, K., & Traynor, S. (1989). High-tech advertising: A status report. *Journal of Advertising Research, 29*(4), 30–36.

Tukey, J. W. (1962). The future of data analysis. *Annals of Mathematical Statistics, 33*, 1–67.

Williams, F. (1979). *Reasoning with statistics*. (2nd ed). New York: Holt, Rinehart & Winston.

CHAPTER 1 2

BASIC STATISTICAL PROCEDURES

Researchers often wish to do more than merely describe a sample; they want to use their results to make inferences about the population from which the sample has been taken. This chapter describes some of the basic inferential statistical methods used in mass media research and suggests ways in which these methods may help answer questions.

HISTORY OF SMALL-SAMPLE STATISTICS

Samples were used in scientific research as long ago as 1627, when Sir Francis Bacon published an account of tests he had conducted measuring wheat seed growth in various forms of fertilizer. In 1763 Arthur Young began a series of experiments to discover the most profitable method of farming; and in 1849 James Johnston published a book called *Experimental Agriculture*, in which he provided advice on scientific research (Cochran, 1976).

One of the best-known investigators of the early twentieth century was William S. Gossett, who in 1908 attempted to quantify experimental results in a paper entitled "The Probable Error of the Mean." Under the pen name "Student," Gossett published the results of small-sample investigations he had conducted while working in a Dublin brewery. The *t*-distribution statistics Gossett developed were not widely accepted at the time; in fact, it was more than 15 years before other researchers began to take an interest in his work. The *t*-test, however, as will be seen, is now one of the most widely used statistical procedures in all areas of research.

Sir Ronald Fisher provided a stepping stone from early work in statistics and sampling procedures to modern statistical inference techniques. It was Fisher who developed the concept of probability and established the use of the .01 and .05 levels of probability testing (Chapter 11). Until Fisher, statistical methods were not generally perceived as practical in areas other than agriculture, for which they were originally developed.

NONPARAMETRIC STATISTICS

Statistical methods are divided into two broad categories: **parametric** and **nonparametric**. Historically, researchers recognized three primary differences between parametric and nonparametric statistics:

1. Nonparametric statistics are appropriate only with nominal and ordinal data. Parametric statistics are appropriate for interval and ratio data.
2. Nonparametric results cannot be generalized to the population. This is possible only with parametric statistics.
3. Nonparametric statistics make no assumption about normally distributed data, whereas parametric statistics assume normality. Nonparametric statistics are said to be "distribution-free."

For the most part, distinctions one and two have vanished. Most researchers argue that both parametric and nonparametric statistics can be used successfully with all types of data, and both are appropriate for generalizing results to the population. The authors of this text agree with this position.

Chi-Square Goodness of Fit

Mass media researchers often compare *observed* frequencies of a phenomenon with the frequencies that might be *expected* or hypothesized. For example, a researcher who wanted to determine whether the sales of television sets by four manufacturers in the current year are the same as sales for the previous year might advance the following hypothesis: "Television set sales of four major manufacturers are significantly different this year from those of the previous year."

Suppose the previous year's television set sales were distributed as follows:

Manufacturer	Percent of sales
RCA	22
Sony	36
JVC	19
Mitsubishi	23

From these previous sales, the investigator can calculate the expected frequencies (using a sample of 1,000) for each manufacturer's sales by multiplying the percentage of each company's sale by 1,000. The expected frequencies are:

Manufacturer	Expected frequency
RCA	220
Sony	360
JVC	190
Mitsubishi	230

Next, the researcher surveys a random sample of 1,000 households known to have purchased one of the four manufacturers' television sets during the current year. Assume the data from this survey provide the following information:

Manufacturer	Expected frequency	Observed frequency
RCA	220	180
Sony	360	330
JVC	190	220
Mitsubishi	230	270

The researcher now must interpret these data in a way that permits a statement of whether the change in frequency is actually *significant*. This can be done by reducing the data to a **chi-square statistic** and performing a test known as the chi-square "goodness of fit" test.

A chi-square (χ^2) is simply a value showing the relationship between expected and observed frequencies. It is computed by means of the following formula:

$$\chi^2 = \Sigma \frac{(O_i - E_i)^2}{E_i}$$

where O_i = the observed frequencies and E_i = the expected frequencies. This means that the difference between each expected and observed frequency must be squared and then divided by the expected frequency. The sum of the quotients is the chi-square for those frequencies. For the frequency distribution above, chi-square is calculated as follows:

$$\chi^2 = \Sigma \frac{(O_1) - E_1)^2}{E_1}$$

$$= \frac{(O_1 - E_1)^2}{E_1} + \frac{(O_2 - E_2)^2}{E_2} + \frac{(O_3 - E_3)^2}{E_3}$$

$$+ \frac{(O_4 - E_4)^2}{E_4}$$

$$= \frac{(180 - 220)^2}{220} + \frac{(330 - 360)^2}{360}$$

$$+ \frac{(220 - 190)^2}{190} + \frac{(270 - 230)^2}{230}$$

$$= \frac{(-40)^2}{220} + \frac{(-30)^2}{360} + \frac{(30)^2}{190} + \frac{(40)^2}{230}$$

$$= \frac{1{,}600}{220} + \frac{900}{360} + \frac{900}{190} + \frac{1{,}600}{230}$$

$$= 7.27 + 2.50 + 4.73 + 6.95$$

$$= 21.45$$

Once the value of chi-square is known, the goodness of fit test is performed to determine whether this value represents a significant difference in frequencies. To do this, two values are necessary: the first is the probability level, which is predetermined by the researcher; the second, called *degrees of freedom* (*df*), is the number of scores in any particular test that are free to vary in value. For example, if one has three unknown values (x, y, and z) such that $x + y + z = 10$, there are two degrees of freedom: any two of the three variables may be assigned any value without affecting the total, but the value of the third will then be predetermined. Thus, if $x = 2$ and $y = 5$, z must be 3. In the goodness of fit test, degrees of freedom are expressed in terms of $K - 1$, where K is the number of categories. In the case of the television sales study, $K = 4$, and $df = 4 - 1 = 3$.

Next, a chi-square significance table is consulted (Appendix 1, Table 4). These tables are arranged by probability level and degrees of freedom. A portion of the chi-square table relevant to the hypothetical study has been adapted here to show how the table is used:

df	.10	.05	.01	.001
		Probability		
1	2.706	3.841	6.635	10.827
2	4.605	5.991	9.210	13.815
3	6.251	7.815	11.345	16.266
4	7.779	9.488	13.277	18.467

If the calculated chi-square value equals or exceeds the value found in the table, the differences in observed frequencies are considered to be statistically significant at the predetermined alpha level; if the calculated value is smaller, the results are nonsignificant.

In the television sales example, suppose the researcher finds a chi-square value of 21.45, with a degree of freedom of 3 and has established a probability level of .05. The chi-square table shows a value of 7.815 at this level when $df = 3$. Since 21.45 is greater than 7.815, the frequency difference is significant, and the hypothesis is accepted or supported: television set sales of the four manufacturers are significantly different in the current year from sales in the previous year.

The chi-square goodness of fit test can be used in a variety of ways to measure changes — for example, in studies of audience perceptions of advertising messages over time, in planning changes in television programming, or in analyzing the results of public relations campaigns. Idsvoog and Hoyt (1977) used a chi-square test to analyze the professionalism and performance of television journalists. The authors attempted to determine whether "professionalism" was related to several other characteristics, including the desire to look for employment, educational level, and job satisfaction. The results indicated that journalists classified on the basis of questionnaire responses differed significantly from those classified as "medium" or "low" professionals.

There are limitations to the use of the goodness of fit test, however. Since this is a nonparametric statistical procedure, the variables must be measured at the nominal or ordinal level. The categories must be mutually exclusive, and each observation in each category must be independent from all others. Additionally, because the chi-square distribution is sharply skewed (Chapter 10) for small samples, Type II error may occur: small samples may not produce significant results in cases that could have yielded significant results if a larger sample had been used. To avoid this problem, most researchers suggest that each category contain at least five observations. Other researchers suggest that 20% of the cells should have expected frequency of at least five, and none should have expected frequencies of zero.

As an alternative to the chi-square goodness of fit test, some researchers prefer the Kolomogorov–Smirnov test, which is considered to be more powerful than the chi-square approach. In addition, a minimum number of expected frequencies in each cell is not required, as in the chi-square test (see Winkler & Hays, 1975, for more information about the Kolomogorov–Smirnov test).

Contingency Table Analysis

Another nonparametric procedure often used in mass media research is the contingency table analysis, frequently called **cross-tabulation** or simply **crosstabs**. Crosstab analysis is basically an extension of the goodness of fit test, the primary difference being that two or more variables can be tested simultaneously. Consider a study to determine the relationship between a person's sex and his or her media usage habits in regard

to obtaining information on new products. Suppose the researcher selects a random sample of 210 adults and obtains the information displayed in Figure 12.1.

The next step is to calculate the expected frequencies for each cell. This procedure is similar to that used in the goodness of fit test, but it involves a slightly more detailed formula:

$$E_{ij} = \frac{R_i C_j}{N}$$

where E_{ij} = expected frequency for cell in row i, column j; R_i = sum of frequencies in row i; C_j = sum of frequencies in column j; and N = sum of frequencies for all cells. Using this formula, the researcher in the hypothetical example can calculate the expected frequencies as follows:

$$\text{Male/radio} = \frac{100 \times 21}{210} = \frac{2,100}{210} = 10$$

$$\text{Female/radio} = \frac{110 \times 21}{210} = \frac{2,310}{210} = 11$$

and so forth. Each expected frequency is placed in a small square in the upper right-hand corner

---

FIGURE 12.1   DESCRIPTION OF RANDOM SAMPLE OF MEDIA USERS IN STUDY OF SOURCES OF NEW PRODUCT INFORMATION

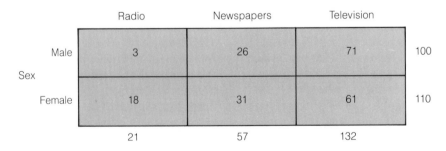

Media Most Used for New Product Information

		Radio	Newspapers	Television	
Sex	Male	3	26	71	100
	Female	18	31	61	110
		21	57	132	

of the appropriate cell, as illustrated in Figure 12.2.

After the expected frequencies have been calculated, the investigator must compute the chi-square, using the following formula:

$$\chi^2 = \Sigma \frac{(O_{ij} - E_{ij})^2}{E_{ij}}$$

Using the same example:

$$\chi^2 = \frac{(3 - 10)^2}{10} + \frac{(26 - 27)^2}{27} + \frac{(71 - 63)^2}{63}$$

$$+ \frac{(18 - 11)^2}{11} + \frac{(31 - 30)^2}{30}$$

$$+ \frac{(61 - 69)^2}{69}$$

$$= \frac{49}{10} + \frac{1}{27} + \frac{64}{63} + \frac{49}{11} + \frac{1}{30} + \frac{64}{69}$$

$$= 4.90 + 0.04 + 1.01 + 4.45 + 0.03$$

$$+ 0.92$$

$$= 11.35$$

To determine statistical significance, the researcher must now consult the chi-square table.

In a crosstab analysis, the degrees of freedom are expressed as $(R - 1)(C - 1)$, where R is the number of rows and C the number of columns. Assuming that $p \leq .05$, the chi-square value is listed in Table 4 of Appendix 1 as 5.991, which is lower than the calculated value of 11.35. Thus, there is a significant relationship between the sex of the respondent and the media used to acquire new product information. The test indicates that the two variables are somehow related, but it does not tell exactly how. To find this out, it is necessary to go back and examine the original crosstab data (Figure 12.1). Looking at the distribution, it is easy to see that females use radio more and television less than do males.

In the case of a 2 × 2 crosstab (where $df = 1$), computational effort is saved when the corresponding cells are represented by the letters A, B, C, and D, such as:

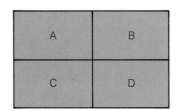

FIGURE 12.2   RANDOM SAMPLE OF MEDIA USERS SHOWING EXPECTED FREQUENCIES

Media Most Used for New Product Information

Sex	Radio	Newspapers	Television	
Male	3 [10]	26 [27]	71 [63]	100
Female	18 [11]	31 [30]	61 [69]	110
	21	57	132	

The following formula can then be used to compute the chi-square:

$$\chi^2 = \frac{N(AD - BC)^2}{(A + B)(C + D)(A + C)(B + D)}$$

Crosstab analysis has become a widely used analytical technique in mass media research, especially since the development of computer programs such as the Statistical Package for the Social Sciences (SPSS-X). In addition to chi-square, various other statistics can be used in crosstabs to determine whether the variables are statistically related.

PARAMETRIC STATISTICS

The sections that follow discuss parametric statistical methods usually used with higher level data (interval and ratio). Recall that these methods assume that data are normally distributed. The most basic parametric statistic is the t-test, a procedure widely used in all areas of mass media research.

The t-Test

In many research studies, two groups of subjects are tested: one group receives some type of treatment, and the other serves as the control. After the treatment has been administered, both groups are tested, and the results are compared to determine whether a statistically significant difference exists between the groups. That is, did the treatment have an effect on the results of the test? In cases such as this, the mean score for each group is compared through the use of a t-test.

The t-test is the most elementary method for comparing two groups' mean scores. A variety of t-test alternatives are available, depending on the problem under consideration and the situation of a particular research study. Variations of the t-test are available for testing independent groups, related groups, and cases in which the population mean is either known or unknown (Champion, 1981; Roscoe, 1975).

The t-test assumes that the variables in the populations from which the samples are drawn are normally distributed (Chapter 10). The test also assumes that the data have homogeneity of variance, that is, that they deviate equally from the mean.

The basic formula for the t-test is relatively simple. The numerator of the formula is the difference between the sample mean and the hypothesized population mean, divided by the estimate of the standard error of the mean (S_m):

$$t = \frac{\overline{X} - \mu}{S_m}$$

where

$$S_m = \sqrt{\frac{SS}{n - 1}} \text{ and } SS = \Sigma(X - \overline{X})^2$$

One of the more commonly used forms of the t-test is the test for independent groups or means. This procedure is used in studying two independent groups for differences (the type of study described at the beginning of this section). The formula for the independent t-test is:

$$t = \frac{\overline{X}_1 - \overline{X}_2}{S_{\overline{x}_1 - \overline{x}_2}}$$

where $\overline{X}_1$ = the mean for Group 1, $\overline{X}_2$ = the mean for Group 2, and $S_{\overline{x}_1 - \overline{x}_2}$ = the standard error for the groups. The standard error is an important part of the t-test formula and is computed as follows:

$$S_{\overline{x}_1 - \overline{x}_2} = \sqrt{\left(\frac{SS_1 + SS_2}{n_1 + n_2 - 2}\right)\left(\frac{1}{n_1} + \frac{1}{n_2}\right)}$$

where SS_1 = the sum of squares for Group 1, SS_2 = the sum of squares for Group 2, n_1 = the sample size for Group 1, and n_2 = the sample size for Group 2.

To illustrate a *t*-test, consider a research problem to determine the recall of two groups of subjects with regard to a television commercial for a new household cleaner. One group consists of 10 males and the other consists of 10 females. Each group views the commercial once and then completes a 15-item questionnaire. The hypothesis predicts a significant difference between the recall scores of males and females. The data are collected at page bottom. Using the *t*-test formula, the next step is to compute the standard error for the groups by using the previous formula:

$$S_{\bar{x}_1 - \bar{x}_2} = \sqrt{\left(\frac{110 + 106}{10 + 10 - 2}\right)\left(\frac{1}{10} + \frac{1}{10}\right)}$$

$$= 1.55$$

The researcher then substitutes this standard error value in the *t*-test formula:

$$t = \frac{8 - 6}{1.55}$$

$$= 1.29$$

To determine whether the *t* value of 1.29 is statistically significant, a *t*-distribution table is consulted. The *t*-distribution is a family of curves closely resembling the normal curve. The portion of the *t*-distribution table relevant to the sample problem is reproduced in Table 12.1. Again, to interpret the table, two values are required: degrees of freedom and level of probability (for a complete *t*-distribution table see Appendix 1, Table 2).

For purposes of the *t*-test, degrees of freedom are equal to $n_1 + n_2 - 2$, where n_1 and n_2 represent the sizes of the respective groups. In the example of advertising recall, $df = 18$ (10 + 10 − 2). If the problem is tested at the .05 level of significance, a *t* value of 2.101 is required for the research to be considered statistically significant. However, since the sample problem is a "two-tail test" (the hypothesis predicts only a difference between the two groups, not that one particular group will have the higher mean score), the required values are actually $t \leq$

Female recall scores			**Male recall scores**		
X	x	x^2 (SS)	X	x	x^2(SS)
4	−4	16	2	−4	16
4	−4	16	3	−3	9
5	−3	9	4	−2	4
7	−1	1	4	−2	4
7	−1	1	4	−2	4
8	0	0	6	0	0
9	1	1	6	0	0
9	1	1	8	2	4
12	4	16	10	4	16
15	7	49	13	7	49
80		110	60		106
$\bar{X} = 8$			$\bar{X} = 6$		

TABLE 12.1 PORTION OF THE t-DISTRIBUTION TABLE FOR THE TWO-TAIL TEST

	Probability			
n	.10	.05	.01	.001
1	6.314	12.706	63.657	636.619
2	2.920	4.303	9.925	31.598
•				
•				
•				
17	1.740	2.110	2.898	3.965
18	1.734	2.101	2.878	3.992
19	1.729	2.093	2.861	3.883
•				
•				
•				

-2.101 or $t \geq 2.101$. The conclusion of the hypothetical problem is that there is no significant difference between the recall scores of the female group and the recall scores of the male group, because calculated t does not equal or exceed the table values.

There are numerous examples of the t-test in mass media research that demonstrate the versatility of the method. For example, Garramone (1985) investigated political advertising by exploring the roles of the commercial sponsor (the source of the message), and the rebuttal commercial (a message that charges as false the claims of another commercial). Among six separate hypotheses that were tested, Garramone predicted that:

H_1 Viewers of a negative political commercial will perceive an independent sponsor as more trustworthy than a candidate sponsor.
H_2 Viewers of an independent commercial opposing a candidate will demonstrate:
   a. a more negative perception of the target's image.
   b. a lesser likelihood of voting for the target than viewers of a candidate commercial.
H_3 Viewers of an independent commercial opposing a candidate will demonstrate:
   a. a more positive perception of the target's opponent.
   b. a greater likelihood of voting for the target's opponent than viewers of a candidate commercial.

Among other findings, Garramone concluded that:

The first hypothesis ... was not supported. [However], hypotheses 2 and 3 ... were supported. Viewers of an independent commercial opposing a candidate demonstrated a more negative perception of the target's image, $t(110) = 2.41$, $p \leq .01$, and a lesser likelihood of voting for the target, $t(110) = 1.83$, $p \leq .05$, than did viewers of a candidate commercial. Also as predicted, viewers of an independent commercial demonstrated a more positive perception of the target's opponent, $t(110) = 1.89$, $p \leq .05$, and a greater likelihood of voting for the target's opponent, $t(110) = 2.45$, $p \leq .01$, than did viewers of a candidate commercial.

Analysis of Variance

The *t*-test allows researchers to investigate the effects of one independent variable upon two samples of people, such as the effect of room temperature on subjects' performance on a research exam. One group may take the test in a room at 70° F, while another group takes the same test in a room at 100° F. The mean test scores for each group are used to calculate *t*. However, in many situations, researchers want to investigate several *levels* of an independent variable (rooms set at 70°, 80°, 90°, and 100° F), or possibly several independent variables (heat and light), and possibly several different groups (freshmen, sophomores, and so on). A *t*-test is inappropriate in these cases because the procedure is valid only for one single comparison. What may be required is an **analysis of variance (ANOVA)**.

ANOVA is essentially an extension of the *t*-test. The advantage of ANOVA is that it can be used to simultaneously investigate several independent variables, also called *factors*. An ANOVA is named according to the number of factors involved in the study: a *one-way* ANOVA investigates one independent variable, a *two-way* ANOVA investigates two independent variables, and so on. An additional naming convention is used to describe an ANOVA that involves different levels of an independent variable. A 2 × 2 ANOVA studies two independent variables, each with two levels. For example, using the room temperature study just described, an ANOVA research project may include two levels of room temperature (70° and 100° F) and two levels of room lighting (dim and bright). This provides four different effects possibilities on test scores: 70°/dim lighting, 70°/bright lighting, 100°/dim lighting, and 100°/bright lighting. ANOVA allows the researcher in this example to look at four unique situations at one time.

ANOVA is a versatile statistic that is widely used in mass media research. However, the name of the statistic is somewhat misleading because the most common form of ANOVA tests for significant differences between two or more group means and has nothing to do with the analysis of variance differences. Additionally, ANOVA breaks down the total variability in a set of data into its different *sources of variation*; that is, it "explains" the sources of variance in a set of scores on one or more independent variables.

An ANOVA identifies or explains two types of variance: systematic and error. **Systematic variance** in data is attributable to a known factor that predictably increases or decreases all the scores it influences. One such factor commonly identified in mass media research is sex: often an increase or decrease in a given score can be predicted simply by determining whether a subject is male or female. **Error variance** in data is created by an unknown factor that most likely has not been examined or controlled in the study. A primary goal of all research is to eliminate or control as much error variance as possible (a task that is generally easier to accomplish in the laboratory — see Chapter 5).

The ANOVA model assumes: (1) that each sample is normally distributed, (2) that variances for each group are equal, (3) that the subjects are randomly selected from the population, and (4) that the scores are statistically independent: they have no concomitant relationship with any other variable or score.

The ANOVA procedure begins with the selection of two or more random samples. Samples may be from the same or different populations. Each group is subjected to different experimental treatments, followed by some type of test or measurement. The scores from the measurements are then used to calculate a ratio of variance, known as the *F* ratio (*F*).

To understand this calculation, it is necessary to examine in greater detail the procedure known as sum of squares (discussed briefly in Chapter 10). In the sum of squares procedure, raw scores or deviation scores are squared and summed, to eliminate the need for dealing with negative numbers. The squaring process does not change the meaning of the data as long as the same procedure is used on all the data; it simply converts the data into a more easily interpreted set of scores.

In ANOVA, sums of squares are computed *between groups* (of subjects), *within groups* (of subjects), and *in total* (the sum of the between and within figures). The sums of squares between groups and within groups are divided by their respective degrees of freedom (as will be illustrated) to obtain a *mean square*: mean squares between (MS_b) and mean squares within (MS_w). The F ratio is then calculated using the following formula:

$$F = \frac{MS_b}{MS_w}$$

where $MS_b df = K - 1$, $MS_w df = N - K$, $K =$ the number of groups, and $N =$ the total sample. The F ratio derived from the data is then compared to the value in the F-distribution table (Table 5 in Appendix 1) that corresponds to the appropriate degrees of freedom and the desired probability level. If the calculated value equals or exceeds the tabled value, the ANOVA is considered to be statistically significant. The F table is similar to the t table and the chi-square table except that two different degrees of freedom are used, one for the numerator of the F ratio and one for the denominator.

The ANOVA statistic can be demonstrated by using an example from advertising. Suppose that three groups of five subjects each are randomly selected to determine the credibility of a newspaper advertisement for a new laundry detergent. The groups are exposed to versions of the advertisement that reflect varying degrees of design complexity: easy, medium, and difficult. The subjects are then asked to rate the advertisement on a scale of 1 to 10, with 10 indicating believable and 1 indicating not believable. The null hypothesis is advanced: "There is no signif-

icant difference in credibility among the three versions of the ad."

To test this hypothesis, the researchers must first calculate the three sums of squares: total, within, and between. The formulas for sums of squares (SS) are:

$$\text{Total}_{ss} = \Sigma X^2 - \frac{(\Sigma X)^2}{N}$$

$$\text{Within}_{ss} = \Sigma X^2 - \frac{\Sigma (\Sigma X)^2}{N}$$

$$\text{Between}_{ss} = T_{ss} - W_{ss}$$

The scores for the three groups furnish the data shown on page 243.

By inserting the figures so obtained in the formulas, the researchers are able to calculate the sums of squares as follows:

$$T_{ss} = \Sigma X^2 - \frac{(\Sigma X)^2}{n_k} = 537 - \frac{(83)^2}{15}$$

$$= 537 - 459.2 = 77.8$$

$$W_{ss} = \Sigma X^2 - \frac{\Sigma (\Sigma X)^2}{n}$$

$$= 537 - \frac{16^2}{5} - \frac{29^2}{5} - \frac{38^2}{5}$$

$$= 537 - 508.2 = 28.8$$

$$B_{ss} = T_{ss} - W_{ss} = 77.8 - 28.8 = 49$$

With this information, the research team can calculate the mean squares between and within groups (SS/df), which can then be divided (MS_b/MS_w) to obtain the value of the F ratio. These results are displayed in Figure 12.3.

Assuming a significance level of .05, the F-distribution data (Table 5, Appendix 1) for degrees of freedom of 2 and 12 indicate that the F ratio must be 3.89 or greater to show statistical significance. Since the calculated value of 10.2 is greater than 3.89, a significant difference in

Group A (easy)		Group B (medium)		Group C (difficult)	
X	X²	X	X²	X	X²
1	1	4	16	6	36
2	4	5	25	7	49
4	16	6	36	7	49
4	16	6	36	8	64
5	25	8	64	10	100
16	62	29	177	38	298

$$\Sigma X = (16 + 29 + 38) = 83$$

$$\Sigma X^2 = (62 + 177 + 298) = 537$$

FIGURE 12.3   VALUES FOR ONE-WAY ANOVA EXAMPLE

Sources of variation	df	Sums of squares	Mean square	F
Between groups	2 $(K-1)$	49	24.50	10.19
Within groups	12 $(n-K)$	28.8	2.4	xxxx
Total	14 $(n-1)$	77.8	xxxx	

credibility among the three types of advertisements does exist, and the researchers must reject the null hypothesis.

Two-Way ANOVA

Researchers must often examine more than one independent variable in a study. For example, if the researchers in the preceding example had wished to investigate simultaneously a second independent variable, product knowledge, they could have used a two-way ANOVA. In a two-way ANOVA, the researchers gather the data and organize them in table form, as with the one-way ANOVA, but the two-way table has both rows *and* columns, where each row and column represents an independent variable. The dependent variable score, represented by the letter X,

FIGURE 12.4   TWO-WAY ANOVA TABLE

	Group A (Easy)	Group B (Medium)	Group C (Hard)
No product knowledge	$X_{111}, X_{112} \cdots \cdots$	$X_{121}, X_{122} \cdots \cdots$	$X_{131}, X_{132} \cdots \cdots$
Product knowledge	$X_{211}, X_{212} \cdots \cdots$	$X_{221}, X_{222} \cdots \cdots$	$X_{231}, X_{232} \cdots \cdots$

X represents a dependent measurement score.

The subscripts identify the subject who received that score.

For example:

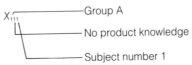

for each subject is entered into each cell of the table. This procedure is demonstrated in Figure 12.4.

The two-way ANOVA can save time and resources, since studies for each independent variable are being conducted simultaneously. In addition, it enables researchers to calculate two types of independent variable effects on the dependent variable: main effects and interactions (one-way ANOVA tests only for main effects). A **main effect** is simply the influence of an independent variable on the dependent variable. **Interaction** refers to the concomitant influence of two or more independent variables on the single dependent variable. For example, it may be found that a subject's educational background has no effect on media used for entertainment, but education and socioeconomic status may interact to create a significant effect.

The main effects plus interaction in a two-way ANOVA create a summary table slightly different from that shown for the one-way ANOVA, as illustrated by comparing Figures 12.3 and 12.4.

Instead of computing only one F ratio as in one-way ANOVA, a two-way ANOVA will compute four F ratios, each of which is tested for statistical significance on the F distribution table (Between columns, Between rows, Interaction, Within cells). "Between columns" (a main effect) represents the test of the independent variable levels located in the columns of a two-way ANOVA (from the preceding example, this would be a test for the differences between groups "easy," "medium," and "hard"). "Between rows" is another main effects test; it represents the significance between levels of the independent variable identified in the rows of the two-way ANOVA (product knowledge and no product knowledge). The "Interaction" section is the test for interaction between both independent variables in the study, and "Within cells" tests for significant differences between each cell in the study to determine how each individual group performed in the analysis. F ratios are not computed for the "Total," which accounts for the X's in the mean square and F columns.

Basic Correlational Statistics

Assume a researcher hypothesizes an association between the number of pictures on the front page of a newspaper and the total number of copies sold at newsstands. If the observations reveal that the more pictures there are, the more papers are sold, a relationship may exist between the two variables. Numerical expressions of the degree to which two variables change in relation with one another are called *measures of association* or *correlation.*

When making two different measurements of the same person, it is common to designate one measure as the *X variable* and the other as the *Y variable.* For example, in determining whether a relationship exists between the size of a subject's family and the frequency with which that person reads a newspaper, the measure of family size could be the X variable and the measure of newspaper reading the Y variable. Note that each subject in the group under study must be measured for both variables.

Figure 12.5 contains hypothetical data collected from a study of 8 subjects. The Y variable is the number of times per week the newspaper is read; the X variable is the number of persons in the household. The scores are plotted on a **scattergram**, a graphic technique for portraying a relationship between two or more variables. The two scores per subject are shown on the scattergram. As indicated, family size and newspaper reading increase together. This is an example of a *positive relationship.*

An *inverse* (or *negative*) *relationship* exists when one variable increases while the other decreases. Sometimes the relationship between two variables is positive up to a point and then becomes inverse (or vice versa). When this happens, the relationship is said to be *curvilinear.* When there is no tendency for a high score on one variable to be associated with a high or low score on another variable, the two are said to be *uncorrelated.* Figure 12.6 illustrates these relationships.

There are many statistics available to measure the degree of relationship between two variables, but the most commonly used is the Pearson product–moment correlation, commonly symbolized as r. It varies between -1.00 and $+1.00$. A correlation coefficient of $+1.00$ indicates a perfect positive correlation: X and Y are completely covariant. A Pearson r of -1.00 indicates a perfect relationship in the negative direction. The lowest value that the Pearson r can achieve is 0.00. This represents absolutely no relationship between two variables. Thus, the Pearson r contains two pieces of information: (1) an estimate of the strength of the relationship, as indicated by the number, and (2) a statement about the direction of the relationship, as shown by the sign. Keep in mind that the strength of the relationship depends solely on the number; strength of relationship must be interpreted in terms of absolute value. A correlation of $-.83$ is a stronger relationship than one of $+.23$.

The formula for calculating r looks foreboding; actually, however, it includes only one new expression:

$$r = \frac{N\Sigma XY - \Sigma X \Sigma Y}{\sqrt{[N\Sigma X^2 - (\Sigma X)^2][N\Sigma Y^2 - (\Sigma Y)^2]}}$$

Where X and Y stand for the original scores, N is the number of pairs of scores, and Σ again is the summation symbol. The only new term is ΣXY, which stands for the sum of the products of each X and Y. To find this quantity, simply

FIGURE 12.5   SCATTERGRAM OF FAMILY SIZE AND NEWSPAPER READING SCORES

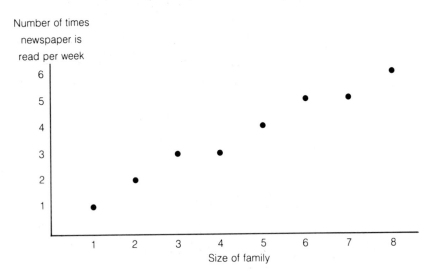

Subject	X: Family size	Y: Number of times newspaper is read per week
A	1	1
B	2	2
C	3	3
D	4	3
E	5	4
F	6	5
G	7	5
H	8	6

multiply each X variable by its corresponding Y variable and add the results. Table 12.2 demonstrates a computation of r. (The use of a calculator or computer is recommended when N is large, since the calculation of r can be tedious when many observations are involved.)

A correlation coefficient is a pure number — it is not expressed in feet, inches, or pounds, nor is it a proportion or percent. The Pearson r is independent of the size and units of measure-

ment of the original data (in fact, the original scores do not have to be expressed in the same units). Because of its abstract nature, r must be interpreted with care. In particular, it is not as easy as it sounds to determine whether a correlation is large or small. Some writers have suggested various adjectives to describe certain ranges of r. For example, an r between .40 and .70 might be called a "moderate" or "substantial" relationship, while an r of .71 to .90 might be

FIGURE 12.6   SCATTERGRAMS OF VARIOUS POSSIBLE RELATIONSHIPS

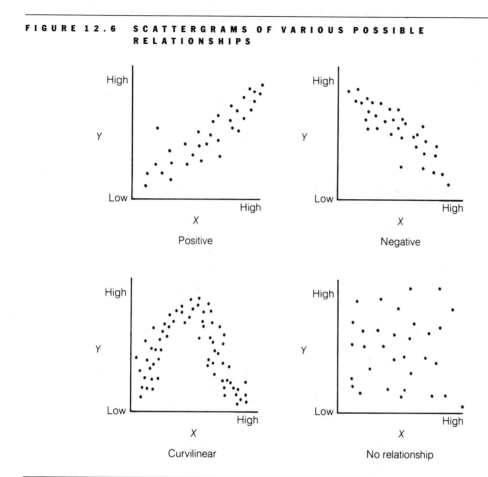

termed "very high." These labels are helpful, but they may lead to confusion. The best advice is to consider the nature of the study. For example, an *r* of .70 between frequency of viewing television violence and frequency of arrest for violent crimes would be more than substantial; it would be phenomenal. Conversely, a correlation of .70 between two coders' timings of the length of news stories on the evening news is low enough to call the reliability of the study into question.

Additionally, correlation does not in itself imply causation. Newspaper reading and income

might be strongly related, but this does not mean that earning a high salary causes people to read the newspaper. Correlation is just one factor in determining causality. Furthermore, a large *r* does not necessarily mean that the two sets of correlated scores are equal. What it does mean is that there is a high likelihood of being correct when predicting the value of one variable by examining another variable that correlates with it.

For example, there may be a correlation of .90 between the amount of time people spend

TABLE 12.2   CALCULATION OF r

Subject	X	X^2	Y	Y^2	XY
A	1	1	1	1	1
B	2	4	2	4	4
C	3	9	3	9	9
D	4	16	3	9	12
E	4	16	4	16	16
F	5	25	5	25	25
G	6	36	5	25	30
H	8	64	6	36	48
$N = 8$	$\Sigma X = 33$	$\Sigma X^2 = 171$	$\Sigma Y = 29$	$\Sigma Y^2 = 125$	$\Sigma XY = 145$

$$(\Sigma X)^2 = 1{,}089$$
$$(\Sigma Y)^2 = 841$$

$$r = \frac{(8)(145) - (33)(29)}{\sqrt{[(8)(171) - 1{,}089][(8)(125) - 841]}}$$

$$= \frac{203}{\sqrt{(279)(159)}} = \frac{203}{(16.7)(12.6)}$$

$$= \frac{203}{210.62} = .964$$

r formula:
$$\frac{N\Sigma XY - \Sigma X\Sigma Y}{\sqrt{[N\Sigma X^2 - (\Sigma X)^2][N\Sigma Y^2 - (\Sigma Y)^2]}}$$

reading newspapers and the amount of time they spend watching television news. That is, the amount of time reading newspapers correlates with the amount of time watching television news. The correlation figure says nothing about the *amount* of time spent with each medium. It suggests only that there is a strong likelihood that people who spend time reading newspapers also spend time watching television news.

Perhaps the best way to interpret r is in terms of the **coefficient of determination**, or the proportion of the total variation of one measure that can be determined by the other. This is calculated by squaring the Pearson r to arrive at a ratio of the two variances: the denominator of this ratio is the total variance of one of the variables, while the numerator is the part of the total variance that can be attributed to the other variable. For example, if $r = .40$, then $r^2 = .16$. One variable explains 16% of the variation in the other. Or, to put it another way, 16% of the information necessary to make a perfect prediction from one variable to another is known. Obviously, if $r = 1.00$, then $r^2 = 100\%$; one variable allows perfect predictability of the other. The quantity $1 - r^2$ is usually called the **coefficient of nondetermination** because it represents that proportion of the variance left unaccounted for or unexplained.

Suppose that a correlation of .30 is found

FIGURE 12.7   BASIC PRODUCT PURCHASE STUDY DESIGN

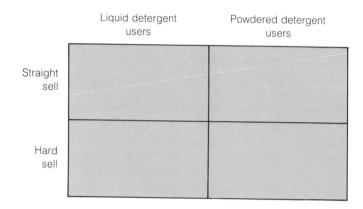

between a child's aggression and the amount of television violence the child views. This would mean that 9% of the total variance in aggression is accounted for by television violence. The other 91% of the variation is unexplained (except to the extent that it is not accounted for by the television variable). Note that the coefficient of determination is not measured on an equal interval scale: .80 is twice as large as .40, but this does not mean that an r of .80 represents twice as great a relationship between two variables as an r of .40. In fact, the r of .40 explains 16% of the variance, while the r of .80 explains 64% — four times as much.

The Pearson r can be computed between any two sets of scores. For the statistic to be a valid description of the relationship, however, several assumptions must be made: (1) that the data represent interval or ratio measurements; (2) that the relationship between X and Y is a linear one, not curvilinear; (3) that the distributions of the X and Y variables are symmetrical and comparable. (Pearson's r can also be used as an inferential statistic. When this is the case, it is necessary to assume that X and Y come from normally distributed populations with similar variances.) If these assumptions cannot validly

be made, the researcher must use another kind of correlation coefficient, such as Spearman's rho or Kendall's W. For a thorough discussion of these and other correlation coefficients, the reader should consult Nunnally (1978).

Partial Correlation

Partial correlation is a method researchers use when they believe that a confounding or spurious variable may affect the relationship between the independent variables and the dependent variable: if such an influence is perceived, they can "partial out" or control the confounding variable. For example, consider a study of the relationship between exposure to television commercials and the purchase of the advertised products. The researchers select two commercials for a liquid laundry detergent (a "straight sell" version, with no special video or audio effects, and a "hard sell" version that does use special effects) and show them to two groups of subjects: people who use only powdered detergent and people who use only liquid detergent. The study design is shown in Figure 12.7.

If the results show a very low correlation, indicating that any prediction made on the basis of these two variables would be very tenuous, the researchers should suspect the presence of a confounding variable. An examination might reveal, for example, that the technicians had problems adjusting the color definition of the recording equipment; instead of its natural blue color, the detergent appeared dingy brown on the television screen. The study could be repeated to control (statistically eliminate) this variable by filming new commercials with the color controls properly adjusted. The design for the new study is shown in Figure 12.8.

The partial correlation statistical procedure would enable the researchers to determine the influence of the controlled variable. Using the new statistical method, the correlation might increase from the original study.

Cutler and Danowski (1981) used partial correlation in their study of older persons' use of television. The authors found it necessary, on the basis of suggestions from previous analyses, to control for sex and education when determining the correlation between political interest and television use. When these variables were partialed out (controlled), they found that media use varied with the subject's age and when the media were used during the campaign.

Simple Linear Regression

Simple correlation involves the measurement of the relationship between two variables. Simple linear regression is used to determine the degree to which one variable changes with a given change in another variable. Thus, linear regression is a way of using the association between two variables as a method of prediction. Let's take the simplest case to illustrate the logic behind this technique. Suppose two variables are perfectly related ($r = 1.00$). Knowledge of a person's score on one variable will allow the researcher to determine the score on the other. Figure 12.9 is a scattergram that portrays such a situation. Note that all the points lie on a straight line, the regression line. Unfortunately, relation-

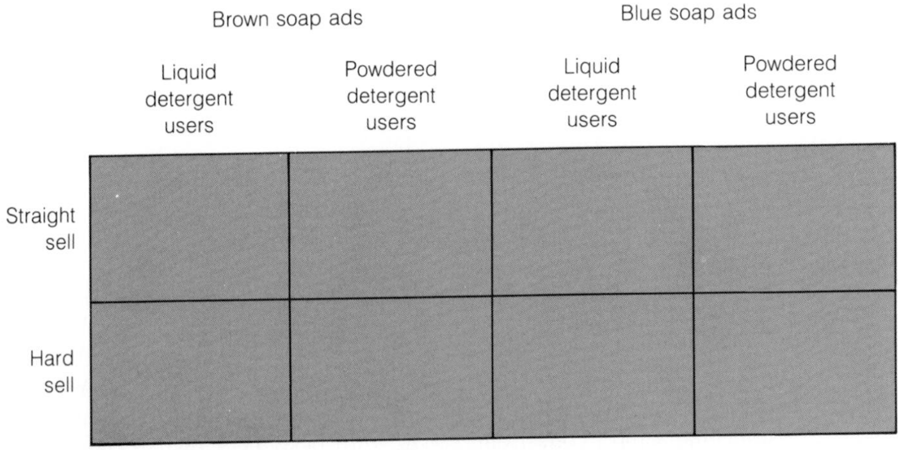

FIGURE 12.8   PRODUCT PURCHASE STUDY DESIGN INCORPORATING PARTIAL CORRELATION ANALYSIS

ships are never this simple, and scattergrams more often resemble the one portrayed in Figure 12.10(a). Obviously, no single line can be drawn straight through all the points in the scatter-gram. It is possible, however, to mathematically construct a line that best represents all the observations in the figure. This line will come the closest to all the dots, although it might not pass through any of them. Mathematicians have worked out a technique to calculate such a line. This procedure, known as the "least squares" method was developed in 1794 by German mathematician Karl Gauss, who used it to successfully relocate Ceres, the first known asteroid, after it was tracked for 41 days.

The least squares technique produces a line that is the best summary description of the re-lationship between two variables. For example, Figure 12.10(a) shows data points representing the relationship between eight x and y variables. The principle of least squares determines the line equation for the data points such that the lines passes through, or near, the greatest number of points. The computed line is then compared to the true, or perfect, line to determine the accuracy of the computed (predicted) line. The closer the computed line is to the true line, the more accurate the prediction.

The solid line in Figure 12.10(b) represents the best fitting line that passes through, or closest to, the greatest number of data points. The broken line connects the actual data points. It is clear that the broken line does not fall on the true line. The data points are some distance away

FIGURE 12.9   PERFECT LINEAR CORRELATION

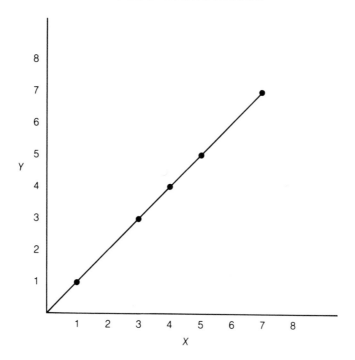

FIGURE 12.10 **(a) SCATTERGRAM OF *X* AND *Y*; (b) SCATTERGRAM WITH REGRESSION LINE**

(a)

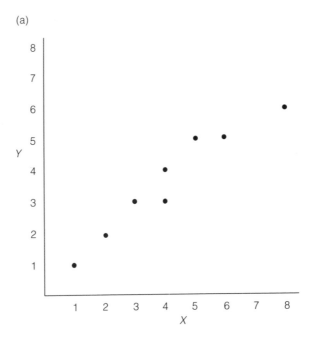

(b)

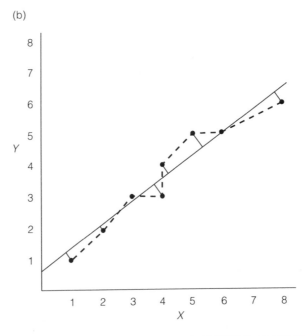

Note: The solid perpendicular lines connecting the data points to the computed line in (b) show the distances that must be determined and squared.

from the true line (showing that the prediction is not perfect).

The principle of least squares involves measuring the distances from the data points to the perfect line, then *squaring* the distances to eliminate negative values, and adding the squared distances together. The computer does this over and over until the sum of the squared distance is the smallest (least squares). The smaller the sum of squared distances, the higher the accuracy with which the computed formula predicts the dependent variable.

At this point it is necessary to review some basic analytical geometry. The general equation for a line is $Y = a + bX$, where Y is the variable we are trying to predict and X is the variable we are predicting from. Furthermore, a represents the point at which the line crosses the y-axis (the vertical axis) and b is a measure of the slope (or steepness) of the line. In other words, b indicates how much Y changes for each change in X. Depending on the relationship between X and Y, slope can be positive or negative. To illustrate, Figure 12.9 (page 251) shows that every time X increases one unit, so does Y. In addition, the a value is zero, since the line crosses the vertical axis at the origin.

Strictly speaking, the equation for a regression line is a little different from the general equation for a line, since the Y in the regression equation does not represent the actual variable Y but rather a predicted Y. Hence, the Y in the regression equation is usually symbolized $\hat{Y}$. Thus, the regression equation is written $\hat{Y} = a + bX$.

Now let's put this general equation into more concrete terms. Pretend that we have data on the relationship between years of education and number of minutes spent looking at the newspaper per day. The regression equation is:

Minutes reading newspaper = 2 + 3
(education)

What can we deduce from this? In the first place, the a value tells us that a person with no

formal education spends 2 minutes per day looking at the newspaper. The b value indicates that time spent with the newspaper increases 3 minutes with each additional year of education. What would be the prediction for someone with 10 years of education? Substituting, we have $\hat{Y} = 2 + 3(10) = 32$ minutes spent with the newspaper each day.

To take an additional example, consider the hypothetical regression equation predicting hours of TV viewed daily from a person's IQ score: $\hat{Y} = 5 - .01(IQ)$. How many hours of TV would be viewed daily by someone with an IQ of 100?

$$\hat{Y} = 5 - (.01)(100) = 5 - 1 = 4 \text{ hours}$$

Thus, according to this equation, TV viewing per day decreases 0.01 hour for every point of IQ.

The arithmetical calculation of the regression equation is straightforward. First to find b, the slope of the line:

$$b = \frac{N\Sigma XY - (\Sigma X)(\Sigma Y)}{N\Sigma X^2 - (\Sigma X)^2}$$

Note that the numerator is exactly the same as that for the r coefficient and the denominator corresponds to the first expression in the denominator of the r formula. Thus, calculation of b is easily determined once the quantities necessary for r have been determined. To illustrate, using the data from Table 12.2 (page 248):

$$b = \frac{8(145) - (33)(29)}{[8(171) - 1,089]} = \frac{203}{279} = 0.73$$

The value of the Y intercept (a) is found by the following:

$$a = \bar{Y} - b\bar{X}$$

Again, using the data in Table 12.2 and the foregoing calculation of b:

$$a = 3.63 - (0.73)(4.125)$$
$$= 3.63 - 3.01$$
$$= 0.62$$

The completed regression equation is: $\hat{Y} = 0.62 + 0.73X$.

Of course, as the name suggests, simple linear regression assumes that the relationship between X and Y is linear. If an examination of the scattergram suggests a curvilinear relationship, other regression techniques are necessary. The notion of regression can be extended to the situation of using multiple predictor variables to predict the value of a single criterion variable.

Multiple Regression

Multiple regression, an extension of linear regression, is another parametric technique used to analyze the relationship between two or more independent variables and a single dependent (criterion) variable. Although similar in some ways to an analysis of variance, multiple regression serves basically to *predict* the dependent variable, using information derived from an analysis of the independent variables.

In any research problem, the dependent variable is considered to be affected by a variety of independent variables. The primary goal of multiple regression is to develop a formula that accounts for, or explains, as much variance in the dependent variable as possible. It is widely used by researchers to predict success in college, sales levels, and so on. These dependent variables are predicted on the basis of *weighted linear combinations* of independent variables. A simple model of multiple regression is shown in Figure 12.11.

Linear combinations of variables play an important role in higher level statistics. To understand the concept of a weighted linear combination, consider the following methods of classroom grading. One instructor determines

---

FIGURE 12.11   MULTIPLE REGRESSION MODEL

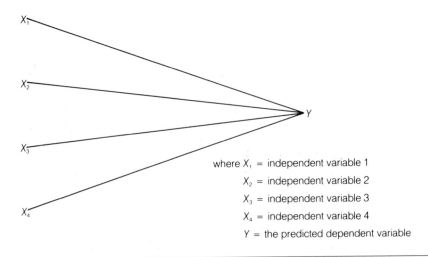

where X_1 = independent variable 1
X_2 = independent variable 2
X_3 = independent variable 3
X_4 = independent variable 4
Y = the predicted dependent variable

each student's final grade by his or her performance on five exams: the scores on these exams are summed and averaged to obtain each final grade. A student might receive the following scores for the five exams: B (3.0); D+ (1.5); B (3.0); B+ (3.5); and A (4.0); thus the final grade would be a B (15/5 = 3.0). This grade is the dependent variable determined by the linear combination of five exam scores (the independent variables). No test is considered more important than another; hence, the linear combination is not said to be weighted (except in the sense that all the scores are "weighted" equally).

The second instructor also determines the final grades by students' performances on five exams; however, the first exam counts 30%, the last exam 40%, and the remaining three exams 10% each in the determination. A student with the same five scores as above would thus receive a final grade of 3.3. Again, the scores represent a linear combination, but it is a weighted linear combination: the first and last exam contribute more to the final grade than do the other tests.

The second grading system above is used in multiple regression: the independent variables are weighted and summed to permit a prediction of a dependent variable. The weight of each variable in a linear combination is referred to as its *coefficient.*

A multiple regression formula may involve any number of independent variables, depending on the complexity of the dependent variable. A simple formula of this type might look as follows (hypothetical values are used):

$$\hat{Y} = 0.89X_1 + 2.5X_2 - 3$$

where $\hat{Y}$ = the predicted score or variable, X_1 = independent variable 1, and X_2 = independent variable 2. The number 3 in the formula, a constant subtracted from each subject's scores, is derived as part of the multiple regression formula. All formulas produced by multiple regres-

sion analyses represent a line in space; that is, the dependent variable is interpreted as a linear combination, or line, of independent variables. The slope of this line is determined by the *regression coefficients* assigned to the variables (Cohen & Cohen, 1975; Thorndike, 1978). The goal of the researcher is to derive a formula for a line that coincides as nearly as possible with the *true* line (a mathematically determined line that represents a perfect prediction) of the dependent variable: the closer the computed line comes to the true line, the more accurate the prediction will be.

Another important value that must be calculated in a multiple regression analysis is the *coefficient of correlation (R),* which represents the product–moment correlation between the predicted $\hat{Y}$ score and the weighted linear combination of the X scores. The square of this coefficient (R^2) indicates the proportion of variance in the dependent variable that is accounted for by the predictor variables. The higher the R^2 (that is, the closer the figure is to 1.00), the more accurate the prediction is considered to be.

Drew and Reeves (1980) conducted a multiple regression analysis to determine what factors affect the way children learn from television news stories. They defined the dependent variable, "learning," in terms of performance on a 10-point questionnaire regarding a news program the children watched in an experimental setting. The selection of independent variables was based on the results of previous studies; they decided to measure: (1) whether the children liked the program, (2) whether the children liked the particular news story, (3) the credibility of the program, and (4) the informational content of the particular story.

The results, shown in Table 12.3, indicate that all the independent variables were statistically significant in their relation to learning. As the beta weights show, "informational content" seems to be the best predictor of learning, while "credibility" accounts for the least amount of

---

TABLE 12.3   DREW AND REEVES' MULTIPLE REGRESSION ANALYSIS

Predictor variables	Beta weights
Like program	.15**
Credibility	.10*
Informational content	.39***
Like story	.25***
Multiple R	.546
R^2	.298

$*p < .05$
$**p < .01$
$***p < .001$

---

variance. The multiple R of .546 could be considered highly significant; however, since it means that only 30% ($.546^2$) of the variance in the dependent variable was accounted for by the four predictor variables, this value may not substantially explain the variance.

S U M M A R Y

Mass media research has made great strides in terms of both number of research studies completed and types of statistical methods used. This chapter has introduced some of the more widely used basic statistical procedures involving one dependent variable and one or more independent variables. The information is intended to help beginning researchers in reading and analyzing published research.

The emphasis in this chapter is on *using* statistical methods rather than on the statistics themselves. The basic formula for each statistic is briefly outlined so that beginning researchers can understand how the data are derived; the goal, however, has been to convey a knowledge of how and when to use each procedure. It is

important that researchers be able to determine not only what the problem or research question is, but also which statistical method most accurately fits the requirements of a particular research study.

Questions and Problems for Further Investigation

1. Design a mass media study for which a chi-square analysis is appropriate.

2. In the chi-square example of television set sales, assume that the observed sales frequencies are 210 (RCA), 350 (Sony), 200 (JVC), and 240 (Mitsubishi). What is the chi-square value? Is it significant?

3. What are the advantages of using an ANOVA over conducting several separate *t*-tests of the same phenomena?

4. How could multiple regression be used to predict a subject's television viewing, radio listening, and newspaper reading behavior?

5. The *t*-test is frequently used in natural science investigations. In the early years of mass media research, the *t*-test was also considered a staple research tool. During the past several years, however, this practice has changed: researchers no

longer seem to rely on the *t*-test. Why do you think this is true?

6. Calculate *r* for the following set of scores:

X	Y
1	8
1	6
3	5
2	4
2	3
4	5
5	2
7	3

References and Suggested Readings

Atwood, L. E., & Sanders, K. R. (1976). Information sources and voting in a primary and general election. *Journal of Broadcasting, 20,* 291–301.

Champion, D. J. (1981). *Basic statistics for social research.* New York: Macmillan.

Cochran, W. G. (1976). Early development of techniques in comparative experimentation. In D. B. Owen (Ed.), *On the history of statistics and probability.* New York: Marcel Dekker.

Cohen, J., & Cohen, P. (1975). *Applied multiple regression/correlation analysis for the behavioral sciences.* Hillsdale, NJ: Lawrence Erlbaum.

Cutler, N. E., & Danowski, J. A. (1981). Process gratification in aging cohorts. *Journalism Quarterly, 57,* 269–276.

Drew, D., & Reeves, B. (1980). Learning from a television news story. *Communication Research, 7,* 121–135.

Garramone, G. (1985). Effects of negative political advertising: The roles of sponsor and rebuttal. *Journal of Broadcasting & Electronic Media, 29,* 147–159.

Genova, B. K. L., & Greenberg, B. S. (1979). Interests in news and the knowledge gap. *Public Opinion Quarterly, 43,* 79–91.

Idsvoog, K. A., & Hoyt, J. L. (1977). Professionalism and performance of television journalists. *Journal of Broadcasting, 21,* 97–109.

Jeffres, L. (1978). Cable TV and viewer selectivity. *Journal of Broadcasting, 22,* 167–178.

Kerlinger, F. N., & Pedhazur, E. J. (1973). *Multiple regression in behavioral research.* New York: Holt, Rinehart & Winston.

Krull, R., & Husson, W. (1980). Children's anticipatory attention to the TV screen. *Journal of Broadcasting, 24,* 35–48.

Metallinos, N., & Tiemens, R. (1977). Asymmetry of the screen: The effect of left versus right placement of television images. *Journal of Broadcasting, 21,* 21–34.

Nie, N. H., Hull, C. H., Jenkins, J. G., Steinbrenner, K., & Bent, D. H. (1975). *Statistical package for the social sciences.* New York: McGraw-Hill.

Nunnally, J. C. (1978). *Psychometric theory.* New York: McGraw-Hill.

Presser, S., & Schuman, H. (1980). The measurement of a middle position in attitude surveys. *Public Opinion Quarterly, 44,* 70–85.

Reeves, B., & Miller, M. (1977). A multidimensional measure of children's identification with television characters. *Journal of Broadcasting, 22,* 71–86.

Roscoe, J. T. (1975). *Fundamental research statistics for the behavioral sciences.* New York: Holt, Rinehart & Winston.

Siegel, S. (1956). *Nonparametric statistics for the behavioral sciences.* New York: McGraw-Hill.

Thorndike, R. M. (1978). *Correlation procedures for research.* New York: Gardner Press.

Wakshlag, J., & Greenberg, B. S. (1979). Programming strategies and the popularity of television programs for children. *Human Communication Research, 6,* 58–68.

Winer, B. J. (1971). *Statistical principles in experimental design.* New York: McGraw-Hill.

Winkler, R., & Hays, W. (1975). *Statistics: Probability, inference, and decision.* New York: Holt, Rinehart & Winston.

RESEARCH IN THE PRINT MEDIA

ethodologies used to study the print media are similar to those employed in most areas of research; academic and commercial research organizations often employ content analysis, experiments, focus groups, and surveys, among other procedures, to study newspapers and magazines. Print media research, however, tends to be more narrowly focused and more oriented toward practical application than is the case in other fields. This chapter provides a brief overview of the most common types of studies in newspaper and magazine research, with a special emphasis on the research most likely to be conducted by advertiser-supported publications.

This chapter does not attempt to deal with *basic market studies* and *advertising exposure studies*. A basic market study provides a statistical portrait of the potential readers of a newspaper or magazine in terms of their demographic or psychographic characteristics. This market research technique is described more fully by Green, Tull, and Albaum (1988). Advertising exposure studies (also called reader traffic studies) are conducted to determine which advertisements are noticed or read by a publication's audience. For more information on these studies see Chapter 15.

BACKGROUND

Research dealing with magazines and newspapers was one of the first areas of mass media research to be developed. The initial interest in such research came from colleges and universities. In 1924 the *Journalism Bulletin* was first published by the Association of American Schools and Departments of Journalism. The first issue contained an article by William Bleyer entitled "Research Problems and Newspaper Analysis," which presented a list of possible research topics in journalism. Among them were the effects of form and typography on the ease and rapidity of newspaper reading, the effects of newspaper content on circulation, and the analysis of newspaper content. Bleyer's article was remarkably accurate in predicting the types of studies that would characterize newspaper and magazine research in the coming years.

Much of the content of early print media research was qualitative. The first volume of *Journalism Quarterly*, founded in 1928 to succeed the *Journalism Bulletin*, contained articles on press law, history, international comparisons, and ethics. Soon, however, quantitative research began to make its appearance in this academic journal: an article published in March of 1930 surveyed the research interests of those currently working in the newspaper and magazine field and found the most prevalent type of study to be the survey of reader interest in newspaper content. The June 1930 issue contained an article by Ralph Nafziger, "A Reader Interest Survey of Madison, Wisconsin," which served as the prototype for hundreds of future research studies.

The 1930s also saw the publication of many studies designed to assess the results of print media advertising. This led to studies in applied research, and several publications began sponsoring their own readership surveys. By and large, however, the results of these studies were considered proprietary.

As the techniques of quantitative research became more widely known and adopted, newspaper and magazine research became more empirical. The growth of this trend was first recognized by Wilbur Schramm (1957) in an **261** article in *Public Opinion Quarterly* that reviewed 20 years of research as reported in *Journalism Quarterly*. Schramm found that only 10% of the 101 articles published between 1937 and 1941 concerned quantitative analyses. By 1952–1956, nearly half the 143 articles published were quantitative, a fivefold increase in only 15 years. The reasons for this growth, according to Schramm, were the growing availability of basic data, the development of more sophisticated research tools, and the increase in institutional support for research.

By 1960 newspapers and magazines were competing with television as well as radio for audience attention and advertiser investment. This situation greatly spurred the growth of private sector research. The Bureau of Advertising of the American Newspaper Publishers Association (now called the Newspaper Advertising Bureau) began conducting studies on all aspects of the press and its audience. In the 1970s, it founded the News Research Center, which reports the results of research to editors. The Magazine Publishers Association also began to sponsor survey research at about this same time. The continuing interests of academics in print media research led to the creation of the *Newspaper Research Journal* in 1979, a publication devoted entirely to research that has practical implications for newspaper management.

In 1976 the Newspaper Readership Project was instituted to study the problems of declining circulation and sagging readership. One major part of the 6-year, $5-million study was sponsoring research into newspaper reading habits. A news research center was set up at Syracuse University to abstract and synthesize the results of more than 300 private and published studies. The Newspaper Advertising Bureau produced dozens of research reports and conducted extensive focus group studies. In addition, regional workshops were held across the country to explain to editors the uses and limitations of research. By the time the Readership Project ended, most editors had accepted research as a necessary tool of the trade.

In fact, research activity in the newspaper business is growing rapidly. In 1977 the Newspaper Research Council (NRC), a subgroup of the Newspaper Advertising Bureau, was incorporated with 75 members. By 1988 this group had expanded its membership to 225 researchers. In the past five years, the NRC has been involved with the American Society of Newspaper Editors in a circulation retention study and with the International Newspaper Marketing Association on how to convert Sunday-only readers to daily readers. Current plans call for the group to put together a research center in Des Moines, Iowa.

Most newspapers with a circulation of at least 100,000 now have an in-house research department. The expansion of group-owned newspapers — about 75% of U.S. dailies in 1990 — has also increased the trend toward research because many small papers can call upon their corporate research staffs for aid. Even some of the individually owned small papers have added researchers to their staff. The Vancouver, Washington, *Columbian* (circulation 48,000) hired a research manager in 1989 as did the Rochester, Minnesota, *Post-Bulletin* (circulation 39,000). The Newspaper Advertising Bureau estimates that the newspaper industry spent about $35–$40 million in 1988 on research, a substantial increase since 1980.

The same trend is found in research conducted for magazines. Jacobson (1988) noted that quantitative studies are playing an increasingly important role in magazine publishing with about 89% of consumer magazines conducting research in 1986 compared to 60% in 1981.

As Veronis (1989) points out, research touches nearly every corner of the publishing industry: advertising, marketing, circulation, readership, and news-editorial. Print media research is conducted by commercial research firms, in-house research organizations, professional associations, and colleges. Print media research is likely to continue its growth. The Associated Press Managing Editors association recently released its "Year 2000" report in which it called for the establishment of an industry-wide research institute. Consensus among industry experts (Veronis, 1989) is that research will remain a vital element of the business as long as newspapers and magazines face heightened competition from other media.

TYPES OF PRINT MEDIA RESEARCH

Newspaper and magazine researchers conduct five basic types of studies: readership, circulation, management, typography/makeup, and readability. Most of their research falls into the first category; circulation studies rank second, followed by management studies, and relatively few studies fall into the last two categories.

Readership Research

Many readership studies were done in the United States in the years immediately preceding and following World War II. The George Gallup organization was a pioneer in the development of the methodology of these studies, namely, a personal interview in which respondents were shown a copy of a newspaper and asked to identify the articles they had read. The most complete survey of newspaper readership was undertaken by the American Newspaper Publishers Association (ANPA), whose *Continuing Studies of Newspapers* involved more than 50,000 interviews with readers of 130 daily newspapers between 1939 and 1950 (Swanson, 1955).

Readership research became important to management during the 1960s and 1970s, as circulation rates in metropolitan areas began to level off or decline. Concerned with holding the interests of their readers, editors and publishers began more than ever to depend on surveys for the detailed audience information they needed to shape the content of a publication.

Today, research into newspaper readership is composed primarily of studies of five types: reader profiles, item-selection studies, reader–nonreader studies, uses and gratifications studies, and editor–reader comparisons.

READER PROFILES   A **reader profile** provides a demographic summary of the readers of a particular publication. For example, a profile of the audience of a travel-oriented magazine might disclose that the majority of the readers earn more than $40,000 a year, are 25–34 years old, hold college degrees, possess six credit cards, and travel at least three times a year. This information can be used to focus the publication, prepare advertising promotions, and increase subscriptions.

Such information is particularly helpful when launching a new publication. For example, when *USA Today* debuted, a reader profile showed that 29% of its readers had annual incomes exceeding $35,000, 67% reported attending college, 32% were 18–29, and 26% had taken six or more round-trip plane trips in the past year. Obviously, such numbers would be of interest to both advertisers and editors.

Because there may be significant differences in the nature and extent of newspaper reading among individuals who have the same demographic characteristics, researchers recently have turned to psychographic and lifestyle segmentation studies to construct reader profiles. Both procedures go beyond the traditional demographic portrait and describe readers in terms of what they think or how they live. **Psychographic** studies usually ask readers to indicate their level of agreement or disagreement with a large number of attitudinal statements. Subsequently, patterns of response are analyzed to see how they correlate or cluster together. People who show high levels of agreement with questions that cluster together can be described with labels that summarize the substance of the questions. For example, people who tend to agree with statements such as "I like to think I'm a swinger," "I'm a night person," and "Sex outside marriage can be a healthy thing" might be called "Progressives." On the other hand, people who agree with items such as "Women's lib has gone too far," "Young people have too much freedom," and "The good old days were better" might be labeled "Traditionalists."

Lifestyle segmentation research takes basically the same approach. Respondents are asked a battery of questions concerning activities, hobbies, interests, and attitudes. Again, the results are analyzed to see what items cluster together. Groups of individuals who share the same attitudes and activities are extracted and labeled. To illustrate, Guzda (1984) reported on a lifestyle segmentation study that resulted in the following group labels: young busy mothers, Mrs. traditionalist, ladder climbers, senior solid conservatives, mid-life upscalers, and winter affluents. Similarly, Ruotolo (1988) identified five types of newspaper readers: instrumental readers, opinion-makers, pleasure readers, ego-boosters, and scanners. Both psychographic and lifestyles segmentation studies are designed to provide management with additional insights about editorial aims, target audiences, and circulation goals. Moreover, they give advertisers a multidimensional portrait of the publications' readers.

ITEM-SELECTION STUDIES   A second type of newspaper readership study, the **item-selection study**, is used to determine who reads specific parts of the paper. The readership of a particular item is usually measured by means of **aided recall**, whereby the interviewer shows a copy of the paper to the respondent to find out which stories the respondent remembers. In one variation on this technique the interviewer preselects items for which readership data are to be gathered and asks subjects about those items only.

Because of the expense involved in conducting personal interviews, some researchers now use phone interviews to collect readership data. Calls are made on the same day the issue of the paper is published. The interviewer asks the respondent to bring a copy of the paper to the phone, and together they go over each page, with the respondent identifying the items he or she has read. Although this method saves money, it excludes from study readers who do not happen to have a copy of the paper handy.

Another money-saving technique is to mail respondents a self-administered readership survey. Hvistendahl (1977) described two variations of this type of study. In the "whole copy" method, a sample of respondents receives an entire copy of the previous day's paper in the mail, along with a set of instructions and a questionnaire. The instructions direct the respondents to go through the newspaper and mark each item they have read by drawing a line through it. A return envelope with postage prepaid is provided. In the "clipping" method, the procedure is identical except that respondents are mailed clippings of certain items rather than the whole paper. To save postage fees, the clippings are pasted up on pages, reduced 25%, and reproduced by offset. Hvistendahl reported a 67% return rate using this method with only one follow-up postcard. He noted that the whole copy and clipping methods produced roughly equivalent results, although readership scores on some items tended to be slightly higher when clippings were used. A comparison of the results of these self-administered surveys with the results of personal interviews also indicated a basic equivalence.

Stamm, Jackson, and Jacoubovitch (1980) suggested a more detailed method of item-selection analysis, which they called a tracking study. They supplied their respondents with a selection of colored pencils and asked them to identify which parts of an article (headline, text, photo, outline) they had read, using a different colored pencil each time they began a new *reading episode* (defined as a stream of uninterrupted reading). The results showed a wide degree of variability in the readership of the elements that made up an item: for one story, 27% of the subjects had read the headline, 32%

the text, and 36% the outline. There was also variation in the length and type of articles read per reading episode.

The unit of analysis in an item-selection study is a specific news article (such as the story on page 1 dealing with a fire) or a specific content category (such as crime news, sports, obituaries). The readership of items or categories is then related to certain audience demographic or psychographic characteristics. For example, Larkin and Hecht (1979) found that readers of nonmetropolitan daily papers read news about local events the most and news about national events the least. Schwartz, Moore, and Krekel (1979) constructed a psychographic profile of frequent newspaper readers that placed each reader into one of four categories—young optimists, traditional conservatives, progressive conservatives, and grim independents—on the basis of which sections of the paper they tended to read. Young optimists, for example, were heavy readers of astrology columns, housing ads, and the classified section; in contrast, grim independents were heavy consumers of sports and business news. In another readership study, Lynn and Bennett (1980) divided their sample according to residence in urban, rural, or farming areas. Their survey found that there was little difference in the type of news content read by farm and rural dwellers, but that urban residents were more likely to read letters to the editor, society items, and local news. More recently, Griswold and Moore (1989) found that readers of a small daily newspaper most often read local news, obituaries, police news, state news, and weather forecasts.

Some item-selection studies have used comprehensive surveys that encompass many newspaper markets. For example, the Newspaper Research Council sponsored a national survey examining selection patterns for approximately 80,000 newspaper items. The study, "Three-quarters of U.S. Adults Read Dailies" (1984) found that item readership nationwide was characterized by a high degree of diversity. In a second study Burgoon, Burgoon, and Wilkinson (1983) surveyed approximately 6,500 adults in 10 newspaper markets to identify clusters of items and topics that interested readers. Respondents were asked how often they typically read items dealing with about 30 topics normally found in the newspaper. Natural disasters/tragedies and stories about the national economy were the most read.

READER–NONREADER STUDIES   The third type of newspaper readership research is call the **reader–nonreader study**. This type of study can be conducted via personal, telephone, or mail interviews with minor modifications. It is difficult, however, to establish an operational definition for the term *nonreader*. In some studies, a nonreader is determined by a "no" answer to the question "Do you generally read a newspaper?" Others have used the more specific question "Have you read a newspaper yesterday or today?" (the rationale being that respondents are more likely to admit they haven't read a paper today or yesterday than that they never read one). A third form of this question uses multiple-response categories. Respondents are asked, "How often do you read a daily paper?" and are given five choices of response: "very often," "often," "sometimes," "seldom," and "never." Nonreaders are defined as those who check the "never" response, or in some studies, "seldom" or "never." Obviously, the form of the question has an impact on how many people are classified as nonreaders. The largest percentage of nonreaders generally occurs when researchers ask, "Have you read a newspaper today or yesterday?" (Penrose, Weaver, Cole, & Shaw, 1974); the smallest number is obtained by requiring a "never" response to the multiple-response question (Sobal & Jackson-Beeck, 1981).

Once the nonreaders have been identified, researchers typically attempt to describe them by means of traditional demographic variables. For example, Penrose and others (1974) found nonreading to be related to low education, low income, and residence in a nonurban area. Sobal and Jackson-Beeck (1981) reported that non-readers tend to be older, to have less education and lower incomes, and to have more often been widowed or divorced than readers. And Bogart (1981) concluded that nonreaders are less likely to have voted in the last presidential election and to believe that their opinions had an impact on local government.

Several nonreader studies have attempted to identify the reasons for not reading the newspaper. The data for these subjects have generally been collected by asking nonreaders to tell the interviewer in their own words why they don't read. Responses are analyzed, and the most frequent reasons reported. Poindexter (1978) found that the three reasons named most often by nonreaders were lack of time, preference for another news medium (especially TV), and cost. Bogart (1981) identified four reasons: depressing news, cost, lack of interest, and inability to spend sufficient time at home. More recently, Lipschultz (1987) discovered that nonreaders relied more on radio and TV for news, found newspapers too costly, perceived papers as neither interesting nor useful, and thought that newspaper reading took up too much time. In addition, similar to the studies just cited, people with less education were more likely to be nonreaders.

Other studies in this area have broadened their focus to include variables that go beyond the control of the newspaper. Chaffee and Choe (1981) in a longitudinal study found that changes in marital status, residence, and employment all had an impact on newspaper readership. Similarly, Einseidel and Kang (1983) found that reading habits are accounted for, at least in part, by civic attitudes. Finally, Grotta and Babbili (1984) questioned the traditional dichotomous division that classifies people as subscribers *or* nonsubscribers. Their study suggested that subscribership is really a continuous variable, exemplified by hard-core subscribers at the positive end of the range through marginal

and potential subscribers to the hard-core non-subscribers at the other extreme.

USES AND GRATIFICATIONS STUDIES   The **uses and gratifications study** is used to study all media content. In the newspaper area, it is used to determine the motives that lead to newspaper reading and the personal and psychological rewards that result from it. The methodology of the uses and gratifications study is straightforward: respondents are given a list of possible uses and gratifications and are asked whether any of these are the motives behind their reading. For example, a reader might be presented with the following item.

> Here is a list of some things people have said about why they read the newspaper. How much do you agree or disagree with each statement?
>
> 1. I read the newspaper because it is entertaining.
> 2. I read the newspaper because I want to kill time.
> 3. I read the newspaper to keep up to date with what's going on around me.
> 4. I read the newspaper to relax and to relieve tension.
> 5. I read the newspaper so I can find out what other people are saying about things that are important to me.

The responses are summed and an average score for each motivation item is calculated.

Several studies have taken this approach to explain readership. For example, McCombs (1979) found three primary psychological motivations for reading newspapers: the need to keep up to date, the need for information, and the need for fun. Reading for information seemed to be the strongest factor. Similarly, Weaver, Wilhoit, and Reide (1979) found that the three motivations most common in explaining general media use are the need to keep tabs on what is going on around one, the need to be entertained, and the need to kill time. The authors also noted differences among demographic groups as to which of these needs were best met by the newspaper. For example, young males, young females, and middle-aged males were most likely to say they used a newspaper to satisfy their need to keep tabs on things, but they preferred other forms of media for entertainment and killing time. A study done in Hawaii (Blood, Keir, & Kang, 1983) reinforced these conclusions. The two factors that were the best predictors of readership were "use in daily living" and "fun to read." In addition, gratifications from reading the newspaper seemed to differ across ethnic groups.

Elliott and Rosenberg (1987) took advantage of the 1985 newspaper strike in Philadelphia to survey the gratifications of readers during and after the strike. They found that people deprived of a daily newspaper turned to other media to fill the surveillance/contact function, but the researchers found no evidence of compensatory media behavior for the entertainment, "killing time," and advertising functions associated with newspaper reading. Payne, Severn, and Dozier (1988) studied uses and gratifications as indicators of magazine readership. They found three main classes of gratifications: surveillance, diversion, and interaction. In addition, readers' scores on these three categories were consistent with the magazines they chose to read.

EDITOR–READER COMPARISONS   In the final area of newspaper readership research, **editor–reader comparisons**, a group of editors is questioned about a certain topic, and their answers are compared to those of their readers to see whether there is any correspondence between the two groups. Bogart (1981) presented two examples of such research. In one study, a group of several hundred editors was asked to rate 23 attributes of a high-quality newspaper. The editors ranked "high ratio of staff-written copy to

wire service copy" first; "high amount of non-advertising content" second; and "high ratio of news interpretations. . . to spot news reports" third. When a sample of readers ranked the same list, the editors' three top attributes were ranked 7th, 11th, and 12th, respectively. The readers rated "presence of an action line column" first, "high ratio of sports and feature news to total news" second, and "presence of a news summary" and "high number of letters to the editor per issue" as a tie for third. In short, there was little congruence between the two groups in their perceptions of the attributes of a high-quality newspaper.

In a related study, Bogart gave readers an opportunity to design their own newspaper. Interviewers presented a sample of readers with 34 subjects and asked how much space they would give to each in a paper tailor-made to their own interests. Major categories of news were omitted from the listings because they were topics over which editors have little control. When the results were tabulated, the contents of a sample of newspapers were analyzed to see whether the space allocations made by editors matched the public's preferences. The resulting data indicated that readers wanted more of certain content than they were getting (consumer news; health, nutritional, and medical advice; home maintenance; travel) and that they were getting more of some topics than they desired (sports news; human interest stories; school news; crossword puzzles; astrology).

Two studies indicate that this technique has been broadened to include journalist–reader comparisons as well as editor–reader matchups. Ogan and Lafky (1983) asked editors, reporters, and the general public to rank the most important news stories from the preceding year. These orderings were compared to the list of the top 10 stories compiled by the Associated Press and United Press International. The results demonstrated that local news stories seemed less important to readers than to professionals but, in general, consumers and newspaper staffers agreed on significant issues. Burgoon, Bernstein, and Burgoon (1983) asked 1,118 journalists (publishers, editors, reporters, and photographers) and 6,112 adults to assign rank order to statements describing the functions of a newspaper. Both the readers and the professionals agreed that the most important functions of a newspaper were to provide a timely account of significant events and to explain how important events and issues relate to the local community. There was one notable disagreement: readers ranked the watchdog function of the press much lower than did journalists.

MAGAZINE READERSHIP RESEARCH   Magazine readership surveys are fundamentally similar to those conducted for newspapers but tend to differ in the particulars. Some magazine research is done by personal interview; the respondent is shown a copy of the magazine under study and is asked to rate each article on a four-point scale ("read all," "read most," "read some," or "didn't read"). The mail survey technique, also frequently used, involves sending a second copy of the magazine to a subscriber shortly after the regular copy has been mailed; instructions on how to mark the survey copy to show readership are included. For example, the respondents might be instructed to mark with a check the articles that they scanned, to draw an X through articles read in their entirety, and to underline titles of articles that were only partly read.

Most consumer magazines utilize audience data compiled by the Simmons Market Research Bureau (SMRB) and Mediamark Research Inc. (MRI). Both companies select a large random sample of households (about 19,000 homes) and interview readers. Company interviewers show respondents cards with magazine logos printed on them and ask if the respondents have read or looked through that particular magazine. If the response is yes, MRI asks more specific questions to pinpoint recent readership whereas SMRB shows respondents a recent issue of the magazine and asks them to indicate what ar-

ticles they have read. Since the two research companies use different techniques, their readership data do not always agree and this discrepancy is a source of some concern in the magazine industry.

Many magazines maintain *reader panels* of 25–30 people who are selected to participate for a predetermined period. All feature articles appearing in each issue of the magazine are sent to these panel members, who rate each article on a number of scales, including interest, ease of readership, and usefulness. Over time, a set of guidelines for evaluating the success of an article is drawn up, and future articles can be measured against that standard. The primary advantage of this form of panel survey is that it can provide information about audience reactions at a modest cost.

Another procedure that is peculiar to magazine research is the **item pretest** (Haskins, 1960). A random sample of magazine readers is shown an article title, a byline, and a brief description of the content of the story. Respondents are asked to rate the idea on a scale from 0 to 100, where 100 represents "would certainly read this article" and 0 represents "would not read this article." The average ratings of the proposed articles are tabulated as a guide for editorial decisions. Note that this technique can be used in personal interviews or with a mail survey with little variation in approach. Haskins also reported a positive correlation between scores obtained using this technique and those determined by postpublication readership surveys.

Other magazine research involves item-selection and editor–reader comparisons. For example, *Glamour* surveys reader response to every issue. Questionnaires are mailed to readers asking them about the articles, the cover, and the respondents' general reading habits. *Travel & Leisure* follows a similar system. The McGraw-Hill magazine group spends approximately $250,000 a year on readership research. *Good Housekeeping* takes a random survey of its subscribers each month to determine what stories were enjoyed and what recipes were tried. Harcourt Brace Jovanovich does both pretesting and posttesting in their health care journals. The company sends the titles of 15 articles printed on a single sheet of paper to 400 or 500 physicians. The respondents are asked to rate each article as having high, moderate, or low interest value. Carlson (1984) summarized some typical questions used in many magazine surveys:

1. Did you find the cover to be
   ____ interesting
   ____ fairly interesting
   ____ slightly interesting
   ____ not interesting
2. What do you like most in this issue? The least?
3. Which regular features are most helpful to you?
4. What do you do with your copy when you finish it?
   ____ save it
   ____ clip and save some articles
   ____ pass it along to another reader
   ____ throw it out

Savvy uses editor–reader comparison research to test staff members' knowledge of their audience. The magazine sends surveys to about 500 readers a month and asks them to list the four best and four worst articles in the previous issue. Editors are asked the same thing. *Savvy* gives a monetary reward to the editors who come the closest to the readers' ranking.

In addition to traditional readership studies, many magazines are conducting focus groups. Harcourt Brace Jovanovich depends particularly on focus groups to help fine-tune the content of new publications. *Farmer* uses focus group sessions for reader reaction to headlines, graphics, and general editorial feedback. Other magazines have started using focus groups as supplements to their monthly questionnaires.

Circulation Research

The term **circulation research** is applied to two different forms of newspaper and magazine study. The first type of circulation research uses a particular group of readers as its unit of analysis. It attempts to measure circulation in terms of the overall characteristics of a particular market, for example, to determine the proportion of households in a given market that are reached by a particular newspaper or the circulation pattern of a magazine among certain demographic groups or in specific geographic areas. Tillinghast (1981), who analyzed changes in newspaper circulation in four regions of the country, found that the greatest decrease had occurred in the East and the South. He also reported that the degree of urbanization in a region was positively related to circulation. Nunn (1979) studied the relationship between circulation and separate editorial management for the morning and evening editions of certain newspapers. He found that papers with different editors for the morning and evening editions had a higher circulation ratio than papers that used the same editor for both editions; this difference was most pronounced in large metropolitan markets. In a study of 69 Canadian daily newspaper markets, Alperstein (1980) discovered that newspaper circulation was positively related to the proportion of reading households within the newspaper's home city. In addition, daily newspaper circulation was found to be inversely related to weekly newspaper circulation.

The recent trend in circulation research has been the identification of other market level or market structure variables that have an impact on circulation. Stone and Trotter (1981) found that the number of households in the local community and measures of broadcast media availability were the two best predictors of circulation. Blankenburg (1981) analyzed market structure variables and determined that county population and distance from the point of publication were strong predictors of circulation.

Hale (1983) concluded from a regression analysis of Sunday newspaper sales in all 50 states that degree of urbanization, population density, and affluence were key predictors of circulation. Moore, Howard, and Johnson (1988) discovered that there was no relationship between viewing television news programs and afternoon newspaper circulation. Market size and location showed a stronger relation to circulation. In sum, it appears from these studies that many factors outside the control of the newspaper publisher have an impact on circulation.

A recent trend in circulation research involves using computer models to predict circulation. *Playboy*, for example, collected data for 52 issues of its publication on number of copies sold, cover price, current unemployment statistics, dollars spent on promotion, number of days on sale, editors' estimates of the cover, number of full-page displays, and several other variables. These figures were subjected to a regression analysis to determine how each factor was related to total sales. Interestingly, the number of copies distributed, the number of days an issue was on sale, and the cover rating proved to be good predictors, but the amount of money spent on promotion was found to have little impact on sales.

More recently, Blankenburg (1987) generated a regression equation to predict circulation after newspaper consolidation. Guthrie, Ludwin, and Jacob (1988) also developed a regression equation, and used theirs to predict metropolitan circulation in outlying counties. They found that the two most important predictor variables were an index of magazine circulation and an index of local newspaper competition for each county.

The second type of circulation research uses the individual reader as the unit of analysis to measure the effects of certain aspects of delivery and pricing systems on reader behavior. For example, McCombs, Mullins, and Weaver (1974) studied why people cancel their subscriptions to newspapers. They found that the primary reasons had less to do with content than with circulation problems, such as irregular delivery and delivery in unreadable condition. Magazine publishers often conduct this type of circulation research by drawing samples of subscribers in different states and checking on the delivery dates of their publication and its physical condition when received. Other publications contact subscribers who don't renew to determine what can be done to prevent cancellations. In recent years, several newspapers have researched the effects of price increases on their circulation. Studies have even been conducted to ascertain why some people don't pay their subscription bills promptly.

The Gannett Company's Newspaper Division conducted research that discovered that customer billing was a prime cause of their newspapers losing circulation. Subsequently, Gannett interviewed a thousand subscribers and conducted several focus groups to come up with a billing system that was more responsive to consumer needs. Some circulation research uncovers facts that management would probably never be aware of. For example, at the Wichita *Eagle*, management was puzzled over circulation losses. A survey found that many subscribers were cancelling because the plastic delivery bags used by the paper on rainy days weren't heavy enough, and many readers were fed up with soggy papers. In short, this type of circulation research investigates the effect on readership or subscription rates of variables that are unrelated to a publication's content.

Newspaper Management Research

Research in newspaper management gained prominence in the late 1980s thanks to several factors. First, newspaper companies expanded their holdings creating a more complicated management structure. Second, media competition became more intense. Newspapers with efficient management techniques had more of an advantage in the new competitive environment. Finally, the newspaper industry became more labor intensive. Skilled and experienced personnel form the backbone of a successful newspaper. More and more managers turned to research to determine how to keep employees the most satisfied and productive.

The techniques used to study newspaper management were the same as used to study any business activity: surveys, case studies, descriptive content analysis, and mathematical models. The main topics that attracted the most research attention in the last half of the 1980s were goal setting by management and employee job satisfaction.

Some representative examples of management research into goal setting include Demers and Wackman's (1988) study of the effect of chain (group) ownership on management's objectives. Secondary analysis of data collected from a sample of 101 newspaper managers revealed that editors at chain-owned daily newspapers were more likely to say that profit was a goal that was driving their organization. In a similar study, Busterna (1989) administered a survey to 42 newspaper executives, most of them from weekly papers, asking them to rate several managerial goals in terms of their relative importance to their newspapers. Managers who also owned their papers placed less emphasis on maximizing profits as a goal, whereas nonowner managers ranked it first. Finally, Connery (1989) conducted a case study of several small daily newspapers and concluded that management commitment was necessary if a newspaper was to achieve its goal of journalistic excellence.

Job satisfaction among newspaper employees has been the topic of several studies. Bergen and Weaver (1988) conducted a secondary data analysis of a survey conducted among 1,001 U.S. journalists. They found that the strongest correlate of individual job satisfaction was how sat-

isfied the journalist was with the performance of his or her news organization. The second strongest correlate was how often employees got feedback on their work. Fedler, Buhr, and Taylor looked at job dissatisfaction. After personal interviews with 62 former reporters, they concluded that journalists who left the field of news media did so because of low pay, poor management, and bad hours. Lastly, Beam, Dunwoody, and Kosicki (1986) conducted a mail survey of 190 working journalists and found that winning a prize for reporting was not related with job satisfaction.

Typography and Makeup Research

Another type of study that is unique to print media research measures the effects of news design elements, specifically typeface and page makeup, on readership and reader preferences. By means of this approach, researchers have tested the effects of dozens of different typography and makeup elements, including amount of white space, presence of paragraph headlines, size and style of type, variations in column width, and use of vertical or horizontal page makeup.

The experimental method (Chapter 5) is used most often in typography and makeup studies. Subjects are typically assigned to one or more treatment groups, exposed to an experimental stimulus (typically in the form of a mock newspaper or magazine page), and asked to rate what they have seen according to a series of dependent variable measures.

Among dependent variables that have been rated by subjects are the informative value of a publication, interest in reading a publication, the image of a page, recall of textual material, readability, and general preference for a particular page. A common practice is to measure these variables by means of a semantic differential rating scale. For example, Siskind (1979) used a nine-point, 20-item differential scale with such adjective pairs as "informative/uninformative," "unpleasant/pleasant," "easy/difficult," "clear/unclear," "messy/neat," "bold/timid," and "passive/active." She obtained a general reader preference score by having subjects rate a newspaper page and summing their responses to all 20 items. Other studies have measured reader interest by using the rating scale technique or the 0–100 "feeling thermometer" (Figure 6.1, page 115). Comprehension and recall are typically measured by a series of true/false or multiple-choice questions on the content that is being evaluated.

Haskins and Flynne (1974) conducted a typical design study to test the effects of different typefaces on perceived attractiveness of and reader interest in the women's section of a newspaper. They hypothesized that some typefaces would be perceived as more feminine than others and that headlines in such typefaces would create more reader interest in the page. The authors showed an experimental copy of a newspaper prepared specially for the study to a sample of 150 female heads of households: one subsample saw a paper with headlines in the women's section printed in Garamond Italic (a typeface experts had rated as being feminine), while a second group saw the same page with Spartan Black headlines (considered to be a more masculine typeface). A third group served as a control and saw only the headline copy typed on individual white cards. The subjects were asked to evaluate each article for reading interest. Additionally, each woman was shown a sample of 10 typefaces and asked to rate them on a semantic differential scale with 16 adjective pairs.

The researchers discovered that typeface had no impact on reader interest scores. In fact, the scores were about the same for the printed headlines as they were for those typed on white cards. Analysis of the typeface ratings revealed that readers were able to differentiate between typefaces; Garamond Italic was rated as the second most feminine typeface while Spartan Black was rated most masculine, thus confirming the judgment of the expert raters.

Studies of page layout have been used to help magazine editors make decisions about the mechanics of editing and makeup. Click and Baird (1979) have provided a summary of the more pertinent research in this area. A few of their conclusions are listed here to illustrate the types of independent variables that have been studied.

1. Large illustrations attract more readers than small ones.
2. Unusually shaped pictures irritate readers.
3. A small amount of text and a large picture on the opening pages of an article increases readership.
4. Readers do not like to read type set in italics.
5. For titles, readers prefer simple, familiar typefaces.
6. Readers and graphic designers seldom agree about what constitutes superior type design.
7. Roman type can be read more quickly than other typefaces.

Recent technological and makeup innovations have sparked renewed research interest in this area. In particular, the advent of *USA Today* with its ground-breaking illustrations and use of color has prompted several studies. Two studies by Geraci (1984a, 1984b) compared the photographs, drawings, and other illustrations used by *USA Today* with those in traditional papers. Click and Stempel (1982) used seven front-page formats ranging from a modular page with a four-color halftone (the format favored by *USA Today*) to a traditional format with no color. Respondents were shown a slide of each page for 15 seconds and were asked to rate the page using 20 semantic differential scales. The results indicated that readers preferred modular pages and color.

More recent studies have continued along these same lines. Smith and Hajash (1988) performed a content analysis of the graphics used by 30 daily newspapers. They found that the average paper had 1 graphic per 17 pages compared to *USA Today*'s average of 1.3 graphics per single page. The authors concluded that the influence of *USA Today* has not been overwhelming. Bohle and Garcia (1987) used the experimental method to gauge reader response to color halftones and spot color usage in newspaper design. Their results indicated that color made a newspaper page more appealing, pleasant, and powerful but had little effect on readers' evaluations of a paper's importance, value, or ethical quality.

Readability Research

Simply defined, **readability** is the sum total of all the elements and their interactions that affect the success of a piece of printed material. Success is measured by the extent to which readers understand the piece, are able to read it at an optimum speed, and find it interesting (Dale & Chall, 1948).

Several formulas have been developed to objectively determine the readability of text. One of the best known is the **Flesch** (1948) **reading ease formula**, which requires the researcher to systematically select 100 words from the text, determine the total number of syllables in those words (*wl*), determine the average number of words per sentence (*sl*), and compute the following equation:

$$\text{Reading ease} = 206.835 - 0.846wl - 1.015 \, sl$$

The score is compared to a chart that provides a description of style (such as "very easy") or a school grade level for the potential audience.

Another measure of readability is the **Fog Index**, which was developed by Gunning (1952). To compute the Fog Index, researchers must systematically select samples of 100 words each, determine the mean sentence length by dividing the number of words by the number of sentences, count the number of words with three or more syllables, add the mean sentence length to the number of words with three or more syllables, and multiply this sum by 0.4. Like the Flesch index, the Gunning formula suggests the educational level required for understanding a text. The chief advantages of the Fog Index are that the syllable count and the overall calculations are simpler to perform.

McLaughlin (1969) proposed a third readability index called **SMOG Grading** (for Simple Measure of Gobbledygook). The SMOG Grading is quick and easy to calculate: the researcher merely selects 10 consecutive sentences near the beginning of the text, 10 from the middle, and 10 from the end, counts every word of three or more syllables, and takes the square root of the total. The number thus obtained represents the reading grade that a person must have reached to understand the text. McLaughlin's index can be quickly calculated using a small, easily measured sample. Although the procedure is related to that for the Fog Index, it appears that the SMOG grade is generally lower.

Taylor (1953) developed yet another method for measuring readability called the **Cloze procedure**. This technique departs from the formulas listed above in that it does not require an actual count of words or syllables. Instead, the researcher chooses a passage of about 250–300 words, deletes every fifth word from a random starting point and replaces it with a blank, gives the passage to subjects and asks them to fill in the blanks with what they think are the correct words, and counts the number of times the blanks are replaced with the correct words. The number of correct words or the percentage of correct replacement constitutes the readability score for that passage. The paragraph below is a sample of what a passage might look like after it has been prepared for the Cloze procedure:

> The main stronghold of the far left ____ to be the large ____ centers of north Italy. ____ is significant, however, that ____ largest relative increase in ____ leftist vote occurred in ____ areas where most of ____ landless peasants live — in ____ and south Italy and ____ Sicily and Sardinia. The ____ had concentrated much of ____ efforts on winning the ____ of those peasants.

Nestvold (1972) found that Cloze procedure scores were highly correlated with readers' own evaluations of content difficulty. The Cloze procedure was also found to be a better predictor of such evaluations than several other common readability tests.

Although they are not used extensively in print media research, readability studies can provide valuable information. For example, Fowler and Smith (1979), using samples from 1904, 1933, and 1965, found that text from magazines had remained constant in readability while text from newspapers had fluctuated. For all years studied, magazines were easier to read than newspapers. Hoskins (1973) analyzed the readability levels of Associated Press and United Press International wire copy and found that both services scored in the "difficult" range; the Flesch indexes indicated that a 13th- to 16th-grade education was necessary for comprehension.

Fowler and Smith (1982) analyzed delayed-reward content (national affairs, science, medicine, business, and economy) and immediate-reward content (sports, people, newsmakers, and movies) in *Time* and *Newsweek*. In general, delayed-reward items were found to be more difficult to read than immediate-reward items. Smith (1984) also found differences in readability among categories of newspaper content, with features and entertainment more readable than national-international or state and local news.

Smith also noted that three popular readability formulas did not assign the same level of reading difficulty to his sample of stories. Porter and Stephens (1989) found that a sample of Utah managing editors consistently underestimated the Flesch readability scores of five different stories from five different papers. They also found that the common claim that reporters write front-page stories at an 8th-grade level was a myth. The hard news stories they analyzed were written at an average 12th-grade level.

PRINT MEDIA RESEARCH: AN OVERVIEW

In 1977 ANPA began to compile, review, and index research studies and private reports dealing with newspaper readership and circulation. The first summary of the project was reported by McCombs (1977) and updated by Poindexter (1979). The research literature was categorized according to 16 major dependent variables that have been studied by newspaper researchers. The most frequent research method was item selection, followed by reader–nonreader studies and studies measuring the amount read in the newspaper.

Readers who are interested in pursuing newspaper research studies can make use of the ANPA computerized bibliography service, which indexes the past 35 years of readership studies. The index contains six pieces of information about each study: independent variables, dependent variables, date of publication, source of the study, whether the report was public or confidential, and whether the study was a major or a minor one. Researchers can request either a bibliography of relevant studies or a set of abstracts. The computerized bibliography is housed at the ANPA News Research Center at Reston, Virginia. A nominal charge for this service covers the cost of computer time used in making the search.

An idea of the types of research done at most newspapers can be obtained from the results of

TABLE 13.1   HOW PERSONAL COMPUTERS ARE USED IN NEWSPAPER RESEARCH

N = 135	
Use	**Percentage**
Secondary data analysis	82
Survey and poll tabulating	62
Syndicated data analysis	52
Ad rate analysis	39
Forecasting	35
Subscriber tracking	19

Source: Data from "PCs and Research" by G. Roberts, Dec. 24, 1988, *Editor & Publisher*, p. 29.

a recent survey of 135 research departments (Roberts, 1988). This survey examined these departments' use of personal computers. As is evident from Table 13.1, the most common research use of PCs is to reanalyze secondary data.

The amount of type of research done in the magazine industry is published by *Folio* magazine. Specifically, *Folio*'s survey is designed to determine how many and what kinds of magazines use research and what types of research methods they use. The results of a recent survey (Hollingsworth, 1987) disclosed that:

1. Ninety percent of consumer magazines and 70% of business magazines conduct research.

TABLE 13.2   TOP TEN TYPES OF RESEARCH CONDUCTED BY MAGAZINES

N = 223	
Use	**Percentage**
Reader profile	79
Market studies	58
Buying influence and intention	57
Marketing and circulation	53
Editorial effectiveness	51
Surveys for article ideas	50
Competitive publication analysis	50
Competitive readership analysis	47
Syndicated readership studies	40
Reader traffic studies	34

Source: Data from "Research Activity of Magazine Publishers" by T. Jacobson, 1988, *Journalism Quarterly*, 65(2), pp. 511–514.

2. The main problem magazines had in conducting research was lack of time, money, and staff.
3. The area that researchers felt deserved more attention was advertising effects.

Folio's survey also revealed that the mail survey was the research method used most often by magazines; 80% of the studies conducted by magazines that did research employed this method. Telephone surveys and in-person interviews tied for second with 10% each, and focus groups were used for 5% of the studies. (The figures total more than 100% because some studies used multiple methods.) Table 13.2 on page 275, adapted from Jacobson (1988), shows all the types of research projects conducted by magazines.

S U M M A R Y

Magazine and newspaper research began in the 1920s and for much of its early existence was qualitative in nature. Typical research studies dealt with law, history, and international press comparisons. During the 1930s and 1940s, readership surveys and studies of the effectiveness of print media advertising were frequently done by private firms. By the 1950s, quantitative research techniques became common in print media research. The continuing competition with television and radio for advertisers and audiences during the past three decades has spurred the growth of private sector research. Professional associations have started their own research operations.

Research in the print media encompasses readership studies, circulation studies, management studies, typography and makeup studies, and readability studies. Readership research is the most extensive area; it serves to determine who reads a publication, what items are read, and what gratifications the readers get from their choices. Circulation studies examine the penetration levels of newspapers and magazines in various markets as well as various aspects of the delivery and pricing systems. Management studies look at goal setting and at job satisfaction. Typography and makeup are studied to determine the impact of different newspaper and magazine design elements on readership and item preferences. Readability studies investigate the textual elements that affect comprehension of a message.

Questions and Problems for Further Investigation

1. Assume you are the editor of an afternoon newspaper faced with a declining circulation. What types of research projects might you conduct to help increase your readership?

2. Now suppose you have decided to publish a new magazine about women's sports. What types of research would you conduct before starting publication? Why?

3. Conduct a pilot uses and gratifications study of 15–20 people to determine why they read the local daily newspaper.

4. Using any five pages from this chapter as a sample, calculate the Flesch reading ease formula, the Gunning Fog Index, and McLaughlin's SMOG Grading.

References and Suggested Readings

Alperstein, G. (1980). *The influence of local information on daily newspaper household penetration in Canada.* (ANPA News Research Report No. 26). Reston, VA: ANPA News Research Center.

Beam, R., Dunwoody, S., & Kosicki, G. M. (1986). The relationship of prize-winning to prestige and job satisfaction. *Journalism Quarterly, 63*(4), 693–699.

Bergen, L. A., & Weaver, D. (1988). Job satisfaction of daily newspaper journalists and organization size. *Newspaper Research Journal, 9*(2), 1–14.

Blankenburg, W. (1981). Structural determination of circulation. *Journalism Quarterly, 58*(4), 543–551.

Blankenburg, W. R. (1987). Predicting newspaper circulation after consolidation. *Journalism Quarterly, 64*(3), 585–587.

Bleyer, W. (1924). Research problems and newspaper analysis. *Journalism Bulletin, 1*(1), 17–22.

Blood, R., Keir, G., & Kang, N. (1983). Newspaper use and gratification in Hawaii. *Newspaper Research Journal, 4*(4), 43–52.

Bogart, L. (1981). *Press and public*. Hillsdale, NJ: Lawrence Erlbaum.

Bohle, R. H., & Garcia, M. R. (1987). Reader response to color halftones and spot color in newspaper design. *Journalism Quarterly, 64*(4), 731–739.

Burgoon, J., Bernstein, J., & Burgoon, M. (1983). Public and journalist perceptions of newspaper functions. *Newspaper Research Journal, 5*(1), 77–85.

Burgoon, J., Burgoon, M., & Wilkinson, M. (1983). Dimensions of content readership in ten newspaper markets. *Journalism Quarterly, 60*(1), 74–80.

Busterna, J. C. (1989). How managerial ownership affects profit maximization in newspaper firms. *Journalism Quarterly, 66*(2), 302–307.

Carlson, W. (1984, September). Researching readers' needs. *Folio*, pp. 63–64.

Chaffee, S., & Choe, S. (1981). Newspaper reading in longitudinal perspective. *Journalism Quarterly, 58*(2), 201–211.

Click, J., & Stempel, G. (1982). *Reader response to front pages with modular format and color*. (ANPA News Research Report No. 35). Reston, VA: ANPA News Research Center.

Click, J. W., & Baird, R. (1979). *Magazine editing and production*. Dubuque, IA: William C. Brown.

Connery, T. (1989). Management commitment and the small daily. *Newspaper Research Journal, 10*(3), 59–67.

Dale, E., & Chall, J. S. (1948). A formula for predicting readability. *Education Research Journal, 27*(1), 11–20.

Demers, D. P., & Wackman, D. B. (1988). Effect of chain ownership on newspaper management goals. *Newspaper Research Journal, 9*(2), 59–68.

Einseidel, E., & Kang, N. (1983). Civic attitudes among non-readers and non-subscribers. *Newspaper Research Journal, 4*(4), 37–42.

Elliott, W. R., & Rosenberg, W. L. (1987). The 1985 Philadelphia newspaper strike: A uses and gratifications study. *Journalism Quarterly, 64*(4), 679–687.

Fedler, F., Buhr, T., & Taylor, D. (1988). Journalists who leave the news media seem happier, find better jobs. *Newspaper Research Journal, 9*(2), 15–24.

Flesch, R. (1948). A new readability yardstick. *Journal of Applied Psychology, 32*(2), 221–233.

Fowler, G., & Smith, E. (1979). Readability of newspapers and magazines over time. *Newspaper Research Journal, 1*(1), 3–8.

Fowler, G., & Smith, E. (1982). Readability of delayed and immediate reward content in *Time* and *Newsweek*. *Journalism Quarterly, 59*(3), 431–434.

Geraci, P. (1984a). Comparison of graphic design and illustration use in three Washington, DC newspapers. *Newspaper Research Journal, 5*(2), 29–40.

Geraci, P. (1984b). Newspaper illustration and readership: Is *USA Today* on target? *Journalism Quarterly, 61*(2), 409–413.

Green, P. E., Tull, D. S., & Albaum, G. (1988). *Research for marketing decisions*. Englewood Cliffs, NJ: Prentice Hall.

Griswold, W. F., & Moore, R. L. (1989). Factors affecting readership of news and advertising in a small daily newspaper. *Newspaper Research Journal, 10*(2), 55–66.

Grotta, G., & Babbili, A. (1984). Daily newspaper subscribing behavior. *Newspaper Research Journal, 5*(2), 3–8.

Gunning, R. (1952). *The technique of clear writing*. New York: McGraw-Hill.

Guthrie, T. L., Ludwin, W. G., & Jacob, S. B. (1988). A parsimonious regression model to predict metropolitan circulation in outlying counties. *Newspaper Research Journal, 9*(3), 59–60.

Guzda, M. (1984, June 9). Lifestyle segmentation. *Editor & Publisher*, p. 16.

Hale, D. (1983). Sunday newspaper circulation related to characteristics of the 50 states. *Newspaper Research Journal, 5*(1), 53–62.

Haskins, J. (1960). Pretesting editorial items and ideas for reader interest. *Journalism Quarterly, 37*(1), 224–230.

Haskins, J., & Flynne, L. (1974). Effects of headline typeface variation on reader interest. *Journalism Quarterly, 51*(4), 677–682.

Hollingsworth, P. (1987, October). Are you getting maximum mileage from research? *Folio*, pp. 166–170.

Hoskins, R. (1973). A readability study of AP and UPI wire copy. *Journalism Quarterly, 50*(2), 360–362.

Hvistendahl, J. K. (1977). Self-administered readership surveys: Whole copy vs. clipping method. *Journalism Quarterly, 54*(2), 350–356.

Jacobson, T. (1988). Research activity of magazine publishers. *Journalism Quarterly, 65*(2), 511–514.

Larkin, E., & Hecht, T. (1979). Research assistance for the non-metro newspaper, 1979. *Newspaper Research Journal*, prototype edition, pp. 62–66.

Lipschultz, J. H. (1987). The nonreader problem: A closer look at avoiding the newspaper. *Newspaper Research Journal, 8*(4), 59–70.

Lynn, J., & Bennett, E. (1980). Newspaper readership patterns in non-metropolitan communities. *Newspaper Research Journal, 1*(4), 18–24.

McCombs, M. (1977). *Newspaper readership and circulation.* (ANPA News Research Report No. 3). Reston, VA: ANPA News Research Bureau.

McCombs, M. (1979). *Using readership research.* Washington, DC: National Newspaper Foundation Community Journalism Textbook Project.

McCombs, M., Mullins, L. E., & Weaver, D. (1974). *Why people subscribe and cancel: A stop-start survey of three daily newspapers.* (ANPA News Research Bulletin No. 3). Reston, VA: ANPA News Research Center.

McLaughlin, H. (1969). SMOG grading: A new readability formula. *Journal of Reading, 22*(4), 639–646.

Moore, B. A., Howard, H. H., & Johnson, G. C. (1988). TV news viewing and the decline of the afternoon newspaper. *Newspaper Research Journal, 10*(1), 15–24.

Nafziger, R. (1930). Reader-interest survey of Madison, Wisconsin. *Journalism Quarterly, 7*(2), 128–141.

Nestvold, K. (1972). Cloze procedure correlation with perceived readability. *Journalism Quarterly, 49*(3), 592–594.

Nunn, C. (1979). *Newspapers with separate editorial managements have higher household penetration.* (ANPA News Research Report No. 17). Reston, VA: ANPA News Research Center.

Ogan, C., & Lafky, S. (1983). 1981's most important events as seen by reporters, editors, wire services, and media consumers. *Newspaper Research Journal, 5*(1), 63–76.

Payne, G. A., Severn, J. J., & Dozier, D. M. (1988). Uses and gratifications motives as indicators of magazine readership. *Journalism Quarterly, 65*(4), 909–913.

Penrose, J., Weaver, D., Cole, R., & Shaw, D. (1974). The newspaper non-reader ten years later. *Journalism Quarterly, 51*(4), 631–639.

Poindexter, P. (1978). *Non-readers, Why they don't read.* (ANPA News Research Report No. 9). Reston, VA: ANPA News Research Center.

Poindexter, P. (1979). *Newspaper readership and circulation: An update, 1977–79.* (ANPA News Research Report No. 22). Reston, VA: ANPA News Research Center.

Porter, W. C., & Stephens, F. (1989). Estimating readability: A study of Utah editors' abilities. *Newspaper Research Journal, 10*(2), 87–96.

Roberts, G. (1988, December 24). PCs and research. *Editor & Publisher*, p. 29.

Ruotolo, A. C. (1988). A typology of newspaper readers. *Journalism Quarterly, 65*(1), 126–130.

Schramm, W. (1957). Twenty years of journalism research. *Public Opinion Quarterly, 21*(1), 91–108.

Schwartz, S., Moore, R., & Krekel, T. (1979). Life style and the daily paper: A psychographic profile of Midwestern readers. *Newspaper Research Journal, 1*(1), 9–18.

Siskind, T. (1979). The effect of newspaper design on reader preference. *Journalism Quarterly, 56*(1), 54–62.

Smith, E. J., & Hajash, D. J. (1988). Information graphics in 30 daily newspapers. *Journalism Quarterly, 65*(3), 714–718.

Smith, R. (1984). How consistently do readability tests measure the difficulty of newswriting? *Newspaper Research Journal, 5*(4), 1–8.

Sobal, J., & Jackson-Beeck, M. (1981). Newspaper nonreaders: A national profile. *Journalism Quarterly, 58*(1), 9–13.

Stamm, K., Jackson, K., & Jacoubovitch, D. (1980). Exploring new options in newspaper readership methods. *Newspaper Research Journal, 1*(2), 63–74.

Stone, G., & Trotter, E. (1981). Community traits and predictions of circulation. *Journalism Quarterly, 58*(3), 460–463.

Swanson, C. (1955). What they read in 130 daily newspapers. *Journalism Quarterly, 32*(3), 411–421.

Taylor, W. (1953). Cloze procedure: A new tool for measuring readability. *Journalism Quarterly, 30*(4), 415–433.

Three-quarters of U.S. adults read dailies. (1984, June). *presstime*, p. 38.

Tillinghast, W. (1981). Declining newspaper readership: Impact of region and urbanization. *Journalism Quarterly, 58*(1), 14–23.

Veronis, C. R. (1989, November). Research moves to center stage. *presstime*, pp. 20–26.

Weaver, D., Wilhoit, C., & Reide, P. (1979). *Personal needs and media use.* (ANPA News Research Report No. 21). Reston, VA: ANPA News Research Center.

CHAPTER 14

RESEARCH IN THE ELECTRONIC MEDIA

During the 1980s, research in the electronic media expanded at a phenomenal rate. The 1990 *Broadcasting/Cablecasting Yearbook* lists no fewer than 100 companies and individuals involved in some type of electronic media research. And the data are not complete: hundreds of college and university professors and private citizens also conduct studies of the electronic media. Add to this the in-house research conducted by stations and networks, and it is easy to see why broadcasting and cable research is now a multimillion-dollar business.

Electronic media research is changing continually, due to advancements in technology as well as improved research methodologies. This chapter introduces some of the more widely used research procedures in this area.

BACKGROUND

Although broadcasting is relatively young compared to other mass media, the amount and sophistication of broadcasting research have grown rapidly. During the initial years of broadcasting (the 1920s), there was little or no concern for audience research. The broadcasters were experimenters and hobbyists who were interested mainly in making sure that their signal was being sent and received. The potential popularity of radio was unknown, and there was no reason to be concerned with audience size at that time.

This situation changed rapidly during the 1930s as radio became a popular mass medium. When broadcast stations began to attract large audiences, concern emerged over how radio would be financed. Eventually it was decided that advertising (as opposed to government financing or taxes on sales of equipment) was the most viable alternative. The acceptance of advertising on radio was the first step in the development of electronic media research.

Advertisers, not broadcasters, were the initiators of broadcast research. Once commercials began to be heard on the air, advertisers naturally wondered how many listeners were exposed to their messages and just how effective the messages were. Broadcasters were thus compelled to provide empirical evidence of the size and characteristics of their audience. This situation still exists — advertisers continually want more information about the people who hear and see their commercial announcements.

In addition to desiring information about audience size, advertisers became interested in why people behave the way they do. This led to the development of the research area known as *psychographics*. But because psychographic data are rather vague, they were not adequate predictors of audience behavior; advertisers wanted more information. Research procedures were designed to study *lifestyle* patterns and how they affect media use and buying behavior. Such information is valuable in designing advertising campaigns: if advertisers understand the lifestyle patterns of the people who purchase their products, they can design commercials to match these lifestyles.

Electronic media research studies today fall into two main categories: *ratings* and *nonratings* research. The remainder of this chapter is devoted to discussion of these two areas of research.

281

RATINGS RESEARCH

When radio first became popular and advertisers began to see its potential for attracting customers, they were faced with the problem of documenting audience size. The print media were able to collect circulation figures, but broadcasters had no equivalent "hard" information — merely estimates. The early attempts at audience measurement failed to provide adequate data. Volunteer mail from listeners was the first source of data, but it is a well-known axiom of research that volunteers do not represent the general audience. Advertisers and broadcasters quickly realized that further information was urgently needed.

Since 1930, when a group called the Cooperative Analysis of Broadcasting conducted one of the first audience surveys for radio, several individuals and companies have attempted to provide syndicated audience information. However, the bulk of syndicated information for radio and television stations and cable has been provided by three companies: A. C. Nielsen and Arbitron for local market and network television and cable TV, and Arbitron and Birch Radio for local market radio.

The A. C. Nielsen Company, founded in 1945, is a subsidiary of Dun and Bradstreet with corporate headquarters in Northbrook, Illinois. Nielsen is one of the world's largest market research corporations, and its television and cable ratings account for only a portion of its business. The American Research Bureau (ARB) was founded in 1949. The name of the company was changed to the Arbitron Company in 1972, then to The Arbitron Ratings Company in 1982, then back to the Arbitron Company in 1989. Arbitron is a subsidiary of the Control Data Corporation and has headquarters in Laurel, Maryland. Birch Radio was founded in 1978 by Tom Birch, a former radio programmer. Birch Radio is now the product of the Birch/Scarborough Research Corporation, based in Coral Springs, Florida.

For more information about the history of broadcast ratings, see Beville (1988).

The Nielsen Company produces several different television ratings reports. The *Viewers in Profile* are the basic market-by-market reports published under the category of *National Station Index* (NSI) estimates. These reports are produced from three to seven times per year, depending on the market, and are based on data collected by diaries (a sample of about 2,500 respondents, which is called the National Audience Composition, or NAC) and electronic meters (a sample of about 4,000 households). The data from these two collection procedures are combined to develop the ratings reports. The *National Television Index* (NTI) provides estimates of network television programs. Nielsen also publishes a summary of network estimates in a publication called *The Pocketpiece*.

Nielsen conducts national audience surveys four times a year, simultaneously surveying all of the more than 200 television markets. These ratings periods — February, May, July, November — are called **sweeps** and are the year's most important surveys. Arbitron conducts television sweeps at the same time as Nielsen. Although other surveys are conducted throughout the year, most advertising rates set by networks and local stations are based on Nielsen's and Arbitron's four "books." Blockbuster movies and special programs are aired during these four ratings periods because of the importance broadcast and cable executives place on the sweeps. The goal is to get the highest audience numbers possible.

Nielsen also has 18 markets that use electronic meters for data collection. The metered data are used not only for NTI and NSI reports, but also for **overnights**, which are preliminary ratings data gathered to give network and station executives, program producers, advertising agencies, and others an indication of the performance of the previous night's programs. Because the sample sizes involved in overnights are small, the actual ratings for the programs do not appear until several days later when an additional sample is added to increase statistical reliability.

Although the Arbitron Company provides ratings for both local market radio and television, the company does not currently provide network ratings information. Arbitron uses diaries to collect radio estimates and both diaries and meters for television estimates; the company also produces overnights in its 18 metered markets. Arbitron is the largest ratings company in the United States that collects radio audience listening estimates. The only network radio ratings are gathered by Statistical Research, Inc., which is hired by networks to produce a RADAR report (Radio's All-Dimension Audience Research). Birch Radio is the only syndicated media ratings company that collects data by personal telephone interviews. No diaries are used in collecting data from the 260 radio markets that Birch Radio surveys.

Broadcast ratings create controversy in many areas: viewers complain that "good" shows are canceled; producers, actors, and other artists complain that *numbers* are no judge of artistic quality (they are not intended to be); and advertisers often balk at the lack of reliable information. Although there may be merit to many of these complaints, one basic fact remains: Until further refinements are made, ratings as they currently exist will remain the primary decision-making tool in programming and advertising.

Since ratings will continue to be used for some time, it is important to understand several basic points about them. First, ratings are only approximations or estimates of audience size. They do not measure either the quality of programs or opinions about the programs. Second, all ratings are not equally dependable: different companies produce different ratings figures for the same market during the same time period.

The key point to remember when discussing or using ratings is that the figures are riddled with error. The data must be interpreted in light of several limitations (which are always printed in the last few pages of every ratings book). Individuals who depend on ratings as though they were facts are misusing the data.

Ratings Methodology

The research methodologies used by Arbitron, Nielsen, and Birch are complex; each company publishes several texts describing its methods and procedures. The data for ratings surveys are gathered by four basic methods: electronic meters, diaries, telephone interviews, and **people meters**. Each method has specific advantages and disadvantages.

Broadcast ratings provide a classic example of the need to sample the population. With about 92.1 million households in the United States, it would be impossible for any ratings company to conduct a census of media use. The companies naturally resort to sampling to produce data that can be generalized to the population. For example, Nielsen's national sample for the NTI and NAC is selected using national census data and involves a procedure known as *multistage area probability sampling*, which ensures that the sample reflects actual population distributions. That is, if Los Angeles accounts for 10% of the television households in the United States, Los Angeles households should compose 10% of the sample as well. Nielsen uses four stages in sampling: selection of counties in the country, selection of block groups within the counties, selection of certain blocks within the groups, and selection of individual households within the blocks. Twenty percent of the NTI metered sample of approximately 4,000 households is reportedly replaced each year.

To obtain samples for producing broadcast listening and viewing estimates, Arbitron, Nielsen, and Birch use recruitment by telephone, which includes calls to both listed and unlisted telephone numbers. Although all the ratings companies begin sample selection from telephone directories, each firm uses a statistical procedure to ensure the inclusion of unlisted telephone numbers, thus eliminating the bias that would be created if only persons or households listed in telephone directories were asked to participate in broadcast audience estimates (Chapter 4). Nielsen calls its procedure a Total Telephone Frame; Arbitron and Birch call their procedures Expanded Sample Frame and Randomization of Last Digits, respectively.

Target sample sizes for local audience measurements vary from market to market. Each ratings service uses a formula to establish a minimum sample size required for a specific level of statistical efficiency, but there is no guarantee that this number of subjects will actually be produced. Although many people may agree to participate in an audience survey, there is no way to force them all to complete the diaries they are given or to accurately use electronic meters. Additionally, completed diaries are often rejected because they are illegible or obviously inaccurate. The companies are often lucky to get a 50% response rate in their local market measurements.

In addition, since participation by minority groups in audience surveys is generally lower than for the remainder of the population, the companies make an extra effort to collect data from these groups by contacting households by telephone or in person to assist them in completing the diary. (These methods are generally used in high-density Hispanic (HDHA) and high-density African-American areas (HDBA); otherwise, return rates could be too low to provide any type of audience estimates.) In such cases where the return (or in-tab) rate is low, statistical weighting or sample balancing is used to compensate for the shortfall. This topic is discussed later.

Perhaps the best-known method of gathering ratings data from a sample is by means of electronic ratings-gathering instruments, in particular the Nielsen *audimeter*, which was introduced in 1936 to record radio usage on a moving roll of paper. Today's audimeter, the storage instantaneous audimeter (SIA), is a sophisticated device that automatically records the time each set in a household is turned on or off, the broadcasting station, how long each set stays on a channel, and all channel switchings. Every day each household in the NTI sample is called by the central computer, located in Dunedin, Florida, which retrieves the stored data and stores them for computation of the National Television Index. All data collection is done automatically and does not require participation by persons in the NTI households.

The Arbitron Company collects metered data via its television meter (TVM), a sensing device very similar to the Nielsen SIA. The TVM records the on/off condition of the set and the channel to which the set is tuned. However, no information is collected about the number of people watching, nor is there any demographic information about the viewers. Arbitron retrieves the household meter data nightly via a direct telephone line attached to the TVM.

For the second major form of data collection, subjects are asked to record in diaries the channels they watch or the stations they listen to, the time periods, and the number of people viewing or listening to each program or **daypart**, a segment of the broadcast day such as "prime time" (8:00 P.M.–11:00 P.M. EST). Arbitron uses diaries for both television and radio. Nielsen uses diaries for the households in its NAC sample to supplement the information gathered from the SIA households because the audimeter cannot record the number of people watching each television set. Examples of the Arbitron television and radio diary instruction pages are shown in Figures 14.1 and 14.2.

The third major type of data collection is by telephone. Birch Radio collects data only in this manner, using a telephone recall methodology. Respondents to the Birch Radio survey are asked to report the previous day's listening activity from 6 A.M. to midnight, along with start and stop times for each listening time period.

According to Tom Birch (1989), telephone interviewing was selected over other data collecting methods for four reasons:

FIGURE 14.1   INSTRUCTION PAGE FROM ARBITRON'S TELEVISION DIARY

Keep this page open to assist you while filling out your diary.

1 List your TV channels.

For all channels this set receives clearly:
- List channel numbers.
- Include call letters/channel identification (WADJ, KABS, etc.) or channel names (HTO, Starvision, etc.).
- Include the city of the TV station or cable company.

2 List all the people who live in your household.

For everyone age 2 or older who lives in this household, write in:
- First Name
- Age
- M (male) or F (female)

If someone who doesn't live in this household watches this set during the week, write in:
- "VISITOR"
- Age (guess if you don't know)
- M (male) or F (female)

When listing **visitors,** give approximate age if not known.

3 Write down what you watch.

Set off or on?
Mark an "X" and lines to show how long.

Set is on for five minutes or more, please tell us what you're watching.

Channel number
From the dial or button you use. Use lines if channel stays the same.

Call letters/channel identification
Write in the call letters or channel name.

Name of program

People watching
Mark an "X" and draw a line to show how long they watched or listened.

Nobody watching or listening while set was on? Write "O" in first column.

Set off all day?
Check (✓) the box at the bottom of the "Evening" page.

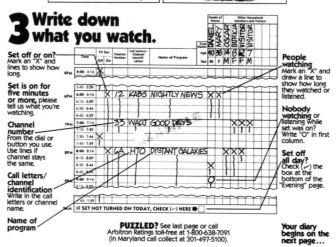

PUZZLED? See last page or call Arbitron Ratings toll-free at 1-800-638-7091 (in Maryland call collect at 301-497-5100).

Your diary begins on the next page...

You count in the radio ratings!

No matter how much or how little you listen, you're important!

You're one of the few people picked in your area to have the chance to tell radio stations what you listen to.

This is *your* ratings diary. Please make sure you fill it out yourself.

Here's what we mean by "listening":

"Listening" is any time you can hear a radio — whether you choose the station or not.

When you hear a radio between Thursday, (Month, Day), and Wednesday, (Month, Day), write it down — whether you're at home, in a car, at work or someplace else.

When you hear a radio, write down:

TIME

Write the time you start listening and the time you stop. If you start at one time of day and stop in another, draw a line from the time you start to the time you stop.

STATION

Write the call letters or station name. If you don't know either, write down the program name or dial setting.

Check AM or FM. AM and FM stations can have the same call letters. Make sure you check the right box.

PLACE

Check where you listen:
- at home
- in a car
- at work
- other place

Write down *all* the radio you hear. Carry your diary with you starting **Thursday, (Month, Day).**

THURSDAY

	Time		Station	Place					
	Start	Stop	Call letters or station name — *Don't know? Use program name or dial setting.*	AM	FM	At Home	In a Car	At Work	Other Place
Early Morning (from 5 AM)	5:45	7:15	KGTU		✓	✓			
	7:15	7:40	108.5 on the dial		✓		✓		
	9:30		WGXP	✓				✓	
Midday									
Late Afternoon		3:00							
	4:20	4:25	Jo Cauvery Show	✓				✓	
Night (to 5 AM Friday)	11:30	12:15	KADV	✓	✓				

If you didn't hear a radio today, please check here. ☐

No listening? If you haven't heard a radio all day, check the box at the bottom of the page.

Questions? Call us toll-free at 1-800-638-7091. In Maryland, call collect 301-497-5100.

1. *Projectability.* Diary methods have high nonresponse rates (as high as 65%), whereas telephone interviews have about 40% nonresponse. According to Birch, the higher response rate corresponds to a more reliable data base.

2. *Reporting accuracy.* Telephone calls do not give respondents time to think about (or plan) their answers as when diaries are used. Respondents' answers are probably more accurate.

3. *Control.* Diaries kept in the home can be filled out by anyone, and may not be completed each day; diary completion may be done at the end of the 7-day diary period instead of each individual day. Significant error may be present because respondents rely on recall. The Birch method limits reports of listening to "yesterday."

4. *Speed.* A complete Birch Radio survey takes only a few minutes to complete. In addition, the company recently installed CATI systems in all of its telephone centers, which allow for immediate access to data for any 24-hour period.

Nielsen and Arbitron also use the telephone to conduct a variety of special studies, allowing clients to request almost any type of survey research project. One of the most frequent types of custom work is the **telephone coincidental**. This procedure measures the size of the medium's audience at a given time — the survey coincides with actual viewing or listening. Basically, the method involves selecting a sample of households at random and calling these numbers during the viewing or listening period of interest. Individuals are simply asked what they are watching or listening to at that moment. This method avoids the necessity of trying to recall information from the previous day. Coincidentals are fairly inexpensive (generally only a few hundred dollars) and are frequently used by station management to receive immediate feedback about the success of special programming. In most cases, coincidental data are used for advertising sales purposes. The Cabletelevision Advertising Bureau (CAB) in New York has prepared a detailed document called "Telephone Coincidental Guidelines."

The fourth method of ratings data collection, people meters, was started in the mid-1980s to have the ability to obtain "*single-source data*," where research companies collect television ratings data, demographic data, and even household member purchasing behavior at one time.

Traditional television meters tell only whether the television set is on or off, and the channel to which the set is tuned; there are no data about *who* is watching. Such information must be obtained by pooling TV meter data with information from households in the diary samples used by Arbitron and Nielsen. People meters attempt to simplify this data collection task by requiring each person in the household, as well as all visitors, to push a specific button on a mechanical unit that records the viewing. Each person in the home is assigned a button on the meter. The meter instantaneously records information about how many people in the household are watching, and the identity of each viewer. The data from each night's viewing is collected via computer. This specific information is valuable for advertisers and their agencies, who now can more accurately target their advertising messages.

Both Nielsen and Arbitron are convinced that using people meters is the way to obtain accurate television ratings information. The companies' interest in people meters was spawned when Audits of Great Britain (AGB) introduced them to the United States in 1987. However, AGB pulled out of the U.S. people meter service in 1988, which leaves only Nielsen and Arbitron to develop a universally accepted system of single-source data collection. The single-source data concept has been expanded by Arbitron in a system called ScanAmerica, a method to collect household purchasing data related directly to television viewing in the household. When purchases are made and brought into the home, a household member passes a scanning wand over the UPC bars on the items and the information is stored in Arbitron's RD-100 people meter for later retrieval. This method, if accepted by consumers involved in the surveys, will provide specific data about television viewing behavior (exposure to commercials) and product purchases (effect of exposure to commercials).

In theory, people meters are quite simple — when a person begins or stops watching television, he or she pushes a button to document the behavior. The button may be located on a hand-held device or enclosed in a small box mounted on top of the television set. However, theory and reality are often misaligned. In late 1989, a survey funded by ABC, CBS, and NBC found that people meters are "turning off" participants, especially with children's programming on Saturday mornings. The Committee on Nationwide Television Audience Measurement (CONTAM), which consists of representatives from the television networks, cable television, and advertisers, recommends three major changes with the people meter system (Donion, 1989):

1. Reduce the fatigue of button pushing by allowing participants to remain in the sample for only two years (Nielsen has families participate for 5 years).
2. Meter all television sets in a household (Nielsen does not meter portable sets).
3. Establish a specific set of research standards for people meter data collection.

The major problem with people meters is that participants get tired of pushing buttons to record when they watch television, and children cannot be depended upon to push the necessary buttons when they turn on the set. The reality is that television ratings produced by people meters are lower than those produced by meters and diaries. Broadcasters and advertisers are concerned. Broadcasters claim the data underestimate actual viewing; advertisers claim the data are probably correct and they are paying too much money (CPM) for their commercials.

Each of the audience estimates procedures is criticized. Simple electronic meters are panned because they do not provide specific audience information. Diaries are blasted because participants may fail to record viewing or listening as it happens and may rely on recall to complete the diary at the end of the week. In addition, many critics contend that diaries are used to "vote" for or against specific shows, and actual viewing is not recorded. Critics of data collection by telephone say that the method favors responses by younger people who are more willing to talk on the phone; older respondents generally do not have the patience to answer the questions about their viewing or listening habits. Finally, people meters are condemned because of participant fatigue, and a failure by many participants (especially children) to remember to push the required buttons when they watch television.

One thing is certain: debate about the accuracy of the various audience ratings methods will continue. Research companies, including Arbitron, Nielsen, and Birch Radio, will be forced to try and develop more valid and reliable research procedures.

Interpreting the Ratings

To explain the ratings interpretation process and its terminology, consider the following hypothetical analysis. (This example uses television networks, but the procedures are the same for radio ratings. In addition, the example has been simplified by using only three commercial television networks; local market ratings books will always include many more stations). Assume that Nielsen has collected the following data for a certain daypart on network television:

Network	Households viewing
ABC	880
CBS	800
NBC	716
Not watching	1,604
	4,000

Recall that Nielsen's NTI sample includes about 4,000 households in the United States and the data collected from them are generalized to the *total* population of about 92.1 million television households.

RATING. An *audience rating* is the percentage of people or households in a population with television or radio tuned to a specific station or network. Thus, the rating is expressed as the station or network's audience divided by the total number of television households or people in the target population:

$$\frac{\text{People or households}}{\text{Population}} = \text{Rating}$$

For example, ABC's rating using the hypothetical data is computed as:

$$\frac{880}{4,000} = 0.22, \text{ or } 22\%$$

This indicates that approximately 22% of the sample of 4,000 households was tuned to ABC at the time of the survey. (Note that although ratings and related statistical values are percentages, the decimal points are eliminated when the data are reported to ease reading.)

The combined ratings of all the networks or stations during a specific time period provide an estimate of the total number of *homes using television* (HUT). Since radio ratings deal with per-

sons rather than households, however, the term *persons using radio* (PUR) is used. The HUT or PUR can be found either by adding together the households or persons using radio or television, or by computing the total rating and multiplying times the sample (or population when generalized). The total rating in the sample data is 59.9, which is computed as follows:

$$\text{ABC} \quad \frac{880}{4,000} = 0.22, \text{ or } 22\%$$

$$\text{CBS} \quad \frac{800}{4,000} = 0.20, \text{ or } 20\%$$

$$\text{NBC} \quad \frac{716}{4,000} = 0.179, \text{ or } 17.9\%$$

$$\text{HUT} = 2,396 \quad \text{Total rating} = 59.9\%$$

In other words, about 59.9% of all households (HH) with television were watching one of the three networks at the time of the survey. As mentioned, the HUT can also be computed by multiplying the total rating times the sample size: $0.599 \times 4,000 = 2,396$. The same formula is used to project to the population. The population HUT is computed as follows: 0.599×92.1 million = 55,167,900 households.

Stations, networks, and advertisers naturally wish to know the estimated number of households in the HUT tuned to specific channels. The data from the sample of 4,000 households are again generalized to find a rough estimate of the households' viewing for each network (or station):

Network rating	×	Population	=	Population HH estimate
ABC: 0.22	×	92.1 million	=	20,262,000
CBS: 0.20	×	92.1 million	=	18,420,000
NBC: 0.179	×	92.1 million	=	16,485,900

SHARE.   A **share** of the audience is the percentage of the HUT or PUR that is tuned to a specific station or network. It is determined by dividing the number of households or persons tuned to a station or network by the number of households or person using their sets:

$$\frac{\text{People or households}}{\text{HUT or PUR}} = \text{Share}$$

In the example, the sample HUT is 2,396 (880 + 800 + 716), or 59.9% of 4,000. The audience share for ABC would thus be:

$$\frac{880}{2,396} = 0.367, \text{ or } 36.7\%$$

That is, of the households in the sample whose television sets were turned on at the time of the survey, 36.7% were tuned to ABC (people may not have been *watching* the set but recorded that they did). The shares for CBS and NBC are computed in the same manner: CBS share = 800/2,396, or 33.4%; NBC share = 716/2,396, or 29.9%.

Shares are also used to estimate the number of households in the target population. The previous example demonstrating how to compute households is considered a rough estimate. However, there is often need for a more exact method for computing households or people.

This is achieved by multiplying the share times the HUT or PUR. The exact households estimates for each network are shown at page bottom (rough estimates are for comparison).

COST PER THOUSAND (CPM). Stations, networks, and advertisers need to be able to assess the efficiency of advertising on radio and television, to be able to determine which advertising buy is the most cost effective. One common way to express advertising efficiency is in terms of **cost per thousand (CPM)**, or what it costs an advertiser to reach 1,000 households or persons. The CPM provides no information about the effectiveness of a commercial message, only a dollar estimate of its reach. It is computed according to the following formula:

$$CPM = \frac{\text{Cost of advertisement}}{\text{Audience size (in thousands)}}$$

Using the hypothetical television survey, assume that a single 30-second commercial on ABC costs $175,000. The CPM for such a commercial would be:

$$\text{ABC CPM} = \frac{\$175,000}{20,246.619} = \$8.64$$

Computing the CPM in the same manner for CBS and NBC, we find CBS = $9.50 and NBC = $10.61.

Network share	×	HUT	=	Population HH exact	Rough estimate
ABC: 36.7	×	55,167,900	=	20,246,619	20,262,000
CBS: 33.4	×	55,167,900	=	18,426,079	18,420,000
NBC: 29.9	×	55,167,900	=	16,495,202	16,485,900
				55,167,900	55,167,900

The CPM is regularly used when buying commercial time. Advertisers and stations or networks often negotiate an advertising contract using CPM figures; the advertiser might agree to pay $8.50 per thousand households. In some cases, no negotiation is involved; a station or network simply offers a program to advertisers at a specified CPM.

The CPM is seldom the only criterion used in purchasing commercial time. Other information, such as audience demographics and type of program on which the advertisement will be aired, is considered before a contract is signed. An advertiser may be willing to pay a higher CPM to a network or station that is reaching a more desirable audience for its product. Cost per thousand should be used as the sole purchasing criterion only when all else is equal: demographics, programming, advertising strategy, and so on.

RELATED RATINGS CONCEPTS. Although ratings and shares are important in audience research, a number of other computations can be performed with the data. In addition, ratings, shares, and other figures are computed for a variety of survey areas and are split into several demographic categories. For an additional fee, ratings companies will also provide custom information such as ratings according to zip code areas.

A **metro survey area** (MSA) generally corresponds to the Consolidated Metropolitan Statistical Areas (CMSA) for the country, as defined by the U.S. Office of Management and Budget. In other words, the MSA generally includes the town, county, or other designated area closest to the station's transmitter. The **area of dominant influence** (ADI), another area for which ratings data are gathered, defines each television or radio market in exclusive terms. Each county in the United States belongs to one and only one ADI, and rankings are determined by the number of television households in the ADI. Radio ratings use the ADIs established from television households; they are not computed separately. (Nielsen uses the term *designated market area*, or DMA, instead of ADI.)

The **total survey area** (TSA) includes the ADI and MSA as well as some other areas the market's stations reach (known as *adjacent ADIs*). Broadcasters are most interested in TSA data because they represent the largest number of households or persons. In reality, however, advertising agencies look at ADI/DMA figures when purchasing commercial time for television stations, and metro figures when purchasing radio time. The TSA is infrequently used in the sale or purchase of advertising time; it serves primarily to determine the reach of the station, or the total number of people or households that listened to or watched a station or channel. Nielsen's equivalent to Arbitron's TSA is the NSI area.

Ratings books contain information about the TSA/NSI, ADI/DMA, and the MSA. Each area is important to stations and advertisers for various reasons, depending on the type of product or service being advertised and the goals of the advertising campaign. For instance, a new business placing a large number of spots on several local stations may be interested in reaching as many people in the trading area as possible. In this case, the advertising agency or individual client may ask for TSA/NSI numbers only, disregarding the ADI/DMA and metro.

The **average quarter-hour** (AQH) is an estimate of the number of persons or households tuned to a specific station for at least 5 minutes during a 15-minute time segment. These estimates are provided for the TSA/NSI, ADI/DMA, and MSA in all ratings books. Stations are obviously interested in obtaining high AQH figures in all demographic areas, since these figures indicate how long an audience is tuned in, and thus how loyal the audience is to the station.

The **cume** (cumulative audience) or **reach** is an estimate of the number of persons who listened to or viewed at least 5 minutes within a given daypart. The cume is also referred to as the "unduplicated audience." For example, a person who watches a soap opera at least 5 minutes a day Monday through Friday would be counted only once in a cume rating, whereas his or her viewing would be "duplicated" five times in determining average quarter-hours.

The **gross rating points** (GRPs) are a total of a station's ratings during two or more dayparts and represent the size of the gross audience. Advertising purchases are often made on the basis of GRPs. For example, a radio advertiser who purchases 10 commercials on a station may wish to know the gross audience they will reach. Using hypothetical data, the GRP is calculated as shown in Table 14.1. The gross rating point indicates that about 32.4% of the listening audience will be exposed to the 10 commercials.

A useful figure for radio stations is the **audience turnover**, or the number of times the audience changes during a given daypart. A high turnover is not always a negative factor in advertising sales; some stations naturally have high turnover (such as "Top 40" stations, whose audiences comprise mainly younger people who tend to change stations frequently). A high turnover factor simply means that an advertiser will need to run more spots to reach the station's audience. Usually such stations compensate by charging less for commercial spots than stations with low turnovers.

Turnover is computed by dividing a station's cume audience by its average persons total (both these figures are reported in ratings books). Consider three stations in the Monday–Friday, 3:00–6:00 P.M. daypart, as shown in Table 14.2. In this market, an advertiser on Station C would

---

TABLE 14.1   CALCULATION OF GRP FOR FIVE DAYPARTS

Daypart	Number of spots		Station rating		GRP (%)
M–F, 6A.M.–9A.M.	2	×	3.1	=	6.2
M–F, 12P.M.–3P.M.	2	×	2.9	=	5.8
M–F, 1P.M.–6P.M.	2	×	3.6	=	7.2
Sat, 6A.M.–9A.M.	2	×	2.5	=	5.0
Sun, 3P.M.–6P.M.	2	×	4.1	=	8.2
	10				32.4

TABLE 14.2   COMPUTATION OF TURNOVER FOR THREE STATIONS

Station	Cume audience		Average persons		Turnover
A	2,900	÷	850	=	3.4
B	1,750	÷	420	=	4.2
C	960	÷	190	=	5.1

need to run more commercials to reach all listeners than one who uses Station A. However, Station C, in addition to having a larger audience, may have the demographic audience most suitable for the advertiser's product.

Reading a ratings book is relatively simple. As mentioned earlier, all decimal points are deleted and all numbers are rounded. A sample page from Nielsen's November 1988 Kansas City NSI ratings book is shown in Figure 14.3. The page is taken from the "Program Averages" section of the book. Only a portion of this page is used because the numbers in the actual book are very small. The page shows the 6:30 P.M. time period.

KCTV is used here to describe how to read the data. First of all, notice that each column is numbered, beginning with Columns 1 and 2 at the left under Metro HH. During the 4-week rating period, KCTV aired *Wheel of Fortune* at 6:30. Each of the days listed represents 4 weeks. That is, "MON" represents the data for four Mondays during the rating period. On Saturdays at 6:30 P.M., KCTV aired *Kansas Lottery Live*. Sundays are not shown here because the program aired at 6:30 P.M. had actually started before 6:30 P.M. This is also why the other stations have slightly different data. The figures display only programs that *started* at 6:30 P.M.

Now, referring to KCTV's Monday performance of *Wheel of Fortune*, the program received a Metro HH rating of 18 and a share of 33, which is usually reported as 18/33. Columns 3, 4, 5, and 6 show the DMA ratings for each of the weeks, with rating and share averages in Columns 7 and 8. The numbers show that the second Monday of the survey (Week 2) was the best performance by *Wheel of Fortune* because its rating was a 21. However, the share trend information (Columns 9–12) shows that the programming at 6:30 P.M. has continued on a downward trend during the last five measurement periods. It started with a share of 42 in November 1987 and had a 34 share in this

book (November 1988). Remember that this discussion refers only to KCTV's Monday performance.

Column 10 shows the DMA HH share number 35X. The *X* means that the programming in May 1988 was the same as the programming in the current measurement. *Wheel of Fortune* was evidently inserted into the programming lineup in May 1988.

Column 13 contains the HUT figure showing that 55% of the television audience was watching television at the time period (Mondays). Finally, Columns 14 through 35 provide specific age/sex cell ratings data. Column 25 refers to working women. Referring to KCTV's Monday performance, more women 18 + (rating = 18) watch *Wheel of Fortune* than men 18 + (rating = 10).

KCTV was chosen as an example for a specific reason. Notice that the women 18 + DMA rating for Mondays is *18*, yet none of the individual age cells come close to this figure (18–34, 18–49, and 25–49 all show 7 ratings; 25–54 shows a 10 rating). The teens and children (Columns 33–35) are not included in the 18 + rating, so where do the viewers come from? Only one place — women who are over the age of 54 — but Nielsen (and Arbitron) do not report these numbers. In other words, looking at the data, more than half of the audience for *Wheel of Fortune* consists of adults (look at the numbers for men to find the same situation) who are over age 54.

A sample page from Arbitron's November, 1989, Denver Television Market Report is shown in Figure 14.4 to demonstrate how it differs from that of Nielsen. This sample comes from the Monday–Friday "Time Period Estimates" section of the book, and shows the 10:00P–10:30P time period. Refer to Figure 14.4. Which station has the lead among ADI HH for the entire half-hour? What type of person is most attracted to each of the stations? (Look at the ADI Ratings.) Incidentally, the symbol "<" means that the

FIGURE 14.3   SAMPLE PAGE FROM A NIELSEN TELEVISION RATINGS BOOK

KANSAS CITY, MO

WK1 11/03–11/09 WK2 11/10–11/16 WK3 11/17–11/23 WK4 11/24–11/30

METRO HH		STATION	DAY	PROGRAM	RATINGS WEEKS				MULTI-WEEK AVG		DMA HH SHARE TREND						PERSONS							WOMEN							FEM PER		MEN							TRS	CHILD	

(Table data — rotated full-page Nielsen ratings chart)

R.S.E. THRESHOLDS 25+% / (1 S.E.) 4 WK AVG 50+%

6.30PM

KCTV MON WHEEL-FORTNE
KCTV TUE WHEEL-FORTNE
KCTV WED WHEEL-FORTNE
KCTV THU WHEEL-FORTNE
KCTV FRI WHEEL-FORTNE
AV5 WHEEL-FORTNE
SAT KS LOTTERY LVE

KMBC MON USA TODAY
TUE FATAL BLAST
WED USA TODAY
THU USA TODAY
FRI USA TODAY
AV5 USA TODAY
SAT CHIEFS-REPORT

KSHB MON NEWHART
TUE NEWHART
WED NEWHART
THU NEWHART
FRI NEWHART
AV5 NEWHART

KZKC SUN CHARLES-CHARGE
SUN LEARNG ROPE SU

WDAF MON ENT TONIGHT 30
TUE ENT TONIGHT 30
TUE EXPLSN-NWS SPC
WED ENT TONIGHT 30
THU ENT TONIGHT 30
FRI ENT TONIGHT 30
AV5 ENT TONIGHT 30

7.00PM

KCT MON DUKAKIS-PLTCL
HW-GRINCH-XMAS
WHART-MON-CBS
AIGN88-CBS
LIVES

PROGRAM AVERAGES

Source: Copyright 1988 A. C. Nielsen Company. Reprinted by permission.

FIGURE 14.4   SAMPLE PAGE FROM AN ARBITRON TELEVISION RATINGS BOOK

Time Period Estimates

DAY AND TIME / STATION PROGRAM	ADI TV HH RATINGS BY WEEKS				ADI TV HH		ADI TV HH SHARE/HUT TRENDS				METRO TV HH		ADI RATINGS PERSONS											WOMEN								MEN						
	NOV 01	NOV 08	NOV 15	NOV 22	RTG	SHR	JUL 89	MAY 89	FEB 89	NOV 88	RTG	SHR	2+	18+	12-24	12-34	18-34	18-49	21-49	25-54	35+	35-64	50+	18+	12-24	18-34	18-49	21-49	25-54	25-54	WW	18+	18-34	18-49	21-49	25-49	25-54
	1	2	3	4	5	6	59	60	61	62	8	9	11	12	13	14	15	16	17	18	19	20	21	22	23	24	25	26	27	28	29	30	31	32	33	34	35
▲ RELATIVE STD-ERR 25% THRESHOLDS (1σ⁻) 50%	3	3	3	3	1						1		−	1	3	1	1	1	1	1	1	1	3	1	7	3	1	1	2	2	2	1	3	2	2	2	2

MON-FRI
10:00P-10:15P

KWGN	HL STRT BLUS	2	2	2		2	4					3	5	1	1	1	2	1	1	2	1	1	1	1	1	2	2	2	2	1	1	1	1	1	1	1
	HL STRT BLU<				2	2	3					2	3	1	1		1	1	1	1	1	1	1	1	1	1	1	1	1	1	1	1	1	1	1	1	1
	--4 WK AVG--					2	4	6	5	5	7	2	5	1	1	1	1	1	1	1	1	1	1	1	1	2	1	1	1	1	1	1	1	1	1	1	1
KCNC	NEWS 4 LT ED	14	14	14		14	26					14	26	8	10	5	6	6	8	9	9	12	12	14	10	5	7	8	9	9	10	9	9	6	8	8	9	9
	VARIOUS				13	13	24					13	24	8	9	5	6	6	8	9	10	12	12	13	10	3	7	9	9	10	10	9	9	5	8	8	9	9
	--4 WK AVG--					14	26	24	27	25	28	14	26	8	10	5	6	6	8	9	10	12	12	13	10	5	7	8	9	9	10	9	9	6	8	8	9	9
KMGH	7 NEWS AT 10	7	5	6		6	11					6	12	3	4	2	2	2	3	3	4	5	5	5	3	3	3	4	4	4	4	4	3	3	3	4	4
	VARIOUS				7	7	12					7	12	4	5	2	3	3	4	3	4	6	5	8	5	3	3	4	4	4	4	4	3	3	3	4	4
	--4 WK AVG--					6	12	12	13	17	14	6	12	3	4	2	2	2	3	3	5	4	7	5	2	3	3	4	4	4	4	3	2	3	3	3	3
KUSA	NINE NWS 10	17		20		19	35					20	38	11	14	6	9	11	12	13	13	16	15	18	14	6	11	12	13	14	14	12	13	10	12	12	13	13
	NINE NWS 10<		18			18	36					20	39	11	13	7	9	10	12	13	13	16	15	17	13	4	10	11	12	13	13	14	12	13	14	14	14
	VARIOUS			19		19	35					19	36	11	13	5	9	11	12	13	14	15	15	17	13	4	10	11	11	12	13	11	14	12	13	14	14
	--4 WK AVG--					19	35	28	31	29	33	20	38	11	13	6	9	11	12	13	13	16	15	17	14	6	11	12	13	13	11	13	10	12	13	14	13
KTVD	NEW T ZONE <	1		2		2	3					2	4	1	1	1	1	1	1	1	1	1	1	1	1	1	1	1	1	1	1	1	1	1	1	1	1
	VARIOUS		2			2	3					2	4	1	1	1	1	1	1	1	1	1	1	1	1	1	1	1	1	1	1	1	1	1	1	2	2
	--4 WK AVG--			2		2	3	2	2	3	**	2	4	1	1	1	1	1	1	1	1	1	1	1	1	1	1	1	1	1	1	1	1	1	1	2	1
KDVR	NGHT COURT-S	3	3	4		3	6					3	6	2	2	3	3	3	2	2	2	2	1	2	2	3	3	3	2	2	2	2	3	2	2	2	2
	NGHT COURT-<				3	3	6					3	6	2	2	3	3	2	2	2	1	1	1	2	3	3	3	2	2	2	2	3	2	2	2	2
	--4 WK AVG--					3	6	8	9	9	7	3	6	2	2	3	3	3	2	2	2	1	2	2	3	3	3	2	2	2	2	3	2	2	2	2
KUBD	HME SHP CLU<																																				
	HME SHP CLUB		−	−							**																										
	--4 WK AVG--																																				
KRMA	PTV	1	1	1	1	1	2	2			1	1	2				1	1	1	1	1			1			1	1	1	1	1					1	1
KBDI	PTV	−	−	−	−																																
	HUT/PVT/TOT	52	52	55	54	53		50	53	52	54	53		32	38	23	29	31	35	36	38	43	42	46	39	24	32	35	35	37	38	34	37	30	35	36	38	37

10:15P-10:30P

KWGN	HL STRT BLUS	2	2	2		2	4					2	5	1	1	1	1	1	1	1	1	1	1		1	1	2	2	2	2	1	1	1	1	1	1	1
	HL STRT BLU<				1	1	3					2	3	1	1		1	1	1	1	1	1	1		1	1	1	1	1	1	1	1	1	1	1	1	1
	--4 WK AVG--					2	4	6	4	5	7	2	4	1	1	1	1	1	1	1	1	1	1		1	1	2	1	1	1	1	1	1	1	1	1	1
KCNC	NEWS 4 LT ED	12	12	13		12	26					13	26	7	9	4	5	5	7	8	9	11	11	12	9	3	5	7	7	8	9	9	8	5	7	7	8	8
	NEWS 4 LT E<				12	12	24					12	23	7	9	4	5	6	8	8	8	11	10	12	9	4	5	7	8	9	9	8	8	5	7	7	8	8
	--4 WK AVG--					12	25	24	25	25	28	13	25	7	9	4	5	5	7	8	9	11	11	12	9	3	5	7	8	9	9	8	8	5	7	8	8	8
KMGH	7 NEWS AT 10	4	4	4		4	9					5	10	2	2	1	1	1	2	2	3	3	5	3	2	1	2	2	2	2	2	2	2	1	1	2	2
	7 NEWS AT 1<				5	5	10					5	10	2	3	1	2	2	2	2	3	3	5	3	2	1	2	3	3	3	3	2	2	2	2	2	3
	--4 WK AVG--					5	9	10	12	14	13	5	10	2	3	1	1	2	2	2	4	3	5	3	2	1	2	2	2	2	3	2	2	2	2	2	2
KUSA	NINE NWS 10	15		17		16	33					18	35	9	11	5	8	9	10	11	11	14	14	16	12	5	9	10	10	10	11	10	12	8	11	12	12	10
	NINE NWS 10<		17			17	35					19	39	10	12	6	8	9	11	11	12	15	14	16	12	7	9	10	10	11	11	12	8	11	12	12	12
	VARIOUS			17		17	35					19	37	10	13	5	9	10	11	12	13	15	14	17	12	5	9	10	11	12	12	13	11	12	13	13	13
	--4 WK AVG--					17	34	28	30	28	31	18	37	10	12	5	8	9	10	11	12	14	13	16	12	5	9	10	11	11	12	10	12	9	11	11	12	12
KTVD	NEW T ZONE	1				1	3					2	4	1	1	1	1	1	1	1	1	1	1		1	2	1	1	1	1	1	1	1	1	1	1	1
	VARIOUS		2			2	3					2	4	1	1	1	1	1	1	1	1	1	1		1	1	1	1	1	1	1	1	1	1	1	1	1
	NEW T ZONE <			2		2	4					2	5	1	1	1	2	2	2	2	1	1	1		1	1	1	1	1	1	1	2	2	2	2	2	1
	--4 WK AVG--					2	3	3	3	3	**	2	4	1	1	1	1	1	1	1	1	1	1		1	1	1	1	1	1	1	1	1	1	1	2	1
KDVR	NGHT COURT-S	3	3	4		4	7					4	8	2	2	3	3	3	3	2	2	2	2	2	2	3	3	3	2	2	2	2	2	3	2	2	2
	NGHT COURT-<				4	4	7					4	9	2	2	4	4	4	3	3	2	1	1	2	2	4	3	3	2	3	2	4	3	3	2	2
	--4 WK AVG--					4	7	9	10	10	8	4	8	2	2	3	3	3	3	3	3	2	2	1	2	3	4	3	3	2	3	2	3	3	2	2	2
KUBD	HME SHP CLU<	−																																			
	HME SHP CLUB		−	−							**																										
	--4 WK AVG--																																				
KRMA	PTV	1	1	1	1	1	2	2		2	1	2				1	1	1	1	1			1		1	1	1	1	1					1	1
KBDI	PTV	−	−	−	−						**																										
	HUT/PVT/TOT	47	47	51	50	49		49	49	49	50	50		29	34	20	26	28	31	32	34	39	37	41	34	20	28	31	31	33	34	30	33	28	32	33	34	34

10:30P-10:45P

KWGN	HL STRT BLUS	2	2	2		2	5					2	6	1	1	1	1	2	1	1		1	1	1	1	1	2	1	1	1	1	1	1	1	1	1
	HL STRT BLU<			2	2	5						3	7	1	1	1	1		1	2	1		1	1	1	1	2	1	1	1	2	2	1	1	2	2
	--4 WK AVG--					2	5	8	6	8	9	3	6	1	1			1		1	1	1			1	1	2	1	1	1	1	1	1	1	1	2	2
	⌐NIGHT SHO<	10			10	10	26					11	⌐			2		9	11	7	3	4	5	6	6	7	5	7	7	4	6		
	⌐US		9		10	9	23									9	9	6	7	6	6	6	7	6	c					
	SHOW			10		10	24										7	3	4	5	6	6	6	7	6	c					
	⌐---	4	4			1C											2	4	5	5	6	6	6						

Source: Copyright 1989 The Arbitron Company. Reprinted by permission.

program aired less than five days, "**" means that share or HUT trends are not available, and "−" means that the program did not achieve a reportable weekly rating.

The Arbitron data shown in Figure 14.4 were gathered by Arbitron's electronic people meter equipment, including its RD-100 Data Collection Unit (DCU), an Infrared Hand-Held Remote Control Unit, a VCR adapter (if necessary), and a Data Wand. The use of these devices is described by Arbitron (Denver Television Market Report, 1989:ii):

> The DCU is installed on a television set. The unit's sensors continuously monitor the television set's on/off condition and the channel tuning. The DCU receives second-by-second information from the television set and stores tuning in the DCU memory.
>
> The DCU also contains hardware that overlays audience identification prompts on the television screen which remind viewers to identify themselves by overlaying a "?" prompt in the upper left-hand corner of the television screen. All viewer responses are stored in the DCU memory.
>
> VCR adaptors alone with DCUs are installed on VCRs to monitor record mode only.
>
> A Data Wand is a scanning device used by householders to scan the Universal Product Code (UPC) symbol on products purchased by the household. . . .
>
> Each night, Arbitron's computer facility in Beltsville, Maryland, polls and retrieves tuning and people data from all eligible households.

Although information on ratings and shares is computed the same way for radio and television audience measurements, the information is presented very differently in these media. Radio books usually contain more than 10 individual sections (such as Target Audience Estimates, Audience Composition, and various trend and rank data), and concentrate on presenting audience estimates in terms of dayparts, not individual programs. Also, because there are so many radio stations in any given market, the emphasis in radio books is on shares, not ratings. Radio broadcasters rarely, if ever, use ratings to sell advertising. In addition, metro shares, not ADI or TSA shares, are the most important numbers in radio.

A portion of an Arbitron radio book (Denver-Boulder, Winter, 1989) is shown in Figure 14.5. The page is taken from the "Target Audience" section for persons 18–34. Interpreting a radio book is somewhat different than the pro-

cedure used in television. For example, refer to KBCO-FM in the first four columns on the left-hand portion of the page (Monday–Friday 6AM–10AM). First note that the AQH and CUME numbers are in 100s; that is, "00" is eliminated from the reported data.

During the "morning drive," KBCO-FM has a *metro* average quarter-hour audience of 20,500 (or an average of 20,500 people 18–34 are listening for at least 5 minutes during any given quarter hour). The number of different people (Cume) who listen to the station is 120,900. The 20,500 AQH number produces an AQH rating (among 18- to 34-year-olds) of 3.2 and an AQH share of 12.3 (the leader in the market in this book). The KBCO A/F TOT line refers to the fact that the station simulcasts its FM program on its AM sister station and combines the two station's numbers to produce one figure.

Figure 14.6 shows a portion of a page from the Spring 1989 Birch Radio Quarterly Summary Report of New York/Northern New Jersey/ Long Island. This page is included to compare to the presentation by Arbitron. The top right-hand portion of the table shows that it is taken from the "Target Demographics" section of the book, and reports data for adults 18–34. The interpretation of the data is the same as for Arbitron. However, notice the difference in audience sizes in New York as compared to those in Denver-Boulder in Figure 14.5. For example, the cume 18–34 leader on this portion of the page during morning drive (Mon–Fri 6:00AM– 10:00AM) is WNEW-FM, with an 18–34 cume audience of 495,300; its total 18–34 AQH audience is 123,600. In addition, about 1,124,000 different people 18–34 tune to WNEW-FM at least once between 6:00AM and 12:00 midnight in a given week (refer to Column 4).

Adjusting for Unrepresentative Samples

Since ratings are computed using samples for the population, there is always a certain amount of error associated with the data. This error,

FIGURE 14.5   SAMPLE PAGE FROM AN ARBITRON RADIO RATINGS BOOK

Target Audience
PERSONS 18-34

Station		MONDAY-FRIDAY 6AM-10AM				MONDAY-FRIDAY 10AM-3PM				MONDAY-FRIDAY 3PM-7PM				MONDAY-FRIDAY 7PM-MID				WEEKEND 10AM-7PM			
		AQH (00)	CUME (00)	AQH RTG	AQH SHR	AQH (00)	CUME (00)	AQH RTG	AQH SHR	AQH (00)	CUME (00)	AQH RTG	AQH SHR	AQH (00)	CUME (00)	AQH RTG	AQH SHR	AQH (00)	CUME (00)	AQH RTG	AQH SHR
KAZY	METRO	130	1001	2.0	7.7	169	1020	2.6	10.4	130	1193	2.0	8.9	53	581	.8	9.5	129	844	2.0	10.2
	TSA	165	1228			230	1296			176	1461			102	829			194	1195		
KBCO	METRO	* 2	13		.1	1	28		.1	2	25		.1					1	23		.1
	TSA	2	13			4	48			6	45							1	23		
KBCO-FM	METRO	205	1209	3.2	12.1	212	1079	3.3	13.1	170	1197	2.7	11.6	49	780	.8	8.8	125	822	2.0	9.9
	TSA	218	1328			222	1202			180	1301			53	830			134	917		
A/F TOT	METRO	207	1222	3.2	12.3	213	1079	3.3	13.1	172	1209	2.7	11.7					126	845	2.0	10.0
	TSA	220	1341			226	1202			186	1313							135	940		
KBPI	METRO	151	1132	2.4	8.9	111	970	1.7	6.9	127	1146	2.0	8.7	60	727	.9	10.7	126	737	2.0	10.0
	TSA	172	1352			131	1149			163	1432			92	973			144	949		
KDEN	METRO		28			1	36		.1									1	13		.1
	TSA		28			1	36											1	13		
KDKO	METRO	17	101	.3	1.0	25	94	.4	1.5	12	102	.2	.8	1	87		.2	8	41	.1	.6
	TSA	17	101			25	94			12	102			1	87			8	41		
KEZW	METRO		14			3	30		.2	1	16		.1	1	16		.2	2	22		.2
	TSA		14			3	30			1	16			1	16			2	22		
KHIH	METRO	58	321	.9	3.4	59	327	.9	3.6	62	360	1.0	4.2	30	231	.5	5.4	39	263	.6	3.1
	TSA	62	357			62	372			64	397			30	247			46	280		
KHOW	METRO	46	206	.7	2.7	7	78	.1	.4	20	192	.3	1.4	4	47	.1	.7	8	50	.1	.6
	TSA	72	350			34	245			39	353			4	47			12	80		
KLZ	METRO	18	134	.3	1.1	12	132	.2	.7	13		.2	.9	4	20	.1	.7	17	130	.3	1.3
	TSA	25	184			21	183							5	27			18	143		
KMJI	METRO	90	486	1.4	5.3	104	484							34	376	.5	6.1	74	488	.6	
	TSA	92	497			114	5..							34	376			78	5..		
~A	METRO	74	386	1.2	4.4										?02	.2	2.3			.3	1.3
	TSA	89	499																		

FIGURE 14.6   SAMPLE PAGE FROM A BIRCH RADIO RATINGS BOOK

NY/N NJ/LONG ISL NY-NJ-CT CMSA
MARCH 1989 - MAY 1989

AVERAGE QUARTER HOUR AND CUME ESTIMATES

Target Demographics — ADULTS 18-34

MON – SUN 6:00AM–12:00 MID

Station	AQH PRS (00)	AQH PRS RTG	AQH PRS SHR	CUME PRS (00)
WABC	78	.2	.8	1716
WADO +	28	.1	.3	635
WALK	1			14
WALK-FM	119	.3	1.2	1890
WBAB-FM	202	.4	2.1	2294
WBGO-FM	4			345
WBLI-FM	114	.2	1.2	1677
WBLS-FM	748	1.6	7.7	8159
WCBS	95	.2	1.0	1529
WCBS-FM	247	.5	2.5	3674
WDHA-FM	134	.3	1.4	1197
WDRE-FM	127	.3	1.3	858
WEBE-FM	72	.2	.7	941
WEZN-FM	34	.1	.3	406
WFAN	158	.3	1.6	3707
WFME-FM	9		.1	146
WHTZ-FM	725	1.5	7.4	10911
WINS	149	.3	1.5	3988
WKDM +	30		.3	595
WKJY-FM	40	.1	.4	518
WLIB*	102	.2	1.0	807
WLTW-FM	321	.7	3.3	3125
WMCA	6		.1	219
WNCN-FM	48	.1	.5	577
WNEW	20		.2	332
WNEW-FM	1004	2.1	10.3	11240
WNSR-FM	311	.7	3.2	3969
WNYC-FM	21		.2	454
WQBM-FM	25	.1	.3	556
VOR	27	.1	.3	581
WPAT				
WPAT-FM	110	.2	1.1	
WPLJ-FM	604	1.3		
?-FM	361			

MON – FRI 6:00AM–10:00AM

Station	AQH PRS (00)	AQH PRS RTG	AQH PRS SHR	CUME PRS (00)
WABC	165	.3	1.5	922
WADO +	53	.1	.5	315
WALK	1			14
WALK-FM	114	.2	1.0	717
WBAB-FM	224	.5	2.0	1158
WBLI-FM	135	.3	1.2	877
WBLS-FM	874	1.8	7.7	3420
WCBS	207	.4	1.8	1023
WCBS-FM	209	.4	1.8	1037
WDHA-FM	206	.4	1.8	680
WDRE-FM	116	.2	1.0	553
WEBE-FM	78	.2	.7	412
WEZN-FM	42	.1	.4	123
WFAN	235	.5	2.1	1886
WFME-FM	12		.1	69
WHTZ-FM	808	1.7	7.1	4780
WINS	534	1.1	4.7	2903
WKDM +	73	.2	.6	328
WKJY-FM	42	.1	.4	280
WLIB*	71	.1	.6	269
WLTW-FM	201	.4	1.8	1229
WMCA	2		.1	44
WNCN-FM	25	.1	.2	142
WNEW-FM	1236	2.6	10.9	4953
WNSR-FM	337	.7	3.0	1828
WNYC-FM	40	.1	.1	277
WQBM-FM	13		.1	177
VOR	82		.7	335

MON – FRI 10:00AM–3:00PM

Station	AQH PRS (00)	AQH PRS RTG	AQH PRS SHR	CUME PRS (00)
WABC	117	.2	.9	575
WADO +	15		.1	259
WALK	4			14
WALK-FM	135	.3	1.1	709
WBAB-FM	285	.6	2.3	969
WBLI-FM	172	.4	1.4	649
WBLS-FM	1023	2.2	8.3	3836
WCBS	99	.2	.8	455
WCBS-FM	368	.8	3.0	1619
WDHA-FM	173	.3	1.4	518
WDRE-FM	129	.3	1.0	437
WEBE-FM	132	.3	1.1	270
WEZN-FM	78	.2	.6	115
WFAN	149	.3	1.2	851
WFME-FM	9		.1	10
WHTZ-FM	880	1.9	7.1	3855
WINS	70	.1	.6	680
WKDM +	21		.2	176
WKJY-FM	64	.1	.5	200
WLIB*	61	.1	.5	219
WLTW-FM	475	1.0	3.8	1325
WMCA	5			74
WNCN-FM	81	.2	.7	139
WNEW			.1	93
WNEW-FM	1339	2.8	10.8	4599
WNSR-FM	514	1.1	4.2	1416
WNYC-FM				44
WQBM-FM	6			198
VOR	20		.2	148
WPAT	82	.2	.7	
WPAT-FM	91			
WPLJ-FM		1.4	5.5	

MON – FRI 3:00PM–7:00PM

Station	AQH PRS (00)	AQH PRS RTG	AQH PRS SHR	CUME PRS (00)
WABC	79	.2	.7	513
WADO +	11		.1	134
WALK-FM	179	.4	1.5	950
WBAB-FM	236	.5	2.0	1182
WBGO-FM	12		.1	171
WBLI-FM	106	.2	.9	692
WBLS-FM	907	1.9	7.7	3537
WCBS	72	.2	.6	611
WCBS-FM	203	.4	1.7	1215
WDHA-FM	191	.4	1.6	813
WDRE-FM	135	.3	1.1	773
WEBE-FM	109	.2	.9	471
WEZN-FM	32	.1	.3	128
WFAN	123	.3	1.0	982
WFME-FM	15		.1	80
WHTZ-FM	1107	2.3	9.4	6407
WINS	97	.2	.8	783
WKDM +	28	.1	.2	77
WKJY-FM	43	.1	.4	259
WLIB*	71	.1	.6	120
WLTW-FM	341	.7	2.9	1403
WMCA	8		.1	99
WNCN-FM	65	.1	.6	202
WNEW	70	.1	.6	257
WNEW-FM	1396	2.9	11.9	6227
WNSR-FM	316	.7	2.7	1483
WNYC-FM	16			

MON – FRI 7:00PM–12:00 MID

Station	AQH PRS (00)	AQH PRS RTG	AQH PRS SHR	CUME PRS (00)
WABC	28	.1	.4	383
WADO +	17		.2	58
WALK-FM	114	.2	1.7	720
WBAB-FM	129	.3	1.9	674
WBGO-FM	6		.1	130
WBLI-FM	46	.1	.7	269
WBLS-FM	569	1.2	8.3	2569
WCBS	68		.6	470
WCBS-FM	125	.3	1.8	700
WDHA-FM	84	.2	1.2	358
WDRE-FM	84	.2	1.2	448
WEBE-FM	12		.2	170
WEZN-FM	4			26
WFAN	135	.3	2.0	1445
WFME-FM	1			10
WHTZ-FM	455	1.0	6.6	2910
WINS	47	.1	.7	465
WKDM +	28	.1	.4	127
WKJY-FM	24		.4	132
WLIB*	14			49
WLTW-FM	172	.4	2.5	914
WMCA	12			31
WNCN-FM	40	.1	.6	141
WNEW	6		.1	29
WNEW-FM	698	1.5	10.2	3792
WNSR-FM	118	.2	1.7	

Source: Copyright 1989 Birch/Scarborough Research Corp. Reprinted by permission.

designated by the notation σ, is known as standard error (introduced in Chapter 4). Standard error must always be considered before interpreting ratings, to determine whether a certain sex/age group has been undersampled or oversampled.

There are numerous approaches to calculating standard error. One of the simpler methods is:

$$SE(p) = \sqrt{\frac{p(100 - p)}{n}}$$

where p = sample percentage or rating, n = sample size, and SE = standard error. For example, suppose a random sample of 1,200 households produces a rating of 20. The standard error can be expressed as follows:

$$SE(p) = \sqrt{\frac{20(100 - 20)}{1,200}}$$

$$= \sqrt{\frac{20(80)}{1,200}}$$

$$= \sqrt{1.33}$$

$$= \pm 1.15$$

The rating of 20 has a standard error of ± 1.15 points, which means the rating actually ranges from 18.85 to 21.15. Standard error formulas are included in all ratings books; Arbitron has simplified the procedure by publishing tables in the back of each book.

Weighting is another procedure used by ratings companies to adjust for samples that are not representative of the population. In some situations a particular sex/age group cannot be adequately sampled, and it becomes imperative that a correction be made.

Assume that population estimates for an ADI/DMA indicate that there are 41,500 men age 18–34 and that this group accounts for 8.3% of the population over the age of 12. The re-searchers distribute diaries to a sample of the ADI/DMA population of which 950 are returned and usable (known as *in-tab* diaries). They would expect about 79 of these to be from men age 18–34 (8.3% of 950). However, they find that only 63 of the diaries are from this demographic group — 16 short of the anticipated number. The data must be weighted to adjust for this deficiency. The weighting formula is:

$$Weight_{sex/group} = \frac{Group\ share\ of\ population}{Group\ share\ of\ sample}$$

In the example, the weighting for men age 18–34 is calculated as:

$$Weight_{MSA\ men,\ 18-34} = \frac{0.083}{0.066}$$

$$= 1.25$$

This figure must be multiplied by the number of persons in the group that each diary would normally represent. That is, instead of representing 525 men (41,500 ÷ 79), each diary would represent 656 men (525 × 1.25). The ideal weighting value is 1.00, indicating that the group was adequately represented in the sample. On occasion, a group may be oversampled, in which case the weighting value will be a number less than 1.00.

Arbitron, Birch and Nielsen all provide detailed explanations of error rates, weighting, and other methodological considerations. Each company includes pages of information in ratings books on how to interpret the data considering different sample sizes and weighting. In reality, however, the vast majority of people who interpret and use broadcast and cable ratings consider the printed numbers as gospel. If they are considered at all, error rates, sample sizes, and other problems are important only when an owner's or manager's station performs poorly in the ratings.

NONRATINGS RESEARCH

Although audience ratings are the most visible research data used in broadcasting, broadcasters, production companies, advertisers, and broadcast consultants use numerous other methodologies. Ratings yield estimates of audience size and composition. Nonratings research provides information about what the audience likes and dislikes, analyses of different types of programming, demographic and lifestyle information about the audience, and much more. All these data are intended to furnish decision makers in the industry with information they can use to eliminate some of the guesswork.

Nonratings research cannot solve all the problems broadcasters face, but it can be used to support decision making. This section describes some of the nonratings research that is conducted in the electronic media.

Nonratings research is important to broadcasters. Steve Berger (1989), president of Nationwide Communications Inc. (a group owner of radio stations), states:

> Most research confirms what most broadcasters already know. However, with the inherent risks in our business, research can become yet another crutch to ease the weight of decision making. Many broadcasters abuse the process by utilizing it to hide from reality and make fuzzier the lines of responsibility.
>
> . . . The ancient philosophers and seers were right when they told us that knowledge does not begin until we know what we don't know. Research is the beginning of the process of discovering "unknowledge."
>
> At Nationwide Communications, we take the "unknowledge" dredged up by research and try to apply it in unusual ways. . . . We use research to confirm or deny our gut feelings and be on the lookout for some feelings we've missed or refused to face.

Berger foresees the future of broadcasting expanding into a variety of areas. He says, "Hopefully, broadcasters will . . . be more interested in the mood a station creates. . . . It will be more necessary than ever to know how people use their radio station(s) and when. . . . In short, we will need to know the exact moods, needs and wants of the largest, hippest and most media assaulted generation ever."

Jim Ehrhorn (1989), operations manager of WSBA-AM in York, Pennsylvania, also perceives a great need for research. He states that

> in the modern world, where the business environment is hyper-competitive, and where the consumer choices are increasing almost exponentially daily, it is no longer wise to base even relatively minor decisions on either experience or intuition.

Ehrhorn, like Steve Berger, sees a need for more exact information: "Research . . . needs to grow to greater and greater levels of sophistication, so that the margin of error, the statistical reliability of the data, and the kinds of data are all of higher quality. . . . Research will have to be able to . . . quantify an emotional experience."

Program Testing

Research has become an accepted step in the development and production of programs and commercials. It is now common practice to test these productions in each of the following stages: initial idea or plan, rough cut, and postproduction. A variety of research approaches can be used in each of these stages, depending on the purpose of the study, how much time is allowed for testing, and what types of decisions will be made with the results. A research director must determine what the decision makers will need to know, and design an analysis to provide that information.

Since major programs and commercials are very expensive to produce, producers and directors are interested in gathering preliminary reactions to a planned project. It would be ludicrous to spend thousands or millions of dollars on a project that would have little audience appeal.

Although most program testing is conducted by major networks, large advertising agencies, and production companies, there is an increasing interest in this area of research at the local level. Stations now test promotional campaigns, prime-time access scheduling, the acceptability of locally produced commercials, and various programming strategies.

One way to collect preliminary data is to show subjects a short statement summarizing a program or commercial and ask them for their opinions about the idea and their willingness to watch the program or buy the product on the basis of the description. The results may provide some indication about the potential success of a show or commercial.

However, program descriptions cannot demonstrate the characters and their relationships to other characters in the program. This can be done only through the program dialogue and the characters' on-screen performance. For example, the NBC-TV program "The Cosby Show" might have been described as follows:

The Cosby Show: A comedy series about the Cliff Huxtable family. Huxtable (Cosby), an obstetrician, and his wife, an attorney, have five children. Each week the program concerns the problems, experiences, and human emotions the Huxtable family faces—with Cosby as ringleader of this typical, yet very comical, middle-class American family.

To many people this statement might seem to describe the type of show generally referred to as a "bomb." However, the indescribable on-screen relationship between Cosby and the other cast members, as well as good story lines, made "The Cosby Show" a hit in 1985. If producers relied totally on program descriptions in testing situations, many successful shows would never reach the air.

If an idea tests well in the preliminary stages (or if the producer or advertiser wishes to go ahead with the project regardless of what the research indicates), a model or simulation is produced. These media "hardware" items are referred to as *rough cuts, storyboards, photomatics, animatics,* or *executions.* The **rough cut** is a simplistic production that usually uses amateur actors, little or no editing, and makeshift sets. The other models are photographs, pictures, or drawings of major scenes designed to give the basic idea of a program or commercial to anyone who looks at them.

Rough cuts or models are tested by companies such as Burke Marketing Research. They do not involve a great deal of production expense, which is especially important if the tests show a lack of acceptance or understanding of the product. The tests provide information about the script, characterizations, character relationships, settings, cinematic approach, and overall appeal. They seldom identify the causes when a program or commercial is found to be unacceptable to the test audience; rather, they provide an overall indication that something is wrong.

When the final product is available, postproduction research can be conducted. Finished products are tested in experimental theaters, in shopping centers (where mobile vans are used to show commercials or programs), at subjects' homes in cities where cable systems provide test channels, or via telephone, in the case of radio commercials. Results from postproduction research often indicate that, for example, the ending of a program is unacceptable and must be reedited or reshot. Many problems that were not foreseen during production may be encountered in postproduction research, and the data usually provide producers with an initial audience reaction to the finished, or partially finished, product.

Each of the major commercial television networks uses its own approach to testing new programs. For example, according to Alan Wurtzel (1989), Senior Vice President of Marketing and Research for ABC, the network does not test program ideas or concepts. Wurtzel believes the approach is inadequate in evaluating a potential program. Instead, ABC begins by testing a completed pilot of the program. This is done by showing the pilot on cable television outlets throughout the country, where viewers are pre-recruited to watch, or by sending viewers video-tapes of the program to view at their leisure. Once a program is on the air, the show is continually tested with various qualitative and quantitative approaches such as focus groups and telephone interviews.

Other companies provide a variety of methods to test commercials or programs. For example, BehaviorScan uses an approach to test commercials as well as new consumer products that operates on cable television systems. It offers the capability to cut in commercials (that is, to replace a regularly scheduled commercial with a test spot) in certain target households. The other households on the cable system view the regular spot. Some time after the airing of the test commercial to the target households, follow-up research is conducted to determine the success of the commercial or the response to a new consumer product.

Nielsen has a similar system called Testsight that began test marketing in Sioux City, South Dakota, in late 1984. A microprocessor called a telemeter is attached to test panel television sets and allows commercials to be cut into normal over-the-air television programs. The telemeter also records viewing activity, much like the standard Nielsen meter. Both BehaviorScan, a system of Chicago-based Information Resources, Inc., and Testsight give test panel households plastic identification cards for use when making purchases at supermarkets or drug stores. The card electronically credits the products purchased by the household members, taking advantage of the UPC bars used in the identification of retail items. The purchasing behavior is then related to television viewing behavior (similar to Arbitron's ScanAmerica).

Music Research

Music is obviously the most important programming element in a music station's schedule. To provide the station's listeners with music they like to hear, and eliminate the songs that listeners don't like or are tired of hearing (*burned out*), radio programmers use a variety of research procedures.

Two of the most widely used music testing procedures are **auditorium music testing** and **call-out research**. Auditorium tests are designed to evaluate *recurrents* (songs that were recently popular) and *oldies* (songs that have been around for years). Call-out research is used to test music on the air (*currents*). New music releases cannot be tested adequately in the auditorium or call-out procedures. If tested at all, new music is oftentimes evaluated on the air during programs titled "Smash or Trash," or something similar, where listeners call in and voice their opinion about new releases.

Auditorium tests and call-out research serve the same purpose: to provide a program director and/or music director with information about the songs that are liked, disliked, burned, or unfamiliar. This information eliminates the gut feeling approach that many radio personnel once used in selecting music for their station.

Both music testing methods involve playing short segments, or hooks, of a number of recordings for the sample of listeners. A **hook** is a 5- to 15-second representative sample of the song—enough for respondents to identify the song if it is already familiar to them and to rate the song on some type of evaluation scale.

Several types of measurement scales are used in music testing research. For example, respondents can be asked to rate a hook on a 5-, 6-, or 7-point scale where 1 represents "hate" and 5 or 7 represents "like a lot" or "favorite." There are also choices of "unfamiliar" and "tired of hearing." Research companies and program directors use a variety of scales for listeners to use in evaluating the music they hear. For example, one type of scale that includes unfamiliar, tired of hearing, and four levels of rating (if the song is familiar) is as follows:

1 = Unfamiliar
2 = Tired of hearing
3 = Hate
4 = Dislike some
5 = Like some
6 = Favorite

Listeners who are not familiar with a hook rate it a 1; those who are familiar with the hook rate it either a 2 for "tired of hearing," or a 3, 4, 5, or 6. Sometimes research companies also ask listeners if they would like radio stations in the area to play the song more, less, or the same amount, but this is a highly inefficient and inaccurate method to determine the frequency with which a song should be played. The reason is that there is no common definition of *more, less,* or *same,* and listeners are extremely poor judges in knowing how often a station currently plays the songs to know whether it's too much or too little.

AUDITORIUM TESTING. In this method between 75 and 200 people are invited to a large room or hall, often a hotel conference room. Subjects are invited to the test because they meet specific requirements determined by the radio station and/or the research company (for example, people between the ages of 25 and 40 who listen to soft rock stations in the client's market). The recruiting of subjects for auditorium testing is generally conducted by a field service company that specializes in recruiting people for focus groups or other similar research

projects. Respondents are generally paid $25–$50 for their cooperation.

The auditorium setting itself — namely, a comfortable location away from distractions at home — enables researchers to test several hundred hooks in one 60- to 90-minute session. Usually between 200 and 400 hooks are tested although some companies routinely test up to 600 hooks in a single session. However, after 400 songs, subject fatigue becomes evident by explicit physical behavior (looking around the room, fidgeting, talking to neighbors), and statistical reliability decreases (standard deviations for song rating grow progressively larger as the number of tested hooks increases). There is definite evidence that summary scores for hooks after the 400 limit are not reliable.

Music testing is designed to test only selections that have been heard for some time. It cannot be used on new releases because people cannot be expected to rate an unfamiliar recording on the basis of a 5- to 15-second hook.

CALL-OUT RESEARCH. The purpose of call-out research is the same as for auditorium testing; only the procedure for collecting the data is changed. Instead of inviting people to a large hall or ballroom, randomly selected or prerecruited subjects are called on the telephone. Subjects are given the same rating instructions as in the auditorium test; they listen to the hook and provide a verbal response to the researcher making the telephone call.

The major limitation to call-out research is that the number of testable hooks is limited to a maximum of about 20, since subject fatigue sets in very quickly over the telephone. Further problems include the distractions that are often present in the home, and the frequently poor quality of sound transmission created by the telephone equipment (the auditorium setting allows subjects to hear the hooks in quality stereo sound).

Even with such limitations, call-out research is used by many radio stations throughout the country. Since call-out research is fairly inexpensive when compared to the auditorium method, the research can be conducted on a continual basis to track the performance of songs in a particular market. Auditorium research, which can cost from $10,000–$100,000 to test approximately 800 songs, is generally conducted only once or twice per year.

Programming Research and Consulting

Some of the largest research companies are The Research Group, Paragon Research, Frank N. Magid Associates, and Strategic Research. Although each research company specializes in specific areas of broadcasting and uses different research procedures, they have a common goal: to provide broadcast management with data to be used in decision making. These companies offer custom research in almost any area of broadcasting, from testing call letters and slogans to air talent, commercials, music, importance of news programs, and the overall sound or look of a station.

Broadcast consultants are equally versatile. Most consultants have experience in broadcasting and offer their services to radio and television stations and cable outlets throughout the country. In some cases their recommendations are based on research, and in some, their suggestions are based on experience in the field. The task of a consultant is probably best described by a real consultant. E. Karl (1989), a well-known and respected radio consultant, was asked to describe what a consultant does for a radio station. He states:

> A consultant works with research data to help plan a strategy for a station. A consultant puts [research] information into a package that will position the station correctly in listeners' minds, and he or she helps market the station to bring listeners in to try out the station . . . from designing music rotations, creating "clock hours" on the station, and selecting air talent . . . to developing

television commercials to advertise the station, executing direct marketing campaigns to ask listeners to listen, to working with the station staff to make sure the "promise" of the station's position stays on track.

Alan Burns (1989), another well-known and respected radio programming consultant, also sees his role as encompassing several areas. Burns says that

> programming consultants need to be able to function in three separate roles: as a student, a teacher, and an innovator. As a student . . . a consultant must observe and learn from programming, ratings, demographics, marketing, and . . . the history [of broadcasting]. As a teacher, the consultant must be able to synthesize . . . information into a body of knowledge that can be passed on to radio stations in a useful fashion. The "innovative" consultant is called upon to help create solutions for new problems, better solutions for recurring problems, and new solutions for old problems.

Performer Q

Producers and directors in broadcasting naturally desire an indication of the popularity of various performers and entertainers. A basic question in the planning stage of any program is "What performer or group of performers should be used to give the show the greatest appeal?" Not unreasonably, producers prefer using the most popular and likable performers in the industry to taking a chance on an unknown entertainer.

Marketing Evaluations, Inc., of Port Washington, New York, meets the demand for information about performers, entertainers, and personalities. The company conducts nationwide telephone surveys using three panels of about 1,250 households and interviewing about 5,400 people 6 years of age and older. The surveys are divided into three sections, Performer Q, Target

Audience Rankings, and Demographic Profiles. The Performer Q portion of the analysis provides Familiarity and Appeal scores for more than 1,000 different personalities. The Target Audience Rankings provide a rank-order list of all personalities for several different target audiences, such as women 18–49. The target rank tells producers and directors which personalities appeal to specific demographic groups. In the third section, each personality is listed according to eight demographic profiles of the survey respondents. This section indicates the types of people that do and do not like the personalities in the survey.

Focus Groups

The focus group, discussed in Chapter 7, is a standard procedure in electronic media research, probably due to its versatility. Focus groups are used to develop questionnaires for further research and to provide preliminary information on a variety of topics, such as format and programming changes, personalities, station images, and lifestyle characteristics of the audience. Data in the last category are particularly useful when the focus group consists of a specific demographic segment.

Miscellaneous Research

Broadcast stations are unique and require different types of research. Research conducted by and for stations includes the following.

1. *Station image.* It is important for a station's management to know how the public perceives the station and its services; hence, "station image" has been mentioned throughout this chapter. Public misperception of management's purpose can create a decrease in audience size and, consequently, in advertising revenue. For example, suppose a radio station that has aired Top 40 music for 10 years switches to a country format. It is important that the audience and advertisers be aware of this change and have a

chance to voice their opinions. This can be accomplished through a station image study, in which respondents to telephone calls are asked questions such as: "What type of music does radio station WAAA play?" "What types of people do you think listen to WAAA radio?" and "Did you know that WAAA now plays country music?" If the research reveals that few people are aware of the change in format, management can develop a new promotion strategy. Or, the station might find that the current promotional efforts have been successful and should not be changed.

Station image studies are conducted periodically by most larger stations to maintain current information on how the audience perceives each station in the market. If station managers are to provide the services that listeners and viewers want, they must keep up to date with audience trends and social changes.

2. *Advertiser (account) analysis.* To increase the value of their service to advertisers, many stations administer questionnaires to local business executives. Some typical questions include: "When did your business open?" "How many people own this business?" "How much do you invest in advertising per year?" "When are advertising purchase decisions made?" and "What do you expect from your advertising?" Information obtained from client questionnaires is used to help write more effective advertising copy, to develop better advertising proposals, and to allow the sales staff to know more about each client. Generally, the questionnaires are administered before a business becomes an advertiser on the station, but they can also be used for advertisers who have done business with the station for several years.

3. *Account executive research.* Radio and television station managers throughout the country conduct surveys of advertising agency personnel, usually buyers, to determine how their sales executives are perceived. It is vitally important to know how the sales people are received by the buyers. The results of the survey

indicate which sales people are performing very well and which ones may need additional help. Many times a survey discloses that a problem between a sales executive and a buyer is purely a personality difference, and the station can easily correct the problem by assigning another sales person to the advertising agency.

4. *Sales research.* In an effort to increase sales, many stations themselves conduct research for local clients. For example, a station may conduct a "banking image" study of all banks in the area to determine how residents perceive each bank and the service it provides. The results from such a study are then used in an advertising proposal for the banks in the area. If it is discovered that First National Bank's 24-hour automatic teller service is not well understood by local residents, for example, the station might develop an advertising proposal to concentrate on this point.

5. *Diversification analyses.* The goals of any business are to expand and to achieve higher profits. In an effort to reach these goals, most larger stations, partnerships, and companies engage in a variety of studies to determine where investments should be made. Should other stations be purchased? What other types of activity should the business invest in? Such studies are used for forecasting and represent a major portion of the research undertaken by larger stations and companies. The changes in broadcast ownership rules made by the FCC have significantly increased the level of acquisition research conducted by individuals, group owners, and other large companies in the broadcasting industry.

6. *Qualitative research.* Several companies offer television program evaluations that go beyond the typical ratings and shares provided by Arbitron and Nielsen. For example, Roger Percy developed a system called Vox Box, an electronic system that allowed viewers to rate programs and commercials as they watched. Percy has since redesigned his system to include not only people meter data and reactions toward programming, but heat sensing devices to determine the number of people actually in the viewing room and additional messages on the screen to remind viewers to respond.

THE FUTURE OF ELECTRONIC MEDIA RESEARCH

Trying to predict the future is no simple task. Certain trends in electronic media research are clear, but long-range predictions must be tenuous because the media change so rapidly. This section discusses some significant topics that have or will have an effect in the research area.

The high degree of audience segmentation created in radio during the 1980s has in turn created extreme competition for radio listeners. Not even the most established stations in the country can continue to rely on tried-and-true methods of the past. Radio listeners are fickle and change their tastes and demands very quickly. Radio managers need to be able to respond with equal speed to keep up with trends and new directions. Their responses have been, and will continue to be (even with more regularity), guided by audience research. For anyone involved in broadcast research, the recent increase in the importance and the sophistication of radio research has been easy to see, and there is no indication that research will become less important in the years to come. Station image studies, music research, personality testing, and general marketing analyses have become commonplace even for radio stations in small markets throughout the country.

In the late 1980s, radio research began using a variety of multivariate statistical procedures to investigate listeners. Two of the most popular methods used are cluster analysis and multidimensional scaling (Appendix 2). These methods have helped radio managers better understand their available audience and determine the positive characteristics of popular radio stations.

The use of multivariate statistics will continue in the 1990s. However, in addition to collecting the typical data used by radio managers (how many listen, when do they listen, and so on), radio research will begin to focus more on the psychology of radio listening. Some of the questions that will be addressed include: What types of moods are listeners in when they select one station over another? What types of feelings do specific radio stations develop when listeners tune in? Do certain types of music segments create unique moods or feelings? How can radio stations create a more enjoyable atmosphere for listeners so they will stay tuned in longer?

Another significant area of radio research in the 1990s will concentrate on the importance of "shock jocks," or announcers (particularly in morning shows) who concentrate on blue humor, off-color jokes, and sexual comments and innuendos. The trend seems to be away from this type of entertainment, and research in the 1990s will more than likely focus heavily on this issue to determine if these types of morning shows help or hinder a radio station's overall performance.

Finally, the 1990s will see additional research on the methods of collecting audience ratings. Is there a better way to collect audience ratings? Are diaries completely inadequate? Is there an electronic device that could solve the problem?

Television offers an even more confusing picture than radio. The decade of the 1970s provided the stepping-stone to the future of television as new technologies paved the way for what was and is to come: direct broadcast satellite transmission; multitiered cable television operations; video games; videotape recorders; videodiscs; television component systems; multiple-use television sets that double as security systems, telephone extensions, and so forth; and multiple-screen sets, which allow viewing of several channels simultaneously.

Some of the questions about television and cable that will be addressed in the 1990s include: Are people meters accurate? How can the systems be improved to provide more valid and reliable data? What kinds of programming will

attract more viewers to commercial television instead of the variety of cable services offered? What types of programming keep viewers most interested? Will VCRs be used more than they are now? What types of programming do viewers want to have on videocassettes? In what other ways can television be used? What types of commercials are most successful in communicating messages to viewers? Are 10-second commercials better than 30-second commercials? Are "soft sell" commercials more effective than "hard sell"? And of course, there will be a continual pursuit of trying to discover what effects television has on viewers, especially children.

Arbitron and Nielsen will work to refine single-source data methods. Electronic meters will become more sophisticated, and these data will be combined with data collected from other sources. One of the major problems that must be solved is how to insure that people meter data are accurate. Recall from earlier in the chapter that people meters have been questioned because many viewers fail to record their presence or absence in front of the television set.

However, this problem may be solved in the early 1990s. Researchers at the David Sarnoff Research Center in Princeton, New Jersey, have developed a system for Nielsen that may eventually solve the people meter problem. The new system, called *smart sensing*, is a sophisticated computer image-recognition system that photographically recognizes viewers who are watching television in a home. According to Hawkins (1990):

> The smart sensing technology will make future Nielsen home installations passive—capable of automatically recognizing family members and combining that information with the time and selected TV channel. . . . The Nielsen box identifies you by matching the characteristics of the faces it has stored in memory.

The smart sensing system offers the possibility of solving current people meter problems.

However, it is possible that viewers may refuse to accept the system in their homes because it is too intrusive, too much like "Big Brother."

The list could continue for several pages. The main point is that many questions need investigation. The electronic media can be a literal gold mine for researchers in search of questions.

S U M M A R Y

This chapter has introduced some of the more common methodologies used in broadcast research. Ratings are the most visible form of research used in broadcasting as well as the most influential in the decision-making process. However, nonratings approaches such as focus groups, music research, image studies, and program testing are all used frequently to collect data. The importance of research is fueled by an ever-increasing desire by management to learn more about broadcast audiences and their uses of the media.

The phenomenon of audience fragmentation has become evident during the past several years. All media now attract smaller, much more narrowly defined groups of people. This competition for viewers and listeners has created a need for research data. Broadcast owners and managers realize now that they can no longer rely on gut feelings when making programming, sales, and marketing decisions. The discussions in this chapter have been designed to emphasize the importance of research in all areas of broadcasting.

Questions and Problems for Further Investigation

1. Assume that a local television market has three stations: Channel 2, Channel 7, and Channel 9. There are 200,000 television households in the market. A ratings company samples 1,200 households at random and finds that 25% of the sample is watching Channel 2, 15% Channel 7, and 10% Channel 9.
   a. Calculate each station's share of the audience.
   b. Project the total number of households in the population watching each channel.
   c. Calculate the CPM for a $1,000, 30-second spot on Channel 2.
   d. Calculate the standard error involved in Channel 2's rating.

2. What are the major data-gathering problems associated with: (a) electronic meters, (b) diaries, (c) telephone interviews, and (d) people meters?

3. Examine a recent Arbitron market radio ratings book. Select a station and a daypart and find that station's: (a) AQH, (b) cume, and (c) turnover.

4. Perform your own music call-out research. Edit several 15-second selections of recordings on a reel or cassette and ask people to rate them on a 7-point scale. Compute means and standard deviations for the results. What can you conclude?

5. Several questions relevant to modern broadcasting trends are listed at the end of the chapter. What type or types of research methods could be used to try to answer these questions?

References and Suggested Readings

Arbitron Ratings Company. (1989). *Description of methodology*. Arbitron Ratings Company.

Berger, S. (1989). Personal correspondence sent to Roger Wimmer.

Beville, H. M. (1988). *Audience ratings: Radio, television, cable* (rev. ed.). Hillsdale, NJ: Lawrence Erlbaum.

Birch Radio. (1989a). *The Birch method of measurement and processing environment*. Birch Research Corporation.

Birch Radio. (1989b). *How Birch measures radio: The complete Birch radio sourcebook*. Birch Research Corporation.

Birch, T. (1989). Anatomy of the Birch radio telephone interview. *Radio & Records, 818,* 30.

Burns, A. (1989). Personal correspondence sent to Roger Wimmer.

Cabletelevision Advertising Bureau. *Telephone coincidental guidelines*. New York: Cabletelevision Advertising Bureau.

Donion, B. (1989, December 14). Glitches in Nielsen's system. *USA Today*, p. 3D.

Ehrhorn, J. (1989). Personal correspondence sent to Roger Wimmer.

Hawkins, W. J. (1990, February). TV views viewers. *Popular Science*, pp. 74–75 + .

Karl, E. (1989). Personal correspondence sent to Roger Wimmer.

McKenna, W. J. (1989). People meters: The search for tomorrow. *Journal of Advertising Research, 29*(4), RC–6–7.

Nielsen, A. C. (1988). *Reference supplement: Nielsen station index*. Nielsen Media Research.

Nielsen, A. C. (1989). *Reference supplement: Nielsen television index*. Nielsen Media Research.

Wurtzel, A. (1989). Telephone conversation with Roger Wimmer.

CHAPTER 15

RESEARCH IN ADVERTISING AND PUBLIC RELATIONS

F or many years, research was not widely used in advertising and public relations; decisions were made on a more or less intuitive basis. However, with increased competition, mass markets, and mounting costs, more and more advertisers and public relations specialists have come to rely on research as a basic management tool.

Much of the research in advertising and public relations is **applied research**, which attempts to solve a specific problem and is not concerned with theorizing or generalizing to other situations. Advertising and public relations researchers want to answer questions such as: "Should a certain product be packaged in blue or red?" Is *Cosmopolitan* a better advertising buy than *Vogue*?" and "Should a company stress its minority hiring program in a planned publicity campaign?"

Advertising and public relations research does not involve any special techniques; the methods discussed earlier—laboratory, survey, field research, and content analysis—are in common use. They have been adapted, however, to provide specific types of information that meet the needs of these industries.

This chapter discusses the more common areas of advertising and public relations research and the types of studies they entail. In describing these research studies, the primary aim is to convey the facts the reader must know to understand the methods and to use them intelligently. A significant portion of the research in these areas involves market studies conducted by commercial research firms; these studies form the basis for much of the more specific research that follows in either the academic or the private sector. The importance of market research notwithstanding, this chapter does not have the space required to treat this topic. Readers who desire additional information about market research techniques should consult Tull and Hawkins (1987) and Boyd, Westfall, and Stasch (1989).

There are three functional research areas in advertising: copy research, media research, and campaign assessment research. Each is discussed in turn, and the syndicated research available in each case is described when appropriate.

COPY TESTING

Everyone who does advertising research agrees that the term *copy testing* is misleading. The word *copy* implies that only the words in the ad are tested. This, of course, is not the case: every element in an ad (layout, narration, music, illustration, size, length, and so on) is a possible variable in copy testing. Leckenby (1984) has suggested that *advertising stimulus measurement and research* (ASMAR) be substituted for *copy testing*, but the new term has not gained wide usage. Likewise, the term *message research* is a less frequently used synonym. Thus we will continue to use the traditional term, despite its shortcomings.

Copy testing refers to that research that helps develop effective advertisements and determines which of several advertisements is the most effective. Copy testing takes place at every stage of the advertising process. Before a campaign starts, it is used to determine what to stress and what to avoid. Once the content of the ad has been established, tests must be performed to ascertain the most effective way to structure these ideas. For example, in studying

311

the illustration copy of a proposed magazine spread, a researcher might show to two or more groups of subjects an illustration of the product photographed from different angles. The headline might be evaluated by having potential users rate the typefaces used in several versions of the ad. The copy might be tested for readability and recall. In all cases, the aim is to determine whether the variable tested significantly affects the recall of the ad.

In TV, a rough cut of an entire commercial might be produced. The rough cut is a filmed or taped version of the ad in which amateur actors are used, locations are simplified, and the editing and narration lack the smoothness characteristic of broadcast (final cut) commercials. In this way, variations in the ad can be tested without incurring great expense.

The final phase of copy testing, which occurs after the finished commercials have appeared, serves to determine whether the campaign is having the desired effects. Any negative or unintended effects can be corrected before serious damage is done to a company's sales or reputation. This type of copy testing requires precisely defined goals. Some campaigns, for example, are designed to draw customers away from competitors; others are conducted for the purpose of retaining a company's present customers. Still others are intended to enhance the image of a firm and may not be concerned with consumers' purchase preferences. As will be discussed later, this type of copy testing blends in with campaign assessment research.

There are several different ways to categorize copy testing methods. Perhaps the most useful, summarized by Leckenby and Wedding (1982), suggests that there are appropriate copy testing methods for each of the three dimensions of impact in the persuasion process. Although, as represented in Table 15.1, the model seems to suggest a linear process starting with the cognitive dimension (knowing) through the affective dimension (feeling) to the conative dimension

---

TABLE 15.1 TYPOLOGY OF COPY TESTING EFFECTS

Dimension of impact	Typical dependent variables	Professional firms conducting research that exemplifies area
Cognitive	Attention Exposure Awareness Recognition Comprehension Recall	Burke Marketing Research (DAR) Gallup & Robinson (MIRS) Starch INRA Hooper
Affective	Attitude change Liking/disliking Involvement	Gallup & Robinson SAMI-BURKE Various firms (physiological measures)
Conative	Intention to buy Purchase behavior	AdTel Nielsen ASI (pre/post intention to buy)

(doing), it is not necessary for the steps to take place in this order. In any event, the model does serve as a convenient guide for discussing copy research testing methods.

The Cognitive Dimension

Turning first to the cognitive dimension, the key dependent variables are attention, awareness, exposure, recognition, comprehension, and recall. Studies that measure attention to advertising can use various methods. One strategy involves a consumer jury. A group of 50 to 100 consumers are shown test ads and then asked which ad was best at catching their attention. A physiological measurement technique, known as an eye tracking study, is also used to determine what parts of an ad are noticed. An eye camera is a device that records the movement of the eye as it scans printed and graphic material. By analyzing the path that the eye follows, researchers can determine what parts of the ad attracted initial attention.

A tachistoscope (or T-scope) is one way to measure recognition of an ad. The T-scope is actually a slide projector with adjustable levels of illumination and with projection speeds that can be adjusted down to a tiny fraction of a second. Ads are tested to determine how long it takes a consumer to recognize the product, the headline, or the brand name.

Ad comprehension is an important factor in advertising research. One study found that all 60 commercials used in a given test were mis-comprehended by viewers (Jacoby & Hofer, 1982). To guard against results such as these, advertising researchers typically test new ads with focus groups (Chapter 7) to make sure their message is getting across as intended. The T-scope is also used to see how long it takes subjects to comprehend the theme of an ad — an important consideration for outdoor advertising where drivers may have only a second or two of exposure.

Awareness, exposure, and recall are determined by several related methods. One measurement technique that taps these variables is used primarily by the print media: subjects are shown a copy of a newspaper or magazine and are asked which advertisements they remember seeing or reading. The results are used to tabulate a "reader traffic score" for each ad. This method is prone to criticism, however, because some respondents confuse the advertisements or the publications in which they were seen, and some try to please the interviewer by reporting that they saw more than they actually did. To control this problem, researchers often make use of aided recall techniques; for instance, they might also show the respondent a list of advertisers, some of whose advertisements actually appeared in the publication and some whose did not.

For obvious reasons, this type of **recall study** is not entirely suitable for radio and television commercials; a more commonly used method in such cases is the telephone survey. Two variations of this approach are sometimes used. In *aided recall*, the interviewer mentions a general class of product and asks whether the respondent remembers an ad for a specific brand. A typical question might be "Have you seen any ads for soft drinks lately?" In the *unaided recall technique*, researchers ask a general question such as "Have you seen any ads that interested you lately?" Obviously, it is harder for the consumer to respond to the second type of question. Only truly memorable ads score high on this form of measurement.

Perhaps a better understanding can be gained by examining the several research companies that offer syndicated services in this area. For example, Burke Marketing offers day-after recall (DAR) testing to measure the effectiveness of TV commercials.

Burke has the capacity to test recall of commercials by consumers in more than 30 cities, although typically only three to five are used in a single test. On the day after the commercial is run, the Burke interviewers conduct a telephone survey to obtain a sample of about 200 people, all of whom have watched the program that contained the commercial. These individuals are asked whether they remember seeing the commercial and, if so, what details they can remember about it. Over the years, Burke has compiled data on numerous commercials and has computed average scores for recall; the scores (called "Burkes") of the commercials that the firm now tests can be considered in light of these norms, thus providing the advertiser with a benchmark for comparison.

Another method of posttesting television commercials is the In-View service provided by Gallup & Robinson. Like Burke, Gallup & Robinson measure the percentages of respondents who remember seeing the commercial and of those who can remember specific points. Additionally, they provide a score indicating the degree of favorable attitude toward the product, based on positive statements made by the subjects during the interview.

Gallup & Robinson also conduct pretests and posttests of magazine advertisements. Their Magazine Impact Research Service (MIRS) measures recall of advertisements appearing in general-interest magazines. Copies of a particular issue containing the advertisement under study are mailed to approximately 150 readers. (In the case of a pretest, the MIRS binds the proposed advertisement into each magazine.) The day after delivery of the magazines, respondents are telephoned and asked which advertisements they noticed in the magazine and what details they can remember about them. These results are reported to the advertiser.

One of the best-known professional research firms is the Starch Readership Report, which conducts posttest recall research. Starch INRA Hooper, Inc., routinely measures advertising readership in more than 100 magazines and newspapers. Using a sample of approximately 300 people, Starch interviewers take a copy of the periodical under study to respondents' homes. If a subject has already looked through that particular publication, he or she is questioned at length. The interviewer shows the respondent an advertisement and asks whether he or she has seen or read any part of it. If the answer is no, the interviewer moves on to another advertisement; if the answer is yes, more questions are asked to determine how much was read. This procedure continues until the respondent has been questioned about every advertisement in that issue up to 100 (at which point the interview is terminated to avoid subject fatigue). Starch places each respondent into one of four categories for each advertisement:

1. *Nonreader* (did not recall seeing the advertisement)
2. *Noted reader* (remembered seeing the advertisement)
3. *Associated reader* (not only saw the advertisement but also read some part of it that clearly indicated the brand name)
4. *Read most reader* (read more than half the written material in the advertisement)

The Starch organization reports the findings of its recall studies in a novel manner. Advertisers are given a copy of the magazine in which readership scores printed on yellow stickers have been attached to each advertisement. Figure 15.1 is an example of a "Starched" advertisement.

The Starch Readership Report provides a measurement of recognition only; for an indication of an advertisement's success in getting its message across, advertisers can request a Starch Reader Impression Study. Such studies also involve in-depth interviews with readers; those who have seen an advertisement in a particular newspaper or magazine are asked a series of detailed questions about it, such as:

1. "In your own words, what did this ad tell you about the product?"
2. "What did the pictures tell you?"
3. "What did the written material tell you?"

FIGURE 15.1 A ''STARCHED'' AD

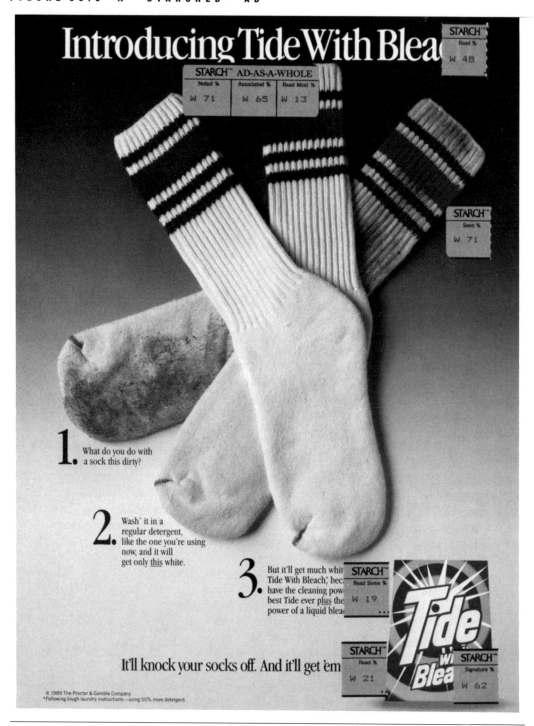

Source: Starch INRA Hooper, Inc. Readership Report of *Southern Living*, October, 1989, p. 129. Reprinted by permission.

The responses are subjected to content analysis, and the results are summarized for clients. Additionally, Starch reports the percentage of favorable and unfavorable comments about each advertisement.

The Affective Dimension

The affective dimension usually involves research into whether a consumer's attitudes toward a particular product have changed because of exposure to an ad or a campaign. Techniques used to study the affective component include projective tests, theater testing, physiological measures, semantic differential scales, and rating scales. Projective tests provide an alternative to the straightforward "Do you like this ad?" approach. Instead, respondents are asked to draw a picture or complete a story that involves the ad or the product mentioned in the ad. Analysis of these responses provides additional insight and depth into the consumer's feelings.

Theater tests involve bringing an audience to a special facility where they are shown television commercials that are imbedded in a TV show. Respondents are given electronic response indicators that allow them to rate instantaneously each commercial they see. The recent trend has been to make theater tests more portable. Specially equipped vans parked outside shopping malls are now filling in for theaters.

Two physiological tests are commonly used in this area. In the *pupillometer test*, a tiny camera, focused on the subject's eye, measures the amount of pupil dilation that occurs while the person is looking at an ad. Changes in pupil diameter are recorded, because findings from psychophysiology suggest that people tend to respond to appealing stimuli with dilation (enlargement) of their pupils. Conversely, when unappealing, disagreeable stimuli are shown, the pupil narrows. The second test measures galvanic skin response, or *GSR* (that is, changes in the electrical conductance of the surface of the skin). A change in GSR rating while the subject is looking at an ad is taken to signify emotional involvement or arousal.

Semantic differential scales and rating scales (Chapter 3) are most often used to measure attitude change. For these measurements to be most useful, it is necessary to accomplish three things. First, a picture of the consumer's attitudes before exposure to the ad should be obtained. Second, the consumer must be exposed to the ad or ads under examination, and third, the attitudes must be remeasured after exposure. To diminish the difficulties associated with achieving all three of these goals in testing television ads, many researchers prefer a **forced-exposure** method. In this technique, respondents are invited to a theater for a special screening of a TV program. Before viewing the program, they are asked to fill out questionnaires concerning their attitudes toward several different products, one of which is of interest to the researchers. Next, everyone watches the TV show, which contains one or more commercials for the product under investigation as well as ads for other products. When the show is over, all respondents again fill out the questionnaire concerning product attitudes. Change in evaluation is the key variable of interest. The same basic method can be used in testing attitudes toward print ads except that the testing is done individually, in each respondent's home. Typically, a consumer is interviewed about product attitudes, a copy of a magazine that includes the test ad (or ads) is left at the house, and the respondent is asked to read or look through the publication before the next interview. A short time later, the interviewer calls back the respondent and asks whether the magazine has been read. If it has, product attitudes are once again measured.

Several research companies offer services designed to measure attitudes. As part of their In-View service, Gallup & Robinson test attitude change by calling eligible respondents and inviting them to participate in the viewing of a test program. During this call, the interviewer records attitudes about six products, three of which will be advertised on the test show. Comparison data are collected from nonviewers of the program. After the program is viewed, respondents are called back and are asked the same attitude questions. Changes in attitude are presumed to be the result of viewing the commercial. The SAMI-Burke company offers a similar service. In magazine measurement, Gallup & Robinson construct a special issue of a magazine containing the ads under consideration. Respondents are randomly selected from the phone book, visited at home, and given a copy of the magazine. The next day, to establish readership, respondents are asked questions about the magazine's contents. The interviewer next reads a list of products and asks whether the magazine contained ads for each product. Each time that a respondent remembers seeing a product ad, the interviewer asks for a description of the ad, as well as the respondent's attitudes toward the product after reading the ad.

The Conative Dimension

The conative dimension deals with actual consumer behavior and, in many instances, it is the most pertinent of all dependent variables. The two main categories of behavior that are usually measured are buying predisposition and actual purchase behavior. In the first category, the usual design is to gather precampaign predisposition data and reinterview the subjects after the advertising has been in place. Subjects are typically asked a question along these lines: "If you were going shopping tomorrow to buy breakfast cereal, which brand would you buy?" This might be followed by: "Would you consider buying any other brands?" and "Are there any cereals you would definitely not buy?" (The last question is included to determine whether the advertising campaign has had any negative effects.) Additionally, some researchers (Haskins, 1976) suggest using a buying intention scale and instructing respondents to check the one position on the scale that best fits their intention. Such a scale might look like this:

_____ I'll definitely buy this cereal as soon as I can.

_____ I'll probably buy this cereal sometime.

_____ I might buy this cereal, but I don't know when.

_____ I'll probably never buy this cereal.

_____ I wouldn't eat this cereal even if somebody gave it to me.

The scale allows advertisers to see how consumers' buying preferences change during and after the campaign.

Perhaps the most reliable methods of posttesting are those that measure actual sales, direct response, and other easily quantifiable behavior patterns. In the print media, direct response might be measured by inserting a coupon that readers might mail in for a free sample. Different forms of an ad might be run in different publications to determine which elicits the most inquiries. Another alternative suitable for use in both print and electronic media advertising consists of including an 800 toll free number that can be called for more information or to actually order the product.

Some research companies measure direct response by means of a laboratory store. Usually used in conjunction with theater testing, this technique involves giving people chits with which they can buy products in a special store (most of the time this is a special trailer furnished to look like a store). They are then shown a program containing some test commercials, given more chits, and allowed to shop again. Changes in preexposure and postexposure choices are recorded.

Actual sales data can be obtained in many ways. They can be obtained directly by asking consumers "What brand of breakfast cereal did you most recently purchase?" However, the findings would be subject to error due to faulty recall, courtesy bias, and so forth; for this reason, more direct methods are generally preferred. If enough time and money are available, direct observation of people's selections in the cereal aisles at a sample of supermarkets can be a useful source of data. Store audits that list the total number of boxes sold at predetermined times are another possibility. Last, and possibly most expensive, is the household audit technique, whereby an interviewer visits the homes of a sample of consumers and actually inspects their kitchen cupboards to see what brands of cereals are there. In addition to the audit, a traditional questionnaire is used to gather further information about the respondent's feelings toward the commercials.

Many professional research firms conduct surveys that deal with purchasing behavior. One such firm, the AdTel Company, a subsidiary of Burke, uses special cable television facilities to test the effectiveness of commercials. The AdTel cable system, which is operated in three separate communities, is designed to carry two signals per channel, so that a household can receive either the A signal or the B signal. The households in these communities are grouped according to key demographic variables, and one group is connected to the A signal and the other to the B signal (the subscribers themselves do not know which channel they are receiving). The A households receive one version of the commercial being tested, while the B group receives either a different version or no commercial. About 1,000 families in each group record the products and services that they purchase by keeping diaries or using electronic scanners that read the Universal Product Codes (UPCs) on the products. The effectiveness of a commercial or campaign is judged by examining the purchasing behavior of the families in each group, as reflected in their records. Measurement bias is eliminated because the families do not realize the connection between their records and their television viewing. The AdTel system also has the advantage of measuring actual purchasing behavior as the dependent variable.

A. C. Nielsen Company uses advanced computer technology to monitor the viewing behavior of 2,500 households. The research company can also electronically cut in test commercials without viewers being aware that something different is being inserted. A tiny device attached to the TV set allows the set to accept these test commercials and to store viewing data for later retrieval. At the supermarket, members of Nielsen's sample present an ID card, and through the use of the UPC all their purchases are electronically recorded and tabulated. Thus, clients are able to monitor actual buying behavior changes in response to test commercials.

Nielsen also offers a Scantrack service that monitors the TV viewing behavior of a panel of households whose members also have their purchases recorded via electronic scanner. Information Resources Inc. (IRI) has a similar service called Infoscan and the Arbitron Ratings Company has recently started a third such service called ScanAmerica.

In the print area, ASI-Market Research, Inc., uses a less expensive technique that measures pseudo-purchase behavior. A test magazine containing the client's ad is left at the house. The respondent is asked to read the magazine, is told there will be a prize for participation, and is asked which brands would be preferred if he or she is a grand prize winner. After the test ads have been looked at, the respondent is again asked about prize preferences. Changes in pre- and postexposure scores are carefully noted.

MEDIA RESEARCH

The two key terms in media research are **reach** and **frequency**. Reach is the total number of households that will be exposed to a message in a particular medium at least once over a certain period of time (usually 4 weeks). Reach can be thought of as the cumulative audience and is usually expressed as a percentage of the total universe of households that have been exposed. For example, if 25 of a possible 100 households are exposed to a message, the reach is 25%. Frequency refers to the number of exposures to the same message that each household receives. Of course, not every household in the sample will receive exactly the same number of messages. Consequently, advertisers prefer to use the average frequency of exposure, expressed by the formula:

$$\frac{\text{Total exposures for all households}}{\text{Reach}} = \text{Average frequency}$$

Thus, if the total number of exposures for a sample of households is 400 and the reach is 25, the average frequency is 16. In other words, the average household was exposed 16 times. Notice that if the reach were 80%, the frequency would be 5. As reach increases, average frequency drops. (Maximizing both reach and frequency would require an unlimited budget, something most advertisers lack.)

A concept closely related to reach and frequency is gross rating points (GRPs), introduced in Chapter 14. GRPs are useful when it comes to deciding between two media alternatives. For example, suppose Program A has a reach of 30% and an average frequency of 2.5 whereas Program B has a reach of 45% and a frequency of 1.25. Which program offers a better reach–frequency relationship? First, determine the GRPs of each program using the following formula:

$$\text{GRPs} = \text{Reach} \times \text{Average frequency}$$

For A:

$$\text{GRPs} = 30 \times 2.5 = 75.00$$

For B:

$$\text{GRPs} = 45 \times 1.25 = 56.25$$

Program A scores better in the reach–frequency combination, and this would probably be a factor in deciding which was the better buy.

Media research falls into three general categories: studies of the size and composition of an audience of a particular medium or media (reach studies), studies of the relative efficiency of advertising exposures provided by various combinations of media (reach and frequency studies), and studies of the advertising activities of competitors.

Audience Size and Composition

Analyses of audiences are probably the most commonly used advertising studies in print and electronic media research. Since advertisers spend large amounts of money in the print and electronic media, they have an understandable interest in the audiences for those messages. In most cases, audience information is gathered using techniques that are compromises between the practical and the ideal.

The audience size of a newspaper or magazine is commonly measured in terms of the number of copies distributed per issue. This number, which is called the publication's **circulation**, includes all copies delivered to subscribers as well as those bought at newsstands or from other sellers. Because a publication's advertising rate is directly determined by its circulation, the print media have developed a standardized method of measuring circulation and have instituted an organization, the Audit Bureau of Circulations (ABC), to verify that a publication actually distributes the number of copies per issue that it claims. (The specific procedures used by the ABC are discussed later in this chapter.)

Circulation figures are used to compute the CPMs of various publications. For example, suppose Newspaper X charges $1,800 for an advertisement and has an ABC-verified circulation of 180,000; Newspaper Y, with a circulation of 300,000, charges $2,700 for the same size space.

TABLE 15.2   DETERMINING ADVERTISING EFFICIENCY FROM AD COST AND CIRCULATION DATA

	Newspaper X	Newspaper Y
Ad cost	$1,800	$2,700
Circulation	180,000	300,000
Cost per thousand circulated copies	$\dfrac{\$1,800}{180} = \$10.00$	$\dfrac{\$2,700}{300} = \$9.00$

Table 15.2 shows that Newspaper Y is the more efficient advertising vehicle.

Note that this method considers only the number of circulated copies of a newspaper or magazine. This information is useful, but it does not necessarily indicate the total number of readers of the publication. To estimate the total audience, the circulation figure must be multiplied by the average number of readers of each copy of an issue. This information is obtained by performing audience surveys.

A preliminary step in conducting such surveys is to operationally define the concept *magazine reader* or *newspaper reader*. There are many possible definitions, but the one most commonly used is fairly liberal: a *reader* is a person who has read or at least looked through an issue.

Three techniques are used to measure readership. The most rigorous is the unaided recall method, in which respondents are asked whether they have read any newspapers or magazines in the past month (or other time period). If the answer is yes, subjects are asked to specify the magazines or newspapers they read. When a publication is named, the interviewer attempts to verify reading by asking questions about the contents of that publication. The reliability of the unaided recall method is open to question (as has been discussed) because of the difficulty respondents often have in recalling specific content.

A second technique involves aided recall. In this method, the interviewer names several publications and asks whether the respondent has read any of them lately. Each time the respondent claims to have read a publication, the interviewer asks whether he or she remembers seeing the most recent copy. The interviewer may jog a respondent's memory by describing the front page or the cover. Finally, the respondent is asked to recall anything that was seen or read in that particular issue. (In a variation on this process, **masked recall**, respondents are shown the front page or the cover of a publication with the name blacked out and are asked whether they remember reading that particular issue. Those who respond in the affirmative are asked to recall any items they have seen or read.)

The third technique, called the **recognition** method, entails showing respondents the logo or cover of a publication. For each publication the respondent has seen or read, the interviewer produces a copy and the respondent leafs through it to identify the articles or stories he or she recognizes. All respondents who definitely remember reading the publication are counted in its audience. To check the accuracy of the respondent's memory, dummy articles may be inserted into the interviewer's copy of the pub-

TABLE 15.3   DETERMINING AD EFFICIENCY FROM AN EXTENDED DATA BASE

	Newspaper X	Newspaper Y
Ad cost	$1,800	$2,700
Circulation	180,000	300,000
CPM	$10.00	$9.00
Number of people	630,000	540,000
who read the issue	(3.5 readers per copy)	(1.8 readers per copy)
Revised CPM	$2.86	$5.00

lication; respondents who claim to have read the dummy items may thus be eliminated from the sample or given less weight in the analysis. Many advertising researchers consider the recognition technique to be the most accurate predictor of readership scores.

Once the total audience for each magazine or newspaper has been tabulated, the advertiser can determine which publication is the most efficient buy. For example, returning to the example of Table 15.2, suppose that Newspaper X and Newspaper Y have the audience figures given in Table 15.3. On the basis of these figures, Newspaper X is seen to be the more efficient choice.

Another variable to be considered in determining the advertising efficiency (or **media efficiency**) of a newspaper or magazine is the number of times a person reads each issue. For example, imagine two newspapers or magazines that have exactly the same number of readers per issue. Publication A consists primarily of pictures and contains little text; people tend to read it once and not look at it again. Publication B, on the other hand, contains several lengthy and interesting articles; people pick it up several times. Publication B would seem to be a more efficient advertising vehicle, since it provides several possible exposures to an advertisement for the same cost as Publication A. Unfortu-

nately, a practical and reliable method for measuring the number of exposures per issue has yet to be developed.

Perhaps the most important gauge for advertising efficiency is the composition of the audience. It matters little if an advertisement for farm equipment is seen by 100,000 people if only a few of them are in the market for such products. To evaluate the number of potential customers in the audience, an advertiser must first conduct a survey to determine certain demographic characteristics of the people who tend to purchase a particular product. For example, potential customers for beer might be typically described as males between the ages of 18 and 49; those for fast-food restaurants might be households in which the primary wage earner is between 18 and 35 and there are at least two children under 12. These demographic characteristics of the typical consumer are then compared with the characteristics of a publication's audience for the product. The cost of reaching this audience is also expressed in CPM units, as shown in Table 15.4. An examination of these figures indicates that Newspaper X is slightly more efficient as a vehicle for reaching potential beer customers and much more efficient in reaching fast-food restaurant patrons.

Determining audience size and composition in the electronic media poses special problems

---

TABLE 15.4   CALCULATION OF AD EFFICIENCY INCORPORATING DEMOGRAPHIC SURVEY RESULTS

	Newspaper X	Newspaper Y
Ad cost	$1,800	$2,700
Circulation	180,000	300,000
CPM	$10.00	$9.00
Number of people who read average issue	630,000	540,000
Number of potential beer drinkers	150,000	220,000
Number of potential fast-food customers	300,000	200,000
CPM (beer drinkers)	$12.00	$12.27
CPM (fast-food customers)	$ 6.00	$13.50

---

for advertising researchers, due to the ephemeral nature of radio and television broadcasts. For a detailed discussion of the techniques involved in this type of audience or ratings research, the reader is referred to Chapter 14.

Frequency of Exposure in Media Schedules

An advertiser working within a strict budget to promote a product or service may be limited to the use of a single vehicle or medium. Often, however, an advertising campaign is conducted via several advertising vehicles simultaneously. But which combination of vehicles and/or media will provide the greatest reach and frequency for the advertiser's product? A substantial amount of recent media research has been devoted to this question, much of it concentrated on the development of mathematical models of advertising media and their audiences. The mathematical derivations of these models are beyond the scope of this book. However, the material that follows describes in simplified form the concepts underlying two computerized models: stepwise analysis and decision calculus. Readers who wish to pursue these topics in more rigorous detail should consult Aaker and Myers (1975) and Moran (1963).

Stepwise analysis is called an iterative model because the same basic series of instructions to the computer is repeated over and over again with slight modifications until a predetermined best or optimum solution is reached. The Young & Rubicam agency pioneered development in this area with their stepwise "high-assay" model. Stepwise analysis constructs a media schedule in increments, initially choosing a particular vehicle on the basis of the lowest cost per potential customer reached. After this selection has been made, all the remaining media vehicles are reevaluated to determine whether the optimum advertising exposure rate has been achieved. If not, the second most efficient vehicle is chosen and the process repeated until the optimum exposure rate is reached. This method is called the "high-assay" model because it is analogous to gold mining. The easiest-to-get gold is mined first, followed by less accessible ore. In like manner, the consumers who are the easiest to reach are first targeted, followed by those consumers who are harder to find and more costly to reach.

Decision calculus models make use of an **objective function**, a mathematical statement that provides a quantitative value for a given media combination (also known as a schedule). This value represents the schedule's effectiveness in providing advertising exposure. The advertising researcher determines which schedule offers the maximum exposure for a given product by calculating the objective functions of various media schedules.

Calculations of objective function are based on values generated by studies of audience size and composition for each vehicle or medium. In addition, a schedule's objective function value takes into account such variables as the probability that the advertisement will be forgotten, the total cost of the media schedule compared with the advertiser's budget, and the "media option source effect" — that is, the relative impact of exposure in a particular advertising vehicle (for example, an advertisement for men's clothes is likely to have more impact in *Gentlemen's Quarterly* than in *True Detective*).

Two computer media models are frequently used to calculate objective functions. MEDIAC (Little & Lodish, 1969), which is designed to maximize sales in a particular market segment by allowing a product's market potential within that segment to be included as an additional variable, calculates the probability that a given person within a market segment will be exposed to an advertisement. This probability depends on such factors as the size of the advertisement, the use of color, and the characteristics of the media vehicle used to deliver the message. It is assumed that exposure to one or more advertisements will affect a person's willingness to buy the advertised product. The advertiser provides MEDIAC with data on the probable sales response to different levels of exposure within all relevant segments of the market; MEDIAC computes the probable sales response for each market segment and totals the response for the entire audience for any given schedule.

A second computer model, called ADMOD (Aaker, 1975), is designed to maximize favorable attitude changes among consumers toward the advertised product. ADMOD evaluates a media schedule by examining its likely impact on each individual in samples drawn from the mar-

ket population. This impact is calculated by taking into account the number and source of exposures for each individual and the effect of these exposures on the probability of obtaining the desired attitude change. The results are then projected to the population. A unique ADMOD feature allows the researcher to include certain data about different message strategies that might be employed. As media schedules increase in complexity and become more expensive, it is expected that computer models such as MEDIAC and ADMOD will be used more widely.

A more limited media model, called exposure estimation or exposure distribution, deals with predicting the reach and frequency of a media schedule. For example, suppose that an advertiser is running an ad in three different issues of both *Time* and *Newsweek*. An exposure estimation model allows the advertiser to estimate the total number of the target market likely to be reached by this schedule and how many of these will be reached after one exposure, two exposures, and so on.

The increased use of microcomputers in advertising agencies has facilitated the computation of the best reach and frequency combinations for the media dollar. The MEDIAC model is available from the Telmar Communications Corporation in an interactive mode. In addition, Telmar and Interactive Market Systems have developed Micronet and Mediapak, two similar software packages designed to calculate reach and frequency data. Current syndicated research data bases are standard with both programs. As new generations of software come on the market, the microcomputer probably will become the media planner's best friend.

Media Research by Private Firms

As mentioned earlier, the Audit Bureau of Circulations (ABC) supplies advertisers with data on the circulation figures of newspapers and magazines. As of 1990, ABC measured the circulation of about 75% of all print media vehicles in the United States and Canada. ABC requires publishers to submit a detailed report of their circulation every 6 months; it verifies these reports by sending field workers to conduct an audit at each publication. The auditors typically examine records of the publications' press runs, newsprint bills, or other invoices for paper, as well as transcripts of circulation records and other related files.

The ABC audit results, as well as overall circulation data, coverage maps, press times, and market data, are published in an annual report and distributed to ABC members and advertisers. ABC now reports data on audience size for certain selected newspapers. Called the "Newspaper Audience Research Data Bank," this report consists of a collection of audience surveys conducted by newspapers in the top 100 markets.

The Simmons Market Research Bureau provides comprehensive feedback about magazine readership. This service selects a large random sample of readers and shows them illustrations of the titles of about 70 magazines to determine which ones they have recently read or looked through. Subjects are shown stripped-down versions of the publications they identified, and readership is verified by further questioning. At the same time, data are gathered about the ownership, purchase, and use of a wide variety of products and services. This information is tabulated by Simmons and released in a series of detailed reports on the demographic makeup and purchasing behavior of each magazine's audience. Using these data, advertisers can determine the cost of reaching potential buyers of their products or services. A portion of a Simmons Report is reproduced in Table 15.5.

Mediamark Research, Inc. (MRI) uses a recent-reading technique to produce audience estimates for magazines and product usage data. More than 25,000 persons are interviewed nationwide about their magazine reading. Additionally, all respondents are given a questionnaire that asks about product usage behavior. Results are summarized in MRI's Magazine Total Audience Report.

Three companies—Arbitron, A. C. Nielsen, and Birch Radio—supply broadcast audience data for advertisers. Arbitron and Birch measure radio listening in about 200 markets across the United States, while Arbitron and Nielsen provide audience estimates for local television markets. (Chapter 14 gives more information on the methods employed by these two companies and others.)

Competitors' Activities

It is often helpful to advertisers to know the media choices of their competitors. This information can help the advertiser to avoid making the mistakes of less successful competitors and to imitate the strategies of the more successful. Moreover, an advertiser seeking to promote a new product who knows that the three leading competitors are using basically the same media mix might feel that their consensus is worthy of consideration.

An advertiser can collect data on competitors' activity either by setting up a special research team or by subscribing to the services of a syndicated research company. Since the job of monitoring the media activity of a large number of firms advertising in several media is so difficult, most advertisers rely on the syndicated service. Such services gather data by direct observation, that is, by tabulating the advertisements that appear in a given medium. For magazines, television, and radio, the complete population of advertisements is studied. For newspapers, samples are observed and the results generalized. In addition to information about frequency of advertisements, cost figures are helpful; these estimates are obtained from the published rate cards of the various media vehicles.

Advertisers also find it helpful to know *what*

competitors are saying. To acquire this information, many advertising agencies conduct systematic content analyses of the messages in a sample of the competitors' advertisements. The results often provide insight into the persuasive themes, strategies, and goals of competitors' advertising. It is because of such studies that many commercials tend to look and sound alike: successful commercial approaches are often mimicked.

The most comprehensive information about advertisers' activities and expenditures in the electronic media is provided by Broadcast Advertiser Reports (BAR). This organization collects data on commercials appearing on network radio and television as well as on local television stations. Advertising activity on network radio is measured by recording all network programs on audiotape. The tapes are played back for coders, who record programs, lengths of commercials, sponsors, brand names, and other details. BAR estimates the cost of each commercial by referring to the network's published rate card. Totals are computed for each brand, and the results are published in BAR's quarterly Network Radio Reports. The reports allow an advertiser to determine competitors' schedules and expenditures.

BAR uses basically the same technique to compile its weekly Network Television Reports. Network programs are recorded and all commercials coded according to brand, length, and program. Rate cards are used to estimate costs. The report also contains a daily log of advertising, indexed by product type, and total of the week's advertising costs per product.

BAR monitors advertising on local television stations by sampling approximately 275 stations located in the top 75 television markets. In the two top markets, New York and Los Angeles, measurements are made every week. In the other 73 markets, BAR selects one week per month for analysis, during which all station programming is recorded or videotaped, and this sample is used to make projections for the entire month. BAR issues two summary reports: a local market report for each city and a cumulative report covering all 75 markets. The types of data and the format are similar to those used for the network summaries.

Local radio advertising is not monitored by BAR. The only data available for advertisers in this area are provided by Radio Expenditure Reports (RER), a firm that sends questionnaires to about 800 stations in the top 150 markets. Each station is asked to provide an estimate of its advertising revenue generated from regional and national commercials. RER tabulates the data and projects a national figure for all such radio advertising. An RER report tells an advertiser how much a competitor spent for radio spots during a certain time period, but it does not show when or on what stations the competitor advertised.

Data about magazine advertising are collected by *Leading National Advertisers* (LNA), in cooperation with the Publishers Information Bureau (PIB). The publishers of magazines that belong to the PIB mark all paid advertising in each issue and send the marked copies to LNA, where trained coders record detailed information about each advertisement. This information is recorded in a report sent to LNA subscribers. The data are arranged according to product type and brand name. By scanning the LNA reports, it is possible to determine which magazines competitors are using, the size of the advertisements they purchase, when they appear, and their approximate cost.

LNA also works with the Outdoor Advertising Association of America to gather data about expenditures in that area. Companies owning billboards in approximately 250 markets send data to LNA about space purchased by national advertisers. LNA publishes this information quarterly.

Information about advertising activity in newspapers is supplied by Media Records. Since

TABLE 15.5 EXAMPLE OF SIMMONS REPORT

TYPE OF VEHICLE PERSONALLY DRIVE
(ADULTS)

	TOTAL U.S. '000	AUTOMOBILE A '000	B % DOWN	C % ACROSS	D INDX	MOTORCYCLE A '000	B % DOWN	C % ACROSS	D INDX	COMPACT PICK-UP A '000	B % DOWN	C % ACROSS	D INDX	PICK-UP TRUCK A '000	B % DOWN	C % ACROSS	D INDX
TOTAL	171205	128002	100.0	74.8	100	8053	100.0	4.7	100	7263	100.0	4.2	100	27941	100.0	16.3	100
AMERICAN HEALTH	2460	1901	1.5	77.3	103	**137	1.7	5.6	118	**97	1.3	3.9	93	*299	1.1	12.2	74
BARRON'S	1012	763	0.6	75.4	101	**46	0.6	4.5	97	**29	0.4	2.9	68	**73	0.3	7.2	44
BETTER HOMES & GARDENS	21887	17470	13.6	79.8	107	771	9.6	3.5	75	1001	13.8	4.6	108	3576	12.8	16.3	100
BON APPETIT	3851	3201	2.5	83.1	111	*158	2.0	4.1	87	*146	2.0	3.8	89	429	1.5	11.1	68
BUSINESS WEEK	4577	3723	2.9	81.3	109	275	3.4	6.0	128	*175	2.4	3.8	90	767	2.7	16.8	103
CAR AND DRIVER	2924	2371	1.9	81.1	108	284	3.5	9.7	206	**172	2.4	5.9	139	696	2.5	23.8	146
CAR CRAFT	2325	1653	1.3	71.1	95	378	4.7	16.3	346	**105	1.4	4.5	106	529	1.9	22.8	139
CBS MAG. NETWORK (GROSS)	18389	14444	11.3	78.5	105	2299	28.5	12.5	266	994	13.7	5.4	127	4313	15.4	23.5	144
CHANGING TIMES	2919	2460	1.9	84.3	113	*117	1.5	4.0	85	**83	1.1	2.8	67	588	2.1	20.1	123
COLONIAL HOMES	1982	1653	1.3	83.4	112	**68	0.8	3.4	73	**85	1.2	4.3	101	331	1.2	16.7	102
CONDE NAST LIMITED (GROSS)	15294	11950	9.3	78.1	105	535	6.6	3.5	74	650	8.9	4.3	100	1851	6.6	12.1	74
CONDE NAST PKG. WOMEN (GROSS)	18803	15064	11.8	80.1	107	634	7.9	3.4	72	1075	14.8	5.7	135	2103	7.5	11.2	69
CONSUMERS DIGEST	2850	2277	1.8	79.9	107	**124	1.5	4.4	92	**94	1.3	3.3	78	545	2.0	19.1	117
COSMOPOLITAN	9563	7466	5.8	78.1	104	*348	4.3	3.6	77	472	6.5	4.9	116	1107	4.0	11.6	71
COUNTRY LIVING	4779	3941	3.1	82.5	110	*246	3.1	5.1	109	*205	2.8	4.3	101	849	3.0	17.8	109
CREATIVE IDEAS FOR LIVING	1780	1422	1.1	79.9	107	**79	1.0	4.4	94	**76	1.0	4.3	101	*246	0.9	13.8	85
CYCLE	1891	1356	1.1	71.7	96	467	5.8	24.7	525	**122	1.7	6.5	152	601	2.2	31.8	195
CYCLE WORLD	1855	1358	1.1	73.2	98	460	5.7	24.8	527	**115	1.6	6.2	146	535	1.9	28.8	177
DISCOVER	1668	1349	1.1	80.9	108	**76	0.9	4.6	97	**101	1.4	6.1	143	*230	0.8	13.8	84
EBONY	8306	5508	4.3	66.3	89	258	3.2	3.1	66	277	3.8	3.3	79	783	2.8	9.4	58
ESQUIRE	2532	1909	1.5	75.4	101	*172	2.1	6.8	144	**80	1.1	3.2	74	332	1.2	13.1	80
ESSENCE	3125	2184	1.7	69.9	93	**72	0.9	2.3	49	**63	0.9	2.0	48	*270	1.0	8.6	53
FAMILY CIRCLE	18770	14929	11.7	79.5	106	532	6.6	2.8	60	712	9.8	3.8	89	3035	10.9	16.2	99
THE FAMILY HANDYMAN	3918	3236	2.5	82.6	110	239	3.0	6.1	130	*170	2.3	4.3	102	975	3.5	24.9	152
FIELD & STREAM	9136	7091	5.5	77.6	104	928	11.5	10.2	216	544	7.5	6.0	140	2898	10.4	31.7	194
FOOD & WINE	1563	1249	1.0	79.9	107	**117	1.5	7.5	159	**26	0.4	1.7	39	*197	0.7	12.6	77
FORBES	2690	2228	1.7	82.8	111	*172	2.1	6.4	136	**118	1.6	4.4	103	352	1.3	13.1	80
FORTUNE	2636	2081	1.6	78.9	106	*179	2.2	6.8	144	*149	2.1	5.7	133	331	1.2	12.6	77
GQ/ GENTLEMEN'S QUARTERLY	2881	2198	1.7	76.3	102	*101	1.3	3.5	75	*129	1.8	4.5	106	315	1.1	10.9	67
GLAMOUR	7232	5711	4.5	79.0	106	*276	3.4	3.8	81	518	7.1	7.2	169	873	3.1	12.1	74

	TOTAL																
GOLF DIGEST	3055	2680	2.1	87.7	117	*207	2.6	6.8	144	**67	0.9	2.2	52	633	2.3	20.7	127
GOLF DIGEST/TENNIS (GROSS)	4394	3715	2.9	84.5	113	288	3.6	6.6	139	*113	1.6	2.6	61	928	3.3	21.1	129
GOLF MAGAZINE	2356	2045	1.6	86.8	116	*159	2.0	6.7	143	**83	1.1	3.5	83	473	1.7	20.1	123
GOLF MAGAZINE/SKI (GROSS)	3785	3188	2.5	84.2	113	285	3.5	7.5	160	*149	2.1	3.9	93	812	2.9	21.5	131
GOOD HOUSEKEEPING	19599	15820	12.4	80.7	108	621	7.7	3.2	67	763	10.5	3.9	92	3165	11.3	16.1	99
GOURMET	2460	2064	1.6	83.9	112	**111	1.4	4.5	96	**110	1.5	4.5	105	329	1.2	13.4	82
GUNS AND AMMO	3062	2320	1.8	75.8	101	414	5.1	13.5	287	*282	3.9	9.2	217	1036	3.7	33.8	207
HARPER'S BAZAAR	3162	2463	1.9	77.9	104	**52	0.6	1.6	35	**118	1.6	3.7	88	328	1.2	10.4	64
HEALTH	3549	2717	2.1	76.6	102	**98	1.2	2.8	59	*120	1.7	3.4	80	423	1.5	11.9	73
HEARST GOLD BUY (GROSS)	11743	9347	7.3	79.6	106	267	3.3	2.3	48	467	6.4	4.0	94	1680	6.0	14.3	88
HEARST HOME GROUP (GROSS)	10886	8814	6.9	81.0	108	368	4.6	3.4	72	391	5.4	3.6	85	1686	6.0	15.5	95
HEARST MAN POWER (GROSS)	8948	7073	5.5	79.0	106	939	11.7	10.5	223	446	6.1	5.0	117	2629	9.4	29.4	180
HEARST WOMAN PWR PLUS(GROSS)	46569	37300	29.1	80.1	107	1513	18.8	3.2	69	1896	26.1	4.1	96	6848	24.5	14.7	90
HOME MECHANIX	3031	2486	1.9	82.0	110	337	4.2	11.1	236	*197	2.7	6.5	153	877	3.1	28.9	177
HOT ROD	3864	3067	2.4	79.4	106	481	6.0	12.4	265	*180	2.5	4.7	110	1147	4.1	29.7	182

Source: Copyright 1986 Simmons Market Research Bureau, Inc. Reprinted by permission.

it is impossible to examine every newspaper in the country, Media Records concentrates on about 220 newspapers published in approximately 85 urban areas. During a specified time period, coders measure the size of every advertisement appearing in each issue of these papers and also estimate costs. The data from this sample are used to project estimates for the top 125 market areas. Media Records publishes this information in its "Bluebooks," which provide data on advertising activity for all comparable products and services.

BAR and LNA combine resources to publish the Ad Dollar Summary, which reports combined advertising expenditures in seven media. Also available is the Company/Brand Dollar Report, which lists expenditures by company and by individual medium.

CAMPAIGN ASSESSMENT RESEARCH

Leckenby (1984) argues that the purpose of campaign assessment research is ". . . to understand the overall response of the consumer to an integrated and executed advertising campaign which itself was the result of copy [and] media . . . research conducted previously." Campaign assessment research builds on copy and media research, but its research strategies are generally different from those used in the other areas. In general, there are two kinds of assessment research. The pretest/posttest method takes measurements before and after the campaign, and **tracking studies** assess the impact of the campaign by measuring effects at several points during the progress of the campaign. Both techniques can be used to examine a wide range of dependent variables: brand name awareness, attitudes toward advertised brands, reported purchase intentions, actual purchases, awareness of advertising. The major advantage of a tracking study is that it provides important feedback to the advertiser while the campaign is

still in progress. This feedback might ultimately lead to changes in the creative or media strategy.

Pretest/posttest studies typically use personal interviews for data collection. At times, the same people are interviewed before the campaign starts and again after its close (a panel study), or two different groups are chosen and asked the same questions (a trend study; see Chapter 9). In any case, changes before and after the campaign are examined to gauge advertising effects. Winters (1983) reports several pretest/posttest studies done for a major oil company. In one study, a pretest showed that about 80% of the sample agreed that a particular oil company made too much profit. Five months later a posttest revealed that the percentage had dropped slightly among those who had seen an oil company newspaper ad but had remained the same among those who had not seen the ad. Additionally, the study disclosed that people who saw both print and TV ads showed less attitude change than those who saw only the TV ads, suggesting that the print ad might have had a dampening effect.

Tracking studies also rely on personal or telephone interviews as their main data collection devices. Technological developments including split cable systems (such as AdTel) and the UPC scanner have allowed researchers to track advertising and sales volume in a way not thought possible a few years ago. In addition, cable and scanners have permitted greater precision in media planning as well. Leckenby (1984) reports the results of a tracking study done for an instant coffee brand. It was determined that most of the TV commercials for the instant coffee were being seen by people who were regular coffee drinkers and, consequently, not good prospects. In response to this, the advertiser decided to shift the ads to reach more instant coffee drinkers. The cable and scanner data allowed researchers to identify the times of day when a high proportion of instant coffee buyers were watching TV, and with this information it was easy to reschedule the ads in more favorable slots.

Tracking studies are tremendously useful but they are not without drawbacks. Perhaps the biggest problem is cost. Tracking studies typically require large samples; in fact, a sample of less than 1,500 cases per year is unusual. If detailed analysis of subgroups is needed, the sample size must be much larger. Furthermore, if the product is a national one, test markets across the country might be necessary to present a complete picture of the results. Finally, the use of sophisticated research methods, such as split cable and scanner, makes the research even more expensive. For those who can afford it, however, the tracking study provides continuous measurement of the effects of a campaign and an opportunity to fine-tune the copy and the media schedule.

PUBLIC RELATIONS RESEARCH

Much like advertising, public relations (PR) has become more research-oriented in recent years. As a leading text points out (Cutlip, Center, & Broom, 1985):

> For years, executives and practitioners alike bought the popular myth that public relations deals with intangibles that cannot be measured. With each passing day it becomes increasingly difficult to sell that position to results-oriented management. . . . Even though it will not answer all the questions or sway all decisions, methodical systematic research is the foundation of effective public relations.

Today techniques such as survey research, content analysis, and focus groups are widely employed in this field. Public relations researchers, however, use these methods for a highly specific reason: to improve communication with various publics.

Types of Public Relations Research

Pavlik (1987) delineated three major types of public relations research: applied, basic, and introspective. Applied research examines specific practical issues; in many instances it is done to solve a specific problem. A branch of applied research, strategic research, is used to develop PR campaigns and programs. A second branch, evaluation research, is done to assess the effectiveness of a PR program. Dozier (1984) identified three common styles of evaluation research in PR: informal, impact, and dissemination.

Basic research in public relations creates knowledge that cuts across PR situations. It is most interested in examining the underlying processes and in constructing theories that explain the public relations process. For example, Grunig (1984) examined the traditional notions of attitude and behavior change, and concluded that a new "situational" view of the process was more useful. The third major type of PR research is introspective research, which examines the field of public relations. To illustrate, Kern-Foxworth (1989) used a survey to provide a profile of the status of minority PR professionals.

Corporate Uses of Public Relations Research

As pointed out by Cutlip, Center, and Broom (1985), informal or exploratory methods are still widely used in public relations research despite the availability of highly developed social science methods. The major problem associated with these informal techniques lies in the selection of respondents. The representativeness of the samples is often questionable. In any event, these methods can be useful provided the researcher recognizes and appreciates their weaknesses. Some of the more common informal methods used in public relations research are personal contacts, expert opinion, focus groups, community forums, call-in telephone lines, mail analysis, and examination of media content.

The more formal methods of research provide objective and systematic information from representative samples. These methods include the familiar survey, tracking study, content analysis, secondary analysis of existing data, and panel studies.

There are five major categories of public relations research: (1) environmental monitoring programs, (2) public relations audits, (3) communication audits, (4) social audits, and (5) evaluation research. The first four were identified by Lerbinger (1977) more than a decade ago.

ENVIRONMENTAL MONITORING PROGRAMS. Researchers use **environmental monitoring programs** to observe trends in public opinion and social events that may have a significant impact on an organization. Generally, two phases are involved. The "early warning" phase, an attempt to identify emerging issues, often takes the form of a systematic content analysis of publications likely to herald new developments. For example, one corporation has conducted a content analysis of scholarly journals in the fields of economics, politics, and science; another company sponsors a continuing analysis of trade and general newspapers. An alternate method is to perform panel studies of community leaders or other influential and knowledgeable citizens. These individuals are surveyed regularly with regard to the ideas they perceive to be important, and the interviews are analyzed to pick out new topics of interest.

Brody and Stone (1989) list other forms of monitoring techniques. One technique is to have the people doing the monitoring look for a **trigger event**, an event or an activity that might focus public concern on a topic or issue. For example, the Chernobyl accident focused public opinion on nuclear safety, and the Exxon oil spill in Alaska brought heavy visibility to environmental concerns. There is no scientific way, however, of determining what is or may become

a trigger event. Monitors are left to trust their own instincts and judgment. The technique of **precursor analysis** is similar to trigger events analysis. Precursor analysis assumes that leaders establish trends and these trends ultimately trickle down to the rest of society. For example, Japanese businesses tend to lead in innovative management techniques, many of which have caught on in the United States. At home, California tends to be a leader in insurance concerns and Florida tends to lead in health issues. Monitors are instructed to pay particular attention to developments in these states.

The second phase of environmental monitoring consists of tracking public opinion on major issues. Typically this involves either a longitudinal panel study, in which the same respondents are interviewed several times during a specified interval, or a cross-sectional opinion poll, in which a random sample is surveyed only once. To illustrate, since 1959 the Roper organization has surveyed public attitudes about media credibility. AT&T, General Electric, General Motors, and the Dow Chemical Company have also conducted elaborate tracking studies.

PUBLIC RELATIONS AUDITS. The **public relations audit**, as the name suggests, is a comprehensive study of the public relations position of an organization. Such studies are used to measure a company's standing both internally (in the eyes of its employees) and externally (with regard to the opinions of customers, stockholders, community leaders and so on). In short, as summarized by Simon (1980), the public relations audit is a "research tool used specifically to describe, measure and assess an organization's public relations activities and to provide guidelines for future public relations programming."

The first step in a public relations audit is to list the segments of the public that are most important to the organization. This is generally accomplished through personal interviews with key management personnel in each department and by a content analysis of the company's external communications. The second step is to determine how the organization is viewed by each of these audiences. This involves conducting a corporate image study, that is, a survey of audience samples. The questions are designed to measure familiarity with the organization (can the respondents recognize the company logo? identify a product it manufactures? remember the president's name?) as well as attitudes and perceptions toward it.

Ratings scales are often used. For example, respondents might be asked to rank their perceptions of the ideal electric company on a 7-point scale for a series of adjective pairs as shown in Figure 15.2. Later, the respondents would rate a specific electric company on the same scales. The average score for each item would be tabulated, and the means connected by a zigzag line to form a composite profile. Thus, in Figure 15.3, the ideal electric company's profile is represented by a broken line and the actual electric company's standing by a solid line. By comparing the two lines, public relations researchers can readily identify the areas in which a company falls short of the ideal. Corporate image studies can also be conducted before the beginning of a public relations campaign and again at the conclusion of the campaign to evaluate its effectiveness.

FIGURE 15.2   A SEMANTIC DIFFERENTIAL SCALE FOR ELICITING PERCEPTIONS OF ELECTRIC COMPANIES

The Ideal Electric Company

good	___:___:___:___:___:___:___	bad
unconcerned	___:___:___:___:___:___:___	concerned
responsive	___:___:___:___:___:___:___	unresponsive
cold	___:___:___:___:___:___:___	warm
big	___:___:___:___:___:___:___	small

FIGURE 15.3   PROFILES OF IDEAL (BROKEN LINE) AND ACTUAL (SOLID LINE) ELECTRIC COMPANIES RESULTING FROM RATINGS STUDY

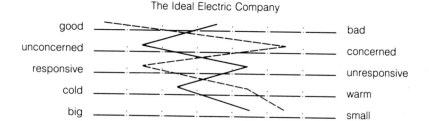

The Ideal Electric Company

COMMUNICATION AUDITS. The communication audit resembles a public relations audit but has narrower goals; it concerns the internal and external means of communication used by an organization, rather than the company's entire public relations program. The three research techniques generally used in conducting such an audit are readership surveys, content analyses, and readability studies. Readership studies are designed to measure how many people read certain publications (such as employee newsletters or annual reports) and/or remember the messages they contain. The results are used to improve the content, appearance, and method of distribution of the publications. Content analyses reveal how the media are handling news and other information about and from the organization; they may be conducted in-house or by private firms that provide computerized studies of press coverage. Readability studies help a company gauge the ease with which its employee publications and press releases can be read. An internal audit would also include an analysis of channels of communication within the organization.

SOCIAL AUDITS. A social audit is a small-scale environmental monitoring program designed to measure an organization's social performance, that is, how well it is living up to its public responsibilities. The audit provides feedback on such company-sponsored social action programs as minority hiring, environmental cleanup, and employee safety. This is the newest form of public relations research and also the most challenging. Researchers are currently studying such questions as what activities to audit, how to collect data, and how to measure the effects of the programs. Nevertheless, several large companies, including General Motors and Celanese, have already conducted lengthy social audits.

EVALUATION RESEARCH. A fifth major category of public relations research has recently achieved prominence and needs to be added to Lerbinger's list: evaluation research. **Evaluation research** refers to the process of judging the effectiveness of program planning, implementation, and impact. Rossi and Freeman (1982) have outlined some basic questions that occur at each of these stages. Some samples are given.

1. *Planning.* What is the extent of the target program? How do the costs of the program relate to the potential benefits?
2. *Implementation.* Is the program reaching the target population or target area?
3. *Impact.* Is the program effective in achieving its intended goals? Is the program having some effects that were not intended?

The specific research methods used at each of these three levels have been mentioned in other chapters. For example, at the planning stage, content analysis (Chapter 8) is used to determine how closely program efforts coincide with the actual plan. Readability tests (Chapter 13) are frequently used to see whether the messages can be read and understood by the target group. During the implementation stage, content analysis is used again to count the number of messages that are placed in the media. Next, the number of people actually exposed to the message is determined by the methods of audience research mentioned earlier in this chapter. Circulation figures and audience estimates from the Audit Bureau of Circulations, Simmons Market Research Bureau, Nielsen, and Arbitron are helpful in measuring exposure.

At the impact level, public relations researchers are interested in the same three levels of effect that are mentioned in the discussion of copy research: cognitive, affective, conative. At the cognitive level, researchers attempt to find out how much people learned from the public relations campaign. At the affective level, measures of changes in attitudes, opinions, or perceptions are used quite frequently. Finally, behavioral change, the conative level, is an

TABLE 15.6   TYPES OF RESEARCH DONE BY PR PRACTITIONERS

Research	Percent Conducting
Employee/management communications	71
Marketing/product public relations	69
Media relations/publicity	65
Corporate image	61
Issue tracking	50
Customer relations	50
Public affairs/government relations	46
Community relations	46
Institutional advertising	43
Investor/financial relations	41

Source: Data from "Talking Research" by M. McGee, Nov. 1988, *Public Relations Journal*, p. 10.

important way to gauge public relations impact. Obviously, the techniques used in advertising campaign effectiveness studies — pretest/posttest and tracking studies — can be applied in measuring the impact dimension of public relations campaigns.

Lindenmann (1988) discusses several examples of evaluation research used by corporations. The Aetna Life and Casualty company has used before and after polling during the last few years as part of a campaign to introduce a long-term health care plan for elderly Americans. Their precampaign polling revealed that a large majority of Americans incorrectly believed that Medicare coverage routinely extended to nursing home stays. After a communication campaign, the company's polls found that more people were aware of Medicare's limitations than they had been before. The California Prune Board used the day-after recall method to gauge the effectiveness of its media campaign designed to promote prunes as a high-fiber food source. A survey of women in Detroit revealed that awareness of prunes as a fiber source increased from 50% to 65%.

Finally, although most public relations professionals appreciate the value of research, a survey by McGee (1988) found that most PR research is still informal, unscientific, and infrequently conducted. More than half of the 245 respondents, however, stated that they thought that research volume is likely to increase in the future. Table 15.6 contains a listing of the most common research done by those responding to this survey.

S U M M A R Y

There are three main areas of advertising research: copy testing, media research, and campaign assessment research. Copy testing consists of studies that examine the advertisement or commercial itself. The three main dimensions of impact examined by copy testing are cognitive (knowing), affective (feeling), and conative (doing). Media research helps determine which advertising vehicles are the most efficient and what type of media schedule will have the greatest impact. Campaign assessment studies examine the overall response of consumers to a complete campaign. The two main types of campaign assessment research are the pretest/posttest and the tracking study. Many private firms specialize in supplying copy, media, and assessment data to advertisers.

Research in public relations involves monitoring relevant developments and trends, studying the public relations position of an organization, examining the messages produced by an organization, measuring how well an organization is living up to its social responsibilities, and evaluating public relations campaigns.

Questions and Problems for Further Investigation

1. Assume you have developed a new diet soft drink and are ready to market it. Develop a research study for identifying the elements and topics that should be stressed in your advertising.

2. A full-page advertisement costs $16,000 in Magazine A and $26,000 in Magazine B. Magazine A has a circulation of 100,000 and 2.5 readers per copy, and Magazine B has a circulation of 150,000 and 1.8 readers per copy. In terms of CPM readers, which magazine is the most efficient advertising vehicle?

3. Select a sample of newspaper and magazine advertisements for two different airlines. Conduct a content analysis of the themes or major selling points in each advertisement. What similarities and differences are there?

4. Assume you are the public relations director for a major automobile manufacturer. How would you go about conducting an environmental monitoring study?

5. How would you assess the public relations impact of an information campaign designed to persuade people to conserve water?

References and Suggested Readings

Aaker, D. (1975). ADMOD, an advertising decision model. *Journal of Marketing Research, 12*, 37–45.

Aaker, D., & Myers, J. (1975). *Advertising management.* Englewood Cliffs, NJ: Prentice-Hall.

Boyd, H. W., Westfall, R., & Stasch, S. F. (1989). *Marketing research: Text and cases* (7th ed.). Homewood, IL: Irwin.

Brody, E. W., & Stone, G. C. (1989). *Public relations research.* New York: Praeger.

Cutlip, S., Center, A., & Broom, G. (1985). *Effective public relations* (6th ed.). Englewood Cliffs, NJ: Prentice-Hall.

Dozier, D. M. (1984). Program evaluation and the roles of practitioners. *Public Relations Review, 10*(2), 13–21.

Dunn, S. W., Barban, A. M., Krugman, D. K., & Reid, L. N. (1990). *Advertising: Its role in modern marketing.* Chicago: The Dryden Press.

Fletcher, A., & Bowers, T. (1988). *Fundamentals of advertising research* (3rd ed.). Columbus, OH: Grid Publishing.

Green, P. E., Tull, D. S., & Albaum, G. (1988). *Research for marketing decisions.* Englewood Cliffs, NJ: Prentice-Hall.

Grunig, J. E. (1984). Organizations, environments, and models of public relations. *Public Relations Research and Education, 1*(4), 6–29.

Haskins, J. (1976). *An introduction to advertising research.* Knoxville, TN: Communication Research Center.

Jacoby, J., & Hofer, W. D. (1982). Viewers' miscomprehension of televised communication. *Journal of Marketing, 46*(4), 12–27.

Kern-Foxworth, M. (1989). Status and roles of minority public relations practitioners. *Public Relations Review, 15*(3), 39–47.

Leckenby, J. (1984). Current issues in the measurement of advertising effectiveness. Paper presented to the International Advertising Association, Tokyo, Japan.

Leckenby, J., & Wedding, N. (1982). *Advertising management.* Columbus, OH: Grid Publishing.

Lerbinger, O. (1977). Corporate use of research in public relations. *Public Relations Review, 3*(4), 11–20.

Lindenmann, W. (1988). Beyond the clipbook. *Public Relations Journal, 44*(12), 22–26.

Little, J., & Lodish, L. (1969). A media planning calculus. *Operations Research, 17*(1), 1–35.

McGee, M. (1988). Talking research. *Public Relations Journal, 44*(11), 10.

Moran, W. (1963). Practical media decisions and the computer. *Journal of Marketing, 27*(3), 26–30.

Pavlik, J. V. (1987). *Public relations: What the research tells us.* Beverly Hills, CA: Sage Publications.

Rossi, P., & Freeman, H. (1982). *Evaluation: A systematic approach.* Beverly Hills, CA: Sage Publications.

Simon, R. (1980). *Public relations: Concepts and practices.* Columbus, OH: Grid Publishing.

Tull, D. S., & Hawkins, D. I. (1987). *Marketing research (4th ed.).* New York: Macmillan.

Winters, L. (1983). Comparing pretesting and posttesting of corporate advertising. *Journal of Advertising Research, 23*(1), 33–38.

CHAPTER 16

RESEARCH IN MEDIA EFFECTS

The preceding three chapters focused on research conducted in a professional or industry setting. However, a great deal of mass media research is conducted at colleges and universities. As mentioned in Chapter 1, there are several differences between research in the academic and the private sectors. To summarize briefly:

1. Academic research tends to be more theoretical in nature; private sector research is generally more applied.
2. The data used in academic research are public, whereas much industry research is based on proprietary data.
3. Private sector research topics are often determined by top management; academic researchers have more freedom in their choice of topics.
4. Projects in private sector research usually cost more to conduct than academic investigations.

The two research settings also have some things in common:

1. Many research techniques and approaches used in the private sector emerged from academic research.
2. Industry and academic researchers use the same basic research methodologies and approaches.
3. The goal of research is often the same in both settings — to explain and predict audience and consumer behavior.

This chapter describes some of the more popular types of research carried out by academic investigators and shows how this work relates to private sector research.

Obviously, not every type of scholarly research used in colleges and universities can be covered in one chapter. What follows is not an exhaustive survey, but rather an illustrative overview of the history, methods, and theoretical development of five research areas: (1) the antisocial and prosocial effects of specific media content, (2) uses and gratifications, (3) agenda setting, (4) cultivation of perceptions of social reality, and (5) advertising and the socialization of children.

ANTISOCIAL AND PROSOCIAL EFFECTS OF MEDIA CONTENT

The study of the *antisocial* effects of viewing television and motion pictures is one of the most heavily researched areas in all mass media. Comstock, Chaffee, and Katzman (1978) reported that empirical studies focusing on this topic outweighed work in all other problem areas by four to one, and this emphasis is still apparent more than a decade later. The impact of *prosocial* content is a newer area and grew out of the recognition that the same principles underlying the learning of antisocial activities ought to apply to more positive behavior. Applied and academic researchers share an interest in this area: all the major networks have sponsored such research, and the effects of antisocial and prosocial content have been popular topics on college and university campuses for the past 30 years. Not surprisingly, there has been

History

a certain amount of friction between academic researchers and industry executives.

Concern over the social impact of the mass media was evident as far back as the 1920s when many critics charged that motion pictures had a negative influence on children. In 1928 the Motion Picture Research Council, with support from the Payne Fund, a private philanthropic organization, sponsored a series of 13 studies on aspects of the movies' influence on children. After examination of film content, information gain, attitude change, and influence on behavior, it was concluded that the movies were potent sources of information, attitudes, and behavior for children. Furthermore, many of the things that children learned had antisocial overtones. In the early 1950s, another medium, the comic book, was chastised for its alleged harmful effects (Wertham, 1954).

In 1960, Joseph Klapper summarized what was then know about the social impact of mass communication (Klapper, 1960). In contrast to many researchers, Klapper downplayed the potential harmful effects of the media. He concluded that the media function most often to reinforce an individual's existing attitudes and predispositions. Klapper's viewpoint, which came to be known as the minimal effects position, was influential in the development of a theory of media effects.

In the late 1950s and early 1960s, concern over the antisocial impact of the media shifted to television. Experiments on college campuses by Bandura and Berkowitz (summarized in Comstock, 1975) showed that aggressive behavior could be learned by viewing violent media content and that a stimulation effect was more probable than a cathartic (or cleansing) effect. Senate subcommittees examined possible links between viewing of violence on television and juvenile delinquency, and in 1965 one subcommittee concluded that televised crime and violence were related to antisocial behaviors among juvenile viewers. The civil unrest and assassinations in the middle 1960s prompted the formation of the National Commission on the Causes and Prevention of Violence, chaired by Milton Eisenhower. The full staff report of the Eisenhower Commission, which concluded that television violence taught the viewer how to engage in violence, made a series of recommendations about reducing the impact of television violence.

The early 1970s saw extensive research into the social effects of the mass media. Just 3 years after the publication of the Eisenhower Commission report came the release of a multivolume report sponsored by the Surgeon General's Scientific Advisory Committee on Television and Social Behavior (1972). In *Television and Growing Up* the committee cautiously summarized their research evidence by stating:

> There is a convergence of fairly substantial evidence on short-run causation of aggression among children by viewing violence . . . and the much less certain evidence from field studies that . . . violence viewing precedes some long-run manifestation of aggressive behavior. This convergence . . . constitutes some preliminary evidence of a causal relationship.

The committee tempered this conclusion, however, by noting that in accord with the reinforcement notion, ". . . any sequence by which viewing television violence causes aggressive behavior is most likely applicable only to some children who are predisposed in that direction."

At about the same time, the three television networks were also sponsoring research in this area. CBS commissioned two studies: a field experiment that found no link between television viewing and subsequent imitation of antisocial behavior (Milgram & Shotland, 1973) and a longitudinal study in Great Britain that found an association between viewing of violence on television and committing antisocial acts such as property damage and hurting others (Belson, 1978). ABC sponsored a series of studies by two mental health consultants who concluded that television contributed only a tiny amount to the stimulation of aggression in children (Heller & Polsky, 1976). NBC began a large-scale panel study, but results were not released until 1983.

In addition to television violence, the potential antisocial impact of pornography was under scrutiny. The Commission on Obscenity and Pornography, however, reported that this material was not a factor in determining antisocial behavior (Commission on Obscenity and Pornography, 1970). The commission's conclusions were somewhat controversial in political circles, but in general they supported the findings of other researchers in human sexuality (Tan, 1981). Subsequent efforts in this area were primarily directed toward examining links between pornography and aggression.

In contrast to violence and pornography, the prosocial effect of television was investigated as well. One stimulus for this research was the success of the television series "Sesame Street." A substantial research effort went into the preparation and evaluation of these children's programs. It was found that the series was helpful in preparing young children for school but not very successful in narrowing the information gap between advantaged and disadvantaged children (Minton, 1975). Other studies by both academic and industry researchers showed the prosocial impact of other programs. For example, the series "Fat Albert and the Cosby Kids" was found to be helpful in teaching prosocial lessons to children (CBS Broadcast Group, 1974).

Studies of these topics continued between 1975 and 1985, although there were far fewer than in the early 1970s. An update to the 1972 Surgeon General's Report, issued in 1982, reflected a broader research focus than the original document; it incorporated investigations of socialization, mental health, and perceptions of social reality. Nonetheless, its conclusions were

even stronger than those of its predecessor: ". . . the consensus among most of the research community is that violence on television does lead to aggressive behavior" (National Institute of Mental Health, 1982). Other researchers, notably Wurtzel and Lometti (1984) and Bear (1984), argue that the report does not support the conclusion of a causal relationship, while Chaffee (1984) and Murray (1984), among others, contend that the conclusions are valid.

Not long after the Surgeon General's report was updated, the results of the NBC panel study begun in the early 1970s were published (Milavsky, Kessler, Stipp, & Rubens, 1983). This panel study, which used state-of-the-art statistical analyses, found a nonsignificant relationship between television violence viewing during the early phases of the study and subsequent aggression. The NBC data have been reexamined by others, and at least one article suggests that the data from this survey do show a slight relationship between violence viewing and aggression among at least one demographic subgroup—middle-class girls (Cook, Kendzierski, & Thomas, 1983). From 1985 to 1990 the controversy subsided but this topic remained popular among academic researchers. Williams (1986) conducted an elaborate field experiment in three Canadian communities. One town was about to receive television for the first time, another received Canadian TV, and the third received both Canadian and U.S. programs. Two years later, Williams and her colleagues found that when compared to the other two communities, children in the town that had just received TV scored higher on measures of physical and verbal aggression.

Additional evidence on the topic of television and violence comes from a series of panel studies conducted by an international team of researchers (Huesmann & Eron, 1986). Data were gathered from young people in the United States, Finland, Australia, Israel, and Poland. Findings from the U.S. and Polish studies reached a similar conclusion: Early TV viewing was related to later aggression. The Finnish study found this same relationship for boys but not for girls. The Israeli study found that TV viewing seemed related to aggression for children living in urban areas but not for those in rural areas. The Australian study failed to find a relationship. In all countries where a relationship between TV viewing and violence was found, the relationship was relatively weak. The practical implications of this weak relationship were examined by Rosenthal (1986) who concluded that even a weak relationship could have substantial social consequences.

Research interest in the antisocial effects of pornography increased in the late 1980s, averaging approximately eight studies per year as listed in *Communication Abstracts*. This increase may have been due in part to reports issued by special commissions on pornography in the United States, Britain, and Canada that used social science research as the basis for some of their recommendations (Einsiedel, 1988). The most controversial research in this area examined whether prolonged exposure to nonviolent pornography had any antisocial effects (Donnerstein, Linz, & Penrod, 1987).

Research interest in the prosocial effects of media exposure decreased in the 1980s. Sprafkin and Rubinstein (1979) reported a correlational study in which the viewing of prosocial television programs accounted for only 1% of the variance in an index of prosocial behavior exhibited in school. The apparent lack of a strong relationship between these two variables, coupled with the absence of general agreement on a definition of *prosocial content*, might have discouraged researchers from selecting this area. In any case, an average of only one study per year appears in the 1986–1989 editions of *Communication Abstracts* and many of these are content analyses (for example, Potter & Ware, 1989).

Methods

Researchers studying the effects of mass media have used most of the techniques discussed in this book: content analysis, laboratory experiments, surveys, field experiments, observations, and panels. Given the wide variety of methods used, it is not possible to describe a typical approach. Instead, this section focuses on four separate studies using different methods as illustrations of some of the research strategies.

THE EXPERIMENTAL METHOD.   A common design to study the antisocial impact of the media consists of showing one group of subjects violent media content, while a control group sees nonviolent content. This was the approach used by Berkowitz and Bandura in their early work. The dependent variable, aggression, is measured immediately after exposure — either by a pencil-and-paper test or by a mechanical device like the one described below. For example, Liebert and Baron (1972) divided children into two groups. The first group saw a 3.5-minute segment from a television show depicting a chase, two fistfights, two shootings, and a knifing. Children in the control group saw a segment of similar length in which athletes competed in track and field events. After viewing, the children were taken one at a time into another room that contained an apparatus with two buttons, one labeled "Help" and the other labeled "Hurt." An experimenter explained to the children that wires from the device were connected to a game in an adjacent room. The subjects were told that in the adjacent room, another child was starting to play a game (there was, in fact, no other child). At various times, by pressing the appropriate buttons, each child would be given a chance to help the unseen child win the game or to hurt the second child. The results showed that children who had seen the violent segment were significantly more likely than the control group to press the "Hurt" button.

Of course, there are many variations on this

basic design. To list just a few, the type of violent content shown to the subjects can be manipulated (for example, cartoon vs. live violence, entertainment vs. newscast violence, justified vs. unjustified violence). Also, some subjects may be frustrated before exposure. The degree of association between the media violence and the subsequent testing situation may be high or low. Subjects can watch alone or with others who praise or condemn the media violence. Media exposure can be a one-time event or manipulated over time. For a thorough summary of this research see Comstock, Chaffee, and Katzman (1978) and Liebert and Sprafkin (1988).

Experimental studies examining the impact of media exposure on prosocial behavior have used essentially the same approach. Subjects see a televised segment that is either prosocial or neutral and the dependent variable is then assessed. For example, Forge and Phemister (1987) randomly assigned preschoolers to one of four conditions: prosocial animated program ("The Get-along Gang"), neutral animated ("Alvin and the Chipmunks"), prosocial nonanimated ("Mr. Rogers' Neighborhood"), and neutral nonanimated ("Animal Express"). The children watched the program and were then placed in a free-play situation where their prosocial behaviors were observed and recorded. The results demonstrated an effect for the program variable (prosocial programs prompted more prosocial behaviors than did neutral programs) but no effect for the animated vs. nonanimated variable.

The operational definitions of prosocial behavior have shown wide variation. Studies have examined cooperative behaviors, sharing, kindness, altruism, friendliness, creativity, and absence of stereotyping.

Almost any behavior with a positive social value seems to be a candidate for study, as exemplified by the experiment by Baran, Chase, and Courtright (1979). Third graders were assigned to one of three treatment conditions. One group saw a condensed version of a segment of "The Waltons" demonstrating cooperative behavior. The second group saw a program portraying noncooperative behavior, and the third group saw no program. After answering a few written questions dealing with the program, each subject left the viewing room only to encounter a confederate of the experimenter who passed the doorway and dropped an armload of books. There were two dependent measures: whether the subject attempted to retrieve the books, and the amount of time that elapsed until the subject began to help. The group that saw the cooperative content was found to be more likely to help, and their responses were quicker than those of the control group. Interestingly, there was no difference in helping behavior or in duration between the group seeing "The Waltons" and the group seeing the noncooperative content.

THE SURVEY APPROACH. Most such studies have used questionnaires incorporating measures of media exposure (such as viewing television violence or exposure to pornography) and a pencil-and-paper measure of antisocial behavior or attitudes. In addition, many recent studies have included measures of demographic and sociographic variables that mediate the exposure–antisocial behavior relationship. Results are usually expressed as a series of correlations.

A survey by McLeod, Atkin, and Chaffee (1972) illustrates this approach. Their questionnaire contained measures of violence viewing, aggression, and family environment. Viewing was tabulated by giving respondents a list of 65 prime-time television programs with a scale measuring how often each was viewed. An index of overall violence viewing was obtained by using independent ratings of the violence level of each show and multiplying it by the frequency of viewing. Aggression was measured by seven scales. One measured respondents' approval of manifest physical aggression (sample item: "Whoever insults me or my family is looking for a fight"). Another examined approval of aggression ("It's all right to hurt an enemy if you are mad at him"). Respondents indicated their degree of agreement with each of the items composing the separate scales. Family environment was measured by asking about parental control over television, parental emphasis on nonaggression punishment (such as withdrawal of privileges), and other variables. The researchers found a moderate positive relationship between the respondents' level of violence viewing and their self-reports of aggression. Family environment showed no consistent association with either of the two variables.

Sprafkin and Rubinstein (1979) used the survey method to examine the relationship between television viewing and prosocial behavior. They used basically the same approach as McLeod, Atkin, and Chaffee (1972), except that their viewing measure was designed to assess exposure to television programs established as prosocial by prior content analysis. Their measure of prosocial behaviors was based on peer nominations of persons who reflected 12 prosocial behaviors, including helping, sharing, rule-following, staying out of fights, and niceness. The researchers found that when the influence of the child's gender, the parents' educational level, and the child's academic level were statistically controlled, exposure to prosocial television explained only 1% of the variance in prosocial behaviors.

FIELD EXPERIMENTS. The imaginative and elaborate fieldwork used to study the antisocial effects of the media by Milgram and Shotland (1973) was discussed in Chapter 5. Parke, Berkowitz, and Leyens (1977) conducted a field experiment in a minimum-security penal institution for juveniles. The researchers exposed groups to unedited feature-length films that were either aggressive or nonaggressive. On the day after the last film was shown, in the context of a bogus learning experiment, the boys were told they had a chance to hurt a confederate of the experimenters who had insulted one group of boys and had been neutral to the other. The

results on an electric shock measure similar to the one described previously revealed that the most aggressive of all the experimental groups were the boys who had seen the aggressive films and who had been insulted. In addition to this laboratory measure, the investigators collected observational data on the boys' aggressive interpersonal behavior in their everyday environment. These data showed that boys who saw the violent movies were more interpersonally aggressive. However, there was no apparent cumulative effect of movies on aggression. The boys who watched the diet of aggressive films were just as aggressive after the first film as after the last.

Figure 5.12 (page 102) illustrates the design of the Canadian field experiment (Williams, 1986) discussed earlier. The dependent variable of aggression was measured in three ways: observations of behavior on school playgrounds, peer ratings and teacher ratings. On the observational measure, the aggressive acts of children in the town labelled A (the town that just received TV) increased from an average of .43 per minute in Phase 1 to 1.1 per minute in Phase 2. Children in the other towns showed only a slight and statistically insignificant rise in the same period. Peer and teacher ratings tended to support the behavioral data. As yet, there have been no large-scale field experiments examining prosocial behavior.

PANEL STUDIES.   Primarily because of the time and expense involved in panel studies, this analysis mode is seldom used to examine the media in relation to antisocial effects. Three studies relevant to this topic are briefly reviewed here. Lefkowitz, Eron, Waldner, and Huesmann (1972), using a catch-up panel design, reinterviewed 427 of 875 youthful subjects 10 years after they had participated in a study of mental health. Measures of television viewing and aggression had been administered to these subjects when they were in the third grade, and data on the two variables were gathered again a decade later. Slightly different methods were used to measure television viewing on the two time occasions. Viewing in the third grade was established on the basis of mothers' reports of their children's three favorite television shows. Ten years later, respondents rated their own frequency of viewing. The data were subjected to cross-lagged correlations and path analysis. The results supported the hypothesis that aggression in later life was caused in part by television viewing during early years. However, the panel study by Milavsky et al. (1983), sponsored by NBC, found no evidence of such a relationship.

The difference between the results of these studies might be due to several factors. The Milavsky study did not vary its measure of "violent television viewing" throughout its duration. In addition, the NBC researchers used LISREL (linear structural equations), a more powerful statistical technique, which was not available at the time of the Lefkowitz study. Finally, the Lefkowitz measures were taken 10 years apart; the maximum time lag in the NBC study was 3 years.

Another panel study of the media and possible antisocial effects was conducted by Huesmann and Eron (1986). The investigators followed 758 children who were in the first and third grades in 1977 and reinterviewed them in 1978 and 1979. Aggression was measured by both peer nominations and self ratings. Multiple regression analyses disclosed that for both boys and girls watching TV violence was a significant predictor of aggression they would later demonstrate. Other variables that were also significant included the degree to which children identified with violent TV characters, the perceived reality of the violence, and the amount of a child's aggressive fantasizing.

SUMMARY. Experiments and surveys have been the most popular research strategies used to study the impact of media on antisocial and prosocial behavior. The more elaborate techniques of field experiments and panel studies have been used infrequently. Interestingly, as pointed out by Andison (1977), the method employed to

study this topic is related to the strength and direction of the results. Laboratory experiments have shown a stronger positive relation between viewing media violence and aggression than have the other techniques.

Theoretical Developments

One of the earliest theoretical considerations in the debate over the impact of media violence was the controversy of catharsis versus stimulation. The *catharsis* approach suggests that viewing fantasy expressions of hostility reduces aggression because a person who watches filmed or televised violence is purged of his or her aggressive urges. This theory has some obvious attraction for industry executives, since it carries the implication that presenting violent television shows is a prosocial action. The stimulation theory argues the opposite: viewing violence prompts more aggression on the part of the viewer. The research findings in this area indicated little support for the catharsis position. A few studies did find a lessening of aggressive behavior after viewing violent content, but these results apparently were an artifact of the research design. The overwhelming majority of studies found evidence of a stimulation effect.

Since these early studies, many of the experiments and surveys have used social learning as their conceptual basis. As spelled out by Bandura (1977), the theory explains how people learn from direct experience or from observation (or modeling). Some of the key elements in this theory are attention, retention, motor reproduction, and motivations. According to Bandura, attention to an event is influenced by characteristics of the event and by characteristics of the observer. For example, repeated observation of an event by a person who has been paying close attention should increase learning. *Retention* refers to how well an individual remembers behaviors that have been observed. *Motor reproduction* is the actual behavioral enactment of the observed event. For example, some people can accurately imitate a behavior after merely observing it, while others need to experiment. The motivational component of the theory depends on the reinforcement or punishment that accompanies performance of the observed behavior.

Applied to the effects area, social learning theory predicts that antisocial or prosocial acts can be learned by watching films or television. The model further suggests that viewing repeated antisocial acts would make people more likely to perform these acts in real life. Yet another prediction involves *desensitization*, to account for the suggestion that people who are heavily exposed to violence and antisocial acts become less anxious about the consequences.

Bandura (1977) summarized much of the research concerning social learning theory. In brief, some of the key findings in laboratory and field experiments suggest that children can easily perform new acts of aggression after a single exposure to them on television or in films. The similarity between the circumstances of the observed antisocial acts and the postobservation circumstances will be important in determining whether the act is performed. If a model is positively reinforced for performing antisocial acts, the observed acts will be more frequently performed in real life. Likewise, when children were promised rewards for performing antisocial acts, more antisocial behavior was exhibited. Other factors that facilitated the performance of antisocial acts included the degree to which the media behavior is perceived to be real, the emotional arousal of the subjects, and the presence of cues in the postobservation environment that elicit antisocial behavior. Finally, as predicted by the theory, desensitization to violence can occur through repeated exposure to violent acts.

More recently, much research has continued to refine and reformulate some of the elements in social learning theory. For example, the arousal hypothesis (Tannenbaum & Zillmann, 1975) suggests that for a portrayal to have a demonstrable effect, increased arousal may be necessary. According to this model, if an angered person is exposed to an arousing stimulus, such as a pornographic film, and is placed in a situation to which aggression is a possible response, the person will become more aggressive (*excitation transfer* is the term used by the researchers). Zillmann, Hoyt, and Day (1979) offer some support for this model. Interestingly, it appears that subjects in a high state of arousal from seeing a violent film will perform more prosocial acts than nonaroused subjects. Like aggressive behavior, prosocial behavior seems facilitated by media-induced arousal (Meuller, Donnerstein, & Hallam, 1983).

Tan (1986) reviewed the literature on TV violence and aggression from a social learning perspective and concluded that the results are exactly what should be expected. Tan presented a three-part model that included the attention process, the retention process, and the reproduction process. This model listed some of the many variables that should be influential in the social learning process.

Other research has shown that social learning theory can be applied to the study of the effects of viewing pornography. Zillmann and Bryant (1982) showed that heavy exposure to pornographic films apparently desensitized subjects to the seriousness of rape and led to decreased compassion for women as rape victims. A similar finding was obtained by Linz, Donnerstein, and Penrod (1984). Men who viewed five movies depicting erotic situations involving violence toward women perceived the films as less violent and less degrading to women than did a control group not exposed to the films. In sum, social learning theory appears to be a promising framework for integrating many of the findings in this area.

Another promising theory, outlined by Berkowitz and Rogers (1986), is based on priming effects analysis. Drawing upon the concepts of cognitive-neoassociationism, priming effects analysis posits that elements of thought or feeling or memories are parts of a network connected by associative pathways. When a thought element is activated, the activation spreads along the pathways to other parts of the network. Thus, for some time after a concept is activated, there is an increased probability that it and other associated parts of the network will come to mind again, creating the priming effect. As a result, aggressive ideas prompted by viewing media violence trigger other semantically related thoughts, increasing the probability that associated aggressive thoughts will come to mind. Berkowitz and Rogers note that priming analysis can explain the fact that much exposure to media violence results in short-term, transient effects. They point out that the priming effect attenuates over time, lowering the probability of subsequent violent effects.

USES AND GRATIFICATIONS

The *uses and gratifications* perspective takes the view of the media consumer. It examines how people use the media and the gratifications they seek and receive from their media behaviors. Uses and gratifications researchers assume that audience members are aware of and can articulate their reasons for consuming various media content.

History

The uses and gratifications approach has its roots in the 1940s when researchers became interested in why people engaged in various forms of media behavior, such as radio listening or newspaper reading. These early studies were primarily descriptive, seeking to classify the responses of audience members into meaningful categories. For example, Herzog (1944) identified three types of gratification associated with listening to radio soap operas: emotional release, wishful thinking, and obtaining advice. Berelson (1949) took advantage of a New York newspaper strike to ask people why they read the paper. The responses were placed in five major categories: reading for information, reading for social prestige, reading for escape, reading as a tool for daily living, and reading for a social context. These early studies had little theoretical coherence; in fact, many were inspired by the practical needs of newspaper publishers and radio broadcasters to know the motivations of their audience in order to serve them more efficiently. (Chapter 13 notes that the uses and gratifications approach is still one of the major types of research performed by those interested in understanding newspaper readership.)

The next step in the development of this research began during the late 1950s and continued into the 1960s. In this phase the emphasis was on identifying and operationalizing the many social and psychological variables that were presumed to be the antecedents of different patterns of consumption and gratification. For example, Schramm, Lyle, and Parker (1961), in their extensive study, found that children's use of television was influenced by individual mental ability and relationships with parents and peers, among other things. Gerson (1966) concluded that race was important in predicting how adolescents used the media. Greenberg and Dominick (1969) found that race and social class predicted how teenagers used television as an informal source of learning. These studies and many more conducted during this period reflected a shift from the traditional effects model of mass media research to the functional perspective.

According to Windahl (1981), a primary difference between the traditional effects approach and the uses and gratifications approach is that a media effects researcher usually examines mass communication from the perspective of the communicator, whereas the uses and gratifications researcher uses the audience member as a point of departure. Windahl argues for a synthesis of the two approaches, believing that it is more beneficial to emphasize their similarities than to stress their differences. He has coined the term *conseffects* of media content and use to categorize observations that are partly results of content use in itself (a viewpoint commonly adopted by effects researchers) and partly results of content mediated by use (a viewpoint adopted by many uses and gratifications researchers).

Windahl's perspective serves to link the earlier uses and gratifications approach to the third phase in its development. Recently, uses and gratifications research has become more conceptual and theoretical as investigators have offered their data in explanation of the connections between audience motives, media gratifications, and outcomes. As Rubin (1985) noted: ". . . several typologies of mass media motives and functions have been formulated to conceptualize the seeking of gratifications as variables that intervene before media effects." For example, Greenberg (1974) ascertained that a positive disposition to aggression characterized children who used television for arousal purposes. Rubin (1979) found a significant positive correlation between viewing television to learn something and the perceived reality of television content: those using television as a learning device thought television content was more true to life. And deBock (1980) noted that people who experienced the most frustration at being deprived of a newspaper during a strike were those who used the newspaper for information and those who viewed newspaper reading as a ritual. These and many other recent studies have revealed that a variety of audience gratifications are related to a wide range of media effects. These "uses and effects" studies (Rubin, 1985) have bridged the gap between the traditional effects approach and the uses and gratifications perspective.

Methods

Uses and gratifications researchers have relied heavily on the survey method to collect their data. As a first step, researchers have conducted focus groups or have asked respondents to write essays about their reasons for media consumption. Closed-ended Likert-type scales based on what was said in the focus group or written in the essays are then constructed. The closed-ended measures are typically subjected to multivariate statistical techniques such as factor analysis (Appendix 2), which identifies various dimensions of gratifications.

Greenberg's (1974) study of British children and adolescents illustrates the usual approach to gathering uses and gratifications data. As a first step, British youngsters wrote essays entitled "Why I Like to Watch Television." These anonymous works were subjected to content analysis and eight general reasons for watching television were identified: passing time, diversion, learning about things, learning about myself, arousal, relaxation, companionship, and habit. Three or four statements were constructed that best appeared to reflect each of these eight reasons. This resulted in a list of 31 items. For example, "I watch television when I'm bored," ". . . because it's a habit," ". . . because it relaxes me," and ". . . because it's most like a real friend." Respondents could indicate that each reason was "a lot," "a little," "not much," or "not at all" like their reason for viewing. After the instrument had been administered to the sample, the data were factor analyzed. Eight separate factors (or functions) appeared: learning, habit, arousal, companionship, relaxation, forgetting, passing time, and boredom. Note that the eight factors derived from the statistical analysis are slightly different from the content analysis of the essays.

Each child or adolescent was given a score on each of the eight dimensions. A score of 4 meant that the child thought the reason was "a lot" like his or hers, while a score of 1 indicated "not at all" like the individual's reason. This analysis revealed that "habit" was the most endorsed reason and "forgetting" the least. In addition, when the average scores per factor were analyzed by age, it was found that each of the eight motives was more strongly present for younger children than for the others. Finally, each of the factor scores was correlated with measures of media use, aggressive attitudes, television attitudes, and demographic variables.

Note that the technique above assumes that the audience is aware of its reasons and can report them when asked. The method also assumes that the pencil-and-paper test is a valid and reliable measurement scale. Other assumptions include an active audience with goal-directed media behavior; expectations for media use that are produced from individual predispositions, social interaction, and environmental factors; and media selection initiated by the individual. Some researchers (see Becker, 1980) suggest that reliability and validity checks should be built into the uses and gratifications approach. For an example of how this has been accomplished, see Rubin (1985).

Dobos and Dimmick (1988) caution that the choice of statistical computer programs and different methods of factor analysis can have an impact on the resulting structure of gratifications. Their reanalysis of existing data found that the results generated from using the Statistical Package for the Social Sciences Program (SPSS) were different from those generated by the Statistical Analysis System (SAS).

The experimental method has not been widely used in uses and gratifications research. When it has been chosen, investigators typically manipulated the subjects' motivations and measured differences in their media consumption. To illustrate, Bryant and Zillmann (1984) placed their subjects in either a state of boredom or a state of stress and then gave them a choice between watching a relaxing or a stimulating television program. Stressed subjects watched more tranquil programs and bored subjects opted for the exciting fare. McLeod and Becker (1981) had their subjects sit in a lounge area that contained public affairs magazines. One group of subjects was told that they would soon be tested about the current situation in Pakistan. A sec-ond group was told they would be required to write an essay on U.S. military aid to Pakistan, while a control group was given no specific instructions. As expected, subjects in the test and essay conditions made greater use of the magazines than did the control group. The two test groups also differed in the type of information they remembered from the periodicals. Experiments such as these two indicate that different cognitive or affective states facilitate the use of media for various reasons, as predicted by the uses and gratifications rationale.

Theoretical Developments

As mentioned earlier, researchers in the academic sector are interested in developing theory concerning the topics they investigate. This tendency is well illustrated in the history of uses and gratifications research. Whereas early studies tended to be descriptive, later scholars have attempted to integrate research findings into a more theoretical context.

In an early explanation of the uses and gratifications process, Rosengren (1974) suggested that certain basic needs interact with personal characteristics and the social environment of the individual to produce perceived problems and perceived solutions. The problems and solutions constitute different motives for gratification behavior that can come from using the media or from other activities. Together the media use or other behaviors produce gratification (or nongratification) that has an impact on the individual or society, thereby starting the process anew. After reviewing the results of approximately 100 uses and gratifications studies, Palmgreen (1984) stated that "a rather complex theoretical structure . . . has begun to emerge." He proposed an integrative gratifications model that suggested a multivariate approach (Appendix 2).

The gratifications sought by the audience form the central concept in the model. There are, however, many antecedent variables such as media structure, media technology, social circumstances, psychological variables, needs, values, and beliefs that all relate to the particular gratification pattern used by the audience. Additionally, the consequences of the gratifications relate directly to media and nonmedia consumption behaviors and perceived gratifications that are obtained. As Palmgreen admits, this model suffers from lack of parsimony and needs strengthening in several areas, but it does represent an increase in our understanding of the mass media process. Further refinements in the model will come from surveys and experiments designed to test specific hypotheses derived from well-articulated theoretical rationales and from carefully designed descriptive studies. For example, Levy and Windahl (1984) examined the assumption of an active audience in the uses and gratifications approach. They derived a typology of audience activity and prepared a model that linked activity to various uses and gratifications, thus clarifying further one of the important postulates in the uses and gratifications process.

Rubin (1986) pointed out that although theory development had progressed, the uses and gratifications approach still had a long way to go. He argued that what was needed was a clearer picture of the relationship between media and personal channels of communication and sources of potential influence. In a similar vein, Swanson (1987) called for more research that would benefit the theoretical grounding of the uses and gratifications approach. Specifically, Swanson urged that research focus on (1) the role of gratification seeking in exposure to mass media, (2) the relationship between gratification and the interpretive frames through which audiences understand media content, and (3) the link between gratifications and media content. In sum, it is likely that the next few years will see an increased emphasis on theory building among uses and gratifications researchers.

The uses and gratifications approach also serves to illustrate the difference in emphasis between academic and applied research objectives. Newspaper publishers and broadcasting executives, who want guidance in attracting readers, viewers, and listeners, seem to be particularly interested in determining what specific content is best suited to fulfilling the needs of the audience. College and university researchers are interested not only in content characteristics, they want to develop theories that explain and predict the media consumption of the public based on sociological, psychological and structural variables.

AGENDA SETTING BY THE MEDIA

Agenda setting theory proposes that "the public agenda — or what kinds of things people discuss, think, and worry about (and sometimes ultimately press for legislation about) — is powerfully shaped and directed by what the news media choose to publicize" (Larson, 1986). This means that if the news media decide to give the most time and space to coverage of apartheid in South Africa, this issue will become the most important item on the audience's agenda. If the news media devote the second most amount of coverage to unemployment, audiences, too, will rate unemployment as the second most important issue to them, and so on. Agenda setting research examines the relationship between media priorities and audience priorities in the relative importance of news topics.

History

The notion of agenda setting by the media can be traced to Walter Lippmann (1922), who suggested the media were responsible for the "pictures in our heads." Forty years later, Cohen (1963) further articulated the idea when he argued that the media may not always be successful in telling people what to think, but they are usually successful in telling them what to think about. Lang and Lang (1966) reinforced this notion by observing, "The mass media force attention to certain issues. . . . They are constantly presenting objects, suggesting what individuals in the mass should think about, know about, have feelings about."

The first empirical test of agenda setting came in 1972, when McCombs and Shaw (1972) reported the results of a study done during the 1968 presidential election. They found strong support for the agenda setting hypothesis. There were strong relationships between the emphasis placed on different campaign issues by the media and the judgments of voters regarding the importance of various campaign topics. This study inspired a host of others, many of them concerned with agenda setting as it occurred during political campaigns. For example, Tipton, Haney, and Baseheart (1975) used cross-lagged correlation (Chapter 9) to analyze the impact of the media on agenda setting during statewide elections. Patterson and McClure (1976) studied the impact of television news and television commercials on agenda setting in the 1972 election. They concluded that television news had minimal impact on public awareness of issues, but that television advertising accounted for a rise in the audience's awareness of candidates' positions on issues.

Lately, agenda setting research has enjoyed increased popularity. *Communication Abstracts* has listed an average of 7.5 articles per year on agenda setting from 1978 to 1989. The more recent articles signal a shift away from the political campaign approach. In the years 1978–1981, about 30% of the agenda setting articles were analyses of political campaigns. From 1982 to 1989, about 11% were of this type. In short, the agenda setting technique is now being used in a variety of areas: history, advertising, foreign news, and medical news. In addition, increased attention is being paid to the methods involved (Roberts & Bachen, 1981), to the time dimension (Salwen, 1988), and to theory building (Williams, 1985; VanLeuven & Ray, 1988).

Methods

The typical agenda setting study involves several of the approaches discussed in earlier chapters. Content analysis (Chapter 8) is used to define the media agenda, and surveys (Chapter 6) are used to collect data on the audience agenda. In addition, since determination of the media agenda and surveying of the audience are not done simultaneously, a longitudinal dimension (Chapter 9) is present as well. More recently, some studies have used the experimental approach (Chapter 5).

MEASURING THE MEDIA AGENDA.   Several techniques have been used to establish the media agenda. The most common method involves grouping coverage topics into broad categories and measuring the amount of time or space devoted to each category. The operational definitions of these categories are important considerations because the more broadly a topic area is defined, the easier it is to demonstrate an agenda setting effect. Ideally, the content analysis should include all media, including television, radio, newspaper, and magazines. Unfortunately, this is too large a task for most researchers to handle comfortably, and most studies have been confined to one or two media, usually television and the daily newspaper. For example, Williams and Semlak (1978a) tabulated total air time for each topic mentioned in the three television network newscasts for a 19-day period. The topics were rank ordered according to their total time. At the same time, the newspaper agenda was constructed by measuring the total column inches devoted to each topic on the front and editorial pages of the local newspaper. McLeod, Becker, and Byrnes (1974) content analyzed local newspapers for a 6-week period, totaling the number of inches devoted to each topic, including headlines and pertinent pictures on the front and editorial pages. Among other things, they found that the front and editorial pages adequately represented the entire newspaper in their topical areas.

Other content analytic approaches have included counting the number of articles that have appeared in major news magazines over a number of years. Funkhouser (1973) used the *Reader's Guide to Periodical Literature* to identify the major topics on the agenda of news magazines from 1960 to 1970. Williams and Semlak (1978b) analyzed the agenda setting impact of the visual dimension in a television newscast. They categorized stories according to their use of chromakey, sound on film, rear-screen projection, and videotape. They found that static visuals (such as chromakey, where two pictures are electronically combined) had an impact on setting personal agendas.

MEASURING PUBLIC AGENDAS. The public agenda has been constructed in at least four ways. First, respondents have been asked an open-ended question such as, "What do you feel is the most important political issue to you personally?" or "What is the most important political issue in your community?" The phrasing of this question can elicit either the respondent's intrapersonal agenda (as in the first example) or interpersonal agenda (the second example). A second method asks respondents to rate in importance the issues in a list compiled by the researcher. The third technique is a variation of this approach. Respondents are given a list of topics selected by the researcher and asked to rank order them according to perceived importance. The fourth technique uses the paired-comparisons method. In this approach, each issue on a preselected list is paired with every other issue and the respondent is asked to consider each pair and to identify the more important issue. When all the responses have been tabulated, the issues are ordered from the most to the least important.

As with all measurement, each technique has its associated advantages and disadvantages. The open-ended method gives respondents great freedom in nominating issues, but it favors those people who are better able to verbalize their thoughts. The closed-ended ranking and rating techniques make sure that all respondents have a common vocabulary, but they assume each respondent is aware of all the public issues listed and restrict the respondent from expressing a personal point of view. The paired-comparisons method provides interval data, which allows for more sophisticated statistical techniques, but it takes longer to complete than the other methods, and this might be a problem in some forms of survey research.

There are three important time frames used in collecting the data for agenda setting research: (1) the duration of the media agenda measurement period, (2) the time lag between measuring the media agenda and measuring the personal agenda, and (3) the duration of the audience agenda measurement. Unfortunately, there is little in the way of research or theory to guide the investigator in this area. To illustrate, Mullins (1977) studied media content for a week to determine the media agenda, but Gormley (1975) gathered media data for 4.5 months. Similarly, the time lag between media agenda measurement and audience agenda measurement has varied from no time at all (McLeod et al., 1974) to a lag of 5 months (Gormley, 1975).

Not surprisingly, the duration of the measurement period for audience agendas also has shown wide variation. Hilker (1976) collected a public agenda measure in a single day, while McLeod et al. (1974) took 4 weeks. Eyal, Winter, and DeGeorge (1981) suggested that methodological studies should be carried out to determine the optimal effect span or peak association period between the media emphasis and public emphasis. Winter and Eyal (1981), in an example of one of these methodological studies found an optimal effect span of 6 weeks for agenda setting on the civil rights issue. Similarly, Salwen (1988) found that it took from 5 to 7 weeks of news media coverage of environmental issues before they became salient on the public's agenda.

Other variables that appear to be important in considering the proper longitudinal dimension for agenda setting studies are the nature of the issues and the media under study. It is conceivable that the electronic media and the print media influence the public agenda at different rates and that some issues take longer than others to show an agenda setting effect. Further study of the methods used in agenda setting should provide further information on these complicated topics.

Several researchers have used the experimental technique to study the causal direction in agenda setting. For example, Wanta (1988) showed groups of subjects newspaper stories with a dominant photograph, a balanced photograph, or no photo. The results were mixed but the dominant photograph did seem to have an effect on the subjects' agenda. Another experiment (Heeter, Brown, Soffin, Stanley, & Salwen, 1989) examined the agenda setting effect of teletext. One group of subjects was instructed to abstain from all traditional news media for 5 consecutive days and instead spend 30 minutes each day with a teletext news service. The results indicated that a week's worth of exposure did little to alter subjects' agendas.

Theoretical Developments

The construction of a theory of agenda setting is still at a formative level. In spite of the problems in method and time span mentioned above, the findings in agenda setting are consistent enough to permit some first steps toward theory building. To begin, the longitudinality of agenda setting has permitted some tentative causal statements. Most of this research has supported the interpretation that the media's agenda causes the public agenda; the rival causal hypothesis — that the public agenda establishes the media agenda — has not received much support (Behr & Iyengar, 1985; Roberts & Bachen, 1981). Thus, much of the recent research has attempted to specify the audience-related and media-related events that condition the agenda setting effect.

It is apparent that constructing an agenda setting theory will be a complicated task. Williams (1985), for example, posited eight antecedent variables that should have an impact on audience agendas during a political campaign. Four of these variables (voter interest, voter activity, political involvement, and civic activity) have been linked to agenda setting (Williams & Semlak, 1978a). In addition, several studies have suggested that a person's "need for orientation" should be a predictor of agenda holding. (Note that such an approach incorporates uses and gratifications thinking.) For example, Weaver (1977) found a positive correlation between the need for orientation and a greater acceptance of media agendas.

These antecedent variables define the media scanning behavior of the individual (McCombs, 1981). Important variables at this stage of the process include media use (see Weaver, 1977) and the use of interpersonal communication (Winter, 1981). Other influences on the individual's agenda setting behavior include the duration and obtrusiveness of the issues themselves and the specifics of media coverage (Winter, 1981). Finally, Lang and Lang (1981) suggest that the potential of the topic to affect many or few in the audience (called "issue threshold") has a bearing on agenda building.

Despite the tentative nature of the theory, many researchers continue to develop models of the agenda setting process. Manheim (1987), for example, developed a model of agenda setting that distinguished between content and salience of issues. VanLeuven and Ray (1988) presented a five-stage model of public issue development that includes agenda setting as one of its key dimensions. Most models use the media as a starting point and examine the ways by which they influence the public's agenda. Some researchers, however, are extending these models one step farther by trying to identify what forces are important in setting the media's agenda (Turk & Franklin, 1987; Megawa & Brenner, 1988; Wanta, Stephenson, Turk, & McCombs, 1989).

CULTIVATION OF PERCEPTIONS OF SOCIAL REALITY

How do the media affect audience perceptions of the real world? The basic assumption underlying the cultivation, or enculturation, approach is that repeated exposures to consistent media portrayals and themes will influence our perceptions of these items in the direction of the media portrayals. In effect, learning from the media environment is generalized, sometimes incorrectly, to the social environment.

As was the case with agenda setting research, most of the enculturation research has been conducted by investigators in the academic sector. Industry researchers are aware of this work and sometimes question its accuracy or meaning (Wurtzel & Lometti, 1984), but they seldom conduct it or sponsor it themselves.

History

Some of the early research studies indicated that media portrayals of certain topics could have an impact on audience perceptions, particularly if the media were the main information sources. Siegel (1958) found that children's role expectations about a taxi driver could be influenced by hearing a radio program about the character. DeFleur and DeFleur (1967) found that television had a homogenizing effect on children's perceptions of occupations commonly shown on television. On a more general level, Greenberg and Dominick (1969) discovered that lower-class teenagers were more likely than middle-class ones to believe that the middle-class world commonly portrayed on television programs was true to life.

The more recent research on viewer perceptions of social reality stems from the Cultural Indicators project of George Gerbner and his associates. Since 1968, they have collected data on the content of television and have analyzed the impact of heavy exposure on the audience. Some of the many variables that have been content analyzed include the demographic portraits of perpetrators and victims of television violence, the prevalence of violent acts, the types of violence portrayed, and the contexts of violence. The basic hypothesis of cultivation analysis is that the more time one spends living in the world of television, the more likely one is to report conceptions of social reality that can be traced to television portrayals (Gross & Morgan, 1985).

To test this hypothesis, Gerbner and his associates have analyzed data from adults, adolescents, and children in cities across the United States. The first cultivation data were reported a decade ago (Gerbner & Gross, 1976). Using data collected by the National Opinion Research Center (NORC), Gerbner found that heavy television viewers scored higher on a "mean world" index than did light viewers. (Sample items from this index included: "Do you think people try to take advantage of you?" and "You can't be too careful in dealing with people [agree/disagree].") Data from both adult and child NORC samples showed that heavy viewers were more suspicious and distrustful. Subsequent studies reinforced these findings and found that heavy television viewers were more likely to overestimate the prevalence of violence in society and their own chances of being involved in violence (Gerbner, Gross, Jackson-Beeck, Jeffries-Fox, & Signorielli, 1978). In sum, their perceptions of reality were cultivated by television.

Not all researchers have accepted the cultivation hypothesis. In particular, Hughes (1980) and Hirsch (1980) reanalyzed the NORC data using simultaneous rather than individual controls for demographic variables and were unable to replicate Gerbner's findings. Gerbner responded by introducing *resonance* and *mainstreaming*, two new concepts to help explain inconsistencies in the results (Gerbner, Gross, Morgan, & Signorielli, 1986). When the media reinforce what is seen in real life, thus giving an audience member a "double dose," the resulting increase in the cultivation effect is attributed to resonance. Mainstreaming is a leveling effect. Differences in perceptions of reality usually caused by demographic and social factors are washed out by heavy viewing, resulting in a common viewpoint. These concepts refine and further elaborate the cultivation hypothesis but they have not satisfied all the critics of this approach.

Recent research into the cultivation hypothesis indicates that the topic may be more complicated than first thought. Weaver and Wakshlag (1986) found that the cultivation effect was more pronounced among active TV viewers rather than among low involvement viewers and that personal experience with crime was an important mediating variable that affected the impact of TV programs on cultivating an attitude of vulnerability toward crime. Additionally, Potter (1986) found that the perceived reality of the TV content had an impact on cultivation. Other research (Rubin, Perse, & Taylor, 1988) demonstrated that the wording of the attitude and perceptual questions used to measure cultivation influenced the results. Finally, Potter (1988) found that such variables as identification with TV characters, anomie, IQ, and informational needs of the viewer had differential effects on cultivation. In other words, different people react in different ways to TV content and these different reactions determine the strength of the cultivation effect.

Method

There are two discrete steps in performing a cultivation analysis. First, descriptions of the media world are obtained from periodic content analyses of large blocks of media content. The result of this content analysis is the identification of the messages of the television world. These messages represent consistent patterns in portrayal of specific issues, policies, and topics that are often at odds with their occurrence in real life. The identification of the consistent portrayals is followed by the construction of a set of questions designed to detect a cultivation effect. Each question poses two or more alternatives. One alternative is more consistent with the world as seen on television, while another is more in line with the real world. For example, according to the content analyses performed by Gerbner et al. (1977), about 60% of television homicides are committed by strangers. In real life, according to government statistics, only 16% of homicides occur between strangers. The question based on this discrepancy was, "Does fatal violence occur between strangers or between relatives and acquaintances?" The response "strangers" was considered to be the television answer. Another question was, "What percentage of all males who have jobs work in law enforcement and crime detection? Is it 1% or 5%?" According to census data, 1% of males in real life have such jobs, compared to 12% in television programs. Thus, 5% is the television answer.

The second step involves surveying audiences with regard to television exposure, dividing the sample into heavy and light viewers (4 hours of viewing a day is usually the dividing line) and comparing their answers to the questions differentiating the television world from the real world. In addition, data are often collected on possible control variables such as gender, age, and socioeconomic status. The basic statistical procedure consists of correlational analysis between the amount of television viewing and scores on an index reflecting the number of television answers to the comparison questions. Also, partial correlation is used to remove the effects of the control variables. Alternatively, sometimes the cultivation differential (CD) is reported. The CD is the percentage of heavy viewers minus the percentage of light viewers who gave the television answers. For example, if 73% of the heavy viewers gave the television answer to the question about violence being committed between strangers or acquaintances compared to 62% of the light viewers, the CD would be 11%. Laboratory experiments use the same general approach, but they usually manipulate the subjects' experience with the television world by showing an experimental group one or more preselected programs.

Theoretical Developments

What does the research tell us about cultivation? After an extensive literature review in which 48 studies were examined, Hawkins and Pingree (1981) concluded that there was evidence for a link between viewing and beliefs regardless of the kind of social reality in question. Was this link real or spurious? The authors concluded that the answer to this question did, in fact, depend on the type of belief under study. Relationships between viewing and demographic aspects of social reality held up under rigorous controls. Correlations between viewing and value-system measures (for example, "Are you [the respondent] afraid to go out at night?") were less robust, and the findings have been mixed. As far as causality was concerned, the authors concluded that most of the evidence went in one direction, namely, that television causes social reality to be interpreted in certain ways.

How does this process take place? Research in this area is so recent that there has been relatively little systematic effort to build a theory on the media's influence on social perception. As Tan (1981) suggested, the principles of social learning theory can be applied to this area, since learning from watching a television program is being generalized to a new situation. Nonetheless, there has been little effort to interpret the results of cultivation research in this context. This may be partly because researchers have not specified all the intervening variables that might affect cultivation.

At a general level, there are probably three classes of variables that might influence the way the mass media shape a person's social perceptions: individual differences, situational variables, and content differences (most cultivation studies are based on measures of total television viewing, but as Hawkins & Pingree, 1981, noted, differences in content in patterns of action and characterization might temper the cultivation impact).

As more researchers uncover other variables important in the process (for example, Potter, 1988), the next step in the theoretical development of the cultivation hypothesis seems to be a greater emphasis on the apparently complicated process that underlies the phenomenon. In his review of the field, Bryant (1986) observed:

> Most of the cultivation research to date seems to have had greater concern with impact than with process, with patterns of cultivation results than with mechanisms. Another earmark of intellectual maturity seems to be a focus on the "whys" and "hows" of a theory as opposed to gathering normative data as to the "whats," "whos," and "wheres." This . . . is a challenge to the next generation of cultivation research.

Moreover, the very act of TV viewing has changed since the cultivation hypothesis was originally formulated. Gone are the days when the networks commanded 90% of the prime-time audience and when the cultivation hypothesis's assumption that viewers were being exposed to homogeneous content was more appropriate. Today, with cable, computers, and VCRs providing more diversity of programming into the home, the audience is much more selective. Again to quote Bryant (1986), "If cultivation research is to remain current, it will have to accommodate, rather than subordinate, notions of program diversity and audience selectivity."

ADVERTISING AND THE SOCIALIZATION OF CHILDREN

The concern over the impact of advertising on children stems from the sheer magnitude of their exposure to such communications. By the time a child reaches high school, he or she has been exposed to approximately 350,000 commercial messages. Not surprisingly, this area has drawn research attention from both academic and applied researchers. There is a large body of applied research in which small samples of children were exposed to commercials to determine comprehensibility and persuasiveness (Griffin, 1976). Many of these studies are proprietary and not open for review. In the academic sector, the research has been conducted for two purposes: to develop theory concerning children and consumer socialization, and to provide guidelines for public policy. In fact, both the Federal Trade Commission (FTC) and the Federal Communications Commission (FCC) have undertaken inquiries into the impact of advertising on children, and academic research played a key part in the deliberations of both agencies.

History

Concern over the effects of television advertising on children can be traced to the 1960s when the National Association of Broadcasters adopted guidelines concerning toy advertising. It was not until the 1970s, however, that this issue gained wide national attention. Action for Children's Television (ACT), a group of concerned parents, petitioned the FCC in 1970 for a new set of rules concerning children's television. Among other things, ACT requested a ban on commercials on children's programs. At about the same time, members on the Council on Children, Media, and Merchandising appeared before Congress to complain about the advertising of high-sugar cereals on television.

This public concern was quickly followed by research into the effects of advertising directed at children. First to appear were content analyses of Saturday morning commercials (Winick, Williamson, & Chuzmir, 1973). The first behavioral studies were included as part of the Surgeon General's report on television and social behavior (Ward, 1972). A few additional studies appeared over the next few years, but research interest did not significantly increase until regulatory agencies used the results of existing studies to formulate new policy. The FTC, for example, cited research findings to support its prohibition of the use of premium offers in advertising.

The number of studies examining the socialization impact of television advertising increased markedly in the mid-1970s. A review of the literature of the period summarized 21 key studies in the area and reported that most were done between 1974 and 1976 (Adler et al., 1977). The main findings of these studies indicated that age was a crucial variable in determining children's understanding of television advertising. Young children (ages 3–5) had trouble separating the commercial messages from the program content. Older children (ages 6–8) could better identify commercials as distinct from the program but did not understand the selling motive behind their presentation. In 1978, in a report on children and television advertising, the FTC called for the banning of all commercials directed at children too young to understand their intent. In making this recommendation, the FTC used the results of many research studies that examined the age variable and its relationship to the understanding of commercials.

On the other hand, defenders of children's advertising have suggested that it helps the child become a better consumer because it contributes to general economic understanding and knowledge of different products. Research into these claims conducted in the late 1970s turned out to be inconclusive (Ward, 1980).

The shift toward deregulation of the media during the early 1980s de-emphasized the policy-making aspects of this research. Research interest in children's advertising leveled off during this period. Many of the more recent studies have been concerned with developmental influences on children's understanding of commercials and their relation to Piaget's theory of cognitive development.

In 1984 the question of regulating ads directed at young people surfaced again when congressional hearings were held concerning the impact of liquor commercials on adolescent drinking behavior. The research evidence in this area suggested that young people who were heavily exposed to liquor and beer ads drank more frequently or reported that they expected to start drinking sooner than did those who were not as heavily exposed (Atkin, Hocking, & Block, 1984). There was no immediate federal action as a result of the hearings, but broadcasters and advertisers promised to present messages that would promote the responsible use of alcohol.

These topics continued to receive research attention during the rest of the decade. Investigators were particularly interested in the impact of cognitive development on the understanding of commercials. Macklin (1985) found that improved nonverbal measures cast doubt on the idea that preschoolers understand the selling intent of commercials. Costley and Brucks (1987) compared the effects of age and knowledge of product on responses to deceptive advertising and found that age differences were more important. A more recent area of concern is program-length commercials. These are programs that are based on existing toys and, according to critics, are merchandising vehicles designed to increase sales of the featured toy or, more frequently, toys. Only a few studies of this phenomenon have been carried out. Bryant (1985) conducted an experiment that disclosed that children who had seen a program featuring an existing toy with embedded commercials for the toy were more likely to show a preference for that toy than were children who had seen shows

that were neutral with regard to a product. Bolenbaugh (1988) conducted a content analysis that found that cartoon shows based on existing toys contained more violent and antisocial acts than did other cartoons. Because these programs may be the focus of future policy decisions by the FCC, more research on their impact is likely.

Methods

The most popular methods used to study this topic have been the survey and the laboratory experiment. Of the 26 key studies reviewed by Adler et al. (1980), half were surveys and half were done in the laboratory. Accordingly, this section examines several illustrative experiments and surveys.

The three dependent variables that have been examined by much of the research are (1) conditions concerning the identification and function of television advertising, (2) the impact of advertising on product preferences, and (3) the impact of advertising on the parent–child relationship. The survey technique has been widely used to study the first of these variables. Ward, Reale, and Levinson (1972) conducted a survey of 67 children, ranging in age from 5 to 12 years, concerning their knowledge of television commercials. Each child was asked a series of 16 questions and the answers were transcribed. The responses were content analyzed and placed in categories according to the degree of awareness exhibited by the child. For example, children were asked, "what is a commercial?" Those whose answers showed confused perceptions and low discrimination between commercials and program were categorized as having "low awareness." Answers from "medium-awareness" children showed an understanding of the advertising content and some information about product. "High-awareness" children gave answers characterized by an understanding of the sponsor concept and the motive of the seller. The results of this analysis showed that more than 50% of those 5–7 years old, but only about 13% of those 8–12 years old, were in the low-awareness category, suggesting that understanding increases with age.

In a related study, Ward, Levinson, and Wackman (1972) used unobtrusive techniques to study children's attention to television commercials. Mothers were trained to record information about their children's normal viewing behaviors. Using code sheets, they noted whether the child was paying full attention, partial attention, or not watching commercials and programs. Analysis of the resulting data indicated a tendency for all children to exhibit a drop in attention when a commercial was shown, but the youngest group (5–7 years) showed the smallest drop. The researchers suggested that this more stable attention pattern among the youngest children demonstrated the difficulty they have in differentiating between program and commercial. Wartella and Ettema (1974), however, in a more controlled situation with trained observers, found an increase in attention among their youngest age group (nursery children) when the commercials came on. This observation suggested that the discrepancy in findings with the study by Ward et al. might be due to the visual complexity of the ads that were shown in the respective investigations.

More recently, Kunkel (1988) performed an experiment that examined if children understood a TV commercial that featured the same primary characters as those in the surrounding program content (a technique known as host selling). Kunkel looked at three dimensions of understanding: ability to differentiate the commercial from the program, ability to attribute persuasive intent to the ad, and attitudes about commercial appeals. In the experiment, younger children (ages 4–5) and older children (ages 7–8) saw either a cartoon and a commercial with the same characters or a cartoon with a commercial featuring other cartoon characters. The results indicated that both age groups were less likely to distinguish commercial from program when host selling was used, but that host

selling had no impact on discerning commercial intent. Finally, older children were more influenced by commercials that used host selling. Kunkel concluded that concern about the effects of host selling should be expanded to older as well as younger children.

The second dependent variable, advertising impact, has been studied using both experimental and survey techniques. Experimental studies that contrast children exposed to television commercials with those not so exposed demonstrate some of the dimensions of this impact. Goldberg and Gorn (1978) showed one group of children commercials for a new toy, while a control group saw no commercials. To examine the ability of commercials to enhance the value of the toy in comparison with the value of being with peers, children were asked to choose between playing with a "nice" child without the advertised toy or with a "not so nice" child with the toy. Almost twice as many children in the control group chose to play with the nice child without the toy; those who saw the commercial more often opted to play with the other child who had the toy.

In a related experiment, Goldberg, Gorn, and Gibson (1978) showed different groups of children: (1) a television show with ads for products high in sugar content, (2) a television show with public service announcements stressing a balanced diet, or (3) an entire program stressing the value of eating a balanced diet. The children were then given a chance to select various snacks and breakfast foods that varied in nutritional value. The group that saw the entire program on a balanced diet selected only a few items that were low in nutrition. The group that saw the ads for the sugared products selected the least nutritional foods. Kohn and Smart (1984) showed college students a videotape edited into three different versions. One program had nine beer commercials, the second had four such commercials, and the third had none. Subjects could choose beer and other refreshments while watching. Exposure to the first few beer commercials increased consumption, but continued exposure had no further effects.

The survey method investigates impact by correlating respondents' consumption patterns with exposure to ads. For example, Atkin, Reeves, and Gibson (1979) measured preferences in food brands among children 5–12 years old. There was a strong positive relationship between viewing television commercials for the food item and liking the food item. Atkin, Hocking, and Block (1984) sampled teenagers in four different regions of the country. They measured exposure to liquor advertising in several ways. In one method respondents were shown specimen ads and asked how often they remembered seeing the commercial messages represented. Alcohol consumption was measured by asking how many different brands of liquor the respondent had drunk, or how much beer and wine were consumed in a typical week. A regression analysis showed that advertising exposure was the strongest correlate of liquor drinking and ranked second behind peer influence in predicting beer drinking. Advertising exposure showed little relation to wine drinking.

The survey approach has also been used in studying the impact of advertising on parent–child relationships. To illustrate, Atkin (1975) found that children heavily exposed to Saturday morning commercials argued more with their parents when requests for an advertised product were turned down than did light viewers. Ward and Wackman (1972) asked a sample of 109 mothers of children 5–12 years old to report the number of times their children asked them to buy an advertised product, and to estimate the number of times these requests resulted in conflicts. The two variables were significantly related.

Researchers have also relied upon the experimental approach. In the study by Goldberg and Gorn (1978), children were asked how a hypothetical child would respond if his/her parents denied his/her request to purchase a particular toy. A significantly greater proportion of children who saw ads for the toy reported that they would express rejection toward their parents than did those who did not see the ads. Galst and White (1976) allowed children in a nursery school setting to regulate their own viewing of commercials. Subsequently, trained observers followed the children and their mothers to the supermarket and recorded each time a child tried to influence a purchase. There was a significant relationship between viewing television commercials and the number of purchase attempts made at the store.

In sum, both laboratory and survey studies of young consumers have demonstrated that age is an important factor in understanding the purpose of commercials, that ads do have an influence on product desirability, and that television commercials can be a source of friction in the parent–child relationship.

Theoretical Developments

Two main theoretical perspectives have been associated with research dealing with advertising and young people. Predictions from the first, *social learning theory*, suggest that behaviors observed in the media, such as eating certain foods or playing with certain toys, will be imitated by observers, resulting in more consumption of advertised products. In addition, investigators expect to be able to discern conditions that either facilitate or inhibit the social learning process.

As the foregoing discussion of research methods and results indicates, the main predictions of this theory are substantiated. Watching television commercials for various products apparently leads to children's preferences for and consumption of the advertised products. Additionally, such factors as the presence of a celebrity endorser of the product (Atkin & Block, 1983) or specific audiovisual techniques (Meringoff & Lesser, 1980) can facilitate modeling.

On the other hand, alerting the child audience to the persuasive intent of a commercial message seems to inhibit its effects (Sprafkin, Swift, & Hess, 1983). Further research that more accurately defines other contingent influences will make social learning theory more valuable as a predictive tool.

The other theoretical formulation is the *cognitive development theory* associated with Swiss psychologist Jean Piaget. This theory posits that children go through stages of development, one following another in a set pattern, but the age at which a child reaches any given stage depends on the individual. Thus these developmental stages are correlated with, but not synonymous with, the chronological age of the child. Piaget postulated four major stages in cognitive development: (1) the sensorimotor stage, characterized by the child defining his or her environment by behavior (grasping, sucking, and so on) without symbolic representation of objects; (2) the preoperational stage, during which the child develops some reasoning ability; (3) the concrete operations stage, characterized by the use of basic logical operations; and (4) the formal operations stage, in which the child achieves adultlike thought patterns such as abstract thought and hypothetical reasoning.

Much of the research in children's consumer socialization is devoted to applying this developmental mode to the comprehension of television messages. For example, Tada (1969) found that young children (those in the preformal operations stage) did not understand the various editing and production techniques used in an instructional film. Noble (1975) reported that preschool children had difficulty in understanding that television programs are "make believe" and that the characters seen on television are actors. Wartella (1980) sums up the results of many of the studies looking at advertising and children. She reported that the development of an understanding of the differences between programs and commercials begins at about age 4, and by kindergarten, most children are able to distinguish between them. Higher level understanding of the functional differences between programs and commercials occurs between kindergarten and third grade.

Recent research has been directed at modifying and refining Piaget's formulations. For example, the theory suggests that the four stages of development are fixed and unchanging, but some evidence suggests that there may be variation. In contrast to the findings of the studies summarized by Adler et al. (1977), as well as his own earlier work with associates (1972), Ward (1980) reported that some kindergarten children could identify the selling purpose of advertising and displayed other consumer-related skills beyond what would be expected from the cognitive stage typically observed in 5-year-olds. Soldow (1983) found greater cognitive ability than predicted by Piaget's theory among his subjects in a test of product recall. More recently, Stutts and Hunnicutt (1987) found evidence that supported Piaget's theory regarding verbal responses, but the evidence did not support it when nonverbal responses were considered. Acker and Tiemens (1981) found that logical operations concerning television images occurred among elementary school children at a later age than predicted. In addition, there is evidence that children can be taught to acquire some cognitive abilities earlier than the theory's guidelines predict (Wackman, Wartella, & Ward, 1979). It is likely that much of the future research in this area will further refine cognitive development theory.

SUMMARY

Academic research and private sector research possess similarities and differences. They share common techniques and try to predict and explain behavior, but academic research differs from private sector research in that the former is public, more theoretical in nature, is generally determined more by the individual researcher than by management, and usually costs less than private sector research. Five main areas that exemplify mass media effects research conducted by the academic sector are (1) prosocial and antisocial effects of specific media content, (2) uses and gratifications, (3) agenda setting, (4) perceptions of social reality, and (5) advertising and the socialization of children. Each of these areas is typified by its own research history, method, and theoretical formulations.

Questions and Problems for Further Investigation

1. List some topics in addition to those mentioned in this chapter that might interest both private sector and academic researchers.

2. What problems arise when the experimental technique is used to study agenda setting? Describe how this might be done.

3. Assume that as a consultant for a large metropolitan newspaper, you are designing a uses and gratifications study of newspaper reading. What variables would you include in the analysis? If you were instead an academic researcher interested in the same question, how might your investigation differ from the private sector study?

4. List some perceptions of social reality, in addition to those discussed in the chapter, that might be cultivated by heavy media exposure.

References and Suggested Readings

Acker, S., & Tiemens, R. (1981). Children's perception of changes in size of TV images. *Human Communication Research, 7*(4), 340–346.

Adler, R., Lesser, G. S., Meringoff, L. K., Robertson, T. S., Rossiter, J. R., & Ward, S. (1977). *Research on the effects of television advertising on children.* Washington, DC: U.S. Government Printing Office.

Adler, R., Lesser, G., Meringoff, L., Robertson, T., Rossiter, J., & Ward, S. (1980). *The effects of television advertising on children.* Lexington, MA: Lexington Books.

Andison, F. (1977). TV violence and viewer aggression: A cumulation of study results, 1956–76. *Public Opinion Quarterly, 41*(3), 314–331.

Atkin, C. (1975). *Effects of TV advertising on children* (tech. rep.). East Lansing: Michigan State University.

Atkin, C., & Block, M. (1983). Effectiveness of celebrity endorsers. *Journal of Advertising Research, 23*(1), 57–62.

Atkin, C., Hocking, J., & Block, M. (1984). Teenage drinking: Does advertising make a difference? *Journal of Communication, 34*(2), 157–167.

Atkin, C., Reeves, B., & Gibson, W. (1979). Effects of television food advertising on children. Paper presented to the Association for Education in Journalism, Houston.

Bandura, A. (1977). *Social learning theory.* Englewood Cliffs, NJ: Prentice-Hall.

Baran, S., Chase, L., & Courtright, J. (1979). Television drama as a facilitator of prosocial behavior. *Journal of Broadcasting, 23*(3), 277–284.

Bear, A. (1984). The myth of television violence. *Media Information Australia, 33*, 5–10.

Becker, L. (1980). Measurement of gratifications. In G. Wilhoit & H. deBock (Eds.), *Mass communication review yearbook* (Vol. I). Beverly Hills, CA: Sage Publications.

Behr, R., & Iyengar, S. (1985). TV news, real-world clues and changes in the public agenda. *Public Opinion Quarterly, 49*(1), 38–57.

Belson, W. (1978). *Television violence and the adolescent boy.* Hampshire, England: Saxon House.

Berelson, B. (1949). What missing the newspaper means. In P. Lazarsfeld & F. Stanton (Eds.), *Communication research, 1948–49.* New York: Harper & Row.

Berkowitz, L., & Rogers, K. H. (1986). A priming effect analysis of media influences. In J. Bryant & D. Zillmann (Eds.), *Perspectives on media effects* (pp. 57–82). Hillsdale, NJ: Lawrence Erlbaum.

Bolenbaugh, B. C. (1988). Program length merchandising and children's television: A content analysis. M.A. thesis, College of Journalism and Mass Communication, University of Georgia, Athens, Georgia.

Bryant, J. (1985, October 28). Testimony at hearings before the U.S. House of Representatives' Subcommittee on Telecommunications, Consumer Protection and Finance.

Bryant, J. (1986). The road most traveled: Yet another cultivation critique. *Journal of Broadcasting and Electronic Media, 30*(2), 231–235.

Bryant, J., & Zillmann, D. (1984). Using television to alleviate boredom and stress. *Journal of Broadcasting, 28*(1), 1–20.

CBS Broadcast Group. (1974). Fat Albert and the Cosby kids. New York: CBS Office of Social Research.

Chaffee, S. (1984). Defending the indefensible. *Society, 21*(6), 30–35.

Cohen, B. (1963). *The press, the public and foreign policy.* Princeton, NJ: Princeton University Press.

Commission on Obscenity and Pornography. (1970). *The report of the commission on obscenity and pornography.* Washington, DC: U.S. Government Printing Office.

Comstock, G. (1975). *Television and human behavior: The key studies.* Santa Monica, CA: Rand Corporation.

Comstock, G., Chaffee, S., & Katzman, N. (1978). *Television and human behavior.* New York: Columbia University Press.

Cook, T., Kendzierski, D., & Thomas, S. (1983). The implicit assumptions of television research. *Public Opinion Quarterly, 47*(2), 161–201.

Costley, C. L., & Brucks, M. (1987). The roles of product knowledge and age on children's responses to deceptive advertising. In P. N. Bloom (Ed.), *Advances in marketing and public policy.* Greenwich, CT: JAI Press.

deBock, H. (1980). Gratification frustration during a newspaper strike and a TV blackout. *Journalism Quarterly, 57*(1), 61–66.

DeFleur, M., & DeFleur, L. (1967). The relative contribution of television as a learning source for children's occupational knowledge. *American Sociological Review, 32,* 777–789.

Dobos, J., & Dimmick, J. (1988). Factor analysis and gratification constructs. *Journal of Broadcasting and Electronic Media, 32*(3), 335–350.

Donnerstein, E., Linz, D., & Penrod, S. (1987). *The question of pornography: Research findings and policy implications.* New York: Free Press.

Einsiedel, E. F. (1988). The British, Canadian and U.S. pornography commissions and their use of social science research. *Journal of Communication, 38*(2), 108–121.

Eyal, C., Winter, J., & DeGeorge, W. (1981). The concept of time frame in agenda setting. In G. Wilhoit & H. deBock (Eds.), *Mass communication review yearbook* (Vol. II). Beverly Hills, CA: Sage Publications.

Forge, K. L., & Phemister, S. (1987). The effect of prosocial cartoons on preschool children. *Child Study Journal, 17*(2), 83–86.

Funkhouser, G. (1973). Trends in media coverage of the issues of the 1960s. *Journalism Quarterly, 50*(3), 533–538.

Galst, J., & White, M. (1976). The unhealthy persuader: The reinforcing value of television and children's purchase influence attempts at the supermarket. *Child Development, 47*(4), 1089–1096.

Gerbner, G., Gross, L., Eleey, M. F., Jackson-Beeck, M., Jeffries-Fox, S., & Signorielli, N. (1977). TV violence profile no. 8. *Journal of Communication, 27*(2), 171–180.

Gerbner, G., Gross, L., Jackson-Beeck, M., Jeffries-Fox, S., & Signorielli, N. (1978). Cultural indicators: Violence profile no. 9. *Journal of Communication, 28*(3), 176–207.

Gerbner, G., & Gross, L. (1976). Living with television: The violence profile. *Journal of Communication, 26*(2), 173–179.

Gerbner, G., Gross, L., Morgan, M., & Signorielli, N. (1986). Living with television: The dynamics of the cultivation process. In J. Bryant & D. Zillmann (Eds.), *Perspectives on media effects* (pp. 17–40). Hillsdale, NJ: Lawrence Erlbaum.

Gerson, W. (1966). Mass media socialization behavior: Negro-white differences. *Social Forces, 45,* 40–50.

Goldberg, M., & Gorn, G. (1978). Some unintended consequences of TV advertising to children. *Journal of Consumer Research, 5*(1), 22–29.

Goldberg, M., Gorn, G., & Gibson, W. (1978). TV messages for snack and breakfast foods. *Journal of Consumer Research, 5*(1), 48–54.

Gormley, W. (1975). Newspaper agendas and political elites. *Journalism Quarterly, 52*(2), 304–308.

Greenberg, B. (1974). Gratifications of television viewing and their correlates for British children. In J. Blumler & E. Katz (Eds.), *The uses of mass communication.* Beverly Hills, CA: Sage Publications.

Greenberg, B., & Dominick, J. (1969). Racial and social class differences in teenagers' use of television. *Journal of Broadcasting, 13*(4), 331–344.

Griffin, E. (1976). What's fair to children? *Journal of Advertising, 5*(2), 14–18.

Gross, L., & Morgan, M. (1985). Television and enculturation. In J. Dominick & J. Fletcher (Eds.), *Broadcasting research methods.* Boston: Allyn & Bacon.

Hawkins, R., & Pingree, S. (1981). Using television to construct social reality. *Journal of Broadcasting, 25*(4), 347–364.

Heeter, C., Brown, N., Soffin, S., Stanley, C., & Salwen, M. (1989). Agenda-setting by electronic text news. *Journalism Quarterly, 66*(1), 101–106.

Heller, M., & Polsky, S. (1976). *Studies in violence and television.* New York: American Broadcasting Company.

Herzog, H. (1944). What do we really know about daytime serial listeners? In P. Lazarsfeld & F. Stanton (Eds.), *Radio research, 1942–43.* New York: Duell, Sloan & Pearce.

Hilker, A. (1976, November 10). Agenda-setting influence in an off-year election. *ANPA Research Bulletin*, pp. 7–10.

Hirsch, P. (1980). The "scary world" of the non-viewer and other anomalies. *Communication Research, 7*, 403–456.

Huesmann, L. R., & Eron, L. D. (1986). *Television and the aggressive child: A cross-national comparison.* Hillsdale, NJ: Lawrence Erlbaum.

Hughes, M. (1980). The fruits of cultivation analysis: A re-examination of some effects of television viewing. *Public Opinion Quarterly, 44*(3), 287–302.

Klapper, J. (1960). *The effects of mass communication.* Glencoe, IL: Free Press.

Kohn, P., & Smart, R. (1984). The impact of TV advertising on alcohol consumption. *Journal of Studies on Alcohol, 45*(4), 295–301.

Kunkel, D. (1988). Children and host selling television commercials. *Communication Research, 15*(1), 71–92.

Lang, G., & Lang, K. (1981). Watergate: An examination of the agenda-building process. In G. Wilhoit & H. deBock (Eds.), *Mass communication review yearbook* (pp. 447–468). Beverly Hills, CA: Sage Publications.

Lang, K., & Lang, G. (1966). The mass media and voting. In B. Berelson & M. Janowitz (Eds.), *Reader in public opinion and communication.* New York: Free Press.

Larson, C. U. (1986). *Persuasion* (4th ed.). Belmont, CA: Wadsworth.

Lefkowitz, M., Eron, L., Waldner, L., & Huesmann, L. (1972). Television violence and child aggression. In G. Comstock & E. Rubinstein (Eds.), *Television and social behavior: Vol. III. Television and adolescent aggressiveness.* Washington, DC: U.S. Government Printing Office.

Levy, M., & Windahl, S. (1984). Audience activity and gratifications. *Communication Research, 11*, 51–78.

Liebert, R., & Baron, R. (1972). Short-term effects of televised aggression on children's aggressive behavior. In J. Murray, E. Rubinstein, & G. Comstock (Eds.), *Television and social behavior: Vol. II. Television and social learning.* Washington, DC: U.S. Government Printing Office.

Liebert, R. M., & Sprafkin, J. (1988). *The early window.* New York: Pergamon Press.

Linz, D., Donnerstein, D., & Penrod, S. (1984). The effects of multiple exposure to film violence against women. *Journal of Communication, 34*(3), 130–147.

Lippmann, W. (1922). *Public opinion.* New York: Macmillan. (reprint, 1965). New York: Free Press.

Macklin, M. C. (1985). Do young children understand the selling intent of commercials? *Journal of Consumer Affairs, 19*(2), 293–304.

Manheim, J. B. (1987). A model of agenda dynamics. In M. L. McLaughlin (Ed.), *Communication yearbook* (Vol. 10, pp. 499–516). Beverly Hills, CA: Sage Publications.

McCombs, M. (1981). The agenda setting approach. In D. Nimmo & K. Sanders (Eds.), *Handbook of political communication*. Beverly Hills, CA: Sage Publications.

McCombs, M., & Shaw, D. (1972). The agenda-setting function of mass media. *Public Opinion Quarterly 36*(2), 176–187.

McLeod, J., Atkin, C., & Chaffee, S. (1972). Adolescents, parents and television use. In G. Comstock & E. Rubinstein (Eds.), *Television and social behavior: Vol. III. Television and adolescent aggressiveness*. Washington, DC: U.S. Government Printing Office.

McLeod, J., & Becker, L. (1981). The uses and gratifications approach. In D. Nimmo & K. Sanders (Eds.), *Handbook of political communication*. Beverly Hills, CA: Sage Publications.

McLeod, J., Becker, L., & Byrnes, J. (1974). Another look at the agenda setting function of the press. *Communication Research, 1*(2), 131–166.

Megawa, E. R., & Brenner, D. J. (1988). Toward a paradigm of media agenda setting effect. *Howard Journal of Communication, 1*(1), 39–56.

Meringoff, L., & Lesser, G. (1980). The influence of format and audiovisual techniques on children's perceptions of commercial messages. In R. Adler, G. Lesser, L. Meringoff, T. Robertson, J. Rossiter, & S. Ward (Eds.), *The effects of television advertising on children*. Lexington, MA: Lexington Books.

Milavsky, J., Kessler, R., Stipp, H., & Rubens, W. (1983). Television and aggression. New York: Academic Press.

Milgram, S., & Shotland, R. (1973). *Television and antisocial behavior*. New York: Academic Press.

Minton, J. (1975). The impact of "Sesame Street" on readiness. *Sociology of Education, 48*(2), 141–155.

Mueller, C., Donnerstein, E., & Hallam, J. (1983). Violent films and prosocial behavior. *Personality and Social Psychology Bulletin, 9*, 183–189.

Mullins, E. (1977). Agenda setting and the younger voter. In D. Shaw & M. McCombs (Eds.), *The emergence of American political issues*. St. Paul, MN: West.

Murray, J. (1984). A soft response to hard attacks on research. *Media Information Australia (33)*, 11–16.

National Institute of Mental Health. (1982). *Television and behavior: Ten years of scientific progress and implications for the 1980s*. Washington, DC: U.S. Government Printing Office.

Noble, G. (1975). *Children in front of the small screen*. Beverly Hills, CA: Sage Publications.

Palmgreen, P. (1984). Uses and gratifications: A theoretical perspective. In R. Bostrom (Ed.), *Communication yearbook 8*. Beverly Hills, CA: Sage Publications.

Parke, R., Berkowitz, L., & Leyens, J. (1977). Some effects of violent and nonviolent movies on the behavior of juvenile delinquents. *Advances in Experimental Social Psychology, 16*, 135–172.

Patterson, T., & McClure, R. (1976). *The unseeing eye*. New York: G. P. Putnam's.

Porter, W. C., & Stephens, F. (1989). Estimating readability: A study of Utah editors' abilities. *Newspaper Research Journal, 10*(2), 87–96.

Potter, W. J. (1986). Perceived reality and the cultivation hypothesis. *Journal of Broadcasting and Electronic Media, 30*(2), 159–174.

Potter, W. J. (1988). Three strategies for elaborating the cultivation hypothesis. *Journalism Quarterly, 65*(4), 930–939.

Potter, W. J., & Ware, W. (1989). The frequency and context of prosocial acts on prime time TV. *Journalism Quarterly, 66*(2), 359–366.

Roberts, D., & Bachen, C. (1981). Mass communication effects. In M. Rosenzweig & L. Porter (Eds.), *Annual Review of Psychology*. Palo Alto, CA: Annual Reviews.

Rosengren, K. (1974). Uses and gratifications: A paradigm outlined. In J. Blumler & E. Katz (Eds.), *The uses of mass communication*. Beverly Hills, CA: Sage Publications.

Rosenthal, R. (1986). Media violence, antisocial behavior, and the social consequences of small effects. *Journal of Social Issues, 42*(3), 141–154.

Rubin, A. (1979). Television use by children and adolescents. *Human Communication Research, 5*(2), 109–120.

Rubin, A. (1985). Uses and gratifications: Quasi-functional analysis. In J. Dominick & J. Fletcher (Eds.), *Broadcasting research methods*. Boston: Allyn & Bacon.

Rubin, A. M. (1986). Uses, gratifications, and media effects research. In J. Bryant & D. Zillmann (Eds.), *Perspectives on media effects* (pp. 281–302). Hillsdale, NJ: Lawrence Erlbaum.

Rubin, A. M., Perse, E. M., & Taylor, D. S. (1988). A methodological examination of cultivation. *Communication Research, 15*(2), 107–136.

Salwen, M. B. (1988). Effect of accumulation coverage on issue salience in agenda setting. *Journalism Quarterly, 65*(1), 100–106.

Schramm, W., Lyle, J., & Parker, E. (1961). *Television in the lives of our children*. Stanford, CA: Stanford University Press.

Siegel, A. (1958). The influence of violence in the mass media upon children's role expectations. *Child Development, 29*, 35–56.

Soldow, G. (1983). The processing of information in the young consumer. *Journal of Advertising Research, 12*(3), 4–14.

Sprafkin, J., & Rubinstein, E. (1979). Children's television viewing habits and prosocial behavior. *Journal of Broadcasting, 23*(7), 265–276.

Sprafkin, J., Swift, C., & Hess, R. (1983). *Rx television: Enhancing the preventative impact of TV*. New York: Haworth Press.

Stutts, M. A., & Hunnicutt, G. G. (1987). Can young children understand disclaimers in television commercials? *Journal of Advertising, 16*(1), 41–46.

Surgeon General's Scientific Advisory Committee on Television and Social Behavior. (1972). *Television and social behavior. Television and growing up* (summary report). Washington, DC: U.S. Government Printing Office.

Swanson, D. L. (1987). Gratification seeking, media exposure, and audience interpretations. *Journal of Broadcasting and Electronic Media, 31*(3), 237–254.

Tada, T. (1969). Image cognition: A developmental approach. *Studies in Broadcasting, 7*, 105–174.

Tan, A. (1981). *Mass communication theories and research*. Columbus, OH: Grid Publications.

Tan, A. S. (1986). Social learning of aggression from television. In J. Bryant & D. Zillmann (Eds.), *Perspective on media effects* (pp. 41–56). Hillsdale, NJ: Lawrence Erlbaum.

Tannenbaum, P., & Zillmann, D. (1975). Emotional arousal in the facilitation of aggression through communication. In L. Berkowitz (Ed.), *Advances in experimental social psychology*. New York: Academic Press.

Tipton, L., Haney, R., & Baseheart, J. (1975). Media agenda setting in city and state election campaigns. *Journalism Quarterly, 52*(1), 15–22.

Turk, J. V., & Franklin, B. (1987). Information subsidies: Agenda setting traditions. *Public Relations Review, 13*(4), 29–41.

VanLeuven, J. K., & Ray, G. W. (1988). Communication stages and public issue coverage. *Newspaper Research Journal, 9*(4), 71–83.

Wackman, D., Wartella, E., & Ward, S. (1979). *Children's information processing of television advertising*. Washington, DC: National Science Foundation.

Wanta, W. (1988). The effects of dominant photographs: An agenda setting experiment. *Journalism Quarterly, 65*(1), 107–111.

Wanta, W., Stephenson, M. A., Turk, J. V., & McCombs, M. E. (1989). How president's state of union talk influenced news media agendas. *Journalism Quarterly, 66*(3), 537–541.

Ward, S. (1972). Effects of television advertising on children and adolescents. In E. Rubinstein, G. Comstock, & J. Murray (Eds.), *Television and social behavior: Vol. IV. Television in day-to-day life: Patterns of exposure*. Washington, DC: U. S. Government Printing Office.

Ward, S. (1980). The effects of television advertising on consumer socialization. In R. Adler, G. Lesser, L. Meringoff, T. Robertson, J. Rossiter, & S. Ward, (Eds.), *The effects of television advertising on children*. Lexington, MA: Lexington Books.

Ward, S., Levinson, D., & Wackman, D. (1972). Children's attention to television advertising. In E.

Rubinstein, G. Comstock, & J. Murray (Eds.), *Television and social behavior: Vol. IV. Television in day-to-day life: Patterns of exposure*. Washington, DC: U.S. Government Printing Office.

Ward, S., Reale, G., & Levinson, D. (1972). Children's perceptions, explanations, and judgments of television advertising. In E. Rubinstein, G. Comstock, & J. Murray (Eds.), *Television and social behavior: Vol. IV. Television in day-to-day life: Patterns of exposure*. Washington, DC: U.S. Government Printing Office.

Ward, S., & Wackman, D. (1972). Television advertising and intrafamily influence. In E. Rubinstein, G. Comstock, & J. Murray (Eds.), *Television and social behavior: Vol. IV. Television in day-to-day life: Patterns of exposure*. Washington, DC: U.S. Government Printing Office.

Wartella, E. (1980). Children and television: The development of the child's understanding of the medium. In G. Wilhoit & H. deBock (Eds.), *Mass communication review yearbook*. Beverly Hills, CA: Sage Publications.

Wartella, E., & Ettema, J. (1974). A cognitive developmental study of children's attention to television commercials. *Communication Research, 1*(1), 46–49.

Weaver, D. (1977). Political issues and voter need for orientation. In M. McCombs & D. Shaw (Eds.), *The emergence of Amerian political issues*. St. Paul, MN: West.

Weaver, J., & Wakshlag, J. (1986). Perceived vulnerability in crime, criminal victimization experience, and television viewing. *Journal of Broadcasting and Electronic Media, 30*(2), 141–158.

Wertham, F. (1954). *The seduction of the innocent*. New York: Holt, Rinehart & Winston.

Williams, T. B. (1986). *The impact of television*. New York: Academic Press.

Williams, W. (1985). Agenda setting research. In J. Dominick & J. Fletcher (Eds.), *Broadcasting research methods*. Boston: Allyn & Bacon.

Williams, W., & Semlak, W. (1978a). Campaign '76: Agenda setting during the New Hampshire primary. *Journal of Broadcasting, 22*(4), 531–540.

Williams, W., & Semlak, W. (1978b). Structural effects of TV coverage on political agendas. *Journal of Communication, 28*(1), 114–119.

Windahl, S. (1981). Uses and gratifications at the crossroads. In G. Wilhoit & H. deBock (Eds.), *Mass communication review yearbook*. Beverly Hills, CA: Sage Publications.

Winick, C., Williamson, L., & Chuzmir, S. (1973). *Children's television commercials: A content analysis*. New York: Praeger.

Winter, J. (1981). Contingent conditions in the agenda setting process. In G. Wilhoit & H. deBock (Eds.), *Mass communication review yearbook*. Beverly Hills, CA: Sage Publications.

Winter, J., & Eyal, C. (1981). Agenda setting for the civil rights issue. *Public Opinion Quarterly, 45*(3), 376–383.

Wurtzel, A., & Lometti, G. (1984). Researching TV violence. *Society, 21*(6), 22–30.

Zillmann, D., & Bryant, J. (1982). Pornography, sexual callousness, and the trivialization of rape. *Journal of Communication, 32*(4), 10–21.

Zillmann, D., Hoyt, J., & Day, K. (1979). Strength and duration of the effect of violent and erotic communication of subsequent aggressive behavior. *Communication Research, 1*, 286–306.

THE COMPUTER AS A RESEARCH TOOL

INTRODUCTION

As in most industries, computers are now commonplace instruments in mass media research. Researchers rely on them for solving both simple and complex problems, building databases, and for retrieving and analyzing archival data such as Arbitron and Nielsen ratings. Much of the reliance on computers is a result of the introduction of the **personal computer** (PC) in the early 1980s, an event that literally reshaped scientific research in only a few years. PCs allow researchers at all levels access to powerful machines previously available only to a select group of scientists.

Before the early 1980s, computers were basically perceived as intimidating devices used only by equally intimidating people. The machines were expensive, gigantic contraptions that had limited capabilities and ran according to sets of complex and arcane rules established by groups of computer scientists who had yet to understand the term *user-friendly*. Then came the personal computer. Advances in technology and a concern about computer *users* eliminated many of the early problems associated with computers. The new easy-to-use PC systems, some of which cost well under $1,000, can quickly perform tasks that were tedious and sometimes impossible for their cumbersome ancestors. Using a computer no longer requires either a formal education in computer science, nor a plastic shirt-pocket protector for pens and pencils.

Dramatically reduced prices, technological advances, and ease of use have made computers a necessity in all types of mass media research. Most mass media employers consider computer experience as a prerequisite for all prospective job applicants. Most media employers expect job applicants to know enough about computers to allow them to quickly learn the system used by the company.

One of the tasks in learning how to use computers is learning the language of computers. As with any technical field, computers involve the use of a great number of acronyms and special terms. The new vocabulary may be confusing at first, but it becomes second nature after exposure to computers.

This chapter is only an introduction to computers and data analysis; therefore, it is not intended to be an exhaustive discussion of these topics. Innovations in computer technology and the use of computers are announced almost daily, and no textbook can be completely up-to-date. At the end of the chapter several publications are listed that provide additional information for readers interested in learning more about the latest advances in computers and computer applications.

A BRIEF HISTORY OF COMPUTERS

One of the earliest types of computing instruments was the *abacus*, a Chinese invention used more than 2,000 years ago. The abacus is a wooden frame with several parallel wires on which beads are moved to perform a calculation (much like the scoring system used for billiards). In 1640 mathematician Blaise Pascal is said to have developed the first digital calculating machine. Other earlier developers of calculating machines include Gottfried Wilhelm von Leibniz who, in the late 1600s, built a machine that could multiply, Charles Xavier Thomas

(1820), who built the first commercially used calculating machine, and Charles Babbage (c. 1830), who presented ideas for a sophisticated steam-powered machine that was never built.

Computer development took a dramatic turn when Herman Hollerith and James Powers used punched data cards for the 1890 U.S. census. The data cards increased speed and decreased errors. However, during World War II, the use of missiles and rockets led to the need for fast and accurate trajectory measurements. To solve the need, in 1942 John Eckert and John Mauchly and their colleagues at the Moore School of Electrical Engineering at the University of Pennsylvania developed a high-speed computer called the ENIAC (Electrical Numerical Integrator and Calculator). Even though the machine used 18,000 vacuum tubes, took up about 1,800 square feet of space, and weighed about 30 tons, it was about 1,000 times faster than any previously built device. The development of modern computers changed dramatically.

However, even to this day, there is debate about who first developed the prototype of the modern computer. Many people feel credit should go to the ENIAC, and they grant the title of "Father of Computers" to Eckert and Mauchly. Yet, many people credit John Atanasoff from the University of Iowa as the father of computers. This credit is bestowed on him because in 1973 a judge ruled that John Mauchly had stolen ideas from Atanasoff when the two men met at a convention in 1940. The argument will no doubt continue for years (Burks, 1988).

Computer development grew rapidly during the 1950s with the invention of magnetic memory and transistors, which were then used in the 1960s to produce commercially available computers. During the 1960s, the development of the **printed circuit board** (a piece of flat plastic that contains electrical circuits) substantially increased speed and decreased the size of components. The advancements in electronic miniaturization continued in the 1970s and 1980s and brought the development of microcompu-

ters, laptop computers, and even smaller machines. The 1990s will include even more developments in computer speed and size. New printed circuit technology, fiber optics, laser optics, and other new developments will allow manufacturers to produce machines that we cannot even imagine at this time.

HOW A COMPUTER WORKS

The title of this chapter suggests the role a computer plays in research. For all the mystique surrounding the machine, a computer is no less a tool than a hammer or a food processor. It is a device built to perform a specific task and like any other tool, it is necessary to understand how it works before it is possible to understand what to do with it. For example, understanding how a hammer works as well as the many types of hammers available makes building something easier. Likewise, when a researcher understands the basic elements of a computer and how it works, it is much easier to use. Most of the problems people have with computers have less to do with the machine than with the expectations and fear people have of them.

At its most basic level, a computer very rapidly performs repetitive alphanumeric tasks, or jobs dealing with words and/or numbers. However, regardless of the task, a computer is doing nothing more than performing a series of calculations. Computers do not think, although some people feel recent developments in *artificial intelligence* (AI) may allow computers to do so on an elementary level. Everything a computer "knows" must be input by a human. A computer simply performs human tasks with much greater speed, efficiency, and accuracy than a human typically can.

In short, computers save researchers time and energy. Repetitive mathematical tasks, data manipulation, and word processing are perfect tasks for the computer. Many researchers wonder how their colleagues from the past (even the early 1980s) got along without computers.

CLASSIFICATION OF COMPUTERS

Computers are generally classified in one of four sizes: micro, mini, mainframe, and super. Historically, the identification of a computer was based on its physical size, but technological advancements have moved so rapidly that clear distinctions between types of computers have essentially disappeared. Currently, classification of computers refers to the processing power of the computer rather than its physical size. All sizes of computers have **multitasking** (several jobs performed at once) or **multiuser** (many users on one machine) ability.

The personal computer, which is technically called a **microcomputer**, or micro, is the smallest type of computer. Probably the most popular micros are the IBM XT, AT, and PS/2, and the Apple Macintosh and Apple II. Several companies, such as Compaq and Tandy, produce micros known as PC *compatibles* or *clones* because they copy the design and functions of IBM. Laptop and portable computers are usually considered as personal computers.

Minicomputers are the next in line and are about the size of a typical apartment or dormitory refrigerator. One common minicomputer is the Digital Equipment Corporation (DEC) VAX system, such as the PDP 11/73.

The **mainframe** computer is the next largest computer. Mainframes can be quite large (several large refrigerators), although they no longer occupy the huge space as in the past. Mainframes are constructed by several companies including IBM, Control Data, and Unisys.

The **supercomputer** is the most powerful of all computers, and is considered the epitome of technological advancement. The "super" designation refers to the number of calculations it can perform, a rate that is measured in millions or billions of instructions per second (MIPS or BIPS). The physical size of supercomputers is deceiving since they are often smaller than a typical mainframe.

Historically, the cost of supercomputers (about $2–$40 million) has limited their use to the federal government and large companies involved in such fields as engineering, physics, chemistry, aerospace, and astronomy. However, recent developments in supercomputer technology may make them accessible to colleges, universities, and small businesses. The major breakthrough in technology relates to how supercomputers solve problems. For example, the typical Cray-2 supercomputer uses only one processor to solve calculations at an astonishing rate of about 1.2 billion instructions per second. The new supercomputer design uses a procedure known as **parallel processing**, where several small processors are connected together. These processors break down a problem or set of instructions into small parts and solve them simultaneously. The speed of these parallel processor supercomputers is currently substantially slower than a typical Cray-2, but the machine sells for only about $500,000. Another example of the new supercomputer design is the CM-2a supercomputer developed by the Thinking Machines company in Massachusetts. It strings together 4,000 processors that collectively handle about 150 million instructions per second.

Regardless of the size of computers mass media researchers may use, it is necessary for anyone involved in research, or who plans to become involved in research, to keep up-to-date with the new technology.

ANATOMY OF A COMPUTER

Any discussion of how computers operate involves two broad topics: **hardware**, which essentially refers to the visible parts of a computer (the machinery), and **software**, which refers to the programs that allow the computer to operate. These two broad classes of elements are the basis for our discussion of the anatomy of a computer.

All computers share certain characteristics. Regardless of size and specific engineering characteristics, every computer system consists of five basic components that are controlled by an **operating system** (OS).

COMPUTER COMPONENTS.   The five basic computer system components are: **input** and **output**, or input/output (I/O), **processing**, **memory**, and **storage**. The I/O components allow a user to get information into a computer and produce the results in some form. The processing component involves the computations a computer makes to solve a problem, which, in turn, requires memory to operate. Finally, the storage component saves data to allow for additional manipulation or retrieval. These five basic components, along with software, enable a computer to function. Figure 17.1 is a simple diagram demonstrating the relationship among the components and software.

Additional hardware pieces help the computer operate and make using a computer easy. Some of these include the keyboard, **monitor** (also known as a CRT, for cathode ray tube, or VDT, for video display terminal), printers, plotters, and cables. All hardware, excluding the computer's **central processing unit** (CPU) and main memory, are called **peripherals**. A computer's CPU is the heart of a computer because it controls the entire system according to a set of guidelines provided by specialized software.

OPERATING SYSTEMS.   In order to allow the computer components to work together smoothly, a software operating system oversees the process. An operating system, usually referred to as the **disk operating system** (DOS), is essentially a computer program that acts like a traffic cop: it translates user commands to computer language, designates when and how instructions should be interpreted, computed, and output, and controls the operation according to a specific set of guidelines. Operating systems are loaded into the computer's memory when the machine is turned on (or *booted*). Operating systems are machine-specific, which means that an OS for one type of machine will not work on another type. Software such as spreadsheets or word processors are usually written to operate with only one type of OS, which is why IBM software will not run on an Apple computer, and vice versa without modification of the software or hardware.

The most common operating systems for PCs are **MS-DOS** (Microsoft disk operating system) and **PC-DOS** (personal computer disk operating system) developed by the Microsoft Corporation. Both systems are essentially the same, except that PC-DOS is sold with IBM machines and MS-DOS is sold with compatibles and clones. In the late 1980s, Microsoft produced the OS/2 operating system for the IBM PS/2 and

FIGURE 17.1   RELATIONSHIP BETWEEN COMPUTER COMPONENTS AND SOFTWARE

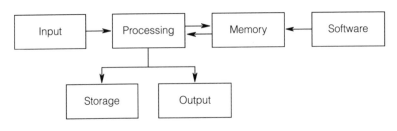

other machines. There are also several mainframe and microcomputer operating systems used for specific computers, such as Cyber NOS, UNIX, Xenix, and TSX.

THE COMPUTER SYSTEM

INPUT. The standard input devices for computers come in three broad categories: keyboards, pointing devices, and scanners. A typical keyboard resembles a standard typewriter keyboard in form and function, but usually includes several other keys that perform specific functions depending on the software being used. The more advanced *enhanced* keyboard includes a separate number pad for data entry and other unique keys. A pointing device allows users to select and manipulate characters and figures on the monitor. The most popular pointing device is the **mouse**, which is about the size of a deck of playing cards. Movement of the mouse corresponds to movement of a cursor on the monitor. Data are input, moved, or manipulated by buttons on top of the mouse. Most graphics packages, spreadsheets, and word processing programs are designed to be used with a mouse.

Finally, scanners are versatile input devices and come in a variety of styles and sizes. Mini-scanners are hand-held devices that, when passed over numbers, pictures or other data, transmit the information to the computer. Large scanners allow for input of an entire page of information. One type of simple scanner is the **optical character reader** (OCR), or **mark-sense reader**, which scans the types of sheets often used for educational exams. More advanced scanners are used to read Universal Product Codes, pictures, and graphics. Scanners are incredibly quick. A typical OCR machine can read two sides of an 8½- by 11-inch paper in about two seconds or less.

Other input devices include joysticks, magnetic strip readers to read such things as the back of credit cards, touch sensitive screens where users literally touch areas of the monitor to enter data, and light pens and graphic pads where users draw or write information on an electronic pad. Input by speech recognition has recently made significant improvements, and may be one of the major sources of data input in the future.

PROCESSING. Computer processing is accomplished through the cooperation of hardware and software. The primary hardware component is the **microprocessor chip**, or **microchip**. The chip is a thin slice of silicon (or other element) about ¼-inch square that has electronic circuitry printed directly on it. Microchips are produced for various functions. For example, a chip called a math **coprocessor** is often installed by users who use their computer for complicated mathematical problems. The coprocessor speeds the computing process because the chip is designed only for "number crunching."

One chip recently developed by the Intel Corporation, called the 80486, contains more than one million transistors and combines *cache* (pronounced "cash") memory (where the most frequently used instructions are stored), data processing, and central processing all on one chip. Previously, the three operations required three individual microchips that communicate between each other to perform calculations. The 80486 combines these operations into one chip.

The microprocessor and its associated support circuitry compose the computer's CPU. The CPU expresses and uses numbers in a *binary* system, a system of two numbers, 0 and 1. Each symbol in a binary number is called a *binary digit*, or **bit**. Bits have been coded into various schemes to represent different numbers or characters. The most commonly used code is called the **American Standard Code for Information Interchange**, or ASCII (as'-key). Each of the 128 codes uses 7 bits to represent one number, letter, or character. For example, the ASCII code for the number 4 is 0110100 and for the letter D it is 1000100. There is also an extended ASCII code that includes a variety of different scientific and mathematical symbols.

Each letter, number, or character in an instruction is called a **byte**, which is made up of 8 bits. In most cases, only 7 bits are used to communicate specific information. The 8th bit is usually used for *parity*, that is, a check for errors in the byte. The computer's CPU reads or stores data 1 bit at a time. How fast a computer reads 1 bit is known as *bit speed*. The original PCs were relatively slow 8-bit systems, meaning that they read 8 bits in a single cycle. New computers can now simultaneously process 16, 32, or 64 bits.

In addition to bit speed, computers are differentiated by their *clock speed*. The clock speed is an expression of the number of cycles a CPU can read in a single second, and is expressed in terms of megahertz (MHz), or millions of cycles per second.

Information is processed by computers in one of two basic ways: batch and interactive (also called on-line). **Batch processing** occurs when a list of instructions is given to the computer by one or more users. The individual instructions are executed in a priority order established by the computer, and the results are output to the user(s). A set of instructions executed in this way is known as a *batch job*, which is similar to being given a list of chores to do around the house and told not to come back until they are done. **Interactive processing**, or on-line processing, involves putting data directly into the computer, usually via a CRT. This type of processing is best exemplified by commercially available software packages where users are not required to enter program instructions. Using the software involves following a set of instructional menus that appear on the screen.

Batch processing is most common in a computer system where several people share the use of one CPU. *Time-sharing* describes batch processing when one mainframe is used by unrelated researchers who are at remote locations.

The users are charged a fee for the amount of time spent on the computer. The term **local area network**, or LAN, refers to batch processing when one computer serves as a host for several users, usually located in one large office or in the same building.

MEMORY.   Computer memory is described in terms of size, which is generally expressed in increments of 1,000 bytes (1,000 bytes = 1 kilobyte, expressed as Kb or K). In reality, one K of memory is actually 1,024 bytes, but it is rounded to 1,000 for convenience. A computer with a memory of 64K is capable of storing or working with 65,536 (64 × 1,024) bytes of information. A typical personal computer usually has 640K on its **motherboard** (the factory-installed primary memory in the computer), but it's common for users to upgrade memory into the millions (1 million bytes is designated 1 Mb, or simply "one meg"). Memory sizes into the billions, gigabytes, are common in large computers.

Computers use several types of memory systems. **Random access memory** (RAM) stores information and data input by the user. RAM is volatile memory, meaning that it is usable or addressable only when the computer is turned on; RAM memory is lost when the computer is off. RAM is the memory number used to identify the size of a computer (such as 64K or 640K). A second type of memory is **read-only memory** (ROM), which is permanently stored in the computer and is nonvolatile; it is not erased when the computer is turned off. ROM usually contains sets of operating instructions that are called upon when the computer is turned on, such as the computer's operating system information.

Another form of memory is called **programmable read-only memory** (PROM), a microchip that is used to store information permanently. Generally speaking, users cannot write into PROMs, although some PROMs allow users access to writing on one occasion to set the chip to meet specific standards or uses.

An *erasable programmable read-only memory* (EPROM) microprocessor allows users to change information as often as is necessary.

STORAGE.   Because RAM information is lost when the computer is turned off, the ability to save information is important. The most popular forms of data **storage** are magnetic disks and tapes. Disks are usually associated with PCs, and tapes with larger computers, although all computers can use one or both media.

The types of disks most commonly used with computers are the **floppy disk** and the **hard disk**. Both are similar in that information is encoded on them by selectively magnetizing tiny particles of a metallic oxide bonded to a solid base material, similar to the process used in audio- and videotape. The floppy disk is a thin piece of plastic material coated with an oxide and enclosed in either a flexible or rigid case that is inserted into a drive unit when needed. The disks come in several sizes and storage capacities, ranging from 3.5 inches to 8 inches. A typical PC floppy is 5.25 inches and stores 360K on a *double-sided, double-density* disk to 1.2 Mb on a *double-sided, high-density* disk.

Hard disks range in storage capacity and are available in increments of 10 Mb. They are usually not removable from the drive unit since they are contained in airtight, dust-free, non-accessible cases. Inside a hard disk unit, the disks look like typical audio CDs stacked one on another, and are rather fragile. A hard disk can "crash" and become unusable (all data are lost) rather easily, which is why researchers who use hard disks make backup copies of the information. All disks must be formatted to the computer's DOS before they can be used.

Some forms of data storage are not based on magnetic storage. One of the more common forms is the *CD-ROM* (compact disc–read-only memory), which is also similar to an audio CD. The CD-ROM uses a laser beam to read information from the disk, which currently stores about 500 Mb of information. CD-ROM users cannot change the data on the disk, but a device known as a WORM (write once, read many) allows users to write and permanently store information on the disc. WORMs are especially useful for libraries and other data archives that store information. The NeXT computer system developed by Steve Jobs (the founder of Apple computers) reportedly features a full read-and-write laser disk drive, but the current cost of the system is prohibitive for general use.

Other types of storage devices include the thermo-magneto-optical (TMO) disk, which stores information by laser beam, mass storage devices such as the Maynard system, which stores information on specially made cassette tapes, and magnetic bubble memory.

OUTPUT.   The effort put into input, processing, and storage is of no use if the outcome is not available to the user. Output from processing is usually sent to a monitor, printer, plotter, disk, video- or audiotape, or a combination of devices.

Excluding the monitor and disk, all output devices provide a hard copy of the computed information. The most common type of **printer** is the dot matrix impact printer (a character is impacted onto the paper), which uses ribbons similar to a standard typewriter. Another popular type of printer is the ink-jet, where characters and numbers are jet-sprayed onto paper. The laser printer, quickly becoming the most popular type of printer, produces high-quality print and allows users to select from a wide variety of print fonts. One of the newest developments in computer output is videotape, an exciting technology made popular by the Amiga computer.

COMPUTER COMMUNICATIONS

It is possible for computer systems to communicate with one another, even if they are of differing types. This is useful when information stored on a PC needs to be transferred (uploaded) to a larger computer, or vice versa (downloaded). One way to transfer data from one computer to another, even over long distances, is with a **modem** (*modulate-demodulate*), which uses standard telephone lines for communication purposes.

An important characteristic of a modem is the rate at which it sends or receives information, known as **baud rate**. Early modems operated at 300 baud, but current modems now transfer data at rates up to 9,600 baud. For two computers to exchange data successfully, they must use the same communication file exchange *protocol*, which means they must "speak" the same language. File exchange protocols are included in various telecommunications software packages, such as Bitcom and Procomm. Not all telecommunications software supports all protocols.

USING COMPUTERS IN RESEARCH

Computers are well suited to statistical analysis because they are designed to make the same types of repetitive calculations found in statistical procedures. The ability to do these calculations rapidly can be either an advantage or a disadvantage to researchers, depending on their knowledge of the problem under consideration. The computer may be able to perform many intricate mathematical tasks, but the responsibility for its correct usage lies with those who use them. In short, it is always important for researchers to be sure that what is asked of a computer is actually what is needed.

The remainder of this chapter deals with two widely available statistical software packages designed specifically to analyze social science research data: *SPSS-X* (for mainframes) and *SPSS/PC+* (for PCs). Both programs are produced by the same company. These software packages, like all others available for commercial use, are constantly updated; new releases are announced periodically to reflect changes in the program. Major releases, such as from Version 1 to Version 2, usually involve substantial changes in the program. Minor releases, usually

issued to eliminate "bugs" in the program, are noted by a decimal digit added to the version number, such as Version 2.1 or 2.2. For this chapter, SPSS-X release 3.0 and SPSS/PC+ 2.0 were used.

It is important for researchers to know which release of a software program is most current. Sometimes new releases are issued without the knowledge of those who use the software. Computer users can keep up-to-date by receiving newsletters published by computer centers at colleges and universities, or by getting on the software company's mailing list. Generally, there is no problem using an old users' manual with newer releases, but the opposite is not true. Old manuals will not describe the enhanced features available in the new releases. Because of the popularity of the SPSS software, the program is usually available at most large computing centers. If any problems are encountered in trying to rerun the data included in this chapter, readers are urged to consult the appropriate SPSS users' manuals.

Basic Characteristics of SPSS-X and SPSS/PC+

Data analysis using either of the SPSS software packages proceeds through four basic steps after the data are collected and coded. First, the coded data are entered into the computer and stored as a file with a unique name. When the data are checked for accuracy, another file is written that tells SPSS how the data are entered and what they mean. Once the data are entered and properly defined in separate files, the two files are combined into one single file. Finally, sets of commands are input that tell the computer to perform various analyses on the data. Each step involves some rules and concepts that must be understood before successfully using the software.

To help understand the SPSS process, the radio listening study presented in Chapter 6 is used here to illustrate some of the rules and concepts. The data are included in Appendix 4, and are also available on diskette from Wadsworth Publishing. Because this is a general discussion of both SPSS-X and SPSS/PC +, the generic *SPSS* is used to refer to characteristics common to both packages.

DATA ENTRY.   In the radio listening survey, 200 respondents between the ages of 18 and 34 were asked 36 questions dealing with their listening habits and preferences. Each person was also assigned an identification code, which means that a total of 37 pieces of information was coded for each respondent. In the parlance of SPSS, the data consist of 200 *cases* with 37 *variables* per case. Figure 17.2 shows the data for the first 10 cases taken from the complete data set in Appendix 4. The position of each number can be expressed in terms of its *record* and *column* position. Records are contained in rows, variables are contained in columns. Figure 17.2 shows that the data are arranged in 10 records and 71 columns.

The first three digits of each record represent the case identification number. Note that they increase by one for each record, and that each lines up under one another. This shows how each column represents the value of one variable for 10 different people. In most situations, each record can contain no more than 80 columns of data. If each case required 96 columns for complete description, they would be split between two records, 80 on the first record and 16 on the second. This is known as having two records per case. In this example, only one record is required because only 71 columns are used.

Figure 17.2 shows how SPSS data are generally entered. The file is an ASCII file containing nothing but rows and columns of numbers. Although this example leaves spaces between columns of variable, SPSS does not require researchers to do so. As long as the values representing a single variable are not broken (such as the respondents' identification number), one or more spaces is usually included only for ease of reading by the researcher.

DATA DEFINITION.   The process of reading this book is possible because we have learned specific rules on how to organize sets of symbols. If letters and words were randomly displayed, it would be impossible to decipher their meaning. Letters and words mean something to us only because we follow a specific set of rules.

This same situation is true for any software package. The letters and words must be arranged according to a set of guidelines established for the computer—all else is meaningless.

The method by which SPSS communication rules are established with a computer is done through a set of instructions known as a *control file*, an example of which is shown in Figure 17.3 for SPSS/PC +.

The first SPSS command is the DATA LIST command, which designates how data are defined. DATA LIST tells SPSS where to find the relevant data file (\DATA.ASC) and how to read it once it does. It also establishes a unique name for each variable in the study (DEMO), and where to find the variable in the file ("5" = column 5). The variable name/column identification continues through all variables in the study. These locations are important for researchers to know since they are used later in writing analysis instructions.

There are some general rules about naming variables. Names cannot exceed eight characters and must begin with a letter or one of a limited number of symbols. The SPSS manual describes which symbols cannot be used for variable names. It is useful to use variable names that are as descriptive as possible to make interpretation of the printout much easier.

The VARIABLE LABELS section in Figure 17.3 is optional in SPSS. This command, however, is useful for providing additional information for the variables in the study, and they make reading the printout much easier. VARIABLE LABELS is typed at the beginning of the command, followed by the variable to be labeled and the desired label enclosed in quotation marks ("DEMO GROUP"). A forward slash (/)

FIGURE 17.2   FIRST 10 CASES FROM DATA CONTAINED IN APPENDIX 4

Case	V1	V2	V3	V4	V5	V6	V7	V8	V9	V10	V11	V12	V13	V14	V15	V16	V17	V18	V19	V20	V21	V22	V23	V24	V25	V26	V27	V28	V29	V30	V31	V32	V33	V34
001	1	2	1	1	2	2	1	1	1	2	2	2	2	1	1	1	2	2	1	1	5	0	2	0	2	1	1	2	1	3	1	1	1	1
002	1	2	1	3	2	2	1	3	1	1	2	2	2	2	1	2	2	2	2	1	2	0	2	0	2	2	1	2	1	1	1	2	1	2
003	1	2	1	1	2	2	1	2	1	1	2	2	2	1	1	2	1	1	1	1	2	0	2	0	2	2	1	3	1	0	2	0	2	3
004	1	1	2	1	1	1	1	1	1	1	1	2	1	1	1	1	2	2	1	1	5	0	2	2	1	1	1	2	1	2	1	2	1	4
005	2	2	1	2	2	2	2	2	1	1	2	2	2	1	1	2	2	2	1	2	2	0	2	0	2	3	1	0	2	3	1	3	1	4
006	1	1	2	1	1	1	1	1	1	1	1	2	2	1	1	2	1	1	1	2	5	0	2	0	2	1	1	2	1	2	1	0	2	1
007	2	1	1	2	2	2	1	2	2	2	2	2	2	2	1	2	2	2	2	2	9	0	2	3	2	3	1	1	1	3	1	3	1	1
008	1	2	1	1	2	2	3	1	1	1	2	2	2	1	1	1	2	2	1	1	2	0	2	0	1	2	1	2	1	2	1	1	1	1
009	1	1	1	1	1	1	1	1	1	2	1	2	2	1	1	1	2	2	1	1	2	0	2	0	2	2	1	1	1	2	1	3	1	1
010	1	2	1	2	2	2	1	2	1	1	2	2	2	2	1	2	1	1	1	1	9	0	2	0	2	2	1	2	1	3	1	2	1	1

separates each of the variables in the VARIABLE LABELS command section.

The VALUE LABELS command assigns additional information to each variable. For example, the value "1" of the variable DEMO means "male 18–24." If this value label were not included, the only way to know the meaning of the value would be to refer to the codebook. As with other commands, VALUE LABELS is typed first, followed by the names of all variables for which the value labels will apply. Each value is then listed with its label immediately following in single quotation marks.

If several variables share the same value labels and are defined in order in the DATA LIST command, the word "TO" between the first and last similar variable is used to eliminate unnecessary typing. For example, the last 21 items defined in the DATA LIST command shown in Figure 17.3 share the same two value labels (1 = agree; 2 = disagree). Instead of naming all 21 variables in the VALUE LABELS command, it is only necessary to type AMT_NEW (the first variable in the group) TO AMT_MUS (the last variable) and define the value labels only once. The "TO" command can also be used in other commands.

Sometimes researchers wish to eliminate some answers given by respondents, such as the "Don't know/No answer" response to the Favorite Station question (FAV_STA). In this case, a value can be declared a missing value, which is accomplished with the MISSING VALUES command (see Figure 17.3).

The control file is one of the most important tasks involved in conducting an SPSS study. Accuracy is important. A single letter, comma, or other misplaced letter or number can cause problems — the program will "blow."

SYSTEM FILES.   After the data are defined in one file, and the control statements placed in another separate file, the information is combined into one file to make running the program more efficient for SPSS and the researcher if addi-tional computations are necessary. With the use of the SAVE OUTFILE command, a special file containing the data and control files is created (shown as \SPSS\RAD_SYS in Figure 17.3).

PROCEDURE COMMAND STRUCTURE.   The data analysis commands are made possible through the use of procedure commands, which include command keywords and specifications. Command keywords tell SPSS what statistical procedure(s) is/are to be performed. The specifications are instructions that appear with the command keyword. These statements are used to modify the way the program operates or define what variables are to be analyzed.

Before any data analysis is possible, SPSS must be told which file to analyze. In SPSS terminology, this is called defining the *active file*. This is accomplished by the GET FILE command shown in Figure 17.4. The command GET FILE is followed by an equal (=) sign and the name of the file to be called into memory. A GET FILE command must precede any procedure statement in cases when a system file is being called into memory.

The GET FILE command usually appears in the first line of the batch job and is followed by the other commands. Figure 17.4 is an example of a batch job written for SPSS/PC + . Procedure statements are submitted one at a time in interactive mode. Usually the GET FILE command is issued and acknowledged by SPSS, then other commands are issued, one at a time. Output is returned immediately to the screen and to another file called a *listing file*. The listing file is useful because it can be printed out after all the analyses are complete.

Figure 17.4 shows the general structure of procedure commands. The command keyword (for example, CROSSTABS) is followed by the first specification (TABLES =) separated by at least one space from the keyword. Other specifications are set apart by slashes. This command structure will vary slightly depending on the

FIGURE 17.3 CONTROL FILE FOR RADIO LISTENING SURVEY

```
DATA LIST FILE='\SPSS\DATA.ASC'/ID 1-3  DEMO 5  WAAA_LIS 7  WAAA_AM 9
WBBB_LIS 11  WBBB_AM 13  WCCC_LIS 15  WCCC_AM 17  WDDD_LIS 19  WDDD_AM 21
WEEE_LIS 23  WEEE_AM 25  WFFF_LIS 27  WFFF_AM 29  FAV_STA 31  AMT_NEW 33
QUAL_NEW 35  AMT_OLD 37  QUAL_OLD 39  AM_SHOW 41  ENERGY 43  CONTESTS 49
FRIENDS 47  PM_JOCKS 49  LOC_ACT 51  FAV_SONG 53  ATTITUDE 55  AM_JOCKS 57
TEMPO 59  NEWS 61  TRAFFIC 63  NEW_MUS 65  VARIETY 67  SOURCE 69
AMT_MUS 71.

VARIABLE LABELS ID     'CASE ID'/
               DEMO     'DEMO GROUP'/
               WAAA_LIS 'WAAA LISTENS'/
               WAAA_AM  'WAAA MORNING'/
               WBBB_LIS 'WBBB LISTENS'/
               WBBB_AM  'WBBB MORNING'/
               WCCC_LIS 'WCCC LISTENS'/
               WCCC_AM  'WCCC MORNING'/
               WDDD_LIS 'WDDD LISTENS'/
               WDDD_AM  'WDDD MORNING'/
               WEEE_LIS 'WEEE LISTENS'/
               WEEE_AM  'WEEE MORNING'/
               WFFF_LIS 'WFFF LISTENS'/
               WFFF_AM  'WFFF MORNING'/
               FAV_STA  'FAVORITE STATION'/
               AMT_NEW  'AMOUNT OF NEW MUSIC'/
               QUAL_NEW 'QUALITY OF NEW MUSIC'/
               AMT_OLD  'AMOUNT OF OLD MUSIC'/
               QUAL_OLD 'QLTY OF OLD MUSIC'/
               AM_SHOW  'MORNING SHOW'/
               ENERGY   'UPBEAT FEELINGS'/
               CONTESTS 'CONTESTS-PRIZES'/
               FRIENDS  'FRIENDS LISTEN'/
               PM_JOCKS 'PM ANNOUNCERS'/
```

```
            LOC_ACT    'LOCAL ACTIVITIES'/
            FAV_SONG   'FAVORITE SONGS'/
            ATTITUDE   'ATTITUDE-LISTENER'/
            AM_JOCKS   'AM ANNOUNCERS'/
            TEMPO      'PACE OR TEMPO'/
            NEWS       'NEWS AND INFO'/
            TRAFFIC    'TRAFFIC REPORTS'/
            NEW_MUS    'HEAR NEW MUSIC'/
            VARIETY    'MUSIC VARIETY'/
            SOURCE     'LOCAL INFO'/
            AMT_MUS    'AMOUNT OF MUSIC'/.
VALUE LABELS  DEMO 1 'MALE 18-24'  2 'MALE 25-34'  3 'FEMALE 18-24'
              4 'FEMALE 25-34'/
              WAAA_LIS WBBB_LIS WCCC_LIS WDDD_LIS WEEE_LIS WFFF_LIS
              1 'YES'  2 'NO'/
              WAAA_AM WBBB_AM WCCC_AM WDDD_AM WEEE_AM WFFF_AM
              1 'FREQUENTLY'  2 'SOMETIMES'  3 'NEVER'/
              FAV_STA 2 'OTHER'  3 'WAAA'  4 'WBBB'  5 'WCCC'  6 'WDDD'
              7 'WEEE'  8 'WFFF'  9 'WGGG'/
              AMT_NEW TO AMT_MUS 1 'AGREE' 2 'DISAGREE'.
MISSING VALUE  FAV_STA (1)/
               AMT_NEW TO AMT_MUS (3).
SAVE OUTFILE=\SPSS\RAD_SYS'.
```

FIGURE 17.4   SPSS/PC+ CROSSTABS COMMAND FILE FOR RADIO LISTENING SURVEY

```
GET FILE='\SPSS\RAD_SYS'.
CROSSTABS TABLES=WCCC_LIS BY DEMO/STATISTICS=1.
```

version of SPSS. Some SPSS/PC+ commands differ from SPSS-X commands, and there are variations between releases of SPSS-X.

There is an important difference between commands written in batch mode and those written in interactive mode. This difference applies to the data definition commands mentioned earlier as well (for example, DATA LIST). The command keywords of batch mode commands *must* begin in the first column of the line in which they appear. This is so the program can recognize where one command stops and another begins. If a command takes more than one line to write, which is often the case, other lines must be indented. To summarize as a general rule, only command keywords may appear in the first column if SPSS is being used in batch mode.

There is no requirement to start command keywords in the first column when issuing commands in interactive mode. Commands should be ended by a period so that SPSS can recognize where one command stops and another begins. A command requiring more than one line can continue onto the next without indenting.

SPSS/PC+ is capable of both batch and interactive processing, as is SPSS-X (as of release 3.0; earlier releases are batch mode only). Generally speaking, however, SPSS/PC+ accepts commands in the interactive format no matter how they are to be processed. For example, all commands are required to end in a period regardless of what mode is used. On the other hand, SPSS-X is probably most often used in batch mode since it was the only way it could be used for many years.

DATA ANALYSIS. This section deals primarily with explaining the content of the command file shown in Figure 17.4 and showing the results of its execution. Data analysis is actually quite simple once the data are declared. It is not unusual for a procedure command to be only one line long as is the case in Figure 17.4. SPSS offers a large number of analysis procedures ranging from simple procedures, such as CROSSTABS, to more complex procedures such as FACTOR, the factor analysis command. Other commonly used procedures are ANOVA, CORRELATIONS, FREQUENCIES, T-TEST, and REGRESSION. To keep the example simple, only CROSSTABS is used for illustration.

The command file in Figure 17.4 will produce a crosstabulation table to show the demographic characteristics of respondents who report listening to station WCCC. The command file accomplishes this in a relatively straightforward manner. First, the GET FILE command calls up the system file \SPSS\RAD_SYS. On the next line the CROSSTABS keyword is invoked. SPSS/PC+ now knows that a crosstabulation procedure is desired. The next thing it expects is what variables are involved in the analysis, which are provided by the TABLES specification followed by the two variable names. The analysis could stop here, but there is also an interest in determining if a relationship exists between reported WCCC listening and demographic characteristics. This is accomplished through the use of a STATISTICS specification.

The output for this procedure is shown in Figure 17.5. The top of the page shows the names and variable labels for the two items included in the analysis. The numbers in each cell represent the number of respondents whose responses fit those categories. The figures on the margins of the table represent the number of responses and percentage of total responses for each row and column. The chi-square results are located below the table. The chi-square statistic, its associated degrees of freedom, and its significance level are reported. The small significance level indicates that demographic characteristics are related to WCCC listening habits in some manner. Note that this analysis was chosen for its simplicity. These findings may or may not have practical significance. The lowest expected frequency in any cell, as well as the number of cells with expected frequencies lower than five, are also reported. These figures are useful for assessing the appropriateness of the

FIGURE 17.5   OUTPUT FROM SPSS/PC + CROSSTABS PROCEDURE SHOWN IN FIGURE 17.4

Crosstabulation: WCCC_LIS WCCCLISTENS
                By DEMO   DEMO GROUP

Count	MALE 18-24 1	MALE 25-34 2	FEMALE 1 8-24 3	FEMALE 2 5-34 4	Row Total
WCCC_LIS					
YES 1	22	24	53	40	139 69.5
NO 2	3	14	13	31	61 30.5
Column Total	25 12.5	38 19.0	66 33.0	71 35.5	200 100.0

Chi-Square	D.F.	Significance	Min E.F.	Cells with E.F. <
14.19371	3	.0027	7.625	None

Number of Missing Observations =   0

chi-square procedure for a particular distribution. Since all of the cells shown here have expected values greater than five, there does not seem to be a problem with using this procedure. Finally, the number of missing cases is shown on the last line of the output.

This is a simple example of an analysis procedure, but it is not too far removed from the most sophisticated procedures. All of the commands are similar. For example, let's suppose we wanted a frequency distribution of our data. We would examine the manual and find that what we want is a procedure command called FREQUENCIES. We would then write the command "FREQUENCIES VARIABLES = AMT_NEW TO AMT_MUS." There are also a number of specifications that could be added to produce bar charts or print simple descriptive statistics. The wide variety of specifications available on most commands requires that researchers have a clear understanding of the procedure. Otherwise, it is quite easy to produce mountains of output that mean nothing.

S U M M A R Y

Any discussion of computers always neglects something. This is due to the complex nature of computer technology. Students in mass media research must pursue more up-to-date materials to keep abreast of the current technology. Much of the information discussed in this chapter is becoming obsolete as it is being written.

The focus of this chapter has been an introduction to computers. Like other areas of media research, computers may initially appear to be difficult or confounding. Once some exposure is gained, however, computers and their applications usually become less intimidating.

This chapter discusses the various components of computers and how they work together to form a system. Learning the vocabulary related to computers is necessary for media researchers to understand and use computers.

The final portion of the chapter demonstrates how to run an SPSS program. As indicated, readers should consult the appropriate SPSS users' manual for any additional information because the discussion presented here is very brief. Many of the topics related to statistical software packages are best learned through experience.

The future of computers offers an extremely interesting scenario. New technology will rapidly change all hardware and software, making computers even more useful in mass media research.

Questions and Problems for Further Investigation

1. Consult the following list for further information:
   PC Week
   Byte
   Personal Computing
   MacUser
   Computerworld
   PC Computing
   PC Magazine

2. Use the data in Appendix 4 to run additional SPSS analyses.

3. When can computers be a hindrance in media research?

4. Consult the following manuals and guides published by SPSS Inc. to learn more about the software:
   SPSS-X Users' Guide
   SPSS/PC + Base Manual
   SPSS-X Basics
   SPSS-X Introductory Statistics Guide

5. The following computer-related terms were not used in this chapter. Find the definitions for each one in a computer textbook or in periodicals.

Acoustic coupler	Icon
Analog computer	Keypunch
BASIC	LED printer
CAD	Multiplexer
COBOL	Raster graphics
Compiler	Soft boot
Daisy wheel printer	Superconductor
Digital computer	Truncate
Expansion slots	Virtual memory

References and Suggested Readings

Asimov, I. (1984). *How did we find out about computers?* New York: Walker.

Burks, A. R. (1988). *The first electronic computer: The Atanasoff story.* Ann Arbor: University of Michigan Press.

Lawlor, S. C. (1990). *Computer information systems.* New York: Harcourt Brace Jovanovich.

Ritchie, D. (1986). *The computer pioneers: The making of the modern computer.* New York: Simon & Schuster.

Shurkin, J. N. (1984). *Engines of the mind: A history of the computer.* New York: W. W. Norton.

CHAPTER 18

RESEARCH REPORTING, ETHICS, AND FINANCIAL SUPPORT

C hapters 13–16 discussed mass media research from the planning stages of a study to the selection of the most appropriate statistical methods for testing purposes. Chapter 17 introduced the computer as a research tool. This chapter focuses on three other areas that are not part of the research process itself but are nevertheless vital to the execution of any research project: reporting, ethics, and financial support.

RESEARCH REPORTS

The first step in writing any research report is to identify the intended readers. This is an important decision because the organization, style, and even the mode of presentation depend on the target audience. In mass media research, there are typically two types of audiences and two types of research reports:

1. Reports aimed at colleagues and intended for publication in scholarly and professional journals or for presentation at a convention
2. Reports aimed at decision makers and intended for in-house use only

The format, length, style, and organization of a published report will have to conform to the guidelines of the journal in which it appears. Since colleagues are the target audience for such reports and papers, the writer must pay close attention to the theory underlying the research, the methods used, and the techniques of analysis. In the second instance, there is more flexibility. Some decision makers prefer to be briefed orally by the researcher. In such cases the verbal presentation might be supplemented by a written summary, handouts, visual aids, and, on request, a detailed report. In other circumstances, the researcher might prepare a written report with a short executive summary, confining most of the technical material to appendixes. No matter what the situation or audience, the primary goal in all research reports is accuracy.

The Need for Accurate Reporting Procedures

Researchers need to report research accurately for two reasons. First, a clear explanation of the investigator's methods provides an opportunity for readers to more completely understand the project. Researchers should keep in mind that in most cases, a reader's knowledge of a given project is based solely on the information contained in the report. Since readers do not instinctively understand each procedure used in a study, these details must be supplied. Second, an accurate report provides the necessary information for those who wish to replicate the study. As Rummel (1970) suggested:

> Enough information must be included or filed somewhere in public archives to enable reproduction of the study without the necessity of personal contact with the investigator. This is to ensure that a study is always replicable regardless of the decades or generations that may pass.

Rummel has even argued that researchers should be able to replicate a published study from the information contained therein. Realistically speaking, however, this is not always possible. Mass media journals have limited space, and journal editors do not have the luxury of

387

printing all raw data, tables, and graphs generated by a study; they are forced to eliminate some essential information. Therefore, Rummel's alternative — **data archives** — is very important. Unfortunately, the mass media field has yet to establish its own data archive service for researchers to use.

The conclusion, then, is that individual researchers must take full responsibility for accurately reporting and storing their own research data. To facilitate this task, the following subsections describe the important elements of research that should be included in a published study. The lists may appear long in some cases, but in reality, most of the information can be contained in a few short sentences. At any rate, it is better to include too much information than too little.

The Mechanics of Writing a Research Report

Beginning researchers may find the writing style used for research reports awkward or unaesthetic, but there is a definite purpose behind the rules governing scientific writing: clarity. Every effort must be made to avoid ambiguity.

Given the wide variety of approaches to research, it stands to reason that the approaches to writing a research report are equally varied. Most research reports, however, include only five basic sections or chapters: introduction, literature review, methods, results, and discussion.

INTRODUCTION. The introduction should alert the reader to what is to follow. Most introductions usually contain the following:

1. *Statement of the problem.* The first job of the report writer is to provide some information about the background and the nature of the problem under investigation. If the research topic has a long history, then a short summary is in order. This section should also discuss any relevant theoretical background that pertains to the research topic.

2. *Justification.* Another important area to be covered in this initial section is the rationale and justification for the project. This section should address the question of why it is important for us to spend time and energy researching this particular problem. Research can be important because it deals with a crucial theoretical issue, because it has practical value, or because it has methodological value.

3. *Aims of the current study.* Most introductory sections conclude with an unequivocal statement of the hypothesis or research question to be answered by the study.

LITERATURE REVIEW. The second major section is the review of the literature. (In some formats, the literature review is incorporated into the introduction.) As the name suggests, the literature review section briefly recapitulates the work done in the field. This review need not be exhaustive; the writer should summarize only those studies most relevant to the current project. All literature reviews should be accurate and relevant.

1. *Accuracy.* A concise and accurate distillation of each study in your review is a prerequisite for any literature review. The main points of each study — hypotheses that were tested, sample, method, findings, and implications — should be briefly summarized. The review should be selective but thorough.

2. *Relevance.* A literature review should be more than a rote recitation of research studies. It must also contain analysis and synthesis. The writer is obligated to discuss the relevance of the past work to the current study. What theoretic development can be seen in past work? What major conclusions have recurred? What were some common problems? How do the answers to these questions relate to the current study? The ultimate aim of the review is to show how your study evolved out of past efforts and how the prior research provides a justification for your study.

METHODS.   The methods section describes the approach used to confront the research problem. Some of the topics that are usually mentioned in this section are as follows.

1.   *Variables used in the analysis.* This includes a description of both independent and dependent variables, explaining how the variables were selected for the study, what marker variables, if any (Chapter 3) were included, and how extraneous variables were controlled. Each variable also requires some justification for its use — variables cannot be added without reason. The mean and the standard deviation for each variable should be reported when necessary.

2.   *Sample size.* The researcher should state the number of subjects or units of study and also explain how these entities were selected. Additionally, any departure from normal randomization must be described in detail.

3.   *Sample characteristics.* The sample should also be described in terms of its demographic, lifestyle, or other descriptor characteristics. When human subjects are used, at least their age and sex should be indicated.

4.   *Methodology.* Every research report requires a description of the methods used to collect and analyze data. The amount of methodological description to be included depends on the audience; articles written for journals, for instance, must contain more detailed information than reports prepared in private sector research.

5.   *Data manipulation.* Often the collected data are not normally distributed, and researchers must use data transformation to achieve an approximation of normality. If such a procedure is used, a full explanation should be given.

RESULTS.   The results section contains the findings of the research. It typically contains the following:

1.   *Description of the analysis.* The statistical techniques used to analyze the data should be mentioned. If the analysis used common or easily recognized statistics, a one-sentence description might be all that is needed, such as "Chi-square analyses were performed on the data" or "Analysis of variance was performed. . . ." If appropriate, the particular statistical program used by the researcher should be identified. Finally, this part should include an overview of what is to follow: "This section is divided into two parts. We will first report the results of the analysis of variance and then the results of the regression analysis."

2.   *Description of findings.* The findings should be tied to the statement of the hypotheses or research questions mentioned in the introduction. The author should clearly state whether the results supported the hypotheses or whether the research questions were answered. Next, any peripheral findings can be reported. Many researchers and journal editors suggest that interpretation and discussion of findings be omitted from this section and that the writer should stick solely to the bare facts. Others think that this section should contain more than numbers, suggesting the implications of the findings as well. In fact, for some short research articles, this section is sometimes called "Findings and Discussion." The choice of what model to follow depends upon the purpose of the report and the avenue of publication.

3.   *Tables.* Tables, charts, graphs, and other data displays should be presented parsimoniously and, if the article is being submitted to a journal, in the proper format. Remember that many readers turn first to the tables and may not read the accompanying text; consequently, tables should be explicit and easily understood by themselves.

DISCUSSION.   The last section of a research report is the discussion. The contents of this section are highly variable but the following elements are common.

1.   *Summary.* A synopsis of the main findings of the study often leads off this section.

2. *Implications/discussion/interpretations*. This is the part of the report that discusses the meaning of the findings. If the findings are in line with current theory and research, the writer should include a statement of how they correspond with what was done in the past. If the findings contradict or do not support current theory, then some explanation for the current pattern of results is provided.

3. *Limitations*. The conclusions of the study should be tempered by a report of some of its constraints. Perhaps the sample was limited or the response rate was low or the experimental manipulation was not as clean as it could have been. In any case, the researcher should list some of the potential weaknesses of the research.

4. *Suggestions for future research*. In addition to answering questions, most research projects uncover new questions to be investigated. The suggestions for research should be relevant and practical.

Writing Style

Since the writing requirements for journal articles and business or government reports vary in several ways, the following guidelines are divided into two sections.

There are nine principal guidelines for writing for scholarly journals.

1. Avoid using first person pronouns: I, me, my, we, and so on. Research reports are almost always written in third person ("Subjects were selected randomly." "Subject A told the researcher . . . ," and so on). First person pronouns should be used only when the article is a commentary.

2. When submitting a paper for professional publication, place each table, graph, chart, and figure on a separate page. This is done because if the article is accepted, these pages will be typeset by one department of the printing company and the text by another. (In manage-

ment reports, tables, graphs, and other displays are included in the text unless they are too large, in which case they should be placed on separate pages.)

3. Read the authors' guidelines published by each journal. They provide specific rules concerning acceptable writing style, footnote and bibliography formats, the number of copies to submit, and so forth. A researcher who fails to follow these guidelines may decrease the chance that his or her report will be accepted for publication — or at least substantially delay the process while alterations are made.

4. Be stylistically consistent with regard to tables, charts, graphs, section headings, and so forth. Tables, for example, should follow the same format and should be numbered consecutively.

5. Clearly label all displays with meaningful titles. Each table, graph, chart, or figure caption should accurately describe the material presented and its contribution to the report.

6. Keep language and descriptions as simple as possible by avoiding unnecessary and overly complex words, phrases, and terms. The goal of scientific writing is to explain findings clearly, simply, and accurately.

7. When possible, use the active rather than passive voice. For example, "The researchers found that . . ." is preferable to "It was found by the researchers that. . . ." Writing in the active voice makes reading more pleasant and also requires fewer words.

8. Proofread the manuscript carefully. Even researchers who are meticulous in their scientific approach can make errors in compiling a manuscript. All manuscripts, whether intended for publication or for management review, should be proofread several times to check for accuracy.

9. Miscellaneous considerations:
   a. Avoid phrases or references that could be interpreted as sexist or racist.

b. Check all data for accuracy. Even one misplaced digit may affect the results of a study.

c. Use acceptable grammar; avoid slang.

d. Provide acknowledgments whenever another researcher's work is included in the report.

e. Include footnotes to indicate where further information or assistance can be obtained.

Guidelines for writing a report for business or government decision makers include the following.

1. Provide an executive summary at the beginning of the report. Since busy decision makers may not read anything else in the report, great care must be taken in constructing this section. Some useful hints are:

a. Get right to the point and state conclusions quickly.

b. Keep the language simple and concise. Don't use jargon, clichés, or overly technical terms.

c. Be brief. Keep the summary to no more than a page — surely no more than two pages. Anything else ceases to be a summary.

2. Place detailed and complicated discussions of methods in a technical appendix. Summarize the procedures in the body of the report.

3. Use clearly defined and easily understood quantitative analysis techniques. Most decision makers are not familiar with complicated statistical procedures. Keep the basic analysis simple. If it becomes necessary to use advanced statistical procedures, explain in the body of the report what was done and what the results mean. Include another technical appendix that describes the statistical technique in detail.

4. Use graphs and charts wherever appropriate to make numerical findings more understandable and meaningful. Never let tabular material stand alone; to ensure that its impor-

tance is not overlooked, mention or explain each such item.

5. Decision makers like research that provides answers to their questions. Put the conclusions reached by the investigators and, if appropriate, recommendations for action, in the last section of the report.

RESEARCH ETHICS

The majority of mass media research involves observations of human beings — asking them questions or examining what they have done. Since human beings have certain rights, the researcher must ensure that the rights of the participants in a project are not violated. This requires a consideration of ethics: distinguishing right from wrong and the proper from the improper. Unfortunately, there are no universal definitions for these terms. Instead, a series of guidelines, broad generalizations, and suggestions has been endorsed or at least tacitly accepted by most in the research profession. These guidelines will not provide an answer to every ethical question that may arise, but they can help make researchers more sensitive to the issues.

Before discussing these specific guidelines, we list some hypothetical research situations that involve ethics.

1. A researcher at a large university hands questionnaires to the students in an introductory mass media course and tells them that if they do not complete the forms, they will lose points toward their grade in the course.

2. A researcher is conducting a mail survey about attendance at X-rated motion pictures. The questionnaire states that responses will be anonymous. Unknown to the respondents, however, each return envelope is marked with a code that enables the researcher to identify the sender.

3.   A researcher recruits subjects for an experiment by stating that participants will be asked to watch "a few scenes from some current movies." Those who decide to participate are shown several scenes of bloody and graphic violence.

4.   A researcher shows one group of children a violent television show and another group a nonviolent program. After viewing, the children are sent to a public playground, where they are told to play with the children who are already there. The researcher records each instance of violent behavior exhibited by the young subjects.

5.   Subjects in an experiment are told to submit a sample of their newswriting to an executive of a large newspaper. They are led to believe that whoever submits the best work will be offered a job at the paper. In fact, the "executive" is a confederate in the experiment and severely criticizes everyone's work.

These examples of ethically flawed study designs should be kept in mind while reading the following guidelines to ethics in mass media research.

General Ethical Principles

General ethical principles are difficult to construct in the research area. There are, however, at least four principles from the study of ethics that have relevance. First, is the principle of autonomy, or the principle of self-determination. Basic to this concept is the demand that the researcher respect the rights, values, and decisions of other people. The reasons for a person's action should be respected and the actions not interfered with. This principle is exemplified by the use of informed consent in the research procedure. A second ethical principle important to social science research is that of nonmaleficence. In short, it is wrong to intentionally inflict harm on another. A third ethical principle — beneficence — is usually considered in tandem with nonmaleficence. Beneficence stipulates a positive obligation to remove existing harms and to confer benefits on others. These two principles operate together, and often the researcher must weigh the harmful risks of research against its possible benefits (for example, increase in knowledge, refinement of theory).

A fourth ethical principle that is sometimes relevant to social science is the principle of justice. At its general level, this principle holds that people who are equal in relevant respects should be treated equally. In the research context, this principle should be applied when new programs or policies are being evaluated. The positive results of such research should be shared with all. It would be unethical, for example, to deny the benefit of a new teaching procedure to children because they were originally chosen to be in the control group rather than the group that received the experimental procedure. Benefits should be shared with all who are qualified.

Although it is difficult to generalize, it is clear that mass media researchers must follow some set of rules to fulfill their ethical obligations to their subjects and respondents. Cook (1976), discussing the laboratory approach, offers one such code of behavior.

1. Do not involve people in research without their knowledge or consent.
2. Do not coerce people to participate.
3. Do not withhold from the participant the true nature of the research.
4. Do not actively lie to the participant about the nature of the research.
5. Do not lead the participant to commit acts that diminish his or her self-respect.
6. Do not violate the right to self-determination.
7. Do not expose the participant to physical or mental stress.
8. Do not invade the privacy of the participant.
9. Do not withhold benefits from participants in control groups.

10. Do not fail to treat research participants fairly and to show them consideration and respect.

Voluntary Participation and Informed Consent

An individual is entitled to decline to participate in any research project or to terminate participation at any time. Participation in an experiment, survey, or focus group is always voluntary, and any form of coercion is unacceptable. Researchers who are in a position of authority over subjects (as in the situation where the researcher hands the university students questionnaires) should be especially sensitive to *implied* coercion: even though the researcher might tell the class that failure to participate will not affect their grades, many students may not believe this. In such a situation, it would be advisable to keep the questionnaires anonymous and to have the person in authority be absent from the room while the survey is administered.

Voluntary participation is a less pressing ethical issue in mail and telephone surveys, since respondents are free to hang up the phone or to throw away the questionnaire. Nonetheless, a researcher should not attempt to induce subjects to participate by misrepresenting the organization sponsoring the research or by exaggerating its purpose or importance. For example, phone interviewers should not be instructed to identify themselves as representatives of the "Department of Information" to mislead people into thinking the survey is government-sponsored. Likewise, mail questionnaires should not be constructed to mimic census forms, tax returns, social security questionnaires, or other official government forms.

Closely related to voluntary participation is the notion of *informed consent*. For people to volunteer for a research project, they need to know enough about the project to make an intelligent choice. Researchers have the responsibility to inform potential subjects or respondents of all features of the project that can reasonably be expected to influence participation. Respondents should understand that an interview may take as long as 45 minutes, or that a second interview is required, or that upon completing a mail questionnaire, they may be singled out for a telephone interview.

In an experiment, informed consent means that potential subjects must be warned of any possible discomfort or unpleasantness that might be involved. Subjects should be told if they are to receive or administer electric shocks, be subjected to unpleasant audio or visual stimuli, or undergo any procedure that may cause concern. Any unusual measurement techniques that may be used also must be described. Researchers have an obligation to answer candidly and truthfully, as far as possible, all the participant's questions about the research.

Experiments that involve deception (see the following subsection) cause special problems with regard to obtaining informed consent. If deception is absolutely necessary to conduct an experiment, is the experimenter obligated to inform subjects that they may be deceived during the upcoming experiment? Will such a disclosure affect participation in the experiment? Will it also affect the experimental results? Should one compromise by telling all potential subjects that deception will be involved for some participants but not for others?

A second problem is deciding exactly how much information about a research project must be disclosed in seeking to achieve informed consent. Is it enough to explain that the experiment involves rating commercials, or is it necessary to add that the experiment is designed to test whether subjects with high IQs prefer different commercials from those with low IQs? Obviously, in some situations the researcher cannot reveal everything about the project for fear of contaminating the results. For example, if the goal of the research is to examine the influence of peer pressure on commercial evaluations, alerting the subjects to this facet of the investigation might change their behavior in the experiment.

Problems might occur in research examining the impact of mass media in nonliterate communities, for example, if the research subjects did not comprehend what they were told regarding the proposed investigation. Even in literate societies, many people fail to understand the implications for confidentiality of the storage of survey data on computer disks or tape. Moreover, an investigator might not have realized in advance that some subjects would find part of an experiment or survey emotionally disturbing. Since it is impossible for informed consent to apply to all situations, the American Psychological Association has suggested that researchers have a responsibility to continue their attention to subjects' welfare after the completion of data collection.

Research findings provide some indication of what research participants should be told. Epstein, Suedefeld, and Silverstein (1973) found that subjects wanted a general description of the experiment and what was expected of them; they wanted to know whether danger was involved, how long the experiment would last, and the experiment's purpose. As far as informed consent and survey participation are concerned, Sobal (1984) found wide variation among researchers about what to tell respondents in the survey introduction. Almost all introductions identified the research organization and the interviewer by name and described the research topic. Less frequently mentioned in introductions were the sponsor of the research and guarantees of confidentiality or anonymity. Few survey introductions mentioned the length of the survey or that participation was voluntary. More recently, Greenberg and Garramone (1989) reported the results of a survey of 201 mass media researchers that disclosed that 96% usually provided guaranteed confidentiality of

results, 92% usually named the sponsoring organization, 66% usually told respondents that participation is voluntary, and 61% usually disclosed the length of the questionnaire.

Finally, one must consider the form of the consent to be obtained. Written consent is a requirement in certain government-sponsored research programs and may also be required by many university research review committees, as discussed next in connection with guidelines promulgated by the federal government. In several generally recognized situations, however, signed forms are regarded as impractical. These include telephone surveys, mail surveys, personal interviews, and cases in which the signed form itself might represent an occasion for breach of confidentiality. For example, a respondent who has been promised anonymity as an inducement to participate in a face-to-face interview might be suspicious if asked to sign a consent form after the interview. In these circumstances, the fact that the respondent agreed to participate is taken as implied consent.

Concealment and Deception

Concealment and deception techniques are encountered most frequently in experimental research. Concealment is the withholding of certain information from the subjects; deception is deliberately providing false information. Both practices raise ethical problems. The difficulty in obtaining consent has already been mentioned. A second problem derives from the general feeling that it is wrong for experimenters to lie or otherwise to deceive subjects.

Many critics argue that deception transforms a subject from a human being into a manipulated object and is therefore demeaning to the participant. Moreover, once subjects have been deceived, they are likely to expect to be deceived again in other research projects. At least two research studies seem to suggest that this concern is valid. Stricker and Messick (1967) reported finding a high incidence of suspicion among subjects of high school age after having been deceived. Fillenbaum (1966) found that about one third to one half of subjects were suspicious at the beginning of an experiment after deception in a prior research experience.

On the other hand, some researchers argue that certain studies could not be conducted at all without the use of deception. They claim that the harm done to those who are deceived is outweighed by the benefits of the research to scientific knowledge. The same arguments can be used both for and against concealment. In general, however, concealment is a somewhat less worrisome ethical problem, provided enough information is given to subjects to allow informed consent and all the subjects' questions are answered candidly.

Obviously, deception is not a technique that should be used indiscriminately. Kelman (1967) suggested that before the investigator settles on deception as an experimental tactic, three questions should be examined:

1. How significant is the proposed study?
2. Are alternative procedures available that would provide the same information?
3. How severe is the deception? (It is one thing to tell subjects that the experimentally constructed message they are reading was taken from the *New York Times*; it is another to report that the test a subject has just completed was designed to measure latent suicidal tendencies.)

Another set of criteria was put forth by Elms (1982), who suggested five necessary and sufficient conditions under which deception can be considered ethically justified in social science research.

1. When there is no other feasible way to obtain the desired information

2. When the likely benefits substantially outweigh the likely harms
3. When subjects are given the option to withdraw at any time without penalty
4. When any physical or psychological harm to subjects is temporary
5. When subjects are debriefed as to all substantial deception and the research procedures are made available for public review

Together the suggestions of Kelman and Elms offer researchers good advice for the planning stages of investigations.

When an experiment is concluded, especially one involving concealment or deception, it is the responsibility of the investigator to debrief subjects. Debriefing should be thorough enough to remove any lasting effects that might have been created by the experimental manipulation or by any other aspect of the experiment. Subjects' questions should be answered and the potential value of the experiment stressed. How common is debriefing among mass media researchers? In the survey cited in Greenberg and Garramone (1989), 71% of the researchers reported they usually debrief subjects, 19% debrief sometimes, and 10% rarely or never debrief subjects. Although necessary in most experiments, the practice of debriefing has yet to spread to all investigators.

Protection of Privacy

The problem of protecting the privacy of participants usually occurs more often in survey research than in laboratory studies. Subjects have a right to know whether their privacy will be maintained and who will have access to the information they provide. There are two ways to guarantee privacy: by assuring anonymity and by assuring confidentiality. A promise of anonymity is a guarantee that a given respondent cannot possibly be linked to any particular response. In many research projects anonymity is an advantage, since it encourages respondents to be honest and candid in their answers. Strictly speaking, personal and telephone interviews cannot be anonymous because the researcher can link a given questionnaire to a specific person, household, or telephone number. In such instances, the researcher should promise confidentiality; that is, the respondents should be assured that even though as individuals they can be identified, their names will never be publicly associated with the information they provide. A researcher should never use "anonymous" in a way that is or seems to be synonymous with "confidential."

Additionally, respondents should be told who *will* have access to the information they provide. The researcher's responsibility for assuring confidentiality does not end once the data have been analyzed and the study concluded. Questionnaires that identify persons by name should not be stored in public places, nor should other investigators be given permission to examine confidential data unless all identifying marks have been obliterated.

Federal Regulations Concerning Research

In 1971 the Department of Health, Education, and Welfare (HEW) drafted rules for obtaining informed consent from research participants, which included full documentation of informed consent procedures. In addition, the government set up a system of institutional review boards (IRBs) to safeguard the rights of human subjects. As of 1990 there were more than 700 IRBs at medical schools, colleges, universities, hospitals, and other institutions. At most universities, IRBs have become part of the permanent bureaucracy. They have regular meetings and have developed standardized forms that must accompany research proposals that involve human subjects or respondents.

In 1981 the Department of Health and Human Services (successor to the Department of Health, Education, and Welfare) softened its regulations concerning social science research. The Department's Policy for the Protection of Human Research Subjects exempted studies using existing public data, research in educational settings about new instructional techniques, research involving the use of anonymous education tests, and survey, interview, and observational research in public places, provided the subjects are not identified and sensitive information is not collected. Signed consent forms were deemed unnecessary when the research presented only a minimal risk of harm to subjects and involved no procedures for which written consent was required outside the research context. This meant that signed consent forms were no longer necessary in the interview situation, because a person did not usually seek written consent before asking a question.

Although the new guidelines apparently exempt most nonexperimental social science research from federal regulation, IRBs at some institutions still review all research proposals that involve human subjects and some IRBs still follow the old HEW standards. In fact, some IRBs might have regulations even more stringent than the federal guidelines. As a practical matter, a researcher should always build a little more time into the research schedule to accommodate IRB procedures.

Ethics in Data Analysis and Reporting

Researchers are also responsible for maintaining professional standards in the analysis and reporting of their data. The ethical guidelines in this area are less controversial and more clearcut. One cardinal rule is that researchers have a moral and ethical obligation to refrain from tampering with data: questionnaire responses and experimental observations may not be fabricated, altered, or discarded. Similarly, researchers are expected to maintain resonable care in processing the data to guard against needless errors that might affect the results.

Researchers should never conceal information that might influence the interpretation of their findings. For example, if 2 weeks elapsed between the testing of the experimental group and the testing of the control group, this delay should be reported so that other researchers can discount the effects of history and maturation on the results. Every research report should contain a full and complete description of method, particularly of any departure from standard procedures.

Since science is a public activity, researchers have an ethical obligation to share their findings and methods with other researchers. All questionnaires, experimental materials, measurement instruments, instructions to subjects, and other relevant items should be made available to those who wish to examine them.

Finally, all investigators are under an ethical obligation to draw conclusions from their data that are consistent with those data. Interpretations should not be stretched or distorted to fit a personal point of view or a favorite theory, or to gain or maintain a client's favor. Nor should researchers attribute greater significance or credibility to their data than they justify. For example, when analyzing correlation coefficients obtained from a large sample, it is possible to achieve statistical significance with an r of only, for example, .10. It would be perfectly acceptable to report a statistically significant result in this case, but the investigator should also mention that the predictive utility of the correlation was not large, and specifically, that it explained only 1% of the total variation. In short, researchers should report results with candor and honesty.

A Professional Code of Ethics

Formalized codes of ethics have yet to be developed by all professional associations involved in mass media research. One organization that has developed its own ethical code is the American Association for Public Opinion Research. The code is reproduced on page 398.

FINDING SUPPORT FOR MASS MEDIA RESEARCH

Research costs money. Finding a source for research funds is a problem that confronts both quantitative and qualitative researchers in all fields of mass media. This section mentions some organizations that have supported mass media research projects. A researcher in need of funding should contact these organizations for details about the types of studies they support and the amount of funds available, as well as instructions for preparing research proposals.

University or college researchers should determine whether the institution has a program of research grants for individual faculty members. Many colleges award such grants, often on a competitive basis, for research in mass media. Typically these grants are modest in size — usually under $5,000 — but they are among the easiest to apply for and to administer. In many cases grants are available for student research, as well.

Several philanthropic foundations sponsor mass media research. Among the better known are the Ford Foundation, the John and Mary Markle Foundation, the Kellogg Foundation, and the Alfred P. Sloan Foundation. The amounts these organizations give to support research range from about $5,000 to as much as $150,000. Competition is stiff, and the researcher should be certain that his or her

American Association for Public Opinion Research
Code of Professional Ethics and Practices

I. Principles of Professional Practice in the Conduct of our Work

    A. We shall exercise due care in gathering and processing data, taking all reasonable steps to assure the accuracy of results.

    B. We shall exercise due care in the development of research designs and in the analysis of data.

        1. We shall recommend and employ only research tools and methods of analysis which, in our professional judgment, are well suited to the research problem at hand.

        2. We shall not select research tools and methods of analysis because of their capacity to yield a misleading conclusion.

        3. We shall not knowingly make interpretations of research results, nor shall we tacitly permit interpretations, which are inconsistent with the data available.

        4. We shall not knowingly imply that interpretations should be accorded greater confidence than the data actually warrant.

    C. We shall describe our findings and methods accurately and in appropriate detail in all research reports.

II. Principles of Professional Responsibility in our Dealings with People

    A. The Public

        1. We shall cooperate with legally authorized representatives of the public by describing the methods used in our studies.

        2. When we become aware of the appearance in public of serious distortions of our research we shall publicly disclose what is required to correct the distortions.

    B. Clients and Sponsors

        1. When undertaking work for a private client we shall hold confidential all proprietary information obtained about the client's business affairs and about the findings of research conducted for the client, except when the dissemination of the information is expressly authorized by the client or becomes necessary under terms of Section II-A-2.

        2. We shall be mindful of the limitations of our techniques and facilities and shall accept only those research assignments which can be accomplished within these limitations.

    C. The Profession

        1. We shall not cite our membership in the Association as evidence of professional competence, since the Association does not so certify any persons or organizations.

        2. We recognize our responsibility to contribute to the science of public opinion research and to disseminate as freely as possible the ideas and findings which emerge from our research.

    D. The Respondent

        1. We shall not lie to survey respondents or use practices and methods which abuse, coerce, or humiliate them.

        2. Unless the respondent waives confidentiality for specified uses we shall hold as privileged and confidential all information that tends to identify a respondent with his or her responses. We shall also not disclose the names of respondents for nonresearch purposes.

research area is one for which these foundations provide funding. As an alternative, there may be smaller foundations located near the researcher's base of operations that could be investigated.

Certain departments of the federal government sponsor mass media research. Among the departments that have been active in supporting media research are the National Institute of Mental Health, the National Science Foundation, and the National Endowment for the Humanities. Other funding agencies can be identified by looking through the *Federal Grant Register*. Applying for a government grant tends to be complicated, and there are many guidelines and regulations. In addition, there is the usual problem of government red tape. Nonetheless, these agencies have been known to make sizable grants to investigators.

Many professional media associations sponsor continuing programs to support research relevant to their particular field. In radio and television, the National Association of Broadcasters awards annual grants for research in broadcasting. The competition is keen: approximately half a dozen grants of $5,000 are made each year to professors and students interested in broadcasting research. The Dowden Center for Telecommunication Studies at the University of Georgia offers two $1,000 awards to support dissertation research dealing with cable TV and other new electronic media. In the print media, ANPA sponsors research having to do with readership and circulation. The Gannett Foundation also provides research funding, and the Magazine Publishers Association (MPA) sponsors magazine-related research.

The American Academy of Advertising sponsors an annual competition to award a $1,500 grant to a new faculty member (one who has been teaching less than 5 years) to conduct research studies in the field of advertising. The American Association of Advertising Agencies has also funded research projects. Similarly, the Foundation for Research in Education and Public Relations has a program of small grants ($1,000–$3,000) to support research in public relations.

Many researchers have obtained money to finance their research by working with the media industry. The three television networks have research departments that are willing to examine proposals from outside investigators that might be of interest to them. Occasionally, they will even sponsor a research program themselves. The American Broadcasting Company in the mid-1970s funded five separate research projects submitted by academic researchers, providing $20,000 for each. The Columbia Broadcasting System recently sponsored a lengthy audience survey conducted among British youngsters. In addition, the larger group owners in broadcasting have research departments that might be approached. The Corporation for Public Broadcasting, for example, has sponsored several audience studies relating to their programs. Similarly, large newspaper chains are potential funding sources. In the public relations field, many researchers have obtained support by contacting the professional organization of the industry they are studying or by working with a private company or corporation.

Industry support can be a mixed blessing. On the one hand, working with industry backing makes it easier for a researcher to enlist the cooperation of people or organizations within that industry and also facilitates obtaining data about the inner workings of the industry. On the other hand, many media industries are interested in limited research areas that may not have much theoretical attraction for the researcher. A company may specify the focus of the study and the variables to be examined. Therefore, when approaching a media organization or any other private company for support, it is wise to determine in advance what control, if any, the private organization will have over the design, execution, and subsequent publicizing of the project.

Finally, most colleges and universities have an Office of Contracts and Grants (or some similar title) that can be of great help to researchers. In addition to aiding the researcher with the bureaucratic requirements necessary for a grant application, this office can offer valuable assistance in other areas. For example, this office might offer computerized searches for sponsoring agencies, information about current grants, budget advice, preparation of abstracts, and even word-processing services. Researchers in the academic setting should take advantage of this resource.

S U M M A R Y

Writing a research report is naturally an important step in the scientific process, since the report places the research study in the public domain for consideration and confirmation. Beginning researchers generally find the process much easier after they have completed one or two studies. A key to successful writing is to follow the guidelines developed by journal editors, or styles developed by individual companies or businesses. The same basic five-section format is used for all reports.

Ethical considerations in conducting research should not be overlooked. Nearly every research study has the potential of affecting subjects in some way, either psychologically or physically. Researchers dealing with human subjects must take great care to ensure that all precautions are taken to alleviate any potential harm to subjects. This includes carefully planning a study as well as debriefing subjects upon completion of a project.

The final part of this chapter describes financing research projects. This topic is relevant to all researchers because lack of funds often cancels good research projects. The chapter describes a variety of sources that provide financial assistance; none should be overlooked.

Questions and Problems for Further Investigation

1. Read an article in a recent academic journal of mass media research. See how well the authors follow the reporting guidelines discussed in this chapter.

2. Using the five examples on pages 391–392, provide, if possible, an alternate way of conducting the study that would be ethically acceptable.

References and Suggested Readings

Beauchamp, T., Faden, R., Wallace, R. J., & Walters, L. (Eds.). (1982). *Ethical issues in social science research*. Baltimore: Johns Hopkins University Press.

Bower, R., & de Gasparis, P. (1978). *Ethics in social research*. New York: Praeger.

Cook, S. (1976). Ethical issues in the conduct of research in social relations. In C. Sellitz, L. Wrightsman, & S. Cook (Eds.), *Research methods in social relations*. New York: Holt, Rinehart & Winston.

Elms, A. (1982). Keeping deception honest. In T. Beauchamp, R. Faden, R. J. Wallace, & L. Walters (Eds.), *Ethical issues in social science research*. Baltimore: Johns Hopkins University Press.

Epstein, Y., Suedefeld, P., & Silverstein, S. (1973). The experimental contract. *American Psychologist, 28*, 212–221.

Fillenbaum, S. (1966). Prior deception and subsequent experimental performance. *Journal of Personality and Social Psychology, 4*, 532–537.

Greenberg, B. S., & Garramone, G. M. (1989). Ethical issues in mass communication research. In G. H. Stempel & B. H. Westley (Eds.), *Research methods in mass communication* (2nd ed.). Englewood Cliffs, NJ: Prentice-Hall.

Kelman, H. (1967). Human use of human subjects: The problem of deception in social psychological experiments. *Psychological Bulletin, 67*, 1–11.

Kelman, H. (1982). Ethical issues in different social science methods. In T. Beauchamp, R. Faden, R. J. Wallace, & L. Walters (Eds.), *Ethical issues in social science research*. Baltimore: Johns Hopkins University Press.

Rubin, R. B., Rubin, A. M., & Piele, L. J. (1990). *Communication research: Strategies and sources* (2nd ed.). Belmont, CA: Wadsworth.

Rummel, R. J. (1970). *Applied factor analysis.* Evanston, IL: Northwestern University Press.

Sobal, J. (1984). The content of survey introductions and the provision of informed consent. *Public Opinion Quarterly, 48*(4), 788–793.

Stricker, L., & Messick, J. (1967). The true deceiver. *Psychological Bulletin, 68,* 13–20.

APPENDIXES

TABLES

Table 1   Random Numbers

```
0 8 9 5 6 4 4 8 9 4 0 7 5 9 7 0 4 5 3 1 2 7 8 6 6
8 2 4 4 8 8 0 2 6 5 5 0 3 5 9 1 3 8 6 8 8 3 1 8 5
3 1 2 3 7 6 4 1 1 4 3 5 2 7 4 9 3 2 7 5 5 4 7 6 2
2 3 8 1 8 6 6 1 0 8 4 1 0 5 0 4 8 5 3 7 8 7 6 5 7
0 0 4 3 6 5 5 2 3 5 2 4 3 3 9 3 2 5 2 0 8 4 6 2 1
1 2 8 9 7 5 8 9 7 8 6 7 4 0 4 0 4 9 7 8 5 0 2 9 8
9 8 4 6 9 9 0 8 0 2 3 2 8 0 5 4 5 0 6 7 6 2 3 9 8
0 7 3 6 9 5 1 6 3 8 0 5 9 0 0 2 0 9 3 6 8 8 2 4 3
2 2 3 9 5 7 9 4 0 6 7 3 6 9 6 4 1 7 3 6 5 1 8 2 6
4 9 5 6 9 3 1 4 7 8 1 5 6 7 2 2 4 6 3 6 5 4 2 1 2
4 0 6 6 8 5 4 3 7 8 3 2 6 8 1 2 2 7 0 6 5 3 5 8 4
6 3 3 2 0 3 9 7 0 2 3 6 9 5 3 4 1 6 1 8 3 9 4 3 3
0 6 1 8 4 2 1 8 6 7 5 4 1 9 0 3 2 4 1 5 7 7 4 0 8
2 2 4 2 9 6 8 5 8 2 6 1 0 7 6 1 7 9 2 0 9 2 8 7 8
8 3 2 3 0 7 4 3 5 8 9 0 8 0 5 8 8 7 1 3 6 0 1 3 9
2 3 1 8 2 3 1 0 9 0 0 8 9 1 2 0 3 7 0 2 0 1 8 1 7
0 8 7 3 4 4 5 1 8 7 4 5 1 9 9 0 3 2 2 3 1 2 6 4 6
5 8 5 6 7 6 1 0 1 6 7 0 2 1 9 1 6 3 2 0 1 1 5 5 9
6 1 1 0 5 1 3 6 7 7 7 8 2 4 5 9 3 0 7 6 7 9 1 1 6
5 3 6 1 2 7 2 6 2 7 3 3 6 8 2 6 5 5 8 4 2 4 2 1 8
8 7 3 9 5 1 1 8 4 1 8 5 6 6 0 6 9 2 2 6 8 2 5 8 5
2 9 1 9 9 5 6 1 8 6 6 4 0 5 0 0 8 8 2 5 9 2 0 1 2
8 1 0 2 1 7 2 0 2 7 6 8 4 8 0 2 6 2 8 0 8 3 6 0 7
9 7 1 5 5 7 4 6 1 5 6 5 9 9 2 2 7 1 2 7 0 0 5 0 9
6 3 7 9 8 8 7 4 9 5 0 3 3 0 3 7 0 7 5 8 1 2 8 3 1
9 4 2 2 1 3 2 0 5 6 0 6 0 9 0 9 3 1 7 8 1 2 3 1 1
5 2 8 5 1 0 2 4 6 0 8 3 4 2 9 0 2 4 0 5 2 7 8 8 8
7 9 7 1 3 7 2 4 6 3 8 4 0 2 5 5 4 6 1 6 5 4 6 3 0
0 1 5 0 6 5 1 1 8 0 9 4 1 1 2 6 1 4 2 0 8 6 3 1 0
5 8 1 7 4 7 5 6 2 1 9 3 7 4 0 4 6 4 6 9 6 7 5 0 6
2 5 0 7 5 1 6 0 4 0 4 1 9 4 9 8 3 6 3 8 0 0 1 7 9
8 8 3 7 8 1 4 6 3 8 0 5 6 4 4 3 5 0 6 9 5 5 0 6 0
4 3 1 8 7 3 4 1 7 1 6 1 5 2 7 9 4 0 2 9 9 6 8 7 6
9 1 4 7 7 4 3 7 4 2 5 5 0 2 1 1 1 4 0 6 4 7 5 9 6
8 6 0 8 2 9 3 4 3 4 7 6 9 6 1 8 2 3 3 8 3 4 6 8 3
3 3 0 6 2 3 8 7 4 3 8 3 1 1 5 9 7 4 4 4 9 7 6 0 9
1 8 2 0 2 9 8 8 0 1 6 8 0 7 5 6 0 8 3 9 2 1 1 2 0
4 7 4 1 1 8 5 9 6 9 7 7 8 0 8 0 8 5 7 2 6 9 4 6 7
7 2 8 1 1 0 4 0 5 0 0 8 2 5 7 4 9 4 0 6 9 7 1 8 0
8 4 0 0 8 1 8 7 1 5 0 1 3 7 3 1 1 4 1 9 7 1 7 8 5
1 5 0 5 3 1 9 7 5 0 3 7 6 3 4 7 2 2 0 5 0 0 7 5 1
6 8 5 1 2 4 1 0 4 6 2 5 9 9 3 2 5 6 0 1 2 0 6 7 7
7 6 5 5 4 6 1 9 1 1 7 9 9 9 6 6 7 1 3 7 7 4 8 8 2
7 8 2 4 2 1 6 4 3 9 7 2 6 6 5 7 0 1 2 8 9 7 1 4 5
9 0 3 3 8 1 3 5 1 4 2 8 7 7 0 3 5 8 0 8 4 2 6 6 4
5 5 4 8 6 5 6 8 0 3 2 0 4 8 4 5 6 6 5 4 7 1 3 1 2
0 6 4 9 7 7 9 8 0 6 4 0 9 2 4 7 8 2 5 1 7 2 3 5 2
6 0 6 7 8 0 8 7 6 8 5 0 1 3 4 3 0 4 7 0 5 2 4 1 3
1 6 3 6 4 9 6 5 3 5 5 3 0 3 3 8 3 7 9 1 1 5 8 2 2
2 1 5 9 7 1 2 6 4 4 5 0 2 1 4 5 1 1 7 0 4 0 1 3 0
```

Table 1 Random Numbers (*continued*)

```
5 0 3 9 1 8 3 8 9 5 5 6 7 3 0 6 7 9 7 1 4 9 2 3 3
3 5 8 1 8 1 6 3 4 7 0 6 7 7 8 9 6 2 0 8 5 0 4 3 7
7 0 6 4 0 6 9 0 5 9 3 3 7 7 1 1 4 4 3 8 0 6 2 1 8
1 0 4 9 2 7 8 1 6 4 4 9 3 2 9 6 7 3 2 4 2 6 4 9 6
7 7 7 0 3 2 5 7 9 3 0 5 6 6 5 8 7 6 2 8 5 2 5 3 8
3 1 4 2 0 1 2 3 5 8 0 4 9 9 9 5 6 4 8 6 4 3 5 0 8
8 7 9 8 4 6 4 1 7 0 8 6 0 0 6 1 7 0 9 0 2 9 8 4 2
5 0 6 9 7 6 4 6 4 9 6 6 0 5 3 2 7 9 2 4 4 4 0 6 5
0 9 7 6 2 3 7 3 6 5 7 7 4 8 5 9 4 9 6 6 0 9 5 6 3
1 1 2 9 9 4 6 0 0 6 3 7 1 3 1 9 1 2 6 6 0 8 7 5 2
9 5 5 5 1 9 7 5 9 0 3 2 1 5 6 1 1 1 2 8 3 5 9 5 5
5 6 2 2 6 5 2 0 4 0 5 8 1 8 6 1 2 3 9 0 3 4 3 0 3
3 0 8 5 5 8 7 5 1 7 1 0 7 0 2 7 4 9 9 5 4 9 3 4 6
1 9 4 1 2 5 8 1 2 4 4 9 7 5 9 7 5 8 8 6 2 2 2 4 0
1 6 0 1 7 5 6 9 4 1 7 3 2 2 6 5 1 4 5 9 8 9 9 2 4
9 4 3 4 6 5 3 2 3 0 8 5 6 6 1 1 0 6 6 6 9 6 0 1 1
3 8 5 2 2 5 3 1 3 4 8 8 2 8 7 5 4 6 4 6 4 0 3 3 4
6 5 9 8 7 5 1 5 0 1 3 1 3 5 7 1 1 7 6 6 6 6 8 4 5
9 9 7 6 9 8 8 7 0 6 1 5 7 9 7 1 5 9 7 9 2 6 7 1 1
3 2 8 0 3 7 7 6 8 3 1 2 6 3 0 8 1 4 8 6 1 2 6 6 8
8 9 9 2 9 7 7 4 2 3 3 5 9 2 3 5 8 6 7 3 0 6 4 9 9
5 2 2 0 3 2 8 7 3 4 1 2 6 8 9 6 8 9 4 1 7 6 8 2 9
9 3 7 1 9 8 3 6 0 2 8 6 3 5 3 0 1 6 1 3 3 8 3 4 8
0 6 7 9 9 0 3 7 7 2 6 0 7 7 1 1 8 1 2 9 9 7 8 0 6
6 5 3 1 0 4 2 4 5 1 4 9 5 3 9 0 2 2 4 5 9 9 9 0 0
4 1 8 9 1 7 4 3 6 4 4 6 6 6 0 7 6 3 2 5 8 2 0 6 8
4 5 4 7 1 1 4 5 0 4 7 9 4 0 6 1 2 1 9 4 9 9 0 2 3
2 5 4 3 3 6 3 1 4 0 9 3 7 9 1 1 8 8 1 8 0 3 1 9 5
4 3 6 4 0 1 7 8 2 0 4 9 5 9 7 9 0 3 3 7 2 9 9 4 0
2 3 8 5 4 4 3 3 0 6 1 0 7 3 5 3 1 3 2 0 6 0 9 1 7
1 6 4 8 7 9 9 9 1 3 1 0 8 6 7 5 6 9 0 3 1 6 8 2 0
4 8 1 6 3 4 5 0 2 7 5 7 0 8 3 2 4 8 5 3 2 9 6 8 1
4 2 1 9 4 6 2 3 0 1 1 6 1 0 7 2 2 3 4 8 7 9 1 4 6
4 0 7 6 5 4 2 9 5 3 3 9 0 6 3 0 2 5 4 9 5 3 6 0 8
8 4 9 3 0 8 2 8 4 0 4 5 6 9 0 6 8 1 1 4 6 7 4 8 1
1 7 6 3 8 1 4 6 2 2 9 4 5 0 3 5 7 0 0 2 4 1 7 1 2
5 6 4 6 9 0 1 5 1 5 5 0 3 1 4 5 1 2 7 0 2 4 9 9 6
0 3 6 0 7 1 4 8 0 3 5 4 8 8 0 4 0 6 7 3 3 1 1 7 4
6 7 2 9 0 4 2 9 2 6 4 6 4 6 4 6 9 4 6 2 3 9 4 8 8
0 3 1 4 5 9 5 0 8 2 6 5 0 8 5 8 0 7 5 0 9 5 3 1 5
7 3 0 9 3 6 1 9 3 1 3 9 8 3 9 7 7 6 6 5 3 0 2 6 8
8 6 7 9 6 6 8 3 4 0 5 9 5 1 7 8 0 1 0 8 9 7 1 4 6
4 9 5 8 6 8 0 4 4 4 5 6 7 4 8 1 7 1 4 9 2 9 5 1 9
6 0 3 9 9 5 8 4 4 1 5 4 0 6 8 6 0 2 0 0 1 8 8 8 0
4 1 0 5 3 6 3 5 0 6 4 0 0 1 2 1 8 2 9 5 4 8 7 2 5
5 2 7 9 6 5 7 4 5 1 3 3 8 8 4 4 0 4 1 8 9 1 1 6 5
3 4 6 1 2 1 8 7 4 7 6 3 3 5 0 0 7 9 1 6 4 0 7 4 6
8 2 2 0 8 8 8 7 3 8 3 1 5 8 4 9 5 1 9 1 7 9 7 9 9
4 8 7 0 7 8 9 4 3 0 9 2 3 5 4 7 2 1 4 6 6 8 6 3 2
9 0 4 3 8 0 1 5 7 6 7 1 6 3 0 5 7 3 7 1 0 9 5 6 6
```

Table 1 Random Numbers (*continued*)

```
8 2 8 9 7 9 6 9 7 9 0 8 2 9 8 1 5 6 9 3 2 9 2 3 3
9 4 6 9 2 6 8 4 4 7 8 3 5 1 0 1 3 9 9 2 9 0 4 0 8
5 6 7 4 2 7 4 1 2 7 3 1 5 8 3 1 0 7 3 8 7 5 2 5 1
8 0 9 9 8 3 2 9 7 5 5 8 0 5 2 1 3 4 2 3 8 6 8 3 6
6 7 0 3 7 9 8 8 2 0 9 1 0 6 0 7 2 4 5 1 3 3 5 1 0
8 1 3 0 0 8 3 4 8 8 3 4 8 9 9 2 0 4 3 9 6 7 6 5 7
1 7 6 2 5 8 6 2 6 6 8 0 8 3 9 8 8 7 4 2 1 3 3 3 2
9 9 7 1 7 5 9 1 3 2 4 6 0 5 9 0 7 3 8 2 3 5 4 7 1
0 4 6 4 0 1 7 9 9 3 6 8 1 5 3 7 1 1 9 5 1 0 1 4 8
9 7 8 2 1 2 9 7 2 0 6 4 2 5 2 7 0 8 1 1 9 7 7 7 0
2 4 6 4 6 3 6 7 5 2 0 0 5 4 7 3 3 4 1 0 7 4 4 0 9
8 5 4 5 4 7 7 4 0 0 5 0 6 4 2 8 8 0 8 0 9 9 0 5 8
5 8 6 7 6 6 4 7 0 1 4 9 9 5 7 2 1 4 1 1 9 7 7 3 5
1 3 8 1 4 7 0 7 4 8 8 4 4 0 1 2 5 1 4 8 1 7 7 3 2
4 1 5 9 7 9 5 6 6 7 4 5 6 1 8 8 8 2 8 9 0 0 9 2 5
9 5 4 7 0 6 8 1 2 1 4 0 4 5 8 3 1 6 0 1 9 7 5 6 0
3 7 2 7 4 1 4 8 3 6 4 1 6 1 9 0 4 1 3 2 6 8 9 2 5
9 7 1 8 1 0 8 3 6 0 1 7 5 0 6 3 2 7 9 2 5 6 2 9 9
9 9 9 9 1 9 4 2 6 9 5 8 5 6 8 3 9 8 6 9 9 6 8 2 5
9 3 0 1 8 1 5 8 8 1 1 4 4 6 6 4 1 0 9 6 6 7 5 5 8
7 9 4 6 8 9 0 6 6 9 5 4 3 1 9 5 1 9 5 6 2 8 2 7 4
3 5 5 4 5 2 5 2 2 1 4 8 2 0 9 1 8 4 3 5 0 3 2 6 5
6 7 2 1 9 0 5 4 3 3 9 8 9 0 1 2 6 6 1 3 0 4 5 4 1
4 0 5 3 9 2 6 3 2 2 0 4 2 0 9 1 0 0 8 8 8 0 2 8 1
2 1 5 7 3 7 3 6 2 8 9 3 2 8 7 9 6 7 9 5 1 9 5 5 4
8 2 9 1 7 6 5 0 5 7 4 2 4 7 5 1 4 2 8 4 0 2 0 4 5
0 4 9 2 5 9 9 8 7 4 7 3 2 2 1 7 7 1 9 5 1 4 4 9 4
3 8 6 7 5 6 1 5 3 0 9 0 8 4 0 4 6 7 2 2 6 8 4 3 5
7 1 8 8 3 6 3 7 4 3 6 3 3 0 1 3 4 9 7 3 8 9 2 3 6
2 3 0 4 7 4 6 9 9 9 8 7 4 4 2 8 1 4 4 4 0 0 6 0 8
8 6 4 4 0 7 1 2 9 6 3 1 3 4 9 1 6 2 9 3 7 6 1 1 0
0 5 5 4 6 7 7 9 6 9 0 2 5 5 3 5 8 5 1 2 9 6 9 3 9
5 7 4 3 2 8 8 4 4 2 0 8 9 6 3 0 5 1 1 2 7 3 7 8 0
8 3 2 7 1 2 7 0 2 9 1 1 7 1 5 4 8 1 9 1 2 5 0 5 3
3 1 2 1 0 7 7 3 0 4 7 1 3 8 9 3 8 7 2 7 5 1 4 8 9
0 7 9 7 0 6 4 5 3 0 5 8 2 7 3 7 3 0 6 2 4 3 3 9 1
9 0 3 4 4 3 1 8 2 1 0 4 5 9 7 2 9 0 5 5 4 7 1 5 9
1 5 7 9 2 9 5 2 8 9 1 8 6 4 2 3 4 0 6 1 4 1 7 9 9
7 3 8 2 7 8 4 7 5 9 3 4 2 9 9 4 8 3 1 1 6 5 1 5 6
2 4 0 4 4 0 4 5 0 7 6 4 9 2 0 5 3 9 2 8 1 1 8 0 2
2 9 9 9 6 6 8 0 6 9 4 0 8 4 2 4 0 4 6 0 2 1 2 2 4
5 8 2 2 2 1 7 7 2 5 9 4 2 1 7 2 1 7 7 9 3 3 5 9 8
7 3 7 4 3 6 3 0 9 9 1 6 3 9 2 3 0 2 6 8 9 8 9 0 7
8 8 9 7 6 2 9 9 0 1 2 0 0 1 0 2 4 7 8 9 6 6 9 7 8
1 4 0 9 6 1 0 9 8 7 0 5 8 0 6 5 8 0 5 0 1 9 3 0 1
1 6 4 2 4 7 6 7 7 3 5 9 3 2 2 9 2 7 8 6 3 7 7 8 1
1 2 9 8 1 2 5 7 7 9 6 8 4 4 0 6 3 3 1 1 6 7 2 5 8
5 7 7 5 3 5 5 5 6 7 9 4 3 1 5 7 2 7 6 9 7 6 1 0 3
2 4 7 9 1 7 2 8 3 4 4 1 1 1 3 0 6 9 1 4 8 8 7 5 6
0 2 5 9 4 0 8 2 5 6 0 4 7 1 6 3 6 5 5 6 1 1 6 7 6
```

Table 1   Random Numbers (*continued*)

```
8 9 0 8 8 8 7 4 1 9 9 9 5 5 1 8 2 1 3 7 5 7 8 7 1
1 1 0 4 2 7 2 3 9 9 5 7 5 0 9 5 3 9 6 8 6 7 4 9 0
0 0 6 6 6 3 1 5 6 3 8 9 7 2 9 0 9 8 4 9 4 2 5 0 0
2 8 5 9 9 3 5 2 5 2 1 1 7 4 0 7 9 0 1 4 9 1 9 8 9
7 5 8 0 7 9 4 5 7 9 3 2 0 7 6 3 2 6 3 6 0 9 7 8 5
2 8 1 2 4 9 9 2 0 1 9 7 9 7 2 0 8 1 4 9 2 8 6 5 9
1 6 5 9 5 2 6 8 5 8 1 8 0 6 1 2 2 7 1 0 8 6 1 9 9
3 8 0 2 2 2 0 4 5 5 5 4 5 6 9 9 1 4 2 6 7 3 9 3 5
7 0 7 8 2 1 9 6 3 1 1 8 1 1 7 8 1 6 0 3 9 6 7 1 0
9 5 9 2 6 6 6 7 4 1 9 5 1 9 8 4 2 7 9 3 8 5 5 0 8
9 9 3 7 7 0 5 3 1 2 2 4 7 0 2 2 4 0 2 1 4 5 2 6 9
2 8 6 7 5 0 2 8 7 0 4 2 5 4 1 5 3 3 7 0 7 8 8 0 8
5 8 4 6 5 0 3 6 4 5 2 4 7 9 6 7 7 3 1 5 9 7 7 4 2
2 7 9 4 0 0 1 7 0 7 2 0 0 5 1 8 6 4 9 7 9 7 0 4 8
3 2 0 4 1 5 9 2 4 0 8 3 9 0 6 9 8 3 7 7 2 6 0 6 8
9 4 4 2 4 3 1 3 1 3 0 2 2 8 2 7 5 6 8 5 3 2 9 9 9
1 4 7 7 0 3 1 3 3 5 9 6 5 1 6 4 0 6 9 7 3 9 2 1 6
2 7 4 6 7 2 6 2 7 2 5 1 3 8 7 7 8 2 1 9 2 5 0 9 0
5 3 2 1 6 4 9 4 4 6 2 5 3 3 3 5 2 5 4 9 5 7 4 4 6
6 0 9 6 4 0 0 9 3 2 7 7 6 6 7 9 7 8 1 8 0 4 1 8 1
6 8 6 5 0 5 3 4 2 3 3 7 5 7 7 9 7 4 7 0 5 6 5 1 3
7 2 1 3 4 1 7 8 1 8 4 4 1 6 6 6 2 5 6 6 2 0 4 1 9
7 5 9 1 3 2 7 1 2 6 3 1 3 3 1 2 9 0 9 8 9 8 6 9 8
8 7 7 6 8 8 8 1 6 8 6 1 8 8 6 1 7 5 6 8 6 4 3 6 9
0 4 6 4 6 1 9 6 1 4 5 9 1 1 3 6 1 4 5 7 0 8 2 5 4
9 6 8 6 1 6 3 0 3 7 0 4 9 8 8 7 7 6 8 1 7 1 5 0 8
7 6 9 7 0 9 8 7 1 2 0 9 0 3 8 5 3 9 3 7 4 1 1 5 7
3 2 7 0 9 2 7 5 8 0 4 7 8 1 4 2 4 0 0 9 6 5 9 2 5
4 2 6 8 9 1 9 0 4 2 1 3 4 3 2 0 6 7 4 7 1 3 9 7 9
6 8 6 5 1 4 1 3 0 6 7 0 9 5 2 8 7 0 9 3 8 5 1 3 5
6 3 5 7 2 0 2 8 6 3 3 8 5 3 1 0 4 6 6 3 1 7 9 9 7
7 3 7 7 3 4 5 2 3 6 2 3 6 5 5 3 9 2 1 7 0 6 4 2 0
6 0 1 2 5 0 2 9 4 9 8 3 5 9 5 7 4 5 2 8 4 7 6 6 4
2 6 6 8 6 5 0 7 7 5 5 4 9 1 2 0 3 4 8 9 6 4 9 8 9
3 6 8 7 2 9 9 2 7 5 6 0 9 0 6 5 8 8 2 8 3 4 7 4 0
4 2 5 5 7 2 6 5 9 4 3 8 7 5 6 5 3 6 3 4 3 8 5 4 7
3 2 3 1 1 5 6 5 8 3 9 6 2 2 0 2 9 0 9 3 1 1 3 1 4
0 2 3 6 6 9 4 4 6 6 0 9 9 7 4 0 1 3 2 5 6 9 4 5 1
6 5 6 9 4 1 6 8 8 6 7 0 0 6 0 8 8 3 9 7 8 4 1 7 6
7 3 1 3 9 1 2 0 7 1 5 2 1 2 0 7 0 1 7 8 6 4 6 6 3
3 5 2 5 5 9 9 0 1 5 3 2 1 7 0 1 9 3 6 3 3 4 5 0 9
2 7 6 2 3 9 6 7 5 3 6 1 5 0 2 0 3 2 9 1 6 2 1 4 6
7 8 9 1 3 0 3 0 0 2 8 5 5 4 3 8 9 6 8 2 2 1 8 8 1
1 1 0 8 2 7 9 9 8 5 5 1 9 0 7 1 2 5 7 6 8 5 8 2 8
9 6 3 9 6 2 1 1 1 0 3 2 1 7 5 0 6 9 0 6 2 0 9 5 1
1 0 3 2 4 6 1 9 9 8 8 6 5 7 6 9 8 9 1 2 4 9 1 3 5
2 3 7 1 5 7 2 5 8 1 1 7 6 6 4 9 1 3 0 3 5 2 6 3 3
2 3 6 4 7 5 3 4 7 7 7 6 4 3 5 9 6 3 8 7 8 0 1 3 2
9 3 6 1 5 4 4 5 3 3 5 4 1 5 2 3 4 6 4 5 3 7 6 9 2
0 4 0 4 6 7 0 2 9 4 3 5 9 9 7 4 9 0 6 8 7 5 9 3 6
```

Table 1 Random Numbers (*continued*)

```
9 3 6 4 8 6 5 9 2 6 4 5 1 6 9 9 0 8 6 7 4 5 7 2 8
1 1 5 8 8 6 9 0 3 3 6 8 4 1 8 1 3 9 0 8 3 4 5 6 5
7 2 8 1 8 8 3 7 4 4 3 5 0 2 1 3 1 9 9 1 1 1 7 0 0
1 8 4 9 4 8 6 2 6 5 1 7 6 9 5 8 8 2 8 4 0 6 2 7 8
2 7 3 0 6 1 3 6 4 1 9 2 4 5 4 4 9 5 4 7 1 4 2 0 0
2 1 0 3 9 9 3 2 8 0 0 3 4 6 2 9 2 5 5 9 6 5 0 7 8
5 1 2 1 7 3 1 5 7 1 5 8 7 7 5 7 9 8 0 8 5 3 2 5 8
2 5 3 5 4 8 4 5 2 5 7 7 2 8 7 1 8 2 3 9 3 1 5 9 9
0 6 1 5 3 1 9 8 0 4 3 2 0 1 4 5 4 2 9 8 2 9 1 5 5
4 7 0 9 2 7 5 8 6 1 5 4 0 9 9 7 3 9 6 5 5 4 0 1 4
4 6 1 4 8 5 7 1 9 7 0 9 4 2 8 0 1 3 6 4 0 4 9 7 2
8 5 2 7 5 0 5 6 6 3 3 3 1 8 1 6 7 3 2 4 9 6 6 8 9
1 9 5 1 2 4 1 4 7 2 9 8 7 7 4 9 5 1 2 8 6 7 0 0 7
1 1 7 5 2 6 4 7 5 9 2 9 2 7 0 9 3 3 1 6 2 1 0 8 2
6 0 4 0 7 7 9 9 5 0 3 8 6 9 8 9 1 2 5 2 6 3 3 6 5
4 2 8 8 4 2 2 6 5 9 7 6 4 5 2 4 4 4 7 2 3 3 8 0 1
6 3 1 3 5 0 4 8 3 4 1 7 2 9 0 6 3 3 5 0 4 0 4 5 1
4 9 9 6 2 8 3 1 8 4 8 1 1 0 9 4 6 4 2 1 5 9 4 8 6
5 5 8 5 7 3 5 3 1 0 8 9 8 0 1 0 6 2 1 6 9 7 3 5 1
0 8 3 6 4 9 7 5 6 2 8 7 3 8 9 0 2 2 0 0 4 9 9 0 9
5 6 2 1 3 3 7 4 0 7 1 9 3 8 7 6 5 8 9 0 8 3 7 1 4
6 7 6 6 5 2 7 1 5 0 1 5 8 3 1 5 3 5 5 2 2 4 2 5 4
1 0 2 9 2 0 9 5 4 1 6 9 6 8 4 0 2 6 5 3 2 2 1 3 9
9 7 3 0 4 1 8 8 6 5 9 3 9 1 2 2 0 7 2 3 8 9 9 7 8
3 6 6 7 1 6 5 6 6 9 6 7 8 6 2 1 4 1 1 0 8 8 5 4 0
2 4 3 9 7 6 0 0 6 2 8 4 3 4 4 1 1 5 9 3 7 9 4 8 3
0 4 7 0 4 1 0 7 2 9 6 4 5 2 7 2 9 8 3 4 5 6 8 8 2
6 0 5 9 1 1 1 4 4 6 9 7 8 8 6 3 6 7 6 0 5 1 0 5 5
1 1 5 1 6 6 0 5 1 5 6 0 7 5 2 7 3 7 2 4 8 6 2 5 4
3 4 2 3 2 5 9 4 7 1 7 8 4 1 3 8 8 5 3 7 6 8 8 6 4
8 3 3 6 5 8 0 5 9 6 6 1 3 4 5 4 2 8 3 9 5 0 8 9 1
9 2 1 2 4 7 6 5 9 3 6 0 5 0 7 5 3 7 9 3 8 5 1 7 6
2 6 6 8 4 7 5 4 7 0 8 4 2 6 8 3 1 4 5 9 8 7 5 0 6
6 6 4 6 5 8 8 5 9 8 5 9 4 6 5 2 4 0 7 1 4 1 8 7 0
1 1 6 5 4 5 4 0 4 1 7 2 1 5 7 5 8 5 7 4 4 8 2 6 2
3 0 8 3 7 1 3 1 9 0 7 7 5 2 2 7 6 3 9 9 9 0 3 8 6
8 0 2 6 1 8 5 9 3 1 7 9 4 7 5 5 4 9 6 4 6 1 6 0 1
4 5 2 7 5 1 0 6 4 2 1 6 2 4 9 1 8 3 1 8 8 2 7 4 1
0 5 6 1 3 8 3 9 8 3 6 9 4 9 1 5 2 5 6 5 8 4 5 1 9
7 4 1 5 0 4 4 3 4 8 7 4 8 7 4 5 1 3 9 2 4 1 2 2 5
7 4 5 7 0 9 8 3 4 9 7 8 1 3 2 2 8 3 7 3 8 5 2 6 1
5 8 8 2 4 5 4 9 5 6 5 5 0 1 7 6 3 6 1 6 6 5 6 8 9
1 4 9 9 2 0 5 4 1 2 6 4 3 8 4 3 4 3 2 4 4 2 9 5 6
2 3 5 4 3 3 6 9 2 8 2 1 1 5 5 0 7 1 4 5 0 5 6 3 0
9 6 1 5 9 9 1 2 9 2 5 3 9 9 4 1 6 2 3 4 0 8 8 6 9
0 7 2 9 3 7 5 5 5 0 5 7 3 3 6 8 6 2 7 2 1 5 0 0 3
6 2 8 1 5 1 1 4 8 2 9 5 5 6 5 2 0 6 7 3 3 9 2 2 2
2 7 8 8 9 0 4 1 4 6 9 7 5 4 9 2 4 4 0 6 9 5 4 4 4
4 3 3 9 1 2 1 3 6 3 4 3 4 8 8 6 9 3 2 3 3 4 7 1 2
8 8 0 5 2 2 8 0 8 5 3 0 3 7 4 9 6 0 1 8 5 3 8 6 4
```

Table 2 Distribution of *t*

df	Level of significance for one-tailed test					
	.10	.05	.025	.01	.005	.0005
	Level of significance for two-tailed test					
	.20	.10	.05	.02	.01	.001
1	3.078	6.314	12.706	31.821	63.657	636.619
2	1.886	2.920	4.303	6.965	9.925	31.598
3	1.638	2.353	3.182	4.541	5.841	12.941
4	1.533	2.132	2.776	3.747	4.604	8.610
5	1.476	2.015	2.571	3.365	4.032	6.859
6	1.440	1.943	2.447	3.143	3.707	5.959
7	1.415	1.895	2.365	2.998	3.499	5.405
8	1.397	1.860	2.306	2.896	3.355	5.041
9	1.383	1.833	2.262	2.821	3.250	4.781
10	1.372	1.812	2.228	2.764	3.169	4.587
11	1.363	1.796	2.201	2.718	3.106	4.437
12	1.356	1.782	2.179	2.681	3.055	4.318
13	1.350	1.771	2.160	2.650	3.012	4.221
14	1.345	1.761	2.145	2.624	2.977	4.140
15	1.341	1.753	2.131	2.602	2.947	4.073
16	1.337	1.746	2.120	2.583	2.921	4.015
17	1.333	1.740	2.110	2.567	2.898	3.965
18	1.330	1.734	2.101	2.552	2.878	3.992
19	1.328	1.729	2.093	2.539	2.861	3.883
20	1.325	1.725	2.086	2.528	2.845	3.850
21	1.323	1.721	2.080	2.518	2.831	3.819
22	1.321	1.717	2.074	2.508	2.819	3.792
23	1.319	1.714	2.069	2.500	2.807	3.767
24	1.318	1.711	2.064	2.492	2.797	3.745
25	1.316	1.708	2.060	2.485	2.787	3.725
26	1.315	1.706	2.056	2.479	2.779	3.707
27	1.314	1.703	2.052	2.473	2.771	3.690
28	1.313	1.701	2.048	2.467	2.763	3.674
29	1.311	1.699	2.045	2.462	2.756	3.659
30	1.310	1.697	2.042	2.457	2.750	3.646
40	1.303	1.684	2.021	2.423	2.704	3.551
60	1.296	1.671	2.000	2.390	2.660	3.460
120	1.289	1.658	1.980	2.358	2.617	3.373
∞	1.282	1.645	1.960	2.326	2.576	3.291

Table abridged from Table III of Fisher and Yates, *Statistical Tables for Biological, Agricultural, and Medical Research*, published by Longman Group Ltd., London (previously published by Oliver and Boyd Ltd., Edinburgh), by permission of the authors and publishers.

Table 3 Areas Under the Normal Curve: Proportion of Area Under the Normal Curve Between the Mean and a z Distance from the Mean

$\frac{x}{o}$ or z	.00	.01	.02	.03	.04	.05	.06	.07	.08	.09
.0	0000	.0040	.0080	.0120	.0160	.0199	.0239	.0279	.0319	.0359
.1	0398	.0438	.0478	.0517	.0557	.0596	.0636	.0675	.0714	.0753
.2	.0793	.0832	.0871	.0910	.0948	.0987	.1026	.1064	.1103	.1141
.3	.1179	.1217	.1255	.1293	.1331	.1368	.1406	.1443	.1480	.1517
.4	.1554	.1591	.1628	.1664	.1700	.1736	.1772	.1808	.1844	.1879
.5	.1915	.1950	.1985	.2019	.2054	.2088	.2123	.2157	.2190	.2224
.6	.2257	.2291	.2324	.2357	.2389	.2422	.2454	.2486	.2517	.2549
.7	.2580	.2611	.2642	.2673	.2704	.2734	.2764	.2794	.2823	.2852
.8	.2881	.2910	.2939	.2967	.2995	.3023	.3051	.3078	.3106	.3133
.9	.3159	.3186	.3212	.3238	.3264	.3289	.3315	.3340	.3365	.3389
1.0	.3413	.3438	.3461	.3485	.3508	.3531	.3554	.3577	.3599	.3621
1.1	.3643	.3665	.3686	.3708	.3729	.3749	.3770	.3790	.3810	.3830
1.2	.3849	.3869	.3888	.3907	.3925	.3944	.3962	.3980	.3997	.4015
1.3	.4032	.4049	.4066	.4082	.4099	.4115	.4131	.4147	.4162	.4177
1.4	.4192	.4207	.4222	.4236	.4251	.4265	.4279	.4292	.4306	.4319
1.5	.4332	.4345	.4357	.4370	.4382	.4394	.4406	.4418	.4429	.4441
1.6	.4452	.4463	.4474	.4484	.4495	.4505	.4515	.4525	.4535	.4545
1.7	.4554	.4564	.4573	.4582	.4591	.4599	.4608	.4616	.4625	.4633
1.8	.4641	.4649	.4656	.4664	.4671	.4678	.4686	.4693	.4699	.4706
1.9	.4713	.4719	.4726	.4732	.4738	.4744	.4750	.4756	.4761	.4767
2.0	.4772	.4778	.4783	.4788	.4793	.4798	.4803	.4808	.4812	.4817
2.1	.4821	.4826	.4830	.4834	.4838	.4842	.4846	.4850	.4854	.4857
2.2	.4861	.4864	.4868	.4871	.4875	.4878	.4881	.4884	.4887	.4890
2.3	.4893	.4896	.4898	.4901	.4904	.4906	.4909	.4911	.4913	.4916
2.4	.4918	.4920	.4922	.4925	.4927	.4929	.4931	.4932	.4934	.4936
2.5	.4938	.4940	.4941	.4943	.4945	.4946	.4948	.4949	.4951	.4952
2.6	.4953	.4955	.4956	.4957	.4959	.4960	.4961	.4962	.4963	.4964
2.7	.4965	.4966	.4967	.4968	.4969	.4970	.4971	.4972	.4973	.4974
2.8	.4974	.4975	.4976	.4977	.4977	.4978	.4979	.4979	.4980	.4981
2.9	.4981	.4982	.4982	.4983	.4984	.4984	.4985	.4985	.4986	.4986
3.0	.4987	.4987	.4987	.4988	.4988	.4989	.4989	.4989	.4990	.4990
3.1	.4990	.4991	.4991	.4991	.4992	.4992	.4992	.4992	.4993	.4993
3.2	.4993	.4993	.4994	.4994	.4994	.4994	.4994	.4995	.4995	.4995
3.3	.4995	.4995	.4995	.4996	.4996	.4996	.4996	.4996	.4996	.4997
3.4	.4997	.4997	.4997	.4997	.4997	.4997	.4997	.4997	.4997	.4998
3.5	.4998									
4.0	.49997									
4.5	.499997									
5.0	.4999997									

Table 4 Distribution of Chi-Square

df	.20	.10	.05	.02	.01	.001
1	1.642	2.706	3.841	5.412	6.635	10.827
2	3.219	4.605	5.991	7.824	9.210	13.815
3	4.642	6.251	7.815	9.837	11.345	16.266
4	5.989	7.779	9.488	11.668	13.277	18.467
5	7.289	9.236	11.070	13.388	15.086	20.515
6	8.558	10.645	12.592	15.033	16.812	22.457
7	9.803	12.017	14.067	16.622	18.475	24.322
8	11.030	13.362	15.507	18.168	20.090	26.125
9	12.242	14.684	16.919	19.679	21.666	27.877
10	13.442	15.987	18.307	21.161	23.209	29.588
11	14.631	17.275	19.675	22.618	24.725	31.264
12	15.812	18.549	21.026	24.054	26.217	32.909
13	16.985	19.812	22.362	25.472	27.688	34.528
14	18.151	21.064	23.685	26.873	29.141	36.123
15	19.311	22.307	24.996	28.259	30.578	37.697
16	20.465	23.542	26.296	29.633	32.000	39.252
17	21.615	24.769	27.587	30.995	33.409	40.790
18	22.760	25.989	28.869	32.346	34.805	42.312
19	23.900	27.204	30.144	33.687	36.191	43.820
20	25.038	28.412	31.410	35.020	37.566	45.315
21	26.171	29.615	32.671	36.343	38.932	46.797
22	27.301	30.813	33.924	37.659	40.289	48.268
23	28.429	32.007	35.172	38.968	41.638	49.728
24	29.553	33.196	36.415	40.270	42.980	51.179
25	30.675	34.382	37.652	41.566	44.314	52.620

Table 4 Distribution of Chi-Square (*continued*)

df	.20	.10	.05	.02	.01	.001
			Probability			
26	31.795	35.563	38.885	42.856	45.642	54.052
27	32.912	36.741	40.113	44.140	46.963	55.476
28	34.027	37.916	41.337	45.419	48.278	56.893
29	35.139	39.087	42.557	46.693	49.588	58.302
30	36.250	40.256	43.773	47.962	50.892	59.703
32	38.466	42.585	46.194	50.487	53.486	62.487
34	40.676	44.903	48.602	52.995	56.061	65.247
36	42.879	47.212	50.999	55.489	58.619	67.985
38	45.076	49.513	53.384	57.969	61.162	70.703
40	47.269	51.805	55.759	60.436	63.691	73.402
42	49.456	54.090	58.124	62.892	66.206	76.084
44	51.639	56.369	60.481	65.337	68.710	78.750
46	53.818	58.641	62.830	67.771	71.201	81.400
48	55.993	60.907	65.171	70.197	73.683	84.037
50	58.164	63.167	67.505	72.613	76.154	86.661
52	60.332	65.422	69.832	75.021	78.616	89.272
54	62.496	67.673	72.153	77.422	81.069	91.872
56	64.658	69.919	74.468	79.815	83.513	94.461
58	66.816	72.160	76.778	82.201	85.950	97.039
60	68.972	74.397	79.082	84.580	88.379	99.607
62	71.125	76.630	81.381	86.953	90.802	102.166
64	73.276	78.860	83.675	89.320	93.217	104.716
66	75.424	81.085	85.965	91.681	95.626	107.258
68	77.571	83.308	88.250	94.037	98.028	109.791
70	79.715	85.527	90.531	96.388	100.425	112.317

Table abridged from Fisher and Yates, *Statistical Tables for Biological, Agricultural, and Medical Research*, published by Longman Group Ltd., London (previously published by Oliver and Boyd Ltd., Edinburgh), by permission of the authors and publishers.

Table 5 . Distribution of *F*: .05 Level

df_1 \ df_2	1	2	3	4	5	6	7	8	9	10	12	15	20	24	30	40	60	120	∞
1	161.4	199.5	215.7	224.6	230.2	234.0	236.8	238.9	240.5	241.9	243.9	245.9	248.0	249.1	250.1	251.1	252.2	253.3	254.3
2	18.51	19.00	19.16	19.25	19.30	19.33	19.35	19.37	19.38	19.40	19.41	19.43	19.45	19.45	19.46	19.47	19.48	19.49	19.50
3	10.13	9.55	9.28	9.12	9.01	8.94	8.89	8.85	8.81	8.79	8.74	8.70	8.66	8.64	8.62	8.59	8.57	8.55	8.53
4	7.71	6.94	6.59	6.39	6.26	6.16	6.09	6.04	6.00	5.96	5.91	5.86	5.80	5.77	5.75	5.72	5.69	5.66	5.63
5	6.61	5.79	5.41	5.19	5.05	4.95	4.88	4.82	4.77	4.74	4.68	4.62	4.56	4.53	4.50	4.46	4.43	4.40	4.36
6	5.99	5.14	4.76	4.53	4.39	4.28	4.21	4.15	4.10	4.06	4.00	3.94	3.87	3.84	3.81	3.77	3.74	3.70	3.67
7	5.59	4.74	4.35	4.12	3.97	3.87	3.79	3.73	3.68	3.64	3.57	3.51	3.44	3.41	3.38	3.34	3.30	3.27	3.23
8	5.32	4.46	4.07	3.84	3.69	3.58	3.50	3.44	3.39	3.35	3.28	3.22	3.15	3.12	3.08	3.04	3.01	2.97	2.93
9	5.12	4.26	3.86	3.63	3.48	3.37	3.29	3.23	3.18	3.14	3.07	3.01	2.94	2.90	2.86	2.83	2.79	2.75	2.71
10	4.96	4.10	3.71	3.48	3.33	3.22	3.14	3.07	3.02	2.98	2.91	2.85	2.77	2.74	2.70	2.66	2.62	2.58	2.54
11	4.84	3.98	3.59	3.36	3.20	3.09	3.01	2.95	2.90	2.85	2.79	2.72	2.65	2.61	2.57	2.53	2.49	2.45	2.40
12	4.75	3.89	3.49	3.26	3.11	3.00	2.91	2.85	2.80	2.75	2.69	2.62	2.54	2.51	2.47	2.43	2.38	2.34	2.30
13	4.67	3.81	3.41	3.18	3.03	2.92	2.83	2.77	2.71	2.67	2.60	2.53	2.46	2.42	2.38	2.34	2.30	2.25	2.21
14	4.60	3.74	3.34	3.11	2.96	2.85	2.76	2.70	2.65	2.60	2.53	2.46	2.39	2.35	2.31	2.27	2.22	2.18	2.13
15	4.54	3.68	3.29	3.06	2.90	2.79	2.71	2.64	2.59	2.54	2.48	2.40	2.33	2.29	2.25	2.20	2.16	2.11	2.07
16	4.49	3.63	3.24	3.01	2.85	2.74	2.66	2.59	2.54	2.49	2.42	2.35	2.28	2.24	2.19	2.15	2.11	2.06	2.01
17	4.45	3.59	3.20	2.96	2.81	2.70	2.61	2.55	2.49	2.45	2.38	2.31	2.23	2.19	2.15	2.10	2.06	2.01	1.96
18	4.41	3.55	3.16	2.93	2.77	2.66	2.58	2.51	2.46	2.41	2.34	2.27	2.19	2.15	2.11	2.06	2.02	1.97	1.92
19	4.38	3.52	3.13	2.90	2.74	2.63	2.54	2.48	2.42	2.38	2.31	2.23	2.16	2.11	2.07	2.03	1.98	1.93	1.88

20	8.10	5.85	4.94	4.43	4.10	3.87	3.70	3.56	3.46	3.37	3.23	3.09	2.94	2.86	2.78	2.69	2.61	2.52	2.42
21	8.02	5.78	4.87	4.37	4.04	3.81	3.64	3.51	3.40	3.31	3.17	3.03	2.88	2.80	2.72	2.64	2.55	2.46	2.36
22	7.95	5.72	4.82	4.31	3.99	3.76	3.59	3.45	3.35	3.26	3.12	2.98	2.83	2.75	2.67	2.58	2.50	2.40	2.31
23	7.88	5.66	4.76	4.26	3.94	3.71	3.54	3.41	3.30	3.21	3.07	2.93	2.78	2.70	2.62	2.54	2.45	2.35	2.26
24	7.82	5.61	4.72	4.22	3.90	3.67	3.50	3.36	3.26	3.17	3.03	2.89	2.74	2.66	2.58	2.49	2.40	2.31	2.21
25	7.77	5.57	4.68	4.18	3.85	3.63	3.46	3.32	3.22	3.13	2.99	2.85	2.70	2.62	2.54	2.45	2.36	2.27	2.17
26	7.72	5.53	4.64	4.14	3.82	3.59	3.42	3.29	3.18	3.09	2.96	2.81	2.66	2.58	2.50	2.42	2.33	2.23	2.13
27	7.68	5.49	4.60	4.11	3.78	3.56	3.39	3.26	3.15	3.06	2.93	2.78	2.63	2.55	2.47	2.38	2.29	2.20	2.10
28	7.64	5.45	4.57	4.07	3.75	3.53	3.36	3.23	3.12	3.03	2.90	2.75	2.60	2.52	2.44	2.35	2.26	2.17	2.06
29	7.60	5.42	4.54	4.04	3.73	3.50	3.33	3.20	3.09	3.00	2.87	2.73	2.57	2.49	2.41	2.33	2.23	2.14	2.03
30	7.56	5.39	4.51	4.02	3.70	3.47	3.30	3.17	3.07	2.98	2.84	2.70	2.55	2.47	2.39	2.30	2.21	2.11	2.01
40	7.31	5.18	4.31	3.83	3.51	3.29	3.12	2.99	2.89	2.80	2.66	2.52	2.37	2.29	2.20	2.11	2.02	1.92	1.80
60	7.08	4.98	4.13	3.65	3.34	3.12	2.95	2.82	2.72	2.63	2.50	2.35	2.20	2.12	2.03	1.94	1.84	1.73	1.60
120	6.85	4.79	3.95	3.48	3.17	2.96	2.79	2.66	2.56	2.47	2.34	2.19	2.03	1.95	1.86	1.76	1.66	1.53	1.38
∞	6.63	4.61	3.78	3.32	3.02	2.80	2.64	2.51	2.41	2.32	2.18	2.04	1.88	1.79	1.70	1.59	1.47	1.32	1.00

Table 6　Distribution of F: .01 Level

df_2 \ df_1	1	2	3	4	5	6	7	8	9	10	12	15	20	24	30	40	60	120	∞
1	4052	4999.5	5403	5625	5764	5859	5928	5982	6022	6056	6106	6157	6209	6235	6261	6287	6313	6339	6366
2	98.5	99.00	99.17	99.25	99.30	99.33	99.36	99.37	99.39	99.40	99.42	99.43	99.45	99.46	99.47	99.47	99.48	99.49	99.50
3	34.12	30.82	29.46	28.71	28.24	27.91	27.67	27.49	27.35	27.23	27.05	26.87	26.69	26.60	26.50	26.41	26.32	26.22	26.13
4	21.20	18.00	16.69	15.98	15.52	15.21	14.98	14.80	14.66	14.55	14.37	14.20	14.02	13.93	13.84	13.75	13.65	13.56	13.46
5	16.26	13.27	12.06	11.39	10.97	10.67	10.46	10.29	10.16	10.05	9.89	9.72	9.55	9.47	9.38	9.29	9.20	9.11	9.02
6	13.75	10.92	9.78	9.15	8.75	8.47	8.26	8.10	7.98	7.87	7.72	7.56	7.40	7.31	7.23	7.14	7.06	6.97	6.88
7	12.25	9.55	8.45	7.85	7.46	7.19	6.99	6.81	6.72	6.62	6.47	6.31	6.16	6.07	5.99	5.91	5.82	5.74	5.65
8	11.26	8.65	7.59	7.01	6.63	6.37	6.18	6.03	5.91	5.81	5.67	5.52	5.36	5.28	5.20	5.12	5.03	4.95	4.86
9	10.56	8.02	6.99	6.42	6.06	5.80	5.61	5.47	5.35	5.26	5.11	4.96	4.81	4.73	4.65	4.57	4.48	4.40	4.31
10	10.04	7.56	6.55	5.99	5.64	5.39	5.20	5.06	4.94	4.85	4.71	4.56	4.41	4.33	4.25	4.17	4.08	4.00	3.91
11	9.65	7.21	6.22	5.67	5.32	5.07	4.89	4.74	4.63	4.54	4.40	4.25	4.10	4.02	3.94	3.86	3.78	3.69	3.60
12	9.33	6.93	5.95	5.41	5.06	4.82	4.64	4.50	4.39	4.30	4.16	4.01	3.86	3.78	3.70	3.62	3.54	3.45	3.36
13	9.07	6.70	5.74	5.21	4.86	4.62	4.44	4.30	4.19	4.10	3.96	3.82	3.66	3.59	3.51	3.43	3.34	3.25	3.17
14	8.86	6.51	5.56	5.04	4.69	4.46	4.28	4.14	4.03	3.94	3.80	3.66	3.51	3.43	3.35	3.27	3.18	3.09	3.00
15	8.68	6.36	5.42	4.89	4.56	4.32	4.14	4.00	3.89	3.80	3.67	3.52	3.37	3.29	3.21	3.13	3.05	2.96	2.87
16	8.53	6.23	5.29	4.77	4.44	4.20	4.03	3.89	3.78	3.69	3.55	3.41	3.26	3.18	3.10	3.02	2.93	2.84	2.75
17	8.40	6.11	5.18	4.67	4.34	4.10	3.93	3.79	3.68	3.59	3.46	3.31	3.16	3.08	3.00	2.92	2.83	2.75	2.65
18	8.29	6.01	5.09	4.58	4.25	4.01	3.84	3.71	3.60	3.51	3.37	3.23	3.08	3.00	2.92	2.84	2.75	2.66	2.57
19	8.18	5.93	5.01	4.50	4.17	3.94	3.77	3.63	3.52	3.43	3.30	3.15	3.00	2.92	2.84	2.76	2.67	2.58	2.49

	1	2	3	4	5	6	7	8	9	10	12	15	20	24	30	40	60	120	∞
20	4.35	3.49	3.10	2.87	2.71	2.60	2.51	2.45	2.39	2.35	2.28	2.20	2.12	2.08	2.04	1.99	1.95	1.90	1.84
21	4.32	3.47	3.07	2.84	2.68	2.57	2.49	2.42	2.37	2.32	2.25	2.18	2.10	2.05	2.01	1.96	1.92	1.87	1.81
22	4.30	3.44	3.05	2.82	2.66	2.55	2.46	2.40	2.34	2.30	2.23	2.15	2.07	2.03	1.98	1.94	1.89	1.84	1.78
23	4.28	3.42	3.03	2.80	2.64	2.53	2.44	2.37	2.32	2.27	2.20	2.13	2.05	2.01	1.96	1.91	1.86	1.81	1.76
24	4.26	3.40	3.01	2.78	2.62	2.51	2.42	2.36	2.30	2.25	2.18	2.11	2.03	1.98	1.94	1.89	1.84	1.79	1.73
25	4.24	3.39	2.99	2.76	2.60	2.49	2.40	2.34	2.28	2.24	2.16	2.09	2.01	1.96	1.92	1.87	1.82	1.77	1.71
26	4.23	3.37	2.98	2.74	2.59	2.47	2.39	2.32	2.27	2.22	2.15	2.07	1.99	1.95	1.90	1.85	1.80	1.75	1.69
27	4.21	3.35	2.96	2.73	2.57	2.46	2.37	2.31	2.25	2.20	2.13	2.06	1.97	1.93	1.88	1.84	1.79	1.73	1.67
28	4.20	3.34	2.95	2.71	2.56	2.45	2.36	2.29	2.24	2.19	2.12	2.04	1.96	1.91	1.87	1.82	1.77	1.71	1.65
29	4.18	3.33	2.93	2.70	2.55	2.43	2.35	2.28	2.22	2.18	2.10	2.03	1.94	1.90	1.85	1.81	1.75	1.70	1.64
30	4.17	3.32	2.92	2.69	2.53	2.42	2.33	2.27	2.21	2.16	2.09	2.01	1.93	1.89	1.84	1.79	1.74	1.68	1.62
40	4.08	3.23	2.84	2.61	2.45	2.34	2.25	2.18	2.12	2.08	2.00	1.92	1.84	1.79	1.74	1.69	1.64	1.58	1.51
60	4.00	3.15	2.76	2.53	2.37	2.25	2.17	2.10	2.04	1.99	1.92	1.84	1.75	1.70	1.65	1.59	1.53	1.47	1.39
120	3.92	3.07	2.68	2.45	2.29	2.17	2.09	2.02	1.96	1.91	1.83	1.75	1.66	1.61	1.55	1.50	1.43	1.35	1.25
∞	3.84	3.00	2.60	2.37	2.21	2.10	2.01	1.94	1.88	1.83	1.75	1.67	1.57	1.52	1.46	1.39	1.32	1.22	1.00

MULTIVARIATE STATISTICS

The discussions of statistics in Chapters 10–12 dealt with *univariate* procedures, which are used to investigate the relationship between one or more independent variables and a single dependent variable. This appendix is a preliminary discussion of **multivariate statistics**, methods that allow analysis of several independent variables *and* several dependent variables in a single study.

The rationale for using multivariate statistics in mass media research is quite simple. Both human behavior and the media are complex systems of interacting variables. There are probably few situations, if any, in which one dependent variable accurately represents a phenomenon or is solely responsible for a particular attitude or behavior. Instead, a series of dependent variables, correlated to some degree, act together to produce or represent a phenomenon, or create an attitude or behavior.

Because they accept the idea of interacting variables affecting interrelated phenomena, many researchers select multivariate statistical methods to analyze data rather than the more traditional, and limited, univariate approaches. This does not mean that univariate procedures are invalid, but rather that multivariate statistics are generally more useful in media research.

The reliance on multivariate analysis in research is based on insights made several years ago: (1) any given experimental manipulation affects several different, but partially related, areas of an individual's behavior, and univariate analysis is capable of investigating only one of these relationships at a time (Harris, 1975); (2) because human beings are multidimensional, it seems reasonable to study them on several dimensions simultaneously, rather than to focus on a single, often arbitrarily chosen variable (Tucker, 1982); (3) measurements taken on the same individual are correlated by virtue of their common origin and thus lend themselves to simultaneous study (Tucker, 1982); (4) multivariate statistical methods are parsimonious and save time, money, and resources, since it is much simpler to investigate several correlated variables simultaneously than to study them one at a time; and (5) multivariate analysis allows researchers to investigate variables as *structures* or *constructs* rather than as the individual components of a structure or construct (Cattell, 1966).

Multivariate statistics, however, do have some disadvantages. First of all, they are difficult to use compared to univariate methods. It is not possible to sit down and learn the procedures involved in factor analysis, for example, as one can do with a *t*-test; multivariate methods require extensive reading and trial-and-error work with a computer. The interpretation of multivariate results is equally difficult in many instances. The results of a *t*-test are relatively straightforward; two groups are either similar or different. In multivariate procedures, however, researchers are often faced with dozens of variable combinations to interpret, and intuitive abilities may become taxed.

Another disadvantage of the multivariate approach is that it is easy to include so many variables that no sense can be made of the results. Although researchers are often tempted to include many potentially relevant variables in a multivariate study, guidelines must be established and followed to restrain this tendency. Finally, it should be noted that multivariate statistics are useful when a question calls for such

419

analysis, but they are not a panacea for all research problems.

The bulk of this appendix is devoted to discussions of four of the most widely used multivariate statistical methods and examples of how they are used in mass media research. The simplified explanations ignore many controversial aspects of each method for the sake of brevity. Readers interested in learning more about multivariate statistics should consult works listed in the "References and Suggested Readings" section.

BASICS OF MULTIVARIATE STATISTICS

The usefulness of multivariate statistics can be demonstrated by an example using the method called **multivariate analysis of variance (MANOVA)**. Assume that researchers are interested in measuring the effects of television viewing and newspaper reading on academic exams in English, history, and economics. Their study design would look like Figure 1. This design offers four situations to examine: "no paper/no TV," "no paper/TV," "paper/no TV," and "paper/TV." More important, however, it allows the researchers to investigate the effects of the independent variables on all three exams simultaneously;

univariate ANOVA would require three individual studies of each exam. It is clear that the multivariate procedure represents a significant savings in time, money, and resources.

All multivariate statistics are designed to reduce an original "test space," or group of data, into a minimum number of values or dimensions that describe the relevant information contained in the data; this is in accordance with the principle of parsimony. Thus, instead of using 20 dependent variables to describe a phenomenon, a researcher might use multivariate methods to reduce the number to 3 summary variables (weighted linear combinations) that are nearly as accurate as the original 20. Data reduction involves little loss of information and makes the data easier to handle. It is an especially useful process in mass media studies dealing with almost limitless numbers of variables.

MATRIX ALGEBRA

Multivariate procedures solve the problem of comparing multiple criterion variables by establishing *weighted linear combinations* of two or more such scores. These composite scores are represented as lines in space called **vectors**. Thus in multivariate statistics one or more vec-

---

FIGURE 1   STUDY DESIGN TO MEASURE EFFECTS OF TV VIEWING AND NEWSPAPER READING ON ACADEMIC EXAMS

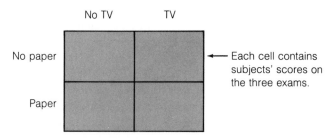

tors are manipulated, usually in an attempt to predict an outcome or event through the principle of least squares. This manipulation of vectors requires a different type of analysis, involving what is known as *matrix algebra*.

Because all multivariate statistics deal with multiple measurements of data in multidimensional space, they depend on matrix algebra. A complete knowledge of matrix algebra is not necessary to understand multivariate statistics, but familiarity with several frequently used terms is essential.

A **scalar** is a single-digit number, such as 6, 9, or 7. A column of scalars is called a *column vector* and is denoted by a lowercase letter:

$$a = \begin{bmatrix} a_1 \\ a_2 \\ \cdot \\ \cdot \\ \cdot \\ a_n \end{bmatrix}$$

(The subscript represents the scalar's location in the column.) A row of scalars is referred to as a *row vector* and is denoted by a lowercase letter followed by a prime symbol:

$$a' = [a_1 \, a_2 \cdots a_n]$$

A **matrix** is a two-dimensional array of scalars, having p rows and n columns, and is denoted by a capital letter:

$$A = \begin{bmatrix} a_{11} & a_{12} & \cdots & a_{1n} \\ a_{21} & a_{22} & \cdots & a_{2n} \\ a_{p1} & a_{p2} & \cdots & a_{pn} \end{bmatrix}$$

The most common matrix used in multivariate statistics is the **intercorrelation** (or simply correlation) **matrix**, which is denoted as R. This matrix contains the coefficients of correlation between pairs of variables. For example, a 3 × 3 correlation matrix (the first number refers to the number of rows, the second to the number

of columns) is used to display the relationship between three variables:

$$R = \begin{bmatrix} 1.0 & .64 & .29 \\ .64 & 1.0 & .42 \\ .29 & .42 & 1.0 \end{bmatrix}$$

This is a **square matrix**: the number of rows equals the number of columns. It contains the value 1.00 in the principal diagonal (top left to bottom right) because the correlation of a variable with itself is usually considered to be 100%. The term *usually* is necessary because in some multivariate models it is assumed that even a correlation of a variable with itself includes some error and hence must be valued at less than 1.00.

A **diagonal matrix** is a square matrix whose elements equal zero except in the principal diagonal. If in addition all the elements in the principal diagonal are 1, the array is known as an **identity matrix** and is denoted by a capital I:

$$I = \begin{bmatrix} 1 & 0 & 0 \\ 0 & 1 & 0 \\ 0 & 0 & 1 \end{bmatrix}$$

An identity matrix indicates that there are no correlations between the variables in the analysis except for the correlation of each variable with itself. Essentially, the identity matrix form implies that the data are of poor quality. Identity matrices are common in research studies that use random numbers (usually in demonstrations of statistical procedures).

Associated with every square matrix is a single number that represents a unique function of the numbers contained in the matrix. This scalar function is known as a **determinant** and is denoted as A. In addition, each square matrix has an associated characteristic equation that represents the information contained in the matrix. The results from the characteristic equation (when computed) reproduce the matrix from which the equation was developed. Several values can be used to calculate a characteristic equation for a matrix; each of these includes a value or number known as an eigenvalue. Each eigenvalue has an associated eigenvector (a column of numbers); the eigenvalue is actually the sum of the squared elements in the eigenvector. In short, eigenvalues and eigenvectors are used to construct a formula that duplicates the information contained in a matrix. Each matrix has a number of characteristic equations, but only one is appropriate for a particular type of analysis.

Multivariate statistics involve two basic algebraic operations. The first is *partitioning* of a matrix, whereby the original matrix is divided into submatrices for analysis. The second operation, *transposition*, involves changing the matrix columns to rows and the rows to columns for further analysis (Horst, 1966). For example, the "transpose" of Matrix A is Matrix A':

$$A = \begin{bmatrix} 1 & 4 \\ 2 & 5 \\ 3 & 6 \end{bmatrix} \qquad A' = \begin{bmatrix} 1 & 2 & 3 \\ 4 & 5 & 6 \end{bmatrix}$$

SIX MULTIVARIATE PROCEDURES

Although there are several multivariate statistics available, six methods appear to be used most often in mass media research. These are factor analysis, canonical correlation, discriminant analysis, multivariate analysis of variance (MANOVA), cluster analysis, and multidimensional scaling. Each method is discussed in terms of how it works and what it can do in media research.

Factor Analysis

Factor analysis is a generic term for a variety of statistical procedures developed for the analysis of the intercorrelations *within* a set of variables.

These relationships are represented by weighted linear combinations known as **factor scores** (or variates), which, in turn, are used in the development of constructs and theories. Factor analysis is divided into several techniques, each of which is appropriate to a specific type of investigation. However, two major techniques are used most often in mass media research: *R-technique* and *Q-technique*. The R-technique is used to factor a set of variables collected at the same time from a number of individuals. The Q-technique is used to factor a number of individuals from variables collected at the same time from those individuals.

Each technique includes a variety of approaches. Some types of R-technique factor analysis are common factor analysis (CFA), principal components analysis (PC or PCA), and minimum residuals (minres). The most often used procedure in the Q-technique is cluster analysis, which seeks to identify types of individuals, not groups of variables as in the R-technique.

Factor analysis is the most widely used multivariate statistic in mass media research, due to its flexibility. Some of the more common uses for factor analysis include the following (Rummel, 1970).

1. Investigating patterns of variable relationships
2. Reducing data
3. Analyzing the structure of a phenomenon
4. Classifying or describing individuals, groups, or variables
5. Developing measurement scales (Chapter 3)
6. Testing hypotheses or research questions
7. Making preliminary investigations in new areas of research
8. Developing theories

As Rummel suggested, factor analysis is appropriate in any phase of research, from pilot studies to theory development. This is not true of other multivariate statistical procedures. The development of the LISREL program (Joreskog, 1973) has made factor analysis much easier to use.

Researchers who use factor analysis assume that any group of variables has some inherent order that, once discovered, can make the description of a concept or construct less complicated. As Thurstone (1947) noted:

> A factor problem starts with the hope or conviction that a certain domain is not so chaotic as it looks. Factor analysis was developed primarily for the purposes of identifying principal dimensions or categories of mentality; but the methods are general, so that they have been found useful for other psychological problems and in other sciences as well. . . . [F]actor analysis is especially useful in those domains where basic and fruitful concepts are essentially lacking and where experiments have been difficult to achieve.

As Thurstone suggested, factor analysis is useful in all types of scientific research. This does not imply, however, that the results of a factor analysis in any particular area are necessarily *meaningful*; any matrix of variables can be factorially analyzed, but not all will yield scientifically useful or meaningful information (Gorsuch, 1974). It is necessary to understand the purpose of factor analysis in order to determine its appropriateness for a specific mass media problem.

Factor analysis includes a wide variety of alternatives. Because of the complexity of many of these methods, it is not possible to discuss each one here. This is left to multivariate statistics books and other more detailed texts.

The two most widely used forms of factor analysis are *principal components* and *principal factors* (also called common factor analysis). The methods are identical except for the initial step: the principal components model uses *unities* (1.00) in the principal diagonal of the correlation matrix, while the principal factors technique assumes that each variable's correlation with itself contains some degree of error and therefore cannot be 100%. These correlations, called *communalities*, replace the unities in the principal diagonal of the original matrix. Communalities are a bit more complicated than unities, since they are only *estimates* of the correlations of variables and themselves. Although choosing the communality estimates to insert into the principal diagonal may sound simple, it is one of the most controversial decisions in factor analysis.

A typical factor analysis begins with the collection of data on a number of different variables (usually at the interval or ratio level). These quantified variables are then transformed via computer into a *product–moment correlation matrix*, the matrix that is usually chosen for factoring. To illustrate, consider the problem of determining which medium, or combination of media, a subject uses for news and information. A questionnaire is designed to collect this information with regard to five media sources: (1) radio, (2) television, (3) magazines, (4) newspaper, and (5) books. The correlation matrix developed from these data may look as shown in Figure 2. The matrix shows the correlations between all five variables. The principal diagonal divides the matrix into two parts, each a mirror image of the other. The diagonal itself is composed of unities, indicating that the method of principal components is being employed.

Note that although any matrix can be factored, even a matrix of random numbers, there are procedures that can help researchers determine whether a particular correlation matrix is valid. Two tests are particularly useful: Bartlett's sphericity test and Kaiser's measure of sampling adequacy (MSA). Both are used to determine the quality of the correlation matrix and to indicate whether the information is adequate for analysis.

In mathematical terms, factoring a matrix consists of extracting eigenvectors and their associated eigenvalues. These two sets of values are used to mathematically reproduce the

FIGURE 2   EXAMPLE OF CORRELATION MATRIX (*R*)

	1	2	3	4	5
1	1.00	.92	.70	.38	.05
2	.92	1.00	.95	.71	.26
3	.70	.95	1.00	.88	.33
4	.38	.71	.88	1.00	.14
5	.05	.26	.33	.14	1.00

correlation matrix. Eigenvectors are factor loadings, or numerical values from −1.00 to +1.00, indicating the amount of contribution each variable makes toward defining a factor. A factor loading is a quantified relationship — the farther its value is from zero, the more relevant the variable is to the factor. The eigenvalues are used to determine which factors are relevant, and hence should be analyzed. (Recall that an eigenvalue is computed by squaring and summing the elements in its eigenvector.) One common procedure is to interpret only the factors with eigenvalues greater than 1.00 (although other methods are used).

The eigenvectors and eigenvalues for the hypothetical study are displayed in Table 1. This example shows that two factors "fell out" (were significant as determined by the eigenvalue cutoff of greater than 1.00) and may be used in explaining the media used for news and information. The eigenvalues are computed by squaring and summing each element in the eigenvector:

$$.85^2 + .66^2 + .37^2 + .52^2 + .29^2 = 1.65$$

The analysis does not stop with this initial extraction of factors; the initial factor loadings are generally too complex to be used for interpretation. Instead, researchers generally perform a second step, factor *rotation*, which essentially involves changing the multidimensional space in which the factors are located. Recall that eigenvectors (a vector of factor loadings) represent lines in space — a space visually constructed by *x*- and *y*-axes. The unrotated factor loadings are often in complex form; that is, there may be several complex variables such that one variable loads significantly on more than one factor. Rotation attempts to clear this problem by changing the space in which the factor loadings are placed. The new factor loadings are mathematically equivalent to the original unrotated matrix, but more often they represent a more meaningful set of factors — where the goal is to have each variable load significantly on only one factor. This additional ease of interpretation makes rotation appealing in behavioral research. A rotated factor matrix is shown in Table 2.

The rotated factor matrix is mathematically equivalent to the unrotated matrix, as witnessed by identical eigenvalues, and the factors are now easier to interpret. The first step in interpretation is to identify the variables that are associated with one and only one factor. Here, it is

TABLE 1   UNROTATED FACTOR MATRIX

Medium	Factor 1	Factor 2	
Newspaper	.85	.53	
Magazines	.66	−.09	
Books	.37	.73	Eigenvectors
Radio	−.52	.34	
Television	.29	.63	
	1.65	1.33	Eigenvalues

TABLE 2   ROTATED FACTOR MATRIX

Medium	Factor 1	Factor 2
Newspaper	.87	.15
Magazines	.66	−.03
Books	.61	.22
Radio	.17	.85
Television	.20	.74
	1.63	1.34

evident that Variables 1, 2, and 3 "load" more heavily on Factor 1, while Variables 4 and 5 load more heavily on Factor 2. Three variables (1, 2, 3) are said to "define" Factor 1, and two variables (4, 5) define Factor 2.

The next step is to categorize the factors on the basis of the variables that define it. In this case, Factor 1 might be classified as "print media" and Factor 2 as "electronic media." In reality, however, Factor 2 might be eliminated altogether at this point, since it is defined by just two variables. It is customary when classifying factors to select only factors that have at least three variables with significant loadings. Some researchers consider this practice controversial, but three significant loadings are necessary to establish the direction of the factor. If a factor has only two significant variable loadings — one

positive and the other negative — it cannot be determined whether the factor itself is positive or negative; a third variable is required to provide the direction. Even when both variables are positive or both are negative, however, a two-variable factor may be inadequate to explain the variance in the factor. As a general rule, it is best to consider only factors that are defined by at least three variables.

Researchers must also consider which type of rotation to use. There are many procedures available, but the two used most often by behavioral researchers are *orthogonal* and *oblique* rotation. The names refer to the angles of the axes on which the data points (factor loadings) are located. Orthogonal rotation keeps the angles at 90° and assumes that the factors are not intercorrelated (that is, orthogonal = uncorrelated).

Oblique rotation allows the axes to take any angle that will produce the most interpretable results; researchers using this approach assume that the factors are correlated to some degree (that is, oblique = correlated). The choice of a rotation method depends on the researcher's likes and dislikes as well as the purpose of the study.

Of the many possible uses of factor analysis mentioned earlier, the three that are most prominent in research studies are data reduction, the search for order in variable structures, and the exploration of uncharted phenomena.

Data reduction, as noted earlier, is essential when investigating research problems that contain large numbers of variables. Factor analysis is often used as a preliminary narrowing device because it allows the selection of salient variables from a large group: it provides a simplification of a particular domain of variables by replacing them with a small number of hypothetical variates (weighted linear sums of the original variables, or factor scores). These variates can then be used in other analyses that employ different statistical methods without a substantial loss of information. For example, consider a 50-item questionnaire designed to measure attitudes toward commercials on television and their effects on buying habits. A factor analysis of the 50 variables would produce a substantially smaller number of representative variates, for factor scores, thus providing an opportunity for a much simpler explanation of the phenomenon being investigated.

The *search for order* in a domain of variables via factor analysis is referred to by several different names: it can be said that factor analysis identifies variable patterns, dimensions of variable domains, underlying constructs, factor dimensions, or factor structures. Whatever terminology is used, the meaning is the same: factor analysis allows the identification from a large group of variables of a smaller number of composite variables that help order and define the phenomenon under study.

A construct such as "program success" may be defined by an infinite number of variables. It may be difficult, if not impossible, to intuitively determine which variables contribute significantly to the construct. Factor analysis, by reducing the number of variables, makes it easier to identify patterns and underlying structures. However, one factor analysis does not produce conclusive results concerning the composition of a construct; different samples, different factor analysis methods, and different variables must be used to verify that the initial results were not sample- or method-specific. That is, replication is necessary to ensure that results are not dependent on some condition external to the relationship among the variables.

Finally, factor analysis can help to provide *explanations of previously unstudied phenomena*. Every research area has many concepts and constructs that have eluded investigation. One reason for this is that the concepts are obscured by large numbers of variables. An example is the question of what characterizes a successful television program. Television executives still do not know; there are simply too many variables. Factor analysis can play a significant (albeit preliminary) role in solving problems of this nature by isolating salient variables from those that will add nothing to the accuracy of a prediction.

Factor analysis allows researchers to take a panoramic view of a variable domain and to isolate important variables. However, it should be used only when a research project is well constructed and meets the prerequisite assumptions discussed above. It should *not* be used in an attempt to salvage a poorly planned study. As mentioned earlier, any matrix of variables can be factorially analyzed, but there is no guarantee that the results will be meaningful.

Canonical Correlation

Canonical correlation (R_c) is essentially multivariate extension of linear multiple regression: a group of independent variables is analyzed to predict multiple criterion variables. However, no distinction is actually made between independent and dependent variables; there are simply two *sets* of variables.

A canonical correlation begins with the formation of an intercorrelation "supermatrix" composed of both sets of variables. For example, if three variables are included in one set and two variables in the second set, the intercorrelation matrix is formed as in Figure 3.

Note that the correlation matrix is divided into four areas: R_{11} represents the intercorrelations among the elements of Set 1; R_{22} denotes intercorrelations among the elements of Set 2; and R_{12} and R_{21} are the cross-correlations between the elements of Sets 1 and 2. This "supermatrix" of intercorrelations provides the information necessary to compute the basic R_c relationship matrix by means of the formula:

$$R_c = [R_{22}^{-1}R_{21}R_{11}^{-1}R_{12}]$$

The canonical correlation matrix formed by the formula is a square matrix and therefore contains eigenvectors and eigenvalues (each unique solution is called a root; each root has a canonical correlation). A *pair* of eigenvectors is extracted from each variable set and normalized;

the resulting scalar values are the sets' beta weights. Finally, for each variable set, the subject's standardized raw scores are multiplied by the beta weight and the products summed. This process yields a pair of scores called *composite canonical variates* (weighted linear combinations of variables). The R_c is the product–moment correlation between these variates.

A researcher interprets three basic values in canonical correlation analysis: the canonical correlation for each root, the canonical components, and the redundancy index. The canonical correlation, since it is merely a product–moment correlation, is interpreted in the same way as any correlation value: the closer the value to 1.00, the stronger the relationship between the composite variates (canonical correlations cannot be negative). The R_c model allows the extraction of as many roots as there are variables in the smaller of the two sets (in the example above, the researcher could extract two unique roots), and each of these is orthogonal (uncorrelated) to all other roots in the analysis. This can provide several possibilities for interpretation (although not all the roots may be statistically significant).

Interpretation of the individual variables in a canonical correlation involves analyzing their

FIGURE 3 R_c INTERCORRELATION ''SUPERMATRIX''

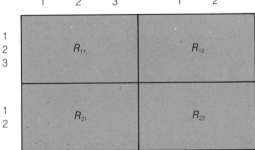

canonical components, that is, each variable's correlation with the canonical variate corresponding to its particular set. Thus, the canonical components are also correlations and interpreted as such: the components whose values are farthest from zero are considered most significant. However, not all researchers agree on what constitutes a significant component value; many consider .30 to be significant, while others use .35, .40, or some different value.

The **redundancy index** provides the direction in which the canonical results should be interpreted; that is, it determines whether the R_c is to be interpreted as "Set 1 given Set 2" or "Set 2 given Set 1," or, possibly, whether it should be interpreted in both directions. The redundancy index increases the interpretive value of canonical correlation by allowing researchers to interpret relationships within canonical components, as well as between the variable sets. In fact, relationships between sets should never be interpreted without first computing the redundancy index.

The formula for computing a redundancy index ($\overline{R}$) is simple: square each component value in a variable set, add the squares, divide the sum by the number of variables in the set, and multiply this value by the canonical correlation squared:

$$\overline{R} = \frac{\Sigma (R_{cc})^2}{M} (R_c^2)$$

where $\overline{R}$ = the redundancy index; R_{cc} = a canonical component; and M = the number of variables in the set.

The importance of these three values in canonical correlation analysis can be illustrated by a research problem shown in Table 3, which asked the question: "What, if any, relationship exists between the mass media actually used for political information and the media considered to be most informative?"

First consider the four canonical correlations for the four roots. Each root has a value of

at least .30, indicating that all may be interpreted unless the component loadings and redundancy index indicate otherwise (.30 is usually the cutoff value for interpretation of a canonical root; however, this depends on the nature of the study and the requirements established by the researcher). In most cases the roots in a canonical analysis do not all have a value of .30 or higher, but such values are common in studies using extremely large samples.

The second step is to examine the significant canonical components, which are considered to be those with absolute values of .30 or greater (again, this limit is at the discretion of the researcher). Referring to Root 1, the variables in Set 1 (also known as the *left set*) show a high positive component value for television (.53) and a very low value for the variable "none" ($-.30$); the remaining variables have values too minimal to be considered significant. The left variable set of Root 1 thus suggests a degree of dichotomy: a great many subjects considered television the most informative medium for political information, but a smaller number indicated that none was most informative, possibly meaning that all were regarded as equally informative (the negative value means that those subjects who responded "television" as most informative did not respond "none"). All the variables in Set 2 (the *right set*) surpassed the .30 cutoff value for Root 1, indicating that the subjects in the study used all these media for political information.

Before the computation can be continued, redundancy indexes must be computed. Without redundancy figures, one can interpret only the relationships within sets, not those between sets. This point is repeated because of its importance: many researchers incorrectly interpret the relationships between sets because they have neglected to compute redundancy indexes.

The general cutoff level for redundancy is .05. That is, a canonical root must account for at least 5% of the variance in the set before interpretation can continue. The redundancy indexes

TABLE 3   CANONICAL CORRELATION EXAMPLE

Variables	Root 1 $(R_c = .85)$	Root 2 $(R_c = .45)$	Root 3 $(R_c = .31)$	Root 4 $(R_c = .31)$
	Left set (media considered most informative)			
Newspaper	.28 (1.00)*	− .63 (− .29)	− .33 (− .07)	− .06 (− .03)
Radio	.02 (.35)	− .08 (.01)	.42 (.50)	− .87 (− .84)
Television	.53 (1.30)**	.53 (.62)	− .30 (.10)	.01 (.02)
Magazines	.16 (.54)	− .46 (− .31)	.64 (.72)	.46 (.45)
Paper and TV	.07 (.27)	− .02 (.03)	− .15 (− .10)	.05 (.05)
2 Combination	.06 (.22)	− .10 (− .05)	.13 (.17)	− .10 (.09)
3 Combination	.04 (.13)	− .09 (− .01)	.10 (.12)	− .02 (− .02)
People	.01 (.08)	.06 (.09)	− .05 (− .03)	.01 (.01)
None	− .30 (.50)**	.49 (.65)	.46 (.59)	.19 (.18)
	Right set (media used for political information)			
Newspaper	.85 (.41)**	− .41 (− .82)	− .30 (− .99)	.02 (− .05)
Radio	.62 (.15)**	− .03 (.07)	.32 (.43)	− .70 (− 1.10)
Magazines	.63 (.52)**	− .38 (.45)	.56 (.97)	.35 (.57)
Television	.90 (.52)**	.41 (1.10)	.02 (− .05)	.11 (.39)

Root 1: $x^2 = 5,460.32$; $df = 36$; p<.01
Root 2: $x^2 = 1,358.26$; $df = 24$; p<.01
Root 3: $x^2 = 635.01$; $df = 14$; p<.01
Root 4: $x^2 = 313.93$; $df = 6$; p<.01

Redundancy indexes

Left set		Right set	
Root 1:	.0470	Root 1:	.4308
Root 2:	.0273	Root 2:	.0258
Root 3:	.0117	Root 3:	.0126
Root 4:	.0111	Root 4:	.0154

*Canonical components are listed first with corresponding beta weights in parentheses.
**Indicates a significant canonical component value.

displayed in Table 3 indicate that only Set 2 of the first root achieved a high enough value to qualify for further interpretation; this means that Root 1 is to be interpreted from the right set (media used), given the left set (media considered most informative).

The remaining three roots in the analysis did not receive significant redundancy indexes (even though their R_c values met minimum requirements); these roots must therefore either be eliminated from further discussion or interpreted for heuristic value only. This demonstrates how the redundancy index serves as a cross-validation for the canonical roots extracted from the analysis; it serves as a back-up test for significance.

Applying this information to the data, the results show that individuals who used all the media for political information tended to feel that television was the most informative. In addition, a smaller group of individuals who used all the media felt that all were equally important.

Discriminant Analysis

Mass media researchers frequently are interested in examining or predicting the attitudes or behavior of subjects who are members of a particular group. For example, a researcher might wish to examine the differences between subjects who subscribe to certain magazines or newspapers, or to predict the characteristics of individuals occupying management level positions in the media. **Discriminant analysis** can be a useful tool in research situations of these types.

In discriminant analysis, linear combinations of continuously scaled variables are derived from measurements made on groups of subjects. The model is used to define a vector that represents the variables for each group so that the separation between groups is maximized. In other words, the researcher uses all the variables in the discriminant analysis to compute a weighted linear combination (var-

iate) for each group, from which it can be determined which of the variables are most helpful in separating or distinguishing the groups. These variables are known as the *discriminating variables*.

The discriminant analysis procedure is shown in graphic form in Figure 4. Here, a *bivariate* example is used (two groups). The two ellipses represent data *swarms* for each group, and the dot at the center of each ellipse denotes the group mean, or *centroid*. The two points at which the ellipses intersect define a line, designated as *A*. If a second line, *B*, is constructed perpendicular to Line *A*, and the points from the intersection of Groups 1 and 2 are projected onto Line *B*, the overlap between the groups is smaller along Line *B* (indicated as *a*) than any other possible line (Cooley & Lohnes, 1971). The discriminant analysis procedure attempts to define this *true* line along which the groups are maximally separated.

Discriminant analysis can serve two purposes, analysis and classification. The data are analyzed by means of statistical tests designed to measure the significance of the combined variables. In classification, which takes place after the data have been analyzed, categories of membership are created for the subjects in the study. A particular study may involve one or both procedures.

Discriminant analysis is closely related to factor analysis and canonical correlation in that each model extracts "factors" from a battery of variables. The factors, which are linear combinations in all models, are referred to as *discriminant functions*. Each discriminant function is orthogonal to all others in the analysis; that is, each function is an independent representation of the analysis in question. In discriminant analysis, the number of functions is one less than the number of groups involved, unless the number of variables in the analysis is smaller. In that case, the number of discriminant functions is equal to the number of original variables.

Interpreting a discriminant analysis involves

FIGURE 4   DISCRIMINANT ANALYSIS PROCEDURE

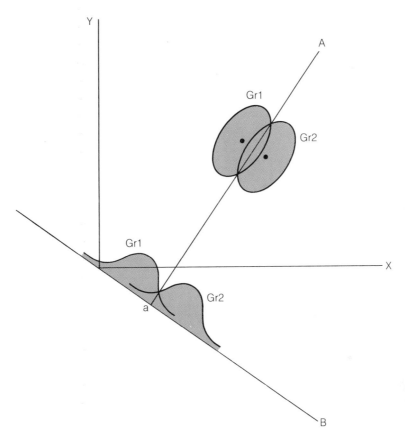

examining the discriminant functions and the weights assigned to each of the variables used in forming those functions. These observations taken together allow researchers to analyze the nature of group differences. As in factor analysis, the dimensions represented by the discriminant functions may be susceptible to meaningful interpretation. However, even if the interpretation is not meaningful, parsimony is achieved by reducing the original space in which the group differences existed (Tatsuoka, 1971).

Another procedure involved in discriminant analysis is plotting the centroids of the discriminant functions. Each group has a mean for the linear combination it creates; these means are plotted to determine the nature of the distance between the groups — the plot provides a visual representation of group differences. Tests are also available to indicate whether the distance separating the groups is statistically significant (Klecka, 1980; Tatsuoka, 1970).

Haynes (1978) used discriminant analysis to test two hypotheses related to children's perceptions of comic and authentic violence in cartoons. A "comic" cartoon was defined as one that portrayed a violent act in a comical manner, and the victim suffered no true or lasting ill effects. An "authentic" cartoon depicted a violent act as "true to life," with no comic effect intended. The two hypotheses were: (1) that children would perceive the violence in a comic cartoon as being more violent than that in an authentic cartoon, and (2) that females would perceive all the cartoons as being more violent than would males.

Haynes's first step was to administer a 12-item questionnaire to a group of 120 children, asking them to describe how they felt about a cartoon they viewed in an experimental situation. These responses were factor analyzed and the factor scores used in the discriminant analysis to determine whether group differences existed. (In this study, Haynes used discriminant analysis solely as a classification procedure, since he had no knowledge about group membership beforehand.)

The first discriminant function (DF I, Table 4) revealed that the males and females who viewed the comic cartoons (Group 1) were most clearly distinguishable from the males and

TABLE 4   HAYNES'S DISCRIMINANT ANALYSIS OF MALE AND FEMALE PERCEPTION OF ''COMIC'' AND ''AUTHENTIC'' CARTOON VIOLENCE

	Discriminant function coefficients	
	Function I	**Function II**
Perceived violence	−.997	.079
Acceptability of violence	.093	.994

DF I–perceived violence	Centroids
Male/authentic	.35
Female/authentic	.42
Male/comic	−.48
Female/comic	−.51

DF II–acceptability	Centroids
Male/authentic	.61
Female/authentic	.65
Male/comic	−.17
Female/comic	−.12

Source: "Children's Perception of 'Comic' and 'Authentic' Cartoon Violence" by Richard B. Haynes, Winter 1978, Journal of Broadcasting, p. 68. Reprinted by permission.

females who viewed the authentic cartoons (Group 2) in terms of a function described as "perceived violence" (so named because of the nature of the most significantly weighted variables in the function). The second discriminant function, DF II, showed that Group 1 was most different from Group 2 with regard to a function described as "acceptability of violence." The centroids for each group showed that no sex differences existed. However, Haynes did find that the comic cartoons were perceived as being more violent than the authentic cartoons, and that the comic violence was perceived as being more unacceptable than authentic violence.

Discriminant analysis is a useful research tool in all areas of mass media. The method is often used as a secondary phase of research, such as was done by Haynes: The researcher may conduct a factor analysis or other statistical procedure that produces summary scores, and use these scores in a discriminant analysis to determine whether group differences exist.

Multivariate Analysis of Variance

Multivariate analysis of variance (MANOVA) was introduced briefly earlier to demonstrate the utility of multivariate statistics over univariate methods. As mentioned, MANOVA is an extension of the simple ANOVA model to situations involving more than one dependent variable. Specifically, MANOVA allows researchers to test the differences between two or more groups on multiple response data.

The distinctive feature of MANOVA is that the dependent variables are represented as a vector, or weighted linear combination, instead of as a single value, as in ANOVA. ANOVA involves testing for group differences along a continuum formed by the dependent variable, as is shown in Figure 5 (Cooley & Lohnes, 1971).

The MANOVA model extends this idea by testing for group differences in a multidimensional space, as depicted in Figure 6.

The test used in MANOVA to determine the equality of centroids (compared to the test for equality of group means in ANOVA) involves forming an F-ratio between the within groups' and total groups' *dispersion matrices*. This concept is beyond the scope of an introductory text; suffice it to say that the procedure is similar to that used in ANOVA except that matrices are used instead of sums of squares.

Lambert, Doering, Goldstein, and McCormick (1980) performed a study that illustrates how several dependent variables can be simultaneously analyzed using MANOVA. The project demonstrates that not only are time and resources saved, but also several characteristics of an individual can be considered simultaneously, thus providing a closer approximation

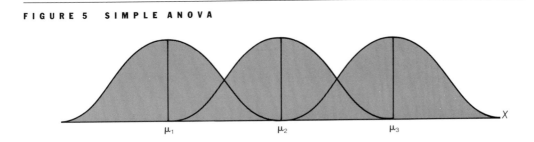

FIGURE 5   SIMPLE ANOVA

FIGURE 6　SIMPLE MANOVA

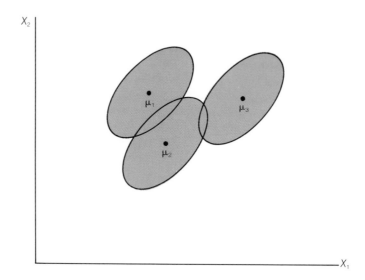

of reality than could a univariate statistical approach.

Lambert and his colleagues were interested in examining the attitudes of consumers generally, and of the elderly in particular, toward the exploitation of opportunities to save money by substituting lower priced generic drugs for brand name products prescribed by their physicians. The authors used a multistage quota sampling procedure to select 510 respondents from four cities in Florida. The subjects completed a questionnaire containing 18 dependent variables. An interesting aspect of the study was the refusal of several of the respondents over age 65 to cooperate with the researchers for one reason or another (such as poor eyesight or fear of being victimized by salespeople). The study offers excellent examples of the problems that can occur in some research studies.

The authors divided the sample into two groups: people who accepted the idea that generic drugs are equivalent to brand name drugs, and those who did not. The groups were compared with respect to their scores on the 18 variables, which included demographics, mobility, general drug knowledge, age, and income. The design is illustrated in Figure 7.

The MANOVA results indicated a significant difference ($p < .0001$) between the two groups on the 18 variables taken as a whole. The study allowed the authors to discuss the influence of many variables on consumers' attitudes toward generic drugs and to make recommendations concerning how drug education programs might help individuals, especially older people, take advantage of the lower cost generic drugs that are available.

Cluster Analysis

Cluster analysis is a term used to describe a variety of methods that are used by researchers when the goal is to classify phenomena into groups, or clusters. Essentially, cluster analysis

FIGURE 7 MANOVA EXAMPLE

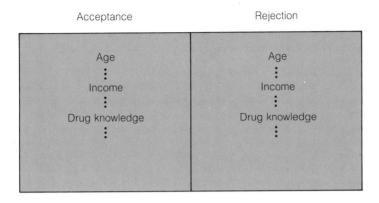

produces clusters of things that are similar in nature. For example, radio listeners in a given market can be placed in clusters by having respondents evaluate different types of music.

Cluster analysis analyzes variables and determines their similarity or dissimilarity, and then places similar variables in groups. The procedure is similar to factor analysis. Most people differentiate between the two methods by stating that factor analysis analyzes columns of data in a data set, whereas cluster analysis investigates the rows of data. However, there are a few cautions when using the various types of cluster analysis. Aldenderfer and Blashfield (1984) discuss three problems. First, most cluster analysis procedures are simple and are not supported by an extensive body of statistical reasoning. Unlike most other multivariate statistics, cluster analysis requires researchers to make a wide variety of subjective judgments in reference to the procedures of conducting the study and the interpretation of the results.

A second problem is that cluster analysis is used by many research disciplines, and each discipline has interpreted what is and what is not required in conducting such a study. These discipline biases mean that cluster analysis in one area of research may not be the same procedure as in another area.

Another problem with cluster analysis is that different clustering methods can generate different solutions to the same set of data. There are at least seven different methods of searching for clusters in a data set. Each one can produce a different analysis of the data. Obviously, the choice of the clustering procedure is important. In fact, using several clustering methods is generally suggested in order to determine which analysis makes the most logical sense.

The final major problem with cluster analysis is that the method imposes clusters on any data set. It is possible to uncover clusters in data that are not actually there. As Aldenderfer and Blashfield state, "The key to using cluster analysis is knowing when these groups are real and not merely imposed on the data by the method."

Multidimensional Scaling

Multidimensional scaling (MDS) is a multivariate technique that identifies proximities, or distances, among a set of data by searching for

FIGURE 8   CLASSIC ROCK CLUSTER: MDS GRAPH OF RADIO STATIONS

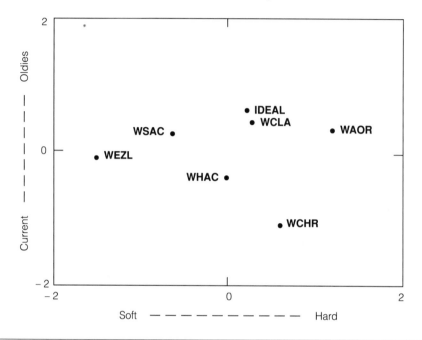

CLASSIC ROCK CLUSTER: MDS Graph of Radio Stations

Source: Paragon Research. Reprinted by permission.

similarities and differences among objects or phenomena. MDS results are displayed in spatial graphs such as the one shown in Figure 8. This figure shows an actual proprietary data set produced by Paragon Research. In this case, 400 respondents were questioned about a variety of radio stations in a midwestern city.

The first step of the study used cluster analysis to place people in categories according to their favorite type of music. The groups were then asked several questions about the radio stations in their market. The graph in Figure 8 shows the evaluations only by listeners who prefer "classic rock" music. Similar graphs were produced for listeners who prefer other types of music. The stations' call letters have been

changed and reflect the type of music played: WEZL = beautiful music, WSAC = soft AC, WHAC = hot AC, WCLA = classic rock, WCHR = CHR, WAOR = AOR, and IDEAL represents the classic rock listeners' evaluations of what an ideal classic rock station would be.

There are two dimensions represented in the graph. The x-axis represents the continuum of "soft to hard" music; the y-axis represents the "current to oldies" continuum. The graph shows that these classic rock listeners rate the local classic rock station very close to their ideal station (notice the closeness of the positions for both IDEAL and WCLA on the graph). However, WAOR plays music that is somewhat too hard (it is to the right of the ideal on the x-axis), but has a good mix of currents and oldies (it is close to the ideal on the *y*-axis); WCHR plays music that is slightly too hard and too current; WHAC, WSAC, and WEZL all play music that has about the right mix of currents and oldies, but all (especially WEZL) are considered too soft.

This graph, and others like it in the analysis, allow the radio station management to visually inspect how their station is perceived by listeners, and what needs to be done to get closer to the ideal. For example, if this study were for WEZL, the management would know immediately that the station would need to play harder music in order to meet the needs of listeners who prefer classic rock music.

References and Suggested Readings

Aldenderfer, M. S., & Blashfield, R. K. (1984). *Cluster analysis*. Beverly Hills, CA: Sage Publications.

Cattell, R. B. (Ed.). (1966). *Handbook of multivariate experimental psychology*. Skokie, IL: Rand McNally.

Comrey, A. L. (1973). *A first course in factor analysis*. New York: Academic Press.

Cooley, W. W., & Lohnes, P. R. (1971). *Multivariate data analysis*. New York: John Wiley.

Duncan, O. D. (1966). Path analysis: Sociological examples. *American Journal of Sociology, 72*, 1–16.

Gorsuch, R. L. (1974). *Factor analysis*. Philadelphia: W. B. Saunders.

Harris, R. (1975). *A primer of multivariate statistics*. New York: Academic Press.

Haynes, R. B. (1978). Children's perceptions of "comic" and "authentic" cartoon violence. *Journal of Broadcasting, 22*, 63–70.

Horst, P. (1966). An overview of the essentials of multivariate analysis methods. In R. B. Cattell (Ed.), *Handbook of multivariate experimental psychology*. Skokie, IL: Rand McNally.

Joreskog, K. G. (1973). A general model for estimating a linear structural equation system. In A. S. Goldberger & O. D. Duncan (Eds.), *Structural equation models in the social sciences*. New York: Seminar Press.

Joreskog, K. G., & Sorbom, D. (1984). *LISREL VI*. Mooresville, IN: Scientific Software.

Klecka, W. R. (1980). *Discriminant analysis*. Beverly Hills, CA: Sage Publications.

Kruskal, J. B., & Wish, M. (1989). *Multidimensional scaling*. Beverly Hills, CA: Sage Publications.

Lambert, Z. V., Doering, P., Goldstein, E., & McCormick, W. (1980). Predisposition toward generic drug acceptance. *Journal of Consumer Research, 7*, 14–23.

Rummel, R. J. (1970). *Applied factor analysis*. Evanston, IL: Northwestern University Press.

Tatsuoka, M. M. (1970). *Discriminant analysis*. Champaign, IL: Institute for Personality and Ability Testing.

Tatsuoka, M. M. (1971). *Multivariate analysis*. New York: John Wiley.

Thurstone, L. L. (1947). *Multiple factor analysis*. Chicago: University of Chicago Press.

Torgerson, W. (1958). *Theory and methods of scaling*. New York: John Wiley.

Tryon, R. C., & Bailey, D. E. (1970). *Cluster analysis*. New York: McGraw-Hill.

Tucker, R. K. (1982). *Basic multivariate research models*. San Diego, CA: College Hill Press.

BRIEF GUIDE FOR CONDUCTING FOCUS GROUPS

PLANNING THE GROUPS

CHOOSING A FIELD SERVICE AND A FACILITY LOCATION

RECRUITING

BEFORE THE GROUPS BEGIN

CONDUCTING THE GROUPS

HANDLING RESPONDENTS

F ocus groups can be very valuable research tools; however, they are double-edged swords. The method looks deceptively simple: invite 6–12 people from a homogeneous group to a research location and have a 2-hour, controlled discussion. But despite their simplicity, focus groups have gremlins hiding around dozens of corners. Researchers who are unaware of the potential problems in conducting a focus group may reap disastrous results. Even the simplest focus group topic can become impossible to handle. Here we discuss some of the problem areas that require consideration both before a focus group meets and while the group is in progress.

First, the investigator needs to be sure that the focus group methodology is the correct approach for the research problem at hand. Focus groups are intended to collect qualitative information and nothing more. But all too often this intention is altered, and people (including some researchers) attempt to interpret focus group data as quantitative information. Indeed, the most serious error associated with the conduct of focus groups is using the method for the wrong reason(s).

PLANNING THE GROUPS

Any research project requires a great deal of careful planning. The best way to accomplish this task is to try to anticipate any condition or situation that might complicate the completion of the groups. Two important considerations in planning focus groups are date and time.

Date

Similar to surveys and experiments, focus groups must be planned with careful consideration of the groups' scheduling. Any conflict with major holidays or other officially recognized days away from work may create severe problems in recruiting participants. In addition to religious holidays, the Fourth of July, Labor Day, and other long-established holidays, researchers need to anticipate problems that may be created by less well-known events.

Depending on the city and the time of year, some or all of the following may create havoc with recruiting: Monday Night Football, the World Series, the Stanley Cup, or even local high school or college games; blockbuster television shows or other widely publicized TV programs that create a great deal of viewer interest; county or state fairs; major musical events or concerts; and political elections.

Problems created by nature obviously cannot be controlled, but consideration should be given to the weather conditions that may exist at the time the groups are scheduled. For example, focus groups planned in the northern part of the United States from January to March have a good chance for cancellation due to snow storms. If research cannot wait until spring, it is wise to plan for an alternative day and possibly an alternative site. Experienced research companies that recruit for focus groups often ask the people recruited about their availability at a later time if the weather forces cancellation of the originally scheduled group.

Friday focus groups should be attempted only in an emergency. Most people do not want to give up one of their weekend nights to participate in a research project. Indeed, few recruiting companies in the country will accept a job of assembling a Friday night focus group. It isn't impossible to conduct Friday night groups, but researchers should plan to pay people more money for their participation and should expect to make many more recruiting phone calls than are normally required.

Time

The time selected to conduct focus groups depends completely on the type of person whose participation is desired. If housewives are needed, late morning or early afternoon is satisfactory. People who work outside the home are best scheduled for evenings. In most cases, back-to-back night focus groups begin at 6:00 P.M. and 8:30 P.M. Since most groups last about 2 hours, the extra half-hour between groups (if two groups are conducted) allows for cleanup of the facility and resetting of tape recorders (if used). Also, it gives the moderator a few minutes to relax before the second group starts.

Just as the date of focus groups can affect the turnout, so can the time. If business travelers are the target group, it might be wise to schedule their group to begin at 8:30 P.M. Researchers need to put themselves in the position of the type of person who is being recruited and try to anticipate the time that would be most convenient.

CHOOSING A FIELD SERVICE AND A FACILITY LOCATION

Researchers who frequently conduct focus groups in the same city tend to use the same field service for respondent recruiting and facility use. In addition to establishing a rapport with the company, the researcher is accustomed to the facilities and is not surprised by anything when the groups begin. It is vitally important to make a complete investigation of *any* company used for the first time. Researchers who do not follow through on this simple task may be headed for serious consequences in the long run.

Veteran researchers have learned very early that just because a company calls itself a research firm does not mean that the people who own and operate the firm know what they are doing. There are incompetents and charlatans in the research field, just as in any other business. Many researchers who plan to use a company new to them consult the lists of affiliates prepared by various marketing research organiza-

tions. For example, the American Marketing Association publishes a list of its members. To the untrained researcher, membership in such an organization may imply that the affiliates listed on the roster are accredited in some way or have passed a series of competence tests. However, the only requirement for listing is payment of annual membership dues. Thus the first caveat in the research field is: Beware of any marketing, research, or consulting group that members can join for a fee.

The best way to investigate a field service, although even this is not 100% effective, is to ask for references and check them out. In addition, one can make one's own inquiries. Veteran researchers have contacts throughout the country and usually can find out about any research company or recruiting firm in one or two phone calls. The value of developing such contacts becomes clear to the novice almost immediately. The truth of the matter is that one can't be too careful. Recently we witnessed a supposedly respectable professional research company convince subjects who were recruited for focus groups to lie about their names, relationships to other members in the group, and addresses. The company apparently had had difficulty in recruiting the required subjects for the groups and committed fraud to save the contract. All researchers, pros as well as novices, need to remember: *Do not rely on any type of membership list as a sign of competence; ask others who have used the firm or know of its operations.*

Once satisfactory references about a field service have been received, it is necessary to investigate the facilities provided by the firm. Is the meeting place easily accessible, or will focus group participants have difficulty finding the building? Is parking nearby and safe? If the groups are to be held in a motel room, it is important to find out about the motel itself. Obviously, a run-down and poorly located motel will hinder recruitment.

Any facility that is used for the groups should be clean and neat. It can be very embarrassing for a researcher to attempt to moderate a serious discussion among strangers who have been invited to an unkempt location. Respondents will base their perceptions on the status of the research project on the quality of the facilities, so every effort should be made to select a facility that enhances the professionalism of the effort.

The focus room should provide enough seating space for up to 14 adults, and the table should allow for easy discussion among all members of the group. The viewing room should have comfortable seating for the observers.

Finally, the researcher must find out about the recording equipment the research company plans to use. The microphones must be sensitive enough to pick up all levels of sound in the room, and a backup system should be provided in the event that the main recording system fails during the groups.

RECRUITING

The recruiting questionnaire, or the screener, used to select people to participate in the groups is one of the most important aspects of the focus group methodology. The screener defines who will and who will not be allowed to participate. If the screener questions do not adequately identify the type of person who should attend, the results of the research will probably be worthless.

Researchers usually work very closely with the recruiting firm in the development of the screener. Every characteristic desired for the participants needs to be covered (age, sex, race, location of residence, type of employment, knowledge of the topic under discussion, and so on). All relevant characteristics must be addressed by the questions in the screener, and the people who will make the recruiting phone calls must understand the requirements precisely. Good research companies will carefully review the screener with their recruiting staff, but it never hurts to ask whether the procedure is planned.

Some guidelines for recruiting include the following.

1.   Always overrecruit. The number of ex-

cess people generally depends on the type of person desired. There is no rule of thumb, but if a researcher needs 10 participants in a group, 14 or 15 should be recruited.

2.   Determine the amount of co-op money to be paid during the initial discussions of recruiting with the research company. As mentioned earlier, co-op fees can range between $10 and $100. Most research companies ask that the co-op money be provided in advance; this is standard procedure. The respondents, however, are always paid after the group, not before or during the session.

3.   Make sure the guidelines for recruiting participants are clearly understood by the field service. These companies often use lists of names in recruiting for focus groups, and it is best to spell out in detail that only one person from each such club, organization, or other group will be allowed to participate. (An unscrupulous field service might simply call the local PTA and ask for volunteers.) In addition, it must be emphasized that relatives of participants will not be allowed in the groups. Finally, it is usually good practice to insist that no person be recruited for a group if he or she has participated in related focus groups during the past year (or other time period the researcher feels is appropriate). This restriction serves to eliminate the "professional" focus group member — the person who is constantly called by the field service to participate.

4.   Always ask the field service for the screeners used in recruiting the groups. Professional field services will have no hesitation about providing the researcher with the screeners; the companies that claim the screeners are private property, have been destroyed, or are proprietary information, are generally trying to hide something (such as the practice of recruiting members from the same club or organization).

BEFORE THE GROUPS BEGIN

The major items researchers must attend to before the focus groups begin are enumerated below. Some jobs involve a great deal of time, and others can be completed in a few minutes.

1.   Prepare the moderator's guide. The moderator uses the guide to be sure that all relevant questions are asked, but not to force a group into a set pattern of questioning and answering. Researchers must be prepared to skip around the prepared questions depending on how the group reacts.

2.   Make arrangements with the field service for any audio- or videotaping that will be required. Audiotaping is generally considered compulsory; videotaping is an option. Most research companies do not charge for audiotaping, but there is usually a substantial additional fee for videotaping.

3.   Check all electronic equipment and other mechanical devices that will be used during the groups. Assume that nothing will work and check everything. The items (for example, tape machines) that aren't checked are the ones that will not work when they are supposed to (Murphy's law).

4.   In most focus group situations, respondents are offered a light dinner or snack. Catering arrangements need to be discussed with the recruiting company and depend on how much money the client wishes to spend.

5.   Although respondents are reminded several times of the group's starting time, one or two people are sure to arrive late. It is the researcher's responsibility to instruct the recruiting company how to handle late arrivals. Some focus groups may suffer no harm if one respondent arrives a few minutes late. If, however, the session begins with the playing of informational audio- or videotapes, a late respondent cannot participate meaningfully in the group. In such cases, it is best to pay the late respondent the co-op money and allow him or her to go home.

Many "professional" focus group respondents have learned that if they arrive about 15 minutes late they will still receive the co-op money. It is up to the researcher to decide the time limit; in most cases, people who are more than 15 minutes late for the session should not be paid co-op.

6.   Researchers need to establish with the recruiting company the course of action when there are not enough respondents for a group. The course of action (such as not paying for the recruiting of the group) depends on the reason for the low turnout. If bad weather or another unpredictable natural event makes it difficult for people to get to the facility, the research company should not expect to avoid paying the recruiting fee. However, if the weather is fine, and there are no unexpected disrupting influences, the researcher may request that recruiting charges be waived. Fortunately for researchers, good field services who face shortfall problems generally offer to reschedule the groups for no additional charge.

7.   There is one basic rule for the people who will view the groups behind the two-way mirror: no loud noises. The only thing that separates the viewing room from the focus room is a thin sheet of glass, and loud talking, laughing, or other noises from behind the barrier are very annoying to the moderator as well as to the respondents. Viewers should also refrain from lighting cigarettes, cigars, or pipes if the flame may be detected by those on the other side of the mirror. This sounds like a minor detail, but the quick flash of light can distract a respondent who is unaware of the presence of viewers behind the mirror. Other rules for the viewers are established by the moderator on an ad hoc basis.

CONDUCTING THE GROUPS

The type of introduction to a focus group, and the amount of information provided to the respondents, depend on the purpose of the group and the sponsor of the research. In some cases it is important for the respondents to have no preliminary information in the introduction; in other cases concepts or procedures must be explained before actual questioning can begin.

Most focus groups start by allowing each respondent to give a very brief self-introduction. Then the moderator generally identifies the purpose of the group and summarizes the goals of the project. Some guidelines for preparing an introduction to a focus group are as follows.

1.   Explain that there are no right or wrong answers to the questions that will be asked. Respondents should feel free to make relevant comments, whether positive or negative.

2.   Advise respondents that the session is being taped for future reference. If the explanation of the taping procedure is handled quickly and professionally, most respondents will be unconcerned with the process.

3.   Be prepared to mention the two-way mirror. Some researchers immediately explain that the respondents are being watched, other researchers believe that the mirror and the viewers should not be discussed except in response to a specific question. If someone does ask whether there is a two-way mirror, a brief answer along these lines is appropriate: "The people who are sponsoring the research have told me that they may view the group, to get as much information as possible. At this time, I cannot really say whether the sponsors are in the room." (This is not lying, since sponsors enter and leave the room periodically, out of sight of the moderator.)

4.   Remind the respondents that they should treat the discussion as a very informal gathering; they should not hesitate to ask questions, and they should feel free to speak up without being invited. The more relaxed the respondents are, the more responsive they will be to the questions asked of them.

5.   Listen closely to respondents' answers, to ensure follow-up on potentially relevant information. The researcher should not be restricted to the order of questioning in the moderator's guide if respondents are providing comments that are relevant to the questions developed before the group began.

HANDLING RESPONDENTS

All things considered, there are basically five types of people who participate in focus groups:

1. The active participant who is interested in providing relevant answers to the moderator's questions.
2. The shy person who is embarrassed to speak out or feels inhibited for some reason.
3. The person who knows too much or has answers to every question. Such people tend to try to dominate the group.
4. The person who rambles on and gives a speech with every response. The "overtalker" will answer a question adequately and then forge ahead: "By that I mean. . . ."
5. The obnoxious person, who does not really wish to participate and attempts to hinder the moderator by making sarcastic remarks or irrelevant comments.

People of the first two types are easy to deal with in a focus group. Even the shy person can be coaxed to provide valuable information by a good moderator. The last three types, however, can ruin a project, and they must be eliminated from the group before they can affect the other participants.

Getting people out of a group that is already in session calls for a prior arrangement with the field service. For example, it may be agreed that when the moderator believes it is necessary to terminate the participation of a group member, the moderator will leave the focus room and give the name of the offending person to the field service representative. A few minutes after the moderator has returned to the group, the unwanted group member is summoned for a phone call. Outside the focus room, the company representative very politely dismisses the person. ("You seem to be an expert in the area, and your input may affect the other respondents' answers" is one approach.)

The goal is to eliminate the know-it-all, the overtalker, or the bully as soon as he or she is identified as a problem. The moderator cannot allow an individual to destroy the group. Speed is most important in getting rid of an unwanted respondent.

SAMPLE DATA

Note: The codebook for the following data is included in Chapter 6.

Column...>Respondent	4	5	6	7	8	9	10	11	12	13	14	15	16	17	18	19	20	21	22	23	24	25	26	27	28	29	30	31	32	33	34	35	36	37
0 0 1	1	1	1	1	3	1	2	1	1	2	0	2	2	5	1	1	2	2	1	1	1	2	2	2	1	1	1	1	2	2	1	1	2	1
0 0 2	2	1	2	1	1	1	2	1	2	2	0	2	0	2	1	1	2	2	2	1	2	2	2	2	1	1	3	1	2	2	1	1	2	1
0 0 3	3	2	2	2	1	1	3	1	2	2	0	2	0	2	1	2	2	1	1	1	1	2	2	2	1	1	2	1	2	2	3	1	2	1
0 0 4	3	2	3	1	0	1	2	1	1	1	2	2	0	5	2	1	2	2	1	1	2	1	2	2	1	1	2	2	1	1	1	1	1	2
0 0 5	4	1	1	1	3	2	2	1	1	2	0	2	0	2	1	1	2	2	2	1	1	2	2	2	1	1	2	1	2	2	2	2	2	2
0 0 6	4	2	0	1	2	1	2	1	1	2	0	2	0	5	2	1	1	1	1	1	1	2	2	2	1	1	1	1	2	2	2	2	2	2
0 0 7	1	1	3	1	3	1	1	1	3	1	3	3	0	9	2	1	2	2	2	1	2	2	2	1	2	1	2	1	2	2	1	2	1	2
0 0 8	2	1	1	1	2	1	2	1	1	2	0	2	0	2	2	1	2	2	1	1	2	2	2	2	1	1	1	3	2	2	1	2	2	1
0 0 9	1	1	3	1	2	1	1	1	1	2	0	2	0	2	1	1	2	1	2	1	2	2	2	1	2	1	1	1	1	3	1	1	1	1
0 1 0	1	1	2	1	3	1	2	1	2	2	0	2	0	9	1	2	1	2	2	1	1	2	2	2	1	2	2	1	1	2	2	2	2	1
0 1 1	1	1	2	1	3	1	2	2	2	1	2	1	2	5	1	1	1	1	1	1	2	2	2	1	1	2	2	1	1	2	1	1	1	1
0 1 2	2	2	2	1	2	2	0	1	2	2	3	2	0	5	1	1	2	2	2	1	1	2	2	2	1	1	1	3	2	2	1	1	2	1
0 1 3	2	1	2	1	2	2	1	1	2	2	0	2	0	9	1	1	1	1	1	1	2	2	2	1	1	1	1	1	1	3	1	1	1	1
0 1 4	2	1	3	1	1	1	2	1	1	2	0	1	3	5	1	1	1	2	2	1	1	2	2	3	1	2	1	1	2	3	1	1	1	1
0 1 5	3	2	2	1	2	1	2	1	2	2	0	2	0	2	1	1	2	1	2	1	1	2	2	1	2	2	2	3	1	1	2	2	1	1
0 1 6	3	1	0	2	3	2	0	1	1	2	0	2	0	5	1	1	2	2	2	1	1	2	2	2	1	2	1	1	1	2	1	1	1	1
0 1 7	3	1	2	2	2	2	0	1	2	1	0	2	0	2	1	1	1	1	1	1	1	2	2	1	1	1	2	1	2	2	1	2	1	1
0 1 8	3	1	2	1	2	1	3	1	3	2	0	2	0	5	1	1	2	2	2	1	2	2	2	2	2	1	1	1	2	2	1	1	2	1
0 1 9	3	2	1	1	3	1	1	1	3	2	0	2	0	2	1	1	1	1	1	1	1	2	2	3	1	2	2	1	1	2	1	1	2	1
0 2 0	3	1	2	2	0	1	1	1	1	2	0	2	0	2	1	1	2	2	1	1	1	2	2	1	1	2	1	1	2	1	1	1	1	1
0 2 1	3	1	2	1	2	1	3	1	1	2	0	1	3	5	1	1	2	1	2	1	1	2	2	2	1	1	1	1	2	3	1	2	2	1
0 2 2	3	2	2	1	2	2	0	1	1	2	0	2	0	2	1	2	2	2	1	1	1	1	2	2	1	2	2	1	1	2	1	2	2	1
0 2 3	3	1	1	1	2	1	3	1	2	2	0	2	0	3	1	1	2	2	2	1	2	2	2	2	1	1	1	1	2	2	1	1	2	1
0 2 4	3	3	3	1	1	2	3	1	2	2	0	2	0	3	1	1	2	2	2	1	2	1	2	3	1	1	1	1	3	3	1	1	2	1
0 2 5	4	1	1	1	2	1	2	1	1	1	2	1	2	9	1	1	1	1	1	1	2	1	1	1	1	2	1	1	3	3	3	1	2	1

026 027 028 029 030 031 032 033 034 035 036 037 038 039 040 041 042 043 044 045 046 047 048 049 050 051 052 053 054 055

056
057
058
059
060
061
062
063
064
065
066
067
068
069
070
071
072
073
074
075
076
077
078
079
080
081
082
083
084
085

146	3	1	3	1	3	1	2	1	3	1	3	1	3	5	1	1	1	1	2	1	2	2	2	2	1	1	2	1	1	2	1	1	1	1
147	3	2	0	2	0	1	2	1	1	2	0	2	0	5	1	1	1	1	1	1	2	2	2	2	1	1	1	1	1	2	1	1	1	1
148	3	1	2	2	0	1	2	1	1	2	0	2	0	9	1	1	2	2	1	1	2	1	1	2	1	1	2	2	2	2	1	2	2	1
149	3	1	3	1	3	2	0	1	1	1	1	1	1	5	1	1	1	1	1	1	1	1	1	3	1	1	1	1	2	2	1	1	2	1
150	3	2	0	2	0	1	3	1	1	1	3	1	3	5	1	1	2	2	2	1	2	2	2	1	1	1	1	1	2	2	1	1	2	1
151	3	1	2	1	2	1	2	1	1	1	2	1	2	5	1	1	2	2	1	1	1	2	1	1	1	1	1	1	2	1	2	1	1	1
152	4	2	0	2	0	1	2	1	1	1	2	2	0	5	1	1	2	2	2	1	2	2	2	1	1	1	2	2	1	2	1	1	1	1
153	2	1	1	1	2	1	2	1	2	1	2	2	0	2	1	1	2	2	2	1	1	2	1	1	1	1	1	1	1	1	1	1	1	1
154	2	1	1	2	0	2	0	1	3	1	3	2	0	2	2	2	1	1	1	1	1	2	1	1	1	1	1	1	1	1	1	1	1	1
155	2	1	2	2	0	1	3	1	2	2	0	2	0	9	1	1	2	2	1	1	1	2	1	1	2	1	2	1	1	1	1	1	1	1
156	2	1	3	1	2	2	0	1	3	1	3	2	0	8	2	2	1	1	2	1	3	2	2	2	2	3	2	1	2	2	1	2	2	2
157	2	1	3	1	3	1	3	1	2	1	1	1	2	5	1	1	2	2	1	1	2	2	1	1	1	1	1	1	1	1	1	1	1	1
158	2	2	0	1	2	2	0	1	2	2	0	2	0	2	2	1	1	1	2	1	2	2	1	1	1	1	2	1	2	1	1	1	1	2
159	2	1	1	1	3	1	1	1	2	2	0	2	0	9	1	1	1	1	1	1	1	2	2	2	1	1	1	1	2	1	1	2	2	1
160	3	1	1	1	2	1	2	1	3	2	0	2	0	2	1	1	2	1	2	2	1	2	3	3	2	1	2	3	1	1	1	2	3	1
161	3	1	1	1	2	1	3	1	2	2	0	2	0	2	1	1	2	1	1	1	1	2	2	2	1	1	3	1	2	1	1	1	2	1
162	3	1	3	2	0	1	2	1	1	1	3	2	0	5	1	1	1	2	1	1	1	2	1	1	1	1	1	1	2	2	1	1	1	1
163	3	1	3	1	3	1	3	1	1	2	0	1	3	5	1	1	2	2	1	1	1	2	1	1	1	1	1	1	1	2	2	1	1	1
164	3	1	3	1	3	1	3	1	2	2	0	2	0	5	1	1	2	2	1	1	2	1	1	3	1	1	1	1	1	1	1	1	1	1
165	3	1	3	1	3	1	3	1	3	2	0	2	0	5	1	1	2	2	1	1	1	2	2	1	2	1	1	1	1	1	1	2	1	1
166	4	2	0	2	0	1	1	1	1	1	1	2	0	2	2	1	2	1	1	1	1	2	1	1	1	1	1	1	1	1	1	1	1	1
167	4	1	3	1	3	1	3	1	2	1	3	2	0	2	1	1	1	1	1	2	1	2	1	1	1	1	1	1	1	1	1	1	1	1
168	4	1	1	1	2	1	2	1	2	1	1	1	2	2	1	1	1	1	1	1	1	2	1	1	1	1	1	1	1	1	1	1	1	1
169	4	1	2	1	1	2	0	1	1	2	0	2	0	2	1	1	1	1	2	1	2	2	2	2	1	1	2	1	1	1	1	1	2	1
170	4	1	3	1	3	2	0	1	3	1	2	1	2	5	1	1	1	1	2	2	2	2	2	1	2	1	1	1	1	2	2	1	1	1
171	4	1	2	1	2	2	0	1	1	2	0	2	0	5	1	1	1	1	1	1	1	2	2	1	1	1	1	1	2	1	1	2	1	2
172	4	1	1	1	2	1	2	1	1	2	0	2	0	5	1	1	2	2	1	2	2	2	2	1	1	1	1	1	2	2	1	2	1	2
173	4	1	2	1	2	2	0	1	1	2	0	2	0	5	1	1	1	1	1	2	2	2	2	2	1	1	1	1	1	1	1	1	1	1
174	4	2	0	1	3	1	3	1	1	2	0	2	0	5	2	2	1	1	1	1	2	2	1	2	3	3	1	1	1	1	2	2	2	1
175	4	1	3	1	2	1	3	1	2	2	0	2	0	2	1	1	2	2	2	1	2	2	2	2	1	2	2	1	1	1	1	1	1	1

176	177	178	179	180	181	182	183	184	185	186	187	188	189	190	191	192	193	194	195	196	197	198	199	200
1	1	1	1	1	1	1	1	1	1	2	1	1	1	1	1	1	1	2	1	1	1	1	1	1
1	1	1	2	2	1	1	1	1	1	1	1	1	2	2	2	1	2	1	1	1	1	1	2	1
2	1	2	2	1	1	1	1	1	1	1	2	1	1	1	1	1	1	1	1	1	1	2	2	1
1	2	2	1	1	1	1	1	1	1	2	1	1	1	1	1	1	1	1	1	1	1	1	1	3
1	1	1	2	1	1	1	2	1	1	1	2	2	2	1	1	1	1	1	2	1	1	1	1	1
2	2	1	1	2	1	1	1	1	1	2	2	1	1	2	1	2	1	1	1	1	3			
1	1	1	1	1	1	1	1	1	1	2	1	2	1	1	1	1	1	1	1	2	1	1		
2	2	2	1	1	1	1	2	1	2	1	1	2	1	3	1	2	1	2	2	1	3			
2	2	2	1	1	1	1	1	1	2	1	1	2	1	1	1	2	1	2	1	1				
1	2	2	1	1	1	1	1	1	2	2	1	1	2	1	1	1	1	1	1	1				
1	2	1	2	1	2	2	1	2	1	2	1	2	2	1	1	1	2	2	1	2	1			
2	2	1	1	1	2	2	2	2	1	2	1	1	2	1	2	2	2	2	2	2	1			
2	2	2	2	2	2	2	2	2	1	2	1	2	2	2	2	1	2	2	2	2	2			
2	1	1	1	2	2	3	2	2	2	1	2	2	1	2	1	2	1	2	2	2	1	1	2	
1	1	2	1	1	1	1	1	1	2	1	1	1	1	1	1	1	1	1	1	1	3			
2	2	1	2	1	1	1	1	2	1	2	1	1	2	2	1	1	2	1	2	2	1			
2	2	2	2	1	2	2	1	1	2	1	2	1	2	1	1	2	2	1	2	1	2	1		
2	2	2	2	1	2	2	1	1	2	1	2	1	2	1	1	2	1	2	1	2	2	1		
1	2	1	1	1	1	1	1	1	2	1	1	1	1	1	1	1	1	1	1	1	1			
1	2	1	1	1	1	1	1	1	2	1	1	1	1	1	1	1	1	1	1	1	1			
5	2	6	5	2	5	5	3	9	5	6	2	5	9	5	2	5	3	5	3	5	5	3	5	5
3	2	1	3	0	0	0	0	3	0	1	0	1	0	0	0	0	0	2	0	3	0	0	0	0
1	1	1	1	2	2	2	2	1	2	1	2	1	2	2	2	2	1	2	1	2	2	2	2	2
0	1	2	3	2	0	0	3	3	0	1	0	2	0	0	3	0	2	2	0	2	0	0	0	0
2	1	1	1	1	2	2	1	1	2	1	2	1	2	2	1	2	1	1	2	1	2	2	2	2
3	2	3	3	2	1	3	3	2	1	3	1	2	2	2	3	1	2	3	1	3	1	1	1	
1	1	1	1	1	1	1	1	1	1	1	1	1	1	1	1	1	1	1	1	1	1	1		
0	3	0	3	1	2	2	0	1	0	2	2	2	2	3	3	3	0	3	0	3	0	3	2	
2	1	2	1	1	1	2	1	2	1	1	1	1	1	1	2	1	2	1	2	1	1			
0	2	0	3	2	1	2	3	2	1	2	2	3	2	3	1	2	3	2	3	1	3	2		
2	1	2	1	1	1	1	1	1	1	1	1	1	1	1	1	1	1	1	1	1	1			
1	2	3	3	1	3	2	0	1	0	2	1	2	0	0	2	3	1	2	0	2	3	2	0	2
1	1	1	1	1	1	2	1	2	1	1	2	2	1	1	1	2	1	1	1	2	1			
4	4	1	1	1	1	2	2	2	2	4	3	3	3	3	3	4	4	4	4	4	4	4		

G L O S S A R Y

acceptance rate: the percentage of the target sample that agrees to participate in a research project

agenda setting: the theory that the media provide topics of discussion and importance for consumers

aided recall: a survey technique in which the interviewer shows the respondent a copy of a newspaper, magazine, television schedule, or other item that might help him or her to remember a certain article, program, advertisement, and so on

algorithm: statistical procedure or formula

American Standard Code for Information Interchange (ASCII): the standard machine language used by microcomputers; each letter, number, or special character is represented by 7 bits of information

analysis of variance (ANOVA): a statistical procedure used to decompose sources of variation in two or more independent variables

analytical survey: a survey that attempts to describe and explain why certain conditions exist (usually by testing certain hypotheses)

antecedent variable: (1) in survey research, the variable used to predict another variable; (2) in experimental research, the independent variable

applied research: research that attempts to solve a specific problem rather than to construct a theory

area of dominant influence (ADI): a region composed of a certain number of television households; every county is assigned to one and only one ADI

artifact: a variable that creates a rival explanation of results (a confounding variable)

audience turnover: in radio research, an estimate of the number of times the audience changes stations during a given daypart

auditorium music testing: testing procedure where a group of respondents simultaneously rates music hooks

available sample: a sample selected on the basis of accessibility

average quarter-hour (AQH): the average number of persons or households tuned in to a specific channel or station for at least 5 minutes during a 15-minute time segment

bar chart: see *histogram*

batch processing (batch job): computer operating procedure in which several users input instructions that are computed in order of input or priority

baud rate: the rate at which a modem sends or receives information

beta weight: a mathematically derived value representing a variable's contribution to a prediction or weighted linear combination (also called *weight coefficient*)

bit: a single piece of information in computers; 8 bits typically represent one character or number, called a *byte*

bit processing: term used to identify the type of information processing system used by a computer; most common is the 8-bit processor in microcomputers

byte: a unit of computer storage, which is typically one character or number; a byte consists of 8 bits

call-out research: a procedure used in radio research to determine the popularity of recordings; see also *hook*

canonical correlation: a multivariate statistic used to investigate the relationship between two sets of variables

case study: an empirical inquiry that uses multiple sources of data to investigate a problem

catch-up panel: members of a cross-sectional sample done in the past who are relocated for subsequent observation

CATI: computer-assisted telephone interviewing; video display terminals are used by interviewers to present questions and enter responses

census: an analysis in which the sample comprises every element of a population

central limit theorem: the sum of a large number of independent and identically distributed random variables that has an approximate normal distribution

central processing unit (CPU): the control and co-ordination system of a computer that decides the order in which computations are made and where to store information, sends information to peripherals, and regulates the entire system operation

central tendency: a single value that is chosen to represent a typical score in a distribution such as the mean, the mode, or the median

checklist question: a type of question in which the respondent is given a list of items and is asked to mark those that apply

chi-square statistic: a measurement of observed versus expected frequencies; often referred to as *crosstabs*

circulation: in the print media, the total number of copies of a newspaper or magazine that are delivered to a subscriber plus all copies bought at newsstands or from other sellers

circulation research: (1) a market-level study of newspaper and magazine penetration; (2) a study of the delivery and pricing systems used by newspapers and magazines

closed-ended question: a question the respondent must answer by making a selection from a prepared set of options

Cloze procedure: a method for measuring readability or recall in which every *n*th word is deleted from the message and readers are asked to fill in the blanks

cluster analysis: a multivariate statistic that classifies phenomena into groups or segments

cluster sample: a sample selected in groups or categories

codebook: menu or list of responses used in coding open-ended questions

coding: the placing of a unit of analysis into a particular category

coefficient of determination: in correlational statistics, the amount of variation in the criterion variable that is accounted for by the antecedent variable

coefficient of nondetermination: in correlational statistics, the amount of variation in the criterion variable that is left unexplained

cohort analysis: study of a specific population as it changes over time

communication audit: in public relations, an examination of the internal and external means of communication used by an organization

concept: a term that expresses an abstract idea formed by generalization

confidence interval: an area within which there is a stated probability that the parameter will fall

confidence level: probability (for example, .05 or .01) of rejecting a null hypothesis that is in fact true (also called the *alpha level*)

constitutive definition: a type of definition in which other words or concepts are substituted for the word being defined

construct: a combination of concepts that is created to describe a specific situation (for example, "authoritarianism")

constructive replication: an analysis of a hypothesis taken from a previous study that deliberately avoids duplication of the methods used in the previous study

continuous variable: a variable that can take on any value over a range of values and can be meaningfully broken into subparts (for example, "height")

control group: subjects who do not receive experimental treatment and thus serve as a basis of comparison in an experiment

control variable: a variable whose influence a researcher wishes to eliminate

convenience sample: nonprobability sample consisting of respondents or subjects who are available, such as college students in a classroom

co-op (incentive): payment given to respondents for participating in a research project

coprocessor: a computer microchip designed for a specific function

copy testing: research used to determine the most effective way of structuring a message to achieve desired results (also known as *message research*)

cost per interview (CPI): dollar amount required to recruit or interview one respondent

cost per thousand (CPM): the dollar cost of reaching 1,000 people or households by means of a particular medium or advertising vehicle

criterion variable: (1) in survey research, the variable presumed to be the effects variable; (2) in experimental research, the dependent variable

cross-lagged correlation: a type of longitudinal study in which information about two different variables is gathered from the same sample at two different times. The correlations between variables at the same point in time are compared with the correlations at different points in time.

cross-sectional research: the collection of data from a representative sample at only one point in time

cross-tabulation analysis (crosstabs): see *chi-square statistic*

cross-validation: a procedure whereby measurement instruments or subjects' responses are compared to verify their validity or truthfulness

cultivation analysis: a research approach that suggests that heavy television viewing leads to perceptions of social reality that are consistent with the view of the world as presented on television

cume: an estimate of the number of different persons who listened to or viewed a particular broadcast for at least 5 minutes during a given daypart (see also *reach*)

data archives: data storage facilities where researchers can deposit data for other researchers to use

daypart: a given part of the broadcast day (for example, prime time = 8:00 P.M.–11:00 P.M. EST)

demand characteristic: the premise that subjects' awareness of the experimental condition may affect their performance in the experiment (also known as the *Hawthorne effect*)

dependent variable: the variable that is observed and whose value is presumed to depend on the independent variable(s)

descriptive statistics: statistical methods and techniques designed to reduce data sets to allow for easier interpretation

descriptive survey: a survey that attempts to picture or document current conditions or attitudes

design-specific results: research results that are based on, or specific to, the research design used

determinant: a scalar that represents a unique function of the numbers in a square matrix

diagonal matrix: a square matrix whose elements all equal zero, except for those along the principal diagonal

discrete variable: a variable that can be conceptually subdivided into a finite number of indivisible parts (for example, the number of children in a family)

discriminant analysis: a multivariate statistic used to classify groups according to variable similarities or to analyze the statistical significance of a weighted linear combination of variables

disk-by-mail (DBM) survey: a survey questionnaire on computer disk sent to respondents to answer at their leisure

disk operating system (DOS): computer program that controls the operation of the CPU

dispersion: the amount of variability in a set of scores

disproportionate stratified sampling: overrepresenting a specific stratum or characteristic

distribution: a collection of scores or measurements

double-barreled question: a single question that in reality requires two separate responses (for example, "Do you like the price and style of this item?")

double blind experiment: a research study in which experimenters and others do not know whether a given subject belongs to the experimental or the control group

dummy variable: the variable created when a variable at the nominal level is transformed into a form more appropriate for higher order statistics

editor–reader comparison: a readership study in which the perceptions of editors and readers are solicited

environmental monitoring program: in public relations research, a study of trends in public opinion and events in the social environment that may have a significant impact on an organization

equivalency: the internal consistency of a measure

error variance: error created by an unknown factor

evaluation apprehension: a fear of being measured or tested that may result in invalid data

exhaustivity: a state of a category system such that every unit of analysis can be placed into an existing slot

experimental design: a blueprint or set of plans for conducting laboratory research

external validity: the degree to which the results of a research study are generalizable to other situations

factor analysis: a multivariate statistical procedure used primarily for data reduction, construct development, and the investigation of variable relationships

factorial design: a simultaneous analysis of two or more independent variables or factors

factor score: a composite or summary score produced by factor analysis

feeling thermometer: a rating scale patterned after a weather thermometer on which respondents can rate their attitudes on a scale of 0 to 100

field service: a research company that conducts interviews and/or recruits respondents for research projects

field observation: a study of a phenomenon in a natural setting

filter question: a question designed to screen out certain individuals from further participation in a study (also called *screener question*)

Flesch reading ease formula: an early readability formula based on the number of words per sentence and the number of syllables per word

floppy disk: an external computer storage device

focus group: an interview conducted with 6–12 subjects simultaneously and a moderator who leads a discussion about a specific topic

Fog Index: a readability scale based on sentence length and the number of syllables per word

follow-back panel: research technique in which a current cross-sectional sample is selected and matched with archival data

forced-choice question: a question that requires a subject to choose between two specified responses

forced exposure: describing the test situation in which respondents are required to be exposed to a specific independent or dependent variable

frequency: in advertising, the total number of exposures to a message that a person or household receives

frequency curve: a graphical display of frequency data in the form of a smooth, unbroken curve

frequency distribution: a collection of scores, ordered according to magnitude, and their respective frequencies

frequency polygon: a series of lines connecting points that represent the frequencies of scores

gross incidence: percent of qualified respondents reached of all contacts made

gross rating points: the total of audience ratings during two or more time periods, representing the size of the gross audience of a radio or television broadcast

group administration: conducting measurements with several subjects simultaneously

hard disk: an external computer storage device capable of storing several million bytes of information

hardware: any type of computer equipment; the physical components of a computer

histogram: a bar chart that illustrates frequencies and scores

homogeneity: equality of control and experimental groups prior to an experiment (also called *point of prior equivalency*)

hook: a short representative sample of a recording used in call-out research

hypothesis: a tentative generalization concerning the relationship between two or more variables that predicts an experimental outcome

identity matrix: a square matrix whose elements equal zero except for those along the principal diagonal, which equal one

incidence: the percentage of a population that possesses the desired characteristics for a particular research study

independent variable: the variable that is systematically varied by the researcher

input: information placed into a computer

instrumental replication: the duplication in a research study of the dependent variable of a previous study

instrument decay: the deterioration of a measurement instrument during the course of a study, which reduces the instrument's effectiveness and accuracy

intensive interview: A hybrid of the one-on-one personal interview

interaction: a treatment-related effect dependent on concomitant influence of two independent variables on a dependent variable

interactive processing (on-line processing): inputting data directly into a computer, usually via a cathode ray tube

intercoder reliability: in content analysis, the degree of agreement between or among independent coders

intercorrelation matrix: a matrix composed of correlations between pairs of variables

internal consistency: the level of consistency of performance among items within a scale

internal validity: a property of a research study such that results are based on expected conditions rather than on extraneous variables

interval level: a measurement system in which the intervals between adjacent points on a scale are equal (for example, a thermometer)

isomorphism: similarity of form or structure

item pretest: a method of testing subjects' interest in reading magazine or newspaper articles

item-selection study: a readership study used to determine who reads specific parts of a newspaper

leading question: a question that suggests a certain response or makes an implicit assumption (for example, "How long have you been an alcoholic?")

Likert scale: measurement scale where respondents strongly agree, agree, are neutral, disagree, or strongly disagree with the statements

literal replication: a study that is an exact duplication of a previous study

local area network (LAN): computer batch processing when one computer serves as a host for several others

longitudinal research: the collection of data at different points in time

mailing list: a compilation of names and addresses, sometimes prepared by a commercial firm, that is used as a sampling frame for mail surveys

mail survey: the mailing of self-administered questionnaires to a sample of people; the researcher must rely on the recipients to mail back their responses

main effect: the effect of the independent variable(s) on the dependent variable (no interaction is present)

mainframe: computer larger than a mini or micro, but smaller than a supercomputer

manipulation check: a test to determine if the manipulation of the independent variable actually had the intended effect

marker variable: a variable that highlights or defines the construct under study

mark-sense reader: see *optical character reader*

masked recall: a survey technique in which the interviewer shows respondents the front cover of a newspaper or magazine with the name of the publication blacked out to test unaided recall of the publication

matrix: a two-dimensional array of scalars

mean: the arithmetic average of a set of scores

measurement: a procedure whereby a researcher assigns numerals to objects, events, or properties according to certain rules

measurement error: an inconsistency produced by the instruments used in a research study

media efficiency: reaching the maximum possible audience for the smallest possible cost

median: the midpoint of a distribution of scores

medium variables: in a content analysis, the aspects of content that are unique to the medium under consideration (for example, typography to a newspaper or magazine)

memory: the amount of information a computer can store and work with, excluding external storage devices

method of authority: a method of knowing whereby something is believed because a source seen as an authority says it is true

method of intuition: a method of knowing whereby something is believed because it is "self-evident" or "stands to reason" (also called *a priori reasoning*)

method of tenacity: a method of knowing whereby something is believed because a person has always believed it to be true

method-specific results: research results based on, or specific to, the research method used

metro survey area: a broadcasting region representing one of the Consolidated Metropolitan Statistical Areas (CMSA), as defined by the U.S. Office of Management and Budget

microcomputer: see *personal computer*

microprocessor chip (microchip): primary computer hardware processing component

minicomputer: computer that is larger than a microcomputer but smaller than a mainframe

mode: the score that occurs most often in a frequency distribution

modem: an electronic device used to transfer computer data via telephone lines (acronym for *modulate-demodulate*)

monitor: a television-type screen that allows a user to view what is entered into the computer as well as the results of any calculations or word processing; also known as a *CRT* (cathode ray tube)

mortality: a problem in panel studies and other forms of longitudinal research caused by original sample members who drop out of the research project for one reason or another

motherboard: a computer's factory-installed primary memory board

mouse: computer device used to input and manipulate data

MS-DOS: Microsoft disk operating system

multidimensional scaling: a multivariate statistic that identifies distances among a set of data by searching for similarities and differences among objects

multiple regression: an analysis of two or more independent variables and their relationship to a single dependent variable (used to predict the dependent variable)

multistage sampling: a form of cluster sampling in which individual households or persons, not groups, are selected

multitasking (multiuser): a computer system designed to allow for simultaneous use by several users

multivariate analysis of variance (MANOVA): an extension of analysis of variance used to study more than one dependent variable

multivariate statistics: statistical methods that investigate the relationship between one or more independent variables and more than one dependent variable

mutually exclusive: a state of a category system such that a unit of analysis can be placed in one and only one category

net incidence: number of respondents or subjects who actually participate in a research project

nominal level: the level of measurement at which arbitrary numerals or other symbols are used to classify persons, objects, or characteristics

nonparametric statistics: statistical procedures used with variables measured at the nominal or ordinal level

nonprobability sample: a sample selected without regard to the laws of mathematical probability

normal curve: a symmetrical, bell-shaped curve that possesses specific mathematical characteristics

normal distribution: a mathematical model of how measurements are distributed. A graph of a normal distribution is a continuous, symmetrical, bell-shaped curve.

null hypothesis: the denial or negation of a research hypothesis

objective function: a mathematical formula that provides various quantitative values for a given media schedule of advertisements; used in computer simulations of advertising media schedules

one-on-one interviews: respondents are interviewed one at a time

open-ended question: a question to which respondents are asked to generate an answer or answers with no prompting from the item itself (for example, "What is your favorite type of television program?")

operating system: set of instructions that control a computer's operation

operational definition: a definition that specifies patterns of behavior and procedures in order to experience or measure a concept

operational replication: a study that duplicates only the sampling methodology and experimental procedures of a previous study

optical character reader (OCR): an input device that electronically reads information from a printed page for entering into a computer

ordinal level: the level of measurement at which items are ranked along a continuum

output: information a computer computes and displays

overnights: ratings surveys of a night's television viewing computed in five major U.S. cities by the A. C. Nielsen Company

panel study: a research technique whereby the same sample of respondents is measured at different points in time

parallel processing: computer system design where several small processors are connected together to act as one unit

parameter: a characteristic or property of a population

parametric statistics: statistical procedures appropriate with variables measured at the interval or ratio level

parsimony principle: the premise that the simplest method is the most preferable (also known as *Occam's razor*)

partial correlation: a method used to control a confounding or spurious variable that may affect the relationship between independent and dependent variables

PC-DOS: personal computer disk operating system

people meter: an electronic television audience data-gathering device capable of recording individual viewing behavior

periodicity: any form of bias resulting from the use of a nonrandom list of subjects or items in selecting a sample

peripheral: any add-on device to a computer system such as a printer

personal computer (PC): the smallest size computer and technically called a microcomputer

personal interview: a survey technique in which a trained interviewer visits the respondent and administers the questionnaire in a face-to-face setting

pilot study: a trial run of a study conducted on a small scale to determine whether the research design and methodology are relevant and effective

population: a group or class of objects, subjects, or units

population distribution: the frequency distribution of all the variables of interest as determined by a census of the population

power: the probability of rejecting the null hypothesis when an alternative is true

precursor analysis: a study that assumes that leaders establish trends, and these trends ultimately trickle down to the rest of society

predictor variable: see *antecedent variable*

prerecruits: respondents who are recruited ahead of time to participate in a research project

prestige bias: the tendency of a respondent to give answers that will make him or her seem more educated, successful, financially stable, or otherwise prestigious

printed circuit board: a piece of flat plastic that contains electrical circuits

printer: a typewriterlike device controlled by a computer

probability level: a predetermined value at which researchers test their data for statistical significance

probability sample: a sample selected according to the laws of mathematical probability

processing: calculations made by a computer

programmable read-only memory (PROM): information stored on a computer chip that is used over and over again, as in cable television channel converters

proportionate stratified sampling: representing population proportions of a specific stratum or characteristic

proposition: a statement of the form "if A then B," which links two or more concepts

proprietary data: research data gathered by a private organization that are available to the general public only if released by that organization

protocol: a document containing the procedures to be used in a field study

psychographics: an area of research that examines why people behave and think as they do

public relations audit: a comprehensive study of the public relations position of an organization

purposive sample: a sample deliberately chosen to be representative of a population

qualitative research method: a description or analysis of a phenomenon that does not depend on measurement of variables

quantitative research method: a description or analysis of a phenomenon that does involve specific measurements of variables

quasi-experiment: a research design that does not involve random assignment of subjects to experimental groups

quota sample: a sample selected to represent certain characteristics of interest

random access memory (RAM): a computer's main memory that is erased when the computer is turned off

random digit dialing: a method of selecting telephone numbers that ensures that all telephone households have an equal chance of being selected

random error: error in a research study that cannot be controlled by the researcher

random sample: a subgroup or subset of a population selected in such a way that each unit in a population has an equal chance of being selected

range: a measure of dispersion based on the difference between the highest and lowest scores in a distribution

rating: an estimate of the percentage of people or households in a population that are tuned to a specific station or network

ratio level: a level of measurement that has all the properties of an interval level scale and also has a true zero point

reach: in advertising, the total number of people or households exposed to a message at least once during a specific period of time (see also *cume*)

reactivity: a subject's awareness of being measured or observed and its possible impact on that subject's behavior

readability: the total of all elements in a piece of printed material that affect the degree to which people understand the piece and find it interesting

reader–nonreader study: a study that contrasts nonreaders of newspapers or magazines with regular readers

reader profile: a demographic summary of the readers of a particular publication

read-only memory (ROM): permanent memory stored in a computer

recall study: a study in which respondents are asked to remember what advertisements they remember seeing in the medium being investigated

recognition: a measurement of readership in which respondents are shown the logo of a magazine or newspaper

redundancy index: a mathematical procedure used in canonical correlation to aid in interpreting relationships between variable sets

region of rejection: the proportion of area in a sampling distribution that equals the level of significance; the region of rejection represents all the values of a test statistic that are highly unlikely, provided the null hypothesis is true

reliability: the property of a measure that consistently gives the same answer at different points in time

repeated measures design: a research design wherein numerous measurements are made on the same subjects

replication: an independent verification of a research study

research question: a tentative generalization concerning the relationship between two or more variables

research supplier: a company that provides various forms of research to clients, from data collection only to a final written analysis and summary of the data

retrospective panel: a study in which each respondent is asked questions about events and attitudes in his or her lifetime

rough cut: a model or simulation of a final product

sample: a subgroup or subset of a population or universe

sample distribution: the frequency distribution of all the variables of interest as determined from a sample

sample-specific results: research results that are based on, or specific to, the research sample used

sampling distribution: a probability distribution of all possible values of a statistic that would occur if all possible samples of a fixed size from a given population were taken

sampling error: the degree to which measurements obtained from a sample differ from the measurements that would be obtained from the population

sampling frame: a list of the members of a particular population

sampling interval: a random interval used for selection of subjects or units in the systematic sampling method

sampling rate: the ratio of the number of people chosen in the sample to the total number in the population (for example, if 100 fraternity members were systematically chosen from a sampling frame of 1,000 fraternity members, the sampling rate would be 10%, or 1/10)

scalar: a single digit (used in matrix algebra)

scattergram: a graphic technique for portraying the relationship between two variables

scientific method: a systematic, controlled, empirical, and critical investigation of hypothetical propositions about the presumed relations among natural phenomena

screener: a short survey or portion of survey designed to select only appropriate respondents for a research project

secondary analysis: the use of data collected by a previous researcher or another research organization (also called *data reanalysis*)

semantic differential: a rating scale consisting of seven spaces between two bipolar adjectives (for example, "good __ : __ : __ : __ : __ : __ : __ bad")

share: an estimate of the percentage of persons or households tuned to a specific station or network

shopping center interview (intercept): a nonprobability study where respondents are recruited and interviewed in a shopping mall

sigma (Σ): the Greek capital letter symbolizing "the sum of"

skewness: the degree of departure of a curve from the normal distribution (curves can be positively or negatively skewed)

SMOG Grading: a measure of readability based on the number of syllables per word

social audit: in public relations research, an analysis of social performance of an organization

software: any type of ready-to-use computer program designed for mathematical computations, word processing, graphics, spreadsheets, and so on

square matrix: a matrix in which the number of rows equals the number of columns

stability: the degree of consistence of the results of a measure at different points in time

staged manipulation: researchers construct events and circumstances so they can manipulate the independent variable

standard deviation: the square root of the variance (a mathematical index of dispersion)

standard error: an estimate of the amount of error present in a measurement

standard score: a measure that has been standardized in relation to a distribution's mean and standard deviation

statistics: science that uses mathematical methods to collect, organize, summarize, and analyze data

storage: forms of saving computer data, such as magnetic disks and tapes

straightforward manipulation: materials and instructions are simply presented to respondents or subjects

stratified sample: a sample selected after the population has been divided into categories

structured interview: an interview in which standardized questions are asked in a predetermined order

summary statistics: statistics that summarize a great deal of numerical information about a distribution such as the mean and the standard deviation

supercomputer: the most powerful computer currently made that computes billions of instructions per second (BIPS)

sweep: a nationwide survey of every television market conducted by the A. C. Nielsen Company and Arbitron

systematic sampling: a procedure to select every *n*th subject for a study, such as every 10th person in a telephone directory

systematic variance: a regular increase or decrease of all scores or data in a research study by a known factor

telephone coincidental: a broadcasting research procedure in which random subjects or households are called and asked what they are viewing or listening to at that moment

telephone survey: a research method in which survey data are collected over the telephone by trained interviewers who ask questions and record responses

theory: a set of related propositions that presents a systematic view of phenomena by specifying relationships among concepts

total observation: in field observation, a situation in which the observer assumes no role in the phenomenon being observed other than that of observer

total participation: field observation in which the observer becomes a full-fledged participant in the situation under observation

total survey area (TSA): a region in which an audience survey is conducted

tracking study: a special readership measurement technique in which respondents designate material they have read (using a different color of pencil for each reading episode)

trend study: a longitudinal study in which a topic is restudied using different groups of respondents (for example, the Roper studies of the credibility of the media)

triangulation: using a combined quantitative and qualitative approach to solve a problem

trigger event: an event or activity that might focus public concern on a topic or issue

t-test: a statistic used to determine significance between group means

Type I error: rejection of the null hypothesis when it should be accepted

Type II error: acceptance of the null hypothesis when it should be rejected

unit of analysis: the smallest element of a content analysis; the thing that is counted whenever it is encountered

unstructured interview: an interview in which the interviewer asks broad and general questions but retains control over the discussion

uses and gratifications study: a study of the motives for media usage and the rewards that are sought

validity: the property of a test of actually measuring what it purports to measure

variable: a phenomenon or event that can be measured or manipulated

variance: a mathematical index of the degree to which scores deviate from the mean

vector: a series of data points represented by a line in space

volunteer sample: a group of people who go out of their way to participate in a survey or experiment (for example, by responding to a newspaper advertisement)

weighting: a mathematical procedure used to adjust the sample to meet the characteristics of a given population (also called *sample balancing*)

NAME INDEX

SUBJECT INDEX